6761

American Writers for Children Since 1960: Fiction

Dictionary of Literary Biography

American Writers for Children Since 1960: Fiction

6761

Edited by
Glenn E. Estes
Graduate School of Library and Information Science
University of Tennessee

A Bruccoli Clark Book
Gale Research Company • Book Tower • Detroit, Michigan 48226

Manufactured by Edwards Brothers, Inc.
Ann Arbor, Michigan
Printed in the United States of America

Copyright © 1986
GALE RESEARCH COMPANY

Library of Congress Cataloging-in-Publication Data

American writers for children since 1960.

(Dictionary of literary biography; v. 52)
"A Bruccoli Clark book."
Includes index.
1. Children's stories, American—History and criticism.
2. Children's stories, American—Bio-bibliography. 3. American fiction—20th century—History and criticism. 4. American fiction—20th century—Bio-bibliography. 5. Authors, American—20th century—Biography—Dictionaries.
I. Estes, Glenn E.   II. Series.
PS374.C454A4   1986   813'.54'099282   86-14885
ISBN 0-8103-1730-3

In Memory Of

Elnora M. Portteus

whose professional influence cannot be measured

Requiem aeternam dona eis Domine, et lux perpetua luceat eis.

Contents

Contents

Plan of the Series

. . . Almost the most prodigious asset of a country, and perhaps its most precious possession, is its native literary product—when that product is fine and noble and enduring.

Mark Twain*

The advisory board, the editors, and the publisher of the *Dictionary of Literary Biography* are joined in endorsing Mark Twain's declaration. The literature of a nation provides an inexhaustible resource of permanent worth. It is our expectation that this endeavor will make literature and its creators better understood and more accessible to students and the literate public, while satisfying the standards of teachers and scholars.

To meet these requirements, *literary biography* has been construed in terms of the author's achievement. The most important thing about a writer is his writing. Accordingly, the entries in *DLB* are career biographies, tracing the development of the author's canon and the evolution of his reputation.

The publication plan for *DLB* resulted from two years of preparation. The project was proposed to Bruccoli Clark by Frederick G. Ruffner, president of the Gale Research Company, in November 1975. After specimen entries were prepared and typeset, an advisory board was formed to refine the entry format and develop the series rationale. In meetings held during 1976, the publisher, series editors, and advisory board approved the scheme for a comprehensive biographical dictionary of persons who contributed to North American literature. Editorial work on the first volume began in January 1977, and it was published in 1978.

In order to make *DLB* more than a reference tool and to compile volumes that individually have claim to status as literary history, it was decided to organize volumes by topic or period or genre. Each of these freestanding volumes provides a biographical-bibliographical guide and overview for a particular area of literature. We are convinced that this organization—as opposed to a single alphabet method—constitutes a valuable innovation in the presentation of reference material. The volume

plan necessarily requires many decisions for the placement and treatment of authors who might properly be included in two or three volumes. In some instances a major figure will be included in separate volumes, but with different entries emphasizing the aspect of his career appropriate to each volume. Ernest Hemingway, for example, is represented in *American Writers in Paris, 1920-1939* by an entry focusing on his expatriate apprenticeship; he is also in *American Novelists, 1910-1945* with an entry surveying his entire career. Each volume includes a cumulative index of subject authors and articles. The final *DLB* volume will be a comprehensive index to the entire series.

With volume ten in 1982 it was decided to enlarge the scope of *DLB* beyond the literature of the United States. By the end of 1985 twenty-one volumes treating British literature had been published, and volumes for Commonwealth and Modern European literature were in progress. The series has been further augmented by the *DLB Yearbooks* (since 1981) which update published entries and add new entries to keep the *DLB* current with contemporary activity. There have also been occasional *DLB Documentary Series* volumes which provide biographical and critical background source materials for figures whose work is judged to have particular interest for students. One of these companion volumes is entirely devoted to Tennessee Williams.

The purpose of *DLB* is not only to provide reliable information in a convenient format but also to place the figures in the larger perspective of literary history and to offer appraisals of their accomplishments by qualified scholars.

We define literature as the *intellectual commerce of a nation:* not merely as belles lettres, but as that ample and complex process by which ideas are generated, shaped, and transmitted. *DLB* entries are not limited to "creative writers" but extend to other figures who in this time and in this way influenced the mind of a people. Thus the series encompasses historians, journalists, publishers, and screenwriters. By this means readers of *DLB* may be aided to perceive literature not as cult scripture in the keeping of cultural high priests, but as at the center of a nation's life.

DLB includes the major writers appropriate to each volume and those standing in the ranks im-

---

*From an unpublished section of Mark Twain's autobiography, copyright © by the Mark Twain Company.

mediately behind them. Scholarly and critical counsel has been sought in deciding which minor figures to include and how full their entries should be. Wherever possible, useful references will be made to figures who do not warrant separate entries.

Each *DLB* volume has a volume editor responsible for planning the volume, selecting the figures for inclusion, and assigning the entries. Volume editors are also responsible for preparing, where appropriate, appendices surveying the major periodicals and literary and intellectual movements for their volumes, as well as lists of further readings. Work on the series as a whole is coordinated at the Bruccoli Clark editorial center in Columbia, South Carolina, where the editorial staff is responsible for the accuracy of the published volumes.

One feature that distinguishes *DLB* is the illustration policy—its concern with the iconography of literature. Just as an author is influenced by his surroundings, so is the reader's understanding of the author enhanced by a knowledge of his environment. Therefore *DLB* volumes include not only drawings, paintings, and photographs of authors, often depicting them at various stages in their careers, but also illustrations of their families and places where they lived. Title pages are regularly reproduced in facsimile along with dust jackets for modern authors. The dust jackets are a special fea-

ture of *DLB* because they often document better than anything else the way in which an author's work was launched in its own time. Specimens of the writers' manuscripts are included when feasible.

A supplement to *DLB*—tentatively titled *A Guide, Chronology, and Glossary for American Literature*—will outline the history of literature in North America and trace the influences that shaped it. This volume will provide a framework for the study of American literature by means of chronological tables, literary affiliation charts, glossarial entries, and concise surveys of the major movements. It has been planned to stand on its own as a vade mecum, providing a ready-reference guide to the study of American literature as well as a companion to the *DLB* volumes for American literature.

Samuel Johnson rightly decreed that "The chief glory of every people arises from its authors." The purpose of the *Dictionary of Literary Biography* is to compile literary history in the surest way available to us—by accurate and comprehensive treatment of the lives and work of those who contributed to it.

The *DLB* Advisory Board

Acknowledgments

This book was produced by BC Research. Karen L. Rood is senior editor for the *Dictionary of Literary Biography* series. Jefferson M. Brook was the in-house editor.

Art supervisor is Patricia M. Flanagan. Copyediting supervisor is Patricia Coate. Production coordinator is Kimberly Casey. Typesetting supervisor is Laura Ingram. The production staff includes Rowena Betts, David R. Bowdler, Tara P. Deal, Mary S. Dye, Kathleen M. Flanagan, Joyce Fowler, Pamela Haynes, Judith K. Ingle, Judith E. McCray, Janet L. Phelps, Joycelyn R. Smith, and Lucia Tarbox. Jean W. Ross is permissions editor. Joseph Caldwell is photography editor. James Adam Sutton and Joseph Matthew Bruccoli did photographic copy work for the volume.

Walter W. Ross and Rhonda A. Marshall did the library research with the assistance of the staff at the Thomas Cooper Library of the University of South Carolina: Lynn Barron, Daniel Boice, Connie Crider, Kathy Eckman, Michael Freeman, Gary Geer, David L. Haggard, Jens Holley, Marcia Martin, Dana Rabon, Jean Rhyne, Jan Squire, Ellen Tillett, and Virginia Weathers.

The editor expresses his thanks to John Cech, Professor, University of Florida, for his initial outline of the contents of this volume and his assignments to the contributors; to Anita Trout, his graduate assistant, and Lisa Welch, staff secretary, for their careful attention to every detail that supported the preparation of the copy for this volume; and to Ann E. Prentice, Professor and Director, Graduate School of Library and Information Science, University of Tennessee, Knoxville, for her willingness to modify schedules so that this editorial task could be completed.

American Writers for Children Since 1960: Fiction

Dictionary of Literary Biography

Lloyd Alexander

(30 January 1924-   )

Laura Ingram

BOOKS: *And Let the Credit Go* (New York: Crowell, 1955);

My Five Tigers (New York: Crowell, 1956; London: Cassell, 1956);

Janine Is French (New York: Crowell, 1958; London: Cassell, 1960);

Border Hawk: August Bondi, illustrated by Bernard Krigstein (New York: Farrar, Straus & Cudahy, 1958);

My Love Affair with Music (New York: Crowell, 1960; London: Cassell, 1961);

The Flagship Hope: Aaron Lopez, illustrated by Krigstein (Philadelphia: Jewish Publication Society, 1960);

Park Avenue Vet, by Alexander and Dr. Louis J. Camuti (New York: Holt, Rinehart & Winston, 1962; London: Deutsch, 1962);

Time Cat: The Remarkable Journeys of Jason and Gareth, illustrated by Bill Sokol (New York: Holt, Rinehart & Winston, 1963); republished in Great Britain as *Nine Lives* (London: Cassell, 1963);

The Book of Three (New York: Holt, Rinehart & Winston, 1964; London: Heinemann, 1966);

Fifty Years in the Doghouse (New York: Putnam's, 1964); republished in Great Britain as *Send for Ryan* (London: W. H. Allen, 1965);

The Black Cauldron (New York: Holt, Rinehart & Winston, 1965; London: Heinemann, 1967);

Coll and His White Pig, illustrated by Eveline Ness (New York: Holt, Rinehart & Winston, 1965);

The Castle of Llyr (New York: Holt, Rinehart & Winston, 1966; London: Heinemann, 1968);

Taran Wanderer (New York: Holt, Rinehart & Winston, 1967);

The Truthful Harp (New York: Holt, Rinehart & Winston, 1967);

The High King (New York: Holt, Rinehart & Winston, 1968);

The Marvelous Misadventures of Sebastian (New York: Dutton, 1970);

The King's Fountain, illustrated by Ezra Jack Keats (New York: Dutton, 1971);

The Four Donkeys, illustrated by Lester Abrams (New York: Holt, Rinehart & Winston, 1972; Kingswood, Surrey: World's Work, 1974);

The Cat Who Wished to Be a Man (New York: Dutton, 1973);

The Foundling and Other Tales of Prydain, illustrated by Margot Zemach (New York: Holt, Rinehart & Winston, 1973);

The Wizard in the Tree, illustrated by Laszlo Kubinyi (New York: Dutton, 1975);

The Town Cats and Other Tales, illustrated by Kubinyi (New York: Dutton, 1977);

The First Two Lives of Lukas-Kasha (New York: Dutton, 1978);

Westmark (New York: Dutton, 1981);

The Kestrel (New York: Dutton, 1982);

The Beggar Queen (New York: Dutton, 1984);

The Illyrian Adventure (New York: Dutton, 1986).

RECORDING: *Fantasy and the Human Condition* (New York Children's Book Council, 1976).

SELECTED PERIODICAL PUBLICATIONS: "The Flat-Heeled Muse," *Horn Book*, 41 (April 1965): 141-146;

"Wishful Thinking—Or Hopeful Dreaming?," *Horn Book*, 44 (August 1968): 383-390;

photograph by Alexander Limont

"A Personal Note By Lloyd Alexander on Charles Dickens," *Top of the News*, 25 (November 1968): 11-14;

"High Fantasy and Heroic Romance," *Horn Book*, 47 (December 1971): 579-584.

In the thirty-odd years of his writing career, Lloyd Chudley Alexander has proven himself a master in the field of modern children's literature. His numerous literary awards both in the United States and Europe, as well as his widespread readership, which includes children as far away as Japan, attest to his international popularity. One reason for Alexander's universal appeal may be that his stories reflect an awareness of the basis upon which all literature is built. Even as a child, he "loved all the world's mythologies," from the tales of the Arabian nights to the didactic animal stories of Aesop.

Although the five-part Prydain cycle, which includes the Newbery award-winning *The High King*, is perhaps his best-known and most highly acclaimed work to date, his contributions to children's literature span a wide range of genres, from richly illustrated fables for very young readers to a trilogy for young adults which explores philosophical questions about political ideals and personal values. Whatever his subject matter and intended audience, however, Alexander manages to incorporate both practical and ethical lessons as well as historical information into his delightful tales.

Lloyd Chudley Alexander was born on 30 January 1924 to Alan Audley and Edna Chudley Alexander. He spent his youth in Philadelphia, where he attended the local public schools until the age of sixteen, when he graduated from Upper Darby Senior High School in 1940. A self-proclaimed bookworm since early childhood, his "best friends and dearest teachers" were the authors who first inspired his love of literature. Shakespeare, Mark Twain, Charles Dickens, and Victor Hugo are a few of his favorites, and their influence, especially that of Dickens, is apparent in Alexander's works.

In a November 1968 article in *Top of the News*, "A Personal Note by Lloyd Alexander on Charles Dickens," he describes the impact Dickens's work had on him as a young boy. Reading *Nicholas Nickleby*, Alexander felt a bond with the book's unhappy schoolboy protagonist: "Charles Dickens somehow put my real one [world] into focus, showing me a way of seeing and feeling I had never known before." He was also fascinated by the stories of King Arthur and often played at being the legendary hero, fighting make-believe battles armed with a trash-can lid shield and a walking cane, borrowed from his rheumatic uncle, which his active imagination easily transformed into the sword Excalibur.

The Alexander family was not wealthy: "Dickens showed me that my own family was Dickensian!," Alexander admits. His father arrived in Philadelphia from Kingston, Jamaica, British West Indies, as a young man. He became a stockbroker, but was bankrupted by the Depression. He then engaged in a series of unsuccessful business ventures—dealing in imported Oriental objets d'art; selling box lunches, packed by his family each morning, to factory workers; attempting to start an auction firm; and operating a gas station. Having experienced firsthand the difficulties of supporting a family, Alan Alexander was not at all impressed when his fifteen-year-old son, soon to graduate from high school, announced his intention to become a poet. Though his father considered his literary ambitions frivolous and impractical, Lloyd Alexander's mother was sympathetic, and through her intervention father and son reached a compromise: Lloyd would be permitted to "have a try" at writing poetry on the condition that he would also engage in some kind of practical work as well.

Unfortunately, Alexander "had no idea how to find work, useful or otherwise. In fact," he confessed, "I had no idea how to become an author." His parents could not afford to finance a college education, and since he had neglected his schoolwork to write poetry and study verse forms, his grades were too low for a scholarship, so he reluctantly secured employment as a messenger boy for a bank. He found life as a bank employee miserable, likening his situation to that of "Robin Hood chained in the Sheriff of Nottingham's dungeon." As soon as he had saved enough money, Alexander quit his job and enrolled in a local school, West Chester State Teachers College. After one term he left that school. Higher education had disap-

pointed him; he felt that his studies were not bringing him any closer to being a writer, and he dropped out of school without earning a degree.

The United States had just entered World War II, and Alexander decided that enlisting in the army would provide the opportunity for high adventure, the perfect preparation for his career as a writer. The army, however, thwarted Alexander's plans for heroism: much to his chagrin, he was stationed in Texas and assigned positions as an artilleryman, a cymbal player in the band, a chapel organist, and a medic. Finally, after this discouraging series of unsoldierly jobs, Alexander was sent to Lafayette College, Easton, Pennsylvania, then to Maryland for training in the United States Army Combat Intelligence and Counter-Intelligence Corps. There he came into contact with individuals who had lived the adventurous life-style Alexander craved; his barrack mates included a wide variety of interesting figures such as veterans of the Spanish Civil War, ex-Foreign Legionnaires, Cherokee Indians, and war refugees, as well as writers, painters, and scholars. Even more promising, the excitement he had hoped to find seemed close at hand: his team was to work with the Resistance after parachuting into France. "This, to my intense relief, did not happen," Alexander later admitted. "Adventurous in imagination, a real parachute jump would have scared me out of my wits. . . ."

Instead, a journey to Wales, where the team continued training, unexpectedly provided the literary fodder that he had hoped to find. The Welsh countryside, with its legendary castles and mountains, as well as its ancient musical language, enchanted Alexander and planted seeds of inspiration that would remain dormant for several years.

From Wales Alexander was sent to the Seventh Army in Alsace-Lorraine, "armed to the teeth with typewriters and machine guns." There he served as a translator-interpreter. After the war, he held the position of staff sergeant with a counterintelligence unit in Paris.

A turning point came for Alexander when he met Janine Denni. Their first encounter occurred when Alexander, in an act of gallantry now standard in World War II movies and novels, stopped his jeep to offer a lift to a soaked and grocery-laden young Parisian woman during a thunderstorm. The two were married three months later, on 8 January 1946. The newlyweds spent two "wickedly delightful" weeks in a *Maison de rendezvous*, the only accommodations available in the postwar housing shortage, until they were able to rent a small, overpriced hotel room where they lived for several weeks.

Around this time he requested a discharge from the service to continue his education. "The Army was as happy to grant it as I to receive it." A scholarship from the French Foreign Ministry enabled him to attend the Sorbonne University of Paris, and there he resumed his studies. He also adopted Janine's small daughter, Madeleine.

The Alexanders' finances shrank, and the French winter grew colder. Despite the excitement of European life, Alexander missed Pennsylvania and felt that he would not be able to write anything of value unless he worked closer to the home of his childhood and youth. Even so, he was determined to complete his studies at the Sorbonne. Because of worsening conditions and the possibility that transportation to the United States might not be available to Janine in the future, she reluctantly agreed to live with her in-laws in Philadelphia, where Alan Alexander was now comfortably installed as an office manager.

When Alexander returned home, the trio continued to live in the attic apartment of his parents' house for several months. Eventually, they saved enough money to buy an old farmhouse in Drexel Hill, near his hometown of Philadelphia. The house is, in Alexander's own words, "the most ancient on the street, and looks it. The flooring has a tendency to sag. Doors and windows operate according to climatic condition. . . ." Even so, the Alexanders found the surrounding woods, nearby creek, and expanse of lawn and gardens adequate compensation for these shortcomings. As well, the community had remained "countrified" in spite of its proximity to a large city and the infringement of the modern world. There, closer to his roots and away from the crowded, noisy home of his parents, he was at last able to write.

Still interested in publishing fiction for adults, Alexander had not yet tried his hand at writing for children, and would not do so for several years to come. He pursued his literary endeavors "grimly . . . , in a stubborn kind of hopeless hopefulness, ready to admit I was no writer at all." Indeed, at this point, Alexander had reason to be discouraged: after seven years and three novels, he had only rejection slips to show for his efforts. During this time, he supported himself by working in various fields which enabled him to utilize his creative inclinations, though not as fully or as autonomously as he would have liked. He found employment as a cartoonist, an advertising copywriter, a layout artist, and an associate editor for an industrial mag-

azine. Between 1948 and 1952, he translated several French works: *Uninterrupted Poetry* by Paul Eluard, *The Wall* and *Nausea* by Jean-Paul Sartre, and *The Sea Rose* by Paul Vialar. Though these occupations brought him closer to the world of publishing, he was still not a writer.

A change in attitude was the first step toward Alexander's success as a writer. He began to see his situation—his desperate desire and cheerless determination to write a novel that would be accepted by a publisher—as "deeply funny." Able, finally, to find humor, and even enjoyment, in his past failure, he chose it as material for his final attempt at novel writing. This novel, *And Let the Credit Go,* was published in 1955.

Having broken into the field, Alexander produced five books for adults in the next ten years. His second published work was *My Five Tigers* (1956), the story of how Alexander, who had always considered himself a "dog person" and had never spent much time in feline company, was persuaded by his wife to take in a stray cat. A collection of anecdotes, *My Five Tigers* chronicles the lives of the first five cats to be part of the Alexander household with humor and an implicit understanding of the feline temperament. Although sometimes grouped with adult books, *My Five Tigers* is appropriate reading for all ages and especially enjoyable for cat lovers.

Alexander's Parisian wife, Janine, and the first years of their marriage provide the subject matter for his next book, *Janine Is French* (1958). Similar in style to *My Five Tigers, Janine Is French* is just as amusing. This account of the humorous escapades of a bright and energetic Frenchwoman transported to the Pennsylvania countryside and of her husband, a struggling writer helpless in the face of female logic and determination, is a warm and romantic story of love and culture shock.

Having, by this time, learned "to write about things I knew and loved," Alexander wrote *My Love Affair with Music* (1960). This account of his experiences as an amateur musician introduces an old Welsh harp, with strings that break unexpectedly (which would later find its way into the hands of one of his characters) as well as Alexander's other "mistresses" in his love affair with music: the piano, the guitar, and the one he still enjoys the most, the violin.

Fifty Years in the Doghouse (1964) tells the true story of William Michael Ryan, special agent of the American Society for the Prevention of Cruelty to Animals and his fight against animal abuse in New York City. This portrait of a social crusader and animal lover includes lions in distress, recalcitrant monkeys, and trapped cats, as well as some more sober encounters that occur in the day-to-day life of an ASPCA special agent. Reprinted in Great Britain as *Send for Ryan*, the book enjoyed popular exposure when excerpts were reprinted in the February 1964 issue of *McCall's* magazine.

Lloyd Alexander's first books for young adults were *Border Hawk: August Bondi* (1958) and *The Flagship Hope: Aaron Lopez* (1960). Both are biographies of two often forgotten Jewish Americans who helped to shape the history of the United States.

August Bondi, a Kansas pioneer of Austrian birth, was one of the men who rode with the famous abolitionist John Brown. Upon a background of pre-Civil War unrest and Kansas's fight for statehood, Alexander paints a noble picture of a man dedicated to his religion as well as to the ideals of personal and political liberty. Despite the violence implicit in a story of political conflict, the book's major themes are those of freedom, patriotism, and religious faith. It was for *Border Hawk: August Bondi* that Alexander won his first book award, the Isaac Siegel Memorial Juvenile Award, in 1959.

Set in pre-Revolutionary Rhode Island, *The Flagship Hope: Aaron Lopez* is the story of a young Jew who flees Portugal, where the practice of his faith has been outlawed, for the freedom he hopes to find in the New World. Rising quickly to prominence as a businessman and importer, he uses his wealth to help promote the Revolutionary War. Though too old for combat, Lopez aids the success of the freedom fighters by contributing food and supplies, incurring great personal losses for his sacrifice. Despite his relative obscurity, Lopez's generosity, reputation for honesty, conviction in his beliefs, and dedication to Judaism earn him a place among the heroes of the American Revolution.

Time Cat (1963) was Alexander's first work of fiction for children. This is the story of a boy, Jason, and his pet, a magical black cat named Gareth, whose powers enable the two to travel backward in time. They first visit ancient Egypt, where cats are worshipped as gods. Subsequently their journey takes them to the year 55 B.C., where they observe the war between Gaul and Rome, then to Ireland, where they meet the legendary Saint Patrick. The book's only Oriental episode takes place in eighth-century Japan, during the reign of the boy-emperor Ichigo. From there they go to fifteenth-century Italy, where they encounter and encourage Leonardo da Vinci, who is still a boy. Their next stop is Peru, under siege by the conquistadors, fol-

lowed by a short stay on the Isle of Man in the year 1588. One of the most harrowing adventures they face takes place in Germany during the time of the witch-hunts. Their last stop before returning to the present is colonial America, immediately prior to the Revolutionary War. These nine episodes provide an informative, if fanciful, introduction to history for young readers, and to the feline role in various time periods. The stark and scratchy illustrations by Bill Sokol complement and successfully reflect the mood of the text.

Alexander considers *Time Cat* "a fantasy perhaps more realistic than otherwise," explaining that "basically, only one fantastic premise moved the story," the power of Gareth to transport himself and the boy through time. This story is not one of a truly magical world where enchantment is commonplace, as the later imaginary Prydain would be, and time travel is partially disguised as a dream which Jason suspects, and hopes, may have actually been real. "*Time Cat* is as bald as a table when it comes to the conjuring of any magical atmosphere," Eleanor Cameron asserts in *The Green and Burning Tree: On the Writing and Enjoyment of Children's Books* (1962), but most critics agree that as a story of adventure and imagination, it is a success.

Time Cat, according to Stevie Smith in her review for *New Statesman*, "has the true-blue classic touch of success," but Miriam S. Mathes of *Library Journal* contends that "the episodic treatment fails to sustain excitement throughout." The book's historical subject matter pleased many critics, who see it as a "fresh, humorous insight into history," which presents a "good delineation of the character of the peoples living in the various historical periods" and "leaves the reader with some interesting reflections of human conduct."

The success of this book showed Alexander that he had finally found his place in the literary world. He found writing for children "the most creative and liberating experience of my life. In books for young people, I was able to express my own deepest feelings far more than I could ever do in writing for adults."

So far, Alexander's most important work has been the Prydain cycle, a series of five novels inspired by the Welsh Mabinogion. As originally planned, the novels were to be simple adaptations of these legends, a special interest for Alexander since he encountered them in his research for *Time Cat*. When he began to dig more deeply into the roots of Welsh mythology, however, the project "grew into something much more ambitious." He had "discovered that place which was, for him, the spiritual expression of something hidden." So, Prydain grew into something much more than a thinly disguised ancient Wales; undeniably, it was similar to that land, but reshaped by the addition of contemporary realism, modern values, and a generous dose of humor, as well as the special depth and insight provided by characters who not only act, but think, feel, and struggle with the same kinds of problems that confuse and trouble people in the twentieth century. In addition to human characters, the novels contain magical creatures both good and evil, including members of an ancient line of enchanters, the Sons of Don, who share the Earth with the human race.

The first novel of the series, *The Book of Three* (1964), is named after a legendary magical book which contains between its covers the wisdom of all time. It is the story of the orphan Taran, Assistant Pig-Keeper, who is bored with his peaceful life under the care of the farmer Coll and the old magician Dallben. He longs for adventure and the chance to perform heroic deeds and finds them sooner than he expects when the search for the runaway oracular pig, Hen Wen, draws him into a battle between good and evil. Taran's companions in his quest for the porcine fugitive are Gurgi, an unkempt creature who speaks in rhymes and whose loyalty compensates for his apparent cowardice; Eilonwy of the red-gold hair, sarcastic but practical heroine of the series; Fflewddur Fflam, a boastful king-turned-bard whose harp strings break whenever he strays from the truth; and the dwarf Doli, whose inability to turn himself invisible accounts for his cynical ill humor. Prince Gwydion, legendary warrior both in Prydain and in authentic Welsh tales, serves as an inspiration for the aspiring hero; though he is in captivity throughout most of the novel, his influence is a major contribution both to the plot and mood, as well as to the overall message of the story.

Evil is personified here by three major figures: the wicked enchantress Queen Achren of the Spiral Castle; King Arawn, the yet unseen death-lord who seeks to enslave all of Prydain; and Arawn's ally, the Horned King. Other antagonists include the gwythaints, once gentle birds, now under the power of Arawn, and the "Cauldron Born," dead men brought back to life as wraiths—soulless, indestructible, and able to do only evil.

From the outset of his adventures, Taran finds his naive notions of heroism, and heroes, proven false. Prince Gwydion, gray-haired and weathered, is hardly the great warrior he expected, and he is amazed to learn that the plump, balding

Coll had been a brave hero in his youth. Gurgi, whom Taran immediately despises and mistrusts, turns out to be a faithful friend and resourceful companion. Eilonwy, whom he first condescendingly dismisses as a "little girl," then accuses of treason, reveals herself as the most sensible among the companions. Taran's meeting with Medwyn, an ancient man resembling the biblical Noah, who rules over a peaceful valley populated by gentle animals, teaches him that "every living thing deserves our respect . . . , be it humble or proud, ugly or beautiful," and Taran's subsequent kindness to a wounded young gwythaint, against the protests of his companions, is repaid in kind much later when the creature aids Gwydion in the final rescue of Hen Wen.

Though the majority of critics responded to *The Book of Three* with high praise, calling it "an enchanting fantasy . . . peopled with an intriguing cast of characters" and finding it "completely convincing," the novel has its detractors as well. A reviewer for the *Junior Bookshelf* charged that "this sample fails to come up to expectations" and found the characters so "trivial . . . that the menace is rendered ineffectual by their reactions." Eilonwy is berated as "a most irritatingly girlish girl" and Fflewddur Fflam as a "petty king turned funny bard." The assertion that the novel is a "mixture of comic-book elements . . . with legendary elements" seems undeservedly harsh and overlooks the book's intended audience.

The second book of the series, *The Black Cauldron* (1965), chronicles the search for the cauldron which transforms slain bodies into the dreaded warrior-wraiths, the Cauldron Born. In addition to the companions who accompanied Taran in *The Book of Three*, two new major characters are introduced: Adaon, whose iron brooch enables the wearer to intuit events about to occur; and Prince Ellidyr, an arrogant and hostile youth whose obsession with obtaining "honor" drives him to behave most dishonorably. He and Taran immediately become rivals. Early in the quest, Adaon is slain by the Huntsmen of Annuvin—ghoulish servants of Arawn who travel in small groups and gain strength when one of their band is killed, but who weaken as they travel away from Annuvin—while saving Taran from certain death at their hands. The party finds the cauldron in the possession of three comical but frightening witches—Orwen, Orgoch, and Orddu—and Taran trades the enchanted brooch, Adaon's dying gift to him, for the cauldron. The witches reveal that there is only one way to destroy the cauldron: "A living person must climb into it . . . , willingly, knowing full well what he does," going on to say that "the poor duckling who climbs in will never climb out again alive." Stealing the cauldron and claiming the glory of discovering it, Ellidyr, nearly mad in his lust for honor, turns it over to King Mordant, one of the expedition's leaders, unaware that the king, overcome by greed, has defected to Arawn. When it seems that all the companions are doomed to become Cauldron Born, it is Ellidyr who redeems himself by leaping into the cauldron, thus destroying it and freeing the companions.

Here, in addition to the basic motif of the quest, Alexander adds two new themes. The first is that of sacrifice—illustrated first by Adaon, then by Taran, and finally and most dramatically by Ellidyr—and the idea that unselfishness is of equal or greater importance than prowess on the battlefield. A second new theme, the notion that most individuals are neither purely evil nor totally good and that these elements are a source of conflict within the individual, is exemplified by King Mordant's treachery and by Ellidyr's last-minute heroism.

Though the story is basically a serious one, *The Black Cauldron* has its share of comic relief. The three witches, who constantly bicker among themselves and take a humorous matter-of-fact attitude toward everything from what (or whom) to eat for their dinner to what kind of creature to turn their captives into, provide amusement for the reader, if not for the companions. The minor character Gwystyl, a gloomy hypochondriac dwarf who complains incessantly, and Kaw, a cocky talking crow, display human traits familiar to all readers.

Once again, critics were divided in their assessment of *The Black Cauldron*. Cameron complains of the abundance, "strangeness, and difficulty of the y-fraught names," and a reviewer for the *Times Literary Supplement* finds the "forced flippancy out of keeping with the main theme." On the other hand, *Horn Book*'s critic sees nothing offensive or inconsistent in Alexander's comic undertones: "The same kind of engagingly fantastic nonsense lightens this story as it did the first one."

One negative review in *Junior Bookshelf* questions the appropriateness of the "unkillable dehumanized" Cauldron Born, deeming their plight "not a subject to introduce lightly into a child's book," and adding, "once introduced it should be honestly and seriously dealt with." The implication that Alexander fails to do this is debatable: It is impossible to treat an imaginary subject with any form of honesty that would prove acceptable to all

readers, and the numerous grave speeches on the horror of the plight of the Cauldron Born and the inherent evil in the practice of creating them surrounds these characters with a seriousness that should satisfy even the staunchest moralist. Disapproval of the Cauldron Born is by no means unanimous among critics: Marion Carr, in her article *Classic Hero in a New Mythology*, found them appropriate to the tale, dubbing them "monsters of marvelous invention."

The Black Cauldron has been called "a wise and wonderful tale written in epic fashion" by *Booklist* and, conversely, "a thin, strained tale with no music in it at all" by the *Junior Bookshelf*. A third viewpoint is put forth by Margery Fisher in her review for *Growing Point*, who asserts that "there is always room for this kind of magical-heroic tale, even if this one does not reach the literary heights which have occasionally been claimed for it."

The Castle of Llyr (1966), the third of the Prydain series, opens with Eilonwy, a princess of Llyr, reluctantly preparing to travel to the Isle of Mona for training befitting her status under the supervision of King Rhuddlum and Queen Teleria. Taran has become very much aware of his tender feelings for the tomboy princess, and is distressed at her leaving. Accompanying her on her journey, Taran and Gurgi find Prince Gwydion in the guise of a shoemaker, Fflewddur Fflam residing in the palace stables, and a new villain, the Chief Steward Magg. To Taran's chagrin, he is faced with another rival, the foolish but good-natured Prince Rhun, whose parents intend for him to marry Eilonwy.

When Eilonwy mysteriously disappears, Taran, Fflewddur Fflam, Gurgi, and the hapless Prince Rhun set out to find her. Their adventures center around a giant cat, Llyan, who is charmed by Fflam's harp and becomes his faithful pet, and the proud giant Glew, whose experiments with potions are responsible for his extreme size and that of the huge feline. In Glew's possession they discover the long-lost book of spells belonging to the House of Llyr, but are not aware of its great power. The crow Kaw, who joins the band in mid search, is the one who finally locates the kidnapped princess, held prisoner on the island of Caer Colur, the ancient fortress of Llyr, by her old nemesis Achren. The companions find Eilonwy physically unharmed but, even more distressingly, she is bewitched, with no memory of her former life or of her friends. Through Eilonwy's powers as an enchantress, Achren and her accomplice Magg plan to overthrow Arawn and gain control of Prydain for themselves. When Achren forces Eilonwy to use the objects of power—the book of spells and the Golden Pelidryn (a luminous sphere which Eilonwy has played with all of her life, calling it her "bauble"), the castle shatters around them, and good once again triumphs over evil. The story ends with Eilonwy and Taran's farewell before the princess returns to the Isle of Mona to continue her education. Eilonwy vows that she will refuse to be married off to Prince Rhun, and presents Taran with an ancient silver battle horn, all that is left of Caer Colur, as a sign of her promise.

The Castle of Llyr is filled with adventure, leaving less opportunity for the kind of personal introspection Taran indulged in during the first two novels. Even so, as he approaches manhood and his feelings for Eilonwy mature into love, he continues to grow in bravery and inner strength. Despite the rivalry between Taran and Prince Rhun, and the advantage Rhun's death would afford him, the Assistant Pig-Keeper risks his own life repeatedly to protect and rescue the bumbling, trouble-prone prince. Although the comic elements in *The Castle of Llyr* are not as strong as those in the first two novels, there are some light moments. It is Rhun, with his cheerful calls of "Hullo, hullo," along with little Glew, who finally attains his wish to be a giant and is upset that nobody recognizes his new importance, that provide the humor in this tale.

In his introductory note to this novel, Alexander states that the story is intended to be "bittersweet rather than grandly heroic," but Ruth Hill Viguers, in a review for *Horn Book* magazine, credits it with reaching "dramatic heights." Margery Fisher, usually an Alexander advocate, dismisses *The Castle of Llyr* as "in the main padded and inflated but basically pedestrian," with "one or two exciting moments," but N. Danischersky points out in *Children's Book News* that although it can claim "neither the simplicity of *The Book of Three* nor the tremendous dramatic power of *The Black Cauldron,* . . . it has its own strong identity."

Taran Wanderer (1967) is the next installment in the series, and it signals a departure from the theme of heroism in the legendary sense. Once again, a quest is the story's main subject, but here Taran searches for *himself* instead of a runaway pig, a lost princess, or an enchanted cauldron. Accompanied by the ever-loyal Gurgi, Taran, desiring to prove himself worthy of a princess, wanders the land seeking to discover his hopefully noble ancestry. He first consults the three hags, Orwen, Orgoch, and Orddu, who recommend that he go to the Mirror of Llunet in the Llawgadarn Mountains.

As he journeys, he outwits a horse-thieving lord, is befriended by a simple farm couple and soon finds the opportunity to repay their kindness tenfold, and is offered reign over the kingdom of Cadiffor by King Smoit, his old friend from the search for the black cauldron. Tempted to accept Smoit's offer and attain noble status the easy way but determined to complete his quest, Taran refuses kingship and resumes his course, joined by Fflewddur Fflam and Kaw. Doli, the grumpy dwarf, makes an appearance here, in the form of a frog bewitched by the evil and power-hungry wizard Morda, whom Taran defeats by breaking the splinter of bone in which the sorcerer had hidden his life force, confident that it would be safe in that shape.

Taran's travels are halted temporarily when he meets a shepherd, Craddoc, whom he believes to be his father. While Taran remains with the old man, his companions, with the exception of Gurgi, scatter. Craddoc's death, his confession that he is not truly Taran's father as he had deliberately misled the boy to believe, and Taran's failure in his attempt to save the life of this man he has come to love leave him uninterested in what the Mirror of Llunet might have to tell him. Instead he chooses to seek his fortune among the common people of Prydain, spending some time with a fisherman's family, then apprenticing himself, in turn, to a metalsmith, a weaver, and a potter. Finding himself unsuited and untalented in each of these trades, he finally reaches the Mirror of Llunet and there discovers only what he would have eventually realized on his own had he only taken the time to think of it: "I saw myself as a man like any other. . . . Now I know who I am: myself and no other. I am Taran. . . . As for my parentage . . . , it makes little difference. True kinship has naught to do with blood ties . . . , life is . . . clay to be shaped, as raw clay on a potter's wheel." Thus Taran ends his quest, at peace with himself at last and ready to return to Caer Dallben to propose marriage to Eilonwy.

Taran Wanderer differs from its companion novels in several major aspects. It is a story with little magic and adventure, concentrating instead on an inward search, symbolized by Taran's wanderings through Prydain. Here, tragedy and self-realization replace the blend of comedy and derring-do found in the first three books. Humorous moments are downplayed. Though there are several armed confrontations, the heroic deeds in *Taran Wanderer* are, for the most part, undertaken not because of the necessity of the situation but as

Dust jacket for Alexander's Newbery Medal-winning novel that concludes the Prydain cycle (Holt, Rinehart & Winston)

a means of fulfilling an inner need to reach out to others as well as within the self, a need that stems not from heroic yearnings, but from merely human ones.

The absence of Eilonwy, though she is ever-present in Taran's thoughts and, in fact, the cause for his quest, adds more than it takes away from the novel, for despite the comings and goings of the companions, without her Taran is essentially alone. Even Gurgi, his most faithful friend who never leaves his side, cannot understand the need which drives his search, though he supports Taran in all his undertakings. Unlike the other three novels, which spare little time for mourning, the fourth tale of Prydain has a tragic strain which lingers, primarily in the pathos of Craddoc's life and death. Even so, independence and alienation ultimately merge in self-realization, which creates a satisfying conclusion to Taran's wanderings.

Critics received *Taran Wanderer* favorably, finding few flaws and great depth in what a reviewer for *Booklist* called "this poignant and spirited fourth chronicle of Prydain." Brian Attebery, au-

thor of *The Fantasy Tradition in American Literature: From Irving to LeGuin* (1980), sees Taran as "a hero in the American grain . . . , an experimenter, a seeker after an identity that always seems to lie over the next hill," who "finds his identity, as Americans have throughout our literary history, in the future rather than in the past." Attebery compares him with Nathaniel Hawthorne's Holgrave and Mark Twain's Huckleberry Finn. That Alexander achieves the "old-fashioned ideals of craftsmanship and its demands" and successfully presents the notion of honesty to oneself without being didactic or obvious is an outstanding accomplishment.

The conclusion of the Prydain cycle, *The High King* (1968), returns to the pattern of the earlier tales as Taran, along with the people of Prydain, unite to defeat Arawn. The plot is a complex account of numerous battles, betrayals, and alliances involving characters from all four of the earlier novels.

When Taran returns home to Caer Dallben after his wanderings, his plans to propose marriage to Eilonwy are forestalled by the news that Arawn

PRYDAIN PRONOUNCING GUIDE

Achren -- AHK-ren
Adaon — ah-DAY-on
Aeddan — EE-dan
Angharad — an-GAR-ad
Annuvin — ah-NOO-vin
Arawn — ah-RAWN
Arianllyn — ahree-AHN-lin
Briavel — bree-AH-vel
Brynach — BRIHN-ak
Caer Cadarn — kare KAH-darn
Caer Colur — kare KOH-loor
Caer Dathyl — kare DA-thil
Coll — kahl
Dallben — DAHL-ben
Doli — DOH-lee
Don — dahn
Dwyvach — DWIH-vak
Dyrnwyn — DUHRN-win
Edyrnion — eh-DIR-nyon
Eiddileg — eye-DILL-eg
Eilonwy — eye-LAHN-wee
Ellidyr — ELLI-deer
Fflewddur Fflam — FLEW-der flam
Geraint — GHER-aint
Goewin — GOH-win
Govannion — go-VAH-nyon
Gurgi — GHER-ghee
Gwydion — GWIH-dyon
Gwythaint — GWIH-thaint
Islimach — iss-LIM-ahk
Llawgadarn — law-GAD-arn
Lluagor — lew-AH-gore
Llunet — LOO-net
Llyan — lee-AHN
Llyr — leer
Melyngar -- MELLIN-gar
Melynlas — MELLIN-lass
Oeth-Anoeth — eth-AHN-eth
Orddu — OR-doo
Orgoch — OR-gahk
Orwen — OR-wen
Prydain — prih-DANE
Pryderi — prih-DAY-ree
Rhuddlum — ROOD-lum
Rhun — roon
Smoit — smoyt
Taliesin — tally-ESS-in
Taran — TAH-ran
Teleria — tell-EHR-ya

*Glossary from a promotional pamphlet for Alexander's Prydain
cycle (by permission of the author)*

has, by means of trickery, gained possession of the enchanted blade of power, Dyrnwyn. Hen Wen's prophecies of speaking stones, noon at night, and burning rivers raise doubts that the sword and Prydain's freedom will ever be regained. Despite her ominous forewarnings, Taran and his companions embark on a quest to recover the stolen sword.

Some old villains reappear: Queen Achren—humble and reformed and now a servant at Caer Dallben—and the twisted, ambitious Magg, who has seized control of Smoit's kingdom. Highlights of the novel include the rescue of Eilonwy and Gurgi by two wolves from Medwyn's hidden valley; the death of the traitorous King Pryderi when he attempts to steal the *Book of Three;* Eilonwy's magical fulfillment of Hen Wen's prophecies; the return of the gwythaint whose life Taran once saved to repay his kindness one last time; Gwydion's presentation of the recovered Dyrnwyn to Taran and the pronouncement that he is rightfully High King as revealed by the sword's inscription; and the final defeat of Arawn, who appears in the form of a serpent and is killed by Taran and Achren. In addition to the moments of triumph, there are sad ones as well: the death of Prince Rhun and of Coll, both killed in battle.

The defeat of Arawn signals the time for the Sons of Don to return to the Summer Country from where they came, a magical land of immortality "where all the heart's desires are granted." Taran declines to join them, feeling a responsibility to Prydain and its people, and chooses to spend his life helping to rebuild the land devastated by Arawn. Eilonwy gives up her powers as an enchantress in order to stay behind with Taran. In *The High King* "the many and devious threads of mystery are adroitly knitted together and there is a gratifying sense of resolution and fulfillment." This conclusion to the Prydain chronicles, which Lillian N. Gerhardt praises in the *School Library Journal* as "a tremendously satisfying finish to what was so well begun in *The Book of Three* four years ago," shows Prydain as no longer a land of magic but a world on the edge of a new age in which people must "guide their own destiny." Ruth Hill Viguers, in a review for *Horn Book,* credits it with being "more than a series of exciting adventures . . . , having the philosophical depths and overtones of great fantasy."

There is, of course, controversy among critics regarding the overall success of the Prydain series. Even so, *The Book of Three* was an American Library Association Notable Book, *The Black Cauldron* was a 1965 Newbery Honor Book, and *The High King* was winner of the Newbery Medal in 1969, as well as finalist for the National Book Award. Many scholars and critics, including Gerhardt, regard the chronicles of Prydain as among "the strongest fantasy written for children in our times." Houston L. Maples called it "a rich and varied tapestry of brooding evil, heroic action, and great natural beauty . . . , romantic in mood but curiously contemporary in its immediacy" in his review for *Book World.*

A major point of contention among critics is the humorous component in the novels. Maples finds Alexander's "weakness for opera bouffe comic relief . . . inconsistent with the eloquence and grandeur of the best episodes." A reviewer for *Junior Bookshelf* charges that "the jokes, especially those about the hero's status as Assistant Pig-Keeper and the similes with which his girl-friend ends practically *every* sentence, are too contrived." Other critics find his "enduring wit" and "the humor of the dialogue" a delightfully whimsical touch which relieves, although does not diminish, the seriousness of the conflicts. Marcus Crouch, author of *The Nesbit Tradition* (1972), considers it "important that there is also fun, a rare element which seldom manages to fight to the surface of the heroic fantasy."

The contemporary tone of the novels, especially in characterization and dialogue, is another subject on which critics and scholars disagree. Some feel that the "imperfect marriage of ancient and modern . . . creates an atmosphere of anachronism which works against credibility." Another contends that "the strength, and also, far too often, the weakness of these books is that Alexander's young hero and heroine are very much contemporary Americans." The flaw, they agree, is that Alexander overextends the modern tone. Although "the democratic exuberance of . . . Taran and Eilonwy breathes a new life into the old Welsh stories, Taran's soul-searching and Eilonwy's liberated motormouth," as well as the "obtrusively contemporary-colloquial" dialogue are seen by John Rowe Townsend, author of *Written for Children: An Outline of English Language Children's Literature* (1975), as too extreme to seem natural. Despite these judgments, many find the characterization quite effective and well done, especially in the cases of Taran and Eilonwy. It is important to keep in mind that the young audience for which the novels were written is unlikely to find this discrepancy offensive. Indeed, the contemporary tone of the work may provide a vehicle for introducing children to a body of ancient lore which would otherwise be uninteresting to a modern child.

The tales draw much of their power from Alexander's characterization of Eilonwy. Rather than wait and worry, as do many traditional, "cardboard" heroines, she is active from the moment that she rescues Taran in the first book of the series to her fulfillment of Hen Wen's prophecies and her sacrifice of her powers at the conclusion of *The High King.* Supporting characters, though initially considered tiresome and foolish by some critics, grow and develop as the chronicles progress. Alexander handles them wisely, rarely discarding characters, but saving them to be reintroduced in later episodes in his first two picture books, *Coll and His White Pig* (1965) and *The Truthful Harp* (1967), and in his first anthology, *The Foundling and Other Tales of Prydain* (1973). The Prydain novels, despite their flaws, constitute a rich and strong fantasy, well written, tightly woven, and "laden with symbolic relationships to Welsh and Celtic mythology, which adds to their power and beauty." The collateral production of picture books and the short story anthology reflect the success of the series, proving the marketability of Alexander's Prydain myth.

After completion of the Prydain series, comparisons between Alexander and J. R. R. Tolkien were inevitable. According to one scholar, "while Tolkien remains the master of the art of sub-creation, Alexander rivals him on an only slightly smaller scale—a scale intended for younger readers." Despite a "strong sense of time and place . . . there is not the historical and philosophical detail of Middle-Earth" in Prydain. Also absent are Tolkien's excessive and detailed descriptions of landscape, that retard the action of the *Lord of the Rings* and which would become tiresome to a young reader. Marshall B. Tymn, Kenneth J. Zahorski, and Robert H. Boyer contend in *Fantasy Literature: A Core Collection and Reference Guide* (1979) that Alexander outdoes Tolkien in that his battle scenes are described in length and detail, avoiding "gruesome butchery" but involving the reader more closely in the action.

Alexander has also been compared with Joan Aiken, Peter Sendal, Alan Garner, and perhaps most often, C. S. Lewis, whose Narnia series share with the Prydain books "a preoccupation with the nature of good and evil and the necessity of sacrifice."

Alexander followed the Prydain series with several less ambitious works, both novels for older children as well as short, simple fables for very young readers. Many of these return to the familiar setting of Prydain, either supplementing the mythology of this imaginary land or providing an introduction for children too young to read the five novels.

Coll and His White Pig (1965), Alexander's first picture book, relates the story of Hen Wen's kidnapping by Arawn and her rescue by warrior-turned farmer, Coll. Through his kindness to Ash-Wing the owl, Oak-Horn the stag, and Star-Nose the mole, whose languages he can understand after eating the Hazel Nuts of Wisdom, Coll has earned the help he needs to free Hen Wen and escape Arawn. Upon his return home, he finds the enchanter Dallben, who had come to warn him of Arawn's plans to abduct Hen Wen but arrived too late. Foreshadowing the arrival of Taran and the events that take place in the Prydain series, Dallben remains with Coll and Hen Wen, and Coll concludes that "it is better raising things up than smiting things down." The earthy illustrations by Eveline Ness combine with a story both simple and skillful to provide an exciting "glimpse into the mythical land" of Prydain.

Another picture book, *The Truthful Harp* (1967), also illustrated by Ness, does for Fflewddur Fflam what *Coll and His White Pig* did for Coll and Hen Wen. Fflam, ruler of a tiny kingdom, longs to be a bard and wander the countryside leading a life full of music and adventure. Although Fflewddur fails miserably before the Council of Bards, the Chief Bard makes him a gift of a beautiful harp and sends him on his way. In his travels, Fflam gives away his coat to a poor old man, rescues a child from drowning, and defends an arrogant and abusive lord from bandits. Throughout his adventures, he is chagrined to find that his harp strings constantly break. When he returns the instrument to the Chief Bard, Fflewddur realizes that it is only when he alters the truth that the strings snap. By the end, his lesson is learned: that deeds of kindness are nobler than fantasies of grandeur and true heroism is found in the day-to-day actions of regular individuals, not on a battlefield.

Critics praised *The Truthful Harp*, with its "sly but innocently smiling prose," and pronounced its message a valuable one for both children and adults. Fflewddur Fflam, despite, or perhaps due to, harmless embroidering of the truth, is a likable character with a good heart. Through him, Alexander reiterates his message that true courage and wisdom are not heroism in the legendary sense, but are gained through selflessness and concern for others. The illustrations are not as richly colored or vibrant as those for *Coll and His White Pig*, but the more subdued style is better suited to the subtle tone of *The Truthful Harp*. The spiky drawings of Fflewddur Fflam are similar in appearance to Alexander himself.

Another tale of fantasy and adventure is *The Marvelous Misadventures of Sebastian* (1970), a tongue-in-cheek account of the wanderings of a bumbling young man who has been fired from his position as fiddler in a nobleman's orchestra. In the world outside the baron's estate, an oppressive ruler, Regent Grinssorg, tyrannizes the land. Se-bastian takes up with a runaway princess intent on escaping marriage to the tyrant, a wise white cat, and a leader of the resistance group opposing the Regent. The story's turning point pivots on the acquisition of an enchanted violin which "produces music of unearthly beauty and power" and helps Sebastian determine his future. *The Marvelous Misadventures of Sebastian* closes with the regent dethroned, the princess reinstated, and Sebastian beginning a quest to prove himself worthy of her love, much like Taran's search to discover whether he deserves Eilonwy's hand.

For Alexander, an amateur violinist who plays with a local Sunday afternoon quartet, *The Marvelous Misadventures of Sebastian* is a "very personal book." To him, aside from being a lighthearted tale of enchantment, the book explores the importance of art in artists' lives and the dedication necessary to pursue an artistic goal.

Several reviewers charged that the characters in *The Marvelous Misadventures of Sebastian* were stereotypical, but also agreed that despite this, Alexander makes them amusing and likable. The story's success, however, is due to the lively adventure, twists in the action, and the whimsical style. This book won the National Book Award in 1971. It has been produced, in serial form, for Japanese television.

The King's Fountain (1971), an illustrated fable about a king who intends to build a fountain which would deprive the surrounding areas of water, is filled with simple wisdom. Though the strong man with his muscles, the scholar with his learning, and the "silver-tongued" merchant fail to confront the king with a plea not to build the fountain, this deed is accomplished by a poor man whose concern for his family and fellows gives him the courage to face the king. The king recognizes the man's wisdom, eloquence, and brave heart and agrees to his request.

Ezra Jack Keats's acrylic illustrations supplement the lyrical text. His "rich painterly style" has been criticized as being "altogether too heavy" for Alexander's tale, but this judgment is by no means unanimous. Its lushness provides an effective contrast to the simplicity of Alexander's lyrical tone, and many find the shadowy textured paintings appropriate to the gravity of the story's theme. Stylistically, *The King's Fountain* has been praised for its poetic style, with suggestions that it be read aloud, and for the ease with which it unobtrusively states its message.

Another picture book, *The Four Donkeys* (1972), relates the story of a baker, a tailor, and a cobbler who set out for the market to sell their wares. From the outset their hindrances are many, beginning with the Baker's torn jacket, grudgingly mended by the Tailor; the Tailor's sore feet, which he blames on the Shoemaker; and the Shoemaker's early start, which tires him so that he has to stop for a nap. When the Baker, after a second breakfast, gets underway, the Tailor and the Shoemaker convince him to carry them and their loads on his wagon. As they insultingly quibble over how much the Baker should be paid for this service, the donkey, overcome with exhaustion after pulling so heavy a load, sits down in the road unable to go on. Finally, the three men haul the donkey into town, only to find that the marketplace is empty—everyone has gone home.

The Four Donkeys is a sly and humorous fable. The human characters exhibit a wide range of less than noble traits including greed, bad temper, selfishness, vanity, pride, and egocentrism. It is not difficult for even the youngest readers to recognize the four donkeys of the tale's title. Lavishly illustrated in the style of the nineteenth century by Lester Abrams, the book is enhanced by colorful, ornate, and humorous depictions of the foolish tradesmen both at home and on the road.

In the lighthearted and high-spirited *The Cat Who Wished to Be a Man* (1973), a wizard's cat, Lionel, wishes to become a man in order to discover the nature of humanity. Despite the wizard's warning that he will find nothing but wickedness, he grants the cat's wish, and Lionel, now a man, sets out to Brightford. There he finds not only greed and corruption but nobler traits as well: independence and fortitude in the innkeeper Gillian whose business is in danger of a takeover by the tyrannical Mayor Pursewig; and kindness and honesty in Dr. Tudbelly, a Latin scholar. By the end of the story, Lionel realizes that he loves Gillian and wishes to remain human. The wizard's attempt to turn him back into a cat against his will fails, and Lionel keeps his humanity.

Reviewers were mostly positive, but June Goodwin considered *The Cat Who Wished to Be a Man* "slightly pretentious—trying too hard to be a fantasy—and fails to hold the reader's interest." Others see the novel as compassionate and humorous, with a message that is understated in its profundity: "people can be corrupt and mean, but . . . it's wonderful to be a person after all." An adaptation of this novel has been performed on the stage in Tokyo.

The Foundling and Other Tales of Prydain (1973) is Alexander's first anthology. Readers of the Pry-

dain series will recognize many characters who were only briefly mentioned in passing in the five novels, as well as some major figures. These eight tales, which "enlarge upon and explain 'certain threads left unraveled in the longer weaving,' " are also independent stories, with strong messages about human nature. In addition to the previously published *Coll and His White Pig* and *The Truthful Harp*, there are six new stories. "The Foundling," the title piece, tells of how the young Dallben, an orphan, was found and taken in by the three enchantresses (Orddu, Orwen, and Orgoch), how he attained his wisdom by accidentally sucking a magic potion from his burnt finger, and how he acquired *The Book of Three*. In "The Stone," a poor farmer soon comes to grief when a trapped dwarf he frees from a fallen log reluctantly complies with his demand for eternal youth. "The True Enchanter" tells of how one of Eilonwy's foremothers recognized the real magic in the words of a bard and chose him for her husband. Kadwy, the title character in "The Rascal Crow," changes his attitude when the other forest animals, whom he ridicules and harasses, join efforts to save him from a hunter. "The Sword" is the story of the enchanted blade Drynwyn, its power-hungry owner Rhitta, its bloody history, and how it came to be buried in the dungeons of the Spiral Castle. In "The Smith, the Weaver and the Harper," all but the harper succumb to greed and are thus tricked out of their livelihoods by Arawn.

The Foundling and Other Tales of Prydain was received positively by reviewers, whose only complaint was that Alexander offered only eight stories in this collection ("It's awfully slight," lamented one critic). Alexander's understated satire and valuable, if sometimes obvious, morals are conveyed easily and effectively in his usual simple and engaging fashion.

Set in the days of an industrial revolution in a land not too different from our own, *The Wizard in the Tree* (1975) features the feisty orphaned scullery maid, Mallory, and Arbican, an even feistier wizard whom she rescues from entrapment in an old tree stump. Eager to make his way to Vale Innis, home of magic folk, Arbican is hampered by his malfunctioning powers and despairs when he recalls an old incantation: "To gain all power lost of old, a maid must give a circle of gold." To compound the displaced wizard's problems, the evil Squire Scrupnor, former assistant to the previous Squire, who has killed his predecessor and plans to exploit the town by establishing and operating a coal mine, shrewdly names Arbican as the previous squire's murderer. Complications arise continuously as Arbican, aided by Mallory, attempts to elude Scrupnor. A colorful variety of characters—the shrewish and greedy Mrs. Parsel and her basically good but easily intimidated husband, the honest and levelheaded notary Rowan, the stupid and antagonistic gamekeeper Bolt, and numerous grasping neighbors both help and hinder the fugitive. When they are finally captured by Scrupnor and are at his mercy, the gold ring the Squire took from the hand of his victim ironically provides the "circle of gold" needed to restore Arbican's powers. After destroying the evil squire, Arbican disappears, leaving Mallory to claim the dead man's estate as reward for discovering the murderer. After appearing for a brief farewell, the wizard sails for Vale Innis.

The critical response to *The Wizard in the Tree* was overwhelmingly good. Reviewers praised its "quick-witted melodrama and nimble-tongued romanticism" and its "quotable bits of wisdom about the real nature of wisdom." Like *The Cat Who Wished to Be a Man*, *The Wizard in the Tree* has been dramatized on the stage in Tokyo.

Drawings by Laszlo Kubinyi illustrate some of the book's most exciting and humorous scenes, such as Mallory kicking the unsavory Bolt, and Arbican, in the form of a stag, carrying Mallory on his back. Kubinyi's depictions of the characters' faces enhance Alexander's descriptions of their personalities, especially in the cases of the less virtuous ones.

The Town Cats and Other Tales (1977), Alexander's second anthology, is a collection of stories about remarkable cats, all creative and clever. Pescato, the wisest cat in Valdoro, saves the town from a greedy official by having the townspeople behave as cats and the cats as people; Quickset tricks a stingy grocer into stocking his mistress's pantry free of charge; Baraka, cat of the Shaipur Bazaar, plays chess with a spoiled king and teaches him the meaning of the word "no"; a cobbler's cat shows his master the folly of vanity; a painter's cat reveals the true nature of three egomaniacs; the feline Master of Revels, Baron Sternbraue, helps a fiddler win the hand of a princess; a sympathetic cat named Margot helps thwart a tyrannical king; and Witling, the apprentice cat, after failing miserably at several trades, learns that the best trade of all for him is being "a master at being a cat."

These "eight fanciful, sparkling fairy tales" resemble folklore, and their settings include Russian towns and Oriental palaces as well as antiquated European villages. Both sly and sensible,

the feline characters always seem to be several steps ahead of their human companions and use their talents to help the honest and thwart the greedy, the unkind, and the proud. Alexander has a genius for portraying cats, and one reviewer for the *Kirkus Review* has described him as "a light-footed master of graceful entertainment." Sara Miller, in her review for *School Library Journal*, called the collection "an enjoyable grouping, slyly humorous and treated lightly."

Laszlo Kubinyi, who also illustrated these stories, used his own two cats as models and "placed a lot of importance on capturing the period and time of each story visually, and in a way I think adds to the humor of it."

The First Two Lives of Lukas-Kasha (1978) begins with a young man, Lukas, putting his face in a dish of water as part of a magic act, only to find himself washed up on a river bank, mysteriously transported to the Oriental kingdom of Abadan. There, he is mistaken for Kasha, a prophesied king, and finds his new role as sultan troublesome and distressing: he is surrounded by fawning courtiers and treacherous advisors, and his life is ruled by the Court Astrologer. The pacifist Lukas finds his kingdom's war with a neighboring country for control of the ore-laden Mountains of Ramayan even more disturbing, and, realizing how little power he has as king, sets out to right matters in his own way. In league with a runaway slave girl, Nur-Jehan, who turns out to be the enemy queen, and Kayim, a rogue poet, Lukas embarks on a search for the famed Bishangari King Ardashir, whom Lukas respects greatly as a military genius. It is only after a series of adventures, including capture by Shugdad, his own evil Grand Vizier, that he learns that Ardashir has been dead for years and that it is Nur-Jehan who has been commanding the Bishangari troops. Unfortunately, soon after Lukas finishes reforming the harsh laws of the now peaceful Abadan, he slips on a rock by the river and lifts his head from the magician's bowl of water. Unsatisfied with his past life as a ne'er-do-well, he takes to the road to begin a new life as a storyteller.

Though most critics hailed *The First Two Lives of Lukas-Kasha* as "not another book but a work of art" and as "Alexander's peak performance," its acceptance was not unanimous. While most reviewers found plot, characterization, and delivery top quality, praising variously the "hilarity, delightful wit, lively dialogue," and "sly observations," Barbara Wersba, in her review for the *New York Times Book Review*, considered it "clichéd, tedious, . . . tiresome," and "less than satisfying," especially in light of Alexander's past accomplishments. Even so, *The First Two Lives of Lukas-Kasha* was nominated for the American Book Award in 1980 and received high honors in the Netherlands, winning the "Silver Slate-Pencil" prize.

Alexander's recent work, the Westmark trilogy, contains many components that will be familiar to readers of his previous books: orphans, journeys, traveling showmen, feisty dwarves, and, of course, evil antagonists. Unlike Alexander's earlier tales, however, these are not fantasy; although Westmark, the land for which the series is named, is an imaginary place which seems to be a cross between colonial America and feudal Europe, there is no enchantment there.

In the first novel of the three, simply called *Westmark* (1981), the land's rightful ruler, King Augustine, has been ill with grief for years over the loss of his daughter, the supposedly dead Princess Augusta. In his misery, he has lost interest in his kingdom, allowing the wicked minister Cabbarus to rule unchecked. Even so, Cabbarus plots to have the king name him heir to the throne.

As *Westmark* opens, the orphan Theo, a printer's devil, has accidentally killed a royal officer during a raid on his master's shop by government agents acting in accordance with Cabbarus's censorship laws. Fleeing for his life, he meets up with an itinerant charlatan, Dr. Absalom, also known as Count Bombas, and his cocky servant, the dwarf Musket. The troupe journeys the countryside, selling elixirs and staging carnival acts, and they are soon joined by a fourth member, Mickle, an amnesiac urchin with numerous theatrical talents. She and Theo become friends immediately, and their relationship, like that of Taran and Eilonwy in the Prydain series, is a mixture of bickering antagonisms and romantic yearnings. Despite his growing fondness for the girl, the inherent dishonesty of his new profession disturbs Theo and his integrity forces him to abandon the troupe. He then falls in with a group of revolutionaries led by Florian, an outspoken and subversive young man who seems to be surrounded by a mysterious immunity to the power of the local authorities. Theo is given the job of printer, along with a clandestine press to operate. In a combination rescue attempt and riot in a nearby town, Theo is reunited with Bombas's band, and the party makes the acquaintance of the exiled Dr. Torrens, once royal physician, and Keller, a journalist whose satirical writings against the government have made him an outlaw as well.

Apparently safe, all go their separate ways; however, a sketch of Mickle drawn by Theo, as well as the girl's performance as an oracle in the traveling show are brought to Cabbarus's attention. Seeing an opportunity to use Mickle's resemblance to the lost princess, he orders Bombas's troupe brought to him and commands a performance in which Mickle, in the role of Augusta's ghost, will advise her father to name Cabbarus heir to his kingdom. The plan fails when Mickle falls into a genuine trance and, subconsciously using her ventriloquistic skills, reenacts Cabbarus's attempt to murder her. The book ends with Mickle reinstated, King Augustine recovered, Cabbarus exiled, and all those wronged by the tyrant pardoned.

There are implications that Mickle and Theo will eventually marry, and Dr. Torrens, newly installed as chief minister, suggests that Theo prepare himself for the role of prince with a fact-finding tour of Westmark. However, Theo is still unable to find peace with himself. Difficult questions have been raised in him: whether killing is acceptable in defense of a friend, or of a belief, and whether monarchy is a fair political system, or, as his friend Florian believes, must be overturned so that the people can rule themselves.

One critic, after reading *Westmark*, proclaimed Lloyd Alexander "a bard who has traveled the roads of many kingdoms, perfecting the act of storytelling and becoming evermore wise in the ways of humankind." Another judged the novel as his "most inventive book in many years." *Westmark* has been cited for its adroitly controlled complex plot, which often delves into the wide gray areas between good and evil; its layers of meaning; its realistic characterization; and the interplay of "carefully built tension and subtly added comic relief." Alexander's much quoted dedication to *Westmark*, "For those who regret their many imperfections, but know it would be worse having none at all," reiterates his running theme that "good does not triumph over evil simply because it is good" and that individuals cannot be perfect, or totally good, but can only try to do what is best.

The Kestrel (1982), the second novel of the Westmark series, begins as an assassination attempt is made on Theo by Cabbarus's spy Skeit. Rescued by his old friend Florian, Theo finds himself becoming involved in defending Westmark against a surprise war waged by the neighboring Regians. The plot of *The Kestrel*—no doubt influenced by Alexander's involvement in military intelligence in World War II—is complex, full of political intrigue, military tactics, espionage, disguised persons, and hidden pasts. Alexander introduces the young wimpish king of Regia, Constantine, and his evil uncle, Conrad, who is plotting with the disgruntled nobles of Westmark and the banished Cabbarus to overthrow the Beggar Queen (the name given Mickle by her people). Mickle, in the meantime, has struck out with Bombas and Musket disguised as a traveling student, teacher, and servant, to locate the missing Theo. Caught in the middle of a Regian attack, she reveals herself, takes command of her armies, and leads the troops in battle. Plot and counterplot unfold as the war rages on. The action shifts from Theo, now known as the bloodthirsty Kestrel in Florian's guerilla army, to Mickle's command of Westmark's army, to the scheming Conrad and his young, not-too-swift nephew. Disguised as a Regian soldier, Mickle accidentally meets King Constantine (Connie) and the two informally negotiate a treaty and end the war. As this segment in the chronicles of Westmark closes, a consulate is formed, leaving Mickle titular head of state, with Florian, his second-in-command Justin, and Theo as the three consuls. Although reunited, Mickle and Theo must postpone their marriage due to the demands of Theo's new position. Once more, all seems to be well in Westmark.

The Kestrel, though it continues the story begun in *Westmark,* takes on a different tone than the previous novel. Animal imagery, especially that of birds, fish, and small mammals, adds meaning as well as color to the story. Clever conversation and humorous description are present, but *The Kestrel* has few lighthearted moments. Theo's conscience suffers further turmoil: his active involvement in the war shows him that he is not the pacifist he once believed himself to be and teaches him that noble goals cannot be achieved without pain and death. His anger and hatred toward the enemy lead him to kill hundreds, despite his inherent pacifism and belief in the good of mankind. The realization that what should be and what is are often in conflict troubles him deeply, as does his conflicting loyalties to Florian, to whom he owes his life, and Mickle, whom he loves above all others.

While the second installment of the Westmark series was well received by critics, Georgess McHargue, reviewing for the *New York Times Book Review,* felt that *The Kestrel* "loses vitality because Lloyd Alexander seems determined to make issues come before character, language, atmosphere or even emotion," and that "the hand of the puppeteer is a little too much in evidence here." Others seemed to agree that though *The Kestrel* deals with increasingly ambiguous, deeper issues and is "more realistic," "more complex and slightly less nimble" than *Westmark,* it is "ultimately no less satisfying."

The work is bound to be troubling, for Alexander proposes a paradox in exploring the confusing demands often made upon the human conscience in times of political upheaval, while once again blasting the "heroics of war" and the equation of power with glory.

In the final novel of the Westmark trilogy, *The Beggar Queen* (1984), the newly established consulate finds itself forcibly disbanded at the hands of Mickle's nemesis, Cabbarus, who, with the help of the treacherous Conrad of Regia and military aid from the Sultanate of Ankar, establishes a directorate in its place, with himself at its head. The Beggar Queen and her allies go underground and form a resistance faction. A plot as circuitous as that of *The Kestrel* takes the deposed consuls and their supporters to the underworld of Westmark, through numerous attacks by and against Cabbarus's once again tyrannical regime.

This novel shows that Westmark is, indeed, a small world. Old friends, as well as old enemies, become involved in the complex scheme of events: the shady pawnbroker, Ingo, who remembers Mickle from her days as an apprentice thief, helps hide the party; Constable Pohn, who allowed Theo to escape years before after his accidental murder of a royal officer, aids him once more by helping him break out of prison; Keller's old companions, "the water rats," Sparrow and Weasel, join wholeheartedly in the cause; and the despicable spy and assassin Skeit unwittingly saves the day in the end by killing Cabbarus in a rage after being cheated by the dictator. The masses, sick of their brutal treatment at the hands of Cabbarus's Ankari mercenaries, rise to help crush the tyrant's forces and are left to form their own government, with Florian and his followers as their advisers. Theo and Mickle, now married, follow the wisdom of statecraft and go into self-imposed exile. United once and for all, the two leave Westmark to fend for itself and set out to see the world, accompanied by their old friends Bombas and Musket.

With an ending similar to that of the Prydain cycle, the *Westmark* series leaves an old world behind and ushers in a new era in which people must undertake both the privilege and responsibility of making fair and practical decisions about the way they will rule themselves.

Like the first two books of this series, *The Beggar Queen* benefits from colorful realistic characters, subtle irony, and sly wit, in addition to a brilliantly constructed, weblike plot. Though in this novel, and *The Kestrel* as well, the battle scenes and circuitous threads of war logistics may become con-

Dust jacket for The Illyrian Adventure, *which, Alexander says, "has something to do with history being transformed into mythology" (Dutton)*

fusing, the fast-paced plot and continuous action move the story quickly to its neat and satisfying climax.

Alexander's latest offering, *The Illyrian Adventure* (1986), is similar to the Westmark trilogy in its realism as well as its political theme. Set in the late nineteenth century, this adventure focuses on the miniscule nation of Illyria and its century-old political turmoil between the original Illyrians and their conquerors, the Zentans. The tale follows the exploits of Professor Brinton Garrett ("Brinnie") and his late colleague's orphaned daughter, Vesper Holly, a roguish sixteen-year-old, as they visit Illyria to prove Professor Holly's theory that the *Illyriad*, the single epic to have come from the tiny nation, was indeed a true account rather than the legend it was believed to be. Soon after their arrival,

Vesper's distress over the oppression of the Illyrians by the Zentans makes her even more determined to uncover the double mystery of the *Illyriad*: the fabled magical warriors and the disappearance of the treasure sent by the twelfth-century Illyrian king Vartan to the Zentan ruler Ahmad in thanks for sparing his life in battle. Despite an attempt made on Vesper's life, she, accompanied by the skeptical and unwilling Brinnie and their seemingly inept Illyrian guide, Nilo, journeys to Mount Albor and the legendary fortress of Vartan. Their progress is slowed but never stopped by a multitude of villains—the evil vizier Ergon Pasha, right-hand man to the young naive King Osman; Dr. Helvitius, a rival scholar; the evasive bureaucrat Colonel Zalik; and the oppressive Zentan army. Falling in with Illyrian rebels, led by the mysterious Nilo, they become involved in the civil unrest that pervades the country, dividing their time between hiding out with the revolutionaries and traveling through the dangerous countryside, constantly patrolled by Zentan troops. Despite these setbacks, they reach their destination, Vartan's Castle, and discover the lost treasure of Vartan, an ancient set of chessmen which time and embellishment have transformed into a mechanical army. After a final showdown with Helvitius, who, in league with Ergon Pasha, plans to murder the oblivious King Osman and assume a tyrannical reign over Illyria, Vesper, Brinnie, and Nilo escape with the chess piece representing King Ahmad and manage to arrive at the palace just in time to warn Osman of the plot against him. When the excitement is over, Vesper, with the help of an ancient peace treaty secreted in the arm of the chessman, persuades Osman and Nilo to honor the wishes of their predecessors and work together to unite the opposing factions of Illyria into a peaceful kingdom.

Thematically and stylistically similar to the Prydain cycle, Alexander's last four books go a step beyond in that there are no magical solutions, only human ones. Geared toward a young adult audience, the books of the Westmark trilogy and *The Illyrian Adventure* are among the few political novels for young people and provide a stimulating look into the complexities of government and the difficulties of establishing a satisfactory system that is just and workable.

Recognized as an authority on children's literature, Alexander has served on numerous boards and committees, including the Library Committee of *World Book Encyclopedia* (1974) and the Friends of the International Board on Books for Young People board of directors (1982). He was author

Alexander -- 98.

The shouts swelled in a furious tide. What had begun as a ~~harmless, rather~~ charming, rustic ritual was (rapidly turning) into something other: if not outright insurrection, certainly open defiance ~~of Zentan authority~~. Had the villagers ~~all~~ gone mad? Did they suppose the Zentans would wink at this rebelliousness?

As it turned out, the police did not intend to wink ~~at such~~ ~~behavior~~. ~~such~~ Colonel Zalik must have foreseen what would happen ~~for,~~ In addition to ~~the~~ constables and troopers, a large portion of his cavalry had been stationed in reserve at the edge of the village. These horsemen came galloping toward the crowd.

The constables, at the same time, drove like a wedge through the mass of onlookers. The villagers, surely, would ~~have to~~ break and fall back. Then I realized ~~that~~ they were, instead, rashly going to make a fight ~~of it~~. The twelve dancers had banded together, fending off the onslaught with their assorted pageant implements. Here and there, knots of Illyrians engaged the troops with ~~whatever~~ makeshift weapons chairs and tables ~~available~~, including ~~broken chairs and legs~~ from the <u>kaffenion</u>.

Vesper and I, by weight of numbers, had been ~~pressed~~ flung closer to the bonfire. I feared ~~that~~, from one moment to the next, that we might ~~would~~ end up in the midst of the flames. I cast around for some escape route; but now a number of the officers had begun seizing whatever Illyrians they could lay hands on ~~and were dragging from~~ ~~away from the square~~

As the officers set upon us, I endeavored to explain that we were ~~simply two~~ bystanders, innocent <u>farenkis</u> on a scholarly expedition.

Page from a draft for The Illyrian Adventure

in residence at Temple University from 1970 to 1974. Presently, he is a member of the editorial board for *Cricket* magazine. His other affiliations include the Philadelphia Children's Reading Round Table and Amnesty International.

In addition to his role as a creative writer, Alexander has gained a reputation as a commentator on the theory of fantasy, inspiration, and writing for children. His articles on these subjects have appeared, most notably, in the *Horn Book* magazine. The best known and most often reprinted of these is "The Flat-Heeled Muse," in which Alexander explores the conflicts that beset the writer between initial inspiration and the actual setting down of words. Most problematic are the practical considerations, such as consistency of plot and the challenge of creating believable characters who encounter believable situations. Alexander concludes that "the less fantastic it is, the stronger fantasy becomes," and because of this "writers of fantasy must be, within their own frame of work, hard-headed realists." In a 1968 article, "Wishful Thinking—Or Hopeful Dreaming?," Alexander discusses the role of fantasy in our increasingly technological world, finding it to be "an essential part of a balanced diet, not only for children but for adults, too." "High Fantasy and Heroic Romance" is a reflection on the basic, unchanging nature of literature. Alexander maintains that "the same questions that preoccupied the ancient Greeks preoccupy us today" and that the writer "must find the essential content of his work within himself." Fantasy, or heroic romance, has always exemplified on a symbolic level the human race's attempt to realize its full potential, to "measure up to the dream" of a better future.

About his career, Alexander says, "writing realism or fantasy, my concerns are the same: how we learn to become genuine human beings."

References:

Brian Attebery, *The Fantasy Tradition in American Literature: From Irving to LeGuin* (Bloomington: Indiana University Press, 1980);

Eleanor Cameron, *The Green and Burning Tree: On the Writing and Enjoyment of Children's Books* (Boston: Atlantic/Little, Brown, 1962);

Marcus Crouch, *The Nesbit Tradition: The Children's Novel in England 1945-1970* (Totowa, N.J.: Rowman and Littlefield, 1972), pp. 125-126;

John Rowe Townsend, *Written for Children: An Outline of English Language Children's Literature* (Philadelphia: Lippincott, 1975), p. 316;

Marshall B. Tymn, Kenneth J. Zahorski, and Robert H. Boyer, *Fantasy Literature: A Core Collection and Reference Guide* (New York: Bowker, 1979), pp. 39-198.

Natalie Babbitt

(28 July 1932-   )

Anita Moss

University of North Carolina at Charlotte

BOOKS: *Dick Foote and the Shark* (New York: Farrar, Straus & Giroux, 1967);

Phoebe's Revolt (New York: Farrar, Straus & Giroux, 1968);

The Search for Delicious (New York: Farrar, Straus & Giroux, 1969; London: Chatto & Windus, 1975);

Kneeknock Rise (New York: Farrar, Straus & Giroux, 1970);

The Something (New York: Farrar, Straus & Giroux, 1970);

Goody Hall (New York: Farrar, Straus & Giroux, 1970);

The Devil's Storybook (New York: Farrar, Straus & Giroux, 1974; London: Chatto & Windus, 1977);

Tuck Everlasting (New York: Farrar, Straus & Giroux, 1975; London: Chatto & Windus, 1977);

The Eyes of the Amaryllis (New York: Farrar, Straus & Giroux, 1977);

Herbert Rowbarge (New York: Farrar, Straus & Giroux, 1982).

BOOKS ILLUSTRATED: Samuel F. Babbitt, *The Forty-Ninth Magician* (New York: Pantheon, 1966; Leicester: Brockhampton, 1968);

Valerie Worth, *Small Poems* (New York: Farrar, Straus & Giroux, 1972);

Worth, *More Small Poems* (New York: Farrar, Straus & Giroux, 1976);

Worth, *Still More Small Poems* (New York: Farrar, Straus & Giroux, 1978);

Worth, *Curlicues: The Fortunes of Two Pug Dogs* (New York: Farrar, Straus & Giroux, 1980).

PERIODICAL PUBLICATIONS: "Between Innocence and Maturity," *Horn Book*, 48 (February 1972): 33-37;

"Happy Endings? Of Course, and Also Joy," in *Children and Literature: Views and Reviews*, edited by Virginia Haviland (Glenview, Ill.: Scott, Foresman, 1973);

"The Great American Novel for Children—And Why Not?," *Horn Book*, 50 (April 1974): 176-185.

Natalie Babbitt

The younger daughter of Ralph Zane and Genevieve Converse Moore, Natalie Zane Moore Babbitt was born on 28 July 1932, in the midst of the Great Depression, and spent the first eighteen years of her life in various towns and communities in Ohio. Though her family suffered economic setbacks during her childhood, she remembers that her parents nevertheless managed to provide a secure and pleasant home for their two daughters. Babbitt has remarked that her mother's early influence was especially important. Although she had been one of the new women of the 1920s, had earned a college degree, and showed promise as a painter, her mother had surrendered her ambitions in the interest of her children. She saw to it that Natalie's imagination and artistic talents were encouraged. While her mother read aloud such children's classics as Charles Kingsley's *The Water-Babies* (1863), which Babbitt detested, and Booth Tarkington's *Penrod* (1914), Babbitt voraciously read myths and fairy tales herself. These stories have clearly exerted a lasting impact upon her imagination, and their powerful influence resonates in the pages of her books.

Originally Babbitt wanted to be an illustrator of children's books rather than a writer. Her secondary school teachers had encouraged her to practice and to polish her skill in drawing at the Laurel School for Girls in Cleveland, and she eventually majored in art at Smith College in Northampton, Massachusetts. After graduation she married Samuel Fisher Babbitt on 26 June 1954. Babbitt's husband spent his early career as a professor of American literature and an administrator at Yale and Vanderbilt and later became president of Kirkland College, the women's division of Hamilton College, in Clinton, New York. For the first ten years of her married life Babbitt was engaged in rearing her three children—Christopher Converse, Thomas Collier II, and Lucy Cullyford—as well as meeting the demanding social obligations which attend the wife of a college administrator.

Fulfilling a long-standing ambition, Natalie Babbitt first entered the field of children's literature as illustrator of *The Forty-Ninth Magician* (1966), an amusing picture book by her husband. In this lighthearted tale, a young king promises to care for all the sons and grandsons of the elderly court magician, to whom the monarch is intensely devoted. The promise turns out to be a rash one, since the magician had seven sons, who each had seven sons, for a total of forty-nine. The king's efforts to restore order to the subsequent chaos make for a pleasantly humorous story. Babbitt illustrated the story in comical black-and-white drawings, which would become her characteristic style. The book was generally well received by readers and reviewers, but, after the couple moved to Clinton, New York, Samuel Babbitt's duties as a college president forced him to give up writing. At that point Babbitt began to write as well as illustrate her own books and soon began to regard writing as the more vital dimension of her creative talent.

Her husband has served as vice-president of Memorial Sloan-Kettering Cancer Center in New York City and currently holds an administrative position in Providence, Rhode Island, where the Babbitts have lived since 1984. They enjoy spending as much time as possible on Cape Cod. In addition to writing books Babbitt has also taught creative writing, reviewed books regularly, and written some perceptive critical articles on the nature and function of children's literature.

With ten children's books to her credit, Natalie Babbitt has earned a distinguished place for herself among contemporary American children's writers. Stating that her motives for writing come from her love of language and the pleasure of exploring its rich possibilities, she has also suggested that the essential issues and themes of her books are the result of incidents which took place in her life before the age of ten, events which underscored for her the "endless moral dilemmas from being human." While much children's literature presents moral dilemmas that are easily resolved, many of Babbitt's best works indicate that neat solutions to the baffling paradoxes of the human situation are unattainable. Her books in fact are notable for introducing complex issues and for exploring these issues from multiple points of view. Yet for all the seriousness of the themes she explores, Babbitt's treatment is apt to be humorous and deftly handled. Clearly she believes that a sense of play, an awareness of the absurdity of existence, and a sense of humor are vital ways that human beings survive ordeals of the flesh and spirit.

Babbitt's characters are usually people who live in the countryside, removed from the artificial urban world. They are close to nature; yet they are more complex, more realistic than folktale characters. They struggle with essential meanings—love, death, immortality, greed, loyalty, and moral choice. While Babbitt is clearly concerned with existential meanings and moral dilemmas, she also expresses amused tolerance for human folly and invariably affirms hope for the human spirit. She expresses, too, delight in the richness of experience, counsels a clear-eyed, tough-minded approach to existence, and celebrates the capacity of art, language, story, and the imagination to help human beings make sense of the world and create a bearable order.

Babbitt's works for children have been consistently praised for their economic yet poetic style, for their carefully wrought structures, and for treating serious themes with an elegantly light touch. She draws rather self-consciously upon the literary conventions of folktale, myth, pastoral, romance, and mystery stories; yet she usually blends the conventions of these traditions so skillfully that she often transcends these genres. Some critics have questioned whether children can easily comprehend Babbitt's complex themes. One may argue, however, that one of her supreme gifts is her ability to make such themes accessible to children through the lucidity of her prose. She never condescends to her young audience. Other critics and reviewers have complained that children in Babbitt's works tend to be two dimensional; yet the author explains that she portrays them in this way because children are in the process of becoming. It is fair to say that in some of her books, however, characters are subordinate to the idea.

Babbitt's skills as a writer have developed substantially since the publication of *Dick Foote and the Shark* in 1967. Babbitt's first solitary venture in both writing and illustrating a book, the story recounts in forty-six quatrains the efforts of a nineteenth-century Cape Cod poet, Dick Foote, to convince his father that writing poetry has practical value. Dick's father, a crusty, no-nonsense fisherman, cannot understand why his son writes verse when he could fish instead. The generation gap is closed happily when Dick finally boards a fishing boat, encounters a vicious shark, and saves the expedition by delivering a mock-heroic encomium in verse to the shark. As a result of Dick's poetic gifts, the Footes escape, and the father finally accepts the son's true identity. Though the book has been criticized for taking so many stanzas to tell a simple story, the narrative poem is graced with bouncing rhythms and ingenious rhymes. The sharp, comic black-and-white ink drawings washed with green help to create the appropriate ambience and tone for the poem.

In 1968 Babbitt wrote and illustrated another picture book in verse, *Phoebe's Revolt*. Phoebe Euphemia Brandon Brown lives with her family in Manhattan in 1904, along with her governess, Miss Trout, and her cat, Elihu. Miserable in flounces, sashes, and lace, Phoebe demands to dress the way her father dresses, a wish she finally is forced to experience for a full seven days. The tone of the story is comic, but Babbitt acknowledges the necessity of living within the conventions of society. Phoebe has a wise mother, though, who knows how to compromise: Phoebe dresses at last in a broadcloth sailor dress which permits her to play freely and to be accepted in her society as well. A strong feature of *Phoebe's Revolt* is the pleasing drawings which depict Manhattan at the turn of the century

and also convey a vivid sense of Phoebe's spirited personality. While the story contains a subdued feminist dimension, it also addresses the fact that people of both sexes are social beings who must search for ways to be true to themselves and at the same time function within society.

Babbitt's first prose work for children, *The Search for Delicious* (1969), is a remarkably complex quest romance, featuring the usual characters and situations of that genre. The fantasy begins with an exquisite creation myth about the essential nature of things before the fall. In this primal order, the narrator tells us, each creature performs its assigned function and keeps the world beautiful. The dwarfs preside in the mountains; woldwellers, wise old woodland creatures, inhabit the forests; and lovely mermaids swim in the lakes, while the winds blow merrily in the air. In one remote spot high in the mountains, a mermaid named Ardis plays with her doll in a well-house submerged in a lake. She loves the doll because it is a gift from her friends the dwarfs, who also give her a whistle that opens and closes the door to the well-house. One

Dust jacket for Babbitt's first prose work for children (Farrar, Straus & Giroux)

day a traveling minstrel inadvertently picks up the whistle. Ardis watches in dismay as he blows it and locks her doll inside the well-house. How she retrieves the whistle becomes a central problem in the complex plot of *The Search for Delicious*.

This framing myth surrounds the quest of the fantasy's young hero, Gaylen, the adopted son of Prime Minister Decree. In writing a dictionary Decree unwittingly foments civil strife, a controversy which threatens to lead to war. The trouble starts when Decree writes that "Delicious is fried fish." Suddenly the entire court begins to argue for their own favorite foods. To settle the dispute, Gaylen is sent on a mission to conduct a survey in the four towns of the kingdom. He is preceded by the villainous Hemlock, who wishes to usurp the king's power and seize the throne. In his quest Gaylen encounters the woldwellers, the mermaids, the dwarfs, and the winds, all of which are far removed from the foolish disputes of human beings, who never seem to change and never learn. Gaylen's quest leads, as it should, to self-discovery. While he is disgusted with the foolishness of humanity, he also realizes that his own fate is inextricably bound up with it. His love for the prime minister and his concern for the people call him back from the remoteness of primal nature to the social concerns of the kingdom. Gaylen learns that Hemlock has been hoarding the kingdom's water supply; with Ardis's help, he releases the water. The people learn too, just in time, what really is most delicious—a refreshing drink of water when one is truly thirsty.

Despite the symbolic and allegorical significance of the fantasy, Babbitt playfully parodies these conventions. For example, the king refuses to adopt the young baby Gaylen, left on his step. On one level, Babbitt is making genial fun of the convention; yet the detail has a function in the plot as well. The people have forgotten the legends and songs and so are too blind to know that a hero has arrived in their midst. While the complicated plot advances a bit slowly, the suspense keeps the reader's attention, and, while Babbitt relies on such archetypal characters as Gaylen, the hero, and Hemlock, the villain, she also renders these characters vividly. Ardis, the enchanting mermaid, is especially appealing, though the reader never knows if she finds her doll.

The theme of *Kneeknock Rise* (1970) is introduced in the prologue: "Facts are the barren branches on which we hang the dear, obscuring foliage of our dreams." In her characteristic introductory frame Babbitt tells the reader how the

Dust jacket for Babbitt's provocative fable about the function of myth and imagination (Farrar, Straus & Giroux)

"Mammoth Mountains" were named and why the people of the village of Instep take so much pride in their mountain, Kneeknock Rise, and its resident monster, the Megrimum. The presence of this terrible creature has imparted grandeur and significance to an otherwise quite ordinary village. Moreover, the monster attracts a large number of tourists each year, who have contributed to the economic well-being of the village.

When the hero of the story, Egan, comes to visit his Uncle Anson, a gentle clock maker, Aunt Gertrude, a highly superstitious but kindly woman, and his cousin, Ada, an arch, superior, red-haired girl whose favorite pet is a spoiled and supercilious cat named Sweetheart, he discovers that the other member of the family, Uncle Ott, an eccentric poet, has mysteriously disappeared, leaving his fat, lovable dog, Annabelle. Ada gleefully claims that Uncle Ott has been eaten by the Megrimum. Gradually Egan is drawn to the mountain and to the monstrous Megrimum. He dreams of climbing Kneeknock Rise, heroically slaying the monster, and returning to receive a hero's glorious reward. When Ada and her cat dare him to climb Kneeknock Rise, he rushes off with Annabelle, thinking, "I'll be famous. . . ." On Kneeknock Rise Egan finds only Uncle Ott and discovers the Megrimum is a figment of Instep's superstitious imagination, an expression of the human need to alleviate boredom and to spice the blandness of existence. Yet when he tries to explain to the people of Instep that the wailings of the Megrimum are only the whistlings of a hot spring on cool, rainy nights, he is chagrined to find that they refuse to believe him and remain faithful to their monster, half convincing him that the Megrimum is up there after all.

Kneeknock Rise is a provocative fable about the function of myth and imagination, about the pride and pretensions of ordinary human beings. Critics of the book have commented that the characters remain too sketchy, that they are manipulated excessively in the service of commenting on the idea. While Uncle Ott, Uncle Anson, Aunt Gertrude, Ada, and Egan are undeniably two-dimensional characters, they are nevertheless memorable. Another notable feature of the book is its spare but almost lyrical descriptive passages. Babbitt uses humorous personification to deflate the pride of the people of Instep and to underscore her theme; the mountains are the only interesting feature "in a countryside that neither rolled nor dipped but lay as flat as if it had been knocked unconscious. . . ." The suspense and atmosphere of mystery in this slender volume captivate the young reader, who is left to exercise the final judgment about the existence of the Megrimum. Another notable feature of the book is its playfully ironic reversal of reader expectations. Egan does not slay the Megrimum and return as a hero. Yet the actual outcome does not disillusion readers but leads them into a more acute awareness of the complexity of reality. Still, as Eudora Welty suggested in an early review of the book, *Kneeknock Rise* touches the intellect, not the emotions. The book was named an ALA Notable Book, was placed on the Horn Book Honors List, and was a runner-up for the John Newbery award.

In *The Something* (1970) Babbitt creates an appealing creature named Mylo, who resembles a prehistoric child with buckteeth. Mylo (who lives in a cave) is afraid of the dark, of unnameable terrors which lurk and wait, of "something." When Mylo tries to fashion the something in modeling clay, his mother is pleased, believing that he has forgotten his fears. In this whimsical tale Babbitt plays with the nature of dream and reality and emphasizes

the child's need to confront terrors and to master them through creative effort. Yet she suggests that we need the something too, that imagined terrors also give us their own piquant pleasure. Babbitt's humorous drawings and comic dialogue distance the terror in this story and also suggest that art can help to exorcise our terrors.

Though not as popular as some of her other books, *Goody Hall* (1970) is perhaps Babbitt's most pleasingly lighthearted story. Drawing upon the traditions of myth, Gothic romance, and picaresque rogue literature, Babbitt creates a humorous mystery about the secrets surrounding a magnificent estate, Goody Hall. The reader learns from a gossipy housekeeper, Dora Tidings, that strange events are afoot at Goody Hall. Mrs. Goody leaves home and goes to the city twice a year, though she never returns with any packages. (The reader later learns that she made these trips to sell jewels stolen by her husband.) She and her son, Willet, remain isolated in their lofty mansion until Mrs. Goody hires an actor, Hercules Feltwright, to become Willet's tutor. With Feltwright the author parodies the twelve labors of Hercules: he has strangled an earthworm, killed a mad cat, and at Goody Hall he descends into Midas Goody's tomb, a mock version of the Gates of Hell, for an extraordinary encounter with the ferocious three-headed dog, Cerberus (a statue), who stands guard there. *Goody Hall* abounds with gypsy seances, mistaken identities, hidden treasures, as well as comic allusions to the Hercules myth, the story of King Midas, and even to Shakespeare's *Macbeth*. Despite all the fun, the story finally endorses traditional values: family, acceptance of one's true self, the pleasure of honest work. Mott Snave, the robber, and Midas Goody, the wealthy miser, are both false identities. In the end the reader learns that Willet's father is actually the hard-working farmer, John Constant, a name suggesting everyday duty and matters of fact.

One of Babbitt's most popular books, *The Devil's Storybook* (1974) portrays, in ten short comic stories, the attempts of a middle-aged and paunchy devil, a would-be trickster who is most often tricked himself, to increase his influence and to swell the ranks of the rather comfortable denizens of hell. As usual, Babbitt uses playful reversals to deflate pomposity and vanity, whether of devil or human origin. The narrator's genial tone assures readers that the stories are good fun, that the devil is beset with human frailty. All of the stories are not equally good. Some are overly sentimental, and the structure of "The Harps of Heaven" is a bit flawed. Yet the better stories are characteristic of Babbitt at her best; readers of *The Devil's Storybook* will enjoy the witty yet tolerant tone, the whimsical play with language and literary convention, delightfully surprising reversals, carefully constructed plots, and Babbitt's typically vigorous style. *The Devil's Storybook* was named an ALA Notable Book and received the Christopher Award and the Lewis Carroll Shelf Award.

To date most critics of children's literature agree that *Tuck Everlasting* (1975) is Babbitt's best book and have praised its style and structure, as well as its perceptive handling of a significant theme. Indeed, in *Tuck Everlasting* Babbitt has blended the traditions of folktale, pastoral, and myth with realism, creating a remarkably original fantasy.

Dust jacket for Babbitt's most widely acclaimed novel in which she draws on the traditions of folktale, pastoral, and myth (Farrar, Straus & Giroux)

In the prologue of *Tuck Everlasting* the narrator introduces the image of a Ferris wheel, which recurs and resonates throughout the narrative, underscoring the poignant recognition that everything is a part of a wheel, the natural life cycle, and that death has its place on the wheel too, as Pa Tuck explains to Winnie in the key episode of the story.

The heroine of *Tuck Everlasting*, Winnie Foster, is an overprotected child who inhabits a no-nonsense house guarded by "a capable iron fence." Unaware that the spring of eternal life quite literally bubbles in the nearby wood, Winnie has lived in the protected oasis of her home for ten years. When she finally ventures into the woods, she is kidnapped by the Tuck family, who have innocently drunk from the fountain of youth with pernicious results. They learn that immortality without growth, change, or death is an infernal paradise—a curse, not a blessing. The Tucks realize that their secret has cosmic implications, that it must be guarded from the villainous "man-in-the-yellow-suit" at all costs. When this evil person threatens to use the secret to acquire wealth and power for himself and to use Winnie as a freak, after he forces her to drink the water, Mae Tuck kills him in an act of violent retribution. While the act resembles the swift justice of a folktale, it has complicated consequences. Winnie in her turn must act to save Mae, whom she loves, and to protect the secret, which she is not sure she believes. Eventually the reader learns that Winnie has embraced her mortality and affirmed her humanity, her place on the wheel, by choosing to become "Winnie Foster Jackson, Dear Wife, Dear Mother."

With admirable economy, in her characteristically understated manner, Babbitt has chosen to treat a potentially tragic theme; yet the fantasy is finally "high comedy" in the sense that it ends on a note of rebirth and renewal. Though Winnie does not drink the water herself, she anoints her friend the toad and makes him safe forever. In this work, the characters are powerfully delineated. *Tuck Everlasting* is one of the most significant works of American children's literature in recent years and was placed on the International Board on Books for Young People Honor List.

In *The Eyes of the Amaryllis* (1977) Babbitt tells the haunting and mysterious story of Geneva Reade, a sea captain's widow, who, with her small son, George, has witnessed the wreck of her husband's ship in a storm. For thirty years Geneva Reade has obsessively waited and watched for a sign of her husband from the sea, which she has identified as her enemy. In pursuing her relentless quest, Geneva has essentially abandoned her son, unable to forgive him because he has been afraid of the sea since the shipwreck. Apparently, she has forsaken the human community altogether, since her only contact is Seward, a ghost who represents the forces of the deep.

The central consciousness in the fantasy is that of George Reade's daughter, eleven-year-old Geneva (called Jenny), who finds herself torn between her grandmother's obsessive madness at the edge of a mysterious other world and the mundane inland world of her father's store. When Jenny visits her grandmother, she experiences strength and freedom for the first time and also enjoys an expanded sense of self and of the world. Eventually Geneva, Jenny, and Seward are implicated in a terrifying contest with the sea, a perilous game which Geneva almost loses. In the end George saves his mother and daughter from the raging sea and conquers his own fear in the process. The powerful tale ends with each character's having undergone transformation and growth. Geneva recovers from her thirty-year obsession and recognizes her son's quiet strength, and Jenny's conflicting loyalties are resolved. The potentially tragic story ends on a note of conciliation and hope.

One of the strengths of this remarkable novel is the power with which Babbitt describes the sea as a living, vital, mysterious force with a will of its own. Geneva's character is powerfully drawn, almost to the point of overshadowing Jenny, a feature which has evoked some unfavorable comment among critics. The novel marks the first time Babbitt has departed from the framing devices which usually surround her narratives. The result is a more organic, less mechanical structure and more compelling characters and settings.

Since the publication of *The Eyes of the Amaryllis,* her third ALA Notable Book, Natalie Babbitt has illustrated two volumes by Valerie Worth and has published a novel for young adults, *Herbert Rowbarge* (1982). This novel marks a departure in style, theme, and audience. Although the book has been marketed as a young-adult novel, it seems in many ways more appropriate for adult readers. In England *Herbert Rowbarge* has in fact been marketed as an adult book and has enjoyed more popular success there than it has in the United States.

In this odd, spare novel Babbitt recounts the illegitimate births and abandonment of Herbert

Dust jacket for Babbitt's third ALA Notable Book (Farrar, Straus & Giroux)

and his twin brother, Otto, and describes Herbert's bleak life in the Gait County Children's Home, in Gaitsburg, Ohio, a town situated on the banks of the Ohio River. When Otto is adopted soon after their arrival at the home, Herbert suffers a permanent sense of loss. Thereafter, the narrator tells us, he feels himself incomplete, half a person: "He had no conception of middles, and did not know, then or ever afterward, that he was whole all by himself, instead of half of a single unit."

In 1889, when Herbert is nine years old, two definitive events occur. Mrs. Frate, the matron of the children's home, acknowledges that the child probably will not be adopted and that he must have a surname. Mrs. Daigle, the cook, noticing that Herbert is both smart and willful, decides that the surname "Rowbarge" suits him. Even more important, Herbert manages to convince Dick Festeen, his only friend in the home, to slip away with him to visit a local carnival. When Herbert first glimpses the splendid Noah's Ark merry-go-round with its gleaming chariots and carved animals and hears the magical music issuing from the steam calliope, he realizes at once that there "had never been anything so fine in all the history of the world." This vision remains bright in Herbert's mind and informs his entire future.

Herbert and Dick eventually establish their own amusement park, and Herbert marries Ruby Nill, the plain daughter of a rich banker, who bears twin girls, Babe and Louisa. When the twins are still toddlers, Ruby is run over and killed by a carriage. Herbert, who has never loved his wife, devotes himself to his amusement park. Rejecting the affections of Babe and Louisa and even of his old and devoted friend Dick, he is haunted by his failure to love and a sense of hollow incompleteness.

In creating the account of Herbert Rowbarge's unhappy life Babbitt begins her narrative from the point of view of Babe and Louisa at age forty-five, on 20 May 1952. The second chapter begins in June 1880, with Herbert's birth, and thereafter the book is composed of chapters with alternating points of view. Babe and Louisa try to please their father and cope with the frustrations of living apart from each other in the present, while the chapters set in the past document Herbert Rowbarge's gradual rise to wealth and fame. At the end of the novel, past and present meet with Herbert's death. Babe and Louisa come together again at last and finally have the courage to admit that their father had never loved them.

The prevailing tone of the novel is comically ironic. Herbert's existence is at once pathetic, absurd, and ordinary. Yet Babbitt manages to suggest enormous emotional waste. Rowbarge barely misses meeting Otto on at least two different occasions. Even more important perhaps is a subdued feminist theme. Ruby's appetite for sexual enjoyment and for intense romantic love are thwarted by Herbert and by society. She feels guilty about her passions, and her death is an emblem for the wasted lives of many other valuable women. In this wry and tough-minded novel, Babbitt asks her readers to take a close look at traditional American values, to examine them without sentimentality and false emotion.

Herbert Rowbarge perhaps marks a shift in Babbitt's writing career but certainly not a falling off. Her readers have learned to expect surprises from this talented writer, who received for the body of her work the George G. Stone Award in 1979 and was the U.S. nominee for the Hans Christian Andersen Medal in 1981.

References:

Geraldine De Luca, "Extensions of Nature: The Fantasies of Natalie Babbitt," *Lion and the Unicorn*, no. 1 (1977): 47-70;

Anita Moss, "Classical Vision and Comic Effect in Natalie Babbitt's *Kneeknock Rise* and *Goody Hall*," *Focus: Teaching English Language Arts*, 11 (Spring 1985);

Moss, "A Second Look at Natalie Babbitt's *The Search for Delicious*," *Horn Book*, 60 (December 1984): 779-783;

Moss, "Varieties of Children's Metafiction," *Studies in the Literary Imagination*, 18 (Fall 1985): 79-92.

Judy Blume

(12 February 1938-   )

Alice Phoebe Naylor

Appalachian State University

and

Carol Wintercorn

BOOKS: *The One in the Middle is the Green Kangaroo* (Chicago: Reilly & Lee, 1969); revised with illustrations by Amy Aitken (Scarsdale, N.Y.: Bradbury, 1981);

Iggie's House (Englewood Cliffs, N.J.: Bradbury, 1970);

Are You There God? It's Me, Margaret. (Englewood Cliffs, N.J.: Bradbury, 1970);

Freckle Juice, illustrated by Sonia O. Lisker (New York: Four Winds Press, 1971);

Then Again, Maybe I Won't (Scarsdale, N.Y.: Bradbury, 1971);

It's Not the End of the World (Scarsdale, N.Y.: Bradbury, 1972);

Tales of a Fourth Grade Nothing, illustrated by Roy Doty (New York: Dutton, 1972);

Otherwise Known as Sheila the Great (New York: Dutton, 1972);

Deenie (Scarsdale, N.Y.: Bradbury, 1973);

Blubber (Scarsdale, N.Y.: Bradbury, 1974);

Forever . . . (Scarsdale, N.Y.: Bradbury, 1975);

Starring Sally J. Freedman as Herself (Scarsdale, N.Y.: Bradbury, 1977);

Wifey (New York: Putnam's, 1978);

Superfudge (New York: Dutton, 1980);

Tiger Eyes (Scarsdale, N.Y.: Bradbury, 1981);

Smart Women (New York: Putnam's, 1984);

The Pain and the Great One, illustrated by Irene Trivas (Scarsdale, N.Y.: Bradbury, 1984);

Letters to Judy: What Your Kids Wish They Could Tell You (New York: Putnam's, 1986).

© *Jerry Bauer*

Judy Blume is in a class by herself among writers of books for children and young adults. In less than two decades her books have sold more than thirty million copies. Part of the Blume phenomenon is that her readers become involved with her as well as with the characters in her books. Two thousand children a month write letters to her. At the same time the books enjoy enormous popularity, they are also highly subject to censorship attempts because of their frankness in sexual content and language and the lack of traditional moralizing and authoritarian pronouncements. Blume's books reflect a general cultural concern with feelings about self and body, interpersonal relationships, and family problems. It is her portrayal of feelings of sexuality as normal, and not rightfully subject to punishment, that revolutionized realistic fiction for children.

Blume's refusal to prescribe solutions or advocate punishment may disturb would-be censors as much as her treatment of sexuality. She believes that bringing thoughts about problems out into the open will contribute to solutions. Much of the conflict over her writing arises from differences in religious values relating not only to sexuality but also to authoritarianism and power. Moral obligations to others are clear, she feels, but often she leaves to the reader the matter of choice and its consequences. Though her stories often deal with such subjects as sibling rivalry, divorce, and death, Blume resists the idea that her books are "problem books." "Life is full of problems," she responds, "Some big and some small."

Blume's writing style is enhanced not only by her ability to recall the most minute details of her childhood, but also by a gift for fantasizing; unspoken thoughts of characters figure in her work and lend it simplicity and authenticity. The point of view in her children's novels is always that of the child, which explains why adult characters are sometimes portrayed as less tolerant or less understanding than children. Blume believes that children need humor in their lives. "If I could write nothing but funny books for children, I would be happy," she has said. The humor in her stories contributes strongly to her popularity.

Blume was born on 12 February 1938 in Elizabeth, New Jersey, to Rudolph and Esther Sussman. Her father, a dentist, shared with her a penchant for fantasy and game-playing and provided emotional support when she was ill, unhappy, or fearful. Blume describes her mother as a traditional homemaker and a reader who spent every afternoon with books. When Blume was in the third grade, she moved with her mother and her older brother, David, to Miami Beach, where the climate would help David recuperate from an illness. Many of the incidents in her books are based on her experiences during the two years she lived in Florida during the school months while her father worked in New Jersey and saw the rest of the family only occasionally. After finishing high school in Elizabeth, Blume went to New York University, graduating in 1961 with a degree in early childhood education. In 1959 Blume had married

John Blume, a lawyer. Their daughter Randy, born in 1961, is now a commercial airline pilot. Larry, their son, was born two years later and is now a filmmaker.

Blume began writing after her children entered nursery school in the mid 1960s. Though she had two short stories published in Westminster Press periodicals, she received as many as six rejection slips a week for two and a half years before Reilly and Lee accepted *The One in the Middle is the Green Kangaroo* (1969). The story begins, "Freddy Dissel had two problems. One was his older brother Mike. The other was his younger sister Ellen." Freddy saw himself as the "peanut butter part of a sandwich." Freddy's part in the school play as a green kangaroo wins him the attention he believes is his due. The feelings of the middle child are simply and successfully conveyed in this book, and the solution is provided by an understanding teacher. *School Library Journal*'s reviewer commented, "Children will see through the suggestion, on the last page, that this success eliminates all of Freddy's middle-child blues, but the story is pleasant, if unexciting." *The One in the Middle is the Green Kangaroo* established the pattern and style of other Blume books which followed in rapid succession.

On the crest of the civil rights movement, Blume enrolled in a class called "Writing for Children and Teenagers." For each session she completed a chapter of *Iggie's House*, which was published by Bradbury in 1970 after having been serialized in *Trailblazer for Juniors* in 1969. In the book, eleven-year-old Winnie spends every Saturday night with Iggie's family from whom she absorbs an attitude of interest in and tolerance for people who are "different." When Iggie's family sells their house to the Garbers, a black family, Winnie stands up to her parents and her white neighbors on the issues of discrimination and acceptance.

In *Are You There God? It's Me, Margaret.* (1970), the central character's thoughts and concerns are what Blume remembered as her own at the age of twelve: Will I be accepted? Will anybody ever know the real me? Margaret has just moved to Farbrook, New Jersey. She soon makes friends with three other girls and they share secrets, gossip on the phone, and worry about boys, their developing figures, and getting their periods. Blume's experiences in having to make new friends in Florida provided some of the flavor of friendship in this book. Margaret's other preoccupation is with religion. She was born to a Jewish father and a Christian mother, and throughout the story she tries in

A NOVEL BY JUDY BLUME

ARE YOU THERE GOD?
IT'S ME, MARGARET.

*Dust jacket for Blume's 1970 novel about a young girl's fears
and anxieties as she approaches adolescence (Bradbury)*

"talks" to God to sort out her own feelings about religion as well as ask for help with her other problems. The *New York Times* called this book one of the outstanding children's books of 1970. Its reception by reviewers was mixed. *Education Digest* praised its "exploration of previously untouched aspects of childhood and adolescent experience." The *New Statesman* reviewer described it as "admittedly gripping stuff no doubt for those wrestling with—or curious about future—bodily changes. . . ." *Book Window*'s writer felt that "when the author rhapsodises about the wearing of a sanitary napkin, the effect is banal in the extreme, and disbelief is total. Suddenly a sensitive, amusing novel has been reduced to the level of some of the advertising blurbs. . . ." The *Times Literary Supplement* reviewer concluded, "Margaret's private talks with God are insufferably self-conscious and arch."

Attempts at censoring the book have continued throughout its lifetime; the *Newsletter on Intellectual Freedom* reports that it has been charged with "denigrating religion and parental authority" and

being "sexually offensive and amoral." Nonetheless, sales have totaled 120,000 hardcover copies and more than a million copies in paperback. *Are You There God? It's Me, Margaret.* received the 1974 Golden Archer Award in Wisconsin, the Nene Award from Hawaiian schoolchildren in 1975, the Young Hoosier Award in 1976, and the North Dakota Children's Choice Award in 1979.

Blume next asked herself what it would be like to be a twelve-year-old boy. In *Then Again, Maybe I Won't* (1971), Tony Miglione's father suddenly becomes a successful, rich businessman. The family moves from a working-class neighborhood into a well-to-do suburb. Tony faces moral problems: his mother's acquiescence to snobbish neighbors; his brother's choice of money over career; the self-imposed "exile" of his grandmother, who is supplanted by a hired cook; and his knowledge that Joel, the boy next door, is shoplifting. In addition to all of that, Tony wonders when he, too, will have wet dreams, how to prevent uncontrollable erections, and if he will be arrested for practicing voyeurism on Joel's sister, the girl next door. He develops severe stomach pains which neither a medical doctor nor a psychiatrist can cure. Here Blume presents the American dream gone awry, where human values are sacrificed for the sake of position and status in an upwardly mobile society, and the harmful effects of it all on children. The characters and events are all viewed through Tony's eyes. *Then Again, Maybe I Won't* has sold fewer copies than any of Blume's other books. Although Tony's preoccupation with sexuality is a minor part of the story, it was the major concern of reviewers and would-be censors. *Booklist*'s reviewer, however, commented, "The first-person story is written lightly but with realism and the facts of the boy's maturation are honestly and naturally treated."

Freckle Juice (1971), which Blume says is "just for fun," is for a younger audience. Its central character, Andrew, envies a classmate's freckles and becomes easy prey to Sharon's convincing sales pitch for a secret freckle juice recipe. As in *The One in the Middle is the Green Kangaroo*, an understanding teacher comes to the rescue. The book was well received by reviewers. *Horn Book* credited it for its "spontaneous humor, sure to appeal to the youngest reader." It remains a favorite easy-to-read, humorous tale.

Blume's ideas for her novels have often come from her own children's concerns. After a rash of divorces in the neighborhood, the Blume children asked whether divorce could ever happen in their family. Blume told them no, not aware of what lay ahead. *It's Not the End of the World* (1972) expresses the feelings of three children faced with their parents' divorce. Karen tries to trick her parents into getting back together; Jeff, an older brother, withdraws and runs away from home; and six-year-old Amy is overcome with fear that the rest of her family will disappear as her father did. The parents' reasons for the divorce are not divulged, although the children do observe angry and antagonistic behavior between them. *Booklist* called *It's Not the End of the World* "a believable first-person story with good characterization, particularly of twelve-year-old Karen, and realistic treatment of the situation."

A house helper who knew that Blume was writing books for children brought her a clipping one day about a boy who swallowed a turtle. "Willie Mae," to whom the book is dedicated, kept Blume informed of developments, and the story found its way into the enormously popular *Tales of a Fourth Grade Nothing* (1972), in which Peter Hatcher's "problem" is his two-year-old brother, Fudge. The episodic chapters of this tale of sibling rivalry are based on conversations Blume heard among her own children and their friends. The events always pit Peter against Fudge for parental approval, personal rights, and the opportunity to do special things. Fudge gets to eat what he wants, and he even swallows Peter's turtle, Dribble. He is chosen as well to star in a television advertising spot. Peter eventually gets a dog for himself alone and names it after the lost turtle. The original idea was for a picture book called "Peter, Fudge and Dribble." It was rejected as a picture book by Bradbury, but Ann Durrell, children's editor of Dutton, suggested the form in which it was finally published. The book enjoys steady popularity. In 1975 it won the Pacific North West Library Association Young Reader's Choice Award, the Sequoyah Children's Book Award in Oklahoma, and the Charlie May Simon Children's Book Award in Arkansas. In 1977 it won Children's Book Awards in Massachusetts, Georgia, and South Carolina.

Blume says that she described all of her own childhood fears in *Otherwise Known as Sheila the Great* (1972). Ten-year-old Sheila Tubman spends the summer away from home with her family in Tarrytown. She brings with her long-standing fears of dogs, thunderstorms, and swimming. To cope, she poses to her new friends there as Sheila the Great, who covers up the truth with hilarious exaggerations about her abilities. The belief that she has to be extraordinary to be liked is convincingly portrayed, especially when Sheila tries to take on

the publishing of a camp newspaper singlehandedly. Mouse Ellis is a sympathetic friend who does not expose Sheila's cover, but instead accepts her the way she is. After a summer of denying her phobias, Sheila's need to pose as the "great" one comes tumbling down. This book is distinguished for humor mixed with genuine pathos. It won the 1982 South Carolina Children's Book Award.

Blume wrote *Deenie* (1973) after meeting a child with scoliosis. It is the only book for which she did research, and since its publication she continually receives letters from children who have scoliosis. Blume's character Deenie Fenner, a thirteen-year-old, is beautiful. She is on the verge of being a cheerleader, getting a boyfriend, and starting a modeling career when she is found to have scoliosis. Her mother has aspirations for her daughter, considering Deenie "the beauty" and Helen, her sister, "the brain." She reacts very immaturely to Deenie's disease, but Mr. Fenner provides the acceptance that calls up Deenie's own strength and helps her to come to terms with her condition.

"*Blubber* [1974] is one of my most important books," says Blume. Her daughter came home from school one day feeling like Rochelle, a character in the book who was frightened by her fifthgrade peers' cruel treatment of a classmate, Linda Fischer. Linda's class report on whales, her being

Dust jacket for Blume's 1974 novel about the frustrations of childhood obesity; she says this is one of her most important books (Bradbury)

overweight, and her passivity are exploited to force her into demeaning situations. But the tables are turned, and one of the chief tormentors becomes the outcast. Profanity in this book has caused some parental objections. However, many teachers read and talk about the story in their classrooms.

The Pain and the Great One (1984), originally appearing in the anthology *Free to Be . . . You and Me* in 1974 and published in book form ten years later, presents sibling rivalry with insight and humor. Six-year-old little brother is "the pain" to big sister; she is "the great one" to him. Blume devotes one chapter to each sibling's complaints, which center on seeming parental favoritism for the other. The book is dedicated "To the original Pain and the Great One with Love," her own children. The complaints are illustrated in delightfully funny watercolor illustrations. It is considered by *School Library Journal* to be "a valuable book about sibling relationships."

With *Forever . . .* (1975), Blume says, she "set out to write a book that didn't equate sex with punishment. . . . My daughter was a reader. At age fourteen she asked me to write a book in which 'they do it and nothing awful happens.' " *Forever*'s dedication reads, "For Randy—as promised—with love." It begins, "Sybil Davison has a genius I.Q. and has been laid by at least six different guys." In the story, high school seniors Michael and Katherine are in love. Katherine's parents attempt to shake her commitment to Michael, her grandmother offers birth control information, and eventually Katherine and Michael have sexual intercourse, described in explicit detail. For Katherine and Michael, "nothing awful happens." Some of their friends are not so fortunate. Sybil becomes pregnant and Erica's boyfriend attempts suicide. During the summer before college, at the camp where she works as a counselor, Katherine is attracted to an older male counselor and realizes that she is not ready for "forever."

A writer for the *Use of English* has called *Forever . . .* "a manufactured sex manual thinly disguised as a novel." The censorship of *Forever . . .* surpassed that of all of Blume's other books, with objectors quoted in the *Newsletter on Intellectual Freedom* as saying it "demoralizes marital sex" and "titillates and stimulates children to the point they could be prematurely awakened sexually." Some literary critics have found the characters stilted and the plot a mere recounting of steps in the process of sexual intimacy. But the book was praised by Joyce Maynard in a *New York Times Magazine* article because it "makes kids' erotic stirrings seem to them

Dust jacket for a later edition of Blume's most controversial novel due to its explicit treatment of teenage sexuality (Bradbury)

more normal." A *School Library Journal* writer has stated, "*Forever* isn't really about sex at all, it's about reassurance. Like many [young adult] novels, it addresses teenagers' feelings, sexual and otherwise, to one point: don't worry, you're normal."

Starring Sally J. Freedman as Herself (1977) is highly autobiographical. A teacher wrote to Blume, among other adults in the arts, asking "what we had been like as children. I answered at great length. It made me think about what kind of child I was. This book is my favorite." Sally J. Freedman, like Blume, left New Jersey in 1947 to spend the school year in Miami Beach. Sally writes letters to "Doey-Bird," her father, telling him how much she loves him. In this book the reader learns more about Blume's childhood fantasizing. In italics Sally records her dreams of becoming a movie star like Esther Williams. She carries on imaginary investigations of an old man living in her apartment building whom she believes to be Adolf Hitler in hiding. Making and relating to friends plays a large part in this story, and Jewish culture and mores are given more importance in it than in Blume's other books. Sally's preoccupation with death is the same as Blume's, caused by the frequency of deaths among Blume's relatives before she was ten. "A lot of kids grow up without dealing with death, but death played a very important part in my life," she says. "My father had six brothers and sisters, almost all of whom died while I was growing up. Two of my father's brothers were dentists; both died at forty-two years of age. So when my father was forty-two, I was scared." (Blume's father died in 1959 at the age of fifty-four.)

The *New York Times* reviewer wrote, "While Mrs. Blume's book is teeming with social value, its redeeming literary qualities are less conspicuous. . . . She describes the 40's in a banal shorthand that misses a good chance to describe what it was really like growing up then." Perhaps the time and setting are only hinted at because Blume never tells more than the child character would have felt or known.

After Blume's first marriage ended, she explored in *Wifey* (1978), her first adult book, the paralysis of a wife in a traditional marriage. In *Wifey*, central character Sandy Pressman, a New Jersey housewife, gradually becomes dissatisfied with the prescribed roles of wife and mother. Sandy resents her safe, predictable husband and the routine, uncommunicative sexuality in her marriage. She blunders into bizarre and hilarious encounters with a best friend's husband, a brother-in-law, an obscene visitor, and a former school flame. "*Wifey* was always in my head," Blume told *People* magazine. "I write out of my real life experiences, but they become fiction." Children ask for *Wifey* because it is a Judy Blume book. However, adults have become as great Blume fans as children. *Wifey* has sold more than most of her children's titles.

Immediately following her divorce from John Blume, Blume married Tom Kitchens. With Kitchens she and her family lived in England for a period and then moved to Los Alamos, New Mexico. Blume divorced Kitchens in 1978 but remained in New Mexico—Santa Fe—until 1985, when she moved to Connecticut. She has maintained an apartment in New York City since 1981.

Superfudge (1980) is a sequel to *Tales of a Fourth Grade Nothing*. It became Blume's best-selling book in hardcover. In *Superfudge*, Peter Hatcher, now in the sixth grade, and Fudge, now four, reappear from the earlier book. They are joined by a baby sister, Tootsie. Fudge is still the biggest pain ever invented, according to Peter, but Fudge now finds

competition for his parents' affection and pretends to be a baby too. Even Peter says, "I know it's stupid, but just for a minute I wished I could be Mom's baby again, too."

Blume's readers continue to ask for more about Fudge. "I wish I could write a book about Fudge every year," she says, "but the ideas are not there." A *Council for Children's Books Bulletin* reviewer called *Superfudge* "better knit" than *Tales of a Fourth Grade Nothing*, "since there are several threads that tie the episodic chapters together—wry but funny, with firm characterization and good dialogue." The *New York Times Book Review* reviewer wrote, "Blume understands the real nature of children's purity, which is in fact not precisely what it has been cracked up to be by some of our more wishful colleagues." *Superfudge* has won many awards, among them the 1982 Colorado Children's Book Award, the 1983 Iowa Children's Choice Award, and both the 1981 and 1985 New Hampshire Great Stone Face Awards.

Blume has called *Tiger Eyes* (1981) "the most adult of my young adult books." In hardcover, its sales have run second only to *Superfudge*. In the story, the father of fifteen-year-old Davey Wexler is shot during a robbery of his 7-Eleven store in Atlantic City and later dies. The emotional trauma facing Davey, her seven-year-old brother Jason, and her mother is depicted in the context of a visit to relatives in Los Alamos, New Mexico. There Davey meets a sensitive young man who helps her through the problems of adjustment. Setting plays a more extensive role in this exploration of personal feelings than in previous Blume books. Also the conflicts of and between adults are elaborated on as well as teenage dilemmas over drugs, alcohol, dating, and boyfriends. The subject of death is presented not only in personal terms, but also in terms of the preoccupation of the population of the "Atomic City" with everything but the destructiveness of the bombs they are helping to create. Blume offers no profound answers in this story, but Davey says, "Each of us must confront our own fears, must come face to face with them. How we handle our fears will determine where we go with the rest of our lives."

Reviewers applauded *Tiger Eyes* as authentic and sensitive. "Blume explores the feelings of children in a non-judgmental way," wrote Robert Lipsyte in the *Nation*. "The immediate resolution of a problem is never as important as what the protaganist . . . will learn about herself by confronting her life." He called it her "finest book—ambitious, absorbing, smoothly written, emotionally engaging

2.

[And] Dad took the lid off the pot on the stove and stirred
up the stew. *You'd have thought we were discussing the weather.*

"How could you?" I shouted. "How could you? Isn't
one enough?"

They both stopped and looked at me.

I kept right on shouting. "Another Fudge! Just what
this family needs." I turned and stormed down the hall.

Fudge, my four year old brother, was in the livingroom,
He was shoving crackers into his mouth and laughing like a loon
at Sesame Street on TV. I looked at him and thought about
having to go through it all over again. *The kicking + the screaming + the slurping and now — much more.* *[And]* I felt so
angry that I kicked the wall. Fudge turned. "Hi, Pee-tah,"
he said. I mumbled something back. My dog, Turtle,
nuzzled up to me and licked my hand. My dog *is* named after
my first pet, Dribble *He was* a tiny green turtle. My brother
swallowed him last year. ~~My brother, who used to eat
under our table, like a dog.~~ My brother, who wanted
to be a bird ~~and tried to fly off the~~ jungle ~~gym~~. My
brother, who ate flowers, who ruined my school projects,
who was the biggest pain ever invented. *My brother, Farley Drexel Hatcher.* ~~I said to
myself, Oh no. No way!~~

I raced to my room and slammed the door so hard my map
of the world fell off the wall and landed on my bed. I
Adidas
pulled my ~~Addidas~~ bag out of the closet and emptied two
dresser drawers into it. Another Fudge, I said to myself.
They're going to have another Fudge!

There was a knock at my door and Dad called, "Peter..."

"Go away," I told him.

"I'd like to talk to you," he said.

Page from a draft for the opening section of Superfudge, *Blume's sequel to her 1972 novel* Tales of a Fourth Grade Nothing
(by permission of the author)

and subtly political." "A hammy moralizer could have made a terrible hash of such material," the *Newsweek* reviewer said. "Blume's delicate sense of character, eye for social detail and clear access to feelings touches even a hardened older reader." This was a new kind of praise for Blume. This book made it past the would-be censors, but only after Blume agreed to change a burst of profanity on page 140 to "I called him every name in the book." Blume also agreed to remove a passage alluding to masturbation. "I was somewhat disappointed at my editor's suggestion, but I understood that paragraph wasn't worth the censor's wrath," she said. Today Blume regrets the decision and says, "I am disappointed in myself that I allowed this to happen. It will not happen again."

Blume's second adult novel, *Smart Women* (1984), is set in Boulder, Colorado, where New Yorker Margo has moved after a divorce. She has two friends, each of whom is smart, successful professionally, and absorbed in her work, children, and relationships with men. At age forty Margo falls in love with Andrew, the ex-husband of her friend B. B. This story came "from real life," Blume states, but not necessarily her own. "I asked myself what could happen when a woman of forty falls in love again. Usually I identify with one character, but in this story I identified with four characters. I had to tell this story from both points of view, children and adult." A *Working Woman* reviewer commented, "All the teenagers are beautifully portrayed—alert, watchful, hostile, exasperated by their parents, wanting to love and be loved." "As in all of Miss Blume's books," said the *New York Times Book Review* writer, "the voices of the children ring loudest and clearest. While her adult characters often seem contrived and non-dimensional (not to mention depressing), the children are splendid in their richness. . . . Blume does not diminish the anger, sadness, confusion and disgust children of divorce can feel." "For once, a book's promotion material says something right and worthwhile," the *Working Woman* reviewer continues. "Smart women put their bad marriages behind them . . . know their own strengths and weaknesses, understand the value of friendship, keep hoping for the respect and affection of their children . . . aren't dumb enough to fall in love again . . . except (sometimes) they do. . . ." As with her children's books, Blume is again chastised for not adding some interpretive comment in this case about the bright, empty lives of smart women. Another suggests that Blume talks about what characters do and "not who they are."

For two years Blume sifted through the letters she had received from children since 1971. *Letters to Judy: What Your Kids Wish They Could Tell You* (1986) includes some of those letters arranged according to the subject addressed. Sexuality, mental illness, divorce, friendship, parents, stepparents, and drugs are some of them. The last ten pages contain a list of organizations and resources that can provide further information on these subjects. Almost half of the book is commentary from Judy Blume interspersed among the letters. She responds to the problems children describe by telling about her own, how she handled them, and what she learned from those times she handled them poorly. The sharing this time is directed toward parents. On the subject of "splitting up" she writes, "Working on this chapter has been very difficult for me because if I am to be honest then I have to write about the worst years of my life and the mistakes I made," which she does. Despite the fact that this is a book for adults, there are frequent asides to "Kids," since Blume knows by now that her child readers will know about the book and read it. An example is "Kids: There is no way that I can say if Annie needs to see a psychologist or not. Some problems persist and grow and make it hard to get on with your life. At those times it's a good idea to ask for help. If you can't ask your parents, you should ask someone at school to help you find a professional." The proceeds from this book are contributed to The Kids Fund, a nonprofit charitable and educational foundation established by Blume to address the needs and concerns of children. It began when Dell Publishing Company issued the Judy Blume Diary, a product Blume was proud to endorse. All royalties from the Diary and *Letters to Judy* go to the fund.

Some critics have expressed the belief that Blume's work has appeal only for upper-middle-class white American children. There was even resistance to reprinting the books in England because they were believed to be culturally specific. However, the translations into German, Scandinavian, French, Dutch, Hebrew, Spanish, Japanese, and other languages, plus sales in England and Australia, have proved otherwise. Fans in the United States include children of all classes and races.

A reviewer for *Signal* has suggested that the theme of all Blume's books is "it's not the end of the world," because "her heroines are given the answers before they have had a chance to grapple with the questions. By reducing, dismissing, or denying the crises, Blume prevents them from occasioning passage. Her heroines adjust and cope;

they do not suffer and change." The thousands of letters written to Blume, however, demonstrate that real children are doing the suffering and changing. Blume's books, and her emerging role as child advocate, indisputably help them along the way.

References:

Diana Gleasner, "Judy Blume," in *Breakthrough: Women in Writing* (New York: Walker, 1980), pp. 15-41;

Betsy Lee, *Judy Blume's Story* (Minneapolis: Dillon, 1981);

Joyce Maynard, "Coming of Age with Judy Blume," *New York Times Magazine*, 3 December 1978, pp. 228-286;

John Neary, "The 'Jacqueline Susann of Kids' Books,' Judy Blume, Grows Up With an Adult Novel," *People*, 10 (16 October 1978): 47-54;

Paula C. Saunders, "Judy Blume as Herself," *Writer's Digest*, 60 (1 January 1980): 18-24;

"A Split Decision: Judy Blume in Peoria," *Newsletter on Intellectual Freedom*, 35 (March 1985);

Justin Wintle, "Judy Blume," in *The Pied Pipers*, by Wintle and Emma Fisher (London: Paddington, 1974).

Sue Ellen Bridgers

(20 September 1942-   )

Theodore W. Hipple
University of Tennessee

BOOKS: *Home Before Dark* (New York: Knopf, 1976);
All Together Now (New York: Knopf, 1979);
Notes for Another Life (New York: Knopf, 1981);
Sara Will (New York: Harper & Row, 1985).

Sue Ellen Bridgers's novels provide young-adult readers with realistic portrayals of life in the small towns of the South, where it is said, "people take care of you when you're sick and talk about you when you're well." The characters in all four of Bridgers's novels are products of their rural roots. Though they are mostly good people—warm, generous, compassionate, and by city standards unsophisticated—they are not simple, nor are their lives uncomplex, and, because Bridgers is a good storyteller, readers are moved by their joys and sorrows, triumphs and failures.

The daughter of Wayland L. and Elizabeth Abbott Hunsucker, Sue Ellen Bridgers was born in Greenville, in eastern North Carolina, and was reared a few miles away in the small town of Winterville. She has spent most of her life in North Carolina, went to school there, and received her B.A. from Western Carolina University in 1976. She now lives in Sylva, a small town in the western tip of the state, with her husband, Ben Oshel Bridg-

ers, and their three children.

Bridgers's three early novels feature as the central character a girl in her adolescence, but, unlike heroines in other young-adult fiction, around whom the entire plot revolves, Bridgers's protagonists become enmeshed in the lives of others whose stories are equally compelling. *Home Before Dark* (1976) is principally about Stella Willis, at fourteen the oldest child of James Earl and Mae Willis, who are returning to James Earl's North Carolina home after sixteen years of migrant work in Florida. James Earl's younger brother Newton allows them to live in a tenant cottage on the family farm that he has inherited and made successful. However, Mae Willis is unable to adjust to a stationary life, and making that house a home—the first she has ever known—becomes more and more Stella's self-appointed responsibility, one she revels in. Mae dies in a lightning storm, and James Earl begins seeing Maggie Grover, whom he eventually marries, leaving his brother's farm and taking his family to town to live in Maggie's house. That is, all except Stella, who refuses to leave the tenant cottage that was her first place to lay down roots. Yet at the end of the book a more mature Stella does join her father and stepmother, arriving home before dark.

All Together Now (1979) is really several small-town stories in one novel. Most important is the story of Casey Flanagan, a twelve year old who comes to North Carolina to live with her grandparents while her father fights in Korea and her mother works in the city. Casey and Dwayne Pickens, a retarded adult, develop a special friendship. Dwayne hates girls, but mistakes Casey, with her short hair and jeans, for a boy. Two much older adults, Hazard Whitaker and Miss Pansy, suitors for twenty-five years, finally get married, though the marriage is off to a predictably rocky start, given Hazard's lifelong image as a loser. After an all night train trip to Washington, D.C., to begin their honeymoon, Hazard meets some of his salesmen friends and goes off drinking with them, leaving Pansy alone in their hotel room. Heartsick, she returns to North Carolina, and it is weeks before

Hazard is able to effect a lasting apology. Additionally there is Casey's uncle Taylor, a stock-car racer, who, with her grandmother Jane, rallies the conscience of the town to prevent Dwayne's being sent to a home. At summer's end Casey, stricken with a fever—the family fears polio—recovers to learn that Dwayne has discovered her true gender, having heard the doctor's report that "she's a sick little girl." However, he is not distressed by this knowledge but eagerly awaits her return the next summer. Bridgers was awarded the Boston Globe-Horn Book Award and Christopher Medal for *All Together Now*.

Notes for Another Life (1981) features Wren, thirteen, and Kevin, sixteen, who live with their grandparents in a small North Carolina town. Their father is in the nearby mental hospital, from which he will return in the novel for a short-lived attempt at a normal life. Their mother is first in Atlanta, then in Chicago, making her way in the world of fashion and business, in contact with her children only by telephone. Wren and Kevin are in effect the children of Bliss, their grandmother, who tries to dispel the talk about the "crazy Jackson family." It is the combination of the fear that he too will become insane, of his inability to endure his father's mental illness, and of the love-hate relationship he has with his mother that causes Kevin to attempt suicide. A young minister provides the counseling Kevin needs and helps bring Wren and Kevin even closer together.

In all of Bridgers's novels an evocative sense of place clothes the action with a special poignancy. Life moves slowly. People linger to pass the time of day. They genuinely listen to Wren's brilliance at the piano or to her choice solos. The whole town holds its breath while Casey battles the fever or Kevin recovers from his overdose of pills. They wonder if James Earl does not begin to date Maggie too soon after Mae's death, but delight in their happy marriage nonetheless. Her descriptions point out the small details—the worn glove Dwayne uses in his and Casey's two-man baseball, the blood-stained mattress on which Stella's cancer-ridden grandmother had shot herself, the songs shared by Bliss and Wren on their way to the mental hospital to visit the son of one, the father of the other. Bridgers's novels are set amid a terrifying realism, though in a place where decency can still prevail. Her uncommon talent in bringing such a place to life makes her novels especially worth the attention of young adults, and, for that matter, adults too.

No less skillful is her rendering of the characters who inhabit these small towns. Her teenagers

Bridgers 48

"I'll do it for you," DeeDee said.

"She'll do it for you," said Newton.

"Well," Anne hesitated for effect. "Well, all right then."

"Now get outa here, Newton Willis. We're busy," DeeDee said with a silly laugh.

"See you later," Newton said into Anne's ear and was gone.

"Newton Willis could have any girl in Montreet County," DeeDee said as happily as if he'd asked to take her home.

I wonder what will happen, Anne thought, lifting the spagetti into the collander. She had always known what her life was about. She'd even reserved a place for Newton Willis, if he were interested. We'll date a few times and that'll be the end of it, she thought, knowing all the time that given the chance she'd spend the rest of her life with him.

Chapter 7

Rodney rode with his left elbow jutting out the window and his right hand gripping the top of the wheel. Pressing his foot on the accelerator, he felt the blue Impala pick up, the hot wind from the window whip up his sleeve and around his head. The speedometer's red arrow edged toward sixty and Rodney smiled. The feel and power of the car were beginning to have an exhilerating effect on him, and he felt his fingers relax on the wheel as the car responded to his lightest carefree touch.

The Impala sped along the country road toward the Willis farm. During the past two weeks, he'd driven the car down this road more times than he could count; now the car seemed to know the road. The bursts of heavy shade and sunlight, the silvery shimmer of the blacktop were familiar to the car itself, and Rodney leaned back, almost stretching, while his fingers hovered around the wheel.

He was happy. Gradually his summer was taking shape without his doing a thing but making himself available. He was acommodating. That was all.

Corrected typescript page from Home Before Dark, *a depiction of life in a small southern town (by permission of the author)*

are seen realistically, especially in their relationships with adults. Unlike their peers in many other novels, Bridgers's teenagers like, love, and respect those adults who deserve this affection. Similarly Bridgers's adults are well drawn and not merely pawns of fictional devices. Bridgers's adults lead lives of their own, apart from the lives of their children or (commonly) grandchildren. They are genuinely interesting, demanding of and getting readers' attention.

Sue Ellen Bridgers, who published an adult novel, *Sara Will,* in 1985, possesses in abundance qualities much needed in young-adult fiction and seldom found there: the ability to tell a good story, to place it in a believable setting, to people it with real teenagers and adults, and to do it all with truly special linguistic talent.

Robert Burch
(26 June 1925-   )

Hugh T. Keenan
Georgia State University

BOOKS: *The Traveling Bird,* illustrated by Susanne Suba (New York: McDowell, Obolensky, 1959);

A Funny Place to Live, illustrated by W. R. Lohse (New York: Viking, 1962);

Tyler, Wilkin, and Skee, illustrated by Don Sibley (New York: Viking, 1963);

Skinny, illustrated by Sibley (New York: Viking, 1964); illustrated by Jan Ribbans (London: Methuen, 1965);

D. J.'s Worst Enemy, illustrated by Emil Weiss (New York: Viking, 1965);

Queenie Peavy, illustrated by Jerry Lazare (New York: Viking, 1966);

Renfroe's Christmas, illustrated by Rocco Negri (New York: Viking, 1968);

Joey's Cat, illustrated by Don Freeman (New York: Viking, 1969);

Simon and the Game of Chance, illustrated by Fermin Rocker (New York: Viking, 1970);

The Hunting Trip, illustrated by Suba (New York: Scribners, 1971);

Doodle and the Go-Cart, illustrated by Alan Tiegreen (New York: Viking, 1972);

Hut School and the Wartime Home-Front Heroes, illustrated by Ronald Himler (New York: Viking, 1974);

The Jolly Witch, illustrated by Leigh Grant (New York: Dutton, 1975);

Two That Were Tough, illustrated by Richard Cuffari (New York: Viking, 1976);

The Whitman Kick (New York: Dutton, 1977);

Wilkin's Ghost, illustrated by Lloyd Bloom (New York: Viking, 1978);

Ida Early Comes Over the Mountain (New York: Viking, 1980);

Christmas with Ida Early, illustrated by Gail Owens (New York: Viking, 1983);

King Kong and Other Poets (New York: Viking, forthcoming 1986).

OTHER: Egon Mathieson, *A Jungle in the Wheat Field,* English version by Burch (New York: McDowell, Obolensky, 1960).

Proficient children's author Robert Burch learned two important lessons early in life: "material possessions are not what matter" and "one must accept the good with the bad." In his eighteen successful books for children and one freely adapted version of a Danish story by Egon Mathieson, Burch has demonstrated the moral truth of the first paradigm and delighted readers with the witty implications of the second. His books are infused with his genial, optimistic view of life while maintaining a realistic, nonsentimental, serious, and moralistic approach.

His best books deal with the period of his own childhood—the Depression years in middle and northern Georgia—and the realistic details of country and small town life during this period come from his experience. His characters are usually in their early teens learning to confront successfully various crises and changes. His readers too are usually young adolescents, though Burch has written for both younger and older children. His best-known and most widely appreciated writing is for the middle grades, and these books generally deal with rural or small town life, usually during the Depression.

Robert Burch was born on 26 June 1925 in Inman, Georgia, to John Ambrose and Nell Graham Burch, and he grew up in the small village of Fayetteville, twenty miles south of Atlanta. He was reared the seventh of eight children on his mother's family farm, performing the usual chores such as feeding chickens, gathering eggs, weeding vegetables, bringing in stovewood, and milking cows. Graduating from high school in the middle of World War II, he served in the U.S. Army from 1943 to 1946. From the rural South, he went to such exotic locations as New Guinea and Brisbane, Australia.

After the war, he returned home and was graduated with a B.S. degree in agriculture, with a major in horticulture, from the University of Georgia. After working unhappily for a year in a commercial greenhouse, he took a clerical job at the Atlanta Ordnance Depot from 1951 to 1953, which led to similar jobs with the army in Yokohama and Tokyo. While in Japan Burch caught the urge for freighter travel and eventually took trips to Asia, Africa, and Europe. When he returned home, Burch settled in New York City for eight years (1955-1963), taking various writing courses as a hobby at Hunter, City College, and New York University and working at clerical jobs with the Muir and Company advertising agency from 1956 to 1959 and with the Walter E. Heller and Company industrial finance organization from 1959 to 1962. A course in writing children's literature taught by Dr. William Lipkind, an anthropologist by training but also the successful writer of a series of books for young children, particularly influenced Burch into becoming a children's author. He continued to do office work and polish his writing skills, receiving a fellowship in juvenile literature to the 1960 Bread Loaf Writers' Conference. In 1962 he returned to live in Fayetteville, Georgia, though he continues to travel extensively. His home in Fayetteville is a modified ranch house in a typical suburban tract, overlooking a pond stocked with large Japanese koi and ringed by beech, sweet gum, and oak trees. Burch, retaining his farm-boy instincts, once said, concerning his wandering over Mexico, Spain, and England, that wherever he went rural Georgia would remain home to him and that when he settled there forever he would start a garden and buy a dog. Now he has the garden and two salukis, an exotic and ancient mideastern breed, whose names, Omar and Willy, perhaps reflect the apparent incongruity between Burch's far-venturing spirit and his down-home manner.

Burch, a sure, economical stylist, excels in establishing principal characters and their conflicts in a few simple words, but they are not flat stereotypes. His farm boys exhibit willfulness, wanderlust, and jealousy along with honesty, industriousness, and charm. Likewise, his villains are not all bad; Alex Folsom in *Wilkin's Ghost* (1978) steals, lies, and frames others for his misdeeds, but he is also a good worker, grateful to Misses Etta and Julia who take him in, and honest in most of his dealings with Wilkin.

Burch typically portrays his characters in a period, time of life, or place of crisis and change: the Great Depression; World War II; old age; puberty; the shrinking farms at the edges of villages or near sprawling cities like Atlanta. In his books, close family ties, neighborliness, trust, and honor seem to flourish better in rural circumstances, and his characters seem happier on marginal farms with few material possessions than they do in prosperous cities.

Portions of his novels have been anthologized in school readers published by Harcourt, Brace and by Scott, Foresman. *Queenie Peavy* (1966) has been translated into Danish and German; *Skinny* (1964) and *D. J.'s Worst Enemy* (1965) into Danish, and *Ida Early Comes Over the Mountain* (1980) into German. His books have been well received by critics, especially by those who review for periodicals designed for teachers and librarians, such as *Instructor, Teacher, Library Journal, Kirkus Reviews, Bulletin of the Center for Children's Books, Language Arts, Childhood Education, Teachers College Record,* and *Grade Teacher.*

Most often the reviewers single out the quiet humor, the accurate and detailed descriptions of rural life, the bittersweet tone, and the nonsentimental, realistic, and sometimes unhappy endings of his stories. In Burch's world miracles do not occur but touching human changes often do. When critics occasionally find fault, it is for episodic plotting, but it is unlikely that children find this the flaw that adults do.

In his first three books, *The Traveling Bird* (1959), *A Jungle in the Wheat Field* (1960, his free adaptation of a literal English translation of the Danish), and *A Funny Place to Live* (1962), Burch adds in small ways to the typical models of picture books for children in the early 1960s. In *The Traveling Bird* he gives a unique and personal twist to the familiar story of a child and a helpful animal. From his Uncle Nathan, David receives a parakeet, a "loquacious and cosmopolitan" traveler, rather than the dog he had hoped for. The bird picks his name, Caesar, and tries to get David a dog. After twice failing he engineers a swap—himself for an airedale, although David soon regrets the exchange. Instead of the boy teaching the bird to speak, Caesar teaches David something about friendship and unselfishness.

Burch's free revision of Egon Mathieson's *A Jungle in the Wheat Field,* another picture book with a conventional plot, was named an Honor Book in the *New York Herald Tribune* Spring Book Festival. In it, the central character, Boy Bandy, searches for his lost cat in a wheat field, which because of the boy's small size looks to him like a forest. When he asks various insects and animals for information, they give different answers and quarrel among themselves. Suddenly Bandy finds this world transformed gigantically. A lizard becomes an alligator and his cat comes crashing toward him like a lion before everything suddenly returns to normal. The realistic description of the predatory nature of animals and insects in this imaginary world saves the book from being just fanciful and sentimental.

Burch's third picture book, *A Funny Place to Live,* repeats the situation of lost children seeking guidance from animals. Here it is Trudy and Vic who are lost in the woods. Various animals try to help them but have an understandable difficulty in reconciling their concept of home with what the children are looking for. When an owl finally shows them the way to their house, all the animals chorus that it is a strange place for someone to live. Despite the educational review of different animal homes and the mildly entertaining squabbles, it is not an outstanding book.

However, with *Tyler, Wilkin, and Skee* (1963), dedicated to Dr. Lipkind, Burch found his appropriate audience—slightly older children—and his proper milieu: the domestic life of children in the Great Depression in rural Georgia. In the book, the episodic adventures of three brothers, Tyler (twelve), Wilkin (eleven), and Skee (seven), follow a seasonal cycle from September to August. Their domestic adventures and exploits show that money is not needed for happiness, though occasionally a vision of the exotic outside world intrudes. A temporary detour brings a road-show Indian down their dirt road in a Buick and then later President Roosevelt on his way to Warm Springs; however, the boys' biggest thrill is attending the county fair.

Each boy is slightly differentiated by only a few, but important, details. Tyler is the quiet, oldest child; Skee is the perennial musician with his made-up songs; Wilkin is delegated the caretaker of the egg money with which the boys do business with Mr. Larson, owner of the country store. Their father, Mr. Coley, is a marginal farmer, dependent on a sawmill job for real income. Though the boys can afford few luxuries such as an occasional Pepsi and candy out of the egg money, the family is happy and supportive. The boys do, however, have disappointments. They fear that their mother has cooked the pet leghorn hen Millie for dinner, but then they discover it has been killed by a car. The boys are excited over Tyler's making a slingshot, but when he accidentally kills a hen with it, all three boys are punished. They miss a trip to the fair at the first of the book because their neighbor Mr. Dawson does not have room for all three boys in his car, but the following August they get to go, this time with their calf Pauline, who has won the third prize ribbon at the local dairy. Throughout the year's adventures, the boys are honest, industrious, optimistic, and courteous without being cute or sentimental. Details of the routine of farm life, chores, and amusements add to the realism of the understated story.

Skinny (1964), which won the Georgia Children's Book Award in 1969, the first year that it was given, and was an Honor Book in the Children's Spring Book Festival Book Week, is named for an illiterate eleven-year-old orphaned son of tenant farmers. This book, which also takes place during the Depression, marks an advance in plot construction as it deals with Skinny's attempts to learn to read and to find a permanent family. Until there is room in the orphanage forty miles away, he is staying temporarily with Miss Bessie, who runs the hotel in a small Georgia town, and her black help, Peachy the cook and Roman the yard man. Skinny acts as the general chore boy. The romance between Frank J. "Daddy" Rabbit, an older traveling construction worker who is a guest in the hotel, and Miss Bessie holds the promise of marriage for them and adoption for Skinny; but when Daddy Rabbit, an incurable ladies' man, moves on, both Skinny and Miss Bessie have to accept their disappointment. The ending of the story has its bittersweet compensations; at the orphanage Skinny begins to learn to read and write and he is to be allowed vacations and summers with Miss Bessie.

The details of life in a small town of the Depression era are well drawn from Skinny's point of view. For him a traveling carnival and the construction of a bridge over the Flint River are momentous occasions. The annual watermelon cutting at the Baptist church is the social event of the season. Such details as the nickname "Daddy" Rabbit, with his attire of flashy ties, "patent-leather shoes, white pants, a striped coat, and one of those flat-top straw hats," clue the reader, but not Skinny, as to the fragile hope to be placed in this aged dandy.

With *D. J.'s Worst Enemy* (1965), Burch presents another trio of Depression era children: D. J. Madison, who is twelve and a jealous bully; Renfroe, his five-year-old brother; and their older sister Clara May, an adult-talking thirteen-year-old. Renfroe is the center of attention because he is the baby and also because he constantly performs imitations of local eccentrics. Andrew Jackson, their hound, the Madison parents, and Nutty, D. J.'s best friend, are others in the cast of characters on a small Georgia farm. The story is told from D. J.'s point of view. A problem child, he is the center of several potentially serious mishaps. At last he realizes that

his vindictive behavior is causing too much pain and expense and he determines to be tolerant and part of the family. The final scene explains part of D. J.'s problem; he is passing through puberty. At the community dance held at the peach-packing shed, he gets the courage to ask a neighbor girl to dance, but as the floor is splintery and they are barefoot, the young couple has to wait. If the book has a fault, perhaps it is that too much is packed into 142 pages, giving the reader more of an outline than a full treatment of the story. As in other novels, the details of country life, such as the communal peach packing, are knowledgeably presented.

Queenie Peavy, which takes place in the 1930s, is a much sparer and more cohesive story which presents a female character similar to D. J. Burch's best-known book, in 1967 it received the Jane Addams Book Award and the Child Study Children's Book Committee at Bank Street College Award for its realistic approach in dealing with juvenile delin-

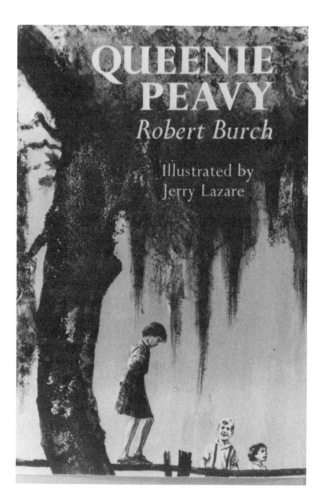

Dust jacket for Burch's best-known book, the story of a country tomboy in the 1930s (Viking)

quency. It was also named an ALA Notable Book and was selected for the Georgia Children's Book Award in 1971. In 1974 *Queenie Peavy* received the George G. Stone Award.

Queenie, a defensive thirteen-year-old tomboy, lives with her family in a two-room shack. Her father is in the Atlanta Federal Penitentiary for armed robbery, and her mother walks daily to town to work at a canning factory. Queenie's closest neighbors, the Corrys, whose young children, Dover and Avis, are her playmates, are a successful black farm family. With the black children, to whom she tells a series of tall tales about their dog Matilda climbing trees, she reveals that she is not as tough as she pretends and is really an industrious and serious student. But in town, she associates with two trouble-making seventh grade boys—Persimmon Gibbs and Floyd Speer. With them, she chews tobacco, smokes, throws rocks, and sasses adults.

Queenie's foil and friend is "Little Mother" Martha Mullins, who though equally poor and even undernourished, talks politely, takes the role of peacemaker, and sacrifices for the younger children in her family. Numerous trips to the principal's office and false charges of vandalism almost get Queenie sent to reform school, and when her father, whom she idolizes, gets paroled and comes home, she and the reader realize his serious shortcomings and the negative effect his influence has had on her. He is cold, curt, short-tempered, and vindictive; he promptly breaks parole by getting drunk and threatening with a gun the people who had previously testified against him.

On her own, Queenie pretends to reform as a joke and a disguise, but when she finds out that actually being a changed character is more rewarding, she determines to stay changed and to think before acting. She is not as sweet and unselfish as "Little Mother" at the end of the book, but she is happier and more feminine than before. As sales of the book and its awards have shown, both adults and children concur that Queenie is an original, totally believable, and appealing country tomboy.

Renfroe's Christmas (1968) shows that the delightful spoiled child of the Madison family from *D. J.'s Worst Enemy* has become older, more selfish, and a bit of a pest. Now a third grader, he has partially outgrown his desire to perform "imitations" to entertain family and friends; he now has grander designs to be an actor. The brief booklet consists of seven interwoven stories set during the Christmas holidays. Early in the book an angel dis-

carded from the tree trimmings is appropriated by Renfroe and nailed over the smokehouse door, becoming the mute barometer to his selfish actions. At the end of the book the angel seems to look up when Renfroe gives his most treasured Christmas present, a Mickey Mouse watch, to Crazy Nathan, a retarded fifteen-year-old.

Joey's Cat (1969) is another of Burch's picture books for young readers and his second book to win the George G. Stone Award, though the slight story is dated by inappropriate, socially conscious illustrations. The plot concerns Joey, who protects a mother cat and her kittens in the garage from another cat, a dog, and a possum. Finally his mother relents and lets Joey bring the cat and kittens inside. One detail lifts the story above the ordinary: as the mother cat winks at Joey, he intuits her message, and both understand that this is the first of many litters that his mother will eventually take in.

In *Simon and the Game of Chance* (1970) Burch ventures into modern times and serious, contemporary family topics: the deaths of a baby and a fiancé; the mental illness of a mother; and the conflict between a righteous, Bible-quoting, and emotionally undemonstrative father and his family. The protagonist, thirteen-year-old Simon, both deliberately baits and unconsciously emulates his father. Clarissa, the eldest daughter, is temporarily caring for the house and children while their mother is in a sanatorium. At the beginning of the book, the mother has a baby girl who dies in the incubator at the hospital. Mrs. Bradley, depressed and withdrawn, is sent away for a cure. The other children in the Bradley family are two boys Ballard (sixteen) and Roy, Jr. (seventeen) and the younger boys, Kleck (nine) and Abner (six).

The setting is Redwood, a small town now fast becoming part of the extended suburbs of Atlanta. The father, Mr. Bradley, a self-made man and the county tax collector, strictly governs the children and his wife with Biblical admonitions and rigid rules.

The story shows that despite the severe conflicts of this family, the rigid small town mores, real domestic tragedies, and the machinations and guilt of Simon, who resents the presence of Clarissa's fiancé, the individual members of the family can find a limited happiness and keep the unit together through compromise and adjustment. Part of that solution comes as they accept life as more a game of chance than predestination. Some of the incidents verge on the melodramatic, such as the death of Clarissa's fiancé when the old boiler in the basement of the barber shop blows up the day before they are to be married. But overall, the author does a good job with basically unattractive characters and an effective resolution of the strained relationship of Simon and his father.

The Hunting Trip (1971), slight but witty, is a lighthearted picture book for young readers. A young wife accompanies her older husband hunting. Each time he proposes shooting some prey, she persuades him to wait for something better. Finally they return home empty-handed to a supper of eggs, biscuits, and milk, and the husband is forced to trade his bullets at the store for peanut butter and cherry jam. After supper the wife remarks ironically that it is fun to go hunting. Unfortunately the illustrator chose to put the characters in central European costumes, a locale that ill suits details of the story such as peanut butter for supper and a skunk in the forest.

With *Doodle and the Go-Cart* (1972), which won the Georgia Children's Book Award in 1974, Burch returned to the rural Georgia scene and the farm boy he writes about best. In this contemporary story, Doodle Rounds rides a two-hundred-dollar go-cart at the fifth grade homeroom party held on the estate of his classmate, Elsie Moreland. Unfortunately, Doodle's father cannot afford such an expensive plaything for his son from his modest living as a cattle rancher, so with eyes only for getting his own go-cart, Doodle sets about various enterprises to earn the money.

The conflict of the story centers about Doodle's apparent willingness to sacrifice his health and finally even his pet mule Addie Flowers for the go-cart; he has bronchitis as a result of his beaver trapping on flooded land, he develops pneumonia from a fall in the water, and he is tempted to sell the mule for seventy dollars. In the background there is the conflict between town and country. The Doodle farm is endangered, as it is nine miles from expanding Ripley, Georgia, and gentlemen farmers like Mr. Maxwell are moving in to take up farming as a hobby. A Christmas visit by the Rounds family to their town relatives, Aunt Peggy, Uncle Roy, and cousin Glenn, sets the two families in sharp contrast. Too much money, too much social ambition, and too many cocktails have combined to make the Carter family unhappy and unadmirable.

Minor characters are delineated succinctly: Gloria Mitchell is crafty and penny-pinching, and Katie Bates is blissfully unaware that if she pays twenty-five cents to ride the mule, she won't have it to spend at the store. The events of the book take place over nearly a year, from the Fourth of July party, where Doodle rides the go-cart, to the following spring, as Doodle makes plans for ways to earn money in the summer. Details of the story are economical yet telling, and there is quiet humor in the unsuccessful money-making projects of Doodle before he hits upon the idea of beaver trapping in his father's bottomland. He is nearly successful, and the seventy dollars he could get for Addie would give him enough money for the go-cart, but he decides to keep her, even though his family will support whatever decision he makes. The moral that family relationships are more important than money is clear but not intrusive.

In *Hut School and the Wartime Home-Front Heroes* (1974), Burch portrays another independent and adventurous female character, but unlike Queenie Peavy, Kate Coleman is admirable from the beginning. Burch sets his characters in Redhill, a small town outside of Atlanta, in the critical period of change and crisis marked by World War II. Kate, a sixth grader, learns how to endure the changes necessary in these times. Her class has to be moved temporarily across the street into a former servant's house because additional classrooms are to be built for the children of parents moving to town to work in the munitions plant; the town children are given a day off to pick cotton because the regular hands have been drafted; the class writes to the serviceman brother of a classmate and then learns he has been killed; Miss Jordan, their beloved sixth grade teacher but a lax disciplinarian, joins the WAVES in the middle of the year; and Kate's father is drafted. Kate learns how to accept these changes like a home-front hero, acting in an independent, cheerful, and resourceful manner. After she joins the town children in the delightful mischief of jumping in the pile of cotton they have picked, she apologizes to the farmer and makes amends by organizing her companions to pick cotton on Saturdays.

In this novel both the town and country families come off admirably, probably a reflection of the united front in wartime, and Burch handles serious topics in both a sensitive and an adult manner. Perhaps Kate's family is a bit too idealistically drawn but other characters, such as the young principal, Mr. Bronson; Miss Dillman, the "drill master" teacher of the seventh grade; and Dinah Myrtle Moore, a sixth grader who is boy crazy, are skillfully developed. The period is convincingly established, and the novel has a contemporaneity the author may not have intended, but the lesson that Kate learns—"nothing stays the same forever, the good or the bad"—is skillfully woven into the narrative.

In *The Jolly Witch* (1975), the heroine is just as independent and self-reliant as Kate, but this picture story for younger readers is more entertaining. Cluny, the jolly witch, is traded by her sisters to a peddler for a boxful of snakes and two iron kettles. Because the peddler is slightly hard of hearing, he leaves this young, pretty, and jolly witch instead of the desired holly switch at the home of a cross old woman who has a son who will not smile, a cat that whines, and a canary that will not sing. By trading the old woman lessons in witchcraft for home economics, Cluny soon puts the house, son, cat, and canary to rights. She gets rid of the old woman as well by getting her to exercise her new powers by riding a broom, which takes her to a witches' den. The story has the charm of wish fulfillment associated with fairy tales reinforced by the droll illustrations by Leigh Grant.

Two That Were Tough (1976), with its striking illustrations by Richard Cuffari which were cited for their excellence by the American Institute of Graphic Arts Book Show in 1977, subtly introduces older children to more serious topics: freedom, independence, and the necessary dependence of the aging are well developed in this book which compares and contrasts the lives and fates of Mr. Hilton, the aged owner of a gristmill, and Wild Wings, a rooster hatched in the wild. The story begins with the York family's wild hen, who raises her brood of ten chicks from a clutch of thirteen eggs in a nest hidden in the mulberry thicket near Mr. Hilton's gristmill. The hen's stoic attitude about her brood is that "they would eat or they couldn't; it was up to them." The tenth chick survives predators, accidents, and attempted capture for the frying pan to become "tall and lean, with slate-colored feathers that shone like satin." When the York family moves away to south Georgia, this rooster stays behind at Mr. Hilton's place.

During the year Mr. Hilton is urged to move in with his daughter in Atlanta. After a year of shared adventures and misadventures with Wild Wings, some of them comic, Mr. Hilton promises to make the move if he can take the rooster with him. But after he finally captures the bird, he releases it in a final gesture toward the independence he is giving up. In the last chapter Mr. Hilton is visited by the new people from Atlanta who have bought the York place. Before he leaves, he gets this family to promise to look after the rooster without trying to make it a pet or take away its freedom.

Two That Were Tough is a more somber story than usual from Robert Burch and would be equally suited for an adult reader. As Paul Heins declared in *Horn Book*, the story has both "understated humor and pathos" and a "simple, colloquial style," both of which can be seen in the description of Mr. Hilton as he sets the trap for the rooster: "he was shaking his fist at the world—at old age, at failing strength and weakened eyesight, and a memory that sometimes became confused."

The Whitman Kick (1977) takes up equally serious topics for junior high students: sexual maturity, teenage romances, breakups, and unwanted pregnancies. Told in the first person by Alan J. Ponder, a seventeen-year-old boy on the verge of manhood who enlists in the U.S. Army in August 1942, the story begins in the barracks of Fort McPherson in Atlanta with the bravado of the other fresh soldiers in Alan's platoon and his own wry reflections: "The kid from Macon is bragging. If he turns out to be as remarkable a soldier as he purports to have been a lover, World War II should not last much longer. He will win it with ease."

This protagonist is again one of Burch's small town boys brought up outside Atlanta. Alan is from the town of Ellenville, twenty miles from Fort McPherson, and having just finished high school, he has joined up after losing his longtime platonic girlfriend Amanda Moore.

Though Alan and Amanda have shared an intellectual affinity and an emotional sympathy since the sixth grade, Alan lacks her sexual maturity. Having experienced a mutual "kick" in the poetry of Walt Whitman, both soon discovered that the passion celebrated in his verse did not carry over into their individual lives. When opportunity presents itself, Amanda finds sexual experience with Hap Jordan, a rich and more sophisticated town boy who has been dating Alan's elder sister Irene. Out of jealousy, Alan takes up with Gloria Mason, an eleventh grader notorious for being easy. Alan gets his experience, but Amanda becomes pregnant by Hap.

In addition to the teenage misalliances of the children there is domestic trouble between Alan's parents. His mother has left his father to live with his cousin in Montgomery, Alabama, under the guise of caring for both the cousin and his ill sister. As Alan and Amanda move farther apart, Mr. and Mrs. Ponder take steps to restore their marriage. Mr. Ponder trades their old family home in the center of town for a new one in the suburbs free of any "ghosts" of the family's troubled times.

The story is marked by the liberal quotations from romantic poets which form much of the interchange between Alan and Amanda, ironically characterizing both its authenticity and shallowness. The enumeration of the bric-a-brac treasured by Amanda's mother is likewise a devastating clue to her materialism. However, the story is lightened by the Ponders' family joke of a sprite named Buddy who sends messages by various birds. Buddy and the birds become the guise through which the Ponder family and their close friends can discuss their feelings and thoughts.

At the end of the book, Amanda has gone to Santa Fe, New Mexico, to have the baby; Hap and Irene elope; Mr. and Mrs. Ponder are reunited; and Alan has learned the lesson of forgiveness given too late. His parting gesture to Amanda is an expensive leather-bound copy of *Leaves of Grass* which he sends to her out west. The story is somber and more bitter than sweet, unlike most of Burch's novels, and the development of the plot seems rather wooden, often insufficiently motivated, but the book does treat serious domestic issues with sensitivity and restraint.

In *Wilkin's Ghost* (1978), Burch returns to his rural trio of Wilkin, Tyler, and Skee, now thirteen, fourteen, and ten, respectively. The well-paced story is told from Wilkin's point of view, revealing his desire to see the world outside the farm and also his inexperience in judging character. As the novel begins, he leaves his brothers and fellow field-workers to take a shortcut home, daring to pass by the hanging tree, scene of an execution ten years before, in 1925, and supposedly the residence of the hanged man's ghost. What Wilkin subsequently takes for the ghost turns out in fact to be Alex Folsom, the sixteen-year-old cousin of the poor, white, and mean Floyd family, who live outside of town. Later, when Alex takes refuge in the house of the town's spinsters, Miss Etta and Miss Julia Todd, which Wilkin is looking after during their absence, Wilkin meets Alex face to face. Alex's mother has remarried, and Alex has run away to live with the Floyds, but he bears an old charge of a robbery at Mr. Larson's store and does not stand well in the community. Despite all of this, Wilkin befriends Alex and gets Miss Julia and Miss Etta upon their return to give him a home in exchange for doing chores. To clear Alex of the old theft charges, he gets Mr. Lawson to employ Alex in the store to make up the amount stolen.

Alex at first seems to justify this trust, for he proves to be a fast, able, and honest worker. The local girls think Alex is "the best-looking person they'd ever seen, maybe because he had blond wavy hair and clear skin," unlike the freckled-faced, stringy-haired country boys they are accustomed to. However, Alex soon excites Wilkin with promises of the money and life-style to be found in Atlanta, and the two boys plan to run away together and work there as bellhops.

When Edgar Rounds, a sailor cousin of Miss Etta and Miss Julia, comes for a visit, the plot gets more complicated. Edgar makes Wilkin realize some of the negative side of being a traveler, such as the loneliness of living a rootless life. Then Edgar's twenty-dollar gold coin is stolen at the welcoming party, and suspicion lights on Alex, though the case cannot be proved. Later Wilkin finds out that Alex is the real thief and is also guilty of both the earlier and a subsequent robbery at Larson's store. He determines not to run away but to wait a while before seeing the world, and thus, the book realistically shows Wilkin maturing in judgment. As in previous books, the details of country life are truthfully and simply drawn, but as a forward step in characterization, the story also shows a mixture of good and bad in characters, including Alex.

With *Ida Early Comes Over the Mountain* (1980), set on the Georgia side of the Blue Ridge Mountains in the late 1930s, Burch introduces his most entertaining character. The rollicking pace of the domestic adventures in this thoughtful novel about family life carries Ida Early, with her folksy speech and straightforward manners, into the Sutton family, making her the catalyst for their recovery from the vacuum left by the recent death of Mrs. Sutton. Ida, a tall, young scarecrow creature in overalls and brogans, appears one morning in mid July at the Sutton home. Hired by the young, widowed Mr. Sutton as temporary help, she promptly becomes the cook, maid, substitute mother, companion, and playmate of the children, Randall, age eleven, Ellen, age twelve, and the five-year-old twins, Clay and Dewey.

Ida promptly routs Aunt Earnestine, who is temporarily taking care of and constantly intimidating the Sutton family, by deliberately capturing the attention of the children with her antics, such as tossing her sweater onto a coatrack as surely as a player putting a basketball through the goal and casually rolling, one-handed, her own cigarettes from Bull Durham tobacco. She also cleverly gets the children to start helping with the cooking and cleaning, as well as the caring for the younger children, by involving them in various games, such as tiddledywinks and checkers. Ida Early is also heroic, when she rescues a small neighbor child from a maddened sow named Mayflower and when she lassos a berserk bear at the school assembly program.

Chapter ~~8~~ 9.

Randall finished reading the twins (*their favorite story*) THE THREE BILLYGOATS GRUFF, *and*
~~their favorite story.~~ Clay ~~took~~ *put* ~~put~~ the book back on the shelf beneath
the window, *He* ~~and~~ brought out another one, *but Randall*
said, "Let's *quit for a while.*" ~~don't read any more,"~~ ~~said Randall, who~~ *He'd* been trying
to keep Clay and Dewey quiet by reading to them.

"Then what can we do?" ~~whispered~~ asked Clay. It was raining, and they
couldn't play outside.

"We can talk if you'll keep your voices down." They'd made so
much noise ~~in the kitchen~~ soon after they'd returned home ~~that×after×~~
from school that Aunt Earnestine ~~x~~ had come into the kitchen and scolded
them. ~~She×was×trying×to~~ ~~She~~'d gone back to her room, *now for the rest of* ~~to try and continue~~
her afternoon nap.

Randall felt sorry for the twins. Naturally, ~~everybody's~~ *their*
spirits were high; *it was a* ~~on a~~ Friday afternoon, *--and* ~~especially when it was~~
close to holiday time, *at that.* Still, he could understand Aunt Earnestine's
wanting them to quiet down. She was under *the* doctor's order*s* to get lots
of ~~bed~~ rest.

"Reckon Santa Claus ~~s~~ will bring anything to Aunt Earnestine?"
whispered Dewey.

"You don't have to whisper," said Randall. "She can't hear
you in her room if you don't talk loud or ~~whop~~ whoop and holler."

"I~~f~~ wouldn't bring her anything," said Clay. "If I were Santa
Claus, I'd skip over Aunt Earnestine."

Ida Early and Ellen came into the kitchen. They'd been
giving the front room--or parlor--~~b~~ what they called its Christmas-
cleaning. The room ~~was~~ was seldom used , except when company came--

Page from a draft for Christmas with Ida Early. *This passage was used as the opening of chapter eleven, "The Checkers Tournament" (by permission of the author).*

*Dust jacket for Burch's forthcoming novel about a young girl
seeking acceptance at a new school (Viking)*

This overgrown and overaged tomboy has a soft, feminine side too. Her feelings are hurt when schoolchildren jeer at her and when Randall and Ellen fail to defend her. She changes her garb for an ill-fitting green dress and tight-fitting Mary Jane shoes in an attempt to fit in. Finally she runs away, but a letter of apology from Randall and Ellen and her love for her adopted family bring her back, though her return on a motorcycle is as startling as her initial appearance; she is dressed in riding pants, a leather jacket, and an aviator's cap. It is just in time, as Thanksgiving is near and Mr. Sutton's critical sisters, including Aunt Earnestine, are coming with their families. Ida Early is in command again of the household as she asks, looking around, "Anybody care for a smoke?" *Ida Early Comes Over the Mountain* was an ALA Notable Book and a Boston Globe-Horn Book Award winner for fiction. Its popularity and Burch's success with the creation of

his memorable heroine led immediately to a sequel.

Set a year later, *Christmas with Ida Early* (1983) covers the holiday season from Thanksgiving to Christmas Day. Events are seen from the point of view of twelve-year-old Randall, but the center of the book continues to be the irrepressible Ida Early. The older children have matured and observe adult behavior with insight and growing tolerance, though Ida continues to make life a game and to lighten the somberness of the motherless family and of the Depression times. Since she is taller than six feet, she is more comfortable using the "top of their icebox as a kitchen counter." When she is making boiled custard, she tosses the egg yolks into the pot by hook shots. Minor and major crises are handled with equal aplomb, and Ida succeeds at last in winning over Aunt Earnestine, who comes for Thanksgiving and has to be nursed through a severe case of the flu until Christmas. Ida uses her talents as a ventriloquist to save the neck of the turkey that the twins Dewey and Clay have made a pet of by making it appear to talk and substitutes a tuna casserole instead with a complementary array of homegrown vegetables.

Ida endures a series of recurring conflicts with Brother Preston; as a fresh seminary graduate, he is a bit pompous and rigid in his first assignment as a preacher. He does not take well to her novel reinterpretations of Sunday School lessons, church festivities, and customs. For example, Ida's version of the feeding of the five thousand as told to the primary class includes "a bucket of peanut shells and a barrel of apple peelings, and a stalk of bananas that had barely been touched" and also "a wagonload of watermelon rinds and half of a big birthday cake with red candles on it." Later Ida turns the Nativity tableau into a sideshow by acting as a barker as well as throwing her voice so that the assembled animals appear to be yodeling.

Critics of both books have noted the resemblance of Ida Early to Mary Poppins, because both characters whimsically appeal to children's imaginations. The story and the exploits of Ida are, however, firmly grounded not in magic but in the realistic details of small town life in Georgia in the 1930s. As the reviewer for *Horn Book* has also observed, her "adventures are in the tall-tale tradition of American humor." In both books, her fantastic tales and amazing adventures are framed by the ordinary domestic duties of daily meal preparation, raising children, and nursing the sick in a home where, along with an assortment of pets, radio programs, games of cards, checkers, tiddledywinks, jigsaw puzzles, and traditional stories such as "The

Three Billygoats Gruff" provide the normal amusements.

Beside the other characters in this homely setting, Ida appears paradoxically both normal and exotic. By the end of the book, accommodation has been made for both her views of life and the quite different ones of Aunt Earnestine and Brother Preston, and all of the members of the Sutton family have learned how to practice tolerance for others without betraying their own ideals.

Christmas with Ida Early was issued as a Puffin paperback in the fall of 1985. At present Burch is at work on two manuscripts. One is a third Ida Early book to be titled either "Ida Early Gives Lessons on Love" or "Valentines for Ida Early." The other, *King Kong and Other Poets,* in which the central character, a twelve-year-old girl, cultivates poetry as her escape from life, will be published in the fall of 1986. His earlier novel, *Queenie Peavy* (1966), was selected by the Children's Literature Association for their Phoenix Award, presented at their annual conference in May 1986.

Robert Burch is associated with the new realism in children's literature, which deals with serious issues and their effects on characters' lives: things such as death, mental illness, sex, unloving or undemonstrative parents, orphans, and delinquency. Burch never sensationalizes or focuses on the subject itself; instead, he shows how the individual and the family must confront the problem. In his best books there are no miraculous solutions, and sometimes the endings are unhappy or mixed, but the characters have learned how to endure.

Since the author focuses on how the individual functions within the family, often the central character is well drawn and the others are more shadowy. Burch has the ability to set characters, conflict, and scene firmly in the reader's mind, but the working of his plots is sometimes episodic and occasionally the resolutions seem too neat. His books are moral and realistic, but they are also very entertaining, with a quiet humor derived from shrewd observations of human nature. His descriptions of country life in the South are authentic and moving; an author who can present aspects of life during the Great Depression in Georgia so that they are entertaining as well as instructive deserves credit for no small achievement. If children realize the human spirit could both persevere and laugh in those times, they can certainly live with the present.

References:

Lee Bennett Hopkins, *More Books by More People* (New York: Citation Press, 1974);

Charlotte Hale Smith, "Bachelor Writes Children's Stories," *Atlanta Journal and Constitution Magazine,* 29 November 1964, pp. 55, 57, 59.

Papers:

Robert Burch has manuscripts and galley proofs on loan at the University of Georgia Library, Special Collections Department.

Betsy Byars

(7 August 1928-   )

Elizabeth Segel

BOOKS: *Clementine,* illustrated by Charles Wilton (Boston: Houghton Mifflin, 1962);

The Dancing Camel, illustrated by Harold Berson (New York: Viking, 1965);

Rama, The Gypsy Cat, illustrated by Peggy Bacon (New York: Viking, 1966);

The Groober (New York: Harper & Row, 1967);

The Midnight Fox, illustrated by Ann Grifalconi (New York: Viking, 1968; London: Faber & Faber, 1970);

Trouble River, illustrated by Rocco Negri (New York: Viking, 1969);

The Summer of the Swans, illustrated by Ted CoConis (New York: Viking, 1970);

Go and Hush the Baby, illustrated by Emily A. McCully (New York: Viking, 1971);

The House of Wings, illustrated by Daniel Schwartz (New York: Viking, 1972; London: Bodley Head, 1973);

The 18th Emergency, illustrated by Robert Grossman (New York: Viking, 1973; London: Bodley Head, 1974);

The Winged Colt of Casa Mia, illustrated by Richard Cuffari (New York: Viking, 1973; London: Bodley Head, 1974);

After the Goat Man, illustrated by Ronald Himler (New York: Viking, 1974; London: Bodley Head, 1975);

The Lace Snail (New York: Viking, 1975);

The TV Kid, illustrated by Cuffari (New York: Viking, 1976; London: Bodley Head, 1976);

The Pinballs (New York: Harper & Row, 1977; London: Bodley Head, 1977);

The Cartoonist, illustrated by Cuffari (New York: Viking, 1978; London: Bodley Head, 1978);

Good-bye, Chicken Little (New York: Harper & Row, 1979; London: Bodley Head, 1979);

The Night Swimmers, illustrated by Troy Howell (New York: Delacorte, 1980; London: Bodley Head, 1980);

The Cybil War, illustrated by Gail Owens (New York: Viking, 1981; London: Bodley Head, 1981);

The Animal, the Vegetable, and John D Jones, illustrated by Ruth Sanderson (New York: Delacorte, 1982; London: Bodley Head, 1982);

The Two-Thousand-Pound Goldfish (New York: Harper & Row, 1982; London: Bodley Head, 1982);

The Glory Girl (New York: Viking, 1983; London: Bodley Head, 1983);

The Computer Nut, computer graphics by Guy Byars (New York: Viking, 1984; London: Bodley Head, 1984);

Cracker Jackson (New York: Viking, 1985);
The Not-Just-Anybody Family (New York: Dell, 1986).

PERIODICAL PUBLICATIONS: "Writing for
    Children," *Signal*, 37 (January 1982): 3-10;
"Leo Edwards and the Secret and Mysterious Or-
    der of the Freckled Goldfish," *Horn Book*, 61
    (October 1985): 533-535.

Betsy Byars has been awarded both the Newbery Medal in 1971 for *The Summer of the Swans* and
the American Book Award in 1981 for *The Night
Swimmers*. Nancy Chambers, editor of the British
critical journal *Signal*, has characterized her as "one
of the ten best writers for children in the world."
Her books have won high favor with children in
the United States and Britain as well: of the twenty-
five books she has published in the United States,
twenty-two are currently in print; sixteen of her
books are listed in *British Books in Print 1985*. Her
books have been translated into at least nine languages, and several of her novels have been dramatized for television.

Betsy Cromer Byars was born in North Carolina in 1928 and grew up during the Depression.
Her parents, George Guy and Nan Rugheimer
Cromer, were well educated and avid readers; her
mother had majored in drama at a small girls'
school. Byars's childhood was spent partly in a small
mill settlement out in the country where her father
worked in the office of a cotton mill and partly in
the city of Charlotte. She felt she had the best of
both worlds—city living and country living. She has
always loved to read, having learned well before
she started school.

The only children's books she recalls reading
as a child were series books of the 1930s: the Bobb-
sey Twins, of course, and her favorites, the Jerry
Todd, Poppy Ott, and Tuffy Bean series of Leo
Edwards (all Grosset). Many of the Edwards books
were humorous adventures of a group of boy detectives.

Thus, she started writing children's books as
someone unfamiliar with the classic works of the
genre. She still reads very few children's books,
although she is an avid reader of adult fiction.
"Most of what I have learned about writing, I have
learned from other authors . . . , everybody from
Thomas Hardy to Françoise Sagan to Toni Morrison, and it's an ongoing thing. Next week I'll be
indebted to somebody else." This unfamiliarity
with the work of established children's writers
probably accounts for the freshness and originality
of her best books, although a knowledge of the

tradition might have spared her one or two failures
with unpromising material.

After high school, Betsy Byars attended Fur-
man University in Greenville, South Carolina, for
two years and then transferred to Queens College
in Charlotte, where she majored in English. After
her graduation in 1950, she married Edward Ford
Byars, a graduate student in engineering at Clemson University. The next six years were spent in
Clemson, living a pleasant graduate-student and
young-faculty life, surrounded by friends. In 1956
the Byarses moved to Urbana, where her husband
pursued further graduate work at the University
of Illinois. They had two small children and were
expecting a third. Byars knew no one in Urbana,
her husband was involved with his studies all day
and often after dinner as well, and most of her
neighbors in the barracks where they lived either
worked or attended school also. She had thought
she would like to try her hand at writing sometime
and now said to herself with characteristic buoy-
ancy: "Well, here is a wonderful opportunity, an
ideal time to try it."

Two years later, the family moved to Morgantown, West Virginia, where Edward Byars
joined the faculty at the University of West Virginia. Betsy Byars's first writing success came with
the publication of short, humorous pieces in the
Saturday Evening Post, Look, Everywoman's Magazine,
and *TV Guide*. Soon she began to write for children,
but many failures preceded her successes. "When
I first began to write, I was terribly prolific," she
has said. "If I thought of it, I wrote it."

Clementine (1962) was her first published book.
It was dedicated to her four children, who ranged
in age from four to eleven. The book takes the
form of a small boy's first-person account of his
imaginative play with a toy dragon named Clementine. "He doesn't look much like a dragon, more
like a fat green sock with eyes on the toe, but a
dragon he is." Clementine is a naive, boastful blus-
terer, constantly revealing the fears he tries to hide,
but he is intended to be lovable all the same because
his foibles mirror those of the very small and vulnerable child. The narrator enjoys feeling superior
and fondly indulges Clementine's foolishness. The
inherent danger of the subject is that the humor,
based on the comical fears and ignorance of the
small child, is in a sense at children's expense. The
young listener, who is trying to put babyish things
behind him, can laugh at Clementine as the adult
does, but to the extent that the work invites this, it
encourages the child to deny the seriousness of his
earlier feelings. More experienced writers than

Byars was have faltered with similar material.

The Bulletin of the Council for Children's Books labeled *Clementine* a marginal book and concluded that "the writing verges on the precious." The quality of preciousness, of archness, that colors the book comes as a surprise to anyone familiar with the unadorned spareness of Byars's novels of the 1970s. Byars put a great deal of her own personality into *Clementine*, and when the book was harshly reviewed she made a decision to retreat to impersonal books—books that anyone could have written.

The Dancing Camel (1965), a slightly plotted picture book, was her next publication. Alice Dalgleish in the *Saturday Review* called it "a pleasant-to-read-aloud book . . . full of good words and good pictures," but another reviewer wrote: "Even as a child I think I would have said 'so what?' to 'The Dancing Camel.' . . . It offers a tidy little moral without much meat."

Rama, The Gypsy Cat (1966), Byars's first novel for children, relates the adventures of a cat who starts off as the pet of a gypsy woman but is inadvertently left behind when her caravan moves on. Rama's journeying up and down the Ohio River is convincingly recorded, and a brisk pace sustains the reader's attention. The open-ended conclusion led one reviewer to suggest the possibility of further adventures of Rama, but, in spite of her success with this form, Byars did not publish a sequel. Nor did she ever again write a novel from an animal's viewpoint. The imaginative exercise of creating Rama's world probably enriched the sensitive portrayals of animals and birds in later books, however.

The Groober (1967), written and illustrated by Betsy Byars, is another negligible picture book—this time about a nebbishlike character who lives in a shallow hole which he loves until he travels and sees other groobers' excavations. Then he digs and digs to reshape his own hole, finally discovering he has ended up with the original shape. "Amiably silly," declared one reviewer; it seems a fair judgment.

At about this time, Byars took a children's literature course at the University of West Virginia and encountered the realistic novel for children for the first time. It seems probable that the increasing assuredness of her writing and her subsequent choice of more promising subjects was related to this exposure.

Trouble River, though published in 1969, was written before *The Midnight Fox* (1968). This is another of Byars's impersonal narratives. Like the animal story *Rama, The Gypsy Cat, Trouble River* falls neatly into a standard category of children's books—the frontier adventure story. Dewey's parents have journeyed to Hunter City for the mother's lying-in, leaving twelve-year-old Dewey Martin and his grandmother alone in the family's cabin on the prairie. One night Dewey and his dog drive off a hostile Indian, but they know he will be back with others to burn them out. Fortunately, Dewey has been building a raft on the nearby Trouble River, and he now takes his grandmother down the muddy river through all sorts of dangers to safety. He sees the events as a test of his courage in adversity, but this aspect of the book does not add very much to a well-worn theme of juvenile adventure stories.

However, the ramrod figure of Grandma on the crude raft in her best bonnet and rocking chair is the first of Byars's varied and perceptive portraits of old people. The growth of respect between boy and old woman, which is the core of the book, is a theme Byars would return to for some of her most successful stories. The book also marks Byars's first use of comic dialogue to control and relieve narrative tension, one of her most characteristic techniques. Reviews were generally favorable, and *Trouble River* was named a Notable Book for 1969 by the American Library Association.

In the meantime, Byars had risked a more personal book, a realistic story set in the present-day mountains of West Virginia, where the Byars family owned a vacation cabin. *The Midnight Fox* had its genesis in the excitement Byars felt in seeing a fox near the cabin. She also turned to her own children's experiences for the details of the book. Unlike some writers who share her gift for evoking the feeling of being a child (Wilder, for instance, or Sendak), Byars says she remembers very little about her own childhood—"just the peaks and the valleys." Fortunately, her own children were exceptionally open and communicative and shared with her the events of their daily lives. When they were young, Byars described herself without hesitation as an ordinary housewife and mother, even though she was putting in a full day of writing while they were at school. She clearly enjoyed those years, and her droll sense of humor and unpretentious manner probably led her children and their friends to tolerate her presence in their private world of "fooling around" from which most adults are barred. Her books from *The Midnight Fox* on are replete with genuine artifacts from that world—endless Monopoly games, heart-to-heart confidences with the family pooch, buried time capsules—and these experiences contribute enormously to their aura of authenticity.

The Midnight Fox is a retrospective first-person account of a memorable summer in a child's life. A brief lyrical passage with a note of foreboding begins the book:

> Sometimes at night when the rain is beating against the windows of my room, I think about that summer on the farm. It has been five years, but when I close my eyes I am once again by the creek watching the black fox come leaping over the green, green grass. She is as light and free as the wind, exactly as she was the first time I saw her.
>
> Or sometimes it is that last terrible night, and I am standing beneath the oak tree with the rain beating against me. The lightning flashes, the world is turned white for a moment, and I see everything as it was—the broken lock, the empty cage, the small tracks disappearing into the rain. Then it seems to me that I can hear, as plainly as I heard it that August night, above the rain, beyond the years, the high, clear bark of the midnight fox.
>
> To begin with, I did not want to go to the farm. . . .

As Tom's mother breaks the news to him that he will be spending two months at Aunt Millie's farm while she and his father take a bicycle tour of Europe, the narrative proper begins. Tom, neither athletic like his parents nor a lover of the outdoors, refuses. "Animals hate me," he insists. "I'll probably be the only kid in the world to be stampeded to death by a bunch of baby lambs." This dialogue rings true to parent-child confrontations and immediately establishes the reality of the two characters. Tom's father, a high school coach, is captured as deftly in the next scene as he expresses his hearty conviction that summer spent on a farm will be the making of his unathletic son. They are typical Byars scenes—at once hilarious and poignant as the well-meaning but blundering adults unintentionally abuse the child's feelings.

Tom concedes but is convinced that Aunt Millie and Uncle Fred are expecting a he-man to help with the heavy farm work (in his vivid imagination he has recast the movie version of *Anne of Green Gables* with himself as protagonist). Although his relatives turn out to be kind and undemanding, Tom is miserable. He will never be able to live up to their sons (now grown), Tom Sawyer types who used to come and go by the tree outside the bedroom window.

Tom is bored and lonely until he sees a black fox. Her beauty and wildness awe him, and from then on his days are spent blissfully exploring the woods and fields, trying to sight her again. He is successful on many occasions; he even finds her den and sees her one pup playing. Byars captures the wonder of each encounter in spare, lucid prose.

Tom's happiness comes to an end when the fox steals one of Aunt Millie's turkeys. Taciturn Uncle Fred, a skilled hunter, agrees to get rid of the fox, and Tom tags along behind, feebly trying to throw his uncle off the trail. Finding the den easily, Uncle Fred digs out the baby fox and cages it to lure the mother within range of his shotgun. That night, Tom musters his courage to climb out his window and down the tree in a storm in order to release the fox cub. Tom's rescue mission succeeds and the two foxes run off in the moonlight to safety. When Tom offers his genuinely felt apology to his aunt and uncle, the book takes an unexpected turn, deepening the meaning of the experience for Tom and for the reader. As Uncle Fred looks at him, Tom realizes,

> he was seeing through all the very casual questions I had been asking all summer about foxes, and seeing through the long days I had spent in the woods. . . . I think all those pieces just snapped into place right then in Uncle Fred's mind and I knew that if there was one person in the world who understood me it was this man who had seemed a stranger.
>
> He cleared his throat. "I never liked to see wild things in a pen myself," he said.

Given this satisfying resolution, the reader may with some justification object to the strong foreshadowing of a tragic outcome that Byars builds up through the book, not only in the prologue but in the downward spiral of events that are apparently leading to the death of the fox. Otherwise, her narrative touch is sure. Tom's friend Petie Burkis appears only in the first and last few pages of the book, but appears through letters and in the frequent memories that sustain Tom in his weeks on the farm. The past and present antics of the two boys not only develop Tom's character but also provide a comic counterpoint to the slow, delicate unfolding of Tom's experience on the farm. This bold mix of humor and sensitivity to the intense emotions of childhood is the keystone of Betsy Byars's originality.

The Midnight Fox was favorably reviewed and has been highly regarded by critics. It is Byars's own favorite among her books: "It came closer to what I was trying to do than any of my other books," she has said. Yet the book did not attract very much attention at the time, and Byars was still not sure that her writing would give her the profession she wanted now that her children were becoming more self-sufficient. During an earlier slump in her writing career, following the publication of *The Groober*, she had gone back to school in Library Science. Now she became interested in mental retardation after a friend suggested that she tell stories to a Brownie troop of exceptional children. She enrolled in a graduate program at the University of West Virginia in 1969, seeking a degree in special education, and began taking courses, though she did not finish. Heeding her husband's advice ("Just don't close the door on your writing"), she did go on writing stories.

In the summers she served as her husband's crew as he pursued his hobby of soaring. This entailed helping assemble and repair the motorless aircraft and driving around the countryside to pick up glider and husband after a landing. In 1968 the family traveled to Texas to take part in a competition. After returning home, Byars began work on a novel set in Texas but found the material intractable, and it was several years and revisions later before it saw print as *The Winged Colt of Casa Mia* (1973). She was more successful with another story, one set in the West Virginia countryside and rooted in the information and insights she was gathering in her work with retarded children. *The Summer of the Swans* was published in 1970 and won the Newbery Medal in 1971, evidence that her writing career was in fact "going to work out" and encouraging her to drop out of graduate school and devote herself to writing.

The Summer of the Swans is the summer of Sara Godfrey's adolescent discontent. She finds herself despondent and irritated—by her own big feet, by her pretty older sister, by her Aunt Willie who has cared for the Godfrey children since their mother died six years earlier—she is even impatient with her younger retarded brother, Charlie. When Sara takes Charlie to see six swans who have appeared on a nearby lake, he is fascinated by the mysterious birds and does not want to leave. That night Charlie cannot sleep and, setting out in search of the swans, becomes lost. In the agonized search and the joyous finding, Sara's passionate protective love for her brother is reaffirmed, her fierce adolescent judgments of others are softened, and her spirits soar

Dust jacket for Byars's novel about a teenage girl's relationship with her younger retarded brother. The book was awarded the Newbery Medal in 1971 (Viking).

with her last glimpse of the swans flying over the trees.

Unfortunately, Joe Melby, a classmate who has helped in the search, at this moment asks Sara to go out with him. Thus her newfound joy and confidence remind one of the facile resolutions of formula teenage romances: all problems cleared up with an invitation to the prom.

A remarkable achievement of the book is Byars's depiction of Charlie, a brain-damaged ten year old who cannot speak. Byars even presents key events from his viewpoint, and these passages, which were based on three case histories, are understated, convincing, and unusually touching.

In this book Byars develops the West Virginia setting as an important component of the story. She has said: "By the time I wrote this book, the State of West Virginia . . . had taken a strong hold on me. It's a place of great individuality and strength, and the setting was very important to me. Most of the land is still untamed and wild: I wanted to give the reader the feeling of the power of the land over the individual. I can't conceive of the book's taking place anywhere else." Over the next decade, Byars built up a dense fictional world of distinctive terrain and inhabitants which readers came to know. On the strength of these novels, Byars deserves a place in the strong regionalist tradition of American realism.

The brief time elapsing in *The Summer of the Swans* and its culmination in a moment of heightened awareness suggest that it is in form closer to the short story than to the novel. Several other of her most successful books are essentially short stories: *The House of Wings* (1972), *After the Goat Man* (1974), and *The Cartoonist* (1978). Byars prefers to depict a crisis in a character's life—"something they have to face"—in a narrative that spans only a few hours or days.

Receiving the Newbery Medal was a great surprise to Byars, who did not yet dare to think of herself as a writer. She had never been in an editor's office, nor did she know any writers. The award did not change her way of life—she went on writing at a desk in her bedroom and serving on her husband's crew on soaring expeditions—yet it made an important difference to her as a writer. She has said that it "seemed to me to be an enormous pat on the back, a sort of you're-on-the-right-track gesture. It encouraged me enormously, and since that time I have been more secure, more willing to try new things, more willing to fail."

Her next published work, *Go and Hush the Baby* (1971), is an appealing picture book. In Byars's brief text a mother's requests that her son amuse the crying baby alternate with his good-natured and inventive attempts. The engaging, imaginative hero is unmistakably a Byars boy, close kin to Tom and Petie of *The Midnight Fox*. Byars, who has often had illustrators who did not do justice to her texts, was blessed in this instance. *Go and Hush the Baby* is one of Emily A. McCully's most successful books; her ink-and-wash sketches elaborate with wit and charm on the simple text. McCully added to the subject of a boy who is good at amusing babies, a mother who is busy painting a picture rather than scrubbing floors. Thus the book was welcomed at a time when many people were looking for books which challenged rigid gender roles without heavy-handed didacticism.

The new confidence Byars felt after receiving the Newbery Medal is evident in *The House of Wings* (1972), the work of an artist who has perfect control of her material and who executes her intention without faltering. It is the first of several explora-

tions into the lives of people who have very little money and live unconventional lives which bear slight resemblance to those of most readers and writers of books; *The TV Kid* (1976), *The Cartoonist* (1978), and *The Night Swimmers* (1980) are others. Byars here uses fiction to help us imagine these unfamiliar lives, yet at the same time to remind us of our kinship with these people by depicting them in difficulties we all have experienced, at least in our fantasies.

In *The House of Wings* the reader is caught up from the first page in the archetypal childhood nightmare—parental abandonment. In the book's first scene, Sammy is running desperately into unknown terrain, pursued by his grandfather. Byars uses flashbacks, which have become a staple of her narrative technique, to explain the cause of Sammy's distress. The boy and his parents have been driving north in an old truck from Alabama to Detroit, where his father hopes to get work. They stop for the night at his mother's old home in Ohio. Her widowed father, who can hardly remember which of his children she is, has let the house go to ruin; his companions are an owl, a parrot, and a flock of geese who wander in and out. The next morning Sammy's grandfather tells him that while he slept, his parents decided to go on without him, planning to send for him later after they got settled. Sammy's dismay and disbelief crystallize into a hatred of the grizzled, bull-necked old man: "Dirty liar!," he sobs and runs off. In the ensuing chase, they come upon an injured crane, and the old man's passionate love for wild things overrides Sammy's outrage and compels him to help in the rescue. Gradually, Sammy comes to share his grandfather's concern for the bird's survival, and he begins to feel at home with the eccentric old man. His temporary abandonment has come to seem a lucky release from the constraints of civilization. That all this transpires in twenty-four hours amazes Sammy himself, but Betsy Byars's unerring instinct for telling details and vivid speech make the emotional curve of the story entirely credible. *The House of Wings* was warmly reviewed and was a finalist for the National Book Award in 1973.

In her next book, *The 18th Emergency* (1973), Byars gave her comic exuberance free rein. In contrast to the previous novels, this has an unparticularized urban setting and a breezy pace. Yet just as the predominately sober novels were leavened with humorous passages, so a fundamentally somber respect for the reality of children's fears and their moral sensitivity undergird the hilarity here. Benjie Fawley, known as "Mouse," has insulted the school bully, Marv Hammerman, by writing his name under the picture of Neanderthal Man on a school chart. Now Marv and his sidekicks are out to get Mouse, and all the solutions to "jungle emergencies" that he and his friend Ezzie have devised will not help. After days of avoiding the encounter, Mouse decides to seek out Hammerman. The confrontation turns out as we expect—Benjie is badly beaten but his courage earns him back his real name and the respect of the other kids. As usual, however, Byars goes beyond the formula. Benjie has glimpsed, by the effect of his mockery, that the terrifying, invincible Hammerman has a vulnerable human psyche. The knightly code of honor which Byars has used as comic hyperbole thus suddenly takes on serious meaning as Benjie allows the wronged Hammerman to exact satisfaction for the insult.

Her next book is less successful; in fact, *The Winged Colt of Casa Mia*, begun in 1968 but published in 1973, is an outright artistic failure. The story tells of an embittered Hollywood stuntman named Coot who has come home to Texas after his error of judgment leads to the destruction of his favorite horse. Returning to the first-person point of view that she had not used since *The Midnight Fox*, Byars decided to make the adult the point-of-view character; unfortunately Coot remains simply a type despite the reader's access to his consciousness. The story begins when Coot's nephew Charles arrives at Casa Mia with little warning for a visit of indefinite length. The boy idolizes, of course, the daredevil uncle he has seen on the movie screen, and the narrative tension of the book comes in part from the painful discrepancy between Coot's own view of himself as a decrepit failure and Charles's idealized view. The other main character is Alado, a winged colt born just hours before Charles's arrival. The basic improbability of a horse with wings, compounded by the coincidental timing, dooms the book.

A soaring competition is briefly described in the course of this story. Perhaps the Byars family's interest in flight was the source of the book's subject as well as its setting. However, the potential excitement is sapped by the book's incongruous elements and by the fact that a secondary character, Mrs. Minney, who seems to have been provided for comic relief, is a shrill caricature without being funny. The book received two enthusiastic reviews among other largely negative ones; Virginia Haviland spoke of a "splendid mixture of high drama, mystery, and often unexpected amusement," and Jane Langton praised "a spare, classic beauty."

Fortunately, the difficulty Byars had writing and rewriting this story did not discourage her from continuing her fictional experiments, for her next book, *After the Goat Man* (1974), is both original and successful. The Goat Man of the title is a fierce eccentric who has been forcibly evicted from the cabin he built himself due to plans for a superhighway. After a few days in the concrete-block house in town to which he and his grandson, Figgy, have been relocated, he takes his shotgun and goes back to make a last stand against the bulldozers. The narrative concerns the impact of the Goat Man's act upon Figgy, a vulnerable, parentless boy who carries a rabbit's foot to ward off the world's dangers, and his two friends: Harold V. Coleman, an overweight boy whose sensitive, self-deprecating consciousness dominates the book; and Ada, a coolly competent child whom both boys look up to.

The children set out to bring Figgy's grandfather back, and on the way Figgy breaks his leg in a bicycle accident. As Ada stays with Figgy, Harold must go alone to get the frightening Goat Man (so called for two goats who had been his constant companions) and bring him to Figgy. Thinking back over his own sad moments as he trudges along the deserted highway, Harold comes to understand the old man's grief and despair. The Goat Man gives up his rebellion to respond to Figgy's need, and the ending is hopeful. As Alice Bach put it in one of the most sensitive reviews written about Byars's work, the characters "become linked by their mutual caring, generosity and gentleness. It is Byars's most affirmative statement: in a world which deals out sudden and often harsh hurts, we can comfort each other."

Harold V. Coleman is one of Byars's funniest and most touching children. She reports, "He was very real to me. I felt that if I were young and male and fat I would be Harold V. Coleman. I wouldn't be *like* him, I would *be* him." The narrative point of view occasionally is transferred to Figgy but never to Ada, who remains a more remote character, in keeping with her more self-sufficient personality. This unorthodox arrangement works well, unobtrusively serving the needs of the story. In form, the narrative is a classic short story. The time span is just over nine hours, but in that time the characters—especially Harold—have been changed forever. The restraint and economy with which Byars tells the story mark it as one of her best.

The Lace Snail (1975) is a picture book written and illustrated by Betsy Byars. In the simple text a snail suddenly begins to leave a trail of lace behind her. Different creatures ask her for lace. To each she says quietly, "You deserve lace as much as anybody," and creates something for each one. Then the trail of lace turns back to an ordinary snail track, because "It's just the way life is, I think," the snail concludes.

What lifts the story above the level of Byars's earliest picture books is the maturation of her special gift for characterization through dialogue, and the bold juxtaposition of the quiet mood (created by the snail's remarks and the cool green, black, and white illustrations), and the comical, boisterous antics of the other animals. The bugs exclaim over their new lace parachutes: "Hey, these things float!," "Look at me, you guys," and "That's nothing, Frog, we got lace, man, LACE!" A mother turtle murmers, "I do not ask to be covered with lace. . . . However—. . . as a mother, I cannot but ask for a bit of lace for my beautiful children." And a happy crocodile in a new lace hammock chortles: "I love it. I love it! I LOVE it! . . . And you can give me a push every time you go by, all right? Everybody BETTER give me a push, if you get what I mean."

Critics have tried to extract philosophic meaning from the snail's comments without very convincing results. As it happens, the book grew out of a course Byars took in etching—not because she intended to do any etching, but so that she would know what good etchings are and how they are created. One of the assignments was to draw something small, and she drew a snail. And then the students were asked to create something using dots. She drew some lace. When her plate came back she saw that if she had moved the lace up a little higher, it would look as if the snail were leaving a trail of lace. (One of her editors has also pointed out that her interest in lace may have had something to do with her involvement at the time in plans for her daughter's wedding.)

Byars has created memorable bright and articulate protagonists—Tom of *The Midnight Fox,* Benjie "Mouse" Fawley, and Harold V. Coleman, for instance. But bright, articulate young characters abound in children's books. A rarer gift is Byars's ability to convincingly portray inarticulate children, ranging from the retarded Charlie, to Figgy, and later, to Thomas J of *The Pinballs* (1977). In her book *The TV Kid* (1976) Byars undertook the difficult task of using such a child as her protagonist.

Lennie and his mother have drifted from job to job, place to place, school to school. Now his mother has inherited the rundown Fairyland Mo-

tel, and the two of them have high hopes of settling down and making a success of it. The nomadic life has not been easy for Lennie, a solitary child and poor student, and he has turned to television for companionship and escape from his troubles. Television shows and commercials, as tacky as the motel itself, feed his imagination as he daydreams about himself as a game-show contestant or a character in a *Bonanza* episode. Lennie's fantasy life also leads him to break into an unoccupied vacation cottage where he imagines a different life for himself. One day when the police come by on a routine check, Lennie crawls under the cottage to hide and is bitten by a rattlesnake. Though he survives, the ordeal he experiences is extraordinarily painful. Out of this suffering comes a dissatisfaction with the television world in which he has been living: "It seemed to him suddenly that every TV person he had ever seen wasn't real. . . . That wasn't life. It was close enough to fool you, Lennie thought, if you weren't careful. . . ." At the book's end, Lennie, for whom schoolwork has been torture, is looking forward to writing a report on rattlesnakes.

Criticism of the book has focused on this abrupt awakening to reality in the conclusion. The *New York Times Book Review* termed it "a copout" and accused Byars of merely lecturing on an old subject, the evils of television. In the *Observer,* Sarah Hayes wrote, "the story is too thin and the formula too near the surface . . . , after the beginning the book becomes predictable and banal." Byars has said that she did not intend the book as a criticism of television (though in *The Cartoonist,* she satirizes its misuse), and indeed if attention is paid to the whole book and not just the flawed ending, it is clear that television, here as in the rest of Byars's fiction, is seen sympathetically—as food for children's agile imaginations—as well as critically. However banal the material, Byars shows the child's imagination transforming it into nourishing fantasies and his wit employing it as a whetstone. Besides, Byars's relish for the oddities of life extends to the foolishness of game-show contestants and dancing pill-bottle commercials. Betsy Byars, who says she always watched television with her children, may be the only writer of children's books who admits to *liking* commercial television. This gives her an edge over other writers in her understanding of how thoroughly the images of that electronic phenomenon permeate the consciousness of today's children. The superior credibility of the contemporary children in her books owes a great deal to her use of television and other manifestations of popular culture in characterization.

When Carlie's new foster mother attempts to greet her in the first chapter of *The Pinballs* (1977) she snaps, "Welcome me during the commercial." She is one of three abused children who find themselves at the Mason home. Carlie is a tough, smart-mouthed adolescent who has been beaten up by her stepfather. Harvey, whose mother left home three years earlier to join a commune and "find herself," arrives with two broken legs. His drunken father has driven his new car over Harvey during an argument. Thomas J is a younger child who was abandoned six years earlier "like he was an unwanted puppy" near the home of elderly twin sisters. They kept him on until they both broke their hips and the child welfare people finally learned of his existence.

Byars's ability to mix the comic and the poignant has never been more striking than in her portrayal of Thomas J and the Benson twins. "They were exactly alike except that one's eyes, nose, and mouth were a little bigger than the other's. They looked like matching salt-and-pepper shakers." Thomas J doesn't talk much because the Benson twins weren't much for conversation. "Sometimes their entire daily speech was 'Water's boiling,' and 'Cronkite's on,' and 'I'm turning in.'" They were not much for touching either. Thomas J longingly remembers the only time they touched him: they patted his head when he found their father's lost gold watch: "'Good boy,' they had said. . . . He had wanted them to lose the watch over and over again so he could keep finding it, the way a dog keeps fetching a stick." From a glimpse in a store of elderly twins dressed exactly alike, Byars skillfully managed to flesh out a bizarre yet plausible existence in her portrayal of the fictional Bensons.

Betsy Byars's willingness to take risks in her writing is much in evidence in *The Pinballs*. She begins the book abruptly with the painful scene of Harvey's accident, then the pathetic histories of Thomas J and Carlie. But before the chapter ends, the sassy vitality of Carlie's wisecracks have punctured the reader's pity and dread; her obvious resilience makes us dare to read on. It is this resilience that renders credible the hopeful resolution of the book against all apparent odds. Carlie starts off believing that she and the boys are "pinballs." "Somebody put in a dime and punched a button and out we came, ready or not, and settled in the same groove. That's all." She becomes so angry at Harvey's father, however, that she resolves to pull Harvey out of his deep depression and succeeds. In the process, she introduces Thomas J to the world of human relationships as well. In the book's

last scene she tells Thomas J that she was wrong about their being pinballs—"as long as we are trying . . . we are not pinballs." Mr. and Mrs. Mason, though kept in the background, are depicted as sensitive, caring people whose low-key understanding and skill at "fostering" also play a part in the happy outcome. The explicitness of the moral deprives the ending of the suggestive resonance that marks the conclusion of *The House of Wings*, for instance, but the optimism of the ending is earned through compelling characterization. Byars herself admits there is something of the fairy tale about the story; it certainly does not depict a typical foster home. Although this may disturb those who rigidly categorize children's fiction as realism or fantasy, it clearly appeals to children, for *The Pinballs* has won many of the awards which children themselves vote, such as the California Young Reader Medal (1980) and the Georgia Children's Book Award (1979), chosen by more than 58,000 children in grades four to seven.

Reviewers on both sides of the Atlantic praised the book highly. Ethel Heins, in *Horn Book*, called "the economically told story, liberally spiced with humor . . . something of a tour de force . . ." and concluded: "A deceptively simple, eloquent story, its pain and acrimony constantly mitigated by the author's light, offhand style and by Carlie's wryly comic view of life." Lance Salway wrote in the *Times Literary Supplement*, that "despite the incidental comedy in this story and the deceptive simplicity of its telling, Betsy Byars has written a serious book about a disturbing subject, investing it with the insight, sympathy and sense of comedy that have distinguished her more recent work. . . ."

Alfie, the protagonist of *The Cartoonist* (1978), is saddled with an idiotic mother who not only watches television all the time but wants everyone else to watch with her: "Well, why don't you come down and study in front of the television? It'll take your mind off what you're doing," she calls to Alfie. She can't see the point of Alfie's witty cartoons; the criminal practical jokes of her other son, Bubba, a former high school football star, are her idea of what is funny. In the tiny ramshackle house that Alfie shares with his mother, his querulous grandfather, and an older sister he has found a refuge in the space under the eaves—a place where he can draw.

When Bubba loses his job his mother invites him and his wife to move in with the family and she plans to fix up Alfie's attic for the couple. Threatened with the loss of his retreat, Alfie bars himself in the attic and refuses to speak or come out. In the lonely hours of his rebellion, Alfie realizes that his mother will never change, will never understand him. In the end, Bubba decides not to move in and Alfie's attic is safe, but he comes down with no illusion of victory.

The book's ending contains an affirmative note, however, as Byars skillfully uses Alfie's art to represent his triumph over pain and isolation. From the start, drawing helps Alfie to face the bleak facts of his life honestly: "Life was very close to cartoons . . . whether you liked it or not. . . . Cartoons took life and sifted out the beauty, the sweetness, the fleeting moments of glory and left you as you really were." By the end of the story, he finds he can at least soften his pain by transmuting it into something of value. As he shakily descends the ladder, he thinks: "maybe it was possible to make a cartoon even of this. The idea surprised him. . . . Not a cartoon of himself—he wasn't ready for that yet. He could do a comic strip about a *man* who had taken himself away from the world. . . . In a balloon, he thought. Balloons were better than attics in a comic strip. He warmed to the idea. . . . Alfie smiled. He was glad there would still be cartoons." This truth is an old one, but new to most children, and Byars presents it in terms a child can appreciate.

The book contains many of Byars's most distinctive elements. The West Virginia milieu is skillfully sketched in—the automobile junkyard Alfie's father had built up before he died, the big game as a major community event. A device she had used in *The 18th Emergency* is further developed: the bumptious, less sensitive friend serving as a foil to the protagonist and providing a measure of comic relief. Alfie's grandfather is another well-observed old person, and, though used primarily as a source of humor, he is nevertheless portrayed with some sympathy, a fellow-sufferer whose understanding sustains Alfie: "I know how you feel up there, Alfie. I have give up a time or two myself. I think about the government rotting away like an apple and senators using our money for trips to China—did I tell you, Alfie, *twenty-seven* senators is going to London, England, to pick up a copy of the Magna Carta? Which they could *mail*, Alfie! And you know who is paying them twenty-seven senators' way, don't you? You and me!"

The book is one of Byars's best and occasioned an admiring and perceptive article in *Horn Book* by the English critic Aidan Chambers. He began, "One of your authors who crosses the Atlantic with great success is Betsy Byars." Byars herself finds this surprising "because I write for American

children and I always think of my books as so American." The popularity of her books in Great Britain testifies to both her skill at bringing to life the distinctively American scene and her perceptive rendering of universal childhood experiences.

Good-bye, Chicken Little (1979), Byars's next book, begins: "Four days before Christmas, Jimmie Little's uncle announced he would walk across the Monday River. It was a sudden decision, made after several beers in Harry's Bar and Grill, and at once the other customers, posse-like, hurried him to the riverbank. Up the hill, in his house, Jimmie Little was standing by the clothes drier, waiting for his jeans to dry." Jimmie's friend Conrad brings him the news, and from this first page, as Jimmie struggles, trembling, into his damp jeans, the reader is impelled with him toward disaster and its aftermath. Jimmie is unable to dissuade his Uncle Pete, a born clown, from attempting the crossing on the thin December ice. Pete drowns and Jimmie is assaulted by painful emotions—guilt (did he do all he could to prevent the accident?), fear (he is paralyzed by an awareness of life's precariousness, as he had been after his father's death in a coal mine), and embarrassment (his is a family of "characters" who, he notices, draw attention to themselves in the wrong way). A few days after the drowning, Jimmie's mother decides to have a family Christmas party. Jimmie is unable to enter into the excitement of the preparations and the party itself: the fond reminiscing about Pete's shenanigans, the carol singing, and the dancing. He goes outside to watch the party through the window and gradually his terrible feelings give way to affection for this unique family. He realizes that the party is indeed an appropriate way to mark Pete's death.

The idea for this book came to Byars from yearly news stories in the Morgantown paper of someone being dared to cross the frozen Monongahela River. Her canniness lies in seeing in this the possibilities for exploring a nearly universal emotion of middle childhood—the growing awareness of how other people view one's family and the dread of family members being labeled as somehow "different." *Good-bye, Chicken Little* also adds another "original" to the Byars' gallery of old people: ninety-two-year-old Uncle C. C., who can hardly wait to get back to the nursing home so the Baptist ladies in the beehive hairdos can make a fuss over him.

Critical reception of the book was largely positive, Elaine Moss noting in the *Times Literary Supplement* that "the reader is being asked . . . to consider some weighty moral issues, lightly suggested." Paul Heins, reviewing the book in *Horn Book,* had reservations, however, feeling that the author "fails to make a successful transition between the tragic and the comic portions of the story."

In spite of the predominantly favorable reviews of Betsy Byars's books in the 1970s and their great popularity with children, she had not won a major critical award since the Newbery Medal in 1971. Ten years later *The Night Swimmers* was awarded the American Book Award in the children's book category. It was also a Boston Globe-Horn Book Honor Book in 1980.

The Night Swimmers depicts a crisis in the lives of three motherless children. Retta Anderson has taken care of her two younger brothers since her mother's death. The children's father works at night as a country-western singer. Retta is determined to be a good mother: to bring up her brothers *right* and to give them the good things of life. "We're going to do all the things rich people do. . . .

Only we have to do them at night . . . ," she tells them. So she drags the nervous boys to swim after dark in the elegant pool of a retired colonel.

Retta has been successful as a no-nonsense surrogate mother modeled on the mothers she observes in the supermarket and on television. But Johnny, her next-younger brother, rebels against her bossiness and begins to make friends and a life of his own. The situation deteriorates as Retta tries harder to control Johnny and ends up hating him. Only the near drowning of Roy, the younger brother, forces the self-absorbed father to admit that he must take more responsibility for his children. The book's conclusion subtly suggests that the burdens of motherhood will be eased from Retta's shoulders by her father's warm and capable girlfriend.

The book's tone is unusually sober for Byars. The father's vanity and his song lyrics are amusing, but the humor has a sharp edge of satire. And though little Roy's fears and misconceptions pe-

Dust jacket for Byars's 1980 novel, which won the American Book Award for Children's Writing (Delacorte)

riodically provide comic moments, these are muted by the reader's awareness of his small-boy vulnerability.

Two compelling images contribute to the underlying somberness of this book. One is the scared but defiant children swimming in the dark and then shivering as they cross the lawn, "past the orchid greenhouse, past the lemon trees from Florida, over the wall made from stone from Mexico." The other is an image from Roy's imagination. He has been told that the sweetish odor he smells from time to time comes from the Bowlwater plant. Not realizing that it is a chemical factory, he envisions it as an enormous bush for children to climb on— "a natural Disney world where everything was real instead of plastic." At the book's end, Roy takes a step toward growing up by facing the truth about the Bowlwater plant. Yet the contrast of his wonderful fantasy with the bleak reality, together with the image of the night swimmers, remain as telling comments on contemporary American life.

As one might guess from the punning title, Byars gives her comic sense free rein in *The Cybil War* (1981). The plot traces the ups and downs of young love. Simon Newton has loved Cybil Ackerman ever since she stood up to an irate teacher on his behalf in second grade. Now his friend Tony has begun telling lies that Simon fears will make Cybil mad at him. Worse than that, Tony seems to want Cybil as a girlfriend himself. Cybil is an appealing enough heroine to be worth the epic battle Simon engages in, and the fourth-grade social dynamics are deftly captured. Tony is the extroverted foil, a familiar character in Byars's fiction, but his vanity distinguishes him from his predecessors: "Tony Angotti was having a hard time believing that Cybil had called him a juvenile. Him, Tony Angotti, who looked like Donny Osmond!"

The comedy is broad in *The Cybil War*: a poodle wets her diaper at a costume pet show; a Miss America contest ends in tears ("Well, I better get to be Miss Congeniality or I'm going home!"). The hyperbolic humor is counterbalanced, though, by a sensitive chronicle, partly in flashbacks, of Simon's reactions to his father's desertion of his family to "get back to the simple life." At first, "It was more than he could stand—that his father, the only person he could not live without, could actually decide to live without him"; then he hopes his father will kidnap him: "He was always at the edge of the street in those days, waiting for the feel of his father's arms as he was lifted into the waiting van and driven away." Finally, though the hurt remains, Simon can see his father dispassionately as a weak figure and be glad that he's not like him.

In May 1980 Betsy Byars and her husband moved back to South Carolina, leaving the Appalachian scene that had nourished her fiction for twenty years. Byars had misgivings about whether she would be able to write anywhere but on the desk in her bedroom which overlooked the West Virginia hills. After the move and a trip to a South Carolina beach where she had vacationed as a child, however, she was soon at work on *The Animal, the Vegetable, and John D Jones* (1982), a disappointing book, perhaps reflecting the difficulty of her transition.

This novel depicts what happens when a divorced father of two daughters and a widowed mother of one son decide to vacation together as one happy family. The girls understandably feel betrayed and angry when it is discovered they will be sharing their father in the scarce time they have with him, but their hostility and self-pity dominate the first two-thirds of the book and become tedious. John D, a bright boy who armors himself against the world in smug cynicism, fails to provide the comic element the book needs. His unpleasantness outweighs his wit. The sports-announcer father and advice-columnist mother are the blandest parents of any Byars book. Only the relationship between the sisters displays the subtlety Byars is capable of.

Much-needed suspense is supplied late in the book when Clara, the younger sister, is swept far out to sea on a rubber float. The chances of rescue appear slight, and the anguish of both Clara and those awaiting word are depicted vividly. Clara does survive, and the event, by changing the dynamics of the group, makes possible a positive ending: John D's worry and sympathy for Clara force him to admit that he cares for someone; Clara asserts herself against her dominant sister by mildly insisting that the vacation not be ended prematurely. The book's predictable ending and its lack of offbeat characters would make it difficult to identify as Byars's work, however, if it did not bear her name.

The Two-Thousand-Pound Goldfish (1982), though, could be no one else's. Warren's hilarious horror-movie scripts weave through the book like "Mouse" Fawley's emergency fantasies and Alfie's cartoons. This affectionate spoof of horror films grew out of Byars's lifelong love of the genre. The rest of the novel is bleak, though, so that Byars's usually successful alternation of humor and poignancy is strained. Warren Otis's mother has had to go underground, a fugitive for years because of her increasingly violent radical politics. Warren longs for her, idealizes her, and fantasizes about her return, projecting his frustrations and anger into his imagined movies. He is cared for by an older sister and by a sour, unattractive grandmother who will not allow his mother's name to be mentioned in her presence. After the grandmother dies, Warren's yearned-for chance to talk to his mother by telephone comes, but the unsatisfactory, tearful call dashes his dreams of his mother's return. A new closeness to his sister and the prospect of living with his favorite aunt soften Warren's disillusionment, but a suggestion that new maturity means less daydreaming works against the reader's sense that Warren's resilient and creative inner life is what has carried him through the harsh traumas of his young life.

By 1983, with the publication of *The Glory Girl*, one senses that Byars's new surroundings have begun to seep into and color her fictions. (The vacation community of her first South Carolina book could have been anywhere from New England to Florida.) This story of the odd child out in a family of traveling gospel singers is skillful and moving. Nonmusical Anna is drawn to her black sheep uncle before she ever meets him, and in a few brief encounters he rewards her caring by persuading her that she, too, has something to offer. Telling details make this eccentric family as credible as any Byars has depicted. Mr. Glory, like some of her earlier creations, is portrayed as an inadequate, difficult adult who nonetheless wins our sympathy. Byars's bad boys reach their apotheosis here in hyperactive twins; the intense energies of their alternating rivalry and mutual dependency invigorate the novel.

Marilyn Kaye's review in the *New York Times* was perceptive: "Byars has a gift for exposing the soul of the lost child—the damaged, the alienated, the unloved. Her stories may not always live up to expectations, but her characters have credibility.... The story is thin, but the tension builds neatly and the writing is polished." In the *Times Literary Supplement* Sarah Hayes called the book "a small sad masterpiece," noting that "the story runs to a lean 114 pages, but it is all meat."

The Computer Nut (1984) was written on and inspired by Byars's new word processor. Her son Guy served as her consultant on technical matters and supplied the computer graphics that figure in this tale of two children's meeting with an extraterrestrial. The book, like many early spin-offs of the computer revolution, is ephemeral. Allowing that questions of credibility may occasionally be finessed by science fiction, one still is left with a silly

premise: BB-9 wants to come to earth, known in the universe as "the laughing planet," to hone his skills as stand-up comic. The fiasco that ensues is only slightly amusing, and the human characters don't ever come alive. The bumptious, insensitive friend, the slapstick humor of a dog's birthday party seem in this case tired recyclings of earlier successes.

Wife-battering might seem too painful a subject for a children's novel. By making the victim a former babysitter of the protagonist, rather than his mother, Byars was able to treat the topic in *Cracker Jackson* (1985). Eleven-year-old Jackson Hunter, affectionately called Cracker by his adored sitter Alma, tries to protect her from her husband he suspects is abusing her. From the first page when Jackson receives the anonymous note, "Keep away, Cracker, or he'll hurt you," the reader is drawn inexorably into the story. Though the comic sidekick, Goat, seems to be lifted bodily from earlier Byars novels, the writer outdoes herself this time: the daring mix of pathos and hilarity has never worked better than when the two boys "borrow" Jackson's mother's car to drive Alma and her baby to the women's shelter.

Alma is a triumph of characterization, with her layaways, her Barbie doll collection, and her simple, affectionate nature, which she lavishes on Jackson and on her baby, Nicole, named for a favorite soap opera character. Her long-standing practice of confiding in Jackson her hopes and dreams makes credible his attempt to assume the role of her protector. The danger to Alma and Nicole is more than a boy can handle, of course, and Jackson's parents relieve him of the burden he has taken on. Yet the courage he has shown figures in the novel's climactic scene: entering the injured Alma's hospital room and comforting her is a continuation of the boy's brave journey to maturity. Though the book will be dismissed by some as another "problem novel," its vivid central characters and resonant conclusion lift it above easy categories. In 1978 Aidan Chambers's only criticism of Byars was that "she has sometimes made her meaning too plain...." He wished she would allow "a little more ambiguity into her work, a little more space for the child to make the meaning with her." *Cracker Jackson* is the first novel since *The Night Swimmers* to provide that space and challenge.

Betsy Byars's distinctive voice and sensitivity to the child's world have earned her a place just below the first rank of contemporary writers of realistic fiction for children—the Katherine Patersons and Paula Foxes. Her well-developed comic

17

Joshua came up out of the leaves slow and mad. "What'd you do that for?" he yelled at his brother. "You made me wreck! You stinking -"

He did not finish his insult because he caught sight of John. He ~~took a step~~ backward. *head got up. He stepped*

John ~~lay without moving, wailing quietly,~~ his hands holding *was twisting like a beached fish, screaming,*

his head. Blood was streaming from each of the fourteen holes. ~~John lifted his hands, and held them in front of his face.~~ *Joshua began wailing too, a quiet sound like snoring.*

~~He saw the blood and wailed louder.~~ He was used to the sight

of ~~his own~~ blood, but not this much. *they both were,*

~~Joshua kept standing there, looking at his brother.~~ He

~~was not able~~ to move. He had ~~never seen so much blood either,~~ *Couldn't*

~~had never~~ known a head could hold so much blood. *not*

"Mommmmmmmmmmmmmmmmmmmmmm!"

He turned ~~finally~~ and began to run down the hill. His

knees were so weak he was ~~staggering.~~ *like a puppet*

"Mommmmmmmmmmmmmmmmmmm."

His voice wavered as he bounced and stumbled over the

uneven ground.

Up~~on~~ the hill John made no attempt to get up. Blood had *He had stopped screaming*

flowed into his eyes, and he felt as if a red curtain had been

drawn between him and the world. ~~Only the pain remained.~~

"Mommmmmmmmmmmmmmmmmmmmmmm." Joshua's voice was far away

now. "Mom, John's ~~been~~ scalped ~~himself!~~" *a siren in the distance*

John heard that. Scalped. One of his greatest fears. He *through his pain* *in the world*

drew in one long shuddering breath and began to ~~scream~~, holding *sob*

his hands beneath his chin so as not to touch his injured head. *tightly*

From a draft for The Glory Girl, *a novel about a family of traveling gospel singers (by permission of the author)*

sense is refreshing. Writing about children under stress, she uses her wit to grapple unsentimentally with subjects ordinarily considered too painful for young readers. Her energy and enjoyment of life, together with her belief in the sensitivity and resilience of ordinary children, endow her books with a fundamental hopefulness.

Her short narratives composed of many dramatized scenes and much dialogue have served her well at a time when children (and therefore publishers) apparently prefer short books. Many writers for children, in trying to pare down their fiction, end up with books thin in substance as well as size because they cut out the details on which fiction has always depended to build up a sense of reality. Byars, on the other hand, by shrinking the time frame of her stories and skillfully selecting telling details, creates works of notable verisimilitude and intensity, which are at the same time remarkably accessible.

References:

Aidan Chambers, "Arrows—All Pointing Upward," *Horn Book*, 54 (December 1978): 680-684;

Lee Kingman, ed., *Newbery and Caldecott Medal Books, 1966-1975* (Boston: Horn Book, 1975), pp. 66-78;

Lois Kuznets, "Betsy Byars' Slice of 'American Pie,' " *Children's Literature Association Quarterly*, 5 (Winter 1981): 31-33;

Ina Robertson, "Betsy Byars—Writer for Today's Child," *Language Arts*, 57 (March 1980): 328-334;

Elizabeth Segel, "Betsy Byars: an Interview," *Children's Literature in Education*, 13 (Winter 1982): 171-179.

Papers:

A corrected typescript and galley proofs of *Goodbye, Chicken Little* and a corrected typescript of *Trouble River* are held by the Kerlan Collection of the University of Minnesota.

Eleanor Cameron
(23 March 1912-   )

Grace Sulerud and Sue Garness
Augsburg College

BOOKS: *Unheard Music* (Boston: Little, Brown, 1950);

The Wonderful Flight to the Mushroom Planet, illustrated by Robert Henneberger (Boston: Little, Brown, 1954);

The Stowaway to the Mushroom Planet, illustrated by Henneberger (Boston: Little, Brown, 1956);

Mr. Bass's Planetoid, illustrated by Louis Darling (Boston: Little, Brown, 1958);

The Terrible Churnadryne, illustrated by Beth and Joe Krush (Boston: Little, Brown, 1959);

A Mystery for Mr. Bass, illustrated by Leonard Shortall (Boston: Little, Brown, 1960);

The Mysterious Christmas Shell, illustrated by Beth and Joe Krush (Boston: Little, Brown, 1961);

The Beast with the Magical Horn, illustrated by Beth and Joe Krush (Boston: Little, Brown, 1963);

A Spell is Cast, illustrated by Beth and Joe Krush (Boston: Little, Brown, 1964);

Time and Mr. Bass, illustrated by Fred Meise (Boston: Little, Brown, 1967);

The Green and Burning Tree: On the Writing and Enjoyment of Children's Books (Boston: Atlantic/Little, Brown, 1969);

A Room Made of Windows, illustrated by Trina Schart Hyman (Boston: Little, Brown, 1971; London: Gollancz, 1972);

The Court of the Stone Children (New York: Dutton, 1973);

To the Green Mountains (New York: Dutton, 1975);

Julia and the Hand of God, illustrated by Gail Owens (New York: Dutton, 1977);

Beyond Silence (New York: Dutton, 1980);

That Julia Redfern (New York: Dutton, 1982);

Julia's Magic (New York: Dutton, 1984).

RECORDINGS: *A Room Made of Windows* (Crane Memorial Library, 1979);

A Branch of the Tree (Children's Book Council, 1979).

PERIODICAL PUBLICATIONS: "Write a Story for Me!," *Wilson Library Bulletin,* 31 (April 1957): 615-617;

"The Unforgettable Glimpse," *Wilson Library Bulletin,* 37 (October 1962): 147-153; revised and republished in *The Green and Burning Tree;*

"Of Style and the Stylist," *Horn Book,* 40 (February 1964): 25-32; revised and republished in *The Green and Burning Tree;*

"The Dearest Freshness Deep Down Things," *Horn Book,* 40 (October 1964): 459-472; revised and republished in *The Green and Burning Tree;*

"Why *Not* for Children?," *Horn Book,* 42 (February 1966): 21-33;

"The Owl Service: A Study," *Wilson Library Bulletin,* 44 (December 1969): 425-433;

"The Art of Elizabeth Enright," *Horn Book,* 45 (December 1969): 641-651;

"Conclusion," *Horn Book,* 46 (February 1970): 26-30;

"High Fantasy: A Wizard of Earthsea," *Horn Book,* 47 (April 1971): 129-138;

"McLuhan, Youth, and Literature," *Horn Book,* 48 (October 1972): 433-440; 48 (December 1972): 572-579; 49 (February 1973): 79-85;

"Sharp Up!" (letter), *School Library Journal,* 19 (January 1973): 4;

"Into Something Rich and Strange; Of Dreams, Art, and the Unconscious," *Library of Congress Quarterly Journal,* 35 (April 1978): 92-107;

"A Response to Perry Nodelman's 'Beyond Explanation,'" *Children's Literature 12,* edited by Francelia Butler (New York: Modern Language Association, 1980), pp. 134-146;

"Fantasy, Science Fiction and the Mushroom Planet Books," *Children's Literature Association Quarterly,* 6 (Winter 1981): 1, 5-9;

"One Woman as Writer and Feminist," *Children's Literature Association Quarterly,* 7 (Winter 1982): 3-6;

"The Inmost Secret," *Horn Book,* 59 (February 1983): 17-24;

"Art and Morality," in *Festschrift: A Ten Year Retrospective,* edited by Perry Nodelman and Jill P. May (West Lafayette, Ind.: Children's Literature Association Publications, 1983), pp. 28-35;

"A Second Look: *Gone-Away Lake,*" *Horn Book,* 60 (September/October 1984): 622-626;

"The Eternal Moment," *Children's Literature Association Quarterly,* 9 (Winter 1984): 157-164;

"With Wrinkled Brow and Cool Fresh Eye," *Horn Book,* 61 (May/June 1985): 280-288; 61 (July/August 1985): 426-431.

Eleanor Cameron's writing is remarkable for both its variety and its quality. She divides her writing career into two parts—the ten works which preceded the publication in 1969 of *The Green and Burning Tree: On the Writing and Enjoyment of Children's Books* and the seven titles which have been published since. Her writing has received much outstanding recognition, especially the later books. *A Room Made of Windows* won the Boston Globe-Horn Book Award in 1971, the year it was published; *The Court of the Stone Children* (1973) won the National Book Award in 1974; and *To the Green Mountains* (1975) was a finalist for that prestigious award in 1976. All three books were also named ALA Notable Books as was *Julia and the Hand of God* (1977). Eight of Cameron's books were chosen as Junior Literary Guild selections: *The Wonderful Flight to the Mushroom Planet* (1954), *The Stowaway to the Mushroom Planet* (1956), *Mr. Bass's Planetoid* (1958), *The Terrible Churnadryne* (1959), *The Mysterious Christmas Shell* (1961), *A Spell is Cast* (1964), *The Court of the Stone Children,* and *Julia and the Hand*

Gale Portrait Gallery

of God. *A Spell is Cast* won the Commonwealth Club
of California's Silver Medal Award in 1964 as did
The Green and Burning Tree in 1969. For her work
published up to that time, the Southern California
Council on Literature for Children and Young
Adults voted her their 1965 Annual Award for Dis-
tinquished Contributions to the Field of Children's
Literature.

The only child of English-born parents,
Henry and Florence Butler, Eleanor Cameron was
born in Canada on 23 March 1912. The family
moved to South Charleston, Ohio, in 1915 and
three years later to Berkeley, California, where the
Carnegie Library became a haven for the young
Cameron, who later worked there as a clerk. Regarding her personal interests at this time, she says,
"I have been preoccupied with the craft of writing
since the age of eleven, and since my teens with
the question of what makes a book memorable."
As early as age twelve, she decided to become a
professional writer and to work as a librarian until
her writing supported her. After a move to Los
Angeles at age sixteen, she finished high school and
then spent two years at UCLA and a year at the
Los Angeles Art Center School. While in school she
worked as a clerk in the literature department of
the Los Angeles Public Library. She married Ian
Stuart Cameron, a printer and publisher, in 1934.
For six years, from 1936-1942, she worked at the
Los Angeles City School Library helping teachers
choose books for their classrooms. Until the birth
of a son, David, in 1945, she was a research librarian
in advertising. Eleven years later she resumed this
career until she realized her early ambition to become a full-time writer.

Work in the public library provided the setting and characters for *Unheard Music* (1950), her
first and only published novel for adults; she
termed it "a critical success if not a financial one."
She began her career as a writer for children in
1954 with the publication of *The Wonderful Flight
to the Mushroom Planet*. Her son David had asked
her to write him a story that would tide him over
until he could go back to his favorite series, Hugh
Lofting's Doctor Dolittle books. He wanted "a story
about himself and his best friend and how they
would build a spaceship and go off and find a
planet just their size, just big enough to explore in
a day or two." Just as he requested, she began with
David Topman and Chuck Masterson answering
an advertisement in the local paper for two boys,
aged eight to eleven, to build an eight-foot spaceship and deliver it to Mr. Tyco M. Bass, 5 Thallo
Street, Pacific Grove, California. After putting fin-

*Cover for Cameron's first children's book and the initial in-
stallment in the Mushroom Planet series (Little, Brown)*

ishing touches on the space ship with some marvelous inventions of his own, Mr. Bass sends them
off to Basidium-X, a tiny satellite of earth only
thirty-five miles in diameter and 50,000 miles away.
Mr. Bass, a member of the race of Basidiumites,
or Mushroom People, who inhabit the satellite, senses that his people are in trouble. How David and
Chuck meet the Great Ta, leader of the Basidiumites, save the Wise Men Mebe and Oru from
death, and discover a way to provide the sulfur
essential to the Mushroom People's diet are some
of the ingredients of the book's fast-paced plot. *The
Wonderful Flight to the Mushroom Planet*, with its skillful blend of fantasy and scientific fact, was well
received by reviewers. Alice Brook McGuire's comment in the *Saturday Review*, which compares Cameron's skill at characterization to Ellen
MacGregor's, is typical: "A new favorite has come
to challenge the popularity of the eccentric and
amusing 'Miss Pickerell!' "

The Wonderful Flight to the Mushroom Planet was
followed in 1956 by *The Stowaway to the Mushroom*

Planet, a sequel even more absorbing than the original. The book's popularity is evidenced by the fact that it was one of the 100 best-sellers on the Scholastic Booklist in 1979, twenty-three years after its first appearance. The stowaway on David and Chuck's second voyage to the Mushroom Planet is Horatio Q. Peabody, an unscrupulous and ambitious young scientist who threatens the destruction of the Basidiumites' simple way of life with plans of scientific excursions and mining expeditions from earth. He fails to carry out his schemes when the Great Ta serves him the Drink of Forgetfulness.

In *Mr. Bass's Planetoid* (1958), the third book in the Mushroom Planet series, David and Chuck must save the earth from destruction without the help of Tyco Bass, who has been transported into another galaxy. The crisis ensues when Prewytt Brumblydge, a scientist at the San Julian Observatory, disappears with the Brumblitron, a preposterous invention which picks up cosmic rays and could start a chain reaction which would unravel the world. David and Chuck travel in their spaceship to a planetoid called Lepton to find Prewytt and prevent the disaster. The story ends rather abruptly, pointing to the next book in the series, *A Mystery for Mr. Bass*, published in 1960.

After a long and somewhat dull introductory chapter to fill the uninitiated reader in on the earlier books, a mystery (and less science fiction) is presented when David and Chuck find the silver-green glowing bones of a Mycetian, or earthborn Mushroom person, in Dr. Austin Shellworthy's backyard in Pacific Grove, California. The curiosity of the worldwide scientific community is aroused, and once again Prewytt Brumblydge is at the center of the controversies. When Prewytt's activities place him under the curse of an ancient Mycetian rune, David and Chuck travel to Basidium-X to seek advice from their old friend Tyco Bass, returned from his sojourn.

The importance of *Time and Mr. Bass* (1967), the fifth and final Mushroom Planet book, lies in Cameron's shift away from science fiction to fantasy in a plot which reveals the history of the Mycetians as a conflict between good and evil. David and Chuck travel with Tyco Bass to Wales for a meeting of the Mycetian League and encounter the sinister figure, Narrow Brain, who plans to destroy the creative energies of the Mycetians.

Although the last two books of the Mushroom Planet series are more confusing and less successful than the first three, as a whole the books are far above the average science fiction fare for children. The series, light and entertaining, was written, according to Cameron, "with a twinkle of the eye in the tone."

The series appeals to the child's desire to have a place of his own, unknown to adults, where he carries out momentous plans to save the world from destruction or to help others fulfill their destinies. Mr. Bass wisely knows that only children can be counted upon to save the Basidiumites with a minimum amount of fuss. " 'You boys wasted no time in doubting. And, Chuck and David, you must *never* doubt anything I tell you. Remember that,' said little Mr. Bass, leaning forward earnestly, 'You must *never doubt*.' " The importance of never doubting is carried throughout the series and constitutes one important theme.

Cameron gives some attention to scientific accuracy in the Mushroom Planet books, but it does not overwhelm the action. The series is curiously both science fiction and fantasy in that Cameron spoofs science and gadgetry with her portrayal of Prewytt Brumblydge and his inventions, but she also presents the wonder and marvel of the universe as revealed by scientific studies. Cameron has said that "the boundary between fantasy and science fiction is of no moment—except perhaps to the critics—only the absorption of the reader. . . ." The continuing popularity of the series is proof that she has succeeded in captivating more than one generation of readers.

Before the last Mushroom Planet book appeared in 1967, Cameron had also published four works ranging from realism to modern fantasy to an original fairy tale. The first of these departures is *The Terrible Churnadryne* (1959), a mystery with a touch of fantasy. During a summer vacation visit to the California coastal town of Redwood Cove, Jennifer and Tom encounter something unusual in the fog at the peak of San Lorenzo, which overlooks the Pacific Ocean. To this mysterious beast they give the name "churnadryne," but their friend, Mr. Looper, curator of the Redwood Cove Natural History Museum, guesses that they have seen an *Elasmosaurus Californicus*. The story portrays story-hungry reporters and skeptical townspeople who try to prove the existence of the creature, but it is Jennifer, who has the wisdom of a child, to whom the truth is finally revealed.

The strength of the story is the creation of a vivid atmosphere in which reality, supported by scientific data, is blended with a wonderful appreciation of the imaginative. The characterizations of the townspeople are lively, even exaggerated, but they add humor to the story. Setting is a very important element; in this book Cameron's talent for sensory description begins to emerge more fully than in her previous books, which emphasize action. In fact, Cameron says that the discovery of the California Big Sur country as the setting for this story made its completion possible. The idea of the story had begun with the word "churnadryne," which a friend's Scottish grandmother had once used to describe a daydreaming child "all laid out like a churnadryne." Disappointed to discover that the phrase did not mean a dead or sleeping dragon but rather the parts of a butter churn laid out to dry, Cameron went on to write a story about the grip an image can hold on a child's imagination. She had enjoyed writing the story but the novel "wavered in places and seemed to lose conviction, . . . too much as to both feeling and intent was unclear and unresolved." The manuscript was put aside for a year; later, when Cameron and her husband were driving through the California terrain which she had explored as a child, Cameron decided to complete the book. This region, with its foggy hills, sea-smelling wind, and echoing caves, is featured in nearly every story she has written. Cameron explains its importance to her writing in her statement that "Place does not give theme . . . only life can give that . . . but without the power of place, without that discovery of a special country of the mind right for this tale, the story could not have been told at all. . . . And yet, it seems to me that in instance after instance it is place that releases whatever feeling is absolutely essential to the writer to enable him to carry out his work of creation. And very often, one discovers, this place lies in childhood or is somehow, perhaps most obscurely, related to childhood."

A sequel, *The Mysterious Christmas Shell*, appeared in 1961, in which Tom and Jennifer return to their grandmother's house in Redwood Cove for a holiday visit. Immediately the spinster Vining sisters enlist their help in a last-minute effort to locate their father's missing will, which would save the scenic Vining estate from becoming a housing development. Jennifer's discovery of a South Pacific court cone shell on the California beach—her mysterious Christmas shell—is the first of several near-miraculous events which occur in this intricate and complicated mystery. Despite some flaws of credibility, the story is carefully written and again evokes a powerful atmosphere of reality. As E. L. Buell of the *New York Times Book Review* put it, "Although their quest is over-extended, the children make use of psychological clues—a phenomenon rare in juvenile mysteries—and there is a fine feeling for both the region and the season's joys."

Drawing upon the literary patterns of the traditional fairy tale, *The Beast with the Magical Horn* (1963) stands as a single work of this type in Cameron's writing. A unicorn helps Allison, a poor but beautiful mountain girl, capture seven fabulous creatures and locate a box the colors of the rainbow which contains the Secret of Life. The success of her quest defeats a wicked queen and wins for her the hand of her beloved Prince Basil. A smoothly written tale which has the authenticity of real folklore, it is not particularly unique except for the character of the king, a romantic yet shrewd fellow who adds a touch of humor to the story.

A Spell is Cast (1964) is realistic although there is an aura of magic in the story and enough mystery to draw readers into it. Ruth Hill Viguers wrote in *Horn Book:* "Here is creative storytelling at its best: style, plot, characterizations, atmosphere, and flavor give importance and intensity to what might have been, in less skillful hands, just another story of an appealing child longing for a home." Orphaned Cory Winterslow arrives at Tarnhelm, a castlelike house overlooking the sea near Carmel, California, where she meets her guardian's family, the Van Heusens. A Scottish couple who maintain Tarnhelm, Fergie and Andrew, envelop Cory with the love and security she has been missing. Mysteries of the Van Heusens' unhappy past are gradually unveiled as Cory finds a happy home and new friends. *A Spell is Cast* has the same setting as *The Terrible Churnadryne* and *The Mysterious Christmas Shell*, again vividly described; it has a deeper significance in the handling of complex emotions and shows definite signs of Cameron's growing skill as a writer.

In 1969 Atlantic/Little, Brown published *The Green and Burning Tree: On the Writing and Enjoyment of Children's Books*, a collection of critical essays by Cameron which say as much about her and her writing as about other writers and their works. The book forms a watershed in her career, as she herself states: *The Green and Burning Tree* "has seemed to divide my work into two so decidedly that some have told me they were surprised to find it was the same Cameron who wrote the earlier books as the late. What has happened is that I have now been basing (but only basing) them on childhood experience, using an actual situation as the takeoff into events that never happened in real life, whereas the earlier books are wholly imaginative."

The gift of a desk from her father and a vivid and complex dream she had as a child are actual situations which provide the takeoff into the events of *A Room Made of Windows* (1971). Julia Redfern's room with its wrap-around windows and skylight is the focal point of her life. Here at the desk her late father had built for her, she strives to emulate him by becoming a writer. From this room she moves out to participate in the lives of family and friends, gathering experiences about which to write. Closest is her family—her mother, who is considering remarriage, and an older brother, Greg, who aspires to become an Egyptologist. Nearby are Daddy Chandler, an eighty-four-year-old writer who encourages her creative efforts, and Mrs. Rhiannon Moore, who helps her understand a heavily symbolic dream which she shapes into a story.

A Room Made of Windows is a wonderfully complex novel, full of unique people who share intricate relationships. Place is as important here as in Cameron's earlier books, and the descriptions of Berkeley, where she lived as a child, are vividly evoked so the realistic atmosphere is reinforced. The theme of an adolescent's growing awareness and understanding is brought out through Julia's insights into the needs of others and the destructive nature of selfishness. The book features skillful characterizations and plot with none of the conspicuous coincidences which mar Cameron's earlier stories. The whole seems to be a slice of life which existed before the book began and will go on after the last incident described is ended: "The writing makes no concessions to a young audience, but is intricate, thoughtful, and mature," commented Zena Sutherland in the *Saturday Review*.

According to critic Brian Attebery, Edward Ormondroyd's *Time at the Top* (1963) and Cameron's *The Court of the Stone Children* (1973) "are the most satisfying American time fantasies to date." Cameron's tale is an artistic exploration of her philosophy that the perception of time as a linear experience of past, present, and future is an illusion of our limited senses. The setting of the story is based on her childhood love of San Francisco and a museum there which evoked for her "the poignancy of human beings hundreds or even thousands of years gone who had made and used these things . . . on which I fed my imagination." Nina, the main character in *The Court of the Stone Children*, also experiences the "museum feeling" when she enters a French museum in San Francisco with its court of stone children. Here she meets Dominique, an inhabitant of Napoleon's France, whose family possessions are on display in the chateaulike museum. Domi appears to Nina several times over a period of weeks; the story of her past and of her father's mysterious disappearance three weeks be-

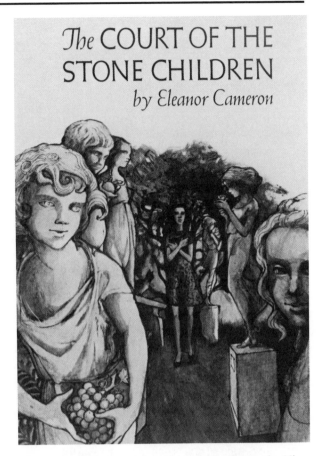

Dust jacket for Cameron's novel in which the protagonist, Nina, encounters a young girl from seventeenth-century France and helps her solve the mystery of her father's disappearance. The novel won a National Book Award in 1974 (Dutton).

fore his execution as a traitor gradually unfolds. The injustice of the execution prompts Domi to enlist Nina's aid in finding proof of her father's innocence. Several remarkable coincidences are required to solve this mystery. Nina meets several people who engage her in discussion about the possibilities of existence out of time; she has access to diaries and documents from the past and discovers the fortuitous location of a nineteenth-century portrait which can provide irrefutable evidence of Domi's father's innocence. However, the coincidental plot is more than redeemed by the poignant evocation of Domi's life in France, the interest of the mystery, and the genuine personalities which inhabit the story. A National Book Award winner in 1974, the book richly deserved this honor.

To the Green Mountains (1975) was first written as a one-act play in 1947. It is the author's most adult novel to date, a very complex treatment of an adolescent's growing awareness that human beings must face what *is* and not fool themselves. A second theme mentioned by the author in a discussion of the work is the idea that human beings should not try to possess one another. The setting is drawn from Cameron's youth, between the ages of three and six, when she lived in a hotel in a small town in southern Ohio.

Kath Rule's recurring dream of returning with her mother to her grandmother's house in the Green Mountains of Vermont provides a temporary escape from the unsatisfying life she lives in one room of a hotel in South Angela, Ohio, during World War I. With assistance from Grant, the black headwaiter, her mother, Elizabeth, manages the hotel and supports her inept husband Jason, who farms nearby. Elizabeth's gift of some expensive law books to Grant sparks ominous gossip in the town and sets in motion a chain of events which ends in the tragic death of Tiss, Grant's wife. Ironically the same events make an eventual return to the Green Mountains possible. The story has a definite air of remembrance of things past, a haunting reality which characterizes Cameron's later work. Just two years after her National Book Award for fantasy, this title was a finalist in the same competition.

A younger Julia Redfern is the central figure of *Julia and the Hand of God* (1977) which ends where *A Room Made of Windows* begins. Her Uncle Hugh's birthday gift of a leather-bound book of blank pages provides a focus for eleven-year-old Julia's struggles to translate her life experiences into written form. The minor disaster which occurs when Julia and her friend Maisie attempt to cremate a mouse in a saucepan, her freeing of a housefinch caught in a bush while she is on an errand for her mother, and her fortuitous waking up in time to escape being burned in the 1923 Berkeley fire are material for what Julia calls her "Book of Strangenesses." Where Julia's dour grandmother sees the ominous Hand of God reaching down to punish Berkeley with a fire just as it had wrecked San Francisco with the earthquake of Uncle Hugh's youth, Julia is captivated by the wonder of her experiences and the strange way one event leads to another.

Julia and the Hand of God is every bit as good as *A Room Made of Windows*. It has the same realistic atmosphere, the rich evocation of a total world which captures Julia's humorous and serious moments at this impressionable age. Having fewer subplots, it is perhaps a tighter, more unified novel than *A Room Made of Windows* in its reflection of

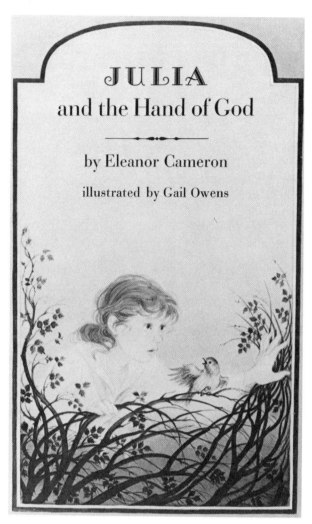

Dust jacket for the second of Cameron's four books featuring Julia Redfern, whom Cameron has identified as "myself as a child, though most of the scenes in these books never happened" (Dutton)

the smaller world of the younger Julia.

In *Beyond Silence* (1980), Cameron's second time-fantasy, Andrew Cames, a troubled young American, travels to Scotland with his father after the accidental death of his beloved older brother, Hoagy. At the castle where his father spent carefree childhood summers on the Cames estate, Andrew encounters Deirdre, a young girl who had lived on the same estate two generations before. These encounters with Deirdre take several forms as she appears to him at different stages of her life. Andy and Deirdre never enjoy a conversation but he sees her and hears her voice, and they act twice to save each other from impending danger in ways which shatter Andrew's sense of time and enable him to face and deal with his own guilt regarding his brother's death.

The story is not as satisfying as *The Court of the Stone Children* for a number of reasons. The character of Andrew, a disturbed young man, is not as appealing as Nina, a bright, motivated young girl. The character of Domi in the earlier book is clearly drawn so that the reader easily identifies with her as a real person whom Nina has encountered. In contrast, Deirdre appears to Andy in a fragmentary way; there is no possibility of a sustained identification with her, leading the reader to suspect that her character may be only hallucination. The interaction of past and present in *The Court of the Stone Children* to solve a mystery holds the reader's attention; Andy's personal dilemma is less interesting and his experience of the past through Deirdre is only tangentially related to his role in the circumstances surrounding his brother's death, the central problem of the book.

With deft verbal strokes Cameron once again succeeds in creating a vivid physical setting inhabited by credible people—even the minor characters in *Beyond Silence* have great depth. However, there are disturbing subplots in the book which do not seem to be relevant to the theme of the story and which jar the reader with their harshness, such as the death of a prominent psychologist who befriends Andrew and the disintegration of his parents' marriage. Cameron uses the first person point of view for the first time in *Beyond Silence;* therefore, the book is not only a time-fantasy but a psychological study as well. In *Children's Literature,* Perry Nodelman has suggested that the apparent loose ends of the novel are really indications that psychological or scientific explanations fall short of describing reality and that beyond explanations there is silence, and, as the title suggests, beyond this silence there is more. Not every reader would be able to explore confusion over the story's apparent weaknesses in such a way. *Beyond Silence* is an extremely sophisticated and unsettling novel.

Two additional books about Julia's earlier years complete the works which Eleanor Cameron has published to date. *That Julia Redfern* (1982) depicts Julia's life just before the time period of *Julia and the Hand of God.* The book covers events which range from the hilarious to the mysterious and sad. Humor erupts when Julia's hefty Aunt Alex sits on Julia's imaginary sister who never again appears to listen to Julia's stories. Aunt Alex's inappropriate gift of a huge doll which Julia promptly names Felony is another cause for amusement. In contrast, an inexplicable dream with a message from her father at the moment of his death gives Julia a link with him which somewhat softens her loss. Her role in locating her father's misplaced story provides her with another vital connection with him. Of central significance to Julia's future is her father's gift of the handmade honey-colored desk, which figured prominently in the earlier novel, and his prediction that she will become a writer.

Julia's Magic (1984) chronicles the guilty fears of six-year-old Julia when she breaks a perfume bottle stopper and the event disrupts relations between Aunt Alex, Uncle Hugh, and their maid Hulda, who is blamed for the accident. The scene of forgiveness between Aunt Alex and Hulda is striking for its authenticity. Julia has two dreams about herself and Hulda which metaphorically picture the isolation her guilt provokes and the later restoration of harmony. Other events include the possibility that the Redferns may have to leave their beloved rented house, Julia's adventures on a trolley ride alone, and her fluctuating friendship with Maisie.

A recital of the high points of plot gives only an inkling of these richly textured stories. They are not merely episodic novels for younger readers; the structure of both books is a skillful interweaving of minor and major events. Both are unified by the strong developing personality of Julia, a child whose sense of self enables her to make independent judgments, suffer through her misjudgments, yet retain her determination and high spirits. Other characters, seen through Julia's eyes, are well delineated, and Cameron is on solid imaginative ground as she draws from the remembered perceptions and emotions of her own childhood. She has said that Julia "is myself as a child, though most of the scenes in these books never happened."

These stories are unusually satisfying as they convey the serious, as well as the lighter, moments in a dynamic child's life. The stories are not simplistic; events are deeply felt, guilts are painfully endured, but the prevailing tone is sometimes humorous and always optimistic. The favorable commentary of the reviewer for the *Bulletin of the Center for Children's Books* on *That Julia Redfern* could apply to both books: "This has more substance than most of the many stage-of-childhood books for children, since it has depth and consistency of characterization, strong dialogue and exposition, and a credible change and growth in the protagonist." These books perfectly bring the younger Julia to life so that the reader is drawn to read again of her eleventh and twelfth years in *Julia and the Hand of God* and *A Room Made of Windows.*

Eleanor Cameron, whose writing has grown from the simpler fast-paced plotting of the Mushroom Planet books to the creation of whole worlds of the past and present, is a writer of outstanding talent and versatility. Her style is rich with beautifully executed descriptions of both characters and settings. She is an expert critic, who examines children's literature by an eclectic, personal method, though she is extremely well read in critical theory and handles many styles of literary interpretation with competence. She also engages in lively critical debates with authors and reviewers who are examining her works and other books written for children. In the course of these discussions, she explores the unique perspective of the writer-critic and the importance of thoughtful, scholarly criticism of children's literature.

Eleanor Cameron's enhanced reputation as an extraordinary writer for children and as an astute critic has provided her with numerous opportunities to publish commentary and criticism in *Horn Book, Wilson Library Bulletin, Children's Literature Association Quarterly,* and other publications. She is also a frequent speaker at children's literature conferences and other events. Of special note was her selection to deliver the annual Whittall Lecture at the Library of Congress in 1977. Other honors include membership to the editorial boards of two publications: *Cricket: The Magazine for Children* (since 1973) and *Children's Literature in Education* (since 1982). She has served as a member of the advisory board for the Study of Children's Literature at Simmons College in Boston since 1977 and was a judge in the children's category for the National Book Awards in 1980. She is now working on a fifth novel featuring Julia Redfern.

References:

Brian Attebery, *The Fantasy Tradition in American Literature* (Bloomington: Indiana University Press, 1980), p. 153;

S. V. Keenan, "WLB Biography: Eleanor Cameron," *Wilson Library Bulletin*, 37 (October 1962): 186;

Perry Nodelman, "The Depths of All She Is: Eleanor Cameron," *Children's Literature Association Quarterly* (Winter 1980): 6-8;

Nodelman, "Beyond Explanation, and Beyond Inexplicability, in *Beyond Silence*," *Children's Literature 12*, edited by Francelia Butler (New York: Modern Language Association, 1980), pp. 122-123.

Ann Nolan Clark

(5 December 1896-   )

Ophelia Gilbert
Central Missouri State University

BOOKS: *Who Wants to be a Prairie Dog?*, illustrated by Van Tishnahjinnie (Phoenix: U.S. Bureau of Indian Affairs, 1940);

Little Herder in Spring, illustrated by Hoke Denetsosie (Phoenix: U.S. Bureau of Indian Affairs, 1940);

Little Herder in Autumn, illustrated by Denetsosie (Phoenix: U.S. Bureau of Indian Affairs, 1940);

Little Boy with Three Names, illustrated by Tonita Lujan (Washington, D.C.: U.S. Bureau of Indian Affairs, 1940);

The Pine Ridge Porcupine, illustrated by Andrew Standing Soldier (Lawrence, Kans.: U.S. Bureau of Indian Affairs, 1940);

In My Mother's House, illustrated by Velino Herrera (New York: Viking, 1941);

A Child's Story of New Mexico, by Clark and Frances Carey (Lincoln, Nebr. & New York: University Publishing, 1941);

About the Slim Butte Raccoon, illustrated by Standing Soldier (Washington, D.C.: U.S. Bureau of

Ann Nolan Clark

Indian Affairs, 1942);

Little Herder in Winter, illustrated by Denetsosie (Phoenix: U.S. Bureau of Indian Affairs, 1942);

Little Herder in Summer, illustrated by Denetsosie (Phoenix: U.S. Bureau of Indian Affairs, 1942);

Buffalo Caller, illustrated by Marian Hulsizer (Evanston, Ill. & New York: Row, Peterson, 1942);

There Still are Buffalo, illustrated by Standing Soldier (Washington, D.C.: U.S. Bureau of Indian Affairs, 1942);

Bringer of the Mystery Dog, illustrated by Oscar Howe (Lawrence, Kans.: U.S. Bureau of Indian Affairs, 1943);

About the Grass Mountain Mouse, illustrated by Standing Soldier (Washington, D.C.: U.S. Bureau of Indian Affairs, 1943);

Young Hunter of Picuris, illustrated by Herrera (Chilocco, Okla.: U.S. Bureau of Indian Affairs, 1943);

Little Navajo Bluebird, illustrated by Paul Lantz (New York: Viking, 1943);

Brave Against the Enemy, by Clark and Helen Post (Lawrence, Kans.: U.S. Indian Service, 1944);

Sun Journey, illustrated by Percy T. Sandy (Chilocco, Okla.: U.S. Bureau of Indian Affairs, 1945);

Singing Sioux Cowboy Primer, illustrated by Standing Soldier (Lawrence, Kans.: U.S. Indian Service, 1945);

Singing Sioux Cowboy Reader, illustrated by Standing Soldier (Lawrence, Kans.: U.S. Indian Service, 1947);

Linda Rita (Washington, D.C.: Government Printing Office, 1948);

Los Patos Son Diferentes (Washington, D.C.: Government Printing Office, 1948);

El Buey Que Querbia Vivir En La Casa (Washington, D.C.: Government Printing Office, 1948);

Juan El Poblano (Washington, D.C.: Government Printing Office, 1949);

El Cerdito Que Fube Al Mercado (Washington, D.C.: Government Printing Office, 1949);

Magic Money, illustrated by Leo Politi (New York: Viking, 1950);

Little Navajo Herder, illustrated by Denetsosie (Phoenix: U.S. Bureau of Indian Affairs, 1951);

Secret of the Andes, illustrated by Jean Charlot (New York: Viking, 1952);

Looking-for-Something, illustrated by Politi (New York: Viking, 1952);

Blue Canyon Horse, illustrated by Allan Houser (New York: Viking, 1954);

About the Hen of Wahpeton, illustrated by Standing Soldier (Lawrence, Kans.: U.S. Bureau of Indian Affairs, 1954);

El Maestro Rural En La Comunidad, by Clark, Manuel Arce, and Miguel Gordillo (Guatemala: Ministerio de Educacibon Publica, 1955);

Santiago, illustrated by Lynd Ward (New York: Viking, 1955);

The Little Indian Pottery Maker, illustrated by Don Perceval (Los Angeles: Melmont, 1955);

Third Monkey, illustrated by Don Freeman (New York: Viking, 1956);

The Little Indian Basket Maker, illustrated by Harrison Begay (Los Angeles: Melmont, 1957);

A Santo for Pasqualita, illustrated by Mary Villarejo (New York: Viking, 1959);

World Song, illustrated by Kurt Wiese (New York: Viking, 1960);

Paco's Miracle, illustrated by Agnes Tait (New York: Bell, 1962);

The Desert People, illustrated by Houser (New York: Viking, 1962);

Tia Maria's Garden, illustrated by Ezra Jack Keats (New York: Viking, 1963);

Medicine Man's Daughter, illustrated by Donald Bolognese (New York: Farrar, Straus, 1963);

Father Kino, Priest to the Pimas, illustrated by H. Lawrence Hoffman (New York: Farrar, Straus, 1963; London: Burns & Oates, 1963);

Bear Cub, illustrated by Charles Fracé (New York: Viking, 1965);

This for That, illustrated by Freeman (San Carlos, Cal.: Golden Gate Junior Books, 1965);

Brother Andre of Montreal, illustrated by Harold Lang (New York: Vision, 1967; London: Burns & Oates, 1967);

Summer Is for Growing, illustrated by Tait (New York: Farrar, Straus & Giroux, 1968);

Arizona Is for Young People, by Clark and Glenna Craw (Lincoln, Nebr.: University Publishing, 1968);

Along Sandy Trails, photographs by Alfred A. Cohn (New York: Viking, 1969);

These Were the Valiant: A Collection of New Mexico Profiles (Albuquerque, N.M.: C. Horn, 1969);

Journey to the People (New York: Viking, 1969);

Circle of Seasons, illustrated by W. T. Mars (New York: Farrar, Straus & Giroux, 1970);

Hoofprint on the Wind, illustrated by Robert Andrew Parker (New York: Viking, 1972);

Year Walk (New York: Viking, 1975);

All This Wild Land (New York: Viking, 1976);

To Stand Against the Wind (New York: Viking, 1978);

In the Land of Small Dragon: A Vietnamese Folk Tale, illustrated by Tony Chen (New York: Viking, 1979).

Ann Nolan Clark, winner of the 1953 Newbery Medal for *Secret of the Andes* (1952), has spent most of her life speaking out for the needs of minority children. She has been one of the few people to write books *for* Indian children as well as about them, extending her creativity to magazine editing and the production of school readers, radio scripts, and braille transliterations. Her books demonstrate her awareness of cultural subtleties; her love and understanding of diverse peoples lies in capturing varied speech patterns, different types of home environment, customs, and attitudes.

She has had firsthand experience with the people about whom she writes. Research for her books has taken her to American Indian reservations, Basque villages in the Pyrenees, Ireland, Central and South America, Canada, and Finland. In her Newbery acceptance speech, she stated: "All children need understanding, but children of segregated racial groups need even more. All children need someone to make a bridge from their world to the world of adults who surround them. Indian children need this; they have the child problems of growing up, but also they have racial problems, the problems of conflicting interracial patterns between groups, and the conflicts of changing racial patterns within the groups. Anyway you look at it, it's rugged to be a child. Often I think more of us did not survive the experience than meets the eye."

Ann Nolan was born in 1896 in Las Vegas, New Mexico, one of four children of Irish-American parents, Patrick Frances and Mary Dunn Nolan. She grew up in the multicultural atmosphere of New Mexico, playing with children whose diverse Indian, French, and Spanish backgrounds made a sharp contrast with her Irish heritage. She attributes the success of her books to this rich and varied cultural mixture, having said of these influences that "all of this gave us understanding, a tolerance and acceptance and appreciation and ease with different people who have other ways of thinking and other ways of living." In her autobiography, *Journey to the People* (1969), she reiterates that "it was the days of early Las Vegas that set the pattern for my acceptance of folkways and traditions. It set the pattern which the years have deepened."

Brought up by strict parents who instilled in their children a high sense of honesty and responsibility, she was a shy, quiet child who attended a convent day school and then the public high school in Las Vegas. During her high school years she was allowed to take some work at the New Mexico Highlands University located in Las Vegas, and during her college years she served as an assistant English instructor at that school.

Soon after the United States entered World War I in 1917, she accepted her first full-time teaching job in a nearby German community in New Mexico. A room in a loft, board, and a cow pony to ride supplemented her meager $60.00 a month salary. Known to the students and members of the community as "Teacher," she disliked the name as well as the attitudes of the pro-German settlement. That first job lasted only a year, although her experiences there helped her learn the necessity of being able to adjust to the different kinds of people she was to be associated with.

The unpleasant experience led her to try new avenues for employment, and in 1918 she went to Tacoma, Washington, where she held a variety of jobs: she operated an elevator, ran a machine in a sash and door factory, worked in a defense plant, and was a society reporter for a newspaper. Home ties proved strong, however, and she returned to Las Vegas. Shortly thereafter she began her second teaching job at an ungraded school in another small town in New Mexico. She graduated from Highlands University in 1919 with a major in education. She married Thomas Patrick Clark on 6 August 1919, and in 1920 her only son, Thomas Patrick, was born.

Her husband died shortly thereafter, and she was left a young widow with a son to support. She found her first job as a substitute teacher with the Bureau of Indian Affairs and taught on two occasions in the Zuñi Pueblo community at the Blackrock Boarding School about forty miles from Gallup, New Mexico, as well as several months at Tesuque, near Sante Fe. In 1923 she was urged by an official of the Bureau of Indian Affairs to take the examination for permanent employment in the

Indian Service. After doing so, and being accepted, her first assignment was at the Santa Fe Boarding School for Indian children; she was soon sent to the Tesuque Pueblo in response to a request from the village representatives, who wanted Clark in particular to teach their children.

Though the superintendent of the branch of Indian Affairs at Santa Fe thought it would be a professional mistake for her to leave the large boarding school, Clark felt differently, and once in her new school, she began to understand the problems of the Indian children, who were expected to learn new ways of thinking, living, and learning totally unrelated to their way of life. She realized that, however good the intentions of the Indian Bureau were, too little consideration was given to the particular needs of the children as Indians. During her four years at Tesuque, Clark began to write new texts suited to the children of this ancient culture and designed to stimulate their desire for reading. The books also have great significance for white children, giving them a truly realistic treatment of Indian ways.

Her first book, "Third Grade Geography," stressed the relationship of people to their locales and ways of living. Because there was little money available to the school, each child illustrated his own copy and bound it with Indian-calico covers. This book eventually found its way to Washington D.C., where someone at the Bureau of Indian Affairs showed it to May Massee at Viking Press. Retitled *In My Mother's House* (1941), this became Ann Nolan Clark's first commercially published book. Small, with a text that reflects the feel and cadence of Tewa Indian speech, the book radiates a deep feeling for the world of the Indian child, whose home, crops, work, festivals, and family are described in this picture book. The illustrations by Velino Herrera incorporate tribal designs along with the familiar routines of living. The book was a Caldecott Honor Book for 1941 and received the *New York Herald Tribune*'s Children's Spring Book Festival Award. Most important, *In My Mother's House* was the first children's book written about American Indian children from their point of view.

Willard Beatty, chief of the Branch of Education, Bureau of Indian Affairs, believed that Indian children should have the opportunity to have books written specifically for them, both in English and Indian languages. In 1940 he chose Ann Clark as the person to write the English versions, and her work with the Bureau changed as she was assigned a series of "Indian Life Readers." Living among the Pueblo, Navajo, Zuni, and Dakota Sioux, co-

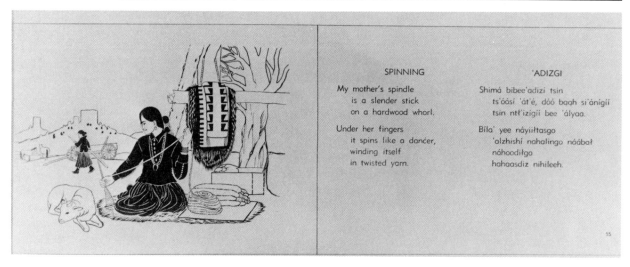

Illustration by Hoke Denetsosie and bilingual text by Clark from Little Herder in Autumn *(U.S. Bureau of Indian Affairs)*

operating with a group of anthropologists and working with translators of various Indian languages, she eventually wrote twenty titles that were printed as paperbacks over a fourteen-year period and were published in English, Sioux, Navajo, and Spanish. Stories of everyday Indian life, they contain easily assimilated information. Most of the readers have effective drawings by Indian illustrators; those of Andrew Standing Soldier are particularly outstanding.

Beatty's next project was a magazine for middle-grade Indian children to be published monthly throughout the United States, and he asked Ann Clark to edit it. She agreed to try, affirming his confidence in her by having the first six issues ready before the publication date.

When World War II began, appropriations for the Indian Bureau were cut and publishing ventures were discontinued, though Clark still worked for the Bureau of Indian Affairs, trying to write a book a year. In 1942 Beatty asked Clark to join an Indian Service team working with Japanese-Americans to help them establish their own educational program in a Japanese rehabilitation center. A short time later, Beatty asked Ann Clark to go to southern Arizona to supervise the teaching of Papago and Pima Indians. While she was there, her son was killed in a flying mission over the Pacific. Clark then went to Santa Fe (where he had grown up) as a supervisor to the Northern Pueblos, though understandably she did not produce any new works during this period.

While working with the children in the Northern Pueblos, she received an invitation to travel to

Central and South America for the Institute of Inter-American Affairs and to write basic reading materials for classroom teaching. Once there, she decided to encourage teachers to write their own books, realizing their work would be more effective than anything she could produce. She toured Guatemala, Honduras, Panama, Costa Rica, Ecuador, and Peru, her travels providing background for later books. Her work in these countries lasted eight years, during which time she went, as the only woman delegate, to Paris for a UNESCO conference on education of underprivileged children and to Brazil to work with newly literate adults.

While she was gone, Beatty started a five-year Special Navajo Program, which ultimately lasted fifteen years. She agreed to return to the United States and help write for this program, with the provision that she could eventually return to Latin America to finish her work.

When Hildegard Thompson succeeded Beatty as Chief of the Branch of Education of the Bureau of Indian Culture, she asked Ann Clark to work with the Adult Indian Education Program. Clark helped train teachers to write their own texts, and as a result, nearly 100 books were produced, primarily vocational manuals on crafts and skills to help prepare Indians for productive work outside their reservations.

During these years, Clark continued to write fiction for children, including *A Child's Story of New Mexico* (1941), which she wrote in collaboration with Frances Carey, and *Little Navajo Bluebird* (1943), an appealing story of a young girl who sees difficulties in adapting to the outside world, which has already changed her older brother and is affecting the attitudes of her older sister. Her decision to leave her hogan to go to school is an agonizing one, but eventually she learns that school may have much to offer, and that cultures may become richer by learning from each other.

In the 1950s Clark began to employ her experiences in Central and South America as the background materials for several books. *Magic Money* (1950) is a story of familial love as seen through the eyes of a small boy whose family works on a coffee plantation in Costa Rica. Wanting to earn money to buy two white oxen for his grandfather's cart so it may win a prize in the annual parade, he discovers that giving can be as rewarding as receiving. Leo Politi's illustrations are colorful and striking, adding warmth and a realistic atmosphere to the story.

The story of a stray burro in Ecuador, *Looking-for-Something* (1952) is told with simple, poetic charm and is about Gray Burro, who lives in a beautiful world, surrounded by the comforts of a mother's love. But he wants something besides the life he lives in the banana grove, so he walks away from the familiar surroundings, despite his mother's pleas. After many days he encounters civilization, in the form of trucks and uncaring people, then is forced aboard a cattle boat, and finally arrives at a city and is taken to work in the gold mines. Everyone he encounters seems to be fulfilling a purpose. He wanders to Indian country, where he is reminded of his homeland, but when an Indian tries to shoot him with a blowgun, he runs away again. Finally, he is found by a small boy who takes him to his house. Although the family is poor and has to work hard, Gray Burro feels at home because he is wanted and loved, and he finally realizes that what he had been looking for during his many adventures was to belong to someone. The drawings of Leo Politi enhance this charming story, which conveys the message of a basic human need while at the same time giving an overview of the landscape, people, and occupations of Ecuador.

The story of Cusi, an Inca boy who lives in a secluded valley in the mountains of Peru, *Secret of the Andes* (1952) is based on historical fact. Unaware of his royal blood, Cusi ultimately discovers he must choose between living in town or remaining in the mountains, caring for the sacred llama herds and guarding his people's heritage. Distinguished by its vivid description of the high Andes and its account of the pride and dignity of the Inca people, this book won the Newbery Medal for 1953.

Blue Canyon Horse (1954), a poetic story of an Indian boy and the young mare he has loved and cared for, describes how the mare, drawn by the lure of a herd of wild horses, runs away. In due time she returns, with her colt, to the boy who has been her loyal friend. The bond which exists between the boy and the animal is expressed in lyrical prose, which is complemented by Allan Houser's illustrations emphasizing the natural beauty of the Indian's homeland.

Santiago (1955) is the story of a Guatemalan boy's search for identity in his world. The protégé of a North American family, he is abruptly claimed by his Indian family when he is twelve and returned to his father's village, where for five years he lives an impoverished life. When the time comes for him to decide his future, he rejects the opportunity to return to the American family and their material success, choosing instead to become a teacher in the village. The book examines the problems which stem from conflicts between the two cultures he knows, as well as the painful process of a boy's maturing into manhood.

Set in New Mexico, *Paco's Miracle* (1962) tells of Paco, brought up by a hermit, who has taught the boy the love of animals as well as of people. When the hermit becomes ill, Paco goes to live with a kindly couple in the nearby village, where, after an accident prevents the purchasing of supplies and decorations for a Christmas Eve celebration, Paco performs a "miracle" by finding appropriate food and decorations in the nearby mountains. Sentimental and tender, the story appeals to sensitive readers.

A beautifully written book about a Papago Indian, *The Desert People* (1962) traces the life of a family in the desert of the American Southwest and describes the pattern of their days, their home life, customs, community life, entertainment, work, and the legends of the desert people. *Tia Maria's Garden* (1963) describes the desert where Tia and her small nephew take early morning walks and focuses on the child's observations of the strange animals and plants.

There is more attention to plot in *Medicine Man's Daughter* (1963), which explores the conflict between the Navajo's ceremonial healing process and modern medicine. Tall-Girl, a fifteen-year-old Navajo, has been chosen to learn the art of healing through rituals and chants. When she discovers that the real power of healing for a burned child must be from the white man, her beliefs are shaken. She finally learns that she may accept the world of the white man without discarding all her traditional

Dust jacket for Clark's Newbery Medal-winning book (Viking)

beliefs.

Set in New Mexico in 1851, when the land has become a territory of the United States and the flag of Mexico has been exchanged for the Stars and Stripes, *Summer Is for Growing* (1968) tells of a young girl who is exposed to new ideas of freedom, equality, and responsibility which her aunt brings back after a trip to Washington, D.C. With her, Lala ventures outside the hacienda walls and sees her new countrymen as they head west by wagon train. She meets Susan, an American girl, and learns that a real American—even a new one like herself—must not only cherish freedom but share it with others.

Between 1970 and 1976 Clark published four books, among them *Circle of Seasons* (1970), a non-fiction account of Pueblo Indian ceremonial customs, and *All This Wild Land* (1976), which is a distinct departure in locale from her previous work, though the theme of conflict between two cultures remains the primary focus. Clark traveled

in Finland and Minnesota to conduct research for this story, which is based on the experiences of early Finnish immigrants. Dealing with an eleven-year-old Finnish girl, whose family finds the courage to withstand the forces of nature in the raw, untamed state of Minnesota, the book depicts their anger, grief, love, and understanding, as well as their excitement over the new land.

Clark's last book, *In the Land of Small Dragon* (1979), is a Vietnamese folktale, retold in blank verse, and is an unusual version of the Cinderella story. Cam is consumed with jealousy of her beautiful older stepsister, Tam, and the mother, siding with her own child, makes Tam work long hours at unpleasant tasks. Tam appeals to her father, who gives his daughters various challenges in order to find out who shall be "Number One." Cam tricks Tam in whatever she tries to do, until finally a magician secretly rewards Tam with a pair of jeweled shoes. A blackbird flies off with one of the shoes and drops it in front of the Emperor's son

Clark's notes on her writing strategy for To Stand Against the Wind *(by permission of the author)*

as he is walking in the palace garden. The prince declares he will marry the possessor of the matching shoe and eventually finds Tam. All ends happily, as good fairy tales do.

Ann Nolan Clark is a quiet, unassuming woman whose primary interests are reflected by the various organizations to which she belongs: P.E.N., the National Council of Women, the International Council for Women, Alpha Delta Kappa, Altrusa International, Mark Twain Society, and Kappa Delta Pi. She lived for many years on her Red Dog Ranch in Tesuque, New Mexico, where she enjoyed painting, gardening, cooking, and raising and training blooded cocker spaniels for their obedience degrees. In 1962 a serious injury kept Ann Clark in the hospital for many months. Recently her health has forced her to reduce many of her activities, and she has moved to an apartment in Tucson, Arizona.

During her professional career Ann Nolan Clark was first a teacher. Besides her books she has also written magazine articles, producing many southwestern historical articles for the *New Mexico Magazine*. She served as educational specialist with the Bureau of Indian Affairs, Washington, D.C.,

from 1920 to 1962, and part of that time was head of the Preparations Materials Department, Adult Division. She also served as educational consultant, Latin-American Bureau (1945-1950), was a materials specialist, Institute of Inter-American Affairs, and served as a U.S. delegate to the UNESCO Conference in Brazil. During all these years she wrote and conducted workshops. Many of her books have been published in braille and some have been reproduced as filmstrips.

Besides the Newbery Medal, her awards include the *New York Herald Tribune* Spring Festival Award for *In My Mother's House* (1941) and *Looking-for-Something* (1952); the Distinguished Service Award, Department of the Interior (1962); and the Regina Medal, Catholic Library Association (1963). *In My Mother's House* and *Little Navajo Bluebird* were also Junior Literary Guild Selections.

Ann Nolan Clark's life and writing have shown her sympathetic awareness of the difficulties involved in intercultural relations. Her books are characterized by humor, understanding, a strong sense of family relationships, knowledge of the past, and the acknowledgment of the dignity of each person as an individual. Few people have

117

131

Grandmother stood up, "But you lied," she said. Then she asked it as a question, "Did you lie?" hoping somehow the answer would be no. Chi-Hai answered, "Yes, Grandmother, I lied. I would have killed if it had been necessary and now I want to go to America to get my baby back."

"We will all go," Em̃ Vŭet said in his new-found strength, and then to his Grandmother, "Are you willing to go little Grandmother?" Without hesitation Grandmother said, "I obey the head of the family. I will go."

Old Uncle asked eagerly, "Will Sam be there? You know he promised to take me. I will go to America with Sam." The old man was confused again.

John said, "I will go with Chi-Bah to get the permits. They will be easy to get excepting the Vietnamese want a sum of money for each permit. I think I can get enough money. Sam had many friends." "We have the money," Grandmother said proudly, dragging out her clay pot and giving John a handful of money. "If there is any left," she told Chi-Bah, "buy perfume pans and bronze bowls for our new altar to our ancestors in America." "That is if you get to America," John said " Many can not make it.

Now instead of nothing to think about, their hours were filled with agonizing worry. They had paid the money and had the paper that permitted them to go. But there was no space available. At first they stood in line, fighting to keep their places and the pushed backward or separated John said this was to draw guards. He got them a place to sit in the hot sun, but it was better than standing and in danger of falling and being trampled upon. John and two of his friends took turns standing in line for them. Then came the day when they actually stepped on the plane. At the last moment Old Uncle refused to go saying he had promised to wait for Sam. John carried him to the sun and got the

Final pages from a draft for To Stand Against the Wind *(by permission of the author)*

118

end page
To Stand Against the Wind

Viet remembered nothing about the trip to America and very little about Camp Pendleton in California where each one was given a number instead of a name. He remembered vividly how they had waited for weeks for some town in America to sponsor them as new neighbors. "What if no group would sponsor them," the boy thought in despair. What if they would be sent back to the barbed wire enclosure in the refugee camp in Vietnam?

At last the boy remembered Sam's letter to his parents and sent them, explaining that some group must sponsor them for a home town in America. In the meantime day after day she went from agency to agency to ask about the Baby Lift and where was the lady that she was to pick up as soon as she got to America. The answer was always the same. Where were her papers? Who was the woman to whom she gave the baby, Baby of no name, no identification of any kind. And always in that face there was the terrible look that they knew she had died.

Grandmother was their only comfort. Over and over she told them, "When the strong wind of sullering blows, the grasses flatten. The wind must stop sometime. Then the grasses can stand upright again. Sam's parents will not fail us. They will find us a group and a town where we can start new lives."

Tom looked up from his paper. It was empty with only marks on it here and there. He had not written a record for those who would come after him. Perhaps it was just a well if they never knew all that happened. His grandmother was looking at him. She expected something to hang on the wall just as he had in Vietnam. "When the strong winds blow." Tom he

given their lives and talents as single-mindedly to a purpose as has Ann Nolan Clark. Few have been able to communicate so clearly the essential brotherhood of man.

References:

C. H. Bishop, "Ann Nolan Clark," *Catholic Library World*, 34 (February 1963): 280-286;

"Friendship Through Understanding," *Oklahoma Librarian*, 3 (Summer 1953);

M. Massee, "Ann Nolan Clark," *Horn Book*, 29 (August 1953): 258-262;

Massee, "Newbery to Ann Clark," *Library Journal*, 78 (15 March 1953);

"Newbery Award Acceptance," *Horn Book*, 29 (August 1953): 258-262;

"Regina Medal to Ann Nolan Clark," *Library Journal*, 88 (15 February 1963): 847-848;

"Regina Medal to Ann Nolan Clark," *School Library Journal*, 10 (February 1963): 35-36;

"Ship's Treasures and Cargo," *Texas Library Journal*, 38 (June 1962);

R. Shor, "Ann Nolan Clark," *Wilson Library Bulletin*, 35 (November 1960): 263.

Papers:

There is a collection of Ann Nolan Clark's manuscripts in the Kerlan Collection at the University of Minnesota and in the de Grummond Collection at the University of Southern Mississippi.

Beverly Cleary

(12 April 1916-   )

Anita Trout
University of Tennessee

BOOKS: *Henry Huggins*, illustrated by Louis Darling (New York: Morrow, 1950);

Ellen Tebbits, illustrated by Darling (New York: Morrow, 1951);

Henry and Beezus, illustrated by Darling (New York: Morrow, 1952);

Otis Spofford, illustrated by Darling (New York: Morrow, 1953);

Henry and Ribsy, illustrated by Darling (New York: Morrow, 1954):

Beezus and Ramona, illustrated by Darling (New York: Morrow, 1955);

Fifteen, illustrated by Joe and Beth Krush (New York: Morrow, 1956);

Henry and the Paper Route, illustrated by Darling (New York: Morrow, 1957):

The Luckiest Girl (New York: Morrow, 1958);

Jean and Johnny, illustrated by Joe and Beth Krush (New York: Morrow, 1959);

The Hullabaloo ABC, illustrated by Earl Thollander (Berkeley: Parnassus, 1960);

Leave It To Beaver, novelization based on television series (New York: Berkley, 1960);

The Real Hole, illustrated by Mary Stevens (New York: Morrow, 1960); republished with new illustrations by Diane De Salvo-Ryan (New York: Morrow, 1986);

Emily's Runaway Imagination, illustrated by Joe and Beth Krush (New York: Morrow, 1961);

Two Dog Biscuits, illustrated by Stevens (New York: Morrow, 1961); republished with new illustrations by De Salvo-Ryan (New York: Morrow, 1986);

Henry and the Clubhouse, illustrated by Darling (New York: Morrow, 1962);

Sister of the Bride, illustrated by Joe and Beth Krush (New York: Morrow, 1963);

Ribsy, illustrated by Darling (New York: Morrow, 1964);

The Mouse and the Motorcycle, illustrated by Darling (New York: Morrow, 1965);

Mitch and Amy, illustrated by George Porter (New York: Morrow, 1967);

Ramona the Pest, illustrated by Darling (New York: Morrow, 1968);

Runaway Ralph, illustrated by Darling (New York: Morrow, 1970);

Socks, illustrated by Darling (New York: Morrow, 1973);

photograph by Margaret Miller

The Sausage at the End of the Nose [play] (New York: Children's Book Council, 1974);

Ramona the Brave, illustrated by Alan Tiegreen (New York: Morrow, 1975);

Ramona and her Father, illustrated by Tiegreen (New York: Morrow, 1977);

Ramona and her Mother (New York: Morrow, 1979);

Ramona Quimby, Age 8 (New York: Morrow, 1981);

Ralph S. Mouse (New York: Morrow, 1982);

Dear Mr. Henshaw (New York: Morrow, 1983);

Lucky Chuck (New York: Morrow, 1984);

Ramona Forever (New York: Morrow, 1984).

Beverly Cleary's overwhelming popularity as a writer for children is attested by the number of state and regional awards voted her by her readers. These have included the Young Readers' Choice Award (1957, 1960, 1968, 1971), the Dorothy Canfield Fisher Children's Book Award (1958), the William Allen White Children's Book Award (1968, 1976), and the Hawaii Association of School Li-

brarians Nene Award (1969, 1971, 1972, 1979). Her recognition from adults was not as immediate but includes such prestigious awards as the Laura Ingalls Wilder Award (1975) for substantial and lasting contribution to children's literature and the American Book Award for paperback (1981). Prior to the naming of *Dear Mr. Henshaw* as the recipient of the 1984 Newbery Medal, two of her books (*Ramona and her Father* in 1978 and *Ramona Quimby, Age 8* in 1982) were chosen as Newbery Honor Books.

Born 12 April 1916 in McMinnville, Oregon, to Chester Lloyd and Mable Atlee Bunn, Cleary spent her early years on a farm in Yamhill. Although the town had no library, her mother presided over a collection of books sent out at intervals from the State Library in Eugene. After her family moved to Portland when she was six, Cleary had her first real contact with a public library, though she remembers not being able to find exactly what she wanted—humorous books about ordinary children similar to herself and the boys and girls in her own neighborhood.

Cleary was educated at the University of California at Berkeley, graduating in 1938. Her interest in children's books led her, quite naturally, into children's library work, and she took a second B.A., in librarianship, at the University of Washington in 1939. As a children's librarian in Yakima, Washington, she had many experiences with children who wanted to read books about children like themselves in situations they could understand, furthering her ambition to become a writer herself.

In 1940 she married Clarence T. Cleary, and they moved to California. During World War II, she served as post librarian at the Oakland Army Hospital. It was not until 1950 and a move to a new house in Berkeley that she sat down and began the story of a boy, a dog, and a bus which was to become *Henry Huggins.* The world of Henry, his family, and his neighbors (some of whom appear in other books) is set in Portland, Oregon, and is partly based on actual places such as Klickitat and Tillamook Streets.

In the first book, eight-year-old Henry finds a stray dog at the drugstore and gets to keep him after managing to smuggle him onto a bus. Ribsy, as he names the dog, becomes his companion in all his later adventures. Henry also learns about the prolific habits of guppies and how to catch nightcrawlers. He has problems with the Christmas play at school, and, in the final chapter, he has to prove that Ribsy is really his in a showdown with the dog's first owner.

Roughly a year is covered in the span of the book, and the chapters are episodic rather than continuously plotted. Because each episode is a mini-story with its own resolution the book has been popular with younger readers who have graduated from primary books but are not ready for longer, more complex plots.

Henry is an average young boy, smart enough to figure out solutions to many of his problems, such as selling his hundreds of guppies to the pet store, but not precociously clever enough to have anticipated the rapid multiplication of the little fish in order to have avoided the problem. He tries to do what his parents want him to do and stay out of trouble, but he does not think to ask before he dusts Ribsy with his mother's pink talcum powder in an effort to clean him up before a dog show.

Because he does not want to be considered different by the other children in his age group he suffers agonies when chosen to play the *little* boy in the Christmas play at school. His horror is compounded when he discovers he will have to wear pajamas on stage and actually be kissed by an older girl. The teasing of his classmates and his embarrassment are effective and convincing.

Henry's story is continued in five other books, including *Ribsy* (1964), told entirely from the point of view of the dog and exploring Ribsy's trials when he becomes separated from Henry. While the books follow the same general pattern as the first, the plotting is more tightly knit. *Henry and Ribsy* (1954) begins with Henry asking his father if he can go along on a proposed fishing trip. After an interesting visit to the garage to have the car greased, Mr. Huggins agrees only if Henry can keep Ribsy out of trouble for the two months preceding the trip. The next four chapters detail Henry's struggle, which is complicated by garbage men, loose teeth, Henry's friend Beezus and her little sister Ramona, and the P.T.A. When the fishing trip finally becomes reality, Henry's troubles are still not over, but he and Ribsy manage to have a completely satisfactory conclusion to the expedition.

After writing *Henry Huggins,* Cleary introduced *Ellen Tebbits* (1951), a girl about the same age, who lives in a nearby neighborhood. Ellen is a female counterpart of Henry and has much of the same charm. She is ordinary in all the ways most children are. She has straight brown hair, which she wishes were curly; she is lonely because her best friend has moved; and she has a secret: her mother makes her wear woolen underwear. Since she thinks she is the only girl in the dance class who wears it, she constantly plots to keep it secret. True to Cleary's form, the underwear paves the way toward friendship with the new girl, Austine. After dance class, Ellen crouches in the broom closet trying to change her clothes when she hears a sound. Austine is also hiding her long underwear from the rest of the girls. The friendship is further cemented when, after Ellen brings an enormous beet to Show and Tell, Austine defends her against the ridicule of her classmates. They have a serious fight when Ellen believes Austine to be the one who tore her new dress, but by the end of the book Ellen and Austine have resolved their problem.

Cleary introduced other characters in these early books and then went on to write more about them. Beezus (Beatrice) Quimby and her younger sister Ramona had a whole series devoted to them after their formal introduction in *Beezus and Ramona* (1955). After Henry Huggins, Ramona became Cleary's best-loved character. Beezus is a well-mannered, practical nine year old whose biggest problem is four-year-old Ramona. She wipes her paint-covered hands on the neighbor's cat, scribbles in library books, and locks Henry's dog in the bathroom. Ramona, who is more imaginative, does not see her behavior as unusual. Beezus has to learn to understand her feelings of dislike and anger toward her sister, and the problem seems aggravated when she compares her sibling relationship with that of her mother and her mother's younger sister.

She cannot understand how things can be so different between members of the same family. The story culminates in disastrous attempts to bake Beezus's birthday cake—attempts ruined twice by Ramona. At the dinner table Beezus blurts out her feelings and is shocked to discover that her mother and aunt had very much the same relationship when they were younger. The fact that her ambivalent feelings toward Ramona are completely normal is brought home to her in such a way that she begins to realize that someday she may even be able to appreciate her sister.

Part of the reason Ramona is so popular is that there is a fascination for children in her almost unrelieved mischief, which is never malicious and which Ramona does not view as mischief. All children have an admiration for the trouble that other children make and seem to live through, and it certainly helps to account for the continued popularity of Ramona.

In *Otis Spofford* (1953), Cleary developed the forerunner of Ramona Quimby. Otis, who lives with his mother in an apartment building, is uncomfortable at school and likes nothing better than to "stir up a little excitement." As the front half of the bull in the Spanish fiesta program, he completely routs the toreador. He throws spitballs in class, so for punishment the teacher makes him chew spitballs all afternoon, without a drink of water. Otis overcomes this seeming defeat by pulling a clove of garlic from his pocket and chewing it, to the horror of the children sitting near him. His ultimate crime is committed against Ellen Tebbits, his favorite target for teasing, when he cuts a big chunk out of her hair while the teacher is absent from the room. Ellen and Austine get revenge that winter when they steal his shoes from the bench while he is ice-skating, leaving him to limp home wearing his ice skates. They force an apology from him, but Otis's unquenchable spirit triumphs as he announces that he had his fingers crossed the whole time.

Otis and Ramona share the ability to come up with unusual ways to challenge the adult rules and conventions which govern their lives. Children are fascinated by their inventiveness and their ability to bounce back in the face of punishment. Otis does not appear again, and readers do not have a chance to see how he grows, but Ramona does mature in later books.

In *Ramona and her Father* (1977) Ramona is seven and in second grade. Her father has lost his job, and she is beginning to understand that grown-ups are not the all-powerful creatures that they seem. While Ramona tries to become cute and adorable in order to make money for her family in commercials, her schemes backfire. She imitates a popular commercial by telling her teacher that her ankles look wrinkled because her stockings are sagging. Her teacher does not appreciate the advice, and her family does not appreciate her constant singing of commercial jingles.

One of the joys of this book is that readers get to see Beezus through Ramona's eyes, a turnabout from the first book. By the age of seven, Ramona is old enough to know that she is fallible and to worry about measuring up to the expectations of parents, teachers, and peers. Beezus is twelve and moody, grumpy, bossy, and usually right.

An important message which Cleary makes through Ramona is how very real are the fears which children have about their parents and family situations. Seven year olds too often hear and know only enough to cause them worry. Ramona is reassured by discovering that, although her life-style has been altered by her father's loss of his job and

Dust jacket for the sixth novel about the Quimby family (Morrow)

the subsequent change in her mother's working hours, these problems have not changed the love her parents have for her. Cleary knows that children need to hear this message often.

Ramona Forever (1984) brings Ramona to several major crossroads in her life. The family cat, Picky-picky, dies; the girls' parents decide that they can stay at home after school by themselves; and their Aunt Beatrice gets married. The biggest change comes with the announcement that Ramona's mother is having another baby.

Change is hard on children, but it is also part of life, and it is important that they be led to see that change may be leaving behind old, familiar things, but it also means new gains. The last sentence in the book, "She was winning at growing up," shows how accurately Cleary has read a child's view of the process—a struggle whose outcome is often in doubt.

Cleary's books are criticized because they do not provide any racial or ethnic mix in the characters and they do not confront any of the serious problems of childhood. It is true that the stories are based on white, middle-class families. Cleary does not attempt to create a world different from that in which she herself grew up, but this does not mean that her books have no value for the many children who do not share this background. The incidents in her books are common to the lives of most children. While not every boy who wants a dog is able to find and keep one as did Henry Huggins, they can still empathize with his desire and enjoy his success. Any girl who has had to wear clothes that are different from what the other girls wear will know full well why Ellen and Austine are hiding in the broom closet.

Cleary's style is clear and plain. She does not embellish the story with elaborate descriptions and details of background and setting. She lets the children speak for themselves. There is a vast difference between looking back on childhood as an adult and being able to reach back and be a child again. Cleary's ability to do the latter gives her books the honesty and humor which reach directly to her readers.

Viewed beside the more aggressive problem novels which abound today, Cleary's teenage stories seem quite tame. But in the context of the years in which they were written, they fare better. All are told from the points of view of young girls, fifteen to seventeen years old, who are just beginning to explore the changes they feel emerging in their relationships with their families and, more important, with boys. Cleary states that she wrote *Fifteen* (1956) in response to requests from junior-high girls who wanted books about people they could recognize.

Cleary's early books for teens portray the immediate concerns of all teenagers. Will members of the opposite sex find me attractive? What will I do with my life? What kind of person am I?

Cleary has surrounded her teen heroines with sympathetic and supportive parents whose constant care is one of the things they, like all teenagers, are fighting. Even if a character is not confronted with a large problem such as divorce, abuse, or alcoholism, she will have a tendency to make things harder than they are by constantly analyzing and second-guessing her reactions.

A good example of this type of painful scrutiny can be found in the characterization of Shelley Latham in *The Luckiest Girl* (1958). An only child, she moves from Oregon to California for a year to live with the family of her mother's college roommate. Her parents feel she needs to try her wings before she goes off to college and that this will be a good experience for her. She meets a handsome boy the first day in her new school and continually replays every word they exchange, searching for the meaning of every nuance. Does Phil really mean to joke when he calls her "webfoot" because she comes from perennially wet Oregon, or does he dislike her?

Jean Jarrett, of *Jean and Johnny* (1959), goes through the same process after she accidentally meets tall, good-looking Johnny Chessler at a dance. The next day she spends hours wondering why he asked her to dance, what he thought of her when he discovered she could not dance, and what he thinks of her now. These situations underline the basic insecurity of teenagers—they are caught between two worlds, childhood and adulthood, and are striving for a sign that they have left behind the former and safely reached the latter. Part of the growth process for all of them is the realization that there is no clear demarcation and that all growth is gradual and continuous.

Much of what forms the backgrounds of Cleary's teen novels seems dated today. Perhaps most obvious are the stereotypical mothers whose primary concerns are with the popularity of their daughters and the upkeep of their homes. Another point is the sameness of the endings of the books. Almost uniformly the handsome boy turns out to have no character or intelligence, and the heroine discovers that the unassuming boy who has been her real friend all along is the right person for her. In spite of these problems, the books are still accurate portrayals of young women discovering themselves and young men. Cleary's warmth and sensitivity are probably prime reasons why the books continue in print.

Another character which stands out from the others is Ralph Mouse, who has appeared in three books since 1965. Ralph is, in mouse fashion, much like Cleary's human characters, and it is no surprise that he was an instant favorite with children. He is spunky, clever, and ambitious, wanting more from life than crumbs and crumpled tissue, and he finds it when Keith and his parents stop at the California motel where Ralph and his family live. Keith brings with him a toy motorcycle, and when Ralph has an accident while trying to ride it, the two meet and are not "the least surprised that each could understand the other. Two creatures who shared a love for motorcycles naturally spoke the same language."

Children who love the adventures of Ralph will cheerfully suspend disbelief. There is perfect logic for them in toy vehicles that move when the

2 5 8
7.

Ralph stopped wiping his paws over his whiskers to look with love at Ryan's teacher. Her long shiney hair fell over her shoulders. It looked so strong that Ralph was sure that just one of thes her hairs would be perfect for tying his exhaust pipe in place.

"Perhaps the custodian has a cage we could keep him in," said Miss K.

Love turned to distrust. This wonderful woman with useful hair was turning out to be like any other grownup.

Ryan spoke up. "I don't think Ralph would be happy in a cage," he told his teacher. "I'll just keep i him in my pocket if it's all right with you." Good old Ryan.

Miss K gently handed Ralph back to Ryan who stuffed him into his shirt pocket. "Thank you for sharing Ralph," she said above the <u>lub-dub</u> of Ryan's heart, steady as a well-oiled motor. "Class, how would you like to draw pictures and write stories and poems about mice? Friday afternoon we could have a mouse exhibit to show off our work. Ryan, you could bring Ralph to school again so he could be our guest of honor." Miss K, who had no idea Ralph was planning to live at school, was a teacher who could turn anything into a project.

Most of the class was enthusiastic. Others though mice were as good a subject as any for drawing and writing. A boy named Gordon said he didn't like to do any of those things. Miss K suggested he could i go to the library, look up facts about mice and write an essay about on them. "And what do you want to do, Ryan?" she asked.

"I would like to tell how smart Ralph is." Ryan's answer

Corrected typescript page from a draft for **Ralph S. Mouse,** *the third book featuring Cleary's resourceful rodent (by permission of the author)*

correct noises are made. It may be easier for them to do because Ralph is such a boylike mouse, and because Cleary enters completely into the spirit of the fantasy. She does not attempt to be cute or coy. She writes as naturally and in as straightforward a manner as if she were relating the new exploits of Henry Huggins. If it may not actually be possible for a mouse to talk, there is very little else that is beyond the means of a resourceful rodent, including bringing an aspirin tablet to Keith when the boy lies ill. In the second book, Ralph runs away to seek adventure in a summer camp but ends up a prisoner until he manages to communicate with a lonely boy named Garf. Finally, in *Ralph S. Mouse* (1982), Ralph befriends two boys, Brad and Ryan. Although Ralph loses his beloved motorcycle, he gains a sports car and the respect of all his relatives.

Part of what enables Ralph to communicate with Keith, Garf, Brad, and Ryan is the boys' insecurity. Cleary has used this as part of each of her books as she shows children at different ages striving to find a place within their families and neighborhoods. All of these children, with perhaps the exception of Otis Spofford, have strong ties to help them achieve their goals.

In *Dear Mr. Henshaw* (1983), Cleary departs from her more usual framework in several ways. First, she has chosen as her main character a boy, Leigh Botts, whose parents are divorced. He lives with his mother and has not really come to terms with his parents' breakup or how he feels about his father, whom he seldom sees. Second, Cleary wrote this book in the first person, so that Leigh speaks directly to the reader. She also gives a glimpse of Leigh in earlier years by including the letters he wrote to Mr. Henshaw, the author of his favorite book, before the actual body of the story begins.

Leigh is not only struggling to understand the divorce but is also having to endure being the new boy in school. He is, like so many of Cleary's other boys, ordinary. He has no special talents to help him over the initial period of trying to fit in. Additionally, someone is stealing the best parts of his lunch from his lunch box, and he has no one to turn to.

In the letters he writes and the diary he keeps, Leigh explores his feelings toward his father—his resentment when he does not call, his worry that his father will marry someone who already has a boy and will perhaps love Leigh less. When Bandit, once the family dog who now travels with his father, disappears, Leigh tries to hate his father but finds that nothing is that simple. Leigh rigs a burglar alarm in his lunch box to stop the thefts. Although

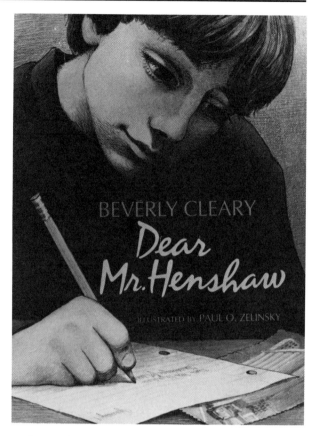

Dust jacket for Cleary's 1984 Newbery Medal-winning novel (Morrow)

he does not catch the thief, the invention gains him the acceptance of his classmates. He also begins to accept himself and his feelings about his father when he realizes that while his parents do not agree on a lot of things, they both love him in their own ways.

In Leigh Botts, Cleary has brought together her years of writing experience and her ability to express the emotions, needs, and humor of a child. She has created a character that is deeper and fuller than her others because she goes further into the child's viewpoint than she has in her earlier books. Cleary has said that part of the reason she wrote *Dear Mr. Henshaw* was the large number of letters she received from children who were going through divorces and moves. She responded to her readers' requests and gave them a book filled not only with people and situations they could recognize but also with a hopeful direction away from their inner problems.

Eleanor Cameron, in her book *The Green and Burning Tree* (1969), states that "a child goes back to characters he loves as if they were his own family or friends." If this is true of all books that children come to know and enjoy, then it must be doubly so for the books of Beverly Cleary, which children come to initially for the fun of reading about their friends.

Vera Cleaver
(6 January 1919-   )
and
Bill Cleaver
(24 March 1920-20 August 1981)

Jane Harper Yarbrough
University of Wisconsin Center, Marinette

BOOKS: *Ellen Grae,* illustrated by Ellen Raskin (New York: Lippincott, 1967);

Lady Ellen Grae, illustrated by Raskin (New York: Lippincott & Crowell, 1967);

Where the Lilies Bloom, illustrated by Jim Spanfeller (Philadelphia: Lippincott, 1969; Harmondsworth, U.K.: Puffin, 1973);

Grover, illustrated by Frederic Marvin (Philadelphia: Lippincott, 1970; London: Hamilton, 1971);

The Mimosa Tree (Philadelphia: Lippincott, 1970; Oxford: Oxford University Press, 1977);

The Mock Revolt (Philadelphia: Lippincott, 1971; London: Hamilton, 1972);

I Would Rather Be a Turnip (New York: Lippincott, 1971; London: Hamilton, 1972);

Delpha Green and Company (Philadelphia: Lippincott, 1972; London: Collins, 1976);

Ellen Grae and Lady Ellen Grae (London: Hamilton, 1973);

The Whys and Wherefores of Littabelle Lee (New York: Atheneum, 1973; London: Hamilton, 1974);

Me Too (New York: Lippincott & Crowell, 1973; London: Collins, 1975);

Dust of the Earth (Philadelphia: Lippincott, 1975; Oxford: Oxford University Press, 1977);

Trial Valley (Philadelphia: Lippincott, 1978; Oxford: Oxford University Press, 1978);

Queen of Hearts (Philadelphia: Lippincott, 1978);

A Little Destiny (New York: Lothrop, Lee & Shepard, 1979);

The Kissimmee Kid (New York: Morrow, 1981);

Hazel Rye (New York: Lippincott, 1983);

Vera and Bill Cleaver

Sugar Blue, by Vera Cleaver (New York: Lothrop, Lee & Shepard, 1984);

Sweetly Sings the Donkey, by Vera Cleaver (New York: Lippincott, 1985).

Vera and Bill Cleaver's novels consistently present young adult readers with realistic characters who are seeking to understand their place within society and the family. The main characters, all between the ages of ten and sixteen, are beset both with the inner conflicts of adolescence and with the external obstacles of difficult family relationships and economic problems. The young heroines and heroes find themselves surrounded by stubbornly stagnant families and communities, mostly in small southern towns, that emit a stifling dullness. Despite what for many would be overwhelming circumstances, they preserve and exert their newly found individuality with uncommon, but not unbelievable, resourcefulness and intelligence. The Cleavers offer young adult readers sensitive, insightful characters with whom to identify, with whom to join on the turbulent voyage of growing up responsible.

Like their most memorable heroine, Mary Call Luther in *Where the Lilies Bloom* (1969) and *Trial Valley* (1978), the Cleavers are self-taught students of human nature. Neither attended schools of creative writing nor had any formal education beyond two years of business school. The Cleavers, Bill from Seattle, Washington, and Vera from Virgil, South Dakota, met during World War II while Bill was in the Air Force and were married in 1945. They describe themselves as graduates of America's public libraries, an education which has served them well. Without fail they appeal to the importance of being well-read, to the pleasures of language play, and to the power of words. The language in their books is not unusually clever or experimental; rather, the narratives are straightforward, lacking descriptive embellishments, and the dialogue rings true without depending on slang or dialect. Not insignificantly, a subtle humorous tone pervades their works. In fact, Vera, who did the actual writing after ideas had been jointly worked out, had a written warning from Bill next to her typewriter. It said: "Don't Be So Serious."

After publishing close to 300 stories, first in pulp magazines and then in such periodicals as *McCall's* and *Woman's Day* (these stories were about, not for, children), they turned to writing for the young adult audience. Their first young adult novel was *Ellen Grae* (1967). Ellen Grae, a precocious eleven-year-old spinner of gory tales, finds herself privy to a true tale even more horrific than the ones she makes up. Peanut vendor Ira, a harmless

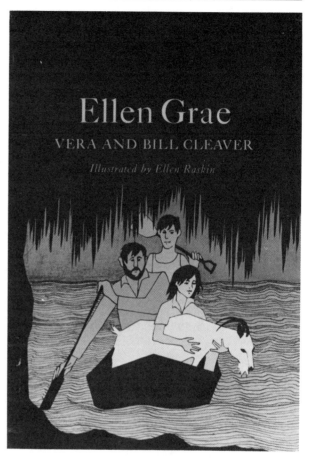

Dust jacket for the Cleavers' first book, illustrated by Ellen Raskin (Lippincott)

mute—or so the townspeople think—grows fond of Ellen Grae and *speaks* to her. One day he tells her that he secretly buried his parents, many years before, in a nearby swamp after they died from rattlesnake bites—a death they intended for him. Carrying this secret becomes an awesome burden for her. She does not want her friend locked in a jail or a mental institution, but she believes that dead people "even bad ones, belonged in cemeteries with markers at their heads to let people know when they had been born and when they had died." When she becomes ill, Mrs. McGruder, whose task it is to educate Ellen Grae in the social graces, summons Ellen Grae's divorced parents, who subsequently wheedle the story out of her. The consequences of telling tall tales, of crying wolf one time too many, are all too apparent; Ellen Grae is not believed. Parental divorce is an underlying theme, but the major dilemma of this short and often amusing book is that between loyal friendship and social responsibility.

From *Ellen Grae* the Cleavers produced two sequels, *Lady Ellen Grae* (1967) and *Grover* (1970). Though well-executed stories, neither has the dramatic impact of the first, the finely woven themes, or the skillful play between light conversation and dark concerns. In *Lady Ellen Grae*, Ellen Grae's parents decide that she is too much the tomboy, even after her desperate attempts to undergo a quick metamorphosis, so she is sent to live with her well-heeled relatives in Seattle. She cannot reconcile herself to exile, and through transparent trickery she is soon warmly greeted by the town folk back home. This contrived solution does not favorably compare to the realistic, though ambiguous, conclusion of *Ellen Grae*.

Ellen Grae's best friend is Grover, who in *Ellen Grae* and *Lady Ellen Grae* has already reconciled himself to his mother's death by suicide. But *Grover* recalls this difficult time, one rendered endurable by Ellen Grae's friendship and by his acceptance

Dust jacket for the Cleavers' most acclaimed novel, the story of an Appalachian girl's attempts to keep her parentless family together (Lippincott)

of his mother's decision to end her cancer-caused suffering. Although Grover is sometimes portrayed less sensitively than the grave circumstances merit, his father's all but complete denial of his wife's suicide is poignantly drawn.

Where the Lilies Bloom is the Cleavers' most critically acclaimed novel; a Newbery Honor Book and an American Library Association Notable Book, it was also nominated for the National Book Award. The novel recreates the exciting contrasts of Appalachian mountain living, the rich abundance and beauty of plant life in the spring, and the stark desolation of the land in winter. But the truly endearing feature of *Where the Lilies Bloom* is the creation of Mary Call Luther, the fourteen-year-old heroine whose inner strength, love of family, irrepressible dignity, pragmatic resourcefulness, indomitable will, and joy for life combine to provide readers with a vividly memorable character whose uplifting story is of one young woman's victories over the oppressive forces of nature and society. After her father dies, Mary Call is left with the responsibility of keeping her family together. In her charge she has two younger siblings, Romey and Ima Dean, and an older sister, Devola, who is gentle, lovable, but "cloudy-headed." Mary Call's responsibilities include keeping her father's death a secret so that the county will not put her brother and sisters in separate foster homes; preventing Devola's marriage to their greedy, superstitious landlord; and providing food and shelter amidst extreme poverty. She teaches herself and the others the art of "wild-crafting" (collecting and selling medicinal plants), and the family remains together through her tact, cunning, and circumventions. Beside the sensitive portrait of Mary Call's development into a young woman of spirited strength, the Cleavers paint a number of impressively moving scenes, in particular the mountainside burial of Roy Luther, the father, and the winter storm which caves in the children's roof.

Nine years and eight novels later, the Cleavers wrote a sequel to *Where the Lilies Bloom*. In *Trial Valley*, Mary Call, now sixteen, continues her courageous struggle to support and educate Romey and Ima Dean. And she faces a new set of problems—caring for an abandoned child and being courted simultaneously by two attractive, but very different young men. Unlike many sequels, *Trial Valley* is as well crafted as its predecessor. In some ways it is the stronger novel, for it attempts to reveal an elusive quality of autonomous characters—the irrepressible drive to become what one knows oneself to be. It is a book about coming of age, of finding and embracing one's direction in life. After questioning her capacity to love the found child and to love either of her suitors, Mary Call realizes that all the time she had "the promise, clean and simple."

In *The Mimosa Tree* (1970), *The Whys and Wherefores of Littabelle Lee* (1973), and *Dust of the Earth* (1975), the Cleavers again create rural characters who struggle against insufferable odds. *The Mimosa Tree* begins and ends on a small farm in the Appalachian mountains, but most of the story takes place in the Chicago slums. Hoping for a better life away from hog-poisoning neighbors, Marvella Proffitt, fourteen, tells herself, "we've got to stay here for a while. Until we can see our way clearer than we can now." But after a series of demoralizing events in Chicago—Marvella's blind father is conned into a get-rich-quick scam, her stepmother (the only family member regularly employed) runs away, the welfare people do not fulfill their promises, Marvella and the oldest boy purse-snatch, and a neighborhood "friend" tries to kill his mother—Marvella concludes that she is afraid "of what's happened to us. What we've become. . . . How we can hear and see and do such terrible things and afterwards go to sleep." Urban poverty, she discovers, is much harder to endure than rural poverty. So the Proffitts go back to Goose Neck. This is a disturbing book on several counts: The children's justification for thievery is all too understandable, but the upgrading of rural poverty and the portrayal of the goodness of country folks, despite their shortcomings, detract from what otherwise could be an incisive story of the socio-economic problems of uprooted rural people in urban slums.

The Whys and Wherefores of Littabelle Lee presents another courageous and determined mountain heroine in the tradition of Mary Call. Littabelle, sixteen, lives in the Ozarks with her aged grandparents and her Aunt Sorrow, a nature doctor and the family's chief provider. After an injurious fall from a horse, Aunt Sorrow gives up her practice and leaves to live with her suitor of many years. The responsibility for the family falls on Littabelle, who now has to meet her "whys and wherefores face to face." With great resolve and vibrant intelligence she meets the daily challenges of survival by first taking a teaching job at Pintail Fork and then by suing her prosperous, citified aunts and uncles for parental neglect, an unusual but effective solution to her dire financial problems. This fast-moving, thoroughly charming book offers young adults the opportunity to reflect, along with Littabelle, on the importance of meeting one's

responsibilities, of meeting one's "whys and wherefores."

The "brooding, primitive land" of South Dakota (the childhood home of Vera Cleaver) is both the setting for and a metaphor for the lonely, haunting family relationships of the characters in *Dust of the Earth*. The days which "drift in a wasteful, hazy way" mirror Fern Drawn's vague but ever-present feeling that something is missing in her family, that, at fourteen, she does not really know her parents or her brothers and sister. Neither parent comes from a close-knit family. But they inherit a run-down sheep farm from Fern's maternal grandfather, Grandpa Bacon, which, as Fern sees it, is the final slap in the face from a pompous old man. When the Drawns move to the farm, Fern resolves to turn Grandpa Bacon's last trick to their advantage. Fern has the pioneer spirit, the dogged courage, and the tough endurance it takes to succeed in this harsh environment. Largely through her efforts and her sheep dog Clyde, the flock stays together, and after a treacherous winter, the lambs come, bringing with them prosperity and family unity for the Drawns. In 1977 *Dust of the Earth* received a much-deserved Golden Spur Award from the Western Writers of America for the best juvenile fiction. Its powerful comparison of environment and emotions is a rare find in young adult literature. As Fern concludes, her family may lose again and again, but "the curtain stays up."

The recurrent theme of meeting one's responsibilities is central to the Cleavers' work. Most of the novels are concerned with family responsibilities, but two novels which address the broader issue of one's responsibilities to the community and to humanity at large are *The Mock Revolt* (1971) and *Delpha Green and Company* (1972). *The Mock Revolt*, set in the late 1930s, is the story of thirteen-year-old Ussy Mock's aborted attempt to escape from the stultifying influence of his father and the other "deadlies" in the small Florida town of Medina. Ussy gets a Mohawk haircut, then a tattoo on his thigh, but his ultimate rebellion requires saving enough money to ride a motorcycle to San Francisco. On his first day working at the Medina Summer Work Camp for Boys, he meets Luke Wilder, the son of ignorant migrant workers, and the meeting changes his life. Although initially Ussy becomes the *unwilling* benefactor of the Wilder family, through conversations with Mr. Suffin, his eccentric friend and teacher, he accepts "his call to humanity."

Delpha, in *Delpha Green and Company*, is an irrepressibly cheerful Pollyanna who, along with her father, an ex-convict and a self-styled preacher, brightens the otherwise dreary lives of the townspeople of Chinquapin Cove. Before the Greens' Church of Blessed Hope welcomed the members of the community to "experience the world" and to be their own "angels," Chinquapin Cove was dominated by the cheerless owner of the town's only industry, a shoe factory. This story, like *The Mock Revolt*, remains lighthearted and entertaining while brushing with a serious philosophical issue, the social obligation of an individual to the rest of humanity. Unfortunately, the Cleavers' use of astrological designations for the chapter titles and character typology detracts from the humorous contrast between the doldrums of the townspeople before, and their vivacity after, meeting Delpha Green.

Three of the Cleavers' novels from the 1970s address contemporary social problems: *I Would Rather Be a Turnip* (1971) looks at illegitimacy; *Me Too* (1973), at autism; and *Queen of Hearts* (1978), at the elderly. In *I Would Rather Be a Turnip*, twelve-year-old Annie Jelks, the somewhat spoiled daughter of a small town pharmacist, worries incessantly, and not without cause, that her reputation will be ruined by the presence of her sister's illegitimate son, eight-year-old Calvin. She is indeed scorned by her erstwhile friends, which leads her to reject her brainy nephew's friendship; but as Calvin slowly grows in her esteem, she endures the ostracism by fantasizing about becoming a famous author. Miss Dishman, the librarian, expresses the more powerful theme of the novel when she tells Annie about Calvin: "He has discovered books. . . . The world will never beat him. It will never hurt him very much. He will conquer the world."

The main characters in *Me Too* are twin girls: Lydia, a normal twelve-year-old, and Lornie, an autistic child. Early in the book their father leaves home, apparently because he wants to escape the fact that he fathered an exceptional child. When the working mother is forced to take Lornie out of the special school, Lydia is saddled with caring for her twin. Lydia believes that her father will return if only she can make her twin like herself. She spends her summer trying to teach Lornie to be normal, but she fails and has to accept Lornie for the gentle, remote child she will always be. Here the Cleavers have produced a sensitive book on a significant social issue—the effects an autistic child can have on the relationships between family members and between the family and their friends. The dialogue between the twins is dramatic and realistic, and equally realistic is the Cleavers' portrayal of

Dust jacket for the Cleavers' last novel, in which an eleven-year-old learns the value of literacy (Lippincott)

Lydia as a vital, self-reliant adolescent who, during her tutelage of Lornie, experiences the delight of unexpected success as well as the frustration of failure.

In *Queen of Hearts*, Wilma Lincoln, twelve, accepts the challenge of staying with her cantankerous, seventy-nine-year-old grandmother who is recuperating from a mild stroke. Except for Granny Lincoln's frequent tantrums, the action in this story is minimal. Instead of relying on surface events, the Cleavers explore the psychological traumas of adjusting to life's passages, the parallel traumas of adolescence and old age. The contrast this novel presents between the frailties of old age and the strength, dignity, and experience of the elderly provides adolescents an opportunity to understand and sympathize with the paradoxes of aging.

In *A Little Destiny* (1979) and *The Kissimmee Kid* (1981) the Cleavers set wild West plots in a southeastern landscape. *A Little Destiny* rambles through the terrain of revenge, unsuccessfully attempting

1061248

Sugar Blue   Cleaver- page 44

econimical at first but expanding as it unfolded. Amy's mother said that she

was relieved to be able to say that Amy's grandfather Harney was out of hospital

and back in his Georgia home, nursing his knee from his own big chair.

Fireflies rose from the dusky grasses just outside the patio to put on

their lantern show, and in a show of her own Ella clapped her hands at this

wonder. She wanted to know if the little luminous beetles pushed buttons

to make their lights wink, and Amy saw the pleasure of instruction in her

father's face.

Her mother went to the bookcase in the living room and came back with

a book that explained fireflies.

Full darkness fell and the lights in the houses around Lake Myrtle came on,

but still the family on the patio lingered. The pages of the book were turned

and the talk was turned to the subject of other insects.

Throughout all of this Amy sat in a state of detachment except when

one of her parents drew her into the conversation. She did not care for insects,

the way they sucked, their bites and stings. Letting her mind drift, she thought

of the coming of Mildred and Brad and hugged her arms.

That night in the wide bed beside Ella she lay coolly wrapped in her privacy

So safe it was, nothing in it, just a comfortable little hiding hole big enough

only for herself.

Ella's wounded heel was a trouble, and the effect of it kept Amy and

Ella confined to the house for several days.

In the kitchen one day, Amy stirred up a batch of quickie pancakes and tried

to flip the first one off the griddle into the air as she had seen the cook

at Sally's Diner do. It was a misadventure in how to make air-borne pancakes

Page from a draft of Sugar Blue *(by permission of the author)*

to tie an adventure story to an introspective exploration of the nature of evil. Early in the novel fourteen-year-old Lucy Commander learns that her father's death was caused by moneylender Tom Clegg, a widower who wants to marry Lucy's mother. Her mother's refusal leads Clegg to claim the Commander property on which he holds the long-overdue mortgage. Lucy does not tell her mother or her older brother Lyman that Clegg let her father bleed to death; instead, she waits for the opportunity for revenge. Meanwhile, Clegg retaliates further for the refusal of his marriage proposal; his thugs kidnap Lucy and Lyman and take them to a hideout in the northern Georgia hills. Shoot-outs, a flash flood, a vanilla-drinking vagabond, and galloping horses all recapture a sense of the old West. But Clegg's rationale for kidnapping the Commander children is never fully revealed. In fact, the entire wild West sequence seems contrived and detracts from the potentially powerful theme of evil enslaving itself.

The Kissimmee Kid, on the other hand, effectively takes an old West plot and transposes it on the contemporary cattle lands of central Florida. Twelve-year-old Evelyn Chestnut visits her older sister Reba and brother-in-law Cam, a former art teacher who is working as a ranch hand for the mean-spirited Major Peacock. Strong, handsome, good-natured Cam remains a hero to Evelyn—despite his failure to withstand the cruelties of high school boys and to provide for Reba better—until she accidentally discovers that Cam is rustling Major Peacock's calves. Like many of the Cleaver characters, Evelyn is forced to choose between protecting the people she loves and following the dictates of her conscience. The pain and resolution of her conflict is perceptively portrayed in the novel's memorable ending.

Hazel Rye (1983) is the last novel on which the Cleavers collaborated. Vera Cleaver completed the novel after her husband's death in 1981. Set in the orange-growing landscape of central Florida—near, no doubt, the Cleavers' home in Winter Haven—the novel shows how an eleven-year-old girl learns the value of being able to read and write well. The Cleavers have artfully avoided a didactic tone while demonstrating the limitations poor literacy skills place on a good intelligence. Hazel's father, whom she admires, is barely literate and has no desire to improve or to tend their little orange grove, which is rapidly going to ruin. Hazel adopts his complacent attitude toward education, until she meets Felder Poole, a twelve-year-old boy who knows all about growing oranges and the value of books. Hazel's father believes that Felder and his ideas are a threat to his friendship with his daughter, and, although he succeeds in driving Felder away, Felder has left Hazel with the desire to know: "At night behind her locked door, working with her pencils, her writing pads, and the dictionary, there were times when she felt the full rumblings of self-doubt," but Hazel has learned the value of the written word and is determined to master it.

Since Bill Cleaver's death, Vera Cleaver has written two novels: *Sugar Blue* (1984) and *Sweetly Sings the Donkey* (1985). Both stories are about girls who take their persistent dissatisfaction with parents and new homes and direct it toward improvement projects. In the first novel, eleven-year-old Amy Blue receives the attention, even adoration, she has been wanting from an unlikely source—her four-year-old niece Ella, who is visiting while her mother prepares to remarry and relocate. Through conniving, Amy seeks to make Ella completely dependent on her. When her schemes fail, Amy turns to friends who were always willing to include her. In *Sweetly Sings the Donkey*, Lily Snow, fourteen, a collector of gifts from the young men she charms, sells her collection and, with the help of new friends, secretly builds a home on a piece of Florida scrubland for her sickly father and two younger brothers. As in many of the Cleaver novels, the oldest daughter is courageous and imaginative while the mother is a weak and shadowy character. Here Lily's mother deserts her family and runs off with the town eccentric.

Vera and Bill Cleaver, in the thirty-six years of their collaboration, produced some of America's best adolescent fiction, portraying characters who overcome the obstacles of parental failure and the conflict of adolescence with courage and resourcefulness. Few, if any, adolescent novelists have continuously provided young adult readers with such an abundance of characters worth emulating, who seek and accept responsibility with uncommon resiliency, intelligence, reflectiveness, and simple, straightforward respect of self and love of family and humanity. The Cleavers have succeeded in giving young adults fiction that respects and extols language used well and stories that are true to human nature.

Barbara Corcoran
(Paige Dixon, Gail Hamilton)
(12 April 1911-   )

Mary Lou White
Wright State University

BOOKS: *Sam,* illustrated by Barbara McGee (New York: Atheneum, 1967);

The Ghost of Spirit River, by Corcoran, Jeanne Dixon, and Bradford Angier (New York: Atheneum, 1968);

A Row of Tigers, illustrated by Allan Eitzen (New York: Atheneum, 1969);

Sasha, My Friend, illustrated by Richard L. Shell (New York: Atheneum, 1969);

The Long Journey, illustrated by Charles Robinson (New York: Atheneum, 1970);

A Star to the North, by Corcoran and Angier (New York: Nelson, 1970);

The Lifestyle of Robie Tuckerman (New York: Nelson, 1971);

Barbara Corcoran

This Is A Recording, illustrated by Richard Cuffari (New York: Atheneum, 1971);

A Trick of Light, illustrated by Lydia Dabcovich (New York: Atheneum, 1972);

Don't Slam the Door When You Go (New York: Atheneum, 1972);

Lion on the Mountain, as Paige Dixon, illustrated by J. H. Breslow (New York: Atheneum, 1972);

All the Summer Voices, illustrated by Robinson (New York: Atheneum, 1973);

Silver Wolf, as Paige Dixon, illustrated by Ann Brewster (New York: Atheneum, 1973);

The Winds of Time, illustrated by Gail Owens (New York: Atheneum, 1974);

The Young Grizzly, as Paige Dixon, illustrated by Grambs Miller (New York: Atheneum, 1974);

Promises to Keep, as Paige Dixon (New York: Atheneum, 1974);

A Dance to Still Music, illustrated by Robinson (New York: Atheneum, 1974);

Meet Me at Tamerlane's Tomb, illustrated by Robinson (New York: Atheneum, 1975);

Titania's Lodestone, as Gail Hamilton (New York: Atheneum, 1975);

May I Cross Your Golden River?, as Paige Dixon (New York: Atheneum, 1975); republished as *A Time to Love, A Time to Mourn* (New York: Scholastic, 1982);

The Clown (New York: Atheneum, 1975); republished as *I Wish You Love* (New York: Scholastic, 1977);

A Candle to the Devil, as Gail Hamilton, illustrated by Joanne Scribner (New York: Atheneum, 1975);

The Search for Charlie, as Paige Dixon (New York: Atheneum, 1976);

Axe-Time, Sword-Time (New York: Atheneum, 1976);

Pimm's Cup for Everybody, as Paige Dixon (New York: Atheneum, 1976);

Cabin in the Sky (New York: Atheneum, 1976);

The Faraway Island (New York: Atheneum, 1977);

Summer of the White Goat, as Paige Dixon (New York: Atheneum, 1977);

Love Comes to Eunice K. O'Herlihy, as Gail Hamilton (New York: Atheneum, 1977);

Make No Sound (New York: Atheneum, 1977);

Ask for Love and They Give You Rice Pudding, by Corcoran and Angier (Boston: Houghton Mifflin, 1977);

Hey, That's My Soul You're Stomping On (New York: Atheneum, 1978);

The Loner: A Story of the Wolverine, as Paige Dixon, illustrated by Miller (New York: Atheneum, 1978);

The Mustang and Other Stories (New York: Scholastic, 1978);

Me and You and a Dog Named Blue (New York: Atheneum, 1979);

Skipper, as Paige Dixon (New York: Atheneum, 1979);

Rising Damp (New York: Atheneum, 1980);

The Person in the Potting Shed (New York: Atheneum, 1980);

Making It (Boston: Little, Brown, 1980);

Walk My Way, as Paige Dixon (New York: Atheneum, 1980);

Beloved Enemy (New York: Ballantine, 1981);

Call of the Heart (New York: Ballantine, 1981);

Abigail (New York: Ballantine, 1981);

Abbie in Love (New York: Ballantine, 1981);

A Husband for Gail (New York: Ballantine, 1981);

Love Is Not Enough (New York: Ballantine, 1981);

Song for Two Voices (New York: Ballantine, 1981);

You're Allegro Dead (New York: Atheneum, 1981);

By the Silvery Moon (New York: Ballantine, 1982);

Child of the Morning (New York: Atheneum, 1982);

A Watery Grave (New York: Atheneum, 1982);

Strike! (New York: Atheneum, 1983);

Which Witch is Which? (New York: Atheneum, 1983);

August, Die She Must (New York: Atheneum, 1984);

The Woman in Your Life (New York: Atheneum, 1984);

Mystery on Ice (New York: Atheneum, 1985);

The Shadowed Path (New York: Archway, 1985);

When Darkness Falls (New York: Archway, 1985);

Face the Music (New York: Atheneum, 1985).

Barbara Corcoran rose to prominence as a prolific author of problem novels for pre- and early teenagers in the 1970s, when contemporary realistic fiction for adolescents was at its zenith. She has written over sixty novels in nineteen years and has been consistently noted by the periodicals which review children's and young adult books.

Corcoran was born in Hamilton, Massachusetts, on 12 April 1911, to Anna Tuck and John Gilbert Corcoran, a physician. She was an only child, which may have prompted her to make up characters and stories out of the need to occupy herself. She has been writing since childhood and recalls that she "used to start stories on my father's prescription pads. My parents were encouraging, although I think my dad thought I'd probably starve to death."

In 1933 she was graduated from Wellesley College with a B.A. degree. In her early twenties she began writing plays and thought she had found her niche in writing, though the endeavor was short lived. She had a few plays produced in Boston and in college theaters, "But although friends told me I reminded them of Lillian Hellman (I think they meant the way I wore my hair), I wasn't having the Hellman effect on Broadway producers. In time, sanity prevailed and I turned to other kinds of writing, always with a feeling that I'd lost something."

Until 1941 she lived in the house in which she was born. With the advent of World War II, she left Hamilton, Massachusetts, to do war work. She was an electronics inspector for the navy and, later, a cryptanalytic aide for the Army Signal Corps. At the end of the war, when she was thirty-four years old, she moved to Hollywood, California, to do managerial work for Celebrity Service from 1945 to 1953. There, she felt, "I didn't have to explain that a grown woman could indeed spend her time writing."

Next she moved to Missoula, Montana, where she worked for a year as a copywriter for Station KGVO. She did graduate work at the University of Montana and received an M.A. in 1955, the same year in which she won the Samuel French Award for an original play. Montana made a lasting impression on Corcoran; she loved the mountains and wanted to stay there but was unable to get a job. Beginning a series of short-term jobs related to writing, she became an instructor in English at the University of Kentucky, Northern Center, from 1956 to 1957; worked for Columbia Broadcasting System Television in Hollywood as a staff member of the story department from 1957 to 1959; was an instructor in English at the University of Colorado, Boulder, from 1960 to 1965; and finally an instructor in English at Palomar College, San Marcos, California, from 1965 to 1969. During this time she practiced many types of writing, including essays, short stories, poetry, radio scripts, television scripts, motion picture documentaries, advertising copy, and more plays.

While at Palomar College, Corcoran wrote her first novel, *Sam* (1967), which began as an adult book but ended as a book for children. The response to *Sam* made up for Corcoran's having lost the theater, for she "got wonderful letters from children who liked and identified with Sam," which "was almost like being in the audience and watching the faces." When Corcoran attended a children's literature conference at Claremont College in California she had the opportunity to talk to children who had read the novel, and found the experience "marvelous," in part because the children "talked about my characters as if they were their own friends." Also at the conference, Corcoran was shown a mural that a group of students from Romana, California, had made of the characters in *Sam:* "I think the moment I saw it was the moment I stopped feeling cheated because I wasn't a playwright. This was just as good, and quite possibly a lot better. The people in the mural looked the way I thought my characters looked. . . . I realized that the book was as alive for them as it was for me." Corcoran was fifty-six years old when *Sam* was published, and she had begun a new career.

Sam was the first of several novels in which Corcoran would use a young person's relationship with an animal as a focal point in a book that primarily deals with the life adjustment of the youth. Sam is a fifteen-year-old girl who has been educated at home by her antisocial father. The family lives on an island in Montana. When Sam enters school for the first time, as a high school junior, she experiences various conflicts in values. Corcoran portrays Sam's problems in making decisions and choices and creates an exciting story and an appealing main character. There are first-novel flaws—an ending that is not entirely credible and a problem that plagues Corcoran through many books: stereotyped secondary characters. The book is popular and continues to be one of her best from both critical and sales perspectives. It has been published in paperback and remains in print after nineteen years.

Before the publication of *Sam*, Corcoran co-authored a book with two other writers, children's author and longtime friend Jeanne Dixon and high school classmate and nature writer Bradford Angier. *The Ghost of Spirit River* (1968) is set in the wilderness of British Columbia as three boys search for wild horses until strange occurrences force them into the deeper parts of the forest. The book received poor reviews and may have been structurally weakened by the input of three writers.

Corcoran's second book of which she was sole author was *A Row of Tigers* (1969). The story of an eleven-year-old girl who becomes a sheep herder with a twenty-seven-year-old hunchbacked man, who seems to be the only one who understands her, is in the words of the *Kirkus Reviews* critic, "a disappointing successor to *Sam*." However, in *Sasha, My Friend*, also published in 1969, Corcoran did manage to build on the success of *Sam*, and produced one of her best-selling books. Hallie is a fifteen-year-old girl who moves from Los Angeles to rural Montana with her widowed father to restore his health. They try to operate a tree farm and Hallie stays home from school to help. She also adopts an orphaned wolf cub, much to the dismay of their neighbors. Themes of hard work, acceptance of people as they are, appreciation of nature, and family love and loyalty are well developed. In 1972 *Sasha* won the William Allen White Children's Book Award.

At this point in her life Corcoran ended her teaching, became a full-time writer, and moved back to Missoula, Montana. She ventured next into the type of novel for which she is best known—contemporary realism in which a young protagonist comes of age through a series of difficult adventures. *The Long Journey* (1970), which won a designation as Child Study Association book of the year, concerns thirteen-year-old Laurie, who has lived with her grandfather in an isolated mining town for ten years since her parents' death. While journeying to Butte to get help for her grandfather, who is going blind, she meets unusual characters and learns about the amenities of modern life that were unknown to her prior to the trip.

Corcoran's next book, *A Star to the North* (1970), published by Thomas Nelson, is another collaboration with Bradford Angier, who was at the time well known for his nonfiction articles and books about the outdoors. The story, drawn from real-life experiences of both writers, follows the adventures of Kimberly, age fourteen, and her brother, Nathaniel, sixteen, who journey through the Canadian north woods to visit their Uncle Seth. The accounts of their adventures such as shooting rapids, the rescue of a malamute pup, and the killing of a moose are well drawn, as is the feeling of love between the brother and sister. *A Star to the North* was favorably received and a Junior Literary Guild Selection.

In 1971 Corcoran published another book with Thomas Nelson, *The Lifestyle of Robie Tuckerman*, about a teenaged girl who travels to Mexico with her parents and must there endure the death of a close friend in a motorcycle accident back home as well as a conflict in values with her parents. Following the publication of this book, Corcoran went back to Atheneum, a Montana setting, and an early teen heroine for *This Is A Recording* (1971), a fast-moving problem novel. Fourteen-year-old Marianne, who narrates the story in the first person, is sent to live with her grandmother, a former actress, in Montana while her parents contemplate divorce. Corcoran's parents divorced when she was thirteen, and this is one of several books in which she explores the effects of parental divorce on teenaged children.

In *A Trick of Light* (1972), a Junior Literary Guild Selection, Corcoran deals with the problem of twins who need to be more independent of each other, and in *Don't Slam the Door When You Go* (1972), she portrays three teenagers who run away from their Florida homes and difficult parents to a small Montana town. At this point Corcoran moved her career in a new direction. Because her publisher felt that she was writing too many books, and that the appearance of overproductivity would damage her reputation, she assumed a pseudonym, Paige Dixon, based on her godson's name. Under the pseudonym she initially wrote a series of shorter books in which animals figure prominently and which usually feature male protagonists, though as Paige Dixon she also wrote more substantial fiction. Corcoran writes very quickly, not even pausing to make an outline. She spends two hours a day at the typewriter and also puts considerable time into revising. She is a compulsive writer, claiming that she is "restless when I'm not doing it."

The first Paige Dixon book, *Lion on the Mountain* (1972), is about Jamie, a sixteen-year-old boy whose brother has recently died as a result of a mountain fall. Jamie believes in hunting only out of necessity; when his father acts as a guide for a city hunter, Jamie's sense of family unity, already shaken by his brother's death, is further weakened. However, both Jamie and his father learn to understand each other in this drama set in the Colorado wilderness.

A second Paige Dixon book, *Silver Wolf* (1973), is an animal story which describes the adventures of a wolf and which is, in fact, a wildlife conservation story. Corcoran enjoys doing research on animals and "turns to animal books now and then as a kind of relief from people problems."

Corcoran moved in still another direction—historical fiction—with *All the Summer Voices* (1973), her first book written under her real name to focus on a male protagonist. The novel is set in Essex, Massachusetts, in 1910 and portrays a boy named David, age fourteen, who takes a summer job working in a shipyard.

The Winds of Time (1974) is a problem novel concerning a runaway. Gail, a thirteen-year-old girl experiencing family problems, strikes out on her own when her uncle, who is taking her to his home in North Dakota, has an accident en route. She is taken in by a kind family, and eventually her father comes to see her with hopes of a reconciliation.

Paige Dixon appears again with *The Young Grizzly*, which describes the first three years in the life of a grizzly bear, and *Promises to Keep*, both published in 1974. *Promises to Keep*, somewhat longer than the other Paige Dixon books, is the story of two cousins who endure great conflict when one—a half-Vietnamese boy, Lon—moves to a conservative New England town long dominated by his wealthy, socially established grandparents. Charles, the other cousin, narrates the story and shares with the reader his divided feelings about Lon's departure and future with his grandparents.

At about this time Barbara Corcoran did a great deal of traveling, incorporating newly visited places into her novels. *A Dance to Still Music* (1974), one of her best books, draws from her visit to Florida. It was published at the height of the period when problem novels concerning persons of various minorities and handicaps were prominent in contemporary adolescent fiction. Margaret, fourteen, is newly deaf and about to be sent to a special school by her insensitive mother, so she runs away from her Key West home, heading for her native Maine. En route she has the good fortune to be cared for by a wonderful woman on a houseboat. For the sensitively told story Corcoran drew from a time in her life when she had an ear infection which resulted in surgery. She was deaf for a period and experienced some of Margaret's reactions. Corcoran grasps the feelings of anger and frustration and skillfully develops the characters.

At this time Corcoran took an extended trip to Finland, the Soviet Union, England, and other European countries. She wrote from abroad, "My past life is somewhat eclipsed by the couple of years that I am spending in Europe. I've been planning this trip since about 1932, and I am at last making the most of it. My advice to the world: travel." This was the first of many long trips taken with her friend, Jeanne Dixon, and several books with international settings emerged. *Meet Me at Tamerlane's Tomb* (1975) is Corcoran's first mystery. Hardy, the protagonist, is an overweight fourteen-year-old girl

Dust jacket for Corcoran's 1974 novel about a fourteen-year-old girl's reaction and adjustment to her recent deafness. A Dance to Still Music *is one of Corcoran's best-selling novels (Atheneum).*

vacationing in Samarkand in the Soviet Union with her parents and younger brother, and she is almost tricked into transporting hashish for a smuggler. The setting is exotic, Hardy's character is fully developed, and the story is amusing, even though the plot is improbable. The book concludes with the two siblings' journal accounts of the adventure, which make an interesting contrast of children's writing styles.

The Clown (1975) also resulted from Corcoran's Russian travels. Lisa is an orphaned sixteen-year-old American girl traveling as a translator for her aunt and uncle in Russia. She befriends a young Russian clown and enables him to impersonate her uncle and use his passport for his escape to the free world, but the problem of stranding the uncle in Moscow without a passport is never solved.

Corcoran's best book under the Paige Dixon pseudonym, and one of her best sellers, is *May I Cross Your Golden River?* (1975). The story concerns eighteen-year-old Jordan Phillips, who has amyotrophic lateral sclerosis, the fatal illness that is known as Lou Gehrig's disease. In the story, which was inspired by the death of one of Corcoran's friends, an English professor, Corcoran constructs a portrait of Jordan through the reactions of his friends and family.

In 1975 Corcoran adopted a second pseudonym, Gail Hamilton, borrowed from the pen name of Abigail Dodge, a nineteenth-century writer who was a friend of Whittier, Hawthorne, Emerson, and the Alcotts and a distant relative of Corcoran. *Titania's Lodestone* (1975) is the first book Corcoran published under the Hamilton name.

In the book, which is dedicated to Corcoran's editor, Jean Karl, fifteen-year-old Priscilla comes back to the United States with her vagabond, hippielike family after wandering for many years through Europe. They settle, by chance, in a small Massachusetts town, very likely similar to Hamilton. Priscilla is plagued with adolescent insecurities, but during the course of the novel she grows in understanding and acceptance of herself and her family and her new situation, a process that is delineated through her journal entries, which are interspersed throughout the novel and which shift and invigorate the pace of the writing.

Corcoran's second Gail Hamilton book, and her second mystery, *A Candle to the Devil* (1975), is based on her travels in England. Daphne, a sixteen-year-old from Wyoming, visits her amateur archaeologist aunt in her old house in Cornwall and relates the story through her letters back home. A theft of a valuable painting and suspicious actions eventually uncover the storage of illegal arms used for supplying gunrunners for Irish radicals. Corcoran strongly denounces the violence on both sides of the Irish unrest in a well-written book which successfully captures the sound of the Cornish dialect.

The Search for Charlie (1976), a short Paige Dixon novel, is a tale of the kidnapping of a college-age woman's younger brother. Jane returns home from college to her home in Montana to search for him with a young Indian friend. The novel focuses on Jane's nonviolent values, which conflict with her rage when she tries, but fails, to kill the kidnapper.

A second effort at historical fiction by Corcoran was well received by the critics. *Axe-Time, Sword-Time* (1976) takes place between September 1941 and February 1942 and tells the story of an eighteen-year-old girl named Elinor who suffers from a learning disability. When her physician father and shallow mother begin divorce proceedings, Elinor takes a war factory job, thus establishing her independence. The home front wartime era is re-created with accuracy, and autobiographical details from Corcoran's early years as a wartime factory worker add to the book's authenticity.

Another Paige Dixon novel, *Pimm's Cup for Everybody*, and Corcoran's third historical novel, *Cabin in the Sky*, were also published in 1976. As in her first historical fiction, *All the Summer Voices*, *Cabin in the Sky* features a male protagonist. In the 1950s eighteen-year-old Tom leaves his small Maine town for a stint in theater work in New York City, staying a few days at the Algonquin Hotel courtesy of his mother. The owner of a night club befriends Tom but is later caught in the web of McCarthy blacklisting and commits suicide. Corcoran's theater background is drawn upon extensively, giving the novel an added appeal to theater-minded young people. In 1976 Corcoran again did more traveling in the U.S. and visited Nantucket

Island for the first time. *The Faraway Island* (1977) draws on this experience and is one of her life adjustment novels that includes problem adults, an orphaned animal, and an adolescent's developing maturity.

After spending almost a year in Hawaii, Corcoran wrote *Make No Sound* (1977), about a young teen named Melody who travels to Hilo with her oddly mixed family and comes to believe that the legends she hears on a late night radio broadcast are real. *Summer of the White Goat* (1977) is another short Paige Dixon nature story, in which Gordon, an eighteen-year-old would-be scientist, observes a mountain goat in Glacier Park in Montana. Gordon deals with his own survival and that of the nanny·goat and kid, narrating the story into a tape recorder and then editing it. The book received a designation as an "Outstanding Science Trade Book for Children" by the National Science Teachers Association. The idea for the story came from a newspaper report about an event that took place in a valley south of Missoula. Corcoran acknowledges that "everything hits as an idea." She files away good ideas that she reads in newspaper articles and that occur as personal experiences.

The third Gail Hamilton book, *Love Comes to Eunice K. O'Herlihy*, about a twelve-year-old girl who gets a crush on a sixteen-year-old Hawaiian, who comes to Montana with his family on a land development scam, was Corcoran's fourth novel published in 1977, and Corcoran again teamed with Bradford Angier in *Ask for Love and They Give You Rice Pudding* to produce another novel that same year. In this novel, Robbie, a rich, friendless seventeen-year-old, has weak parents who are currently absent from his life. He tries unsuccessfully to buy the affection of a girlfriend, though he eventually begins to mature and gain some initial understanding of his parents as adults with problems. By coauthoring the book and by placing it with Houghton Mifflin, Corcoran was able to solve the problem of having too many books published by the same company in any one year in a way other than using a pseudonym.

A visit Corcoran made to Palm Springs, California, prompted the setting for *Hey, That's My Soul You're Stomping On* (1978). This is a typical Corcoran problem novel: parents are problematic; the setting is intriguing; the main character is a teenager experiencing emotional upset; and informative details are woven into the background. The plot involves a sixteen-year-old girl who is sent to stay with her grandparents at a Palm Springs motel while her parents make a decision about divorce.

Also in 1978 Corcoran published a collection of three short stories entitled *The Mustang and Other Stories,* and another animal story published under the pseudonym Paige Dixon, called *The Loner: A Story of the Wolverine.* The book portrays a hunter and his Cree Indian guides as they try to kill a wolverine, about whom there is a superstition. The guides flee and the story becomes a survival tale of the hunter and the wolverine.

Me and You and a Dog Named Blue (1979) capitalized on things that were in vogue in the late 1970s, beginning with the title, taken from a popular song. This problem book concerns teenage Maggie, who lives with her widowed, alcoholic father, and her relationship with Co Co Rainbolt, a wealthy philanthropist who is attracted to Maggie's father.

Corcoran's sole sequel is *Skipper* (1979), written under the Paige Dixon pseudonym as a follow-up to the very popular *May I Cross Your Golden River?* The book is extremely complex—eighteen new characters in one hundred pages. Jordan Phillips's fourteen-year-old brother, Skipper, bicycles through North Carolina searching for his father. Many melodramatic incidents provide suspenseful fare for younger readers, including a fire in Skipper's father's cabin, Skipper's mysterious attempted murder with a cottonmouth snake, and a fight with his evil half-brother, Gerald, who looks like Jordan. A genealogy chart, first person journal writing to Jordan, and short, easy-to-read chapters with smoothly flowing dialogue make it an engaging novel for young adults.

Walk My Way (1980), another Paige Dixon book, is the story of Kitty LeBlanc, who is, at fourteen, nearly six feet tall, broad shouldered, and clumsy. Thinking she has killed one of her drunken father's friends who made advances toward her, she sets off on a fifty-mile hike to the Maine home of her late mother's sister.

In *Rising Damp* (1980), Corcoran again features a foreign setting—Ireland—and another young teen with parental difficulties is shown at a crucial time of her life. The protagonist, Hope, is on vacation with her mother's friend, Eileen, who has just been jilted. They get along miserably at first but after a romance for each they develop a mutual affection and a beneficial understanding of each other.

Two visits to New Orleans provided the background for *The Person in the Potting Shed* (1980), a mystery set in an old plantation house. Preteen brother and sister Dorothy and Franklin spend their summer with their mother, whom they have

Dust jacket for Corcoran's 1980 murder mystery set on an old New Orleans plantation (Atheneum)

not seen in fifteen months, and their new stepfather, whom they have never met. The overriding concern of the novel is the two children's adjustment to their stepfather, though the immediate mystery centers on a recently buried body the children find in the exploration of the plantation.

An incident that occurred with a Missoula family prompted the novel *Making It* (1980). Shy Sissy, seventeen, is one of six children in a minister's family in Colorado. She goes to UCLA on a scholarship, happy to be near Charlotte, the older sister whom she idolizes. She soon learns that Charlotte's gorgeous clothes and high living come from her life as a prostitute and drug dealer, a realization which becomes tragic when Charlotte is murdered. The book's first person style is breezy and appropriate for Corcoran's readership of young teens who enjoy "good reads." Corcoran worked on this book with editor Melanie Kroupa at Atlantic Monthly Press, whom she and Angier had earlier worked with on *Ask for Love and They Give You Rice Pudding.* In writing about her work with Jean Karl and with Kroupa, Corcoran notes that "Both of them were very constructive and encouraging. They both went for as much depth as I could get, but didn't change the course of the book."

A major shift in Corcoran's writing came in 1981, when she began a series of adult paperback romances for Ballantine Books. Few have been reviewed but the Corcoran name apparently caused at least one to be misconstrued as a young adult novel. Corcoran acknowledges that these books were written as money-makers. *Abigail* (1981), which began as a lengthy Civil War romance, was divided into a trilogy, with the second volume entitled *Abbie in Love* (1981), and the conclusion called *A Husband for Gail* (1981). Ballantine published five other historical romances by Corcoran for adults which she describes as "simple and unsophisticated": *Beloved Enemy* (1981), the story of a nurse in the Union Army during the Civil War; *Call of the Heart* (1981), which portrays an Irish governess for wealthy and terrible twins during World War I; *Love Is Not Enough* (1981), about two New England young women who work with celebrities in California at the end of World War II; *Song for Two Voices* (1981), in which a Massachusetts-born young woman goes to New York to find a career as a playwright in the late 1930s; and *By the Silvery Moon* (1982), the story of a musically talented young woman who works on the wealthy Bradenton estate in Florida. Autobiographical similarities are obviously the basis of many of the tales. In all cases the young heroines find adventure, intrigue, and, of course, love.

Along with the Ballantine romances, Corcoran began another series in 1981 with the first of three mysteries which focus on a girl named Stella and her friend Kim. Corcoran enjoys mysteries for her personal reading along with novels by Ernest Hemingway and Eudora Welty. As a child she attended an actual Camp Allegro. In *You're Allegro Dead* (1981), Stella's and Kim's mothers, who had been campers at Camp Allegro years before, send the two girls, both twelve, to the camp's revival. The camping experiences are suspensefully heightened when someone throws rocks at Stella and shoots at Kim. Kim and Stella are believable characters and the clues are well placed.

In *A Watery Grave* (1982), Kim and Stella are not at camp, but in their own New England town staying as houseguests of the Farleys, a new family in town who happen to be observing the anniversary of their son's drug-related death. A murder occurs and Kim and Stella solve the mystery, though not before more violence occurs. The story

has suspense and smooth dialogue.

In *August, Die She Must* (1984), set at Camp Allegro, Kim and Stella are involved in a conflict that leads to the shocking murder of a counselor. Twins who are campers are the murderers, but they are let off totally free. There is a rape, a possible pregnancy, and violence toward another camper. The reviewer for the *Bulletin of the Children's Literature Assembly* notes that readers enjoy a mystery because it is set in a controlled world where people are soundly punished and good succeeds. The orderly progression of a mystery includes people being brought to justice. Another rule of children's mysteries is that the reader is not supposed to be well acquainted with the murdered person. Corcoran breaks all these rules.

Kim and Stella's parents join them for the latest adventure at Camp Allegro in *Mystery on Ice* (1985). A developer wants to buy out the camp and tries to frighten the owners into selling. There is much suspense even though the many characters are confusing and the action seems contrived.

Besides the mystery quartet, Corcoran has written other novels in the 1980s. *Child of the Morning* (1982), a Junior Literary Guild selection, concerns Susan, fifteen, who is having fainting spells. Ignoring her problem, she works on the crew at a summer theater and eventually takes a dancing role. After she collapses during a performance the condition is diagnosed as symptomatic epilepsy. Susan realizes that she must accept her problem and rebuild her life so that she can cope with it.

In the early 1980s a bitter strike by Missoula, Montana, teachers tore apart that community. Corcoran followed accounts of the strike and used it as the basis for *Strike!* (1983). Fifteen-year-old Barry has a workaholic father who is a member of the school board, and they clash on almost every issue, including the teachers' strike. It is never made clear why the teachers are striking although the issues of book censorship and a raise in pay are alluded to. The *development* of the issues is the problem; they are mentioned but not clarified. As in many of Corcoran's books there are several subplots that could be the focus of entire books; Barry and his father argue about his forthcoming career and his lack of interest in baseball; Barry's father is an alcoholic; Barry has a crush on a teacher.

The censorship of books and the limitation of ideas is a topic about which Corcoran has strong feelings. In 1981 she wrote an impassioned letter to the editor of the *Horn Book* which appeared in the October issue and concerned the attempts to ban the use of books that demand children making judgments. She stated, "The essence of education, surely, is the question asked and the answer honestly given." Corcoran's books reflect this spirit as she leads her characters through difficult decisions toward more mature understandings of life.

Atheneum began a new series of mysteries by various authors in 1983, and Corcoran supplied *Which Witch is Which?* (1983) for one of its first installments. Designed for middle grade readers, the book has short chapters and high-interest mysteries. Twins Jennifer and Jack realize that cats are disappearing shortly after they have moved to Salem, Massachusetts. They form a cat detective agency and follow an older woman whom they not only suspect is stealing cats but whom they also think is a witch.

A complete change of pace in writing occurred in *The Woman in Your Life* (1984). Written for an older young adult readership, the story tells of Monty, a college freshman who has been imprisoned for drug smuggling from Mexico. Chapters move back and forth between her italicized first person journals written in prison and the third person narration. While in prison Monty finds women who befriend her and give her a strong sense of self that she has never had before. As she is paroled she has new courage for facing life.

Corcoran's longtime Atheneum editor, Jean Karl, went into semiretirement in 1985. She will still do a few books a year, including one Corcoran book. Because of Karl's retirement Corcoran began looking into other avenues for publishing. She worked with Helen Pyne at the Cloverdale Press on two books for a new paperback series. Of Pyne, Corcoran wrote, "Those books were more subject to tight plotting direction, but Helen was very good indeed." The two books *The Shadowed Path* (1985) and *When Darkness Falls* (1985) are part of the Moonstone Mystery Romance series which is designed for grades five and up. The heroines are bright and curious and the plots combine light romance against the intrigue of mystery. Corcoran's ability for telling a good story may find her a permanent place in this series even though Pyne has left Cloverdale.

Corcoran's latest book, *Face the Music* (1985), concerns a college-age girl, Marcie, and her whiny, dependent mother. During a trip to a family wedding in Austin, Marcie decides to stay in Texas, take a year off from college, and play bluegrass guitar with some new friends. There is difficulty with her mother but Marcie grows to become her own person. This book is illustrative of the main thrust of Corcoran's work. When asked if she had

Dust jacket for Corcoran's 1985 novel about a girl who must make a choice between independence and maintaining a close relationship with her emotionally dependent mother (Atheneum)

hopes for changing parent/child relationships in her writing, she noted, "I don't think I want to change anybody, but I'd like to provide readers with perhaps a new insight, something that makes them say, 'I never thought of that.'" Corcoran likes to think her writing has deepened a bit over the years. *Face the Music* is indicative of her ability to lead young readers to alternative views of adolescent problems and interests.

Corcoran stated in an article published in the 29 August 1981 *Missoulian* newspaper that, "I don't see myself as a great writer so I don't think either the world or I is being cheated of anything. I think I'm a competent writer. I know the tricks of the trade." Professional reviewers and her critical readership view her in much the same way. Most commentaries are mixed: many are quite favorable. Corcoran's strengths in writing are that she can tell an engrossing story and that she can write on many themes. Her main characters are usually well developed, and her animal tales are compassionate. In 1986 Corcoran turned seventy-five. In the preceding nineteen years before reaching that pinnacle she authored sixty-two books that have

received a steady readership as well as critical respect.

Robert Cormier
(17 January 1925-   )

Joe Stines

BOOKS: *Now and at the Hour* (New York: Coward-McCann, 1960);

A Little Raw on Monday Mornings (New York: Sheed & Ward, 1963);

Take Me Where the Good Times Are (New York: Macmillan, 1965);

The Chocolate War (New York: Pantheon, 1974);

I Am the Cheese (New York: Pantheon, 1977);

After the First Death (New York: Pantheon, 1979);

Eight Plus One (New York: Pantheon, 1980);

The Bumblebee Flies Anyway (New York: Knopf, 1983);

Beyond the Chocolate War (New York: Knopf, 1985).

OTHER: "Forever Pedaling on the Road to Realism," in *Celebrating Children's Books: Essays in Honor of Zena Sutherland*, edited by Betsy Hearne and Marilyn Kay (New York: Lothrop, Lee & Shepard, 1981).

PERIODICAL PUBLICATION: "The Cormier Novel, The Cheerful Side of Controversy," *Catholic Library World*, 50 (July-August 1978): 6-7.

photo by Finkle Photography

While Robert Cormier began his career writing fiction for adults, *The Chocolate War* (1974) established his reputation as an author of young adult literature. He says that he writes novels with young people in them rather than stories for young adult readers; however, he acknowledges that his most avid followers are junior and senior high school students.

Cormier began writing as a journalist in 1948, and he twice received the Associated Press award for the best news story in New England (1959, 1973) and won an award sponsored by the K. R. Thomson Newspapers for best column in 1974.

Critical honors for his young adult novels have included the New York Times Outstanding Book of the Year Award for *The Chocolate War* in 1974, for *I Am the Cheese* in 1977, and for *After the First Death* in 1979. *The Chocolate War* received the Lewis Carroll Shelf Award in 1979 and was, along with *I Am the Cheese* and *After the First Death*, named as an ALA Best Book for Young Adults. His fiction elicits empathetic responses from the reader by expressing natural emotions within highly complex and controversial plots. Cormier then thwarts that empathy with negativity and pessimism, his critics claim. Cormier seems to believe that teenagers are more idealistic today than in years past, and he affords them respect and responsibility in his writing while simultaneously awakening them to the harsh realities of life in contemporary America. He enthusiastically describes his young readers as being "responsive, caring, quick to be passionate about a book" and further says they are "so innocently critical and so marvelously appreciative." In reviewing comments by his young readers, one realizes that these teenagers not only read but discuss and question Cormier and his works.

Son of Lucien Joseph and Irma Collins Cormier, Robert Cormier was born into a large family in Leominster, Massachusetts. He married Constance B. Senay in 1948; together with their three daughters and a son, the Cormiers have continued to reside in Leominster.

In 1946 Cormier began writing commercials for a Worcester, Massachusetts, radio station, an experience that taught him economy of words and which led him to newspaper work. From 1948 to 1955, he worked as a reporter for the *Telegram & Gazette* in Worcester. In 1955 Cormier began employment with the *Fitchburg Sentinel* as book reviewer and wire editor. Before leaving the now-consolidated *Fitchburg-Leominster Sentinel and Enterprise* in 1978, he served as reporter, assistant city editor, and finally as associate editor. From 1964 to 1978, using the pseudonym John Fitch IV, Cormier wrote a human interest column, "And So On," which offered readers a cheerful, constructive side to the news. Cormier has written more than seventy-five short stories which have appeared in *McCall's, Redbook, Woman's Day,* and the *Saturday Evening Post,* as well as in such Catholic magazines as *St. Anthony Messenger* and the *Sign.* He recalls having the desire to become a fiction writer as early as the eighth grade; later, he found journalism a good way to earn a living while working and experimenting with words.

Written honestly and without regard for a specific audience, Cormier's novels are Orwellian in theme: his topics, including terrorism, suicide, child murder, betrayal, personality destruction, and governmental and religious corruption, are sometimes difficult to accept in a young adult novel. He offers few happy endings, believing that literature should touch the emotions many readers strive to avoid. His characters are subject to the inevitability of the events that govern their circumstances; they develop in situations that demand the most of them, even more than they realize themselves capable of.

Employing both first person and third person narration, Cormier uses flashbacks within flashbacks, as well as irony, often demanding that the reader detect the meaning behind his undependable narrators' versions of events. His endings are often puzzling, for he strives to make the reader think, feel, and wonder. One young Cormier reader remarked, "This novel did something to me. I'm not sure yet what."

More than half of his published short stories involve teenagers, although they were written as "adult" stories. Cormier acknowledges the influence his own maturing children have had on his writing: "Their lives seesawed between ecstasy and despair, often during one single afternoon. They fell in and out of love as swiftly and flamboyantly as the seasons change. They lived on the knife-edge of emotional crisis. And all of this mattered to them. And I came to write more and more about them, matching their comings and goings with memories of my own." Cormier understands the vulnerability of adolescence, with its special agonies. His writing illustrates the fact that innocence does not provide immunity from evil and the fact that we remain vulnerable at any age.

Now and at the Hour (1960), his first novel, is the story of Alph LeBlanc, a New England mill worker who is dying of cancer. Cormier allows the story to unfold through the thoughts of LeBlanc, creating a minute-by-minute study of pain, fear, and deterioration. From Cormier's depiction of Alph LeBlanc's humanity and courage, the reader discovers that Alph is not as ordinary as he himself thinks. Without the use of sentimentality the author shows that death can be both dignified and life affirming.

Cormier returns to the subject of death in later novels, using a similar approach but dealing with more unusual and complicated circumstances. His use of "hints" to build suspense and his ability to place the reader inside the mind of a principal character are more refined and strategically applied in later works, though *Now and at the Hour* remains one of his most acclaimed novels, establishing the literary style upon which he continues to build.

The protagonist of Cormier's second novel, *A Little Raw on Monday Mornings* (1963), is a widowed mother of three who becomes pregnant. She is one of the "insignificant" people of whom critics speak when describing Cormier's use of honest realism and his ability to portray characters. In his later works, Cormier continues to raise humble characters to heroic stature.

Take Me Where the Good Times Are (1965), the author's third novel, is the story of seventy-year-old Tommy Bartin and his brief but tragic "furlough" from the Monument City infirmary, less euphemistically known as the "poorhouse." Bartin travels from one tragic moment, rejection due to circumstance, to another, entrapment. The plot, though it contains mild humor and bits of nostalgia, also involves suicide, again revealing Cormier's interest in the thematic explanation of death. Its setting, Monument City, is a small New England town similar to Cormier's native Leominster, one that Cormier uses repeatedly in his writings.

In 1974, nine years after the publication of his third critically acclaimed but modestly selling adult work, Cormier published a fourth novel, written about teenagers. In *The Chocolate War* freshman Jerry Renault, still stunned by his mother's recent death, is enlisted to sell candy for Trinity High School's annual fund-raising project, but, as a joke, Archie Costello, leader of a secret prep school so-

ciety, the Vigils, gives Jerry the "assignment" not to sell his candy for two weeks. When Jerry continues not to sell any candy beyond the assigned time, he temporarily becomes a hero. His stand is a threat not only to Archie and the Vigils but also to Brother Leon, the teacher in charge of the candy sale, and to the school. Archie's skill at intimidation finally turns Jerry from hero to outcast and victim, leaving him vulnerable and cornered in a brutal fight with the school bully, Emile Janza.

Cormier underscores the fact that good guys do not always win. He also indicts those who remain indifferent in the face of evil or wrongdoing, pointing out that anyone who takes the risk of challenging evil can be destroyed both physically and psychologically. *The Chocolate War*, characterized by salty language, has no true heroes but is rather a story of brutality, terror, manipulation, entrapment, and rejection, containing a message about the usurpation and misuse of power. The reader sees that growing up is accompanied by the realization that the world can be deceitful, that good and evil are barely distinguishable; each side ex-

Dust jacket for Cormier's controversial novel of brutality, terror, and manipulation (Pantheon)

hibits weakness, fear, and selfishness.

Using paradox, the subjunctive mood, and a chapter-by-chapter switch in viewpoint, Cormier offers the reader, first, a glance inside Trinity, a prep school for Catholic boys. Once inside, the author allows the reader to know not only the actions of the teachers and students but their thoughts as well. Young readers learn some shocking things—men of the cloth are not always pure; youth is not always innocent.

Brother Leon, a distrusting and corrupt priest fascinated by power, runs Trinity High through exploitation and manipulation. He blackmails an honor student, David Caroni, into revealing that Jerry's refusal to sell candy is a Vigil assignment.

It is through Brother Leon's actions that Archie, leader of the Vigils, comes to understand the use of power and corruption. Archie's thoughts portray Brother Leon as "someone riddled with cracks and crevices" and living "proof of what he'd always suspected, not only of Brother Leon" but of most adults. Archie comes to see grown-ups as "vulnerable, running scared, open to invasion."

Archie controls the subculture of the student body with "artistic maliciousness." He uses Carter, the football captain, for muscle and Obie, his friend, as an errand boy. Jerry becomes student body hero by challenging Brother Leon and the Vigils when he refuses to participate in the school's chocolate sale. But the enemy proves too powerful for Jerry and he loses not only the "war" but his self-respect and faith in justice as well. By relinquishing the role of hero, Jerry exits the story leaving street-smart Archie and his evil power triumphant over good.

The Chocolate War and the youth market it attracted brought Cormier popular success as a fiction writer. It remains his most commercially successful novel. However, not every reader appreciates what some consider his pessimistic presentation of contemporary issues. On more than one occasion school boards have met to consider banning the book from school libraries. Critics object to the language of the book, its portrayal of authority as evil, its ugly imagery, and the feeling of hopelessness supported by the somber plot and a "downbeat" ending. Students have banded together, signing petitions to keep the book in their libraries. Cormier's use of "hints," with which he toys with the reader's sense of hope and justice, has also come under attack, though these same critics admit that Cormier has written a compelling, masterfully structured novel. *The Chocolate War*, originating from an idea conceived one afternoon as

Cormier observed his son carrying home boxes of candy for a school sale, has become the cornerstone of his writing career.

Cormier expresses his belief that man is living in terrifying times, that our immense high tech society renders us powerless as individuals, that it "takes an act of faith to live today." Surely his experience as a newspaperman has given him reason to feel this way and has influenced his fictional writing. In 1977 he published his most complex work, *I Am the Cheese*, based on an idea he developed after reading of the U.S. Witness Relocation Program. The novel is more frightening and unnerving than his previous work because the "evil foe" remains unknown until the end. It is the story of fourteen-year-old Adam Farmer, who learns that his real name is Paul Delmonte. When he was three years old his family was given a new identity by the government as a result of his father's testimony against organized crime figures. Eventually his parents reveal their history to him and explain the monthly visit of Mr. Grey, a representative of the relocation

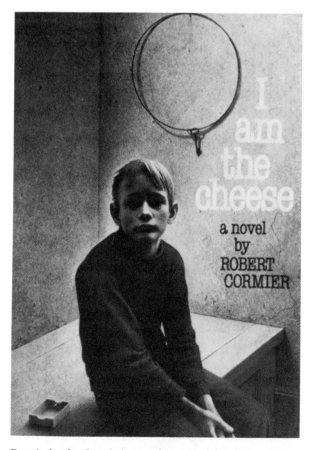

Dust jacket for Cormier's second young adult novel, a psychological nightmare involving government corruption, espionage, and the disintegration of the mind (Pantheon)

program. Not long afterward Grey, who may not be the friend the Farmers think he is, arranges a trip for the family. They are followed by hit men, and Adam's mother and father are killed. Though Adam survives, he is taken to a confinement facility and for three years is subjected to drugs and periodic interrogation by a man pretending to be a psychiatrist.

Highly sophisticated in style, the story unfolds through bits and pieces taken from Adam's imaginings and recollections and the pseudopsychiatrist's tape recordings. Cormier's use of flashback and his "puzzle" approach make this novel a challenge for young readers. As Adam Farmer becomes the victim of his family's circumstances, Cormier uncovers the pain that evil inflicts upon the innocent.

Fear becomes a major theme in the novel, at times so realistic that it overshadows other aspects of the book, including character, plot, and setting. Its overriding presence allows few happy moments for the reader or for Adam, though a break in the gloom comes as Adam remembers his girlfriend, Amy Hertz, to the psychiatrist and what she had once told him: "You don't laugh enough. You have this long look on your face. But there's hope, Ace, there's hope. I see the possibility of laughter in your baby blues." Amy is more than Adam's first love; she represents the stable, pleasant part of his life. Being held prisoner by a horrifying government agency separates Adam from all pleasantness and reality.

Loss, however, dominates the book: loss of identity, loss of parents and girlfriend, and, most tragic, loss of reality. *I Am the Cheese* is a psychological nightmare, involving government corruption, espionage, and the disintegration of the mind.

Cormier's sixth novel, *After the First Death* (1979), was prompted by recent news stories. This story of terrorism represents an undeclared war, with battlegrounds both physical and mental. On a bridge at the outskirts of a New England town, a bus load of drugged preschool children is being held hostage, the ransom being the dismantling of a secret government agency, Inner Delta. The novel's characters include Miro, a sixteen-year-old male terrorist who has no past and possibly no future; Artkin, the terrorist leader who thinks nothing of murder; Kate, a substitute bus driver whose courage and resourcefulness give hope and dignity to the unraveling story; Ben, an innocent messenger; and his father, the General, who victimizes Ben and whose secret could lead to his own destruction.

Cormier's teenage characters possess typical young adult attributes—insecurity, innocence, guilt, peer influence, and sexual awareness. They must, however, deal with these under unusual and difficult circumstances. Miro, for example, has been trained to exhibit no emotion, but he is obviously moved by Kate's gentle touch. Kate realizes she cannot get out of the bus alive, so she plays her last trump card—using her femininity and sexuality to win Miro. Kate dies wanting to ask someone if she had been brave. Ben also dies, but as a result of his father's priority placing love of country before that of family.

Each word, each emotion, each breath is more real than the preceding one. The story shows failure of adults' values and actions and contains brutality, sexual overtones, insensitivity, and fear. Cormier has been accused of misleading his readers by suggesting the false hope—through the revelations that Kate has an extra key to the bus hidden in her shoe and that Raymond, one of the children on the bus, is pretending to be asleep—that justice will finally triumph. Cormier allows the reader to feel tenderness and sympathy for both Kate and Miro, a frustrated youth ripe for a first relationship. But the unexpected happens, and suddenly, with a slip of the trigger by a government sniper, the situation is out of control. Raymond's murder and Miro's loss of Artkin, killed by a sniper, give Kate's murder a sense of inevitability. Even the identity of the story's narrator becomes suspect, for Ben, who appears to be telling the story, is dead; the reader is left to wonder if the General is in fact narrating the events in a state of delusion.

Critics object not just to the story's plot or its unpleasant themes but mainly to its "degree" of terror and reality. *After the First Death* places the reader in a nightmare world where innocence becomes monstrous (Miro), patriotism breeds evil (the General), and courage has many meanings. Its ending is more than unhappiness; it is a realistic view of hopelessness.

Eight Plus One (1980) presents a different side of Robert Cormier. These nine short stories written between 1965 and 1975 probe the feelings and reactions of young people in trying situations: a first love, leaving home for college, handling ethnic prejudice, family disintegration due to divorce, and the realization that a father is no more than human. Through vivid characterizations, the author shares himself with his readers. Using his own New England in the 1930s as well as a more contemporary time period, Cormier gives an adult's viewpoint on situations commonly faced by young adults. Each story is prefaced by a brief introduction which tells as much about the writer as it does about the characters. Using many of the same themes and plot elements from his earlier works, including innocence, emotionality, human relationships, and the complexities of life, Cormier shows himself in these stories to be sentimental and intensely personal.

Cormier's eighth novel, *The Bumblebee Flies Anyway* (1983), was inspired by a poster which described the aerodynamic miracle that the bumblebee, with its heavy body and short wing span, can fly, though the book's setting grew out of an article Cormier read concerning experimental hospitals, where terminally ill patients receive radical and unconventional treatments. It is the story of sixteen-year-old Barney Snow, the only patient in such a hospital who does not appear destined to die. Each youth is there voluntarily, some to serve science, and some, like Mazzo, seeking a quick, private death.

Barney is told that he is the "control," supposedly brought to the complex for scientific research on memory. He is warned by his doctor to keep within his own compartment and form no friendships with the dying around him. With his own memory faltering, he is tormented by a repeated hallucination that he is at the wheel of an out-of-control car with a young girl stepping in its path. Barney finds the individuality and courage of his fellow patients too overwhelming to ignore: Billy the Kidney, whose cries of pain are materialized only through his eyes; Allie Roon, whose body twitches and leaps; and wealthy, once handsome Mazzo, who wants Barney to disconnect his life-support system.

Barney soon falls in love with Mazzo's twin sister, Cassie, who asks him for help because her brother refuses to see anyone from his family. Upon his introduction to Cassie, Barney describes her beauty as "vibrant and compelling." "Her movements were thrillingly sexual to Barney, the way she raised her arms, the fullness of her breasts, the lips wet and slightly parted." Later, Cassie visits Barney to ask, "Would you visit with Mazzo, get to know him better, become friendly with him? Cheer him up?" Although Barney does not like the role of spy, he realizes that he will see Cassie when she comes for her reports. "Look, Cassie, I'll do it," replies Barney. The forthcoming visits with Cassie awaken a new meaning of living for Barney. He is no longer isolated. He enters Mazzo's compartment and begins to feel for him and the other patients as well.

Barney conceives a miracle plan to give Mazzo his final wish; with assistance from Billy and Allie, he steals a life-size model car made of balsa wood—the "Bumblebee"—and takes it apart in the junkyard next door, moving it piece by piece to the hospital attic where he reconstructs it. One night with an unbelievable struggle, he and Mazzo carry the car onto the roof in order to give Mazzo a final glorious ride into space.

As with Cormier's earlier works, the story unfolds from "inside" one of its characters, in this instance Barney Snow. The book is uncompromisingly honest and brutal at times in its exploration of medical ethics, manipulation, attitudes toward dying, and raw courage. Cormier's writing style, marked by distasteful imagery, is once again deceptive, as both the reader and Barney gradually learn that the memory experiments have only twisted the truth; Barney Snow is also dying. Through Barney's and Mazzo's resistance to a passive acceptance of death, *The Bumblebee Flies Anyway* gives meaning to dying and shows it can be an affirmative and spirited act of life in the midst of hopeless despair. Barney Snow is a hero, honest and real.

In a December 1984 interview with Anita Silvey, Robert Cormier says that at first he "resisted a sequel [to *The Chocolate War*]" and goes on to say, "I don't particularly like sequels—mostly because they are usually disappointing." Cormier's most recent novel, *Beyond the Chocolate War* (1985), is anything but "disappointing." His literary style has matured, displaying a remarkable control of pacing, a masterful display of simile and metaphor, and a thoroughly developed and unforgettable character, Archie Costello.

The story line picks up and ends the Trinity High school term begun in *The Chocolate War*. Archie and the devilishness he represents are more vividly drawn and eternally present than ever. Returning characters include Obie, Archie's chief stooge whose loyalty is threatened by Laurie Gundardson, Obie's first love; Jerry Renault; Brother Leon; David Caroni, a tragic soul going through the motions of daily "living"; Roland Goubert (the Goober), burdened with guilt and facing a final test of friendship; Carter, president of the Vigils; and Emile Janza, whose emergence as the new leader of the Vigils leaves the reader mystified.

New to Trinity High is Ray Bannister, a talented magician, who learns of the chocolate sale and the Vigils from Obie. Ray has constructed a guillotine as part of his magic act. The guillotine and Archie are at center stage for the story's stun-

which meant he was now ~~19~~ *is* pounds overweight. Found it hard

to breath going up the stairs, ~~XXXXXX~~ sweated all the time,

perpetually moist, oozing. And ~~top~~ *on* top of all that, the

Vigils.

He was bubbling with sweat now as he stood in the

small storage room in the ~~XXX~~ gym. He had to blink to get rid

of the ~~moisture~~ *perspiration.* gathering in his eyes, ~~from the perspiration~~

~~coming from his forehead.~~ He knew that he looked as if he was

crying. But he wasn't. He didn't want anybody to think he

was a weeper, *or disguise,* Underneath this terrible fat that he couldn't ~~XXX~~

get rid of, he was brave and strong and durable. As he stood

before the members of the Vigils, ~~XXX~~ he was determined to put

up a good front, despite the fat and the sweat. He ~~XXX~~ recognized

some of the guys who sat in the ~~XXX~~ room's dimness, knew their

names but had never ~~XXXXX~~ talked to *any of* them. Freshmen like Tubs

kept out of the way of upperclassmen. He looked around for

the kid called ~~XXX~~ Obie but did not see him here. Obie was the

only Vigil member he ~~knew~~ *had talked with* and he preferred ~~XXX~~ not to think about

their association, the ~~only time they'd talked,~~ because it had

to do with Rita ~~and~~ *the chocolate .*

There was an attitude of waiting in the room, as the

guys talked together in low tones, They ~~XXXXXXXXXXXXXX~~ acted as if

~~XXX~~ Tubs didn't exist. Tubs knew ~~XXXXXX~~ who ~~XXX~~ they were waiting

for. ~~XXX~~ Archie Costello. He dreaded Archie Costello's arrival.

He knew all about him, his power and his assignments. ~~First Rita,~~

~~now XXX thic .~~

Page from the penultimate draft for Beyond the Chocolate War *(by permission of the author)*

ning climax. Obie persuades Ray to perform at Trinity's annual "Fair Day" and manipulates Archie into serving as the magician's assistant. Driven by revenge and regret, Obie confronts his own turpitude by rigging the guillotine so that it will kill.

The themes of *Beyond the Chocolate War* are explicit. Cormier says, "The power of the leader comes from those who allow themselves to be led" and that "choice is always possible." He goes on to state, "Terrible things happen because we allow them to happen."

Cormier allows the reader another disturbing look at the misuse of power and the evil side of human nature. He again writes of suicide. This time, he portrays the doomed character, David Caroni, with documentary reasoning, obviously drawn from the author's newspaper background. He once again returns to the use of ugly imagery and salty language but in a somewhat more direct and strategic style.

By allowing decent people such as Jerry Renault and Ray Bannister to emerge, Cormier provides the reader with the hope that evil, though not defeated, can be at least temporarily controlled. Robert Cormier's themes are controversial, emo-tional, and stark, his style complex and manipulative. He forces his readers to think and feel, made evident by the polarized response his young adult novels have received. Although he was hailed by Tony Schwartz in *Newsweek* as the one youth writer who is "an equivalent to Saul Bellow or William Styron," others have sought to ban his books from high school libraries. Young readers need many books, of many themes, with varied settings, and they are certainly richer for having their visions broadened by the writing skill of Robert Cormier.

References:

Laurel Graeber, "PW Interviews Robert Cormier," *Publishers Weekly*, 224 (7 October 1983): 98-99;

Paul Janeczko, "An Interview with Robert Cormier," *English Journal*, 66 (September 1977): 10-11;

Frank McLaughlin, "Robert Cormier, A Profile," *Media and Methods*, 14 (May-June 1978): 28;

Anita Silvey, "An Interview with Robert Cormier," *Horn Book*, 61 (March-April 1985): 145-155.

Meindert DeJong

(4 March 1906-)

Myra Kibler
Belmont College

BOOKS: *The Big Goose and the Little White Duck,* illustrated by Edna Potter (New York & London: Harper, 1938; London: Heinemann, 1939);

Dirk's Dog, Bello, illustrated by Kurt Wiese (New York & London: Harper, 1939; London: Lutterworth, 1960);

Wheels over the Bridge, illustrated by Aldren Watson (New York & London: Harper, 1941);

Bells of the Harbor, illustrated by Wiese (New York & London: Harper, 1941);

The Little Stray Dog, illustrated by Edward Shenton (New York & London: Harper, 1943);

The Cat That Walked a Week, illustrated by Tessie Robinson (New York & London: Harper, 1943; London: Lutterworth, 1965);

Meindert DeJong

Billy and the Unhappy Bull, illustrated by Marc Simont (New York & London: Harper, 1946; London: Lutterworth, 1966);

Bible Days, illustrated by Kreigh Collins (Grand Rapids: Fideler, 1949);

Good Luck Duck, illustrated by Simont (New York: Harper, 1950; London: Hamilton, 1950);

The Tower by the Sea, illustrated by Barbara Comfort (New York: Harper, 1950; London: Hamilton, 1950);

Smoke above the Lane, illustrated by Girard Goodenow (New York: Harper, 1951);

Shadrach, illustrated by Maurice Sendak (New York: Harper, 1953; London: Lutterworth, 1957);

Hurry Home Candy, illustrated by Sendak (New York: Harper, 1953; London: Lutterworth, 1962);

The Wheel on the School, illustrated by Sendak (New York: Harper, 1954; London: Lutterworth, 1956);

The Little Cow and the Turtle, illustrated by Sendak (New York: Harper, 1955; London: Lutterworth, 1961);

The House of Sixty Fathers, illustrated by Sendak (New York: Harper, 1956; London: Lutterworth, 1958);

Along Came a Dog, illustrated by Sendak (New York: Harper, 1958; London: Lutterworth, 1959);

The Mighty Ones: Great Men and Women of Early Bible Days, illustrated by Harvey Schmidt (New York: Harper, 1959; London: Lutterworth, 1960);

The Last Little Cat, illustrated by Jim McMullen (New York: Harper, 1961; London: Lutterworth, 1962);

Nobody Plays with a Cabbage, illustrated by Tom Allen (New York: Harper, 1962; London: Lutterworth, 1963);

The Singing Hill, illustrated by Sendak (New York: Harper & Row, 1962; London: Lutterworth, 1963);

Far Out the Long Canal, illustrated by Nancy Grossman (New York: Harper & Row, 1964; London: Lutterworth, 1965);

Puppy Summer, illustrated by Anita Lobel (New York: Harper & Row, 1966; London: Lutterworth, 1966);

Journey from Peppermint Street, illustrated by Emily McCully (New York: Harper & Row, 1968; London: Lutterworth, 1969);

A Horse Came Running, illustrated by Paul Sagsoorian (New York: Macmillan, 1970; London: Lutterworth, 1970);

The Easter Cat, illustrated by Lillian Hoban (New York: Macmillan, 1971; London: Lutterworth, 1972);

The Almost All-White Rabbity Cat, illustrated by H. B. Vestal (New York: Macmillan, 1972; London: Lutterworth, 1972).

OTHER: "Acceptance Paper," in *Newbery Medal Books: 1922-1955,* edited by Bertha Mahoney Miller and Elinor Whitney Field (Boston: Horn Book, 1955), pp. 434-439;

"Autobiographical Sketch of Meindert DeJong," in *More Junior Authors,* edited by Muriel Fuller (New York: H. W. Wilson, 1963), p. 63;

"The Cry and the Creation," *Horn Book,* 39 (April 1963): 197-206; republished in *Children and Literature: Views and Reviews,* edited by Virginia Haviland (Glenview, Ill.: Scott, Foresman, 1973), pp. 160-168.

Meindert DeJong's prominent place in children's literature seems assured, although he has passed the peak of his popularity. In thirty-four years (1938-1972) he published twenty-seven books for children, and his work has won major awards, including the Newbery Medal. DeJong's consistent strength as a writer is his power to convey what it is like to be a particular child or animal in that individual's world. He sees the world through his characters' eyes and recreates their experiences from their perspectives. Place is an important part of their experiences and DeJong's skill in evoking the worlds in which his characters live, especially in his well-known Dutch stories, is masterful.

DeJong's own childhood has provided the main source for his stories. He claims never to concern himself with the ages or interests of his readers; instead he focuses inward, on his own subconsciousness. He describes his writing process as becoming rather than just remembering; by becoming a child again, he sees from the child's perspective, whereas remembering simply yields an adult's conception of the child's perspective. His best work is characterized by the intensity of this

limited perspective, sometimes projected into animals in stories such as *Hurry Home Candy* (1953) or *Along Came a Dog* (1958).

Meindert DeJong had, in a sense, two childhoods. With dramatic timing, his birth in Holland on 4 March 1906 coincided with a storm that drove the sea over the dike, flooding the fishing village of Wierum. His parents, Raymond R. and Jennie DeJong, were strict Calvinists, part of a strong family that lived in and near Wierum. He had two older brothers, David and Remmeren, and one younger brother, Corneil, born in the United States. Meindert was a small, sickly child. He had pneumonia three times and came so close to dying on one occasion that the whole village prayed for him. He survived but he was small for his age and not competitive with his peers. His parents left Holland for America when Meindert was only eight, but by that time the land, the culture, and the people had made an indelible impression on him.

Some of his best work depicts his childhood homeland, the flat land of Holland and the village of Wierum, with canals and ditches, which are at times threatening to the safety of children but which, when frozen, also provide arenas for marvelous ice holidays. The sensitivity of place is heightened by the importance of the sea and weather to the people, both real and fictional, who depend on the sea for their livelihood and on the dike that holds back the sea for their safety. The landmarks of this place—the dike, the tower, the school, the church, the roads that link one small village to another—are as integral a part of De-Jong's Dutch stories as the moor in Thomas Hardy's novels. These stories could not have happened in Anytown; they are rooted in the land, the culture, and the time of DeJong's early life.

This world, considerably different from the world of contemporary American children, nevertheless is recreated with such detail that the place itself becomes a major interest in DeJong's Dutch stories. People sleep in beds that have doors; they wear wooden shoes which can become weapons in fights. Vendors travel from village to village in horse- or dog-drawn carts full of wares. Streets are so narrow that neighbors can call back and forth, and a wide cart coming may set women hollering and scrambling to rescue wash hung out to dry on racks in the streets. Children in DeJong's Dutch stories attend school fifty weeks of the year—except for ice holidays—and they work on slates in mixed-grade classes. In church children sit together in back rows, and women carry heaters to warm their feet in the unheated building. Warm breath rises to the ceiling, condenses, and drips down to the tile floors.

Cultural differences also make this fictional world remote from contemporary Americans. The family is a strong, stable unit often with grandparents, aunts, and uncles. The past is remembered in legends, stories, and songs, and religion is a dominant force. Characters in DeJong's books often quote the Bible or sing hymns, and they work, occasionally against their natures, to keep religious observances. Among many people, especially the fishermen, superstition is also a powerful force, and customs, quite different from those in America, reflect the special nature of the place. For example, boys play Over-a-Paper-Ceiling, a game that eventually results in a dunking for someone. Then they carry the unlucky wet one home, wrapped in coats, as they sing a song of ridicule about having caught a pickerel.

That Holland provided such a complete world for Meindert DeJong's work is surprising since he was so young when he left there for America. How much he remembered and how much he learned from family lore probably even the author himself cannot tell. But the place and its people vividly inform seven of his books.

His second childhood was more difficult. His father, wanting to save his sons from being inducted into the military during World War I, immigrated with the family to Grand Rapids, Michigan. He may have saved their lives in doing so, but their quality of life was suddenly reduced. In the years just after the move, they experienced poverty, prejudice, and illness. Their helplessness in a strange country at first kept them from getting proper medical treatment. A fourth child was born and died, and Mrs. DeJong suffered a lengthy illness, which went undiagnosed until her health had been irreparably damaged by diabetes. The children worked for what support they could contribute, and they attended Dutch Christian schools at the insistence of their pious parents despite the abuse they received from the Dutch Christians who had been in America a little longer and despite the fact that the public schools were better academically.

The boys were put back in school several years behind their grade-levels in Holland. This demotion was so humiliating to David that he changed his age to correspond to the grade he was placed in. Meindert in turn changed his to correspond to David's, and some records incorrectly give his altered birthdate, 1910, when in fact, Meindert DeJong was born in 1906. To add further injury,

a teacher urged Remmeren and Meindert to Americanize their names to Raymond and Melvin. Remmeren took her advice, but Meindert not only kept his name but also adopted his brother's cast-off name, signing himself Meindert Remmeren DeJong. Remmeren and Meindert tried to escape mistreatment at school with truancy, letting David cover for them as long as he could. Meindert even forged a letter from his father explaining that they had been sick. With a sick mother who slept on the sofa all day under the effect of drugs and an overworked father who no doubt suffered ego deflation under such conditions, the boys were left to fend for themselves in a hostile community. Although DeJong has written no stories about the immigrant period of his life, he developed a sensitivity to the plight of people and animals who are mistreated just because they are different. It is undoubtedly due to his experiences during this period of his life that he understands how it feels to yearn for a home, a place to be warm and fed and loved. It may also speak for DeJong's sensitivity that he rarely depicts a child in such awful deprivation, the main exception being Tien Pao in *The House of Sixty Fathers* (1956); usually it is an animal that has been abandoned or lost, or for some other reason neglected.

David DeJong did not go directly to high school because the family needed the support he could provide by working, but when Meindert considered dropping out because of low grades and disinterest David made vehement demands that he continue. After that Meindert made top grades and insisted that David take time to read certain books. Eventually David, too, returned to finish high school. The two brothers saw to each other's education and together worked their way through Calvin College.

Both boys tried writing in college, and they wrote with special fervor during their senior year in an effort to earn enough money from their writing to avoid having to take teaching jobs after graduation. Unsuccessful, Meindert, who earned an A.B. in 1928, went off with considerable dread to teach in a small college in Iowa. As he expected, he hated teaching and never tried it again. While in Iowa he also tried farming but found that he could not survive on the meager income it brought him. Farming, however, did provide some pleasurable experiences; he enjoyed raising animals, and it did provide the other setting, besides Holland, that is most frequently used for his stories. Many of his books are set on farms, and frequently the people depicted have recently moved to the country, are only renting, or for some reason are novices at country living. Although this locale lacks the richness and wholeness of the Holland settings, it provides a place where a character may have to deal with loneliness, one of DeJong's major themes. It also provides for a solution for loneliness: frequently the care of a helpless or needy animal eases a character's sense of isolation. DeJong's animal characters include not only dogs and cats but also a duck, a goose, a rabbit, a turtle, a cow, a bull, a horse, and even a skunk.

It was during his farm period that DeJong found his real vocation. A librarian suggested that he write a children's story about a goose he owned that manifested a notable personality. He wrote *The Big Goose and the Little White Duck* (1938) and offered it to Harper, where it was accepted and published. A simple story narrated by an omniscient storyteller, it begins, "It was this way," and the speaker remains in the foreground throughout. He tells what each person or animal thinks and sometimes evaluates their situations: "Maybe it was lucky for the goose that he did not know the grandfather was going to lock him up." There is no effort here, as there would be in later books, to empathize with the animal. The reader may feel for the goose and want it to live (after all, it is a worthy goose), but he is not made privy to the goose's feelings. The little white duck, who is the silent pal of the goose, never attains the importance suggested by his place in the title. The book's human characters are relatively undeveloped, known only as the boy, the little old lady, and Grandpa. The success of the story depends on its repetitive, episodic structure, in which the goose proves its worth on the farm again and again until even the crotchety old grandfather realizes that it is of more value alive than as his birthday dinner.

This first book established DeJong as a successful writer, and, with his wife Hattie Overeinter, whom he had married in 1932, he returned to Grand Rapids, where he took a job with the Federal Writers' Project but also continued writing children's stories. DeJong chose Holland as the setting for his second book, *Dirk's Dog, Bello* (1939), and introduced his readers to Weirom (a re-creation of his birthplace, Wierum), a fishing village on the North Sea which lies below sea level. Only the dike holds the tenuous line between the land and the sea, and, because it is vital to the safety of the villagers, it is of central concern. Jinne, the dike inspector, keeps constant watch over it, monitoring loose stones and watching for debris from the sea that might damage it. Because the dike also affords

Dust jacket for the first of seven DeJong novels to feature the illustrations of Maurice Sendak (Harper)

the highest point in a flat land, it is a lookout place from which people watch for the return of fishermen, a change in the weather, the progress of someone on the roads, or occasionally the distress of ships on the Wiked Wife, an especially treacherous stretch of water between the mainland and an island just offshore.

Such an occasion opens *Dirk's Dog, Bello*. A crew of fishermen escape a sinking ship in a lifeboat, but they abandon a great dane, Bello, to fight for his life in the pounding surf. Dirk rescues the dog as the waves throw it on the pilings at the foot of the dike and then begin to pull it out to sea again. Rescues from the sea happen frequently in DeJong's Dutch stories, and the danger and excitement of making a rescue attempt is heightened by the fact that most people in this northern coastal area do not swim. Having rescued the dog, Dirk's joy gradually gives way to realization that he cannot support such a large animal. The plot develops his efforts to do what must be done to keep Bello alive.

They involve increasingly difficult tasks which require hard work, humiliation, self-sacrifice, and real suffering. There are people who are simply insensitive to the plight of Dirk and Bello, and there are opportunists who exploit Dirk's desperation. Happily the agents of good are larger than the agents of evil—literally. Mighty Pier, the biggest man in the village, is on Dirk's side. Normally a gentle person, Pier becomes violent when he sees someone mistreat an animal, and then only Dikke Trien can control him. Trien is a massive woman, revered in the village for her ability to pick up any man and set him where she wants him.

The attempt of a child to care for an animal is a recurrent DeJong theme, and the need is usually mutual. The animal needs a home, food, love, a sense of belonging; and the child needs to be needed, needs to give, in an essential way, to something dependent on him. The child is most often either an only child or the youngest child in a family; sometimes it is even an adult who is alone, a tramp or a man who has no family. The needs of the person and the animal complement each other as DeJong repeatedly explores this reciprocal relationship between human and animal.

Bells of the Harbor (1941) is a sequel to *Dirk's Dog, Bello*, though it is a much busier book. The complex plot has a full measure of suspense, mystery, and excitement. Mighty Pier has married Dirk's widowed mother, and the family adopts an orphan boy, Jan, who comes, as Bello did, from a shipwreck. Suspicious circumstances surround the ship's sinking and Jan's past life. An investigation ensues, but Dirk's family embraces Jan as brother and son without waiting for information about his former life. When he is suspected of theft, they have only their intuition to support their trust in him.

The community in this book is not only a collection of individuals, as it was in *Dirk's Dog, Bello*. Although Sipke, the village simpleton; the prophesying Old Ott; Uncle Hannes, who hides his money in the sugar barrel; Aage the Roamer; Grandfather Tjerk; and others are very much individuals and are more fully developed than they were in the first book, more important, in *Bells of the Harbor*, the community becomes an entity larger than the individuals who live there. When a crisis arises, they find a solution through cooperation. Though the villagers are poor, they take the stranded sailors from Jan's ship into their homes until an investigation into the sinking is concluded. When the people of Weirom and neighboring villages are on the frozen sea for ice races and the ice

breaks up, they take responsible, coordinated action to rescue everybody. The community functions at its best when it responds to the losses sustained one night when people are forced to flee from their homes because the dike has threatened to break. The greatest loss is to Hannes, the storekeeper, whose savings are stolen during the chaos. In an organized manner, everyone tells what he saw that night. Even Dirk is required to tell what he saw although it implicates Jan, whom he believes to be innocent and who indeed is vindicated in the end. It is his civic responsibility to tell. Assuming that a collective vision is better than an individual's, the community believes that when all the pieces of information are compiled into a whole picture the truth will be known. DeJong escapes the charge of naiveté because, although he shows such positive views of human cooperation and communal effort again in *The Wheel on the School* (1954) and to some extent in *Far Out the Long Canal* (1964), he also shows the reverse when a community is united by fear and superstition, as in *The Tower by the Sea* (1950).

DeJong sustains interest through the long and complex plot of *Bells of the Harbor* by creating exciting episodes, each of which has its own climax. The rescue of the sailors, the adventure of hiding a yellow sailboat that belongs to the captain of the wrecked ship from the dike inspector who wants to claim it, Dirk's race for the doctor after his sister swallows poison, the ice holiday with its impending tragedy, the night flight of the people from Weirom and the subsequent robbery, the chase and capture of the thief, and a trip with the fishing fleet are subplots within the main plot, the story of Jan's escape from the sea and his acceptance by a loving family.

Perhaps the high point of the book is the description of the ice holiday, foreshadowing one which figures prominently in *Far Out the Long Canal*. DeJong is at his best in depicting this occasion of joyful freedom among people who normally lead lives restricted by weather, space, economic hardship, and religion. Rarely does the ice freeze hard enough for skating on the canals, for conditions must be just right. Sometimes several years pass without a good freeze; though the weather is often cold enough, the wind must also be from the right direction. When the combination happens and lasts long enough to produce good ice, the normally self-disciplined, dutiful, religious people celebrate with an ecstasy that lighter hearted folk could not know. School turns out, church services are cancelled, women leave their kitchens and

placent about the sea, begin to worry; when conditions change faster than expected, Pier puts his emergency evacuation plan into action and narrowly saves all the people as the ice breaks up under the awesome power of wind and tide. The juxtaposition of great joy and great danger gives the ice holiday passages in DeJong's stories a level of excitement and vitality usually available only in more contrived situations or more imaginative literature.

Despite the impending threat of the sea and weather on the northern coast of Holland, the people have a strong feeling of permanence which comes largely from their sense of history. Meindert DeJong's parents had just moved to Wierum when a flood destroyed houses and lives. When his father took the older children out to survey the damage, his brother David asked why people continued to live there. His father answered, "Because they've lived here for centuries and centuries." Having been uprooted in his own life, DeJong is perhaps more sensitive to the security that comes from a link to the past. Characters in his stories that take place on midwestern farms or in suburban settings and downtown apartments do not have the same sense of history as characters in his Dutch stories.

History, for DeJong's characters, is fragmentary. It resides in the memories of the living and in songs and legends, but sometimes, as in *The Tower by the Sea,* only a few lines of a song are known, and sometimes no one in the community can remember an event. In *Bells of the Harbor,* the villagers do not know if the sea has ever frozen over before. Their sense of antiquity tells them it would be unlikely for nature to produce a new event, but no one remembers such a freeze in the past. They are conscious of how fragmentary their knowledge of history is because they also have evidence, though no concrete record, of a great flood that wiped out half the town: the tower now stands by the dike rather than in the center of the village, and one time many graves of people of all ages were discovered—undoubtedly victims of a flood which no one alive remembers. Still, the past is a source of wisdom for which old people are especially valued. When Lina in *The Wheel on the School* sets out to solve the problem of why storks do not nest in her village, Shora, she uses clues from the past which she gets from talking with an old woman and from a picture on a piece of old crockery.

Religion is another source of security for the people in DeJong's stories. DeJong's view is special because, having experienced life in the Dutch culture, he can see both from within and, more critically, from his removed perspective as an

Front cover for a later edition of DeJong's Newbery Medal-winning novel (Harper & Row)

everyone goes to the canals for the holiday. Dignity, authority, and obedience have little power on the ice. Races, champions, and prizes, along with colorful tents where concessionaires sell oranges and hot chocolate, contribute to the festive mood. People tour nearby towns via the frozen canals and relatives who do not see each other often are able to visit. However, each such holiday is too short, and even as they revel, skaters realize that before they are ready, the ice will be gone. Their consciousness of the ephemeral quality of an ice holiday creates a seize-the-day attitude that allows them to set aside their normal routine. When the wind shifts or the sun appears, the ice will break up.

In *Bells of the Harbor* the potential for tragedy is greater than usual. For the first time in remembered history, the sea has frozen. At the peak of the festivities, competitors, spectators, concessionaires, even horses and sleighs are on the sea-ice far from land. Tension builds as Grandfather Tjerk and Mighty Pier, who know better than to be com-

American citizen. That DeJong sees religion as a source of strength, character, and cultural roots is evident both from the scenes in his books in which people gather at the church after a crisis to thank God for their deliverance and from the fact that he has written two Bible-story books for children. However, the foolish adherence of his parents to the church schools and community in Michigan, when in fact the Christian Dutch immigrants abused and took advantage of them, must have made young Meindert conscious of a gap between the ideals of religion and some of its practical manifestations. As he depicts religion in his stories, it sometimes is a vehicle for expression of the best in people, as in *Shadrach* (1953); other times it reflects their shortcomings. The minister in *Bells of the Harbor* interprets the threat to the dike from the ice breakup as the wrath of God because people enjoyed an ice holiday instead of going to church. He further endangers their lives by calling on them to demonstrate their faith by kneeling in the square as the ice batters the dike and pushes over the top. Because DeJong offers no support to the minister's interpretation of events, his momentary stand seems foolish, more a function of his sense of guilt than of insight. Insufficient information and an active imagination produce fearful concepts that can be contained only by truth, reason, and fact. Such concepts in their worst form are dangerous.

Bells of the Harbor, DeJong's longest book, is not as good as some of his later work, most notably *The Wheel on the School* and *Far Out the Long Canal*, although it adequately rewards readers who attempt it. It provides an interesting perspective to a student of DeJong's entire canon because it introduces more fully than *Dirk's Dog, Bello* his fictional portrayal of the north coast of Holland and the interaction between its people and their culture.

In 1941, the same year *Bells of the Harbor* appeared, DeJong also published another long novel. *Wheels over the Bridge* is drawn from DeJong's experiences on his midwestern farm. Gone is the security of the big, competent father figure and the permanence of centuries. This world reflects the insecurity of DeJong's American childhood, characterized by poverty and a father who was not powerful, and DeJong's efforts to farm during the Depression. Carl Anderson's family rents a small farm from a miserly man named Mr. Drake. Although Carl's father, Steve, has improved the farm in the few years he has worked it, he cannot get out of debt to Drake. Steve is not a good businessman; when there is no food for the calves, he brings

home from an auction a pet beef cow and a piano, the property of Kelly, a little girl on a nearby farm whose parents have died and who is being sent to relatives in New York. Steve bought the items because Kelly hopes to reclaim them some day. Matters are complicated for the Anderson family by the fact that Mr. Drake is so stingy he will not provide the means necessary for success; without feed, the cows will not thrive. He even denies them use of firewood from the land they rent, and there seems no way they can ever make progress to pay off their debt. Kelly's hopes of returning to the country and Steve's of becoming a successful farmer seem equally improbable. After all their best efforts, including some desperation endeavors, fail and it seems that Steve will have to go back to a factory job he hates, Kelly offers him her family farm. Her relatives, she is sure, will agree to let her return there since they have no need for her or the farm. There the Andersons can escape the tyranny of Drake and will have resources necessary to make a success, and Kelly will have a family again and a place for her cow and piano. The resolution is happy but contrived.

The Cat That Walked a Week (1943) is a sparse depiction of a mother and son who live in a tall apartment building in the city. Except for the white sink and the piano, the reader is not allowed to visualize anything in the home setting. Connected to the ground only by an elevator, these people seem to have no cultural context. There is no other family or community except for the strangers that live in the next apartment and the anonymous radio listeners who follow the radio broadcast announcements about the child's lost cat and then call the station to report sightings of it. Perhaps DeJong isolated the characters to make the child's relationship to his cat more important, or maybe he was writing about a setting he did not know from firsthand experience. Whatever the cause, the result is anemic compared to the richly detailed environments of some of his other books.

The plot involves a simple repetitive structure, which young children enjoy. In that respect it is similar to *The Big Goose and the Little White Duck*. After neighbors, disturbed by the noise of the boy and the cat, drop the cat in the country, it makes its way home across difficult terrain. The improbable manner in which the cat orients itself on the journey by climbing a tree each day for a sighting of the apartment building; the way it crosses a swamp on a log, repeatedly falling off and then climbing back on to push it toward the other side, detract from the book's credibility. There are other flaws in the book too; for example, the author describes a little girl in a dress, but the illustrator shows her on the opposite page dressed in pants. John Rowe Townsend, in *A Sense of Story* (1971), accepts the "superficial realism" of *The Cat That Walked a Week* as having the "logic of a modern fairy tale." Perhaps such logic does make acceptable the succession of calls from all the people the cat encounters on its way, but it does not adequately explain how the cat can see the apartment building in the city across such a long distance. These flaws indicate a distance between the writer and his material too great for him to do his best work.

The Little Stray Dog (1943) is another pale offering, though the situation in the book is characteristic of DeJong's stories. A little boy, Ronnie, wants to help a hungry, stray dog, but he recognizes the dog as one that has angered the neighborhood with his garbage foraging; the child's perspective, more empathetic than the adults' views, is more attuned to the dog's plight. His recognition of the dog, however, causes it to be captured, and he wants to set him free. He is assisted by an old lady and a fat man, who accomplish a generous and improbable solution. Ronnie's world—his life with a single, working mother and a babysitter—is not made real. DeJong does not create that world for us to see as he did in better books. The characters are flat and the joy of an animal who finds a home strikes no sympathetic chord in the reader because the reader has not entered that world with any emotional involvement.

Having escaped military obligation in Holland, Meindert DeJong was inducted into the U.S. Army Air Force in World War II. Instead of being sent to Holland as an interpreter, as he had expected, he went to China and spent three years in Peishiyi as historian for the American Composite Wing of the Fourteenth Air Force. From this experience comes the setting for *The House of Sixty Fathers* (1956), written in China but not published until fifteen years later because the story was considered too realistic and too harsh for a children's book.

In the first book he wrote after returning from China, DeJong discovered the empathic mode which characterizes his best work. The protagonist of *Billy and the Unhappy Bull* (1946) is an only child whose family has recently moved from the city to the country. They are unfamiliar with the new way of life, and their rural neighbors view them disdainfully as "the city people." On a neighboring farm Billy soon discovers a starving bull, which belongs to an elderly couple who have lost

Dust jacket for a later edition of DeJong's novel about a Chinese boy lost behind enemy lines during the Japanese invasion of China (Harper & Row)

most of their property in a fire. They have no means of feeding the huge animal through the winter, but the old man is too sentimentally attached to the bull to do "the kindest thing" and shoot him. The needs of the child and the needs of the bull complement each other and produce a moving relationship between human and animal of the type which characterizes many of DeJong's stories.

Despite some improbable events in the plot, the fictional world of this book seems plausible. DeJong creates the place for us; Billy's house, the root cellar, and the bull's stall are places that we can envision. Characters are developed beyond the flat, nameless figures of *The Little Stray Dog*. The old people, the Shephards, have distinct personalities. Mr. Shephard makes decisions with his heart rather than his head, and his wife tries to be more practical but is really just as softhearted. It is easy to understand the motives of Billy's parents as they try to manipulate him into wanting the bicycle that his father has chosen for his birthday, as a means of lessening his devotion to the bull, and DeJong subtly allows the reader to respond to the loneliness of Billy's mother as she eavesdrops on the telephone party line just to hear other human voices. Here DeJong seems to have found his way into his creation—seems to have found an intuitive approach to his work.

To a greater extent than in any previous book, in *Billy and the Unhappy Bull* DeJong attempts to show the processes of a child's mind. Largely through objective presentation of actions and conversation, the workings of Billy's mind are revealed to the reader. For example, in his first talk with Mrs. Shephard, after she has told of her plan to shoot the bull, should things come to that, Billy learns that her birthday is the day before his. Although the conversation shifts to his father's plan to plant trees on his thirty acres, Billy's concern for the bull is obvious. Lamenting his father's preference for trees over animals, Billy says, "Wish my dad and mom liked animals." And then, still worried about Mrs. Shephard's plan, he exploits the commonality suggested to him by the coincidence of their birthdays: "We do [like animals], don't we?" DeJong uses the word *demanded* to describe the way Billy says that sentence. It indicates Billy's desperate need to see that he and Mrs. Shephard are alike. He would not shoot the bull; therefore Mrs. Shephard will not shoot the bull either. As he leaves he turns back to confirm his conclusion: "You don't really want to shoot the old bull—not really?" She answers, "Why, no, Billy. It would only be because I have to, not because I want to. Why I like the poor old fellow as much as you do." Her negative response has hinged on the word *want*. She will not kill the bull out of any desire to do so; she has not denied that she may do it out of kindness to prevent his further suffering, but Billy's interpretation conforms to his strong desire, and he feels that she has confirmed his prior conclusion: "Oh. Why then you'll never shoot him." DeJong has allowed Billy to reveal himself, a skill that requires the author to see both as Billy would see and as an objective observer would see.

Billy's limited perspective functions within the larger context available to the reader. The reader has the objectivity to see, for example, that Billy's father wants to use the bicycle to distract Billy from his single-minded concern for the bull. The reader sees through the father's threat to box up the bicycle and send it back and his several ploys designed to attract Billy's attention to the bicycle. The intensity of Billy's anguish over the bull's plight is conveyed by his renunciation of such a grand temptation as the bicycle. DeJong's control of the dual perspective in this book marks an achievement in the development of his craft.

Four years passed after the appearance of *Billy and the Unhappy Bull* before the publication of *Good Luck Duck* in 1950. Like *The Big Goose and the Little White Duck, The Cat That Walked a Week,* and *The Little Stray Dog,* it is for the younger child. A storyteller's voice opens this tale in intimate conversational manner: "It is a quiet valley. It is a cozy house. I mean the little white house where Timothy lives with his mother and father. I mean the quiet valley three miles down Cable's Road, past Abraham's Wood, and just beyond the blueberry-sycamore swamp. That valley."

Having established rapport with his listener, the narrator recedes from the foreground, but his description of the quiet valley, where birds sing "only in the morning and a little at night" and where rabbits play (though "rabbits can play the hardest games, and still not make a bit of noise"), has established the idyllic setting. The repetition of sounds and phrases and the simple repetitive sentence structure ("The streetcar does not get there. The bus does not go that far.") create a soothing, lyrical tone, though the opening quickly gives way to the noise, color, and activity of the fair. The contrast between calmness and excitement is the basis for the story about a boy who lives in a valley so quiet that he needs as a companion a duck who hates noise and needs a peaceful home. The bright illustrations in this book and the happy solutions to the problems of the various people Timothy encounters with the duck, capped off by a joyful trolley ride, make this book the lightest of DeJong's stories. Its consistent, contemporary fairy-tale tone does not cause the same credibility problems that the mixture of fairy tale and realism did in *The Cat That Walked a Week.*

DeJong produced another book in 1950, *The Tower by the Sea,* which, other than having a storyteller as narrator, bears little resemblance to *Good Luck Duck.* Perhaps based on a North Sea legend, it is as dark a tale as the other was light, frightening in its glimpse of the evil in human nature. The narrator presents it as a story which the nursemaids of Katverloren tell to explain the unusual weather vane made to resemble a cradle that once stood atop their village tower. On the cradle stood a white cat with a blue jewel eye, its paw pointing into the wind. The cat and cradle no longer exist, but grandmothers in Katverloren still sing two lines from an otherwise forgotten song:

There's a cradle rocking, rocking
There's a cradle gently rocking in the sunlit sea.

As the narrator introduces the story, he transports the reader into the past with the mesmerizing quality of his repetitive sentence structure. The rhythm repeats the motion of the rocking cradle: "It is a sad tale, and a cruel tale, for it happened in the olden days, and they were cruel times, and there was little enough of mercy."

The nursemaids' story is about the powers of superstition and fear and concerns an old woman who lives close to a graveyard. Believing that all God's creatures have a right to live, she has taken in a magpie and a cat with a blue eye and taught them to live in peace. Such an unnatural alliance disturbs the superstitious townspeople. She also befriends Crazy Alice, the lighthouse keeper's wife whose loneliness and childlessness have deluded her to grieve for a dead baby she never had. Alice also frightens the superstitious villagers by wandering in the graveyard at night. Because the old woman is different from the townspeople, she becomes a focus of superstition. When the children in the town become ill, the villagers blame the old woman and tie her to a stake to burn her as a witch, but a miraculous event stops them.

Poor demented Alice had heard rumors that all the children in the village were dying, all but the Burgomaster's child. Because the Burgomaster and his family lived isolated away from the townspeople, his child had not taken the fever that was actually spread by a traveling barber. Alice attempts to further protect the baby by stealing it, cradle and all, and taking it to her island home for safety. She also saves the white cat with the blue eye, who has been tormented by villagers. In a storm on the way to the island, Alice's boat capsizes, and the baby's cradle, with the white cat perched on top, falls into the sea. Trying to keep its feet dry the cat jumps back and forth on the cradle, keeping it steady on the waves. The discovery of the cat and the cradle, with the baby safe inside, stops the people just as they are about to set fire to the stake.

The Burgomaster erects a weathervane depicting the cat and the cradle and commands the people to leave the woodpile and charred rags as a symbol of what they almost did. The villagers are so ashamed that they secretly and gradually dismantle the woodpile. The weathervane, however, lasted many years, and long after it was gone and the tower that held it had crumbled, the fable remains to remind listeners of the potential for evil that resides within them.

The novel tells a compelling story with great skill; its power resides in its universality. As controlled and distanced as the story is, it must have held considerable interest for DeJong; as an immigrant, he himself experienced the cruelty of people toward one who is different. He shows that same kind of behavior among chickens in *Along Came a Dog* (1958). If a chicken looks different for any reason, the others will turn on it and try to destroy it. With chickens such behavior seems a mindless, instinctual act, not so reprehensible as it would be in humans. Even so, DeJong's human character in *Along Came a Dog* expresses the anger that the author himself must sometimes have felt: "it gets you at times—so much stupidity. And so much meanness because of the stupidity."

DeJong frequently alludes in his books to superstitions of the fishermen in Holland. One of their fears was of ghosts, and it is interesting to note that DeJong's grandfather's house, where his parents moved just two weeks before his birth, stood in a cluster of buildings apart from the rest of the town and so close to the cemetery that the villagers would pass along the street there only in pairs. That DeJong places the old woman's house in *The Tower by the Sea* next to the graveyard may be only to heighten the credibility of the villagers' fears, but it may also suggest an emotional identification that DeJong felt to her. He often focuses sympathetically on a character who lives on the fringe of the community, either literally or figuratively, such as the tramp in *Smoke above the Lane* (1951).

Like the tramp in *The Little Cow and the Turtle* (1955), he is a rather idealized figure, who seems to have chosen his life-style for its freedom and independence. DeJong's tramps bear little resemblance to the desperate men who drifted during the Depression looking for work. These fictional tramps seem happy to make do with what comes their way and to share with fellow travelers—in this case, even if that companion is a skunk. *Smoke above the Lane* is an entertaining story for younger children with the distinctive DeJong theme of two lone creatures becoming a kind of family for each other.

With *Shadrach* (1953) DeJong reached the fullness of the empathic process for which he is noted, presenting the intensity of life from a child's level. This aspect of DeJong's writing is supplemented, beginning with *Shadrach,* by the illustrations of Maurice Sendak. Although DeJong had good illustrators for all his books, it was in Sendak that he found his most compatible partner. They worked together on seven books, the last of which DeJong dedicated "To Maurice Sendak, who illuminates my things because we are a pair." DeJong has said that his own childhood was the source for his childlike perspective: "you cannot stare over an adult fence . . . and get back into the essence of childhood." In *Shadrach* he used that "rapport with [his] subconscious" which served him in his best creative work.

DeJong's own childhood experience is evident in *Shadrach* in the character of Davie, a child who has just recovered from an illness and who wants a pet rabbit more than anything else. The Davie in the story seems to be a blend of Meindert and his brother David. A small, sickly child, Davie worries about the sacrilege of his applying the words of a hymn to a rabbit. Rem, the energetic, careless, older brother of the story, who picks up the rabbit by his ears and who helps himself to a pole from Grandpa's secret room, is modeled no doubt after Remmeren, for DeJong dedicated the book to him. Perhaps other characters too had their prototypes in DeJong's childhood: the grandparents, who indulge him and offer a less restrictive alternative to home; the mother who loves her delicate son and insists on his resting for a long period each day; and the father, whose bedtime game suggests the name for the rabbit. (Davie's father would toss him in the air saying "Shadrach," without letting him go. Then he would toss him again, saying "Meshach." The third time his father would say "and A-bed-we-go," and throw him in the air to bounce on the bed.)

In *Shadrach* DeJong completely involves the reader in the wonderful intensity of Davie's world. We learn just how long a week of waiting is for a child; indeed the reader awaits the arrival of Shadrach for half the book because DeJong presents time as Davie perceives it. By the time the rabbit which Davie's grandfather has ordered for him arrives, Davie's anticipation is excruciatingly high. In Davie's mind the rabbit is so marvelous that his feelings find expression in the words from a joyful hymn: "the fairest of ten thousand to my soul." Davie worries that it might be wicked to think of a rabbit in that religious context, but the moment in DeJong's stories when a child apprehends the wonder of life itself in the being of an animal is truly an epiphany for which a religious context is appropriate. Davie experiences a full range of emotions, from anxiety, to joy, worry, guilt, fear, love— all well-grounded in realistic situations—all real enough for the reader to share.

The intensity of Davie's feelings comes in part from the fact that they are his alone; no one else in his world can understand the full extent of his feelings for the rabbit. In fact, only a sophisticated reader will be sensitive to the extent to which DeJong developed the subtle motivation behind Davie's feelings, much of which stems from his working out with the rabbit the feelings of love and anxiety that his mother shows for him.

Despite Davie's loneliness, there are people who care about him, and he has moments of understanding with them that are joyful and touching. As he and his father set off for church, his father is thinking separate thoughts, and Davie is worried about his rabbit escaping from the hutch. From his private thoughts his father eventually becomes aware of how worried Davie is, and he responds: "I've a notion that even if you and I went on to church, that preacher could preach and preach, but I'd be in that farmhouse I'm building, and you'd be in your rabbit hutch with your little rabbit." So they skip church and work on the hutch instead. To find that he and his father are alike and that his father understands his anxiety is an enlightening experience for Davie. DeJong shows how special the feeling is to Davie by having him savor those words of his father's and make a kind of song with them. From within the child's perspective, DeJong is able to portray Davie's realization that he had a kind and loving father. Similar instances of communion happen with his mother and with his grandparents to create a warm feeling of family support.

The plot of *Shadrach* is very simple. A boy waits for arrival of a new rabbit, and when it arrives, he takes care of it. The rabbit escapes and finally is found. On the framework of such simple events, however, DeJong develops the real complexity of Davie's emotional world so masterfully that the reader, too, participates in Davie's experience and shares his feelings.

If a reader stays with *Hurry Home Candy* (1953) until the conclusion, it is not because he is rewarded periodically with warm, happy feelings. It must instead be that the story of a lost dog named Candy is so compelling that a reader cannot forsake it, painful as it is. With Candy, DeJong exercises his process of empathic creativity on an animal. Of course DeJong cannot know how it feels to be a dog, but he may know how it feels to be lost, to be shut away from the comforts of a home, to be an interloper on someone else's turf. It takes only a small leap then to invest those feelings in a dog, a leap DeJong makes so gracefully that it escapes the reader's notice.

His limited third-person point of view works very well to show how the world looks to a puppy—or how DeJong imagines a puppy would see it. From his view, a broom looms large and threatening, and the mother and father who discipline the dog appear terribly insensitive. The realism in this book is unrelenting, revealing even the children who love the puppy to be fickle; after a year they prefer a monetary reward over recovery of the lost dog. The only relief to the sustained suffering and repeated frustrations to this little dog's chances for a place to belong comes at the end of the book when a man who had experienced abuse himself takes Candy home and patiently works to build trust in an animal for whom it was almost too late.

DeJong broadens his perspective in another Dutch story, *The Wheel on the School* (1954), and looks at a whole community as he did in *Bells of the Harbor,* though this time he exercises more control over his material. Beginning with a child's question, the story expands outward, as if the notion of the wheel, which figures so prominently in the story, suggested the structure of the novel. When Lina asks her question about why storks do not nest in the village of Shora, her schoolteacher responds, "When we wonder, we can make things happen." Together they initiate a research project that ultimately involves the whole community. In the process the reader comes to see each child in the school and even members of the community as realized individuals. The children learn from the collective wisdom and experience of people in the village and, in so doing, enlist the villagers in their effort to bring storks to Shora. The sharing experience enriches the lives of all involved as the children successfully prepare a nesting site and rescue two storks from the sea, but by then the storks are only a symbol of making things happen.

As in the other Dutch stories, the characters and the way of life and the landscape are distinctively Dutch. Place is not a separate piece of the book but the fabric of it. The sea and the weather; the tower and the dike and the steep roofs; Grandmother Sibble III, Janus, Douwa, and the tin man are all part of that particular place, and yet, because human nature is the same there as here, then as now, American readers can take pleasure in the interaction between the children and the villagers and in the transformation that occurs in Shora. Because *The Wheel on the School* won the Newbery Medal, it is the best known of DeJong's books and provides a good starting point to introduce a new

reader to DeJong's fiction.

The Little Cow and the Turtle (1955) celebrates life, adventure, and loyalty to a friend. Not the average, complacent, cud-chewing milk cow, the little cow of the book's title likes to play and discover new things. The hard-working farm couple who own it enjoy the antics of their pet even though she does not give much milk. The cow's encounters with hoboes and children provide interesting episodes and develop her friendly nature. The book's main interest, however, develops around the cow's concern for an old mud turtle that she discovers on its journey to a new pond. The overland trip is long and laborious for the turtle. The frisky little cow and the slow, old turtle seem curious companions, and the farm couple enjoy watching the progress of the turtle each day as the little cow patiently accompanies it. Suspense builds as the turtle approaches the railroad tracks where the little cow's devotion to the old turtle is tested and proven. One of the minor books in DeJong's canon, *The Little Cow and the Turtle* is nevertheless a fresh, fun, and warmhearted story.

The House of Sixty Fathers (1956) is a departure from the Dutch and rural American settings of most of DeJong's books, but in other ways it is typical of his work. In his trying to find his way home, Tien Pao is a human version of Candy (in *Hurry Home Candy*). DeJong is again writing from the child's perspective—no matter that this child is Chinese and his home is a sampan. In fact DeJong seems to be at his best in establishing the commonality of people across great distance and cultural differences.

Tien Pao has fled with his family during the Japanese invasion of China. As Tien Pao remembers their escape under Japanese fire, the reader realizes that he is viewing a world remote from his own experience. Part of the interest in this book, as in the Holland stories, is in learning—not in an academic sense but in an experiential way—about an unfamiliar part of the world. Tien Pao is different from the average American child, but he is essentially the same. He has parents who worry about him and make rules that restrict his freedom. He also has pets, even if they are ducks and a pig, and he makes up games to pass time when he is alone. More important, he thinks and feels as all people do, and on the basis of this common ground the book explores what it is like to be a child lost behind enemy lines in a war-ravaged land.

The plot is structured around Tien Pao's journey back home after the sampan on which he is waiting for his parents breaks loose and floats down the river below Japanese lines. Working his way back through occupied territory, Tien Pao witnesses many horrors, but he also gives and receives help, acts of human kindness in the midst of inhuman atrocities.

Tien Pao's perspective is maintained throughout the book. He watches from a mountainside as a plane strafes a line of troops on the road. The troops are Japanese, whose planes had shelled his village just as an American plane now shells them. The horror of killing is awful for Tien Pao no matter which side is suffering: "Tien Pao dug his fingers into his ears, but it was as if the screaming went on inside him. His skin went tight with horror, but he kept looking, he couldn't tear his eyes away." The reader sees what he sees and feels what he feels. At times Tien Pao is shocked beyond interpretation or evaluation: "Men fell, horses fell. Men tumbled off cannon and the cannon went over them behind the madly plunging horses. Horses broke loose from their traces and reared and floundered in the deep, muddy ooze of the rice paddies. One, wounded and maddened, thrashed over the bank into the river and sank from sight. The river turned red where the horse had gone under."

It is as if Tien Pao's mind cannot process such horror, but his eyes cannot turn away, so the reader is barraged with a rapid succession of objective details. Later, as he watches a downed pilot's escape, he is able to think again. From a hillside view he can see the wounded American airman running from approaching Japanese soldiers, and he evaluates the objective details he sees. He thinks, for example, that the soldiers will not expect anyone to escape from the burning wreckage, and, as he sees a Japanese soldier fall, he knows that it is a trick. Tien Pao's screamed warning, although in a foreign language, saves the American's life. DeJong's ability to show how the mind works under stress contributes to the realism of this novel.

Perhaps we are most aware of Tien Pao's point of view when he encounters Americans. Never having seen chewing gum before, he approaches it as a real puzzle:

> Tien Pao put the candy in his mouth. It lay sweet and thin on his tongue, but it did not begin to melt at all. He took it out again to look at it, turned it over—it stuck to all his fingers. Tien Pao stuck his fingers in his mouth to tear the candy off with his teeth. But the moment it was in his mouth it did not stick at all. . . . He chewed and chewed, but the stuff simply would not chew away.

> At last Tien Pao gulped and swallowed it. He rubbed his stomach to show . . . how good it had been.

This limited point of view allows the reader to see not only how a familiar item like gum appears foreign to someone who encounters it for the first time, but also how something unfamiliar—like war—might appear to any child. In this manner DeJong bridges the cultural gap, which is the main theme of the novel. To Tien Pao the house of sixty fathers is a big room with many beds, but the reader recognizes it as a barracks. For Tien Pao it is also a safe place where the airmen give him food, a bed, and assistance in his search. As such, to Tien Pao it is *house* in the larger sense of family.

The "house of sixty fathers" is a symbol of the bridge between cultures; it seems to offer for Tien Pao as much of a homecoming as can be expected amid the chaos of war. This sense of "family," in the larger context of human beings who help each other during a time of crisis, has been prepared for throughout the book—in Tien Pao's encounters with guerillas who lead him through enemy lines, an old hag who gives him not one but two bowls of rice, a young woman who bathes him, a mad woman who leads him to a train, a soldier who makes a place for him on the crowded train, and Tien Pao himself as he helps the downed American airman.

A sense of completion comes when Tien Pao arrives at the barracks and feels safe among the sixty airmen, but DeJong continues the story, and Tien Pao is reunited with his parents after he spots them among thousands of refugees. This ending seems not only improbable but a flaw in the structure of the novel. Added to the other improbability that the airman Tien Pao helps turns out to be the first American he encountered and mistook for a river god is just too much coincidence. Of course had Tien Pao not found his parents there would have been a sense of fracture and permanent loss, but that ending would have been compatible with the reality of war. The contrived reunion is not.

Despite the flawed ending, *The House of Sixty Fathers* is one of DeJong's best books. It well deserves the Children's Book Award it won in 1956 and the critical acclaim it has received. It will undoubtedly be a classic among war stories for children and among fictional views of other cultures.

Nowhere does DeJong display his skill in animal characterization to better advantage than in his next book, *Along Came a Dog* (1958). As in *The Little Cow and the Turtle*, the main characters are animals and adults; there are no children in this book. The relationship that develops between a dog and a hen is based on the sort of mutual need that DeJong explores most often in relationships between animals and humans. The dog is a stray who needs a home, and the hen needs protection because it is an outcast from the flock. The hen belongs to a kind of farmhand who talks to animals and who needs companionship. Because dogs have killed his previous flock of chickens, leaving the red hen as the only survivor, he reluctantly drives away the dog, which he might otherwise have taken in. But the wise old dog, determined to make his home there, finds his way back and hides in a storage bin.

DeJong attributes a rather high degree of rationality to the dog. Having shown that the dog is smart through a series of incidents—such as his finding his way back to the farm, his associating the sound of the car with the man and coordinating his movements with the man's behavior patterns in order not to be discovered, and his shrewdly taking advantage of a hiding place he has discovered by accident—DeJong is then able to show the dog using logical thought in a way that is quite believable.

The man has unwittingly shut an injured chicken in the storage bin where the dog is hiding. The frightened hen hysterically beats her way to a rafter and nervously lays an egg, which lands with a splat and becomes a surprise meal for the hungry dog, but the dog also realizes a truth beyond the immediate fact of the egg: "The dog looked up at the chicken. He looked at the spot where the egg had splattered, stood as if thinking. He looked up at the chicken again, and now his tail waved. He had made a great discovery—chickens laid eggs, and eggs were food, tasty food. And food was his problem—the everlasting, everyday problem." Having identified the egg with the chicken, the dog later tries to help himself to one of the little red hen's eggs, but she puts up a great squawk, asserting her possession of it. The dog then concludes that broken eggs are for eating, but whole eggs belong to the hen. Having figured out that law, he abides by it.

Portraying the hen's perspective would seem to offer a greater challenge because chickens are far less intelligent than dogs, but DeJong creates a believable character and places her in situations that arouse sympathy. When the hen stumbles down the ramp to the chicken yard, she is puzzled, as is the reader, at her difficulty. She stands looking at her feet, none the wiser for her observation. However, the farmhand soon realizes that her toes

have been frozen off, even though she continues, in her ignorance, to try things she is no longer capable of doing. A proud rooster commands the hen to follow where she cannot go and punishes her for not obeying, and the flock attacks her for being different. However, the hen eventually triumphs and leads her chicks from their hidden nest to the barnyard despite the threatening presence of a hawk.

To the dog, the hen's vulnerability provides a duty: to guard the hen, and that duty defines his place in life. He belongs to the hen because she needs him, and he will tolerate his poor living conditions, eating chicken feed and hiding from sight, for the sake of his symbiotic relationship with the hen. Though his lot improves when the man finally discovers him and adopts him, the dog's need to belong, which was strong enough for him to endure deprivation, appeals to the reader's sympathy.

The Last Little Cat (1961) is another homecoming story but one told from a greater distance. A narrator tells the story to a young child, and the rhythm of his speech pattern, his interjections of "believe it!," and his vocal inflections, suggested by dashes and capital letters, "—THERE WAS THE WORLD," continually keep his presence between the reader and the material. A story of rejection, *The Last Little Cat* tells of the search for a home by the runt of a litter. Born in a chicken nest in a kennel barn, the little kitten cannot get enough to eat. As the other kittens grow, the little one gets weaker. He falls into a blind old dog's cage on the shelf below and for a time enjoys the dog's food and the warmth of another creature, but one day he finds himself locked out of the barn, and he gets lost wandering from house to house, looking for a home. Each place rejects him until he finally ends up back where he started and is reunited with the old dog. The harsh indifference of the mother cat is tempered by his adoption by the kind man who owns the place and who celebrates the little cat's arrival on his birthday. While there is some suspense in the story, there is no pain. Although DeJong claims never to think about his readers, he does seem to qualify his realistic approach at times when writing for the very young.

The Singing Hill (1962) is one of his best books, for he deftly and economically develops the world of Raymond, both its inner realm and its external landscape. Raymond is the quintessential DeJong child, but nowhere is this child drawn more sensitively than in *The Singing Hill*. In many ways this book is like *Shadrach* with an American setting. Raymond's family has just moved to the country, not to farm but to live in a rented house on land that is planted in corn right up to their doorstep. Raymond's father is a salesman who travels during the week; his mother, who obviously feels uncomfortable in the country, stays busy with household work. His siblings, Martin and Shirley, go off to school each day, and Raymond, who has no role to play in this new world, is left alone to discover its dimensions and his place in it. His task and his size in relation to it are signified in the image of Raymond returning home through the cornfield after walking part way to school with Martin and Shirley. Afraid of becoming lost, he cannot see the boundaries of the cornfield, nor does he yet realize that corridors can be aids to orientation. The cornfield maze also has imagined dangers, as his brother and sister tease him with the possibility of starving to death if he were to get lost and fall into the "skunk" hole.

Although Raymond is isolated, his environment is not a hostile world like Tien Pao's. In fact, Raymond discovers his own competence; he learns that he can traverse the cornfield and that he can establish relationships with others. He begins in a small way with a game he uses to deal with his fears. Drawing a square around himself, he chants,

Click, clock,
Turn the lock.
Shut the window,
Close the door.
And click-clock,
Turn the lock,
and nothing can get in.

He teaches his technique to his mother, too, when she is afraid of crawling things that she imagines might be in the cellar and learns that not only can he control his own fear but he can help her control hers as well. He also helps his father with a much larger and more awesome danger: an angry bull. When his father is chased by the bull, Raymond climbs the fence and hollers, distracting it long enough for his father to escape. Although he had not known what he was doing at the time, in retrospect he is proud to have saved his father from such a menace. Gradually his experiences give him confidence in his own ability. He takes his biggest step toward independence, however, for the sake of a horse who has no shelter from a storm. Raymond disobeys his parents, an act which, for him, takes considerable motivation, but he acts out of a strong will and he is prepared to accept any consequences. He courageously rides the big horse

through a driving storm to his house, where he intends to shelter him in an old stall. His assertive act indicates his new level of confidence in himself to act in this environment.

His family receives him with understanding and support, and Raymond is happy to have helped the horse and to be understood by his parents. His anxiety gives way to joy and he sings a natural song that celebrates his world—the season, the people, the place, and his own accomplishment in it.

The Singing Hill has elements of both *Shadrach* and *Billy and the Unhappy Bull*. All three depict a young person's independent action motivated by concern for an animal. In each book DeJong creates the child's world in its outer dimensions of landscape, family, and community and in its inner dimensions of fear, love, and joy. Although the outer world may be a different one from the place where most readers live, the inner world of the child may be shared.

Nobody Plays with a Cabbage (1962) stands apart from DeJong's other books and seems the least characteristic of his work as a whole. Intended for the younger child, the story has its genesis in a piece DeJong wrote in college, the elements of which reappeared thirty years later in what DeJong felt was his "most graceful little book yet." Jim Jordan is a solitary child who, instead of caring for a rabbit or a bull, tends a cabbage, the sole survivor in his vegetable garden. Jim is small enough and patient enough to see that a cabbage is the center of a whole cycle of activity. A snail and a toad come to live under it; butterflies lay eggs on it; and the caterpillars that hatch from the eggs become food for a wren to take to her babies. The cabbage also makes a fine hiding place for a rabbit. Jim, with his head under the cabbage, makes friends with them all. When the cabbage is mature all the creatures leave, and Jim knows it is time to harvest it. No one else has noticed the slow progress of the cabbage, just as no one has paid close attention to Jim. But when he produces his amazing cabbage, big and beautiful because it has had such good care, everyone looks "at Jim—and at the beautiful cabbage." The cabbage serves the same function for Jim that animals serve for characters in other DeJong stories. It is dependent on him for its care; it gives him companionship through the life that gathered about it; and Jim gains self-confidence through bringing the cabbage to maturity: "I grew it in my garden."

Far Out the Long Canal (1964) is the best of DeJong's Dutch stories, and it deserves a high ranking in his canon. It vividly evokes the magic of an ice holiday in Wierum and Moonta's intense need to join the community of skaters. The action of the novel is restricted to a two-day period. Moonta has yearned for the appearance of ice on the canals because he was ill when they froze four years before. Therefore he did not learn to skate at the normal time and has reached the age of nine as a nonskater. In the community of Wierum nearly everyone else can skate. Moonta's parents are champion skaters, and in order to feel that he belongs in his family and in the community Moonta needs to learn to skate. As the book opens, the weather seems to be right for ice, and Moonta can hardly contain himself.

Despite his eagerness to learn, obstacles still prevent him. The schoolmaster, not knowing that Moonta was sick during the last freeze, prohibits all but the younger children from getting on the first ice that forms in the area called the skating school. This early ice gives the young ones a chance to learn to skate so that they can go on the canal with everyone else. When Moonta ventures out on the skating school ice, mothers of the younger children shoo him away. Desperate for a chance to learn, he goes too far on the bigger ditches and falls through the thin ice. As punishment and protection against illness, his mother then puts him to bed. However, Moonta's father promises that, if Moonta can learn to skate by then, he will take him on a skating trip to New Church's Pipe the next day after he and Moonta's mother return from the Eleven Towns Tour, an adult skating event. Moonta is thrilled with the prospect because such a trip would be a symbol of his competence as a skater.

Yet another obstacle appears the next day when Moonta's grandfather announces that he wants to go on one last Eleven Towns Tour. Moonta realizes that if his grandfather goes, he will slow his father down, and he will be back too late to go to New Church's Pipe. Although his father's reasoning with Moonta cannot lessen his disappointment, the next day Moonta learns quickly and joins in with the skating community on the canal. In his cockiness, however, he decides to go for New Church's Pipe alone, even though he does not really know what, or where, it is. The ice is already breaking up as Moonta starts on his journey.

The trip is dramatic, and suspense builds as Moonta reaches the pipe and meets his father and grandfather hurrying back from the tour. After his grandfather falls into the icy water, he helps in the rescue, and his chant from atop his father's shoulders sets the pace for a desperate race home. The foolhardiness of his attempt to reach the pipe is

Dust jacket for DeJong's last novel with a Dutch setting, winner of the first National Book Award for children's literature in 1969 (Harper & Row)

tempered by the importance of its meaning to him in the face of so many frustrations. Of equal interest is the description of the ice holiday itself. The contagious joy infects the reader and increases sympathy for Moonta in his desire to be a part of it.

John Rowe Townsend, in *A Sense of Story*, calls *Journey from Peppermint Street* (1968) "the strangest of all [DeJong's] books." The story of a boy named Siebren, it contains many Gothic elements: an old monastery on the edge of a marsh, where a tiny aunt lives with her deaf, giant husband; a lonely night in a room with a well, where a frog is the only company; and a storm that leads Siebren to discover secret passages and a mysterious ointment made by the monks long ago. The strangeness of all these elements is heightened by Siebren's imagination. However extravagant the details might seem, several of them are in fact autobiographical. Meindert was named after a deaf uncle, and when he was born, his brothers were sent to stay with an aunt who lived in an old monastery that had a well in it. Even the storm in the book recalls one which occurred during DeJong's childhood in Wierum. Siebren's father is a builder, as was DeJong's, and the relationship between Siebren and his little brother is similar to the relationship between David and the sickly young Meindert.

The plot of *Journey from Peppermint Street* is structured around a trip that Siebren takes with his grandfather. For Siebren the trip is a vacation from the constant duty of caring for his little brother, Knillis. The plot develops through a series of encounters and external events involving a pack of dogs, a miller, a storekeeper, a woman who lives on the edge of the marsh, and Siebren's tiny Aunt Hinka and deaf Uncle Siebren at the monastery, where a storm hits. An important part of the plot, however, is internal action in Siebren's mind. His mental world is a solitary one, where he struggles with guilt because he erroneously believes he has Knillis's tormenting scalp disorder or worries over the implications of being the "handball of Satan," in his grandfather's words. He works to control his imagination, which runs ungoverned in a place as strange as the monastery at night. The book's eccentric characters and strange events make for good reading, but it is in Siebren's introspection that the reader is most likely to recognize feelings of his own.

Journey from Peppermint Street won the first National Book Award for children's literature, though some critics thought the book too conventional for such distinction. It is true that DeJong worked the same territory that he had explored and developed with earlier books, but that territory was extremely fertile, and DeJong displays in this novel a vitality of vision. It was, however, the last time he went to his native Holland for material.

Critics generally agree that *A Horse Came Running* (1970) is a disappointing book. The events seem interesting enough material: a boy and his beloved, feeble old horse are isolated from the boy's parents when a tornado hits, and they help transport an elderly neighbor to the hospital. Events, however, are not the real material of a DeJong novel; felt experience is. And in this book DeJong fails to make the experiences felt.

In *The Easter Cat* (1971) DeJong again re-creates the magic of childhood when Millicent discovers her Easter cat. She interprets the cat's arrival as a miracle because it appears on Easter morning

Dust jacket for DeJong's 1971 book illustrated by Lillian Hoban (Macmillan)

with her Easter basket, despite the long family restriction against having a cat because of her mother's allergies. The miracle gives way to disappointment as her mother suffers a reaction to the cat, and Millicent runs away, determined not to give up her new pet. The detective who finds Millicent explains rather didactically to the older brothers and the mother what DeJong developed more sensitively and more meaningfully in other books: that as the youngest child in the household, Millicent needs something that needs her. The problem is not solved, but at least Millicent's family has a better understanding of her.

The strained title of *The Almost All-White Rabbity Cat* (1972) suggests the ambiguity of this book. Had DeJong abandoned realism altogether and made this story clearly a fantasy, it might have worked, but, because the book is an uncomfortable blend of realism and the incredible, it does not.

DeJong's last three books, *A Horse Came Running*, *The Easter Cat*, and *The Almost All-White Rabbity Cat*, seem to be unsuccessful attempts to return to the vision which informed his earlier works. Since then DeJong has written nothing else, and he says that he believes he has finished, citing his wife Beatrice's death in 1969 and his own age as reasons for retirement. He lives in Chapel Hill, North Carolina, where he and Beatrice built a home.

The acclaim that DeJong's work received in the 1950s and 1960s has now faded. Though he won the International Hans Christian Andersen Award in 1962 for the body of his work, and the Regina Medal of the Catholic Library Association in 1972 for distinguished work in children's literature, John Rowe Townsend's assessment in *A Sense of Story* probably expresses current opinion: "DeJong is a limited and rather old-fashioned writer whose main springs of inspiration clearly come from a childhood which itself was a good many years ago. He is an adequate technician . . . but not a brilliant stylist."

"Limited" and "old-fashioned" may be more accurate descriptions than they appear to be in the negative connotation of Townsend's statement. Limitation is an essential part of DeJong's creative process. In his own words, the artist's task is to put the creation into his own "particular cage of form." Much of DeJong's power derives from his use of the limited perspective; in the sense of range, however, the term "limited" does not apply, as some of his books are dark and ominous while others are light and joyful. DeJong wrote for both younger children and for older ones, and he wrote successful stories of three different cultures. His characters are common and eccentric, male and female, human and animal, adult and child. He explores the psychology of characters as well as their external environment, and he depicts average families, one-parent families, and single adults as well as the lonely child for which he is noted. What limits his work is his use of the child's perspective. That limitation is the source of the realism and the integrity of DeJong's work, not a restriction of range.

DeJong generally does a better job with characters that live in the time period of his own upbringing and in his stories with rural settings, but in his depiction of the inner child he crosses barriers of time and culture. That he communicates with contemporary children and adults, and the fact that his books have been translated into several languages, speak for the universality of his writing. He would no doubt look with disdain at the contemporary guidelines for writers of children's books which stress marketing concerns that have nothing to do with the creative process.

His old-fashionedness may explain the current disinterest in his books. The current literary climate addresses children as a target audience, focusing on age, sex, skin color, language, and sociological group. Often these books depict children in contemporary settings dealing with contemporary problems in isolation, with no sense of a past or a world outside their own immediate experience. DeJong's books, though, will last, because of the pleasure they provide in being transported outside one's own experience into another person's world—on a farm or in Holland long ago or in war-torn China—and finding there someone like ourselves.

References:

Patricia Jean Cianciolo, "Meindert DeJong," *Elementary English*, 45 (October 1968): 725-730; republished in *Authors and Illustrators of Children's Books*, edited by Miriam Hoffman and Eva Samuels (New York: Bowker, 1972), pp. 115-121;

David Cornel DeJong, "My Brother Meindert," in *Newbery Medal Books: 1922-1955*, edited by Bertha Mahoney Miller and Elinor Whitney Field (Boston: Horn Book, 1955), pp. 427-433;

DeJong, *With a Dutch Accent* (New York: Harper, 1944);

John Rowe Townsend, "Meindert DeJong," in his *A Sense of Story* (Philadelphia: Lippincott, 1971), pp. 68-74;

"When Once a Little Boy," *Times Literary Supplement*, 4 December 1959, p. xxiv; republished in *Children and Literature: Views and Reviews*, edited by Virginia Haviland (Glenview, Ill.: Scott, Foresman, 1973), pp. 277-280.

Papers:
Meindert DeJong's manuscripts are in the Kerlan Collection at the University of Minnesota.

Louise Fitzhugh

(5 October 1928-19 November 1974)

Perry Nodelman
University of Winnipeg

BOOKS: *Suzuki Beame,* by Fitzhugh and Sandra Scoppettone (Garden City: Doubleday, 1961);

Harriet the Spy (New York: Harper & Row, 1964; London: Gollancz, 1974);

The Long Secret (New York: Harper & Row, 1965; London: Gollancz, 1975);

Bang, Bang, You're Dead, by Fitzhugh and Scoppettone (New York: Harper & Row, 1969);

Nobody's Family Is Going to Change (New York: Farrar, Straus & Giroux, 1974; London: Gollancz, 1976);

I Am Five (New York: Delacorte, 1978);

Sport (New York: Delacorte, 1979);

I Am Three, illustrated by Susanna Natti (New York: Delacorte, 1982);

I Am Four, illustrated by Susan Bonner (New York: Delacorte, 1982).

"At times I refuse to be moved"; so says the five-year-old heroine of Louise Fitzhugh's posthumous picture book *I Am Five* (1978). She shares her obstinacy with many of Fitzhugh's characters. The people in Fitzhugh's darkly satiric (and often hilarious) novels are unyielding eccentrics, condemned by their temperaments to repeat the same actions again and again. Fitzhugh savagely criticized the self-indulgence of their inflexibility; but she also sympathized with her young protagonists' growing acceptance of their own rigidity, and of the tragic but exhilarating inability of human beings to ever be anything but themselves. Despite the fading contemporaneity of Fitzhugh's writing, her novels still cleverly express the differences between individuality and eccentricity, and between what one owes others and what one deserves oneself. As her treatment of once-controversial issues becomes less shocking, Fitzhugh's merit as a tough-minded satirist becomes more apparent.

The daughter of Millsaps Fitzhugh and Louise Perkins Fitzhugh, Louise Fitzhugh was born on 5 October 1928 in Memphis, Tennessee. While her father was a wealthy man with an important position in state government, her childhood was not happy. As Ursula Nordstrom, former editorial

Louise Fitzhugh (photo by Susanne Singer)

director of Harper junior books, remembers, "There were many things in Louise's well-born southern upbringing and experiences that she did not like, including her horrified remembrance of teenage friends who, after a date, decided it would be fun to go down to 'coon town' and throw rocks at the heads of young Negro boys and girls. She got out of the South as soon as she could, came north, went to Bard College, and concentrated on losing every single trace of her southern accent— and prejudices."

Louise Fitzhugh attended numerous schools in addition to Bard, including Hutchison School and Southwestern College in Memphis, Florida Southern College in Lakeland, and the School of Education at New York University. She had many talents; throughout her life she played the flute and drew, and her interest in literature started at least as early as the age of eleven, when she first started to write. She majored in literature in college, but when her interest in art temporarily won out, she stopped her literary studies six months short of a degree. She enrolled at the Art Students League in New York, then studied at Cooper Union. But even after a successful show of realistic oil paintings in New York in May 1963, Fitzhugh continued to express herself in diverse ways. While she kept painting, she also wrote plays and adult novels (which were never published). She relaxed by dancing and playing tennis, and she continued to play the flute. She also continued her extensive travels. She had spent six months in Europe in 1954, and a year in Bologna, Italy, studying painting in 1957; she also lived at various times in Washington, D.C., New York City, the north shore of Long Island, and Bridgewater, Connecticut. After her death in 1974 from a ruptured aneurysm she was buried in Bridgewater, in accord with her instructions that she be buried north of the Mason-Dixon line.

Fitzhugh's career as a writer for children was brilliant but spotty; she did not pursue it constantly or consistently. Her first illustrations for a picture book appeared in 1961, her first and second novels in 1964 and 1965. She collaborated on the text for another picture book in 1969. When she died on 19 November 1974 her third novel was set to be published; it appeared eight days later. Another novel and a series of shorter books were still to come.

Fitzhugh's first book was *Suzuki Beame* (1961), for which she illustrated a text by Sandra Scoppettone. Two decades later, this book seems very much a creature of its time—and a little silly. Suzuki's parents are beatniks who live in a pad in the Village and devote themselves to art; according to Suzuki,

we all have a ball here
we don't have much bread but
bread is not very important
when you have good relationships

This was obviously written a long time ago; Suzuki's tongue is nowhere near her cheek when she says, "I dig life the most—I mean like it really swings."

While Fitzhugh did not write this text, it is like much of her later work. The characters, particularly the adult ones, are exaggerated caricatures. They are so self-centered they do not even realize how cruel they are, and they are cruel because they believe people unlike themselves are not quite real. Confronted by this blind self-indul-

gence, Suzuki and her "square" friend Henry Martin do what most of Fitzhugh's children do: they realize that people around them are too rigid to change, and move beyond them. As the book ends, Suzuki and Henry are in the process of running away from home together. In Fitzhugh's illustrations for this attack on anti-individuality her distaste for any sort of prejudice is already apparent. The drawings present a satiric portrait gallery of early 1960s types—beatniks, society poets, dancing teachers. Like all her drawings, they use a strong, definite line to wickedly unmask human silliness.

Fitzhugh had little financial backing from her family (although she inherited a great deal of money after her father's death); the advance from Harper and Row, based on the first few pages of what became *Harriet the Spy*, meant a great deal to her. According to Ursula Nordstrom, "The first material on this book, submitted to Harper by an agent, eventually became the contents of Harriet's notebook." In her report on this manuscript, Charlotte Zolotow, then a senior editor of the depart-

Dust jacket for Fitzhugh's popular story of a young girl's innocent but unflinchingly honest perception of human weakness (Harper & Row)

ment, wrote, "You have to get this writer to come in and talk. This isn't a book but it could be." Fitzhugh expanded the book under editorial guidance, particularly the role and character of the nursemaid Ole Golly.

When Harper and Row published *Harriet the Spy* in 1964, it excited a great deal of controversy. While the book is anything but realistic in style, it does discuss perfectly ordinary things that were not ordinarily discussed in children's books in the early 1960s. Reviewers hated its supposedly unchildlike cynicism and its obvious lack of faith in the supposed delights of childhood innocence. *Harriet the Spy* is just not *nice*; the book won no awards. But like many pioneering books, it was and continues to be an immense success with young readers.

Harriet the Spy describes Harriet M. Welsch's innocent but unflinchingly honest perception of human weakness. The hostility some readers feel toward Harriet, described by one critic as "one of the most fatiguingly ill-mannered children imaginable," is not surprising; as Harriet herself learns, few of us are large-minded enough to appreciate someone who both notices our inadequacies and is honest enough to say so, and the novel itself graphically illustrates how Harriet's talent for observation annoys others. But the way Fitzhugh tells her story engenders much sympathy for Harriet; we find ourselves enjoying in the novel the very things about Harriet we would most likely loathe if she lived next door.

While reviewers insisted on the "devastating" realism of *Harriet the Spy*, its paperback publishers market it as "the zany adventures of a child spy." Book one is undeniably wacky. The zaniest thing about it is that it accounts for almost half the novel, and almost nothing happens. Someone reading *Harriet the Spy* for the first time could easily finish book one convinced that nothing will ever happen. It describes a world comic because it is rigid, a world of "always": "They *always* did this"; "she *always* said"; "Ole Golly *never* went to the movies." This comic rigidity is heightened by exaggeration. Almost everyone in the novel is excessively rich. Neither Harriet nor any of her conveniently small group of schoolmates has brothers or sisters; nor do many of the other characters. Their lives are uncomplicated by poverty or sibling rivalry or other ordinary concerns. The characters all have only one significant, obvious trait. The outlines of their claustrophobic world are simple enough to be clear, exaggerated enough to be exact—like the outlines of a caricature. In her otherwise uncomprehending review in *Horn Book,* Ruth Hill Viguers was quite

right to "challenge the assumption that New York City harbors only people who are abnormal, ill-adjusted, and egocentric." *Harriet the Spy* is not realistic at all, and never pretended to be.

Inflicted with an insatiable curiosity, Harriet wanders through this weird world as a spy, recording in her notebook the zaniness of her New York City neighborhood. She watches total strangers like the Robinsons collect ridiculous objects merely to excite envy in their friends, and she breaks into a house and hides in a dumbwaiter to hear Mrs. Agatha Plumber announce the secret of life: "My dear, it's very simple, you just *take* to your *bed*." The intention is clearly satiric. The people in Harriet's caricatured world are all like the Robinsons, who "had only one problem. They thought they were perfect." In one clever episode, Harriet overhears two different people comment on human perfection in two separate conversations. One says, "I have to admit, I handled that case in a perfect way, a really perfect way," while the other almost simultaneously calls his father "a rat because he thinks he's perfect." Because these people are egocentric enough to think they are already perfect, they cannot change; nobody changes, and that is why nothing happens in book one.

Fitzhugh's wonderfully wicked illustrations cleverly support this comic vision of rigidity. In most of them, one of the characters stands alone, pinned in naked isolation against an uncompromisingly blank background and caught in an intense moment of being uncompromisingly him or her self. Agatha Plumber is a soft, fluffy woman drawn in soft, fluffy lines in a soft, fluffy bed. The enthusiastic dancing instructor, Miss Berry, swoons in a tangle of disconnected lines, her face looking disconnected from everything. Crazed Mrs. Golly, the mother of Harriet's nursemaid, hangs in space as if she has been punched in the stomach by reality—and found it rather enjoyable. If we enjoy these pictures and admire the wicked imagination that sees people so clearly and honestly, then we must also admire Harriet.

Harriet has the same honesty, and sees things in much the same way—and we cannot enjoy what she sees unless we approve of her seeing it that way. Satirists often show us ourselves through the eyes of an uninvolved outsider who reveals our inadequacies because he does not share our values. As a child, Harriet is unfamiliar with adult values; as a particularly curious and observant child, she sees a lot, and her attitude is interested but uninvolved. She is a little like the Greek gods she is studying in school, a comparison she implicitly draws herself: "Talk about spies. Those gods spied on everybody all the time." The novel begins appropriately with Harriet playing God, inventing a town and the people in it and making things happen to them.

But in Harriet's town, "everybody goes to bed at nine-thirty." Harriet is herself as rigid as the people she spies on. That makes her as funny as the people she observes; so does her ingenuousness. Harriet shows us what is ridiculous in what she does not understand, but is herself ridiculous for not understanding it.

While this is all quite delightful, *Harriet the Spy* moves past comic satire. Fitzhugh chose, not just to make Harriet a satiric observer, but to explore what it means to be one. In her excellent discussion of this novel in *Children's Literature,* Virginia L. Wolf says that, "limiting us to Harriet's point of view, *Harriet the Spy* is fundamentally a thorough characterization of Harriet." Harriet becomes psychologically convincing as she confronts the tendencies in her character that make her view others so interestingly.

Harriet's desire to stand back and observe makes her arrogant about the failings of others. As she admits, she likes to hear "what peculiar things people say to each other," and she enjoys the circus because "I LOVE THE FREAKS." Thinking about brothers and sisters, she writes, "ONE THING, WHENEVER THEY YELLED IT WOULDN'T ALWAYS BE AT YOU. SOMETIMES IT WOULD BE AT YOUR BROTHER THEN YOU COULD LAUGH." While Harriet's lack of compassion allows her to see others unfiltered by kindness, it is inhumane. She treats her talent for observation the way she describes her friend Janie's treatment of chemistry experiments: "only Janie understood anything whatever about them, and she wouldn't explain but instead called everyone a cretin who asked her." Triumphant individualists both, Harriet and Janie lack respect for others. With her usual vacuous incomprehension, Ole Golly quotes a passage from Dostoyevski that makes a point about this sort of respect: "Love all God's creation, the whole and every grain of sand in it. . . . If you love everything, you will perceive the divine mystery in things." Harriet's response to this is characteristically obtuse and self-involved: "I want to know everything." Loving only knowledge, Harriet lacks the humility to perceive her own involvement in the human condition.

Appropriately, Harriet learns about love as Ole Golly, the ultimate caricature of the self-controlled nursemaid, falls in love. The rigid caricature turns out to be not so rigid after all; it was mostly just a figment of Ole Golly's imagination, a false picture of herself as a strong-minded intellectual. Ole Golly softens; eventually, she leaves. As book one ends, holes appear in Harriet's comfortable world. By the middle of chapter five, Harriet notes, "something was definitely happening"; a few chapters later, "SOMETHING TERRIBLE IS GOING TO HAPPEN. I KNOW IT."

Harriet does not like what happens in book two at all. Her notebook, which represents her talent for observation, becomes a source of pain. The other children read what she has written about them, and do not like it; adults assume that Harriet's need for the notebook is evidence of abnormalcy. Harriet faces the dilemma inherent in her character: either she can be herself, lose her friends, and be considered freakish; or she can do what others expect, have friends—and stop being herself. Astonishingly, she makes the first choice. Contrary even to the expectations it sets up itself, the novel ends more or less as it began. Harriet remains her own unhumble self, still not terribly charitable, and still doing what she did at the beginning.

When the other children exclude her, Harriet's first panicky response is to consider changing: "I HAVE THE FEELING THIS MORNING THAT EVERYONE IN THIS SCHOOL IS INSANE. I MIGHT POSSIBLY BRING A HAM SANDWICH TOMORROW BUT I HAVE TO THINK ABOUT IT." But even though Harriet's previous insistence on nothing but tomato sandwiches was funny, even though her notebook entries are cruel and her spying obnoxious, most readers have so much sympathy with Harriet's perceptions by this point that they do not *want* her to eat ham. As Harriet quickly realizes herself, "The world went on the same after all. The same things happened every morning. So *what* if they didn't like her? *She* would go on the same. *She* was Harriet M. Welsch, and she would continue to be Harriet M. Welsch, and that was the thing to remember." Fitzhugh supports Harriet's wish to keep on being herself by stressing the cruelty of the others' attempts to punish her, rather than the benefits she might gain by conforming. By the end of book two, Harriet is not the contrite victim of self-indulgence we might have expected, but a martyr.

Not only Harriet does not change. In the long run, nobody does, and as she finally realizes, "SOME PEOPLE ARE ONE WAY AND SOME PEOPLE ARE ANOTHER AND THAT'S THAT." Just about everyone in the novel faces a major disruption: Harriet's friends Janie and Sport become her enemies; on Harriet's spy route, Fabio Dei Santi has an accident, Little Joe Curry's food thefts are discovered, Harrison Withers loses his cats, Mrs. Plumber's doctor confines her to bed. But the irony in these apparent changes is summed up by the big event in the life of the Robinsons—the purchase of a statue of a giant baby holding a tiny mother, which merely expresses symbolically everything we already know about their "perfect" and perfectly sterile lives. The same is true of the others; what seems to be a major change actually just intensifies what went on before. In the long run, the Dei Santis continue on as they were to begin with, Mrs. Plumber keeps thinking only of Mrs. Plumber, the Robinsons are still perfect, and Harrison Withers gets a new cat. Harriet writes, "HEE HEE. THEY AIN'T GOING TO CHANGE HARRISON WITHERS." They ain't going to change Harriet either; at the end she has her friends and her notebook back, and she has settled down to playing God just as she did at the beginning. Only now, she knows she does it, knows that she thinks of real people as if they were figments of her imagination: "They were so far away that they looked like dolls. They made her think of the way she imagined the people when she played Town. Somehow this way she could see them better than she ever had before." Harriet needs her distance and accepts its implications in order to maintain it. Her conclusion that "THINGS ARE BACK TO NORMAL" is ironic; for Harriet, it is normal to be eccentric. She must learn, not to change, but to live with who she is.

Harriet learns that in a letter from Ole Golly that infuriates many adult readers of the novel. Ole Golly tells Harriet that in order to regain her friends, "you are going to have to do two things, and you don't like either one of them: 1) You have to apologize. 2) You have to lie." But this recommendation of hypocrisy is good advice; the only humane way to allow yourself honest perceptions of those you care for is to lie about them, to not always announce what you know or see or understand—to have charity. Ole Golly adds, "Remember that writing is to put love in the world, not to use against your friends. But to yourself you must always tell the truth." What Harriet learns is the difference between writing and mere spying, between a social act and a self-indulgent one. The difference is not in what she does or who she is, but in her reasons for doing what comes so naturally and uncontrollably. As editor of the sixth-grade page of the school newspaper, Harriet gath-

ers information, not just to satisfy her curiosity, but also for the pleasure of others, and that means she is no longer an arrogant observer.

Everyone in *Harriet the Spy* has the quality Harriet admires in her friend Janie: they are "definite"—with one exception. Beth Ellen Hansen, a "mouse" who sometimes acts bravely, is the only person who ever surprises Harriet; her character is the one real mystery in the novel. *The Long Secret*, published in 1965, is a sort of sequel to *Harriet the Spy* that solves the mystery, and reveals who Beth Ellen is both to readers and to Beth Ellen, as it describes the summer after sixth grade that the girls spend in their families' cottages on Long Island.

The Long Secret also reveals who others think Harriet is. Readers who felt compassion for Harriet as perceived by Harriet in *Harriet the Spy*, now see her from the outside, through Beth Ellen's eyes, and understand how difficult she is. Even though Beth Ellen finds Harriet's self-assuredness comforting, "the principle feeling she felt when with

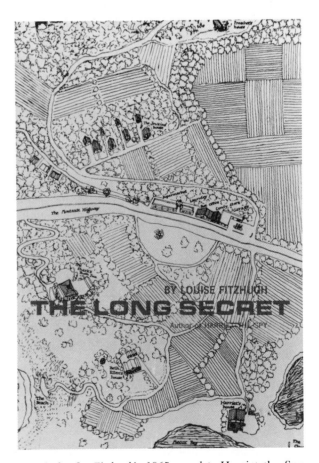

Dust jacket for Fitzhugh's 1965 sequel to Harriet the Spy *(Harper & Row)*

Harriet was one of being continually jarred." In *The Long Secret*, Harriet fluctuates between being an agitating caricature—the person seen by others—and an interesting, sensitive person, seen by herself.

That fluctuation is central both to the shape and the meaning of *The Long Secret*. Harriet always thinks she understands everybody; in this second novel Fitzhugh continually points out that all she understands of others is all anybody ever understands—what we make of them. Not only do we find out that Beth Ellen's idea of Harriet is different from Harriet's; we also learn that Beth Ellen's idea of Beth Ellen is different from Harriet's. Harriet's version of Beth Ellen as reported in *Harriet the Spy* turns out to have been based on incomplete information; here, and again in the later novel *Sport*, Fitzhugh returns to characters from an earlier novel we thought we knew completely, and reveals unexpected facets both of their lives and of their personalities.

Fitzhugh's insistence that we have the humility to acknowledge the limitations of our ideas about other people is expressed constantly in *The Long Secret;* characters repeatedly thwart our expectations of them. Beth Ellen's grandmother, who at first seems strict and unloving, shows real concern for her granddaughter. Jessie Mae Jenkins, an ever-so-born-again and ever-so-dismissable girl from the South who lives with her sizable family in a house nearby, admits she is lonely and merely hiding in her exaggerated sanctity; in fact, the portrait of Jessie Mae and her archetypically southern family is surprisingly sympathetic, considering Fitzhugh's avowed hatred for the South. But above all, Beth Ellen turns out to have kept her own secret so well that readers may be almost as angry when it is revealed as Harriet is.

On first reading, *The Long Secret* seems shapeless. It includes bitter criticism of the sterile inhumanity of international café society, the low comedy of the despicably southern Jenkins getting rich quick by making "toe medicine" out of watermelons, a controversial technical discussion of menstruation, the highly charged melodrama of Beth Ellen's blatantly cruel parents. Fitzhugh gets away with including so many different kinds of characters by focusing on the different ways Harriet and Beth Ellen see them; she alternates between telling the story as Beth Ellen sees it and as Harriet sees it, so that comparisons are inevitable.

At one point, Beth Ellen even has the same fantasy Harriet had in *Harriet the Spy*. Harriet imagined what would happen if the world exploded:

"WHAT WOULD HAPPEN? WOULD WE FLY THROUGH THE AIR? IN SPACE YOU JUST FLOAT AROUND. I WOULD BE LONELY." Harriet fears loneliness because her curiosity feeds on other people; Beth Ellen's reaction to the same idea is quite different: "was that what happened when the bomb dropped and the world was destroyed? Did it split in half like an orange and everyone just float around? Lonely, so lonely it would be. And kind of embarrassing, humiliating for some reason, to be there all alone and no place to put your feet down and walk around." For Beth Ellen, this fantasy is symbolic of her own state of mind. Surrounded by "definite" people like her own mother and like Harriet, and embarrassed by her own inability to be like them, she thinks she has no place to stand.

But the indefinite Beth Ellen she lets herself and others know about is not the real one. Harriet says, "You know, sometimes, Beth Ellen, I wonder where you keep yourself." Beth Ellen is more than she usually shows; since her mother has deserted her, she thinks she must be unlovable, and she has hidden away that unlovable self in order to protect it. It is so well protected that she seems unable to find it, and she says, "I am truly a mouse. I have no desire at all to be me."

But that is not true; she does wish to be herself, if only she can rediscover what that means: "where do I live, she thought, and began to cry." When her mother returns from Europe and turns out to be cruel and self-indulgent, Beth Ellen rediscovers the intense and very definitive feelings she has buried. She finds herself, and she finally exults, "I live somewhere, I live somewhere, I live somewhere." She has a place to stand.

The "long secret" of the title is that it is Beth Ellen, the mouse, who has been distributing anonymous notes to the townspeople. Her grandmother explains why: "shy people are angry people.... You're a very angry little girl." Beth Ellen's notes use familiar quotations, often biblical, to describe the "secret" desires that control other people. Since the notes create immediate recognition in everyone but the person who receives them, they comment on our willingness to ignore our failings. Ironically, a secret Beth Ellen, hidden even from Beth Ellen, has been telling other people where *they* live. Unlike Harriet's self-regarding notes to herself in her notebook, Beth Ellen's notes are an attempt to communicate.

Fitzhugh gets away with something tricky here; the person from whose point of view much of the story is told turns out to be the perpetrator of the mystery of the notes at the heart of the plot. She gets away with that because the double point of view allows her to switch off to Harriet whenever Beth Ellen might be thinking of leaving notes. In any case, the point of the book is that there is much Beth Ellen will not admit, even to herself. For a whole day, she is sick and lazy, and we learn all her thoughts but the important one—that, as she eventually tells Harriet, she is menstruating for the first time. Apparently she has been willing to think about that no more than she thinks about her secret note-leaving.

Symbolically speaking, the secrets we keep longest are the things at the heart of our being— what we really are. Beth Ellen's mother thinks such secrets are dangerous: "It's very hard to tell one fanatic from another these days. They look like ordinary people until you get to know them, and then you find out they're obsessed." But the real secret, which everyone else shares and Beth Ellen eventually learns, is that no one is "ordinary," and everyone is "obsessed." Beth Ellen says that more positively than her mother: "Everyone I know has something like this. Something to love. I need something to love." Fanaticism is merely knowing who you are, being positive about it, and being humble enough to accept the fanaticism of others. By the end of the novel, Beth Ellen is able to admit that, through her secret notes, she was always just as fanatical and just as definite as everybody else. She arrives at exactly the same balanced place Harriet reached, but from an opposite direction; Beth Ellen learns self-love, and Harriet charity.

The Long Secret is a subtle and energetic novel, as good in its own way as *Harriet the Spy*. Unfortunately, Fitzhugh's undeniably brave discussion of menstruation has attracted most of the attention that *The Long Secret* has received. But the interest excited by those few pages is not surprising; commenting on her first reading of the manuscript of this novel, Ursula Nordstrom says, "When I came to the page where the onset of Beth Ellen's first menstrual period occurred, and it was written so beautifully, to such perfection, I scrawled in the margin, 'Thank you, Louise Fitzhugh.' It was the first mention in junior books of this tremendous event in a girl's life."

The emphasis on controversial, realistic issues continues in Fitzhugh's next book, another collaboration with Sandra Scoppettone. Published in 1969, *Bang, Bang, You're Dead* is a strong antiwar statement that exudes the atmosphere of its time; this is a "now" book for the "Now Generation," now past. The text, by both Fitzhugh and Scoppettone, graphically describes a battle between two groups of children, which ends with their overstated realization that they lose more than they gain by fighting: "this isn't any fun. . . . Why did we do it?" Their violence is both verbal and physical; they lunge at each other's throats, poke at each other's eyes, and gush blood, and they say things like, "Give up, puke-face." While there is energy here, there is not much else. One reviewer of *Bang, Bang, You're Dead* made the revealing comment that Fitzhugh's pictures left the large number of characters "somewhat undifferentiated." It was only in her novels that Fitzhugh could add a sense of individual character to the satiric energy and moral conviction of her two collaborations with Scoppettone.

The heroine of *Nobody's Family Is Going to Change*, published soon after Fitzhugh's death in 1974, is Emma Sheridan, "a fat brown girl with funny hair" who thinks herself "truly and completely disgusting." Fitzhugh's profound hatred for the inhumanity of prejudice and its effects on peo-

Dust jacket for Fitzhugh's posthumously published 1974 novel in which she attacks racial and sexual stereotyping (Farrar, Straus & Giroux)

ple like Emma is evident, as the book sizzles with an intense anger that makes Emma an exciting character.

While Emma eventually comes to like herself better, she must realize, like Harriet and Beth Ellen, that she will not change. *Nobody's Family Is Going to Change* is Fitzhugh's most earnest and most paradoxical novel—a savage attack on the rigidity of conventional values that expresses no faith that change is possible. But it does want to change readers' attitudes; it has a point to make, and it makes it energetically and systematically.

Fitzhugh's earlier insistence on respect for individuality here becomes a general attack on discrimination of all sorts, even on shallow categorizing of all sorts. Young, black, and female, Emma is a prime target of discrimination. For Fitzhugh, Emma's father is the ultimate villain, a symbolic representative of everything in human nature that justifies power over others. He is a typical believer in middle-class values, a typical power-mad parent, a typical male chauvinist. He wants his son to be a lawyer, like he is, his daughter a lawyer's wife, like his own wife. He does not care that Emma's brother, Willie, wants to be a dancer and Emma a lawyer, for he considers Willie's pursuit unmasculine, Emma's unfeminine, and both unnecessarily unconventional. Even worse, his faith in conventional values—which, in the book, are conventional white values—makes him look down on the idea of blacks dancing: "You've got to think of all the people who have bled and died so other people don't look at you and see nothing but a minstrel show." In his fear of prejudice he despises anything that might be identified with being black, so that paradoxically, he represses Willie to protect him from repression. Given values that place him, a successful, adult male, utterly in command, Mr. Sheridan is a barrier to his children's selfhood: Emma realizes "she had never thought of her father as a man before. She thought of him rather like one thinks of Boulder Dam. He was something to scale or go over in a barrel."

When she does think of him as a man, as he tells her of his difficult early years, Emma realizes that she has dehumanized him, in her hatred of his rigidity, as much as he has dehumanized her: "Emma's sympathy careened toward her father. . . . She had never thought of her father as *feeling* anything." But the most interesting thing about this novel is its refusal to be simpleminded, even in approval of something so undeniably worthy as charitable thoughts about others. Emma soon realizes that sympathy for her father is a trap. He

has tried to get it only in order to maintain his unreasonable control over her and Willie. He will not change, and she cannot afford to change her feelings toward him. She tells him, "You never think about anybody, but just how you think they should live. You don't even know us. . . ! You just stand up here and tell us what your life was like! Who cares? You don't care what our lives are like!" He does not care—and he never will, for as the novel insists again and again, everyone is stuck with his character. Willie tells his father, "I'm not going to be any different," and Emma's schoolmate Goldin says, "My brother couldn't stop being like himself if the roof fell in on him." Emma's uncle Dipsy says to her mother, "Boy, people don't change, do they. . . ? I don't change and you don't change. You're exactly the way you were as a kid." Emma finally concludes that "fathers don't change and mothers don't change."

Emma has wanted her parents to adapt enough to accept the fact that she herself will not change; when she realizes they will not, her response is, "I can change. I can change myself." She cannot, of course, any more than Harriet could. But she can change her attitude, toward herself and others; she can accept and live with the fact that nobody will ever be anything but what they already are. When Emma's father tells her, "I think any woman who tries to be a lawyer is a damned fool," her response sums up the message of the novel: "That . . . is your problem, not mine."

Nobody's Family Is Going to Change is a product of its thesis. Its characters are deliberately stereotyped, deliberately contrasted with each other, in order to make points; the attempts of Emma to be a "Big Chief Looney Lady Lawyer" and Willie "the nigger Nijinsky" are presented with absolute symmetry. The astonishing thing is that a book so involved with its thesis should have so much energy. The thesis is argued passionately, and the book is saved from mere point-making by Fitzhugh's refusal to be content with easy answers. When Emma contacts the Children's Army, it seems like the solution to her problems—children wresting power from grown-ups who misuse it. But Fitzhugh makes Emma realize the harsh truth: "when it gets right down to it, the Children's Army is no different from any adult organization. Males were in control and would depend on force." While the rhetoric is inflammatory, the idea is humane: there are no easy answers. Human beings are complicated, and no organization or idea that leaves anything human out of consideration is a good one.

Fitzhugh includes everything in this novel, including many things surprising in a children's book. At one point she lets Emma peruse her stool, and at another she actually allows Dipsy to admit that some dancers are indeed gay. Goldin's brother is an unrepentant transvestite; Emma herself has an understandable distaste for white skin that few other children's writers, white or black, would acknowledge: "white faces only looked weak to her, as though white people didn't have as much substance, but were so much protoplasm without much reality." While these things do not transform Fitzhugh's caricatures into believable personalities, they give them astonishing energy as caricatures, completely human eccentrics who live in an eccentric but complete world. In the early 1980s, *Nobody's Family Is Going to Change* saw new life as the basis for a successful Broadway musical, *The Tap Dance Kid*.

The publication of *Nobody's Family Is Going to Change* shortly after Fitzhugh's death did not put an end to the appearance of her books for children. Four years later, Delacorte Press published the first of a series of shorter books. *I Am Five* (1978) was both written and illustrated by Fitzhugh; in it, a child tells us who she is and what she does on the day after her fifth birthday. The text is slight; the child speaking seems to be intended to represent all five-year-olds and to sum up their characteristic behavior. Except for a characteristic refusal to be moved, she is so generalized that she has little individuality. But the pictures are something else again—vintage Fitzhugh sketches that say a hundred times more about who this young girl is than the words do.

Compared to Fitzhugh's earlier novels, *Sport*, which appeared in 1979, seems unfinished and rather thin. It reads like *Harriet the Spy* deprived of its heroine's subtle consideration of what it means to be human. But the boy Sport is not Harriet, and *Sport* is fun simply because it is not subtle. The feeling of the book is summed up by the fact that when Harriet appears in it, she is only a tomato-sandwich-eating and note-making freak, a funny caricature.

Sport, who was Harriet's best friend in *Harriet the Spy*, here turns out to have a whole secret (and rather zany) life of his own, stemming from the death of his grandfather and the inheritance of no less than $32 million. We learn a lot more than the little Harriet knew about him in *Harriet the Spy*, and his personal situation turns out to be much like Beth Ellen Hansen's: both have apparently cold grandparents who actually love them and heartless mothers who have deserted them and gone to Europe to live frivolously; both must confront the ugly fact of their mothers' despicable personalities. But a situation that allowed Beth Ellen to come to terms with herself in *The Long Secret* is only an occasion for comic melodrama in *Sport*. That happens partially because Sport, unlike Beth Ellen, knows himself, likes himself, and can take care of himself. But it is clear that Fitzhugh simply chose not to emphasize the psychological aspects of the situation here. Instead, she makes things deliciously lurid. Sport's mother is not just the thoughtless consumer Beth Ellen's mother is, nasty but dismissable because she is useless. Sport's mother is a pure force of unmitigated, self-regarding evil, who calls her son a "little jerk" to his face and callously arranges for him to be kidnapped.

Melodramatically opposed to this terminally, delightfully awful woman is the paragon Kate, whom Sport's father marries in the course of the book. Kate is pretty, kind, loving, a beacon of normalcy in a wilderness of freaks. As Sport notes: "he had long ago discovered that women who never intended to marry had very sharp, very pointed, very delicate and special shoes and far be it from baby to need anything that would deplete the shoe money. . . . Kate's shoes were just shoes." Kate is perfection—perfectly ordinary; for Sport, she represents the ordinary childhood he lusts after: "I am doing what I have seen families do in comic books, he thought quickly. This is the way they behave when there is a man, a woman, and a child. . . . He sat, feeling a kind of peace, a strange sensation of no worry that he had never felt before."

But before Sport is allowed the pleasant boredom of normal life, the traditional happy ending, he must, of course, go through hell. Fitzhugh dwells lovingly on the grotesque horror of his dying grandfather's "thin, hawklike, yellow hand that traveled crablike toward Sport," and the equally grotesque absurdity of his mother's parties:

> "How old are you, dear?" said another
> woman, shouting above the noise.
> "Forty seven," said Sport.
> "You're tall for your age," trilled the
> woman, not having heard a thing.

Sport is the most Dickensian of Fitzhugh's novels; eventually, Sport achieves a typically Dickensian happy ending, as an ordinary person protected from the freakishness of everyone else by a small group of other normal people.

While this resolution is not profound, it is satisfying. Fitzhugh manages to make these undeniable excesses seem, if not contemporary, at least immediate, mostly because Sport himself is so ordinary and so convincingly contemporary. As a normal boy who wants only to ride his bicycle and hang out with the guys, Sport offers a recognizably contemporary point of view on the excess absurdities he encounters. Consequently, readers can have it both ways: both enjoy the delights of melodramatic and comic grotesquerie and affirm their faith in the pleasures of the ordinary.

Delacorte Press published *I Am Three* and *I Am Four* in 1982. They have the manuscript for "I Am Six"; unfortunately, Fitzhugh did no pictures for these books. *I Am Three* was illustrated by Susanna Natti; *I Am Four* by Susan Bonner. As yet "I Am Six" is not scheduled for publication. Delacorte also has the rights to a picture book by Fitzhugh called "My Friend John."

Ursula Nordstrom recalls that "Louise Fitzhugh adored music and was a superb dancer. She was also a brilliant painter. One of her canvases of a little girl standing alone in a meadow expressed all the essential loneliness I think Louise always felt. She was a brilliant, erratic, moody, often extremely thoughtful and endearing person. And she was intensely committed to her writing and to her drawing and painting." Not surprisingly, her writing and her drawing both express the essential horror and the essential wonder of the inevitable loneliness of being human. Like Harriet the spy, Louise Fitzhugh had an unfailing interest in the oddities of people, an uncanny ability to describe them in words and in pictures. And like Harriet, she had a good moral for her writing: "THAT IS THAT SOME PEOPLE ARE ONE WAY AND SOME PEOPLE ARE ANOTHER AND THAT'S THAT."

References:

Hamida Bosmajian, "Louise Fitzhugh's *Harriet the Spy:* Nonsense and Sense," in *Touchstones: Reflections on the Best in Children's Literature* (West Lafayette, Ind.: Children's Literature Association, 1985), pp. 71-82;

Kate Fincke, "The Breakdown of the Family: Fictional Case Studies in Contemporary Novels for Young People," *Lion and the Unicorn,* 3 (Winter 1979-1980): 86-95;

Francis Molson, "Another Look at *Harriet the Spy,*" *Elementary English,* 51 (October 1974): 963-970;

Molson, "Portrait of the Young Writer in Children's Fiction," *Lion and the Unicorn,* 1 (Fall 1977): 77-90;

Virginia L. Wolf, "*Harriet the Spy:* Milestone, Masterpiece?," *Children's Literature,* 4 (1975): 120-126.

Paula Fox

(22 April 1923-   )

Anita Moss
University of North Carolina at Charlotte

BOOKS: *Maurice's Room,* illustrated by Ingrid Fetz (New York: Macmillan, 1966);

A Likely Place, illustrated by Edward Ardizzone (New York: Macmillan, 1967; London: Macmillan, 1968);

Poor George (New York: Harcourt, Brace & World, 1967; London: Macmillan, 1970);

How Many Miles to Babylon?, illustrated by Paul Giovanopoulos (New York: David White, 1967; London: Macmillan, 1967);

Dear Prosper, illustrated by Steve McLachlin (New York: David White, 1968);

The Stone-Faced Boy, illustrated by Donald A. Mackay (Englewood Cliffs, N.J.: Bradbury Press, 1968; London: Macmillan, 1969);

The King's Falcon, illustrated by Eros Keith (Englewood Cliffs, N.J.: Bradbury Press, 1969; London: Macmillan, 1970);

Portrait of Ivan, illustrated by Saul Lambert (Englewood Cliffs, N.J.: Bradbury Press, 1969; London: Macmillan, 1970);

Hungry Fred, illustrated by Rosemary Wells (Englewood Cliffs, N.J.: Bradbury Press, 1969);

Blowfish Live in the Sea (Englewood Cliffs, N.J.: Bradbury Press, 1970);

Desperate Characters (New York: Harcourt, Brace & World, 1970; London: Macmillan, 1970);

The Western Coast (New York: Harcourt, Brace Jovanovich, 1972; London: Macmillan, 1973);

Good Ethan, illustrated by Arnold Lobel (Scarsdale, N.Y.: Bradbury Press, 1973);

The Slave Dancer, illustrated by Keith (Scarsdale, N.Y.: Bradbury Press, 1973; London: Macmillan, 1974);

The Widow's Children (New York: Dutton, 1976);

The Little Swineherd and Other Tales, illustrated by Leonard Lubin (New York: Dutton, 1978; London: Dent, 1979);

A Place Apart (New York: Farrar, Straus & Giroux, 1980; London: Dent, 1981);

One-Eyed Cat (Scarsdale, N.Y.: Bradbury Press, 1984);

A Servant's Tale (San Francisco: North Point, 1984);

© *Jerry Bauer*

The Moonlight Man (Scarsdale, N.Y.: Bradbury Press, 1986).

OTHER: "Newbery Award Acceptance," in *Newbery and Caldecott Medal Books 1966-1975,* edited by Lee Kingman (Boston: Horn Book, 1975), pp. 116-125.

Paula Fox has earned a deserved reputation as one of America's most outstanding writers for children. Critics and reviewers have praised her capacity to capture the intense emotions and perceptions of young characters, her willingness to explore complex, even tragic, themes and moral issues, her ability to create psychologically realistic characters and vividly realized settings in graceful, even at times poetic, prose. Fox's use of understatement, her ability to evoke significance and to suggest emotional emphases and symbolic resonances through carefully selected details and precisely employed figurative language are among her many achievements as a writer. In addition to the fourteen books she has written for children, Fox has also written five novels for adults, one of which, *Desperate Characters* (1970), has already been acclaimed an American masterpiece among short novels by such eminent critics as Irving Howe and Alfred Kazin.

The daughter of writer Paul Harvey Fox and Elsie de Sola Fox, Paula Fox was born in New York City on 22 April 1923. In 1931, when she was eight years old, the half-Spanish and half-Irish Fox went to live with her grandmother in Cuba. There she attended a one-room school and learned to speak Spanish fluently from other children. She also played on a village baseball team. When Fulgencio Batista began his rise to power in 1934, Fox returned to New York.

Fox has written that both before and after her stay in Cuba, she moved often, seldom living anywhere longer than a year. After returning from Cuba, she hardly saw her parents. By the age of twelve, she had attended nine different schools. Because of the chaotic conditions of her childhood, the young Fox often escaped into the peaceful solitude of the public library, where she read voraciously and began to nurture her writing talent.

Fox began to work at age seventeen and subsequently held many different and unusual jobs. She worked for a newspaper, as a machinist for Bethlehem Steel, for British publisher Victor Gollancz, as a reader for a movie company, and for a British news service in Paris and Warsaw. Probably her most unusual job was punctuating fifteenth-century Italian madrigals.

After leaving her situation with the English news service in the late 1940s, Fox returned to New York and married Richard Sigerson in 1948, by whom she has two sons, Adam and Gabriel. Divorced from Sigerson in 1954, Fox attended Columbia University from 1955 to 1958, after which she worked at a school for emotionally disturbed children in Dobbs Ferry, New York. She has also taught English to Spanish-speaking children. For several years she taught fifth-grade at the Ethical Culture Schools in New York.

In 1962 Fox married Martin Greenberg, former editor of *Commentary* and currently professor of English at C.W. Post College in Greenvale, New York. In addition to her novels, Fox has also written television scripts and several short stories. She lived for six months in Greece in 1962 and 1963 while her husband was on a Guggenheim Fellowship, and it was upon her return to the United States that she began to write for publication. At various times she has conducted writing workshops at the University of Pennsylvania.

Fox has been the recipient of several major literary awards. In 1972 she received a Guggenheim Fellowship and the National Institute and American Academy Award. In 1974 she received the American Library Association Newbery Medal for *The Slave Dancer* and a grant from the National Endowment for the Arts. For the body of her fine work for children, Paula Fox received the distinguished Hans Christian Andersen Award in 1978. In 1981 she received the American Book Award for *A Place Apart*. Fox was awarded the Brandeis Fiction Citation in 1984. In addition, she was a finalist in the National Book Award Children's Book Category in 1971 for *Blowfish Live in the Sea*. She currently resides in Brooklyn, New York.

In her Newbery award acceptance speech Fox remarks that she writes to discover how "to connect ourselves with the reality of our own lives. It is painful; but if we are to become human, we cannot abandon it." In her best children's books Fox manages to discover what it is to be a vulnerable child struggling for a sure sense of self in a bewildering and often alien world. In such a world, Fox suggests, children need caring adults to guide them as well as their own resourcefulness. They need to use all of their human faculties—intelligence, imagination, the gift of language—to endure the world and to make sense of it.

In her first book, *Maurice's Room* (1966), Fox reveals an exceptional understanding of and sympathy for children. Maurice collects things and stores them in his room. At the time the story begins, Maurice's room is full, so that only he and his friend, Jacob, can enter it safely. Mr. Klenk, the janitor of the building where Maurice and Jacob live, has helped by building shelves for the room. When Maurice's mother finally demands that he at least clear the floor, Mr. Klenk again comes to the rescue by hanging different items from the ceiling. Among those exciting and unusual objects are a dried octopus, a bottle full of dead beetles, a raccoon tail, a plate of mealy worms, nuts, bolts, rocks, and many other things which fascinate Maurice and Jacob. Maurice also keeps several turtles, a lizard, a snake, a robin, and an old hamster in his crowded

Dust jacket for a later edition of Fox's first novel, about a young boy who fills his room with a collection of "junk" (Macmillan)

room.

Maurice's parents, who refer to his vast collection as "junk," try to direct his attention to other interests. They force him to take trumpet lessons, and on his birthday they give him a lovely toy sailboat. He loathes the trumpet lessons but likes the boat. However, when Maurice and Jacob take the boat to the pond in the park, they become distracted by some rusty bedsprings submerged in the water and allow the sailboat to crash into the bank.

At last Maurice's parents decide that they must move to the country to give their child more room to play. Maurice gives Jacob his bedsprings but manages to pack the rest of his collection, which is lost when the moving truck goes over a bad bump. He comes to terms with his loss, however, because he discovers that the barn at his new home is full of the type of things he cherishes. Jacob comes for a visit, and the two boys happily make plans to fix up the barn.

Although *Maurice's Room* does not really suggest the power which Fox's writing would soon display, it is nevertheless a delightful book because it captures the hidden and secret world of childhood

and the intensity with which children work at playing. Although the characters are not developed in psychological depth, they are nevertheless believable, humorous, and interesting. The book's humor, its vivid descriptions, its depiction of the child's capacity to create a special place of his own, and the child's ability to evade the constraints of the adult world are all expressed in a style which Fox continues to develop and improve upon.

Many of Fox's child protagonists often feel overwhelmed by the powerful and often well-meaning adults around them. In *A Likely Place* (1967), nine-year-old Lewis contemplates running away because "everyone wanted to help" him. Adults intrude too much into Lewis's life. His teacher wants him to learn the nuances of grammar, which he finds boring, and his parents constantly ask him questions which he does not wish to answer. For example, Lewis has taken to wearing a woolen cap even though the weather is warm. When his mother asks why he wears the cap to bed, he evasively replies that he had forgotten to take it off, though the real reason for his wearing it is that it makes him "feel everything inside his head" is in the right place. When Lewis asks questions, however, his parents usually reply, "Oh, Lewis!" and give him a cookie.

Similarly, adults often take Lewis places where he does not wish to go; they do not bother to ask him what he wants to do. Adults constantly tell him how he feels: "Lewis could have made a list a mile long of all the things people had told him he was feeling." At school he has difficulty remembering dates and places of historical interest in addition to his problems with spelling. He is likewise a failure at playing the recorder, which he does not want to play in the first place. The only activity which gives him pleasure is reading ghost stories to several younger children each afternoon after school, but even in this his mother diminishes his joy by asking why he does not choose friends his own age.

Fox perceptively reveals in *A Likely Place* the piling up of several minor negative experiences which impede Lewis's emotional and intellectual growth. She shows that the adults in Lewis's life are well-meaning but self-absorbed and rather insensitive. Lewis simply has no place of his own, not even his room, where he can take cover and where his dreams may be sheltered and nourished without the intrusions of adults. He takes no interest in schoolwork because his teacher provides him with no room for exploring topics which interest him. Feeling more and more trapped and frustrated,

Lewis glumly contemplates running away.

He decides to postpone his escape when his parents tell him that they are going to Chicago on a business trip. They engage an eccentric but highly interesting young woman, Miss Fitchlow, to stay with Lewis while they are away. Miss Fitchlow treats Lewis as an equal and introduces him to yoga exercises and health foods. She asks him intelligent questions and assumes that he can answer for himself. Most important, she gives him much more freedom than his parents do.

When Miss Fitchlow allows Lewis to go into the park alone, he meets another interesting friend, Mr. Madruga, an elderly gentleman from Barcelona. He tells Lewis how homesick he is and how he needs to be working again as a shoemaker. Barcelona, Mr. Madruga explains, is a magnificent city. Each afternoon after work, says Mr. Madruga, he would drink thick delicious chocolate and watch the people go by. Mr. Madruga's son-in-law, Charlie, does not allow the old gentleman to express his feelings. Mr. Madruga wants to write a letter to Charlie and needs Lewis's help since his English is not quite good enough for letter writing.

Mr. Madruga helps Lewis to achieve a sense of competence and he also helps Lewis to discover "a likely place" of his own, a secret cave in the park where he can hide, think, and imagine. In this secret place Lewis puts a candle and a damp booklet he has found in the park entitled *Mosquito Control in Southeastern Delaware*. In helping Mr. Madruga compose his letter, Lewis discovers a real purpose and a real audience for writing; thus his spelling improves dramatically. Moreover, the letter gets results. Mr. Madruga's son-in-law helps him to get a job in a shoemaker's shop. As a token of their friendship, Mr. Madruga gives Lewis a beautiful umbrella, the handle of which is a carved Spanish dragon. When Lewis's mother remarks that the umbrella is far too big, Lewis remarks confidently, "I'll get bigger."

A Likely Place presents an exceptionally vivid psychological picture of a child's coping with the confining restraints of overly protective adults. Although Lewis travels no farther than the park near his home, he has gone very far by the end of the book in the painful journey toward maturity.

How Many Miles to Babylon? (1967), which borrows its title from a nursery rhyme, represents an important milestone in Fox's writing career and in contemporary children's literature as well. At the time it was published, children's writers had just begun to present complex stories featuring minority characters. In this novel Fox uses the journey

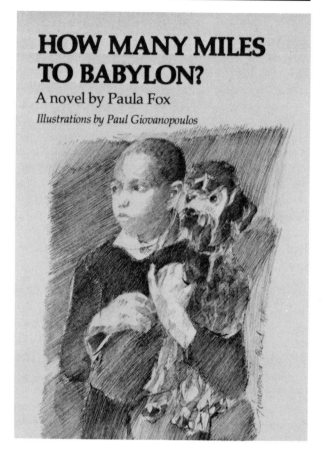

HOW MANY MILES TO BABYLON?

A novel by Paula Fox

Illustrations by Paul Giovanopoulos

Dust jacket for a later edition of Fox's 1967 novel about the fantasy life of a ten-year-old boy from a ghetto and his confrontation with reality (Bradbury)

as a structural device for showing how James Douglas, a young black child who lives in the inner city, comes to terms with his internal and external conflicts. James lives in a tiny room with his three great aunts: "Aunt Grace who kept a towel around her head to keep off the dust, Aunt Althea who ate more than anyone else, Aunt Paul who had lost her own first name when her husband died and had taken his." He resists going to school, wishing that he could "eat peanut butter on soft white bread and watch the television flicker and not think about anything."

James lives in a world where stories are mostly sad or incomplete, "stories that filled up the halls with shouting and then fizzled out like damp firecrackers." When James asks his aunts for stories about their childhood, Aunt Paul tells him how the three aunts had lived long ago in the rural South. Aunt Grace and Aunt Althea, however, insist that James does not need to hear about "the old times." They are more concerned with his future and the fact that he must go to school in order to prepare himself for it.

To endure the harsh circumstances of his life, James tells himself stories. He knows the actual story of his own life; how his father had disappeared and how his mother had succumbed to a nervous breakdown and had been hospitalized. But it is a story too painful for James to bear; he perceives or imagines another beneath or within the actual one. He had found a ruby ring on the street and believed it to be a sign from his absent mother, who had once told him the story of how African princes had been captured and brought across the water to become slaves. The terrible story of his own cultural history helps to inspire James to create his own fantasy which helps him to survive. He was really a prince, he thought, left in the care of three old ladies while his mother returned to Africa to prepare a place for him.

In the basement of an abandoned building James dresses in robes and feathers and dances before the image of a cardboard Santa Claus. This magical ritual puts him in touch spiritually with his mother and warms him against the cold, fear, and emptiness he feels more or less constantly. When three tough street boys—Stick, Blue, and Gino—burst into the basement, James's comforting fantasy is shattered. They fling his ruby ring into a corner. James realized that when the ring was in his pocket, "it was magic but lying in a dusty corner, it was just what Stick had called it, a candy-box ring, good for nothing."

Stick, Blue, and Gino coerce James into participating in their dog-napping scam. He goes into affluent apartment buildings and asks to walk the dogs of wealthy residents. The three boys then keep the dog until they see a reward offered in the paper. Suddenly James finds that he must learn to use new strategies to survive. Inventing stories to tell himself will not suffice. He must lie to Stick, Blue, and Gino. He must make secret plans, exercising forethought and coming to terms with the actual conditions of his existence.

When the police begin to look for the dog-nappers, Stick, Blue, and Gino take James to Coney Island to hide out, and he sees the Atlantic Ocean for the first time. Suddenly realizing the difficulty his mother would have in crossing the ocean to reach Africa, he worries about her: "It was terrible to think of his mother out there in the black night bobbing around on the top of that water by herself." As James comes to terms with his situation, he relinquishes his fantasy but also acquires a deeper and truer understanding of his mother's emotional state. When he escapes from the street boys, he runs home to his aunts, where he finds all the people in the building welcoming him as he realizes that "No story was good enough. He would have to tell them what had really happened." Inside the apartment James finds not only his three aunts but also his mother, who is not a tall regal queen in white robes but a tiny vulnerable woman in a dark dress. Just as James begins to wonder who he really is, he realizes that he is *this* woman's son, and that she loves him.

A descriptive account of *How Many Miles to Babylon?* can hardly convey the eloquent characterizations, the intricate structure, or the poetic language of the novel. James, clearly a storyteller in the making, expresses his perceptions in precise but evocative figurative language which suggests the incredible menacing world in which he must live. For example, "Gino's eyes looked like holes burnt in an oilcloth," wasteland imagery forms a significant symbolic structure in the novel: abandoned buildings, trash on the streets, dilapidated tenements, shuffling wrecks of human beings, the skeleton of an abandoned and stripped automobile. Such imagery culminates in the nightmare world of the Fun House which James visits on Coney Island, with its crazy labyrinth and its distorted images.

The traditional device of the circular journey works especially well in *How Many Miles to Babylon?* Like the character in the nursery rhyme, James can indeed get there and back again. He emerges from his dangerous journey to a community which celebrates his return and joyously acknowledges his new status as hero. But James's psychological journey toward emotional maturity is far more significant. At the end of the novel he has integrated internal and external reality and has acquired a surer sense of himself in the harshly threatening world in which he must live. Even though the story is incredibly dark, Fox nevertheless holds out hope for those who, like James and his mother, can through their own resourcefulness and courage endure in the direst circumstances. The reader is left with a sense that James's mother is home to stay, that James will be able to grow and to accept the responsibilities in the future which had been too much for his father to accept in the past.

While Fox most often creates vivid psychological portraits of child characters, in *Dear Prosper* (1968) she portrays a literate dog who is writing a letter to one of his former owners, a young American boy who had found the dog wandering the streets of Paris. The narrator recounts his life story, beginning with his birth in a packing case behind a general store in Truth or Consequences, New Mexico. Eventually his brothers and sisters are all given away, and the little dog's mother seems only vaguely aware of who he is. At this point he begins to prepare himself for running away: "I ate heartily. I concentrated on developing such dog skills as springing, barking, running in circles, ducking, and stalking." At last his chance comes, and the dog makes his way to the village of San Marcial, where the sheriff adopts him and names him Frank.

At his new home Frank must contend with other dogs—Pal, O'Neill, and Roy, as well as an ill-tempered burro named Taco. Once O'Neill encourages Frank to show off in front of sheep breeders and ranchers. One of the ranchers is so impressed with Frank's herding abilities that he takes the dog far into the mountains to work on his sheep ranch. Frank realizes that O'Neill has deliberately tricked him into showing off in order to get rid of him. Frank's new owner, Mr. Iradi, renames him 'Juanito' and proceeds to work the dog far too hard. Nevertheless Juanito endures his life and does his best until Mr. Iradi brings a lazy dog named Pedro to the ranch. Pedro only pretends to work when his master is around. Otherwise he sleeps and allows Juanito to do all the work. When Juanito is kicked and punished for Pedro's mistakes, he decides to set out on his own.

In Taos, New Mexico, the dog encounters Mrs. Dickey, a rich lady from New York who adopts him, bathes him, pampers him, and names him Anthony. The dog eats sumptuously but hates the perfume, the baths, and the walks on leash, which Mrs. Dickey subjects him to. In particular, he dislikes the sly cruelties of Fred, the chauffeur, who resents the dog's presence. Eventually Anthony runs away from Mrs. Dickey and his pampered soft life with her to join a circus, where he becomes the dancing dog Boffo.

Eventually Boffo travels to Europe with the circus. When he arrives in Paris, he realizes that he has at last found his true home: "From the first whiff I caught of the city, I loved it. What fragrance! What vistas! What parks and avenues, alleys and bridges!" Boffo loves Paris so much that he stays behind when the circus departs for Hungary. In Paris he meets Prosper, who names him "Duke." With the young American boy, Duke experiences the pleasures of Parisian life: "I enjoyed walking with you, poking around the shady, dusty little streets, strolling along the banks of the Seine, sitting outside the cathedrals and museums. . . ."

When Duke realizes that Prosper and his family will soon depart for New Haven, Connecticut, he again runs away, this time to the Tuileries gardens, where he is adopted by a kindly old blind French gentleman who calls him "Chien." At last the dog, in his own old age, has become content: "I have a good job here and one that will, I hope, last. My owner enjoys my company. More important, I am useful to him. He depends on me to help him through the streets, up and down stairs and across the many bridges of Paris."

In this slim volume Fox has imaginatively captured a dog's view of existence. At the same time the dog's long journey through life resembles that of most people. He must try many different identities, overcome obstacles, defy bullies, experience both betrayals and loyal friendships, and confront dangers before he can feel at last that he has arrived at a true home, where he feels at once loved and needed. Fox manages to suggest also in *Dear Prosper* an especially vivid sense of place, especially the sights, smells, and sounds of Paris.

One of Fox's most penetrating works is *The Stone-Faced Boy* (1968), in which the central character, Gus Oliver, lives in a home full of aggressive and confident siblings. To defend himself, Gus has cultivated an impassive and expressionless countenance, which he maintains so persistently that his siblings nickname him "stone face." When Gus's great-aunt Hattie arrives for a visit, she perceives an interesting and sensitive person who is hiding behind the mask. She gives the boy a geode, a symbol of Gus's shining self encased in the stone.

Fox reveals Gus's tensions and pain as he attempts to liberate himself from all that imprisons him. The middle child in a family of five, he feels overwhelmed by his house and especially by his siblings. He feels comfortable only with his younger sister Serena, who brings home stray animals and extends her love and acceptance to her brother. Gus worries about impossible things—that the world will end or that he will fall off the planet, but only Serena will listen to him and take him seriously.

Great-aunt Hattie arrives unexpectedly in January, driving a Stutz Bearcat, smoking cigars, and slipping something from a bottle into her coffee. Her identity remains mysterious, but for Gus, she is like a fairy godmother. She sees the person inside him. While the other family members ignore Gus, even when he has been out in the cold all night looking for Serena's lost dog, Great-aunt Hattie praises his courage and acknowledges his feelings. In this episode she even manages to get Gus to laugh. When she drives away, Gus is holding the geode. The ending is not an unqualified happy one, for the reader realizes that Gus will have a long way to develop the confidence and courage which his great aunt has only begun to instill in him.

Fox continues to explore the consciousness of an isolated child in *Portrait of Ivan* (1969). Eleven-year-old Ivan is having his portrait painted by a genial but mildly eccentric painter named Matt Mustazza. To help Ivan pass the time during the tedious sittings, Matt has engaged his book-loving friend, Miss Manderby, to read to the boy. When Miss Manderby inquires how he came to be named Ivan, he replies that his mother was Russian: "My Uncle Gilbert says that she left Russia in a sled pulled across the snow by horses. After the sled crossed the border, my mother went to Warsaw." During the course of Ivan's sittings, Matt makes a charcoal sketch of the sledge, Ivan's Uncle Vladimir, and his mother. The sketch becomes a more important symbol of Ivan's identity than does the portrait.

Ivan's experiences with Matt and Miss Manderby enlarge and enrich his rather desolate existence in several ways. Ivan learns, for example, that a work of art represents important ways of knowing and seeing. As Matt prepares to paint Ivan's portrait, he explains: "I'm going to paint you. But first I'm going to make some sketches. In that way I'll learn how you look. My hand will learn."

In his first sitting, Ivan reveals that his mother is dead, news which Matt and Miss Manderby accept matter-of-factly. The two eccentric adults treat Ivan as an equal. They do not condescend to him with false sympathy, and they take a genuine interest in his conversation, in contrast to Ivan's father, who is forever answering long distance phone calls and catching airplanes to such exotic cities as Caracas.

As the sittings continue, Matt adds more details to his drawing of the sledge. Matt, Miss Manderby, and Ivan participate in the creation of the drawing. Matt remarks that they have forgotten the sentry box; he draws the soldiers in the box and a soldier who runs to pursue the sledge. Miss Manderby worries that the soldiers may not be wearing the correct uniform for the period. Thus Matt and Miss Manderby help to put Ivan in touch with his mother's experience by helping him to imagine what it was to be alive in the era of her childhood immediately after the fall of Czarist Russia. Ivan knows the flat facts of his mother's childhood escape. Matt's art helps him to know the fullness of the experience as it is rendered lively by human

art and creative imagination. Matt and Miss Manderby are thus enabling Ivan to create the exciting story of his own family history.

Later in the novel Matt explains that he is going to Jacksonville, Florida, to paint a large old plantation house and grounds of the Crown estate since it is about to be sold to make a golf course and country club. Matt emphasizes again that art itself is an important way that human beings have of knowing. When Ivan asks why Mr. Crown does not take photographs of the estate, Matt says Mr. Crown feels that paintings will "show more of what things are really like," and Miss Manderby adds that "nothing is exactly what it looks like."

When Matt perceives how disappointed Ivan and Miss Manderby are that he is leaving for Florida, he invites them to come and even to bring Miss Manderby's cat, Alyosha. Miss Manderby packs a delectable picnic. Matt packs his painting supplies, and after Ivan convinces his father, they all depart in Matt's friend's car, an elegant black automobile with a "little silver statue of a winged lady on its hood."

The trip to Florida becomes an expansive adventure for Ivan. He meets a girl named Geneva who takes him for boat rides and shows him how to scare water moccasins off the dock. She shares cornbread-and-jam sandwiches with him and even convinces him to swim in the terrifying black water of the river where the snakes live. Ivan tells Geneva about his mother, grandmother, and uncle escaping from Russia in the sledge. He makes a real friend in Geneva, who cries when he leaves. When Ivan returns home with his father, his adventure to Florida becomes like a dream. Soon he learns that Matt is leaving for San Francisco, but before he departs, he leaves Ivan's portrait and the drawing of the sledge. As Ivan looks at the drawing, he notices every detail: the powerful horses, the black sledge, the branches of pine trees bowed with snow, the alarmed Russian soldiers. He also sees that, "In the sledge huddled two children, who would not see their father again. The little girl did not know she had begun a journey that led right to this room where her son lay, half asleep. What had she thought, sitting there in the frosty air among the fur robes and the small Oriental rugs? The sledge had been filled up with people he knew, Harry and Matt, Geneva and Miss Manderby. Somewhere in his mind, an empty ghost sledge raced across the snow. But this one would do for now."

In *Portrait of Ivan* Fox reveals her deep reverence for human community, imagination, and art. Interacting with a group of people helps Ivan perceive the concrete and the imagined world and enables him to transform the bare, bleak facts of his existence. Through social interaction and through the shaping forces of the human imagination, Ivan must create a self and fill the empty sledge that represents his future with possibility and meaning. In this complex novel Fox creates exceptionally subtle characterizations as she explores the relationship between life and art and the individual within a community.

The King's Falcon (1969) is a beautifully crafted fairy tale. King Philip rules a country so tiny that he can view all of it from his castle rampart. Philip is lonely, and nothing in the kingdom seems right—poor land, squabbling peasants, and pervasive poverty blight the land. The queen, twenty-two years older than Philip, is shrewish and unpleasant. Thus he lives with a sense of diminishment. He suffers acute boredom, since he cannot read and can find little to interest him. His extraordinary memory does not help; it only makes him sad, "for the stories which had so excited his imagination when he had heard them as a child concerned the great adventures of the old times, the brilliant histories of knights long dead, the forgotten crossroads of far countries where traveling fairs had once lighted up the nights and enlivened the days." The king is troubled also because he can do nothing. When he and an old falconer find a nest of young falcons, Philip realizes that at last he has a chance to achieve mastery in at least one small area of existence.

The old falconer proves to be an excellent teacher. Philip takes his falcon and escapes from his confining kingdom and marriage to become a King's Falconer himself. *The King's Falcon* celebrates the capacity of human beings to change. Fox suggests the redeeming pleasure of work and the need for one to create an identity rather than accepting one ready made. The book's economical but poetic prose, its subtle play with the conventions of fairy tales, and its effortless use of symbolic allegory make it a memorable book. Also the pensive and rather sensitive portrayal of the king suggests a judgment on patriarchal society. King Philip is interested in improving the quality of his life through his own efforts, rather than imposing his authority upon others.

In *Blowfish Live in the Sea* (1970) Fox presents a thirteen-year-old narrator, Carrie, who describes her eccentric eighteen-year-old half brother Ben, who has let his hair grow long and constantly writes the sentence "Blowfish live in the sea." Ben's peculiar behavior and his attempts to deal with his identity crisis have resulted in a tension-ridden

Dust jacket for Fox's 1970 novel about the relationship between a thirteen-year-old girl and her withdrawn and rebellious half brother (Bradbury)

household. The relationship between Carrie's father and Ben is especially strained. Ben has not seen his natural father for many years, and his well-to-do stepfather no longer understands or sympathizes with him. Carrie often finds herself torn between her feelings for her parents and for Ben, especially when the parents try to persuade her to influence him. Carrie, however, refuses to pressure Ben into conforming to her parents' expectations. Rather she tries to understand and to accept him as he is.

Ben's problems reach a crisis after his maternal grandfather dies. Soon after the death, Ben runs away. When he returns, the household becomes even more silent and filled with tension. Carrie seems to feel the tension more acutely than anyone else in the family: "Everything is different now. I feel as if my clothes are held together with safety pins and my shoes don't fit, neither of which is true. How could it all change back again? How could Ben start getting up in the morning again, or go to school or cut his hair or talk with me the way he used to?"

Just as the situation is growing unbearable, Ben receives a letter from his father asking him to come to Boston for a visit. Ben wants Carrie to go with him. Despite the parents' fears, Ben and Carrie set off to Boston on the bus. When they arrive at the appointed room in a disreputable hotel, Ben's father has left another letter saying that he has been called back to his ranch in Arizona. Ben and Carrie wander around Boston all afternoon until Ben decides to return to the hotel room. There they find Ben's father, hopelessly drunk. Eventually the three go out to dinner, and Ben's father describes his latest venture—the attempt to refurbish an old motel near Boston. Ben decides to join his father in restoring the motel, and Carrie returns home. While Carrie packs Ben's belongings, she finds a blowfish, "stiff with varnish, orange and yellow and shiny." The stuffed blowfish has been Ben's only connection with his missing father—hence his compulsion to write the sentence.

In *Blowfish Live in the Sea* Fox manages to show Carrie's affection for Ben in understated, moving terms. Fox also reflects the turmoil of the Vietnam War era in interesting ways. Carrie mentions, for example, that the war has been going on as long as she can remember. Ben believes in natural things and rejects the establishment. More important, Fox's selection of detail and use of diction vividly convey Carrie's consciousness of experience. When Carrie enters the hotel, for example, she says that: "It felt like the place the bad weather was coming from, dark and stale and cold."

Ben's archetypal search for his father is rendered in highly realistic terms as Ben and Carrie encounter lost alienated people such as a pathetic bag lady on the bus, dangerous drug dealers in the park, and a cynical but apparently good-hearted old man, Mr. Krakowski. One senses that Carrie's journey has allowed her to mature by experiencing a more expansive sense of reality and the possibilities in it, even as it permits her the pleasure of returning safely home.

Good Ethan (1973) is a simply told picture book in which Fox begins with an inane warning of parent to child, "Ethan, be a good boy. . . . You must not walk across the street." When Ethan's ball bounces away and rolls across the street, the boy faces a moral dilemma. Since the adult passers-by will not help him, Ethan devises his own resourceful plan. Fox thus celebrates the child's ingenuity with wry humor, as she shows Ethan successful in

the end.

The Slave Dancer (1973), winner of the Newbery Medal, is one of the finest achievements in American children's literature. In this powerful novel Fox has blended the traditions of the sea adventure story and historical fiction to tell the story of Jessie Bollier, a thirteen-year-old boy who is kidnapped and forced to go on board a slave ship, *The Moonlight*, in order to be a "slave dancer." While captured Africans shuffle a pathetically grotesque dance, Jessie plays his fife. In this nightmare voyage Jessie passes several moral tests of character, encounters varieties of evil and returns safely home, but fails to come to terms with his painful experience. His journey thus represents a painful fall from innocence into horrifying experience.

In the opening chapter Fox details Jessie's enclosed life with his mother and ailing sister, Betty. Jessie's father had drowned many years earlier, and Jessie often dreams of the drowning, urging his father in the dream to swim. Mrs. Bollier earns a meager living for herself and her children by sew-

Dust jacket for Fox's historical novel about the New Orleans slave trade, winner of the Newbery Medal in 1974 (Bradbury)

ing elegant gowns for the aristocratic ladies of New Orleans. Jessie's mother forbids him to visit the slave market, for she perceives the horror of it. Innocently curious, however, Jessie often slips to the market and plays his fife for pennies. He stares into the courtyards of the wealthy ladies and gentlemen. Once he sees a slave woman named Star return his stare but does not perceive that the opulent beauty of the city and the gracious leisurely lives of the wealthy depend upon the evil institution of slavery.

Once when Jessie goes to borrow candles from his maiden aunt in order that his mother may sew all night, he ventures again to the forbidden slave market. As he watches the people and looks at the lovely houses, he fantasizes about his own future: "Someday I might become a rich chandler in a fine suit, with a thousand candles to hand if I needed them instead of three grudgingly given stubs. I imagined the splendid house I would live in, my gardens, my carriage and horses." Entranced by his own dreams of power (which depend upon his own support of slavery), Jessie immediately finds himself suffocating in a foul canvas bag. When he sees daylight again, Jessie is aboard *The Moonlight* and bound for Africa to capture slaves.

Fox announces the theme of her starkly powerful historical novel soon after Jessie arrives on the ship. Ben Stout explains that he and all of the other crewmen had also been kidnapped when they had made their first voyage on a slaver. But then the men "got to like it" and thereafter willingly served on the ship. Then Stout remarks to Jessie, "You'll see some bad things, but if you didn't see them, they'd still be happening, so you might as well."

Indeed Jessie does see some bad things. He tries to establish relations with first one and then another crewman, but all have succumbed to the evil of slavery and represent different sinister expressions of it. The most likeable of the crew is Clay Purvis, who tries to befriend and to protect Jessie. Purvis has rationalized his own participation in the horrible mission because he says that his Irish parents have suffered so terribly on their way to America. Captain Cawthorne, whose mad and obsessive character strongly resembles Herman Melville's Captain Ahab, is driven by greed. Ben Stout, however, emerges as a character whose evil appears unmotivated. He seems, like Shakespeare's Iago, to enjoy evil for its own sake. He enjoys torturing the slaves. Since he knows the language of the Africans, he can inflict both psychological and physical pain. In one dark scene, it is also hinted that Stout tor-

tures a woman sexually.

At one point Ben Stout, for reasons known only to himself, steals Jessie's fife and throws it into the hold of the ship where slaves have been crammed together. In order to find the fife, Jessie has to descend into the hold and quite literally walk on the bodies of the Africans. As he is lowered into the hold, the Africans buoy him up and find his fife for him. Earlier Jessie had noticed an African boy about his age. It is the boy, Ras, who retrieves the fife for Jessie.

Jessie's severest moral test occurs when he grows sick and disgusted at the pitiful condition, the very stench of the slaves: "I hated the slaves! I hated their shuffling, their howling, their very suffering. . . . Oh, God I wished them all dead!" Overcome by his feelings of revulsion, Jessie drops his fife and takes refuge in his hammock. As punishment, Captain Cawthorne sentences Jessie to five lashes. Jessie then recognizes his kinship with the Africans, and his humanity is saved. He does not finally participate in supporting slavery but struggles to maintain his own sense of morality in the face of the horror around him. His sense of kinship with his alter ego, Ras, Fox suggests, allows Jessie to perceive what it would be like if he were himself a slave, and in a sense he is also imprisoned in the suffocating world of the ship.

The horrifying climax of the novel occurs when an American ship approaches the slaver. To avoid persecution, Cawthorne orders that the slaves be thrown overboard. During the madness that follows, a violent storm overtakes the ship. Jessie and Ras take refuge in the strangely womblike hold of the ship as it is driven before the storm. All of the slaves and all of the crew members are lost. At last the ship reaches the gulf coast of Mississippi, and the two boys are able to reach the beach safely after an urgent struggle.

Once Jessie and Ras have reached the land, they meet Daniel, a wise old black man who has run away from slaveholders to live alone in the woods. He befriends the boys and feeds and protects them. Yet Daniel is unable to offer Jessie the affection he bestows upon Ras. Though Ras and Jessie have grown as close as twins, Daniel cannot transcend racial barriers in his attitude toward Jessie. Soon Jessie makes his way home to New Orleans, while Ras is conducted north to freedom. Jessie, however, finds himself estranged from home. He cannot bear to remain in New Orleans and later makes his way north to Boston. Perhaps the most telling evidence that Jessie has been in some sense tragically broken by his experience is that he could never again bear the sound of music.

The Slave Dancer is historical fiction at its finest, for Fox has meticulously researched every facet of the slave trade and of the period. More important she allows the reader to perceive the true horror of slavery by showing the sights, sounds, and details of it as they are filtered through Jessie's consciousness. Like Joseph Conrad's *Heart of Darkness, The Slave Dancer* takes the reader on a voyage that reveals a haunting glimpse into the abyss of human evil. Perhaps, Fox suggests, Jessie's baffled and permanent hurt is the only response possible in the face of his experience.

Some readers and critics of *The Slave Dancer* have bitterly criticized the fact that black characters are presented in such a helpless and passive role. Indeed they are portrayed as naked and pathetically helpless in the face of the power of their captors. In an important sense, this criticism seems to miss the point. The story is told from Jessie's point of view. While the Africans were assuredly finding their own resourceful ways to resist their horrifying situation even in the holds of slave ships, Jessie would not have been able to see this. He is, however, able to imagine what it would be like to endure such suffering, just as the sensitive reader of *The Slave Dancer* can imagine what it was to be conscious at such a dark period of American history. Another charge against the novel—that the characters seem to be merely devices for conveying information about the slave trade—seems totally unjustified. The characters in the novel are vividly and specifically realized as Jessie experiences them. *The Slave Dancer* is clearly Fox's masterpiece, and it is fast becoming a classic in American children's literature.

In her collection, *The Little Swineherd and Other Tales* (1978), Fox models her short stories on traditional folktales and upon the literary folktales of Hans Christian Andersen. However, she creates a humorous framework for the tales. An enterprising duck wishes to become the manager of the story-telling goose who narrates five tales to eight frogs sitting on lily pads: "The Little Swineherd," "The Rooster Who Could Not See Enough of Himself," "Circles and Straight Lines," "The Alligator Who Told the Truth," and "The Raccoon's Song." Fox's anthropomorphic animal characters satirize human beings. The stories are memorable for their concrete detail, their subtle plays on folktale conventions, their open endings, and their humor.

A Place Apart (1980) features a thirteen-year-old narrator, Victoria Finch, called "Tory" by her family. After her father's sudden death, Victoria and her mother are forced to sell their home in Boston and move to the small Massachusetts town of New Oxford. Here Tory and her mother refurbish their shabby little house and try to adjust to their grief and loss.

Victoria acquires two friends as she settles into her new life. Elizabeth Marx shares ordinary pleasures with Victoria: eating doughnuts, bicycling, starting a small day-care business in the summer. Victoria's most intense feelings, however, are directed toward Hugh Todd, an arrogant and wealthy young man whose real interest in Victoria is that he believes her to be a writer and therefore special and different from other people. He is particularly interested in producing a play she has written.

Within a few months Victoria must also deal with her mother's plans to remarry. Inevitably she feels a sense of betrayal, but she tries to deal with her ambivalent feelings and get along with her mother's fiancé. The next year, when Victoria turns fourteen and has entered her sophomore year, she finds that Hugh, who has recently returned from Italy, no longer seems interested in her friendship except to try to manipulate her into finishing the play. He now focuses his attention on Tom Kyle, a shy boy who has recently moved from Boston. Gradually Victoria's self-image grows strong enough that she can defy Hugh and resist his manipulations.

Meanwhile Elizabeth Marx's mother has experienced a nervous breakdown just in time to prevent Elizabeth from running away. Elizabeth forms a relationship with Frank Wilson, a boy who had previously asked Victoria to go out. The crisis of the novel occurs when Frank insists upon driving Elizabeth, Victoria, and Tom Kyle to the top of a nearby mountain on a dangerously icy road. All four youngsters are terrified, but Tom Kyle humiliates himself by wetting his pants. The story circulates throughout the school. Tom finally has to prove that he is not a coward and attempts the treacherous drive himself. After Tom is seriously injured and in the hospital, Frank Wilson tells everyone that Hugh has viciously spread the story of Tom's terror and the pants-wetting episode. Hugh becomes increasingly isolated and eventually leaves the school for private tutoring. The novel ends with Victoria's having achieved a surer sense of herself as she anticipates a new life with her mother and stepfather.

A Place Apart is Fox's least successful novel. Victoria's life is crowded with various conflicts, most of which are not sufficiently developed. For example, near the beginning of the novel the reader learns that Mrs. Finch must somehow prepare herself to earn a living, as Mr. Finch had not left much insurance. However, Mrs. Finch continues to stay at home, to smoke, and to play the piano until she conveniently finds an available college professor to marry her. The reader has a sense that Fox offers a conventional and pat solution to the difficult economic and emotional problems faced by a middle-aged single mother. Perhaps the most serious flaw in the novel is that the narrator herself is finally not interesting enough to command a reader's sympathy and attention. She is too entirely like too many other teenaged characters, and she lacks the complex character development of most of Fox's novels.

One-Eyed Cat (1984), however, is one of Fox's finest literary achievements. Ned Wallis, a congregational minister's only child, lives in Tyler, New York, in a house built by his great grandfather in 1846. Ned, his father, and his mother love the house, even though it is too expensive for a minister's salary. Ned must witness the pain of his mother, who suffers from crippling rheumatoid arthritis. He often feels trapped in the house with his mother's illness and his father's patient goodness. But at least the Wallis house is quiet until the arrival of Mrs. Scallop, the new housekeeper "whose voice now intruded in the dining room every morning, as sharp and grinding as the woodcutter's saw when he came in the spring to thin out the pines which grew along the north side of the Wallises' property." To escape from the intrusive Mrs. Scallop, Ned accepts an afternoon job doing chores for Mr. Scully, an elderly neighbor.

Ned's central conflict is initiated by a visit from his rather glamorous Uncle Hilary, a world traveler who brings Ned presents from exotic spots around the globe. On his most recent visit, Uncle Hilary brings Ned an air rifle for his birthday. Ned is aware immediately that his parents disapprove of the gun. Mr. Wallis intervenes and explains that the gun will have to be stored in the attic until Ned is older. Full of anger and resentment, Ned is unable to sleep. Later in the evening he goes to the attic, takes the gun from its hiding place, and hastens out into the night with the gun in his hand, making his way through the darkness to the deserted barn. Seeing a flitting dark shadow from the corner of his eye, Ned impulsively presses the trigger: "There was a 'whoosh,' the sound a bobwhite makes when it bursts out of underbrush, then silence . . . he had heard something, a kind of disturbance in the air. He walked over to the barn.

There was no shadow now. There was nothing." When Ned returns to the house, he is sure that someone is looking down at him from an upper window.

A few days later, while Ned is doing chores for Mr. Scully, the old man tells him about the wild feral cats who live in the woods, noting that there is something wrong with one which had ventured near the house. Ned realizes suddenly that one of the cat's eyes is missing, and he instantly feels "a touch of fear." Mr. Scully remarks that "someone used him for target practice. A boy would do that. A living target is more interesting than a tin can. Or he might have had a bad fight with another animal."

Thereafter Ned becomes obsessed with the one-eyed cat and finds every excuse to spend time with Mr. Scully, who also exhibits unusual concern for the maimed animal. Gradually a deep sense of guilt settles into Ned's soul, eating at him and estranging him from his parents. Even as Ned grows more distant from his parents, however, he grows even closer to Mr. Scully.

Deep in the winter, after a terrible blizzard, Ned and Mr. Scully fear that the cat has not survived, but the cat shows up and sleeps inertly on top of an old icebox in Mr. Scully's utility shed. Clearly the cat is seriously ill, but it does survive.

Meanwhile Ned continues to suffer acutely from his guilt. He grows even more withdrawn and silent. Even the removal of the intrusive Mrs. Scallop to take charge of a nursing home hardly cheers him. He is unable to take joy in a proposed trip to Charleston, South Carolina, with Uncle Hilary. Instead he wishes to remain home, help Mr. Scully, and care for the one-eyed cat.

One day when Ned arrives to do his chores and to check on the cat, he finds Mr. Scully, who has had a stroke, collapsed in the upstairs hall. An ambulance takes him to the hospital, and he is later removed to the nursing home where Mrs. Scallop works. Meanwhile Mr. Scully's daughter permits Ned to continue feeding the cat. His guilt plagues him, as he realizes: "All the lies he had told, the subterfuge, were piled up over the gun like a mountain of hard-packed snow. He felt his secret had frozen around him. He didn't know how to melt it."

At last Ned's guilt makes him physically ill. He feels frantic about the cat and wishes it were dead. After Ned recovers from his illness, he asks his parents if he may visit Mr. Scully. When Ned first sees a greatly diminished and infirm Mr. Scully, he "felt his stomach sink the way it did when he turned over a rock and saw the sudden stirring of insects and worms." As Ned continues his visits, Mr. Scully grows steadily weaker. At last the nurse tells Ned that Mr. Scully cannot last much longer. Feeling desperate about his deep guilt, Ned blurts what he believes to be the truth. Summoning all of his strength, Mr. Scully reaches towards Ned's hand: "He felt the touch of Mr. Scully's fingers, then gradually his whole hand covering Ned's own. There was the faintest pressure, so faint, Ned wasn't sure how he knew there'd been any at all."

Ned suffers most when others misinterpret his attention to Mr. Scully. When his father praises him, Ned cringes and longs to howl out the truth, "It's because of the cat I went to see him." Yet Ned knows that is not the whole truth: "More than the secret of the cat had drawn him to the nursing home. It was Mr. Scully himself. He'd known *him*, his habits, the things he knew how to do, the way he made his bread...." Again and again Ned comes close to confessing to his mother or father.

True release comes for Ned at last one evening in mid-April. He makes his way through the darkness to the old Makepeace mansion. In the shadows of the mansion Ned finds his mother. They discuss Mr. Scully's death, and in a painful moment, Ned becomes aware of his own mortality and that of his mother: "and at that moment as the sorrow of it seemed to lodge in his throat so that it was hard to breathe, a cat walked straight out of the woods and into the moonlight." Ned and his mother watch the one-eyed cat and two kittens frolic in the moonlight. At last Ned tells his mother the truth. She responds by confessing her own act of irresponsibility, and tells Ned that she had once left him and his father, and that during the time of the separation Ned had been left alone to wander about the house in the night. The novel ends as Ned and his mother go home to his father. He is reconciled with himself by seeing the fault of others.

Fox depicts Ned's fall from innocence into bitter experience with exceptional insight. While Jessie Bollier in *The Slave Dancer* consciously resists participating in the evil around him, Ned commits an evil act without even intending it. In the *One-Eyed Cat* Fox creates complex characterization, vividly dramatic scenes, and an evocative sense of place. Among the many strengths of this fine novel is the depth with which Fox treats the mother's character. For all the pain, death, guilt, illness, and suffering portrayed in the novel, *One-Eyed Cat* is nevertheless a profoundly affirmative book. Fox asserts that genuine relationship is possible and that

Dust jacket for Fox's most recent children's book (Bradbury)

making mistakes is an essential part of being human, as is forgiveness.

In her Newbery award acceptance speech in 1974, Fox states that the "effort to connect ourselves with the reality of our own lives" is one of the most essential parts of being human and adds: "It is an effort carried about against formidable enemies: habit; inertia; the fear of change and what it will entail; the wish to preserve our idiot corners of safety, of being 'right'; and self-righteousness— the most dangerous enemy of all, full of a terrible energy that would turn us away from pondering the mystery of existence towards its own barren pleasures."

In *One-Eyed Cat* Fox endorses Ned's efforts to achieve this connectedness with himself, with Mr. Scully and the cat, and with his parents. To do so he must experience painful moral dilemmas and become aware of ambiguities and ambivalence, the highly complex nature of truth and moral choice. Fox contrasts this difficult process against the pat and platitudinous self-righteous morality of Mrs. Scallop, who congratulates herself constantly on her goodness and generosity. On the other hand, Mr. Wallis, the dedicated minister, is truly good, a quality which put pressures on his wife and son. As his mother explains to Ned, she had run away because "I was afraid of your father's goodness. I'm not so very good."

Paula Fox is one of America's finest writers for adults or children. Her novels are marked by their fine craftsmanship, their warm humor, their humanity, and their utter honesty. Readers who admire Fox's work return to it again and again, for it rewards the most demanding critic and also pleases the child reader, a rare achievement in the world of children's literature.

References:

Lois R. Kuznets, "The Fresh-Air Kids, or Some Contemporary Versions of Pastoral," *Children's Literature,* 11 (1983): 156-168;

Christine McDonnell, "A Second Look: *The Stone-Faced Boy,*" *Horn Book,* 60 (April 1984): 219-222;

Anita Moss, "Varieties of Children's Metafiction," *Studies in the Literary Imagination,* 18 (Fall 1984): 79-92;

Perry Nodelman, "How Typical Children Read Typical Books," *Children's Literature in Education,* 12 (Winter 1981): 177-185;

John Rowe Townsend, *A Sounding of Storytellers* (New York: Lippincott, 1979).

Jean Fritz

(16 November 1915-   )

O. Mell Busbin

Appalachian State University

BOOKS: *Bunny Hopwell's First Spring,* illustrated by Rachel Dixon (New York: Wonder Books, 1954);

Help Mr. Willy Nilly, illustrated by Jean Tamburine (New York: Treasure Books, 1954);

Fish Head, illustrated by Marc Simont (New York: Coward-McCann, 1954; London: Faber & Faber, 1956);

121 Pudding Street, illustrated by Sofia (New York: Coward-McCann, 1955);

Hurrah for Jonathan!, illustrated by Violet La Mont (Racine, Wis.: Whitman, 1955);

Growing Up, illustrated by Elizabeth Webbe (Chicago: Rand McNally, 1956);

The Late Spring, illustrated by Erik Blegvad (New York: Coward-McCann, 1957);

The Cabin Faced West, illustrated by Feodor Rojankowsky (New York: Coward-McCann, 1958);

The Animals of Dr. Schweitzer, illustrated by Douglass Howland (New York: Coward-McCann, 1958; Edinburgh: Oliver & Boyd, 1962);

Champion Dog, Prince Tom, with Tom Clute, illustrated by Ernest Hart (New York: Coward-McCann, 1958);

How To Read a Rabbit, illustrated by Leonard Shortall (New York: Coward-McCann, 1959);

Brady, illustrated by Lynd Ward (New York: Coward-McCann, 1960; London: Gollancz, 1966);

December Is for Christmas, as Ann Scott, illustrated by Alcy Kendrick (New York: Wonder Books, 1961);

Tap, Tap, Lion—1, 2, 3, illustrated by Shortall (New York: Coward-McCann, 1962);

San Francisco, illustrated by Emil Weiss (Chicago: Rand McNally, 1962);

I, Adam, illustrated by Peter Burchard (New York: Coward-McCann, 1963; London: Gollancz, 1965);

Magic To Burn, illustrated by Beth and Joe Krush (New York: Coward-McCann, 1964);

Surprise Party, illustrated by George Wiggins (New York: Initial Teaching Alphabet Publications, 1965);

The Train, illustrated by Jean Simpson (New York: Grosset & Dunlap, 1965);

Early Thunder, illustrated by Ward (New York: Coward-McCann, 1967; London: Gollancz, 1969);

George Washington's Breakfast, illustrated by Paul Galdone (New York: Coward-McCann, 1969);

Cast for a Revolution: Some American Friends and Enemies, 1728-1814 (Boston: Houghton Mifflin, 1972);

And Then What Happened, Paul Revere?, illustrated by Margot Tomes (New York: Coward, McCann & Geoghegan, 1973);

Why Don't You Get a Horse, Sam Adams?, illustrated by Trina Schart Hyman (New York: Coward, McCann & Geoghegan, 1974);

Where Was Patrick Henry on the 29th of May?, illustrated by Tomes (New York: Coward, McCann & Geoghegan, 1975);

Who's That Stepping on Plymouth Rock?, illustrated by J. B. Handelsman (New York: Coward, McCann & Geoghegan, 1975);

Will You Sign Here, John Hancock?, illustrated by Hyman (New York: Coward, McCann & Geoghegan, 1976);

What's the Big Idea, Ben Franklin?, illustrated by Tomes (New York: Coward, McCann & Geoghegan, 1976);

The Secret Diary of Jeb & Abigail: Growing Up in America, 1776-1783, illustrated by Kenneth Bald and Neil Boyle (Pleasantville, N.Y.: Reader's Digest, 1976);

Can't You Make Them Behave, King George?, illustrated by Tomie de Paola (New York: Coward, McCann & Geoghegan, 1977);

Brendan the Navigator: A History Mystery About the Discovery of America, illustrated by Enrico Arno (New York: Coward, McCann & Geoghegan, 1979);

Stonewall, illustrated by Stephen Gammell (New York: Putnam's, 1979);

Where Do You Think You're Going, Christopher Columbus?, illustrated by Tomes (New York: Putnam's, 1980);

The Man Who Loved Books, illustrated by Hyman (New York: Putnam's, 1981);

Traitor: The Case of Benedict Arnold (New York: Putnam's, 1981);

The Good Giants and the Bad Pukwudgies, illustrated by de Paola (New York: Putnam's, 1982);

Homesick: My Own Story, illustrated by Tomes (New York: Putnam's, 1982);

The Double Life of Pocahontas, illustrated by Ed Young (New York: Putnam's, 1983);

China Homecoming, photographs by Michael Fritz (New York: Putnam's, 1985);

Make Way for Sam Houston, illustrated by Elise Primavera (New York: Putnam's, 1986).

OTHER: "The Very Truth," in *Celebrating Children's Books: Essays on Children's Literature in Honor of Zena Sutherland,* edited by Betsy Hearne and Marilyn Kaye (New York: Lothrop, Lee & Shepard), pp. 81-86.

PERIODICAL PUBLICATIONS: "Style in Children's Literature," *Elementary English,* 18 (October 1941): 208-212;

"Two-way Story Hours," *Library Journal,* 79 (August 1954): 1372-1374;

"Parents: A Challenge to Librarians," *Library Journal,* 82 (15 April 1957): 1077-1081;

"Are You Sure You Can't Write?," *Library Journal,* 85 (15 October 1960): 3826-3828;

"The House That Jack Built," *Horn Book,* 42 (December 1966): 681-683;

"On Writing Historical Fiction," *Horn Book,* 43 (October 1967): 565-570;

"Make Room for the Eighteenth Century," *Horn Book,* 50 (October 1974): 177-181;

"George Washington, My Father, and Walt Disney," *Horn Book,* 52 (April 1976): 191-198;

"The Education of an American," *Top of the News,* 32 (June 1976): 321-336;

"Making It Real," *Children's Literature in Education,* 22 (Autumn 1976): 125-127;

"An Evening with Richard Adams," *Children's Literature in Education,* 9 (Summer 1978): 67-72.

Jean Fritz has established herself as a writer of historical fiction and biographies for children, two genres which require accuracy, something for which Fritz diligently strives and at which she constantly excels. Many of her noted children's books have been set during the American Revolution. In 1978 she was given the Children's Book Guild Nonfiction Award for the "body of her creative writing."

For the first thirteen years of her life Jean Guttery lived in Hankow, China, where she was born to Arthur Minton and Myrtle Chaney Guttery, who had gone to China in 1913 as a newly married couple to serve as YMCA missionaries. As a child Fritz confided in one of her parents that when she grew up she was going to be a writer. She convinced her parents of the seriousness of this intent while in high school when she began to write poetry, short stories, and essays. Most important, though, she began keeping a journal, which at first consisted primarily of quotes from books and poems she was reading but which soon expanded into more than just a collection of comments on life by great writers; it became a place for her to articulate her feelings about people and life. Years later she drew upon it in her writings for children.

In 1933 Fritz enrolled at Wheaton College in Norton, Massachusetts, where she majored in English, graduating in 1937. While at Wheaton she became a regular writer for the campus newspaper, the *Wheaton News,* and was made an associate editor in her junior year.

During the fall of 1937, with the encouragement of her mother, Fritz enrolled in an advertising course at Columbia University. She began, however, to see the advertising business as irresponsible, and her heightened social consciousness did not permit her continuation in a line of work whose methods she viewed as deceiving, dishonest, and in complete disregard for public interest. In order to broaden her employment skills she then took a secretarial course. By 1939 she had accepted a temporary job with the textbook publisher Silver

Burdett Company, where she remained until 1941. At the encouragement of a Silver Burdett editor, Jean enrolled in a graduate course in children's literature at Columbia University, studying under Jean Betsner. At Betsner's suggestion she submitted her term paper, "Style in Children's Literature," to *Elementary English,* where it was published in the October 1941 issue.

Jean Guttery married Michael Fritz on 1 November 1941. He had just been discharged from the military, but, after the Japanese attack on Pearl Harbor, he was recalled to active duty. Fritz continued with Silver Burdett for a short period of time before taking a job with the research department of the Boy Scouts of America. Eventually, her husband's military assignments led Fritz to San Francisco, where she reviewed children's books for the *San Francisco Chronicle* and gave birth to her first child, David Minto Fritz, on 18 May 1943. Their next temporary residence was Fort Lewis in Tacoma, Washington, where Fritz reviewed adult books for the *Ledger-News-Tribune.*

At war's end, the Fritzes temporarily lived with Jean's parents in New York City. A daughter, Andrea Scott Fritz, was born on 29 April 1947. During this time Fritz served as a ghost writer and prepared teacher's manuals for Macmillan's social studies editor, James Michener. Later she began working for the Prang company, writing educational and promotional materials.

Having located in Dobbs Ferry, New York, Jean Fritz began serving as a volunteer in the local public library in 1953. There was no children's department, and she sought to establish one. During her two years at the library she succeeded in getting children, as well as adults, actively involved with children's books and films. What began as volunteer work later became a part-time, then a full-time paid position, but Fritz gave up the opportunity in order to pursue her writing career.

In the early 1950s Fritz wrote several short stories for *Humpty Dumpty* magazine which dealt with the experiences of young children and which served as her attempt to discover whether she could write about childhood things for children. These stories focus on events that went on around her, mainly the experiences of her young son and daughter, rather than something from within herself.

Between 1954 and 1957 Fritz wrote four "concept" books: *Bunny Hopwell's First Spring* (1954), about a rabbit in springtime; *Help Mr. Willy Nilly* (1954), in which the child must complete aspects of the story as it is read; *Growing Up* (1956), about changes that take place in nature; and *The Late Spring* (1957), about how a robin finally wakes up to his duty of being the first robin of spring in the North, following a winter in Florida. *Help Mr. Willy Nilly* resulted from Fritz's efforts to involve children in books while she was serving as a volunteer in the Dobbs Ferry Public Library.

Fish Head (1954) is a picture book for young children, with an effective balance of text and character-revealing illustrations. The title refers to a cat that lives on a fishing wharf until one of his rat chases results in his becoming a stowaway on a fishing boat at sea. Fish Head soon learns the joys of eating the fish which land on the deck each morning, and he easily adjusts to the joys of his new life. Fritz has indicated this story resulted from one of her "getaway impulses," a sense of the need to be near the sea to feel free.

As Fritz quickly matured in her writing, ideas became more complex and dramatic, and she began to include themes from her introspective journal writing. *121 Pudding Street* (1955) was her first "long" book for children. Focusing on the theme of personal freedom, it depicts what she as a child in China envisioned to be the typical American street, though the main characters are based upon people from the Fritzes' American neighborhood. (The boy who likes to eat is based on her son David; the girl who writes poetry on her daughter Andrea.) Pudding Street is a place where parents are neither seen nor heard and where every child is free to live out his own fantasy. Reflected in this story is what Fritz would like to have had during her childhood in China, for there she was deprived of the idealized American upbringing for which she longed. There is a proper balance between the natural and the highly improbable—but utterly desirable—in this fantasy for young children.

The Cabin Faced West (1958) was Fritz's initial experience with historical fiction. The idea for the novel came from a favorite family story about her great-great-grandmother and the day Gen. George Washington had supper in her home. It portrays the isolation and loneliness of pioneer life, as opposed to the glorious life which is traditionally reflected in children's books. The preteen heroine, Ann Hamilton, lives a lonely life on the Pennsylvania frontier after her family moves there from Gettysburg in 1784, but she eventually overcomes her aversion for "the West" and its life-style. Although much of the story was invented, Jean was able to draw real names and places from county records. This novel is characterized by charm and ever-mounting interest and provides insight into a

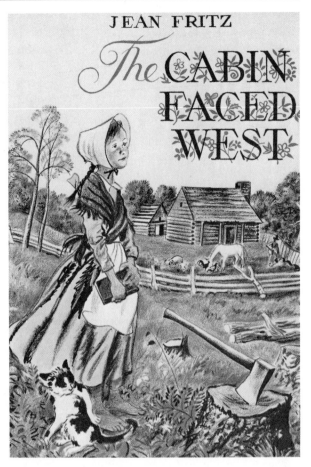

Dust jacket for Fritz's first historical novel, which portrays the isolation and loneliness of pioneer life (Coward-McCann)

child's life in the 1780s. Sales for this novel are reported to be in excess of 57,000.

Champion Dog, Prince Tom (1958) resulted from Fritz's having read an article in the *Saturday Evening Post* about a cocker spaniel. Prince Tom began as the unwanted blond runt in a litter of black puppies and became one of the most famous dogs in the country, who, among other things, pushed baby carriages and eventually won the National Field Trial Championship. The *Post* article motivated Fritz to read as much as she could about dog competitions before she finally went to meet the owner, Tom Clute, with whom she wrote the book. Good adult-children relationships are stressed in this lively true story, which also provides helpful suggestions for dog training.

After seeing a documentary film on Dr. Albert Schweitzer with her fourth grader Andrea, Fritz was intrigued at how his reverence for life extended to his many pets. With the help of Erica Anderson, she conducted the research that went into *The Animals of Dr. Schweitzer* (1958). A good description of Schweitzer's work is effectively interwoven with charming animal anecdotes. The story is sensitively told with gentle humor, resulting in an inspiring glimpse of one man's profound concern for all living things, rather than a nature study as the title might imply.

The idea for *How To Read a Rabbit* (1959) resulted from Fritz's hearing of libraries which loan pets to children in Florida, Ohio, and Connecticut. In this well-written picture book, six-year-old Stephen learns that the sign "Animals Lending Library," which he spies outside the Junior Museum, refers to a library where people can borrow animals, not one where animals take out books. Too young to borrow the animals, Stephen seeks the help of his brother Kenny, who is really interested in skunks and flying squirrels rather than the brown rabbit Stephen desires. The interesting story line—funny and full of surprises—delights young children. The satisfying ending, in which the librarian informs Stephen he may have one of the five baby rabbits which have been born to the one he had wanted Kenny to borrow, suits the relationship being portrayed between Stephen and his older brother Kenny.

By the end of the 1950s, as her children became teenagers, Fritz ventured into writing short stories for teenagers. These stories are about middle- or upper-class churchgoing families in which normal children have normal growing up experiences; several appeared in *Seventeen* magazine. Also in the late 1950s she began writing adult short stories. Most of these seek to demonstrate that one can rise above difficulties, rather than being overcome by them. These adult short stories were published in the *New Yorker*, *McCall's*, *Charm* magazine, *Redbook*, and the *Atlantic Monthly*.

While writing and publishing adult short stories, Fritz began writing book reviews regularly for the *New York Times* and on occasion for the *Chicago Tribune*. As her writing and reviewing became more familiar to the public, she was sought out as a speaker and a teacher.

Eventually the librarian at the Katonah, New York, public library convinced Fritz to organize and direct a writing workshop there. She agreed, and the Jean Fritz Writers' Workshop was established in 1962. For more than a decade she worked with the same basic group of fourteen women, and during that time more than one hundred books were written and published by members of this group.

Brady (1960), Fritz's second historical novel, is set in a rural, 1836 Pennsylvania community bit-terly divided on the slavery question. Earning trust and living with uncertainty are two prevalent themes. The protagonist, Brady Minton, is the son of a white minister who is secretly an agent of the Underground Railroad and is in trouble with his congregation over his sermon against slavery. Although the political conflict is slavery, there is personal conflict between Brady and his father because the father does not trust his son to keep the secret of his underground activities. As Brady struggles to accept the responsibilities of growing up, he learns to form his own opinion about slavery; "It's a sin. . . . And I'm going to do something about it. One way or another, sometime when I'm able." The characters of both Brady and his father are skillfully developed. The background of farm and family activity results in a colorful period flavor, but Fritz is more successful in communicating the growth of the boy than she is in conveying a sense of emotional conflict surrounding the slavery issue. She does, however, express through a multitude of characters every conceivable view about slavery. The book is characterized by good writing, sound values, and smooth pace. Its sales are in excess of 45,000.

December Is for Christmas (1961), a picture book, has as its theme the search for and the maintenance of the true meaning of Christmas. It was originally written as a Christmas card for Alice Torrey and later submitted to Wonder Books under the pseudonym Ann Scott. The main character, a rabbit, is endowed with the power to read, but his family views books as irrelevant and without meaning. When the rabbit begins putting together pieces of information—all of which relate in some way to Christmas—his reading becomes meaningful to his family, as it ultimately represents the magic of Christmas. His family finally applauds his ability to read.

Tap, Tap, Lion—1, 2, 3 (1962) involves four animals who decide to play children's games and allow a real child, Sally, to join them. The five play several games before Sally, playing the mother in the game of "house," sends all to bed. Once the animals are asleep, Sally sneaks off to her own house. The unique reversal, where the animals pretend to be people instead of children pretending to be animals, is an idea children find enjoyable.

Fritz's temporary residence in San Francisco during her husband's military tour there provided her with the firsthand experience needed to write the nonfiction book *San Francisco* (1962) for Rand McNally's Cities of the World series. Essentially a guided tour of San Francisco, this book is filled with interesting information about the history, events, people, and places of the city. Its informative narrative is rich with the sort of humor which permeates so much of her writing, and Fritz succeeds admirably in conveying San Francisco's personality and charm. The Junior Literary Guild chose it as an outstanding book for older readers.

In *I, Adam* (1963), the fifteen-year-old protagonist is a mid-nineteenth-century boy who is struggling to come to grips with his uncertain future. The conflict arises from his concern over the opposition between what he thinks he must do for his family and what he wants to do for himself. Although he feels that his family expects him to choose between whaling and farming, he eventually decides to attend college, overcoming his prejudices toward schooling. This decision, however, is preceded by a bitter experience on a farm, arising from the evil doings of a defaulting owner Sharkey, from whom the farm is being bought by the family, and his father's loss of a leg while whaling. Adam, who displays the qualities of devotion, ability to accept responsibility, courage, perseverance, and self-reliance, learns to live up to the maxim "This above all, to thine own self be true," introduced to him by one of his schoolmasters. Adam's problems, pleasures, and dilemmas are not unlike those of young people today. In this novel Fritz presents a fascinating cross section of life in the East during the 1850s and deals effectively with good father-son relationships.

The Fritzes' trip to the British Isles, Denmark, and Norway provided the groundwork for *Magic To Burn* (1964). The idea for this story of an American family's visit to England for several weeks in the summer resulted from Fritz's desire to linger in the English countryside. The father, a professor, is on a research assignment involving Chaucer. Blaze, a boggart (a ghostly inhabitant of the English bogs), enters the story and discovers that Ann and Stephen, the two children, might be useful in helping him escape. As the family tours England, the old is contrasted with the new, revealing the conflict created when progress overrides the serenity of the countryside. It is this conflict which drives the boggart to leave his home and travel to America as a stowaway on Ann and Stephen's ship. Fritz effectively combines fantasy and magic with realistic character portrayal, moving in and out of fantasy in a skillful manner. The reader can easily accept the boggart because he is believable, his personality is well developed, and his actions are in line with his character.

Fourteen-year-old Daniel, in *Early Thunder* (1967), must choose between the Tories and Whigs in the American Revolution. Torn between respecting his father's Tory politics and his own growing support for the Whig party, Daniel must make an independent decision about his loyalties regardless of the wishes of his father. His conscience will not permit him to follow family tradition unless he believes in it. Living in Salem, Massachusetts, he feels loyalty to England yet understands the position of those who no longer can tolerate England's absorption of their freedoms. In the end, however, he makes a difficult decision: to reject his father's wishes that he go to England for schooling, which would prepare him for a career in law. In a strategically important action, Daniel chops a hole in the bottom of his boat, *Libera*, rendering it useless to the British, who had wanted to use it to steal Salem's cannon. *Early Thunder* weaves fiction with facts about Salem in 1774-1775, as it examines the Whig versus Tory issue. A truly understanding presentation of conflicting issues, the book has implications for decision-making today.

The unraveling of fiction from fact is a characteristic trait of Jean Fritz's writing. She also feels children should participate in the unraveling. In *George Washington's Breakfast* (1969), a sprightly, humorous story, she shows the excitement and rewards of historical research. George Washington Allen, a boy who wants to know what his namesake ate for breakfast, undertakes research that involves much reading, trips to the Smithsonian Institution and Mount Vernon, and rummaging through attic trash. Finally, his research helps him answer the question: Indian hoecakes and tea. However, the story ends with him asking a new question about Washington: what did he have for lunch? The fictional framework is deftly employed and the characterization of the small, determined boy is believable. The book is a good introduction to the intricacies of historical research.

Fritz spent seven years on her history for adults, *Cast for a Revolution: Some American Friends and Enemies, 1728-1814* (1972). Seeking to portray history as an interaction of people and events, she wanted to show how the personalities played upon one another and affected the events of their times. The book is essentially a history of the American Revolution as seen from the viewpoint of Massachusetts historian and dramatist Mercy Otis Warren. Warren emerges as an intellectual, a political radical, and a happily married woman of remarkably independent mind and spirit. The "friends and enemies" include her brother James Otis, her

The
Good Giants
and the
Bad Pukwudgies

by
Jean Fritz

illustrated by
Tomie de Paola

Dust jacket for Fritz's retelling in picture-book format of a legend of the Wampanoag Indians of Massachusetts (Putnam)

husband, James Warren, her children and other relatives, along with such Revolutionary figures as John and Abigail Adams, Gov. Thomas Hutchinson, and assorted Whigs and Tories. *Cast for a Revolution* presents an intimate view of the moral, intellectual, political, and social climate and tensions in Massachusetts prior to, during, and following the Revolution. Fritz used original sources, and the book was well researched. The dramatic setting is somewhat contrived; but the work is well written and the characters are believable.

From writing her adult book Jean Fritz developed an interest in biography. During her extensive research, she found a great deal of material she felt too valuable to keep secret. She realized there were many possibilities for children's biographies of Revolutionary figures. In writing her Bicentennial set of biographies for children she tried to change the textbook image of these traditional political leaders and policymakers of the Revolution.

In her biographies Fritz attempts to get at the truth of the individual through his likes, dislikes, worries, joys, successes, failures. In each case she reveals the humanity of the individual, presenting his life as revealed in his diary, letters, and other original sources. Through her humorous style she paints a full, believable picture of each individual, using specific, exact language and precise detail. She refuses to create fictional dialogue for the characters in her biographies; the only conversation found in these books is that which she has discovered in letters, diaries, journals, and other original sources, which she draws upon plentifully.

A philosophical attitude about presenting history and the people who participate in history is reflected in these biographies for children. She believes that (1) history can be presented to children

Dust jacket for Fritz's 1985 account of the trip she and her husband took in 1983 to Hankow, China (Putnam)

honestly and realistically, showing that motivations behind decisions and events have not always been pure (as textbooks have traditionally suggested) nor in line with what was ultimately for the good of the country; (2) in order to understand history, people must understand humanity and the nature of human interaction; and (3) a sense of humor provides perspective in the recounting of history. Through her research she has discovered that pride, greed, and selfishness were some of the key motives behind what ultimately became major decisions and events in American history. Consequently, her nonfiction writing for children brings new interpretation. Changing history is not her aim; bringing a fresh look at it is.

Fritz began her children's biography series with Paul Revere. As presented in *And Then What Happened, Paul Revere?* (1973), Revere's famous ride is preceded by a description of his life and the political situation in Boston. The conclusion details his adventures upon arriving in Lexington. The ride itself is funny, fast-paced, and historically accurate. Revere, a multitalented man who loved people and excitement, is revealed as busy, bustling, versatile, and patriotic. The causes and effects of his famous ride are presented amusingly and excitingly in this attractive blend of facts and a touch of legend, and her engaging portrait of Revere serves to humanize the man behind the myth. For one bit of information Fritz searched and searched but did not find the answer until after the manuscript had gone to press. The horse Paul Revere rode in his big ride was named Brown Beauty. Sales for her first biography, which was named a *New York Times* Outstanding Book of the Year, exceed 56,000.

Why Don't You Get a Horse, Sam Adams? (1974) exploits the patriot's stubborn reluctance to learn to ride. After an unheroic escape from the Redcoats via horse-drawn carriage, his cousin John Adams persuades Sam through an appeal to his patriotism to forego his pedestrian preferences and get a horse but not before his soles have been worn thin by his treading the cobblestones and wharves of Boston while agitating against the king. Fritz effectively describes the start of colonial dissent as she deftly portrays the reluctant rider; however, the humor implied in the title is not completely borne out in the text. Sales for this biography, Fritz's second *New York Times* Outstanding Book of the Year, exceed 38,000.

In addition to the answers to the title question, *Where Was Patrick Henry on the 29th of May?* (1975), readers learn of his boyhood, marriage, efforts as a beginning lawyer, and growing career as an orator and statesman. Fritz uses Henry's birthday as a focal point for summing up the different stages of his life. The Council of Interracial Books has criticized the contradiction between Henry's cry for freedom and liberty during the Revolutionary War and his holding of large numbers of black people in bondage, which is never addressed by the author. Fritz's prose for this historically accurate but lighthearted and humorous biography creates a conversational tone that is effectively engaging. This book is a biography for fun seekers and was also chosen a *New York Times* Outstanding Book for 1975.

Who's That Stepping on Plymouth Rock? (1975) explodes the myth that Pilgrims actually landed on Plymouth Rock. According to Fritz, this myth began when an elderly man, under pressure, said he

15

just to let him know if he should change his plans because the
stars looked unlucky or because the clouds weren't quite right.
No, Emperor K'ang Hsi *Xi* wasn't interested in that nonsense. "I just
go each day," he said, "in an ordinary way, and concentrate on
ruling properly."

My first peep into the world of dynasties ~~came~~ *had come about* when I was
eight years old, on a visit to ~~Peking~~ *Peking (now called Beijing)*. My father and I were riding
beside each other in rickshas on a broad avenue past a huge oblong
group of temple-like buildings. The grandest building had yellow
tiles on its roof.

"That is the Forbidden City," my father called.

The Forbidden City! It sounded as if it had come straight out
of a fairy tale. It looked that way too.

"That's where the emperors used to live," my father explained.
No one had been allowed in the Forbidden City at night, he said,
except the emperor himself, his family, and those who served him.
And ~~only a favored few~~ *those who came* in the daytime ~~and then they~~ were *generally* expected
to arrive at dawn.

I knew there was no emperor now so I didn't see why we couldn't
go in and look around, but no, it was still forbidden. Even though
the dynasty (the Qhing dynasty) had been overthrown, the ~~last~~ member~~s~~
of the family ~~young Pu Yi~~, had been allowed to ~~stay on~~ *keep on living there. Pu Yi the last emperor,* ~~He~~ was sixteen years old now, my father said. Sixteen! I wondered if he had
any fun under his yellow roof. ~~He had no one to order around now
except his servants and if anyone bumped his head on the floor,~~ it
~~would only be out of politeness.~~ What did he do all day?

Page from the draft for China Homecoming *(by permission of the author)*

thought he remembered hearing that the rock was a landmark. Her research found no proof that the Pilgrims ever landed on it. Through her book children learn something important about fact and fiction in history, how history is made and unmade by those who participated in it and later shared it with others. The real story of Plymouth Rock is made far more interesting than the myth. Meticulously researched, this is a lively work in which Fritz shows how fact and fiction became intertwined and what motivates the intertwining.

In the sprightly book *Will You Sign Here, John Hancock?* (1976) Fritz reveals this good-hearted signer of the Declaration of Independence to have been wealthy, extravagant, quite vain, and much concerned with his popularity. Fritz begins with a description of the Boston Common and then examines Hancock's personality. She reveals that he was always wishing for things—mostly to be accepted and noticed—and that he practiced writing his signature before affixing it on the Declaration of Independence. Fritz includes many interesting facts about her subject, including his disappointment at having no heirs after the deaths of his two children, the criticisms of his ostentatious displays of wealth, and his ambition to become commander in chief of the army. A Boston Globe-Horn Book Honor Book for Fiction, this book is a delightful, well-researched biography, written with a light touch belying the serious scholarship of its author.

In *What's the Big Idea, Ben Franklin?* (1976), Fritz's fourth *New York Times* Outstanding Book of the Year, she expertly personalizes the subject, highlighting his inventiveness. In the description of his multifaceted career are many personal details and some of his pithy sayings. Background information about colonial affairs enables readers to understand the importance of Franklin's contributions to the public good. The manner of presentation is clever; the humor is entertaining; and the style is lively; however, a page of notes is substituted for more detailed footnotes or references.

Can't You Make Them Behave, King George? (1977) is a charming, amiable biography of George III. Beginning as a bashful boy, George emerges as a ruler who was determined to be a good king but who had the not-uncommon viewpoint that those who disagreed with him were traitors or scoundrels. King George is presented as a tidy, thrifty, and resolutely moral man, who lapsed into senility at the end of his life. Fritz includes funny and poignant everyday touches that enable the reader to see the monarch as a person, and she

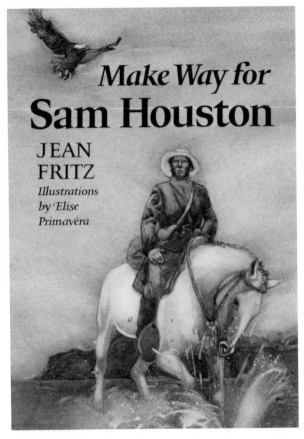

Dust jacket for Fritz's 1986 novel, about the life of the frontier hero, statesman, and soldier (Putnam)

presents an unconventional view of the American Revolution, a view not usually found in children's books.

Fritz wrote *Brendan the Navigator: A History Mystery About the Discovery of America* (1979) for *Cricket* magazine but agreed to rewrite it as a picture book if Enrico Arno, who did the magazine illustrations, would illustrate the book. Retelling the legend of Saint Brendan, who was born on the west coast of Ireland, the story is too outlandish to be accepted as factual, yet it raises questions that suggest to children that perhaps even in legends and myths there may be clues to finding the truth. Did Brendan and his men reach North America 900 years before Christopher Columbus? The reader is reminded that history is indeed a mystery that is not easily solved. While the postscript makes clear that there is no corroboration for the fact that Brendan discovered America—only that a 1976-1977 trip across the Atlantic in a leather boat proves that such a voyage would have been possible—some readers are apt to get the impression that the voyage was actually made in the sixth century.

In *Stonewall* (1979), *Traitor: The Case of Benedict Arnold* (1981), and the recently released *Make Way for Sam Houston* (1986), Fritz has presented analyses of the personalities in more depth. Beyond just presenting the essence of the individual, Fritz has gone deeper into showing who he was and why he did what he did.

In *Stonewall* the focus is on Thomas Jackson's prowess as a military leader. He emerges as rigid, zealous, and in some instances fanatical in this sensitive and emotion-filled interpretation. In the early part of the text the author skillfully establishes Jackson's probity, eccentricity, and toughness while the later part serves to amplify the personal portrait as well as to give a vivid picture of the Civil War years. Humor is downplayed; instead, Fritz gives greater attention to Jackson's humanity, giving considerable dimension to his character. Readers are made aware of the curious mix of circumstances and complex personality that pushed him ever onward to his place in history. An extensive bibliography corroborates the evidence presented in this well-written and carefully structured text. Sales for this book, Fritz's second Boston Globe-Horn Book Honor Book for Fiction, exceed 31,000.

Where Do You Think You're Going, Christopher Columbus? (1980), a finalist for the American Book Award, presents its subject as an excellent seaman but a man blinded by his own convictions and hampered by the geographical ignorance of his time. Columbus emerges as courageous, determined, mercenary, querulous, and self-assured. Interesting details of his four voyages to the New World, which he insisted must be the East Indies, are presented. He is described in his last years as being wealthy and avaricious and still unaware that the American continents existed. This biography is based on thorough research and is written in a smooth, humorous, and informal style. Its facts are interesting; its asides are occasionally startling. Tantalizing insights into historical events and personages are presented in a fresh, colorful manner completely different from the story traditionally presented to children.

The picture book *The Man Who Loved Books* (1981) is based on the story of Saint Columba. While in Ireland doing research for *Brendan the Navigator*, Fritz conceived of the idea for this story, also first published in *Cricket* magazine. Some historical evidence for the legend exists, as Columba was known to have been born in Ireland in 521 and to have immigrated to Scotland as a missionary, to convert the Picts to Christianity. In this version,

Columba is supposed to have left Ireland in repentance for having caused a battle in which thousands of men were killed. The focus is on Columba as a book lover, so avid for reading matter that he illegally copied a manuscript. However, he was denied its possession by the high king. The light, tongue-in-cheek style is just right for the subject matter, and Fritz readily admits that the story was a joy to write.

The vivid and perceptive portrait of the fallen military officer in Fritz's *Traitor: The Case of Benedict Arnold* is one of a man who is hot-tempered, impetuous, and enamored of money. Arnold continually proves himself, out of compulsion to demonstrate his worth supposedly rooted in the shame he felt over an alcoholic father who left his family in financial and social ruin. In this biography, Fritz writes not only about Arnold but she also develops the character of John Andre, the British major hanged for his role in Arnold's traitorous action, in such a way as to evoke compassion from the reader. She is both candid and canny, giving a brilliant picture of the egotistical, ambitious, and unscrupulous soldier who felt his contribution to the commonweal was unappreciated. Final judgment of Arnold's character, however, is left to the reader. The staccato style is appropriate for conveying the truly chaotic state of affairs during the Revolutionary War and results in a brisk unfolding of the events. *Traitor: The Case of Benedict Arnold* was another American Book Award finalist.

The Good Giants and the Bad Pukwudgies (1982) is a retelling in picture-book format of a legend of the Wampanoag Indians of Massachusetts. Combining several tales to explain the formation of Buzzard's Bay, Nantucket, and Martha's Vineyard, as well as some smaller islands, the book also describes such mythic peoples as the pukwudgies—mischievous little people who have a habit of turning themselves into stinging mosquitoes and shooting tiny arrows at the First People (Algonquins)—and the good giants, especially Maushop, who help the First People by controlling the pukwudgies. Much humor is derived from the terse New England speech of dialogues between Maushop and his wife. Because there is no full account of the legend in historical sources, Fritz pieced together references to form the tale. There is some crowding of plot, but this flaw is compensated for by the style and the humor.

Not until the 1980s has Jean Fritz been able to use China, her birthplace, in her writing. *Homesick: My Own Story* (1982), which is partly autobiographical, is a remarkable blend of truth and storytelling which draws readers into scenes of her youth during her last two years in the turbulent China of the mid 1920s. Near the beginning of the book she indicates that her childhood seemed like a story, and consequently she decided to tell it as such, letting events fall as they would into the shape of a story laced together with fictional bits. Allowing herself to take liberties with literal accuracy permitted Fritz the freedom to recreate the emotions she remembered so vividly. Many of her childhood reactions to people and events are timeless and universal. The writing flows smoothly, richly, and intimately, reflecting yearnings and fears and ambivalent loyalties of a young girl strong in character. Told with an abundance of humor, the memoir is vibrant with atmosphere, personalities, and a palpable sense of place. *Homesick: My Own Story* was a Newbery Honor Book and won the American Book Award.

In her first youth biography of a female subject, *The Double Life of Pocahontas* (1983), Fritz includes more history than biography since little is known of the subject. The history is mainly a description of the Jamestown colony and its relations with Powhatan, Pocahontas's father. Pocahontas is presented as the Indian princess who, as a child, loved her adoptive brother, John Smith, and later married John Rolfe, going to live with him in England. Fritz tells the colorful story with polished simplicity, stressing the dichotomy at which the title hints: the divided loyalties of the young, proud girl who loved both her tribe and the English friends with whom the tribe was in conflict. This book is one of the more substantial treatments of Pocahontas.

China Homecoming (1985), a follow-up to *Homesick: My Own Story,* is Fritz's account of a trip she and her husband were permitted to take to Hankow, China, in 1983. Fritz has effectively woven discussions of China's past and present into her narrative in an effort to present information and explanation about the country. Michael Fritz's photographs document the excitement, surprise, and sad moments in their return to his wife's beginnings, some fifty-five years later. Although interesting and informative, the book lacks some of the emotional power of *Homesick: My Own Story.* The effortless and entrancing style, however, will make readers feel they are sharing this trip. This book helps to fill a void of thoughtful children's books on contemporary China.

In November 1985, Jean Fritz indicated she and her husband were seeking a sponsorship for another trip to China. At the end of April 1986, she and her husband departed for China. She would like to create a book for young people about the Long March in China. At that time she envisioned a fictionalized hero serving as a main character. Continuing to write biographies (Narcissa Whitman is a likely subject) is also one of her goals.

References:

Richard Ammon, "Profile: Jean Fritz," *Language Arts,* 60 (March 1983): 365-369;

Elaine Edelman, "Jean Fritz," *Publishers Weekly,* 220 (24 July 1981): 76-77;

Elizabeth Ann Rumer Hostetler, "Jean Fritz: A Critical Biography," Ph.D. dissertation, University of Toledo, 1982;

"How Do You Make History Come Alive, Jean Fritz?," *Early Years,* 12 (February 1982): 34-36.

Papers:

Jean Fritz's manuscripts are on permanent loan to the University of Minnesota, Kerlin Collection; the University of Oregon; and the University of Southern Mississippi.

Jean Craighead George

(2 July 1919-   )

Karen Nelson Hoyle
University of Minnesota

BOOKS: *Vulpes, the Red Fox,* by George and John
Lothar George (New York: Dutton, 1948);
Vision, the Mink, by George and John Lothar George
(New York: Dutton, 1949);
Masked Prowler, the Story of a Raccoon, by George
and John Lothar George (New York: Dutton,
1950);
Meph, the Pet Skunk, by George and John Lothar
George (New York: Dutton, 1952);
Bubo, the Great Horned Owl, by George and John
Lothar George (New York: Dutton, 1954);
Dipper of Copper Creek, by George and John Lothar
George (New York: Dutton, 1956);
The Hole in the Tree (New York: Dutton, 1957);
Snow Tracks (New York: Dutton, 1958);
My Side of the Mountain (New York: Dutton, 1959;
London: Bodley Head, 1962);
The Summer of the Falcon (New York: Crowell, 1962;
London: Dent, 1964);
Red Robin, Fly Up! (Pleasantville, N.Y.: Reader's Di-
gest Services, 1963);
Gull Number 737 (New York: Crowell, 1964);
Animals from A to Z (Pleasantville, N.Y.: Reader's
Digest Services, 1964);
Spring Comes to the Ocean, illustrated by John Wilson
(New York: Crowell, 1965);
Hold Zero! (New York: Crowell, 1966);
The Moon of the Bears, illustrated by Mac Shepard
(New York: Crowell, 1967);
The Moon of the Owls, illustrated by Jean Zallinger
(New York: Crowell, 1967);
The Moon of the Salamanders, illustrated by John
Kaufman (New York: Crowell, 1967);
Coyote in Manhattan, illustrated by Kaufman (New
York: Crowell, 1968);
The Moon of the Chickarees, illustrated by John
Schoenherr (New York: Crowell, 1968);
The Moon of the Fox Pups, illustrated by Kiyoaki Ko-
moda (New York: Crowell, 1968);
The Moon of the Monarch Butterflies, illustrated by
Murray Tinkleman (New York: Crowell,
1968);
The Moon of the Mountain Lions, illustrated by Win-
ifred Lubell (New York: Crowell, 1968);

photo by Ellan Young

The Moon of the Wild Pigs, illustrated by Peter Par-
nall (New York: Crowell, 1968);
The Moon of the Alligators, illustrated by Adrina Zan-
azanian (New York: Crowell, 1969);
The Moon of the Deer, illustrated by Zallinger (New
York: Crowell, 1969);
The Moon of the Gray Wolves, illustrated by Lorence
Bjorklund (New York: Crowell, 1969);

The Moon of the Moles, illustrated by Robert Levering (New York: Crowell, 1969);

The Moon of the Winter Bird, illustrated by Kazue Mizumura (New York: Crowell, 1969);

Beastly Inventions: A Surprising Investigation Into How Smart Animals Really Are (New York: McKay, 1970); republished as *Animals Can Do Anything* (London: Souvenir Press, 1972);

All Upon a Stone (New York: Crowell, 1971);

Who Really Killed Cock Robin? An Ecological Mystery (New York: Dutton, 1971);

Julie of the Wolves, illustrated by Schoenherr (New York: Harper & Row, 1972; London: Hamilton, 1973); republished with new illustrations by Julek Heller (Harmondsworth, U.K.: Puffin, 1976);

Wild Guide to the Everglades, illustrated by Betty Fraser (Washington, D.C.: National Park Service, 1972);

All Upon a Sidewalk, illustrated by Don Bolognese (New York: Dutton, 1974);

New York in Maps, 1972/73, by George and Toy Lasker (New York: New York Magazine, 1974);

Hook a Fish, Catch a Mountain (New York: Dutton, 1975);

New York in Flashmaps, 1974/75, by George and Lasker (Chappaqua: Flashmaps, 1976);

Going to the Sun (New York: Harper & Row, 1976);

The Wentletrap Trap, illustrated by Symeon Shimin (New York: Dutton, 1978);

The American Walk Book; an Illustrated Guide to the Country's Major Historic and Natural Walking Trails from New England to the Pacific Coast (New York: Dutton, 1978);

The Wounded Wolf, illustrated by Schoenherr (New York: Harper & Row, 1978);

River Rats, Inc. (New York: Dutton, 1979);

The Cry of the Crow (New York: Harper & Row, 1980);

The Grizzly Bear With the Golden Ears (New York: Harper & Row, 1982);

The Wild, Wild Cookbook: A Guide for Young Wild-Food Foragers (New York: Harper & Row, 1982);

Journey Inward (New York: Dutton, 1982);

The Talking Earth (New York: Harper & Row, 1983);

One Day in the Desert (New York: Harper & Row, 1983);

One Day in the Alpine Tundra (New York: Harper & Row, 1984);

How to Talk to Your Animals (New York: Harcourt Brace Jovanovich, 1985);

One Day in the Prairie (New York: Harper & Row, 1986).

SELECTED PERIODICAL PUBLICATIONS: "Summer and Children and Birds and Animals and Flowers and Trees and Bees and Books," *Horn Book,* 35 (June 1959): 191-198;

"Chicago, Our Windy Wonderful Crow," *Audubon Magazine,* 64 (September 1962): 260-263; abridged and republished as "Smartest Bird in the World," *Reader's Digest,* 81 (October 1962): 19-20;

"The Sociable Sea Gull," *National Wildlife* (August 1963): 108-113;

"Victory in the Everglades," *Reader's Digest,* 97 (August 1970): 73-77;

"Bicycles Built for Fun," *Reader's Digest,* 108 (March 1976): 168-170;

"Battle to Save Florida's Palms," *National Wildlife,* 14 (June 1976): 17-19;

"White-Water High," *Reader's Digest,* 111 (September 1977): 74-77;

"My Search for Secret Agent #25238," *National Wildlife,* 16 (April 1978): 16-19;

"Consider the Ones Who Lead," *International Wildlife,* 9 (Summer 1979): 38-45;

"Wonder of Waterfalls," *Reader's Digest,* 117 (August 1980): 148-155;

"Lure of the Winter Beach," *Reader's Digest,* 118 (February 1981): 70-72;

"Epic Journey of the Monarchs," *Reader's Digest,* 118 (May 1981): 197-198.

Jean Craighead George was born in Washington, D.C., to an entomologist father, Frank C. Craighead, and a storytelling mother, Carolyn Johnson Craighead. George and her twin brothers, John and Frank, who are now ecologists, were raised in an atmosphere designed to foster an early acquaintanceship with nature. Birds and animals were allowed to share their living quarters, and the family made many field trips and nature excursions.

George earned a B.A. degree in 1941 from Pennsylvania State University, where she studied science, and English under the Pulitzer Prize-winning poet Theodore Roethke. After graduation she attended Louisiana State University in Baton Rouge, where she studied art, and the University of Michigan. In 1944 she married John L. George. Together they strove to introduce their three children—Carolyn Laura, John Craighead, and Thomas Lothar—to nature in much the same way as her parents had their children. George's first six

Masked Prowler

The Story of
A RACCOON

By John and Jean George
Illustrated by Jean George

Dust jacket for the third of the six books George coauthored with her husband (Dutton)

books, which she illustrated, were coauthored with her husband. These books, each of which characterizes a certain type of animal, are best represented by *Dipper of Copper Creek* (1956), which won the Aurianne Award in 1958. The book interweaves facts about the life cycle of the water ouzel with the tale of prospector Whispering Bill Smith and his grandson Doug's yearning for independence. Scientists at the Rocky Mountain Biological Laboratory at Gothic, Colorado, shared their research findings with the Georges, who wrote the book on site. Chapter headings such as "The Nest on the Canyon Wall" and "The Ceremony of Farewell" suggest the drama of the life of the tiny bird living in a subalpine zone.

The couple divorced in 1963, but George and her children continued the family hobby of raising wild animals, eventually raising 173 wild pets, most of which were eventually returned to nature. As a reporter for the International News Service (1942-1944) and the *Washington Post* (1944-1946), as an artist and then art director for *Pageant* magazine

(1946-1947) and staff writer (1969-1974) and roving editor (1974 to 1982) for *Reader's Digest*, George mastered her writing skills effectively while efficiently meeting deadlines. In 1968 she was named Penn State Woman of the Year. She lives in Chappaqua, New York, from where she ventures out in pursuit of subjects for articles and juvenile novels.

Jean Craighead George's books for children, with settings that range from Alaska to the Bahamian island of Bimini, meld accurate natural history with stories about adolescents and younger children. Family trips, research, and wild pets provided the bases for her books and her more than seventy magazine articles. Her timely plots usually involve a portion of the life cycle of both creature and maturing human child or adolescent as they interrelate. Humans often have nicknames, while animal characters often have names related either to their scientific genus or species or to their behavior. *The Hole in the Tree* (1957), George's first book written without her husband, documents the penetration of an old apple tree, initially by a bark beetle, with further enlargements of the beetle's hole by Old Stonehead, a downy woodpecker, and Giant Driller, a pileated woodpecker. The human characters, Scott and Paula Gordon, note that "a hole in a tree is not an easy thing to keep," for increasingly larger animals soon occupy it. By the end of the book it is inhabited by raccoons.

The same sentence—"The snow sprinkled out of the sky one day until the floor of the February woodland was as smooth and white as paper"—both introduces and concludes *Snow Tracks* (1958), in which creatures travel in search of food or shelter, leaving discernible prints. The story moves inside the house of a boy named Trapper, who also leaves a trail: hand and footprints on the refrigerator, cupboard, floor, and staircase.

My Side of the Mountain (1959) takes the form of Sam Gribley's diary. Drawing on George's own childhood experiences with survival living, the book tells how Gribley acquires information in the town library about how to search for and prepare food, build a hut, and train a falcon to hunt. A favorite among readers, *My Side of the Mountain* was an ALA Notable Book, a Newbery Honor Book, and the recipient of the George G. Stone Award. It was the basis for a 1969 film and has had many paperback printings.

June Pritchard trains a sparrow hawk, Zander, in *The Summer of the Falcon* (1962) and simultaneously learns self-discipline. The book is based in part on George's childhood diary, and the heroine even has twin brothers. The training and

Dust jacket for George's popular story of a young boy's attempt at survival living. The novel was the basis for a feature film of the same title (Dutton).

freeing of the falcon parallel her own emergence into self-reliance and womanhood. Up to this point George had illustrated all her books; however, after *The Summer of the Falcon* she decided to devote more time and energy to her writing and to leave the task of illustrating to others.

The author often produces a nonfictional article and a juvenile book about the same subject. For example, an article in the August 1963 issue of *National Wildlife* is entitled "The Sociable Sea Gull"; one of George's books published the next year has the intriguing title *Gull Number 737*. Luke Rivers and his professor father learn enough about bird behavior to recommend to airports a means of preventing further accidents due to planes colliding with birds by using a tape of gull distress calls to lure the birds away from the planes' paths.

Spring Comes to the Ocean (1965) remains George's favorite among her own books. Each of the twelve chapters in this novel concentrates on a species of ocean creature and its response to a change of season in the Atlantic or Pacific Ocean. There is no interference from humans, except for a team of oceanographers who attempt to study a baby whale while assisting him on his continued journey. This book dramatizes the life cycles of several ocean species in chapters such as "The Rock in the Gulf Stream" and "The Festival of the Oysters." One chapter deals with porpoises' courting habits, a "ballet of love." An experienced female in the porpoise harem supervises pregnancy and birth, while the herd vocalizes in celebration. In another, readers learn that while the lowly aceola worm knows only "about one inch of the entire Pacific Ocean, the gray whales migrate seven thousand miles to eat plankton in the Bering Straits." Nature's puzzles and mysteries are also investigated in the narrative; for example, scientists return to the cage in which they have captured a baby whale to take a cardiogram but find the "fence crunched and the whale child gone." A description, inserted later, of a mother whale provides a hint to the disappearance—"the belly of the female bore toothlike gashes as if raked by wire fence."

Rocket building in a Blue Springs, New York, marsh—the subject of *Hold Zero!* (1966)—is an exception to George's usual subject matter. A group of teenagers interact with one another, their family members, and police officer Ricardo as they relay signals and messages. The book focuses on thirteen-year-old Steve and fifteen-year-old Craig Sutton, who have opposing attitudes toward girls, but who are equally precocious and innovative in finding the time to devote to their interest in rockets; they avoid piano practice by using a tape recorder to outwit their parents. Descriptive passages about the environment occasionally delay the otherwise fast action.

Each of the thirteen "Moon" books published during a three-year period (1967-1969) centers on a particular phase in a creature's life cycle: for example, a bear in February in the Smoky Mountains of Tennessee, a mole in December and January in Twin Butte Creek in Kansas, and an amphibious salamander in a Michigan forest. In each of the books, animals coexist in an ecological balance, but no human beings intrude on the scene. Some critics argue that lower forms of animals lack the emotions which George assigns them in this series.

In *Coyote in Manhattan* (1968) Tenny Harkness, from Harlem, releases a wild coyote named Tako from a boat into the urban setting. The coyote eventually establishes a home in Central Park. A map of "Tako's Central Park and Nearby Streets" assists non-New York readers. This book is slightly marred by an inconclusive and incomplete substructure which hinders the plot development, as Tenny yearns to be accepted by both a clique of girls and by her father.

"A stone by a stream in the woods is like a tiny country," George proposes in *All Upon a Stone* (1971), which follows a mole cricket, which hears with its knees and breathes through its belly, as it goes through its daily routine. More successful is a companion volume, *All Upon a Sidewalk* (1974), in which a common yellow ant from 195th Street, named "Lasius flavus" for its genus and species, follows its own lingering chemical trail when returning to the ant community after a search for a sugar-producing insect.

Who Really Killed Cock Robin? An Ecological Mystery (1971) deals with the complicated food chain. Teenage sleuths Tony Isidoro and Mary Alice Lamberty dismiss suspected pollutants such as DDT and PCB and attempt to engage the townspeople in the drama of their search for exactly what caused the death of their town's mascot.

The misleading title *Beastly Inventions: A Surprising Investigation Into How Smart Animals Really Are* (1970) was changed to the more appropriate *Animals Can Do Anything* in the British edition published two years later. Provocative chapter titles, such as "Diners of Unlimited Imagination," describe the adaptations of unusual animals and the peculiarities of courtship and sex, habitats, and senses of living creatures. George provides a bibliography and index to assist the reader, and she uses the first person occasionally to add validity to her observations. For example, the author describes a "nestling grosbeak, one of which I raised." In the first chapter, George expresses her purpose in writing the book. "I was not a scientist like my father and brothers, but without knowing it at the time, I was beginning a long search for unique animals of all kinds. It was not to be as organized a quest as theirs, but rather a hopscotch trip into worlds stretching well beyond my imagination."

Julie of the Wolves (1972), winner of the Newbery Medal in 1973, is George's most significant book. Focusing on the theme of self-reliance, the plot, character development, and setting are epic in dimension. Julie Edward Miyax Kapugen, an Eskimo girl, becomes lost on the Alaskan tundra

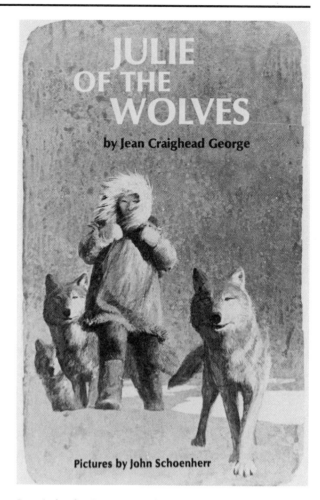

Dust jacket for George's Newbery Medal-winning novel about a young Eskimo girl who is taken in by a wolf pack on the Alaskan tundra (Harper & Row)

and survives by sheer tenacity. Departing from her usual chronological sequence of events, the author divides the book into three parts, using a flashback technique for the central portion. Julie abandons an unwanted marriage and sets out on a journey to meet a pen pal in San Francisco. She encounters and communicates with a wolf pack, particularly the leader, whom she names Amaroq, and the assistance of the wolves is instrumental in her survival. Besides winning the Newbery Medal, *Julie of the Wolves* was a National Book Award Finalist and recipient of the Jugend Prize in Germany and of the Silver Skate Award for the Dutch language edition. It was also selected as one of the ten Best American Children's Books in 200 years by the Children's Literature Association in 1976. Gillwood Productions is currently making a film version.

The Snake River in Jackson Hole, Wyoming, is the setting for *Hook a Fish, Catch a Mountain*

(1975), in which a thirteen-year-old budding New York dancer, Spinner Shafter, delays her return to the city until autumn as she becomes intrigued with the cutthroat trout and decides to assist in their repopulation in the streams of Wyoming. An Indian phrase serves as both motif and title for *Going to the Sun* (1976). Marcus Kulick and Melissa Morgan systematically record observations of Rocky Mountain goats during a summer spent on the mountain peaks and meadows. Among other things, they learn that goats "keep themselves healthy by their social system and . . . hunting destroys nature's delicate balance." Reminiscent of *Romeo and Juliet*, the plot includes the love of teenagers Marcus and Melissa, their feuding fathers, a secret marriage ceremony, and their seeming final separation due to misinformation.

A dramatic picture book, *The Wentletrap Trap* (1978), set on the island of Bimini, describes a boy named Dennis and his search for a rare shell. Though he is disheartened when the spiral-shelled gastropod scurries back into a wave, he rejoices when his "Paw" returns safely on his fishing boat after a storm.

The Arctic tundra, with its snowy owl, white fox, musk ox, and long-tailed jaeger gull, is depicted in *The Wounded Wolf* (1978). A caribou strikes a wolf named Roko and a raven then picks the open wound; however, the leader of Roko's pack, Kiglo, brings the meat to the victim, saving his life. Although the scene was observed and reported to George by Dr. Gordon Haber, the poetic description excludes human interference and dialogue. Likewise, *The Grizzly Bear With the Golden Ears* (1982) is based on a factual situation in which a bear steals fish, first from other bears and then from fishermen. *One Day in the Desert* (1983) and *One Day in the Alpine Tundra* (1984) are reminiscent of Sally Carrighar's *One Day on Beetle Rock* (1944) and *One Day at Teton Marsh* (1947), in that daily episodes in the wilderness are made dramatic, in George's books, even before the heat of the day or the aftermath of the torrential rain.

Jean George floated down the treacherous Colorado River prior to writing *River Rats, Inc.* (1979). In the story, Joe Zero and Crowbar Flood travel the river illegally at night without a license because a widow has hired them to scatter her deceased husband's ashes at a particular set of falls. A wild mute, whom they call Lizard Boy because he is fast and eats lizards, assists them when the boat capsizes. In the progress of the novel, Joe and Crowbar teach Lizard Boy to speak and rename him Walter, and he in turn teaches them skills nec-

essary to survive in the Grand Canyon. Suspense dominates the purpose of the trip, the episodes, and even the final resolution, as Lizard Boy disappears and then emerges to join the boys' community.

The Cry of the Crow (1980) concludes with Mandy Tressel's ultimate choice to champion either her brother, Drummer, or Nina Terrance, the crow she has raised after Drummer shot up its nest in the Florida Everglades. After the crow matures, it continually attacks Drummer, and Mandy is forced to shoot it herself with a shotgun, realizing she should not have made it a wild pet. Another book set in the Everglades, *The Talking Earth* (1983), deals with the reciprocal relationship of man and nature. Billie Wind lacks respect for the legends of her Indian tribe and is temporarily banished. She survives a hurricane by observing the ways animals prepare and protect themselves, and comes to understand the profound legacy of her people.

In *How to Talk to Your Animals* (1985), the author informs the reader of communication patterns within a species and recommends that humans observe and repeat them. A book scheduled for publication in 1987 focuses on the bowhead whales of Barrow, Alaska, and the interrelationship with the Eskimo cultural characteristic of sharing. In the research phase, George spent six weeks in the area, camping for a time on sea ice when the temperature was thirty-five degrees below zero.

At age sixty-three, Jean Craighead George completed her autobiography, *Journey Inward* (1982). Dealing candidly with her divorce and raising children alone, she reminisced about her first-hand investigation of both nature and of human behavior. In addition, she reflected on her role as a roving reporter for *Reader's Digest*, which provided grist for her writing. In 1970 she received the Eva L. Gordon Award from the American Nature Society, and in 1982 she was the recipient of the Kerlan Award at the University of Minnesota, "in recognition of singular attainments in the creation of children's literature and in appreciation for generous donation of unique resources to the Kerlan Collection for the study of children's literature."

George's research and travels have resulted in a prolific outpouring of children's and young adults' books and in periodical publications for adults. Her plots, characters, settings, and themes are convincing, as they emerge with seeming ease and logic. She has matured as a writer, most notably in her characterizations, which in later books reveal more complexity and strength than in earlier works. In *Going to the Sun, The Wentletrap Trap,* and *The Cry of the Crow* especially, the protagonists gain the confidence and skills to survive emotionally, as well as physically.

George continues in her quest to understand nature, incorporating personal observation, research, and opinions of other experts in her nonfiction documentaries and fictionalized accounts. She avoids repetition from book to book, drawing her inspiration from nature's infinite variety. Most important, Jean Craighead George elevates nature in all its intricacies and makes scientific research concerning ecological systems intriguing and exciting to the young reader.

References:

Lee Bennett Hopkins, "Jean Craighead George," *Elementary English,* 50 (October 1973): 1049-1053;

Helen Melvin, "Jean Craighead George," *Horn Book,* 49 (August 1973): 348-351.

Papers:

Jean Craighead George's manuscripts are in the Kerlan Collection, University of Minnesota.

Virginia Hamilton
(12 March 1936-   )

Marilyn F. Apseloff
Kent State University

See also the Hamilton entry in *DLB 33: Afro-American Fiction Writers After 1955.*

BOOKS: *Zeely,* illustrated by Symeon Shimin (New York: Macmillan, 1967);

The House of Dies Drear, illustrated by Eros Keith (New York: Macmillan, 1968);

The Time-Ago Tales of Jahdu, illustrated by Nonny Hogrogian (New York: Macmillan, 1969);

The Planet of Junior Brown (New York: Macmillan, 1971);

W. E. B. Du Bois: A Biography (New York: Crowell, 1972);

Time-Ago Lost: More Tales of Jahdu, illustrated by Ray Prather (New York: Macmillan, 1973);

M. C. Higgins, the Great (New York: Macmillan, 1974; London: Hamilton, 1975);

Paul Robeson: The Life and Times of a Free Black Man (New York: Harper & Row, 1974);

Arilla Sun Down (New York: Greenwillow, 1976; London: Hamilton, 1977);

Justice and Her Brothers (New York: Greenwillow, 1978; London: Hamilton, 1979);

Dustland (New York: Greenwillow, 1980; London: MacRae, 1980);

Jahdu, illustrated by Jerry Pinkney (New York: Greenwillow, 1980);

The Gathering (New York: Greenwillow, 1981; London: MacRae, 1981);

Sweet Whispers, Brother Rush (New York: Philomel Books, 1982);

The Magical Adventures of Pretty Pearl (New York: Harper & Row, 1983);

Willie Bea and the Time the Martians Landed (New York: Greenwillow, 1983);

A Little Love (New York: Philomel, 1984; London: Gollancz, 1985);

Junius Over Far (New York: Harper, 1985);

The People Could Fly: American Black Folktales, illustrated by Leo and Diane Dillon (New York: Knopf, 1985; London: Walker, 1986).

OTHER: *The Writings of W. E. B. Du Bois,* edited by Hamilton (New York: Crowell, 1975);

"Illusion and Reality," in *The Openhearted Audience: Ten Authors Talk About Writing for Children,* edited by Virginia Haviland (Washington: Library of Congress, 1980), pp. 115-131;

"Through the Eyes of an Author: Tapping One's Own Experiences," in *Through the Eyes of a Child: Introduction to Children's Literature,* edited by Donna Norton (Columbus: Merrill, 1983), pp. 500-501.

Cox Studios

PERIODICAL PUBLICATIONS: "Portrait of the Author as a Working Writer," *Elementary English*, 48 (April 1971): 237-240, 302;

"High John Is Risen Again," *Horn Book*, 51 (April 1975): 113-121;

"Newbery Award Acceptance Speech," *Horn Book*, 51 (August 1975): 337-343;

"Writing the Source—In Other Words," *Horn Book*, 54 (December 1978): 609-619;

"Mission to Moscow: The Second International Conference of Writers for Children and Youth," *School Library Journal*, 26 (February 1980): 21-25;

"Ah, Sweet Rememory!," *Horn Book*, 57 (December 1981): 633-640;

"Boston Globe-Horn Book Award Acceptance," *Horn Book*, 60 (February 1984): 24-28.

Virginia Hamilton has established herself as one of the foremost writers for children and young adults. Unlike many authors whose styles and subjects are similar from book to book, Hamilton experiments with techniques and theme; her readers are continually faced with new challenges in her writing. She feels that "every fiction has its own basic reality . . . through which the life of characters and their illusions are revealed. . . . The task for any writer is to discover the 'reality tone' of each work." She is a productive writer, having produced a new book almost every year since 1967, when *Zeely* was published. A dynamic speaker as well as a fine writer, she is in great demand at national and international conferences.

Virginia Hamilton's maternal grandfather Perry escaped from slavery to Yellow Springs, Ohio, where he eventually purchased land and produced the Perry clan, a large, close-knit family. After their marriage, Hamilton's father and mother, Kenneth James and Etta Belle Perry Hamilton, farmed on the Perry land, where Virginia Hamilton was born and grew up, the youngest of five children. Except for fifteen years spent in New York City where she met Arnold Adoff, a poet, whom she married on 19 March 1960, she has continued to make Yellow Springs her home with her husband and two children. That Ohio setting has been a prominent feature of many of her novels.

Zeely, Hamilton's first book, grew out of a short story she wrote as a student at Antioch College (1952-1955) in Yellow Springs. In the book, Elizabeth Perry (note the last name), called Geeder, is visiting her uncle's farm with her brother one summer when she encounters Zeely, a six-and-one-half-foot tall young black woman whom Geeder imagines is a Watutsi queen enslaved by a cruel father to oversee his hundreds of prize hogs. Zeely learns of Geeder's imaginative story and urges Geeder to employ fact for daily life without losing the gift of imagination: "You have a most fine way of dreaming. Hold on to that." It is this understanding of self that is the main theme of the book, as Geeder discovers that it is what a person is rather than what she does that is important.

The setting of *Zeely* is like the Yellow Springs farmland of Virginia Hamilton's childhood. Most of the interior settings are remembered from her Uncle Lee's home, although the pump room that is described, according to Hamilton, was at her Uncle Willie's. The various farm chores mentioned in the novel are those she had seen performed as a child. Local areas that are prominently mentioned in the book are based upon actual places near her

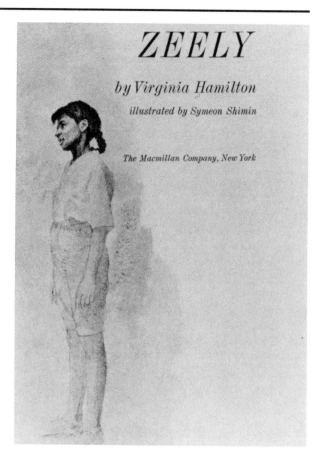

Title page spread for Hamilton's first novel (Macmillan)

present home. The Yellow Springs locale appears in Hamilton's Ohio novels repeatedly, although the town is not specifically named, but the reader never has the feeling of sameness from one book to another: through imagination and craft, Hamilton creates individualized settings.

Another feature of Hamilton's fiction is uniqueness of character and situation. Certainly Zeely is unusual, not only for her height but also for the aloofness that sets her apart from the dirt and smell of the hogs. Geeder's imagination, that makes a Watutsi queen of Zeely, adds to the young black woman's mysteriousness. In the subsequent novels, such characterization plays an even more prominent role, for Hamilton believes that "there is something about the feeling of myth and the unexplainable that I think adds a dimension to the character that one would not have otherwise."

Hamilton's second book, winner of the Edgar Allan Poe Award for the best juvenile mystery of 1969, was a departure from the first. *The House of Dies Drear* (1968) uses information about the Underground Railroad and the now nonexistent Dies

House, a staging post on one of the slave escape routes. The Small Family—father, mother, Thomas, and infant twins—move into Dies House at the beginning of the novel, and the forbidding atmosphere of the place—with its false walls and secret passages—sets the tone. Unusual situations arise as the secret tunnels and passages are discovered and the book's most unusual character, Mr. Pluto, is introduced. Like Zeely, Pluto is larger than life, and his vivid green eyes, white hair, beard, and mysterious manner all add to his overpowering presence. Furthermore, he lives in a cave, an uncommon habitat.

The setting again is based upon Yellow Springs, but the focus this time is on what Hamilton describes in the novel as the "limestone country, and always with limestone in this formation you'll find the water table percolating through rocks into springs. There are caves, lakes, and marshes all around us, all because of the rock formations and the way they fault." A college is also introduced as part of the town, based upon Antioch College which Hamilton not only attended as a young woman but also went to for meals as a child, just as Thomas does in the novel. Much of Thomas's knowledge of the area and its history he learns from his father, as Hamilton had from hers. Together father and son work out the mystery of trespassers in their house and the secret of Pluto's cave.

In *The House of Dies Drear* there is a direct reference to American Indians for the first time— a motif that recurs throughout Hamilton's novels. The references to Indians in her books are probably the result of two factors: Hamilton knew that many Shawnees lived in the Yellow Springs area originally, with Cherokees further south, and her grandmother claimed to be part American Indian. Since both the history of the region and of her family were important to Hamilton, it is not surprising to find the Indian motif in her novels. In *The House of Dies Drear,* Indians had obviously once lived in Pluto's cave, for there were numerous artifacts there.

Virginia Hamilton's third book in part reflects her move to New York in the late 1950s. *The Time-Ago Tales of Jahdu* (1969) is a frame story that begins in the Harlem apartment of Mama Luka, who babysits Lee Edward after school and tells him stories of Jahdu. Four of those tales are in the book. Jahdu encounters the allegorical figures Sweetdream, Nightmare, Trouble, Chameleon, and others and is revealed as clever, mischievous, and witty. These original tales have a timeless quality about them; in addition, they reveal a racial pride, as Jahdu discovers in the last tale that he is happiest when he becomes part of a black family in Harlem.

Hamilton's next novel, *The Planet of Junior Brown* (1971), is a challenging one. The setting is New York City, and again the characters and situations are unique, revealing an interest mainly in survival. Buddy Clark has no family; he is the "Tomorrow Billy," the leader of a group of younger homeless boys who look to him for survival, just as he had depended upon a Tomorrow Billy in another of the groups or "planets" when he was young and alone. Junior Brown, his friend, weighs 262 pounds; his bulk and the situations he encounters isolate him from society and, eventually, from reason. He has parents, but they hinder rather than help him: his father is absent all week and often on weekends, too, and his mother, an asthmatic, has removed the wires from the piano that Junior practices on because she needs her rest. Junior's piano teacher is having a nervous breakdown that finally envelops Junior, too, as his world deteriorates. Only in a special room in the school basement with Buddy, Mr. Pool (a former teacher and now

Dust jacket for Hamilton's novel about an isolated, mentally disturbed youth from New York City and the community which accepts him (Macmillan)

janitor), and the constructed "solar system" does Junior Brown feel at ease. Through Buddy, Junior survives because he is removed from his damaging home life and placed in one of the "planets" under Buddy's care.

Junior Brown is Hamilton's most fully developed character because of his problems. However, as Junior's grip on reality weakens, Buddy matures, comes more sharply into focus. He realizes that living for himself, his old belief, is not the answer: "We have to learn to live for each other. . . . The highest law for us is to live for one another." Mr. Pool, who has befriended both boys and who is a loner himself, also learns about commitment to others; he helps Buddy relocate Junior Brown to one of the planets where he will be cared for. That planet will henceforth be known as "the planet of Junior Brown," named by Buddy to indicate his affection for Junior Brown.

Although the setting is again New York City, *The Planet of Junior Brown* does not have the warm glow of Hamilton's previous book. The realistic descriptions of the stench of the Hudson River and the deserted buildings which provide havens for drug pushers as well as for planets anchor the characters to the actual world and prevent them from becoming imaginative people in a fantasy world.

During this period Hamilton did not confine herself to writing fiction. While she was creating *The Planet of Junior Brown*, she was also working on a biography of the great activist/scholar W. E. B. Du Bois (1868-1963). As Hamilton remarked: "It really works nicely having a nonfiction and a fiction going at the same time: one's a relief from the other, a different kind of writing." Hamilton had been influenced during her childhood by her father, who read *Crisis* magazine, edited by Du Bois, and who thought that, as Hamilton put it, "Du Bois was extraordinary." She discovered that she had to write about the times in order to reveal the whole man, for he was shaped by when and where he lived as well as by his own character and the people he met. Noted for his lifelong fight against oppression and prejudice, Du Bois was also egotistical and sometimes arrogant. In 1961, disillusioned with conditions in the United States, he joined the Communist party and immigrated to Ghana, where he became a revered citizen. He died there at the age of ninety-five. Hamilton's biography portrays Du Bois complete with faults and weaknesses and also brings his era vividly to life. Here one can learn history that is so often omitted from textbooks. *W. E. B. Du Bois: A Biography* (1972) is a first-rate, critical study of the man and his times.

Hamilton returned to fiction with *Time-Ago Lost: More Tales of Jahdu* (1973). The setting is again Mama Luka's Harlem apartment, where she again tells the stories to Lee Edward, but the mood has become somber: she is threatened with urban renewal, with having to find another place to live. The first story reflects the new tone, for it begins in darkness as Jahdu journeys to the East to be reborn so that he can get more magical Jahdu dust that can "put things to sleep and wake them up." The second and third tales are continuations of the first rather than separate stories as they were in the earlier Jahdu book. Through cleverness Jahdu frees Yang, the light, who has been bound, bringing it back to earth. The setting of the last chapter moves from Mama Luka's apartment to the streets of Harlem, as Lee Edward walks with his father, who is part Indian and who works on a rising gang

that brings steel beams to the riveter gangs. He listens to his father describe his job "high up on the girders of a new building," working with some Mohawk Iroquois. Soon after they reach home, Lee Edward has a dream about Jahdu, then learns when he awakens that it will be a long time before Mama Luka has to move. Joyful, Lee Edward begins a Jahdu tale for his parents, the first one he has ever told them.

Time-Ago Lost incorporates African tradition and mythology and Chinese cosmology as Jahdu does restore the balance between Yin and Yang and regains his magical powers through rebirth. Characterization is again memorable as Jahdu encounters crazy Loon, a Fisherman fishing in sand, the giant Trouble, and others. The setting, an eerie darkness seemingly without end, creates and emphasizes the somber, brooding tone; even the restoration of the light at the end of the third tale does not entirely dispel the gloom: that does not happen until the very end of the book.

In 1980 Hamilton wrote *Jahdu*, a single tale created for younger readers. Among the characters are some familiar ones from the earlier Jahdu books, such as Lee Edward, Chameleon, and Shadow, but the technique of the frame story has been dropped: there is no Mama Luka or Harlem. The tale is new, too.

The reader is treated to figurative language: "the cup of night was pouring in a cool, dark spill." The language is predominantly simple, as it was in the other two Jahdu books, and the tone is upbeat, cheerful. The prose is rhythmical, with some repetition that adds to the effect. Although this story is not as rich as the earlier ones, it makes a fine introduction to Jahdu for younger children.

In 1974 *M. C. Higgins, the Great* was published and marked Hamilton's return to the Ohio setting. In this book, the Glen Helen woodland of her childhood has been transformed into hills bordering the Ohio River: here, near the top of Sarah's Mountain, live the Higgins family, just below a sliding stripmining spoil heap that threatens them with destruction. Mayo Cornelius Higgins, called M. C., is thirteen, the oldest child. He alone seems to be aware of the danger to the family, and he tries to get his parents to leave the mountain. By the end of the novel he has come to realize what Sarah's Mountain means to his father especially, and, together with his family and his friend Ben Killburn, he stays and fights the menace by erecting a barrier wall.

Characterization is outstanding, not only of M. C. but also of his father, his mother, the outsider Lurhetta Outlaw, Ben Killburn, and some of Ben's

Dust jacket for Hamilton's novel about a family struggling to protect their home and environment from strip miners. The book was awarded the Newbery Medal, a National Book Award, the Boston Globe-Horn Book Award, and the Lewis Carroll Shelf Award (Macmillan).

family. Father and son are shown to be alike in many ways: in their pride and stubbornness and their love of family. Lurhetta is truly an outlaw, alienated from her family and new to the environment of the hills. Because she has no preconceived notions or prejudices, she challenges M. C.'s beliefs and arouses new emotions in him; however, since she is an outsider, she leaves, but she helps M. C. gain a new awareness before she goes.

M. C.'s best friend, Ben Killburn, stands out for several reasons. First, his appearance is unique: like all the members of his family, he has red hair (he is black), six fingers on each hand, and six toes on each foot. M. C.'s father, Jones, calls the Killburns "witchy" and fears them, and his son has the same superstitions. Through Lurhetta, M. C. learns that the Killburns are not to be feared, and he openly admits his friendship with Ben. Ben's

family also has an unusual life-style, for all of the land in their compound is devoted to a vegetable garden, leaving no room for the children to play. Instead, above the compound is a giant weblike structure of rope on which they spend all of their time out-of-doors.

Characterization, setting, and plot are skillfully woven to create a memorable novel, one that in 1975 was awarded the Newbery Medal and a National Book Award for the excellence of its writing. Here are distinctive but believable characters who speak about a growing concern: the environment and survival. The Higgins family show every sign of enduring through their determination to stay and fight. The future of Sarah's Mountain and the surrounding hills is in doubt, though, for the land and the water may have been poisoned beyond reclamation. That possibility is left for the reader to ponder, a device Hamilton often uses: her novels rarely have a completely finished feeling to them but instead often leave the reader wondering about the future of her characters.

While Hamilton was writing *M. C. Higgins, the Great*, she was also working on a biography of Paul Robeson (1898-1976), another man greatly admired by her father. Robeson, the son of a runaway slave, rose to international prominence as an actor and singer. In her introduction to the book, "The Knowledge," Hamilton states that "he was more than one man, more than a symbol for blacks like my father whose dreams had become thwarted. Through his art and the spoken word, Robeson had the amazing ability to project to the world his profound understanding for his people. For black America, he embodied the age-old spirit of Survival." But, in many ways, Robeson seemed a larger-than-life character, and Hamilton had to work to show realistically his human side. The result is a book that reveals a man of great warmth, intelligence, and physical ability, blessed with a magnificent voice. *Paul Robeson: The Life and Times of a Free Black Man* (1974) portrays how frequently Robeson's hopes were dashed, especially his hopes for equality for blacks, yet he kept trying, jeopardizing his own career by speaking out when people came to hear him sing. Finally branded a Communist, he was shunned by his country and booed abroad. His last years were spent in ill health and retirement.

Like the earlier biography of Du Bois, *Paul Robeson: The Life and Times of a Free Black Man* attempts to give the reader a full understanding of the times as well as of the man. Hamilton succeeds; the reader learns a great deal about the period of

Robeson's life in an interesting, very readable book, which benefits from scholarly notes and bibliographies as well as from well-chosen photographs which show Robeson and his family during several different periods of his life.

The following year, 1975, Virginia Hamilton's edition of *The Writings of W. E. B. Du Bois* was published to introduce his works to adolescents. Providing a biographical framework and selections from his writing, it is an excellent companion to her biography of Du Bois.

Hamilton returned to fiction with *Arilla Sun Down* (1976), a novel with many autobiographical elements that have been expanded and altered through imagination. This time the setting is primarily in a town that Hamilton describes as "a combination of Yellow Springs and Xenia." The Glen Helen woodland of *M. C. Higgins, the Great* again appears in a crucial scene, and, according to Hamilton, another town called Cliffville in the novel was based upon the town of Clifton but with its inhabitants changed to include many Amerindians; "in reality," Hamilton notes, " a town like that would be further south." The Adams family bears a resemblance to Hamilton's, for both the author and Mrs. Adams are black, have interracial marriages, and have two children, a boy and a girl. However, the fictional husband, Sun Stone (called Stony), is an Amerindian, not white, and his son, Jack Sun Run, is preoccupied with his Indian identity, a distinct feature of the novel. The protagonist, the Adamses' daughter, Arilla, tries to discover who she is, where she belongs, and in the process she becomes a survivor.

Arilla Sun Down is told in the first person and shifts back and forth in time as Arilla remembers events from her early childhood in Cliffville in a challenging stream of consciousness. The thoughts and attitudes of the twelve-year-old are revealed: her feelings of unworthiness, jealousy of her brother, and love for her mother and father are all evident. Brother and sister constantly quarrel, yet the bond of love is there, too. Here are characters that develop and fascinate. The reader sees the father's periodic need to get away from the white man's world; the mother's desire to become a settled part of the community again (she was born there and had left for several years, like Hamilton); the son's pride in his Indian heritage; and Arilla's confusion and concern about her own identity.

Actual places in Yellow Springs are used, although sometimes given new names or not named, yet they are often transformed into something else to serve the author's purposes. According to Ham-

ilton, the park in Yellow Springs "in reality isn't as large as Spangler Park in *Arilla*" where a confrontation takes place between Jack and some men from the town on the Fourth of July, and "the skating rink, called the pavillion when I skated there, no longer exists." Like Dies House, it has been torn down. The Municipal Building was the former school Hamilton's mother attended, and the college referred to is based upon Antioch. Through her skill she has blended reality and imagination into a memorable work of fiction.

Again there is a larger-than-life character, Jack, usually inseparable from his horse. Arilla regards him with a mixture of fear, jealousy, and love; she is sure that he hates her. The townspeople are angered by Jack's arrogance, and Arilla, too, regards him with awe. His mother and father argue about him, for his mother feels that her husband, Stony, is too lenient with Jack, gives him his way too often. Not until Arilla saves Jack during a hailstorm in the glen do both children come to a full awareness of each other, of their strengths and weaknesses.

The next novel, *Justice and Her Brothers* (1978), marked the beginning of another literary experiment, for it is the first book of a trilogy that focuses on four children who have the ability to project themselves into the future. The theme is survival. Futuristic novels are one of Hamilton's many interests: "I . . . read an enormous amount of science fiction. . . . I absolutely love it." In her trilogy the four children have extrasensory perception, or ESP. Three of them are siblings: Justice is eleven; her brothers, Levi and Thomas, identical twins but opposites in disposition and temperament, are thirteen. The fourth child is Dorian Jefferson, Justice's friend. One of the main features of *Justice and Her Brothers* is the atmosphere that is created for the present world as heat and dust build to unnatural proportions, though characterization remains a key feature of the novel. Thomas and Levi are mirror twins, one left-handed, the other right-handed, one with hair parted on the left, the other with the part on the right. Their temperaments are also in opposition: Levi is kind and considerate, especially of Justice, but Thomas goes out of his way to confound her, even to attempt bodily harm. Moreover, Thomas is able to control Levi's mind, make him say what he wants him to and make him feel things that are not there. Thomas becomes furious at the end of the book when he discovers that Justice not only has ESP too, but that her power is stronger than his and she will be the leader of their foursome, the "unit," when they journey into the future, a journey foreshadowed in the children's minds in this book. However, the children have very human qualities that give them balanced characterization. Justice loves to ride her bicycle, loves the sense of freedom that it gives her. She wants to join her older brothers and their friends at play. The boys smoke when their parents are away, but they love their parents and each other. Thomas stutters, which, as Levi explains, accounts for some of his rage, and the children race on their bikes the way all children do. Indeed, the last word of the novel emphasizes their human qualities: "Kids."

The second book of the trilogy, *Dustland* (1980), is set in a dust-covered land of the future. Dustland's inhabitants—the giant, the Slakers, the flying females, and the lone canine creature, Miacis, who drinks blood to relieve her thirst—have been imaginatively created by Hamilton to survive in such an environment. Vocabulary has changed, too, for as Hamilton reported, she "had to learn words to express abstractions." The den that Miacis

Dust jacket for the second book in Hamilton's science fiction Justice trilogy, in which four children travel to a dust-covered land of the future (Greenwillow)

digs is called a "dark," and the night is divided into periods such as Nolight and Graylight. Other words are completely imaginative but are understandable through context; "kelm," for example, obviously refers to a tribe, a particular group of Slakers. Hamilton's creation of words, inhabitants, and situations capture the reader's interest and grip him as he wonders what will be encountered next in that strange land.

Characterization of the four children forming the unit—Justice, Thomas, Levi, and Dorian—is similar to that in the first novel, but more of their talents are revealed. Justice, still with the most power, is the Watcher; Dorian is the Healer; Thomas is the Magician; and Levi, Hamilton writes, "suffered for them all." The unit structure is essential: only when the four of them join hands and concentrate can they mind-journey through time. Yet Thomas persists in railing against Justice's control; he rebels, creating problems for the unit.

In 1981 the last book of the Justice trilogy appeared: *The Gathering*. A brief prologue sets the scene for the unit (Justice, Thomas, Levi, and Dorian) to mind-travel to the future, leaving Dorian's mother behind to guard their empty bodies. The four enter Dustland, but this time through an inhabitant's dream. This dreamer, Duster, a human stunted in his growth, "was the leader for a packen of fifteen youngens. The youngens were divided into five trips of three youngens each." The unit, along with Duster and the packens, Miacis, Slakers, and others, gain entrance to Sona, a large domed living area free of dust. Here they learn about Dustland and its inhabitants; they hear that "genetic destruction in human cells caused generations of physical changes," and terrible nuclear accidents caused "catastrophic devastation from radioactivity." Characterization here is based upon what has occurred earlier, although by the end of the trilogy, the children return without their mind-journey powers and each is changed for the better because of the futuristic encounter.

The main theme of *The Gathering*, survival, is handled well, as logical, plausible reasons are given for the changes in the environment, and the reader learns how people and other creatures adapted to them. Hamilton's imaginative creations seem natural to the landscape, believable adaptations of earlier forms of life transmuted by nature and radiation.

When Virginia Hamilton's next novel appeared in 1982, it was another departure from her previous works. *Sweet Whispers, Brother Rush*, set in the Wilberforce area of southern Ohio, has a ghost as one of the characters, yet this is not a traditional ghost story. The appearance of Brother Rush, dead for many years, is explained as a part of tradition, of black folklore: "she [an old woman] told of *mysteries*, the way you learn them and see and feel *them*. . . . Say it's in the blood of centuries, comin down the line, just like health or sickness." The ghost, or *mystery*, is thus put into a historical and cultural context.

Brother Rush appears to Teresa (called Tree) and her older, retarded brother, Dabney (Dab), revealing separate episodes of their past to each. Thus Tree, now fourteen, learns that Dab was an abused child, and she sees hitherto unknown relatives and finds out about an inherited disease that is gradually, painfully, disabling her brother. Dab's illness, porphyria, was a crucial factor in the creation of the novel: " 'I became absolutely fascinated because of a very close association with the defect, and I found a way to work it into a book which I had wanted to do for twenty years.' " As Tree learns about her and her brother's pasts, she becomes better able to deal with the present and its difficulties and tragedies—she matures. Throughout the book, as the various family relationships are explored, past and present are skillfully woven together.

Again Hamilton has created memorable characters and situations which children from various backgrounds can understand. Tree's awakening interest in boys, her love for and sometimes turbulent relationship with her mother, her reaction to her mother's boyfriend, and her love for her brother touch upon relationships that should strike a familiar chord in many children. Here, too, is a one-parent family, the children left alone for long periods because their mother must work.

The novel was named a Newbery Honor Book and received the Coretta Scott King Award and the Boston Globe-Horn Book Award for fiction. To Hamilton's surprise, the ghost did not detract from the realism: "What is amazing to me is that nobody questioned the ghost at all. I'm absolutely astounded by that!" The International Board on Books for Young People (IBBY) awarded Hamilton a Certificate of Honor for *Sweet Whispers, Brother Rush* for its "outstanding example of literature with international importance." The language used in the novel, a variation of black English, is a powerful form of poetic writing.

In 1983 two books were published that varied from each other and their predecessors in subject and style. The first, *The Magical Adventures of Pretty Pearl*, is a long book set nearly a century ago. Pretty

Pearl, a child god, yearns to leave her home on Mount Kenya in Africa. Her brother, John de Conquer, grants her request and together they go to America, changing shapes en route. Once there they stay in the Georgia soil, Pretty Pearl learning about the Civil War with its bloody battlefields and Reconstruction. Finally emerging to join a group of freed slaves and their descendants hidden in the woods with a band of Cherokee Indians, Pretty Pearl assumes a human form and adopts the last name of Perry.

Although dialect is used, it is again unique. Hamilton explains: "I could not use the same language that I would use for contemporary Tree and Dab in *Sweet Whispers*. . . . I tried to imagine what the speech patterns would be like for the first generations of blacks after surrender." The book was special for her: "I think that *Pretty Pearl* is a culmination of all the work I've done and all the things I have tried to do in each book. This time all my love for the mythology and the folklore of black culture and black history and my love for creating characters and plots seemed to come together to such an extent that I felt that it was a completely organic book." *The Magical Adventures of Pretty Pearl* was well received by reviewers, who praised its language and the fine blending of mythology, folklore, and history. In her Boston Globe-Horn Book Award acceptance speech for *Sweet Whispers, Brother Rush*, Hamilton spoke about the new possibilities with language that emerged later in *The Magical Adventures of Pretty Pearl*: "*Sweet Whispers, Brother Rush* represents a turning point at which I discovered that I have many more voices than I realized. It freed me from a set view of what fiction could be for me. . . . I wanted to be more daring in my work. Say more. Reach a different level of life. Speak differently." She obviously succeeded, for there are vast differences in style, content, and setting between *The Magical Adventures of Pretty Pearl* and the books that preceded and followed it.

Willie Bea and the Time the Martians Landed (1983) returns to Ohio for its setting. It is Halloween 1938, the day after Orson Welles's broadcast of "The War of the Worlds," which created a national furor. Willie Bea's extended family, at her home for the holiday, believes that the Martians have invaded the country. Undaunted Willie Bea, convinced by her fortune-telling Aunt Leah that she, Willie, has the Star of Venus in her palm which means that she "will know the strange and the unknown," sets out to meet the creatures whom she believes are from Venus, not Mars. What she encounters—deceiving monstrous harvesters—is

Dust jacket for Hamilton's 1983 novel about a young girl who mistakes harvesting machines for aliens following Orson Welles's 1938 broadcast of "The War of the Worlds" (Greenwillow)

dramatically told as the eerie Halloween atmosphere combines with the terrors created by the broadcast.

Family unity is a strong theme. Aunts, uncles, and cousins have converged for the holiday, the various jealousies and rivalries surfacing as well as love. The family members are distinctive, revealed through conversations and actions as well as through description. The language level is simpler in this book than in many of the others, reminiscent of *Zeely* or *The House of Dies Drear* in its appeal to the middle reader rather than to an older child, and the relationships portrayed are developed with that age level in mind.

In 1984 *A Little Love* was published with a contemporary Ohio setting. Sheema, seventeen, is the protagonist, overweight, a slow learner, filled with a longing for the father who left when her mother died giving birth to her. After Sheema's relationships with her grandparents, with whom

she lives, and her boyfriend, Forrest, are fully explored and her feelings about herself are revealed, Sheema and Forrest leave in his old car to search for Terhan Cruze Hadley the signpainter, Sheema's father. Heading south from the Dayton area, watching for signs and checking telephone books whenever they stop, they stumble upon his name in an old book in Tennessee where the car has broken down. When asked about Hadley, the repairman who is fixing their car tells the teens that Hadley has gone to Georgia. Sheema and Forrest pay Hadley a visit which results in a change in Sheema's attitude about herself and her future.

The theme, the need for "a little love," is shown in many ways. Although Sheema has her grandparents' and Forrest's love, that is not enough. She yearns for the parents she never had, the one unobtainable but the other a possibility. Virginia Hamilton has taken a widely publicized subject, the search for one's parents, and has given it a slight twist since Sheema knows who her father is. Characterization is revealed less by action than through thoughts and conversation. Hamilton has chosen black English, which is modified somewhat during narration, for the dialect. The result is that the reader has a better idea of characterization, of how they sound as well as think. The reading may be more difficult because of it; the content, too, makes *A Little Love* more suitable for an older reader. The psychological interplay of relationships between characters would be understood and appreciated more by young adults.

Junius Over Far (1985) is Hamilton's most sophisticated novel to date. Its juxtaposition of youth and age, its alternating settings, and its language shifts from Caribbean dialect to standard English require a mature reader. The book focuses on the relationship of Junius Rawlings and his paternal grandfather, who eventually returns "over far" to Snake Island in the Caribbean after filling Junius with wonder about that faraway place through stories and legends. The plot alternates between Junius's loneliness after his grandfather's departure and his grandfather's struggle on Snake Island with a run-down estate owned by a distant relative who is both his friend and foe. The story is one of passage—a young man's passage to manhood and an old man's passage to death. Throughout the complex novel Hamilton explores universal themes through well-constructed descriptions of people and place. Her representation of the negative effects of the aging process are particularly noteworthy. Although the book may be outside the reach of most children, Hamilton maintains her consistent portrayal of supportive family relations, her development of loner characters, and her provocative themes—all important features of her writing.

The People Could Fly: American Black Folktales (1985) is an outstanding collection of black folktales written in a cadenced prose that is a pleasure to read aloud. Hamilton has included cogent explanatory notes for the tales, and, where the dialect might be a problem, a glossary is provided. The work includes twenty-four stories divided into four sections: animal tales; tales of the real, extravagant, and fanciful; tales of the supernatural; and tales of freedom. This is a significant collection of folklore, a major contribution to study of the evolution of the black folktale.

Virginia Hamilton is a writer of considerable talent and depth, a skillful experimenter with language who is not afraid to take chances by challenging her readers. She has moved from the simpler first novels to a rich, imaginative, and unique prose style that varies in each of her later books as she suits language to subject. She has created memorable characters in each work of fiction, basically loners, but each vastly different from the others and often haunting. Her work has received extensive critical praise and numerous awards; she is certainly one of the most prominent writers for children today.

Interview:

Marilyn Apseloff, "A Conversation with Virginia Hamilton," *Children's Literature in Education*, 14 (Winter 1983): 204-214.

References:

Marilyn Apseloff, *Virginia Hamilton: Ohio Explorer in the World of Imagination* (Columbus: State Library of Ohio, 1979);

Paul Heins, "Virginia Hamilton," *Horn Book,* 51 (August 1975): 344-348;

Lee Bennett Hopkins, "Virginia Hamilton," *Horn Book,* 48 (December 1972): 563-569;

Hopkins, "Virginia Hamilton," in *More Books by More People* (New York: Citation Press, 1974), pp. 199-207;

Jane Langton, "Virginia Hamilton, the Great," *Horn Book,* 50 (December 1974): 671-673;

John Rowe Townsend, "Virginia Hamilton," in *A Sounding of Storytellers* (New York: Lippincott, 1979), pp. 97-110.

Jamake Highwater
(Piitai Sahkomaapii, tribal name)
(14 February 1942?-   )

Nellvena Duncan Eutsler
East Carolina University

See also the Highwater entry in *DLB Yearbook: 1985*.

BOOKS: *Rock and Other Four Letter Words,* as J Marks (New York: Bantam, 1969);

Mick Jagger: The Singer Not The Song, as J Marks (New York: Curtis, 1973);

Indian America (New York: McKay, 1975; London: Hodder & Stoughton, 1976);

Song From the Earth: American Indian Painting (Boston: Little, Brown, 1976);

Ritual of the Wind: North American Indian Ceremonies, Music and Dances (New York: Viking, 1977);

Anpao: An American Indian Odyssey (Philadelphia & New York: Lippincott, 1977);

Many Smokes, Many Moons: A Chronology of American Indian History Through Indian Art (Philadelphia & New York: Lippincott, 1978);

Dance: Rituals of Experience (New York: A & W Publications, 1978);

Journey to the Sky: A Novel About the True Adventures of Two Men in Search of the Lost Maya Kingdom (New York: Crowell, 1978);

The Sun, He Dies: A Novel About the End of the Aztec World (New York: Lippincott & Crowell, 1980);

The Sweet Grass Lives On: Fifty Contemporary North American Indian Artists (New York: Lippincott & Crowell, 1980);

The Primal Mind: Vision and Reality in Indian America (New York: Harper & Row, 1981);

Moonsong Lullaby (New York: Lothrop, Lee & Shepard, 1981);

Arts of the Indian Americas: Leaves from the Sacred Tree (New York: Harper & Row, 1984);

Legend Days (New York: Harper & Row, 1984);

Words in the Blood: Contemporary Indian Writers of North and South America (New York: New American Library, 1984);

Eyes of Darkness (New York: Lothrop, Lee & Shepard, 1985);

The Ceremony of Innocence (New York: Harper & Row, 1985);

photo by Johan Elbers

I Wear the Morning Star (New York: Harper & Row, 1986);

Shadow Show: An Autobiographical Insinuation (New York: Van de Marck, 1986).

Jamake Highwater is a master storyteller whose books for young people reflect the Native American experience. His books are researched and documented, though his tales, by his own admission, include anecdotes based upon personal experience, and his characters, explored through the device of the private myth, may be composites of relatives or people he has known.

N. Scott Momaday's general remarks on the art of the storyteller in his *Literature of the American Indians* (1975) shed a revealing light, one that helps the reader to comprehend better Highwater's view of himself and his function as a writer. Storytelling, Momaday asserts, is "imaginative and creative in nature. It is an act by which man strives to realize his capacity for wonder, meaning and delight. It is also a process in which man invests and preserves himself in the context of ideas. Man tells stories in order to understand his experience, whatever it may be. The possibilities of storytelling are precisely those of understanding the human experience."

In order to further apprehend Highwater's position as a storyteller it is helpful to understand the insight provided by Momaday as he answers the questions concerning "the relationship between what a man is and what he says—or between what he is, and what he thinks he is." Momaday says, "This relationship is both tenuous and complicated. Generally speaking, man has consummate being in language, and there only. The state of human *being* is an idea, an idea which man has of himself. Only when he is embodied in an idea, and the idea is realized in language, can man take possession of himself."

Highwater says he does not know "where or when he was born." He has no original birth certificate, and the details he does know about his background are kept private. His sense of family privacy is outlined in *Ritual of the Wind: North American Indian Ceremonies, Music and Dances* (1977), where he states that to the Indians "privacy has a highly mystic and deeply significant value," a value often misunderstood by the white man. Highwater contends that to Indians revelation of personal information "debilitate[s] their personal identity."

Since Highwater's childhood is not a matter of public record, it is nearly impossible to assess his works against a biographical background. However, when and where he was born is not as important in viewing his children's stories as is the validity of his themes and messages.

Jamake Highwater understands the importance of metaphor. He emphasizes the necessity for

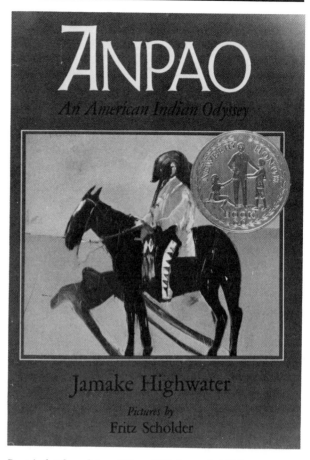

Dust jacket for a later edition of Highwater's 1977 novel about a young Indian on a mystical journey to find himself (Lippincott)

seeing many world views in an attempt to underscore the importance of living in a "multi-verse" rather than in a universe.

In *Anpao: An American Indian Odyssey* (1977), set on the early American frontier, Highwater presents a young hero engaged in a search for his identity. Anpao must find his twin in order to find himself, because he cannot become whole until he is reunited with Oapna, who represents his other half, his contrary side. Yet he must learn that what is "done . . . cannot be undone. That is the way it always is. We are free to do what we wish; but we must also accept whatever comes of it. That is the way it is."

In the beginning Anpao is a whole child. Then he disobeys Grandmother Spider and throws his hoop into the air. When it falls it lands on Anpao's head, splitting his personality in two. Grandmother Spider then sends Anpao and Oapna away: "When you were young," she says, "you were one with my house. But now you have become your own friend. Now there is nothing I can do to keep you here. You must go off, my dear sunshine-children, and find your adventures among the places beyond the world." Only after Anpao recognizes his contrary nature can he reconcile his differences and become whole again.

The story of Anpao is drawn from the oral tradition of the American Indian, old tales that Highwater presents as "an alternative vision of the world and an alternative process of history." His research for Anpao is documented with a bibliography and notes on his sources. The book also includes "The Storyteller's Farewell," in which Highwater says, "These stories, like ancient Indian designs, have been passed from one generation to the next and sometimes have been borrowed by one tribe from another. None of the tales is my own invention; they were born long before I came into the world. The words, like the threads of a weaving, are new, and these are mine, but the stories belong to everyone."

Claudia Lewis has praised *Anpao* for "the creative imagination behind the magical happenings," stating that "whether such story inventions as this come from Indian legend or from the mind of Jamake Highwater," the book is "a treasure to return to again and again." Jill May, professor at Purdue University, who used the book "on a project using literature to instill an appreciation of Native American culture and history," found that *Anpao* gave fifth and sixth graders a "deep understanding" of "the symbolic destruction of Native American cultures through the white man's intrusions of settlers, disease, and religion, and of the Native Americans' heroic journey" that "could not have developed without their literary journey through Highwater's tale."

Many Smokes, Many Moons: A Chronology of American Indian History Through Indian Art (1978), an illustrated book, introduces young readers to the world of the American Indian, discussing artifacts and art to trace the rise of Indian civilization. A selective overview of history, archaeology, anthropology, and cultural information, it emphasizes the many outrages suffered by the Indians at the hands of the early explorers and political forces. The first part of the book presents a view of both Americas, but, beginning with post-Columbian times, it focuses on North America.

In the preface Highwater introduces the reader to the problems posed by cultural differences, suggesting that many could be alleviated by our understanding that different people view objects and events from different perspectives. He cautions that "we must be exceedingly careful not to destroy the diversity of many cultures of man that gives human life meaning, focus, and vitality."

Many Smokes, Many Moons begins with the Navajo creation story then scans through the centuries, highlighting discoveries made by archaeologists and anthropologists and events recorded by historians. This book is a useful tool to introduce children to another culture.

Moonsong Lullaby (1981), illustrated with Marcia Keegan's photographs, is Jamake Highwater's evensong. The focus is on nature, with the soft light of the Moon "streaming through the treetops." The paean here is to the earth and its abundance, which nurtures and sustains man. The nighttime becomes a promise for a good tomorrow:

Listen carefully, child.
The singing is everywhere
The dark trees,
the clouded sky,
the mountains,
the grasslands all echo
the Moon's mellow music
until the last long whisper
that brings the dawn.

Legend Days (1984) is the first part of the Ghost Horse Cycle. Highwater notes that its historical perspective is "based on early accounts of life on the Northern Plains," and identifies his sources as George Bird Grinnell, J. W. Schultz, Walter McClintock, and the oral histories of the Blackfeet Confederacy. He also cites the historical works of John C. Ewers and Beverly and Adolph Hungry Wolf.

The young heroine of *Legend Days* discovers her animus in the beginning of the story. She is in her "tenth winter" when a smallpox epidemic strikes, and she is driven away from the camp so she will not contract the illness. Only by using her "man" strength and her "man" power is she able to survive: "And thus it happened in the time of the white owl and the kit fox that Amana changed into a man" (her name, Amana, reveals the "man" within). During these times Amana dreams the songs and dances that gave the foxes their power. Her eyes are opened in her eleventh springtime. She is filled with the power of the fox and songs come to her on the wind. "I am your dream," one says:

I am the seed that grows. I am the cave of
your heart and the drum that summons legends and dreams. Listen to me and listen to

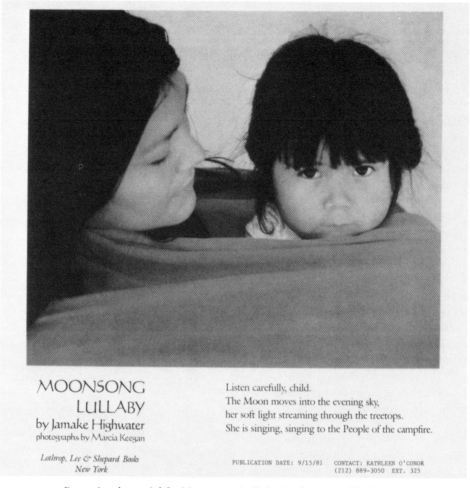

Promotional material for Moonsong Lullaby *(Lothrop, Lee & Shepard)*

me well, for I will not sing this song again in all your days.

By becoming a man, by receiving the strength and by learning the vocational skills of one, Amana becomes what she is capable of being in order to survive. She becomes "utterly transformed." As long as she receives and uses these gifts "in silence" she will be able to survive in her world. The voice within her says, "I am the vision that gives you great strength. I am your warrior; I am your spirit guide. Listen to me and you will prosper. But you must keep me hidden. You must nourish me and honor me. . . ."

When Amana returns to the campsite, she finds no one there except two grandmothers, Crow Woman and Weasel Woman, who teach her all they know so they may all survive. She becomes a hunter, but, because she must be both warrior and woman, they also teach her how to be a woman.

This experience is one she must suffer through, for "Suffering brings vision to those who know how to see through their pain." Being a "man" serves her for the time as a matter of survival, but she is cautioned that "In the days ahead you must come to understand not only your powers as a man but also your powers as a woman."

Finally Amana is reunited with her sister and her sister's husband, Far Away Son. Amana is twelve and, according to the custom of the tribe, Far Away Son marries his wife's orphaned sister. Amana becomes strong "like a warrior," but she also becomes a person "full of gentleness and compassion." She must nurse her sister and, in caring for Far Away Son, learn from him all that she can. He too is an independent person, saying of himself: "I know what I have done . . . , I am too old to worry about what people think of me. . . . I know who I am."

*Dust jacket for the first part of Highwater's Ghost Horse Cycle
in which Amana, a young Indian girl, begins a spiritual quest
after her camp is stricken by a smallpox epidemic
(Harper & Row)*

Amana learns much, including the fact that
a man's world and a woman's world are entirely
different. "How free men are!," she whispers, but
Far Away Son encourages her and includes her in
his male activities. However, the white man's intrusion has been too great. His alien customs, his political and military strength, his religious fervor
combine to overwhelm Amana's people.

After the deaths of Far Away Son and her
sister, Amana is truly alone, but the story ends with
a note of hope when Amana hears a distant sound:
" 'Yes . . . ,' Amana murmured with a gentle smile
as she ran into the deep night. 'It is a fox!' "

The Ceremony of Innocence (1985) is part two of
the Ghost Horse Cycle. Amana's story continues,
but the plot is not easy to follow, and the characters
are not fully drawn and developed.

Now twenty-eight, Amana, whose Indian
world has lost its center, is attempting to survive in
the white man's world when she meets Amalia, a
woman whose courage "was born of arrogance and
anger." For Amana "all dreams of power dried up
and died" with the death of Far Away Son, whose
death becomes symbolic of the Indian ways that
Amana cherished. When Amana tries to "dream
herself back into existence," she is always overwhelmed by the conditions created by the dominance of the white man.

For Amana "the voices of storytellers become
silent. Their tales of destiny feel like leaves in an
endless autumn. The powerful animals withdrew
into the distant land where white men had not
found their way, taking with them the wisdom they
had once shared with Indians." Everything familiar
to Amana, everything she had once loved was gone:
her tribe, her sister, and her husband. "I am not
an Indian anymore," she says, and "I have not
learned how to fight and yet I have not learned
how to give up." Amana knows that she "must have
a reason of my own to live," and Jean-Pierre Bonneville, a trader who appears briefly in *Legend Days*,
becomes her reason.

Having strayed far from her vision, Amana
strays even further with her alliance with Bonneville. Shortly before the birth of their daughter,
Jemina, Bonneville leaves her and returns to his
home in Canada; now there is no one left for
Amana. Her world becomes divided "into two ir-
reconcilable parts." During the winter, and shortly
after Jemina's birth, Amana abandons the trading
post where she has lived with Bonneville, and all
the remaining Indians there are herded off to a
reservation.

Amalia, who had earlier joined the white culture, again befriends Amana and takes her and her
infant to live in an entirely different environment.
Amana becomes a dishwasher in a white man's restaurant, and Jemina grows up and is sent off to a
boarding school. Amana pleads with her daughter
to "dream," but Jemina cannot. Amana realizes that
she herself once had a dream but Jemina, her child,
has nothing. "She was born into a dead land. There
is no center. The world in which we once lived and
into which we brought our children is gone."

The plot rapidly advances through many
years of Jemina's marriage. Her first son, Reno,
seems destined to be the child who assimilates the
ways of the white man, "becoming just what his
mother wanted him to be: an American boy." However, her second son, Sitko, seems to "have a vision
in his fingertips!" He is "in tune with nature." In

the final analysis, Amana realizes, "I must be who I am, and you must try to find out who you are. And eventually it will be all right."

Eyes of Darkness (1985) is a work of fiction based on the life of Charles Alexander Eastman, a pioneer Indian intellectual. David Jackson, writing in the *Village Voice*, has pointed out that Eastman, in his autobiographical works, described "his sense of entrapment," but unlike Highwater Eastman remained "an advocate of the ideals (if not the unpleasant realities) of western civilization as the only route to salvation." Jackson further asserts that Highwater is "aware that whites are often skeptical of their own culture and mass behavior, [and] tries to turn his writing into compelling acts of both self- and tribal discovery." The reader should not view this book as a biography of Eastman, for it is the story of Dr. Alexander East, a fictional character.

Named Hakadah, "the pitiful last," at birth, East remains "the pitiful last" until he earns a new name. When he becomes a "winner," he becomes Yesa; after he enters the world of the white man he becomes Alexander East.

When the story opens Alexander East is confronted with the questions "How did I get here and how is it that I have changed?" and "How is it that I have changed so utterly?" Having entered the white man's world, he is forced to take sides, to make choices. He is faced with understanding himself and finding the center of his life.

This powerful story is told against the backdrop of "the terrible and inevitable catastrophe" of the battle of Wounded Knee. In the beginning the reader knows who Yesa has become, and the following chapters describe his transformation into Alexander East, a man who must resolve the conflicts between the Indian within and the world of the white man without.

While he is growing up, Yesa learns from his grandmother the voices of nature, and as an adult he carries within the "fragile memories of a small red bird." The white man's intrusion, however, forces Yesa's tribe to make one move after another, and Yesa moves closer and closer into the white man's world.

Fortunately, along the way the grandmother sees that Yesa has learned many lessons: "He fell in love with the wings of birds, the bright light of spring dancing upon them in the morning." The grandmother tells him, "When we are wise and when we ponder many questions, it is not truth that we are seeking, my children. What we are seeking is meaning. And meaning and truth are not the same thing."

In Highwater's books the grandmother figure passes down the tradition and teaches the important lessons. Yesa's grandmother provides crucial insight when she tells Yesa: "The greatest wisdom can only be gained with great sorrow. We do not know why it should be so, but that is the way it is with us. From pain we learn courage. From sadness we learn generosity. From shame we learn dignity. From the longest winters come the greenest springs."

When Yesa meets the white man and learns of his ways he cannot hate him. His grandmother has taught him not to fill his mind with death, vengeance, and anger, and had insisted to his uncle, who looked after him because his father was presumed dead, that she would "not allow his thoughts to be filled with rage and vengeance!" Yesa cannot hate white men, but he distrusts them. Having learned of the many remarkable things they could do, he regards them as "a race whose power bordered upon the supernatural," but he has also seen their greed as they collected "things" and their hypocrisy in the practice of their religion.

While Yesa is young, the grandmother is in charge; however, after his father, who has adopted the white man's ways, returns, Yesa is forced to accept the white man's way of life. After years of study, he becomes Dr. Alexander East, the man the reader meets in the opening chapter of the book. He has become the man the reader sees symbolized on the last pages as he looks through the window "watching the tiny red bird flit aimlessly in the blind, dark sky." The reader is left to draw his own conclusion about what Dr. Alexander East will find as he goes "in search of himself and of the center where the sacred tree still grows."

I Wear the Morning Star (1986), part three of the Ghost Horse Cycle, continues Sitko's story from *The Ceremony of Innocence*. Sitko's vision, which Grandmother Amana depends on to make everything "all right," becomes obscured time after time by his feeling of abandonment while he lives at Star of Good Hope, a foster home where Jemina, his mother, leaves him.

In the first part of the book Sitko experiences rejection by his peers because he is different. He is altered by other people's opinions of what is acceptable. He is isolated and retreats into silence, and in his self-imposed exile, realizing that he "could never be anything but an outsider," he discovers that "the imagination was the place where [he] lived!" It was during his experience of playing with the other rejected children, the "leftover people," that he tries to plant a Chinese garden filled with sweet peas which suffocate under the dark earth. Sitko, too, suffers and suffocates "under the heavy folds of earth"; he, too, is trapped and cannot blossom, and his "dream of sweet peas" turns "to ashes."

When Reno, his brother, arrives to live at the home, he tries desperately to encourage Sitko to abandon his vision and be like everyone else. Sitko feels that Reno is the "butterfly," but he, Sitko, is only "a shadow." Sitko does try to change, but cannot. During this period Reno reads to Sitko, who discovers "a succession of bright images which flickered through [his] mind." He surrounds himself with these images, "basking in the brilliant colors and fantastic figures," and begins to draw them.

Because Sitko cannot conform, he suffers emotional torture and extreme physical abuse from the headmaster and is finally removed from the home. Jemina takes him to the house of Alexander Miller, with whom she lives; however, the situation does not improve and again physical abuse and emotional anguish dominate the scene.

Sitko does again have the love and support of Grandmother Amana, who sends him on a vision quest, during which he is "completely surrounded by colors," and receives the imprint which "remains forever upon [his] brow." He can indeed wear the Morning Star.

Shortly after Sitko starts to school in his new environment he meets a teacher, Mrs. Blake, who has a great impact on his life. With Mrs. Blake, Sitko learns that "there are other worlds," and he learns "a remarkable language of images and ideas." He also meets other young people who are "different" and with them explores the world of music, poetry, literature, and art. The more Sitko explores that other world, the greater the strain in his relationship with Alexander Miller and his mother's world, and his association with Reno.

At a party, Sitko meets an old woman and is "stripped naked" by her perception of his "desperation and confusion." Sitko had felt in his new-found intellectual pursuits that he "was independent and free; [he] claimed that [he] didn't care if people accepted [him]. . . ." Through the piercing insight of this old woman he realizes that he could "never escape the profound longing to be loved."

This short novel is more than the story of Sitko and his brother, Reno; it is the story of all children who live outside the circle, those who are not nurtured and fed, but who may some day thrive. In the final analysis Reno is the loser, but the reader knows that Sitko will eventually thrive,

as will his garden:

> *Yet in a brittle soil in some distant time and place, under fragrant eucalyptus trees where children still sometimes play, a herd of brilliant sweet peas rise high above the ground. No water flows to nourish them. No hands extract the weeds that strangle them. Yet miraculously they have survived, making their way through the hard, ungiving land and climbing high into the air. Now in this longest night their blossoms pour a heavy honey into the air.*

Jamake Highwater has earned a secure place among authors of literature for young people. *Anpao*, a Newbery Honor Book, won the Boston Globe-Horn Book Award and the Best Book for Young Adults Award from the American Library Association in 1978. *Legend Days* was cited by the American Library Association in 1984 as Best Book of the Year and Notable Book of the Year. *The Ceremony of Innocence* was placed on the Best Books of the Year list by the American Library Association in 1985.

Highwater, like any other writer, has his detractors. Yet, as David Jackson has noted, "Society is so filled with fantasies about Indians (and other "others") that it notices only part of Indian culture. From the white world, there is resistance to and suspicion of Highwater's cosmopolitanism. And in spite of Highwater's achievements in influencing Native American thought and action there is a violent antagonism toward him among certain Indian nationalities who feel his kind of adaptation is assimilation. . . ." Highwater may have his detractors, but a catalogue of his supporters, who come from a wide range of interests and disciplines, is impressive. They include Joseph Campbell, John Gardner, Edward Albee, Kurt Vonnegut, Jr., and F. S. C. Northrup, as well as a number of influential American Indians. In 1979 Ed Calf Robe, Elder of the Blood Reserve of Blackfeet Indians in Alberta, Canada, and member of the Horns Society, acting on the behalf of the Blackfeet people, honored him with a new name—Piitai Sahkomaapii/Eagle Son—because of his achievements as a scholar and writer on Native Americans.

Madeleine L'Engle has said, "Jamake Highwater's writing helps bring the reader in touch with the earth on which we live, and the interrelationship between the human being and all of creation. This is something we need to recover, and I am grateful to him for emphasizing the unity of all life." Sarah S. Allen has called Highwater an original thinker, with the "rare and awesome gift of the gods." She says, "He made me see and feel for the first time the variations in cultural thinking, the power of visions, and the wonders of subliminal experience."

In speaking of the appeal of Jamake Highwater's books, David Jackson sees in them "valuable additions to the literature of Indian arts and culture; they are schemes for new explorations of old problems." There are many who, with Jackson, "identify with Highwater's dialectic personality, with him and 'others' who are 'us' and 'them' at the same time."

Jamake Highwater's metaphors are meaningful; his symbols are vivid; his imagery is awe-inspiring. Highwater creates for the reader an awareness of the earth and its wonders. His vision is perhaps best expressed in his portrait of Amana in *The Ceremony of Innocence,* as "She sat behind the cash register and stared off into empty air, seeing things that others could not see. She saw flowers bloom from the telephone poles and she saw a cascade of lavender butterflies rain down upon the mud-filled street where misty animals with human faces drifted like smoke among the wildly charging carriages and automobiles."

References:

David Jackson, "Jamake Highwater's Native Intelligence," *Village Voice* (3 May 1983): 37-39;

N. Scott Momaday, "The Man Made of Words," in his *Literature of the American Indians: Views and Interpretations* (New York: New American Library, 1975), pp. 96-110.

Papers:

Jamake Highwater's manuscripts have been donated to the archives of the Native Land Foundation in New York with the stipulation that they are not to be reproduced during his lifetime.

Russell Hoban

(4 February 1925-   )

Alida Allison

BOOKS: *What Does It Do and How Does It Work? Power Shovel, Dump Truck, and Other Heavy Machines* (New York: Harper, 1959);

The Atomic Submarine: A Practice Combat Patrol Under the Sea (New York: Harper, 1960);

Bedtime for Frances, illustrated by Garth Williams (New York: Harper, 1960; London: Faber & Faber, 1963);

Herman the Loser, illustrated by Lillian Hoban (New York: Harper & Row, 1961; Kingswood, Surrey: World's Work, 1972);

The Song in My Drum, illustrated by Lillian Hoban (New York: Harper & Row, 1962);

London Men and English Men, by Hoban and Lillian Hoban, illustrated by Lillian Hoban (New York: Harper & Row, 1962);

Some Snow Said Hello, by Hoban and Lillian Hoban (New York: Harper & Row, 1963);

The Sorely Trying Day, illustrated by Lillian Hoban (New York: Harper & Row, 1964; Kingswood, Surrey: World's Work, 1965);

A Baby Sister for Frances, illustrated by Lillian Hoban (New York: Harper & Row, 1964; London: Faber & Faber, 1965);

Bread and Jam for Frances, illustrated by Lillian Hoban (New York: Harper & Row, 1964; London: Faber & Faber, 1966);

Nothing To Do, illustrated by Lillian Hoban (New York: Harper & Row, 1964);

Tom and the Two Handles, illustrated by Lillian Hoban (New York: Harper & Row, 1965; Kingswood, Surrey: World's Work, 1969);

The Story of Hester Mouse Who Became a Writer, illustrated by Lillian Hoban (New York: Norton, 1965; Kingswood, Surrey: World's Work, 1969);

What Happened When Jack and Daisy Tried To Fool the Tooth Fairy (New York: Four Winds Press, 1966);

Goodnight, illustrated by Lillian Hoban (New York: Norton, 1966; Kingswood, Surrey: World's Work, 1969);

Russell Hoban (© Jerry Bauer)

Henry and the Monsterous Din, illustrated by Lillian Hoban (New York: Harper & Row, 1966; Kingswood, Surrey: World's Work, 1967);

The Little Brute Family, illustrated by Lillian Hoban (New York: Macmillan, 1966);

Save My Place, by Hoban and Lillian Hoban (New York: Norton, 1967);

Charlie the Tramp, illustrated by Lillian Hoban (New York: Four Winds Press, 1967);

The Mouse and His Child, illustrated by Lillian Hoban (New York: Harper & Row, 1967; London: Faber & Faber, 1969);

A Birthday for Frances, illustrated by Lillian Hoban (New York: Harper & Row, 1968; London: Faber & Faber, 1970);

The Stone Doll of Sister Brute, illustrated by Lillian Hoban (New York: Macmillan, 1968; London: Collier-Macmillan, 1968);

The Pedaling Man, and Other Poems, illustrated by Lillian Hoban (New York: Norton, 1968; Kingswood, Surrey: World's Work, 1969);

Harvey's Hideout, illustrated by Lillian Hoban (New York: Parents' Magazine Press, 1969; London: Cape, 1973);

Best Friends for Frances, illustrated by Lillian Hoban (New York: Harper & Row, 1969; London: Faber & Faber, 1971);

The Mole Family's Christmas, illustrated by Lillian Hoban (New York: Parents' Magazine Press, 1969; London: Cape, 1973);

Ugly Bird, illustrated by Lillian Hoban (New York: Macmillan, 1969);

A Bargain for Frances, illustrated by Lillian Hoban (New York: Harper & Row, 1970; Kingswood, Surrey: World's Work, 1971);

Emmet Otter's Jug-Band Christmas, illustrated by Lillian Hoban (New York: Parents' Magazine Press, 1971; Kingswood, Surrey: World's Work, 1971);

Egg Thoughts, and Other Frances Songs, illustrated by Lillian Hoban (New York: Harper & Row, 1972; London: Faber & Faber, 1973);

The Sea-Thing Child, illustrated by Abrom Hoban (New York: Harper & Row, 1972; London: Gollancz, 1972);

Dinner at Alberta's, illustrated by James Marshall (New York: Crowell, 1973; London: Cape, 1977);

Letitia Rabbit's String Song, illustrated by Mary Chalmers (New York: Coward, McCann & Geoghegan, 1973);

The Lion of Boaz-Jachin and Jachin-Boaz (London: Cape, 1973; New York: Stein & Day, 1973);

Ten What?: A Mystery Counting Book, illustrated by Sylvie Selig (London: Cape, 1974; New York: Scribners, 1975);

How Tom Beat Captain Najork and His Hired Sportsmen, illustrated by Quentin Blake (New York: Atheneum, 1974; London: Cape, 1974);

Kleinzeit (London: Cape, 1974; New York: Viking, 1974);

Turtle Diary (London: Cape, 1975; New York: Random House, 1975);

Crocodile & Pierrot: A See-The-Story Book, by Hoban and Selig (London: Cape, 1975; New York: Scribners, 1977);

A Near Thing for Captain Najork, illustrated by Blake (London: Cape, 1975; New York: Atheneum, 1976);

The Twenty-Elephant Restaurant, illustrated by Emily Arnold McCully (New York: Atheneum, 1978);

Arthur's New Power, illustrated by Byron Barton (New York: Crowell, 1978);

La Corona and the Tin Frog, illustrated by Nicola Bayley (London: Cape, 1979);

Flat Cat, illustrated by Clive Scruton (New York: Philomel, 1980);

The Dancing Tigers, illustrated by David Gentleman (London: Cape, 1980);

Ace Dragon (London: Cape, 1980);

Riddley Walker (New York: Summit Books, 1981);

Ace Dragon Ltd., illustrated by Blake (London: Cape, 1981);

The Serpent Tower, illustrated by David Scott (London: Methuen, 1981);

The Great Fruit Gum Robbery, illustrated by Colin McNaughton (London: Methuen, 1981); republished as *The Great Gumdrop Robbery* (New York: Philomel, 1982);

They Came from Aargh!, illustrated by McNaughton (London: Methuen, 1981; New York: Philomel, 1981);

The Battle of Zormla, illustrated by McNaughton (London: Methuen, 1982; New York: Philomel, 1982);

The Flight of Bembel Rudzuk, illustrated by McNaughton (London: Methuen, 1982; New York: Philomel, 1982);

Pilgermann (New York: Summit Books, 1983);

Charlie Meadows, illustrated by Martin Baynton (New York: Holt, Rinehart & Winston, 1984);

Jim Frog, illustrated by Baynton (New York: Holt, Rinehart & Winston, 1984);

Lavinia Bat, illustrated by Baynton (New York: Holt, Rinehart & Winston, 1984).

RECORDINGS: *Frances,* Caedmon (TC 1546, 1977);

A Bargain for Frances and Other Stories, Caedmon (TC 1547, 1977);

The Mouse and His Child, Caedmon (TC 1550, 1977).

OTHER: "Thoughts on Being and Writing," in *The Thorny Paradise,* edited by Edward Blishe (New York: Horn Book, 1975), pp. 65-76.

PERIODICAL PUBLICATION: "Time slip, uphill lean, laminar flow, place-to-place talking and hearing the silence," *Children's Literature in Education,* 9 (November 1972): 33-47.

Russell Hoban is a writer whose genius is expressed with equal brilliance in books both for children and for adults. Since the late 1950s, Hoban has created some of the best-known characters in postwar children's literature: Frances the Badger, Charlie the Tramp, Emmet Otter, the Mouse and His Child, and Manny Rat. In his more than fifty children's books, Hoban has established himself as a writer with a rare understanding of childhood (and parental) psychology, sensitively and humor-

ously portrayed in familiar family situations. He has an unerring ear for dialogue and has recorded some of the funniest lines in children's books; his background as an artist has contributed to his memorable depiction of scenes; his intelligence and skill have crafted wise and warm stories notable for delightful plots and originality of language. Yet Hoban is much more than just a clever and observant writer. His works are permeated with an honest, often painful, and always uncompromising urge toward self-identity, whether the seeker be little Charlie the beaver trying to decide for himself if building dams is what *he* wants to do with his life, or disgruntled Frances the badger insisting on her unusual diet of bread and jam sandwiches, or the mouse and his child, a connected windup toy, discovering on their arduous road to "self-winding" the importance of territory—communal territory, family territory, and internal, personal territory. In his more recent books for children and in the adult novels he began writing in the early 1970s, this theme of identity becomes more apparent, more complex as Hoban's works have become longer and more penetrating. Indeed, Hoban's writing has not so much gradually developed as it has leaped and bounded—paralleling upheavals in his own life. One of his most recent adult novels, *Riddley Walker* (1981), has received acclaim on both sides of the Atlantic as a sui generis masterpiece. In it, twelve-year-old Riddley, setting off on his own in a shattered world far in the postnuclear-war future, learns a fundamental lesson on his way to becoming an adult: Fate cannot be mastered; all we as humans can do is master our response to Fate. The same hard but true lesson is masterfully told in Hoban's *The Dancing Tigers,* a children's book published in 1980.

Russell Conwell Hoban was born 4 February 1925, in Lansdale, Pennsylvania, the third of three children, and the only son of Abram T. and Jeanette Dimmerman Hoban. Hoban himself has described his early life and the influence his parents had on him: "My mother bred pigeons and gardened. My father was advertising manager for the *Jewish Daily Forward* in Philadelphia. He took me hiking, handed out nickels for clever remarks at the dinner table, directed amateur productions of Russian and Yiddish classics and protest plays of the thirties . . . and voted for Norman Thomas. The first two rules of etiquette I learned were never to cross a picket line and always to eat the union label on the pumpernickel for good luck. As a child I drew very well and was expected to be a great artist when I grew up."

Though his father died in 1936, Hoban went on to do what was expected of him by becoming a successful artist and illustrator. Temple University provided him with a partial scholarship, but he dropped out after five weeks of college: "I wanted no part of an educational package," he told Frederic Whitaker of *American Artist* in 1961. "I was sure I could learn by reading and observation all the schools could teach me, and also a good deal more of my own choosing." He chose to attend the Philadelphia Museum School of Industrial Art for a year and a half and, in 1944, married Lillian Aberman, another art student whom he had met at the Graphic Sketch Club when they were both seventeen. Hoban joined the U.S. Army in 1943, went overseas to Italy in 1944, and returned in 1945. He took whatever work he could find: Western Union messenger, freight handler, and silk-screen artist. At one point, the growing family was so broke they put together all they had, two hundred dollars, for Hoban to travel to Detroit, where he hoped to get drawing assignments from auto manufacturers, which he did. From the early fifties until the mid 1960s Hoban worked as a television art director and then as a free-lance illustrator, commissioned by such national publications as the *Saturday Evening Post, Time,* and *Sports Illustrated.* Hoban's particular fascinations during this first career as an artist were machinery and sports. He often attended sports events, sketch pad in hand, interested less in the technical aspects of the play than in the courage and strength of the participants. He has said, were it not for his poor eyesight, that he would have enjoyed being a boxer.

By 1961 Hoban was well-enough known as a commercial illustrator for Whitaker to write the following of him in *American Artist:* "Hoban is now thirty-six, and from the Horatio Alger point of view he has already arrived. But it would appear that his present notable ability places him only at the threshold of a career.... I am curious to know what kind of article may be written about Russell Hoban twenty years from now."

Whitaker's comment was prescient, though Hoban would likely have been as surprised as Whitaker had he known that the career he was on the threshold of was in writing and not in art. Hoban's first children's book, *What Does It Do and How Does It Work?* (1959), was published at the recommendation of Ursula Nordstrom at Harper, followed by *The Atomic Submarine* (1960). Both are technical and explanatory as opposed to the imaginative and domestic books which were soon to come, but Hoban had had his first taste of writing and he

liked it. "Being a published writer, I went on writing, and found that writing was what I liked best." Lillian Hoban began illustrating her husband's books in 1961 with *Herman the Loser.* Her approach to illustration, she notes, was quite different from his: "Russ and I have completely different feelings about illustration. It was always a heavy thing for him—he used to sit at the easel groaning and yawning, and he was glad to give it up when he did. But for me it's completely satisfying and cozy. I have just as good a time as a kid with a coloring book. I'm not a strong draughtsman, but I don't worry about it—I concentrate on getting the right feeling in the pictures...."

Together, the Hobans began to concentrate on their family situations as the subject matter for their books. Lillian Hoban has said, "I don't exactly use our children as models, but whether I'm drawing children or animals I have them in mind, and the expressions on the face of Frances the badger have appeared on various small Hoban faces in our household."

Hoban, too, has commented on the role of his children in the many books he and his wife created together: "Most of the ideas for the Frances stories and the other picture books come from our family life.... Ever since I became a writer there has always been a child of less than three feet around...." Hoban states that because his stories were "mostly about ordinary domestic situations," he had "to pay close attention to whatever is going on in the house, looking for whatever humor there may be in the situation and in the resolution of it; and the resolution has to be one that really works."

Herman the Loser is a good example of a book which reflects the workings of the Hoban family. The book is about a little boy who constantly loses such mundane items as his cowboy hat and a mitten, a habit which fuels the snide commentary of his older sister, Sophie. On a walk with their father, Herman and his sister are led to discover that there are other valuables Herman has a knack for finding, such as round stones, a bicycle valve cap, and the place where he beat up his friend Timmy. The gentle, unobtrusive solicitations of the parents save face for Herman, and even his nasty sister agrees at the end that Herman is not a loser.

Hoban dedicated the book to his mother "who helped me find things," and on the back cover, above pictures of two smiling Hoban children, is written, "Here are the original Sophie and Herman. They are Phoebe and Abrom.... Their third child, Esmé, will make her first appearance in the Hobans' next book, *The Song in My Drum.*"

Tom and the Two Handles (1965), an "I Can Read" book, is, despite the restrictions of vocabulary, an inventive, straightforward book about a boy learning how to deal with a friend who keeps giving him bloody noses. After each one-sided pugilistic encounter, Tom receives well-intentioned but platitudinous advice from his father, who tends more toward philosophy than practicality. "There are two sides to every situation," says Father; "Old friends are the best friends." Tom's worldly wise objection is: "All I know is I lost two fights in a row." Finally Tom accomplishes the necessary by beating his friend in a slugfest—recalling to mind Hoban's own dictum that "the resolution has to be one that really works."

The Hobans' work together was usually well received, with many of their books topping reviewers' lists of favorites: the Frances books, *Charlie the Tramp* (1967), *Herman the Loser, The Sorely Trying Day* (1964), and *The Little Brute Family* (1966) are

BEDTIME
FOR FRANCES

by Russell Hoban
Pictures by Garth Williams

Dust jacket for the first installment of Hoban's popular Frances series, which, according to Jane O'Reilly, "is one of the few post-war children's books which have already become 'classics'" (Harper)

some that are frequently mentioned. Jane O'Reilly wrote in the *New York Times Book Review*, "*Emmet Otter's Jug-Band Christmas* is by the authors of *Charlie the Tramp* and *Bread and Jam for Frances*—my two all-time favorite children's books"; "*Bedtime for Frances* is one of the few post-war children's books which have already become 'classics.'" *Bedtime for Frances* (1960), O'Reilly continued, "is the rarest kind of children's book, rhythmic, natural, unalterable." Hoban's talent for representing the cadence of children's speech, his humor, the sensitive and reassuring parental viewpoint portrayed, and the honesty with which he depicted the motivations of children in *Bedtime for Frances* were especially praised.

And yet, in the midst of the seemingly perfect husband-and-wife collaboration, there were pans as well as paeans, books faulted for excessive coziness, for sentimentality, and for sterotyped male-female roles. *Goodnight*, for example, came out in 1966 to the following assessment in *Children's Book News:* "It is almost impossible to find anything to praise in this unbearably arch production. From its coy, sugar-almond coated colouring to its sickly verse, it is exactly what one most deplores in books for children."

Typical reviews for *The Song in My Drum* (1962) were similar: "Russell Hoban's duologue of a brother and sister will baffle and bore young listeners . . . , the result neither entertains nor sparks the imagination. . . . Like a private joke . . . it is meaningless to all but the originators."

If one overall criticism can be made of the Hobans' work together, it is that it tends toward repetition. The stories of little animals, endearing as they are, soon merge into a sameness, so that there is little difference between Delver Mole in *The Mole Family's Christmas* (1969), any of the animals in *Save My Place* (1967), Hester Mouse in *The Story of Hester Mouse Who Became a Writer* (1965), and Harvey Muskrat in *Harvey's Hideout* (1969). *The Little Brute Family* (1966), an imaginative story about a mannerless and uncaring family of brutes whose life is changed when the littlest brute comes home one day having captured a "wandering good feeling," was followed two years later by *The Stone Doll of Sister Brute* (1968); but whereas the first book is delightful and original, with several pages devoted to details about pre-good-feeling diet and habits, the sequel is stretched thin, relying on a small joke already played out in the first book. *Harvey's Hideout*, about the resolution of a brother-sister rivalry, is much like any one of the Frances books. "Man seems driven," Hoban wrote years later, "in his one-way passage through time, through cycles of order and chaos." But more rut than drive is evident as the Hobans worked more and more together. This is especially true of the illustrations.

Lillian Hoban's art verges toward the garish, and all of her animals look the same—the only difference, for example, between a mouse and a mole is the length of their noses. Despite critical praise for memorable creations such as Charlie the Tramp and the Stone Brute Family, Lillian Hoban's style remained the same although her husband's work was changing, creating opportunities for great rather than "cozy" children's art. "Lillian Hoban . . . is no Garth Williams," who illustrated *Bedtime for Frances*, "but she conveys satisfactorily" a "homely uncloying sweetness" in *A Baby Sister for Frances* (1964), wrote one reviewer. Writing about *Bread and Jam for Frances* (1964), another critic observed, "Let us acknowledge that Lillian Hoban . . . is no badger-master; it is a measure of the text that the illustrations need only position the characters for the message to carry." One rapidly tires of Lillian Hoban's constant use of pink and purple and yellow, and some of her art is muddy, as in *Save My Place*.

The Mouse and His Child, Hoban's first novel, published in 1967, marked a cardinal point in his career. He called the book, the first he had written that was "anything longer than 12 typewritten pages of picture book text," his "favorite." Hoban worked on it for three years—"the whole book went through four complete rewrites"—and he felt that "at the age of 41 it was the fullest response I could make to being alive in the world. . . ."

The controversial book set off an avalanche of reviews, largely laudatory, as was the critique in the *Times Literary Supplement:* "Russell Hoban is best known for his gentle bedtime stories about little Frances. . . . Excellent as they are, they give no hint that the author had in him such a blockbuster of a book as *The Mouse and His Child*. The story is rich in memorable invention, but this would count for nothing if the style were not so exquisitely apt. . . . This is a perfection so flawless as to pass unobserved until, the turmoil and passion of the story over, one thinks back to the masterly means by which these ends were reached."

Not all comment, though, was favorable. Another critic remarked, "For me, cruelty and decay are what the book is really about," and a third claimed that "the intellectual trappings of the story are unnecessary." Most reviewers were captivated by the scope and depth of Hoban's first novel; criticism focused mainly on its suitability for children.

Dust jacket for Hoban's first novel, which he said at the time of its publication "was the fullest response I could make to being alive in the world. . . ." Though highly praised, the book's publication was greeted with controversy due to the claims of some critics that it was intended more for adults than children (Harper & Row).

The *Times Literary Supplement* review concluded, "It may not be a Children's Book but, my goodness, it is a *Book*," and another British critic, Ann Thwaite, challenged parents in her *New Statesman* review, "Buy it and read it aloud to children . . . warmed with mugs of malted milk. Alone, in a cold bedroom, it could be too much for them to take."

The Mouse and His Child are windup toys who start out in a busy city toy store populated by other mechanical toys, all of which come to life after midnight. The child's first question to his father, to whom he is joined at the hands, sets the theme for the book:

"Where are we?" . . .
"I don't know," the father answered.

"*What* are we, Papa?"
"I don't know. We must wait and see."

An answer is provided by a pretentious elephant who considers herself "part of the establishment." She tells the mechanical mice, "One does what one is wound to do"—the first of Hoban's many plays on words and also the first of the elephant's fundamental mistakes. The elephant guards a fabulous dollhouse, brilliantly detailed by Hoban, which she considers her own, another mistake, as is her belief that her self-appointed position of grande dame of the toy shop is inviolate. When the mouse child asks her to be his mother, she haughtily replies that the child had best prepare himself to "go out into the world with his father and dance in a circle," to which the child replies, "But I don't want to," and begins to cry. "No crying on the job," a clock in the store warns him, "no good ever comes of it."

The toy mice are bought, and for five Christmases they entertain children beneath a Christmas tree, until one Christmas the mouse child, remembering the elephant he wanted for his mama and a little tin seal who had befriended him, begins to cry on the job. The family cat notices and swipes the toy, smashing it. The mouse and his child are tossed out with the trash.

The toy mice are providentially uncovered by a tramp who, in one of Hoban's loveliest scenes, had seen them on display in the toy store. The tramp repairs them as best he can, and the father and son are set down and wound and released, no longer to dance in circles but to plod along toward their destiny. It is no easy journey; no sooner have the mice run down than they meet their nemesis: Manny Rat, the brutal, self-serving, and heartless king of the trash dump. "He was there all at once . . . as if he had been waiting just beyond their field of vision, and once let in, would never go away." Manny Rat press-gangs father and son into his broken-down crew of pitiful drone scavengers.

"Where are you taking us?" asked the father.
"To a ball," said the rat. "To a jolly, jolly ball. . . ."

On their first forage, the mice meet an oracular frog who makes an unwilling prediction for them: "Low in the dark of summer, high in the winter light; a painful spring, a shattering fall, a scattering regathered. The enemy you flee at the beginning awaits you at the end."

What the frog prophesies is played out through a cast of characters that ranges from theatrical crows who perform in the "Caws of Art" troupe to a pedantic muskrat to a Brecht-like playwriting turtle to warring bloodthirsty shrews whose battle reminds one of *War and Peace*. When the pair is seemingly stuck forever to rust at the bottom of a murky pond, it is the child's unflagging spirit that revives the father. Realizing ultimately there is nothing to rely on except themselves, together they contrive an ingenious escape from the depths. Later, old friends and new—"a scattering regathered"—join to battle scores of gaudy, taunting rats which have overrun the doll's house, and the child eventually gets his family too. His heroic father falls in love with the elephant, who becomes the mother the child had longed for. A tin seal becomes his sister, and he acquires as well an odd assortment of loving uncles—including the frog seer and, at least apparently, even Manny Rat himself.

In the book there is parody, poetry, song, satire, and even an imaginative use of capitalization and typography which dramatizes the situation. There is cruelty and decay present, but they are the artful rendering of the facts of life. If there is betrayal, there is also self-sacrifice. If there is loss, there is also love. If there is homelessness, there is also destination. The mouse child gets his family in the end; children's literature gets a masterpiece.

The book was a watershed for Hoban: Ian D. Mackillop has stated that "*The Mouse and His Child* was a kind of creative spending-spree after which Hoban began to think more deeply about his purchases." Its themes of "self-winding," of territory of one's own, of leaping—like it or not—into the world signaled a genuine departure from his earlier work. He created a vivid fictional world, and it is no surprise *The Mouse and His Child* was made into a feature-length cartoon in 1976.

Certainly the best illustrations for Hoban's books are found in those published after the early 1970s: James Marshall's hilarious crocodiles in *Dinner at Alberta's* (1973), Nicola Bayley's brilliantly colored art in *La Corona and the Tin Frog* (1979), Clive Scruton's kinky cartoons in *Flat Cat* (1980), Colin McNaughton's exuberant children in *They Came from Aargh!* (1981), and the beautiful work done by David Gentleman for such haunting prose as this from *The Dancing Tigers* (1980): "Ah, but they could dance! Nobody danced like the tigers, nobody could even think of such dances as they did. Moon dances, shadow dances, silence dances, and dances for the starlight and the glimmers on the river. Even the child tigers . . . danced the most complex

Frontispiece and title page for Hoban's 1972 novel, which was illustrated by his son (Harper & Row)

patterns . . . in the bending grasses and the shadows of the jungle under the humming and the hissing of the moon, under the racing clouds under the teeming rain."

Hoban quotes from W. H. Auden's poem "Leap Before You Look" on the opening page of *The Mouse and His Child:*

> The sense of danger must not disappear:
> The way is certainly short and steep,
> However gradual it looks from here;
> Look if you like, but you will have to leap.

And leap Hoban did, across the Atlantic, leaving behind his wife of over twenty-five years and his four children—the foundation of his early writing—and estranging himself from the comfortable life he had known in Connecticut. He eventually married a German woman much his junior and by her fathered three more children.

In a 1981 *Publishers Weekly* interview, Hoban said it was not until he left his first wife that he was free to write adult fiction, "to use all of myself and my experience." He continued in the same article to state that *The Lion of Boaz-Jachin and Jachin-Boaz,* published in 1973, and set somewhere in the Middle East, is his "most autobiographical book," about a father, Jachin-Boaz, and his son, Boaz-Jachin. The father, a mapmaker, promises the son a master map in which everything the father has found, everything the son would ever need to know, is shown. Then, instead of giving the map to his son, the father deserts both son and wife, taking the map with him. The son follows, his rage at his father materializing a lion (though the species is now extinct) which the boy sees in a temple statue; in it, the lion, pierced by arrows and spears, is endlessly crushed beneath the wheel of the king's chariot. Fathers and sons often appear in Hoban's work; both *The Mouse and His Child* and *Riddley Walker*

(1981) feature this relationship. We are reminded of Hoban's own father who left his young son when he died in 1936 when Jachin-Boaz recalls his father's death: "My father lay in his coffin with his beard pointing like a cannon from his chin. While he lived he praised me and expected much of me. From my early childhood I drew maps of clarity and beauty, much admired. My father and mother wanted great things from me. For me. . . . Which I of course wanted too. . . . 'They wanted,' said Jachin-Boaz. 'I wanted. Two wantings. Not the same. No. Not the same.' "

Hoban has written at length in an article that appeared in the 1972 *Children's Literature in Education* about the burden of expectations, the "uphill lean" placed on talented children by misdirected parents. The burden is to keep producing, to look toward future fruits, not to rest in the child's joy of what has just been produced—the delight of the present creation. The poor child is pushed upward, robbed of the now: "*Now* becomes the time that doesn't matter. It's the *going to be* that matters, the time up ahead, the time one isn't in yet. And it's possible to lose all *now*, and always be waiting for the time that never comes, because when it comes it's now, and now doesn't matter. That's time slip. And one can spend a lot of time looking for that lost *now*. . . . the situations [are] drawn from my own experience."

On page ten of *The Lion of Boaz-Jachin and Jachin-Boaz*, Hoban tells why the father left his family: "Jachin-Boaz was at the age called middle life, but he did not believe he had as many years ahead of him as he had behind him. He had married very young, and he had been married for more than a quarter of a century. Often he was impotent with his wife. On Sundays, when the shop was closed and he was alone with her and his son, he tried to shut out of his mind a lifelong despair. . . . He felt the silent waiting of all the seeking and finding . . . journeys to hidden sources of wisdom, passes through mountains to lodes of precious metals, secret ways through city streets to secret pleasures."

Like the father in this autobiographical book, shortly after leaving his wife, Hoban met the woman he was to marry and to whom the book is dedicated, Gundula. Like Hoban's new wife, Jachin-Boaz's lover, Gretel, soon becomes pregnant: "Good God," says Jachin-Boaz, "Another son." The Hobans named their first child, a boy, Jachin-Boaz, and, in an irony more fabulous than fiction, all three children of Hoban's second marriage have been sons.

Dust jacket for Hoban's 1978 story about a young crocodile who continually disturbs his family by playing his new electric guitar (Crowell)

It is a mark of Hoban's honesty that he writes sensitively in *The Lion of Boaz-Jachin and Jachin-Boaz* book of both the new wife, she who waits and wonders, and the old, she who bathes in perfumed oils, meets another man, and weeps. But it is the lion who is the real star of the book, the mighty, roaring, vital, unbroken lion with his rage to be free and to live without expectations:

> For him there were no maps, no places, no time. Beneath his tread the round earth rolled, the wheel turned bearing him to death and life again. Through his lion being drifted stars and blackness, morning sang, night soothed, dawn burst its daylight from the womb of mighty terror. . . . In clocks ticked lion time. . . . He was.
> "What is the sound of not wanting, my lord Lion?"
> The lion rose to his feet and roared.

There is the human urge toward order, but that order is, at any time, likely to be crushed beneath the fact that we are not in control; we are not the movers, but the moved. Yet there is more to the fact of existence, for, if the wheel flattens, it also elevates: the fact remains we are here, on the wheel and amid it. As Jachin-Boaz says, "It's the wheel. . . . Biting it doesn't help, but one has to. That's all there is."

Hoban said in the *Publishers Weekly* interview that he visits his psychoanalyst (who is a character as well in *The Lion of Boaz-Jachin and Jachin-Boaz*) and daily reads to him the previous day's writing. The presence in Hoban's novels of that impersonal, vast, and random power—call it the mindless flow of birth and death and circumstance—reveals itself in images which seem drawn from depth psychology, from a genius who has traveled through his own muck confronting the fact of his helplessness. "Sometimes I wonder," says the clock in Hoban's 1979 children's book, *La Corona and the Tin Frog*, "whether I keep time or time keeps me." That human beings continue in the face of our powerlessness is an existential, a titanic value, not a religious or spiritual one. There are no benign gods in Hoban's writing, no ascent through grace. There are only undergrounds, as in *Kleinzeit* (1974), Hoban's second book for adults, and in *The Lion of Boaz-Jachin and Jachin-Boaz*; oozing pond bottoms as in *The Mouse and His Child*; and primitive powers which kill, such as Aunty in *Riddley Walker*.

The closest figure to a god in Hoban's work is the tramp in *The Mouse and His Child* who sets the windup toys off on their journey with two

PICTURES BY COLIN McNAUGHTON

Promotional material for Hoban's 1981 book about a group of exuberant children (Philomel)

words, "Be tramps," and blesses them at the end with "Be happy." Yet there are no epiphanies; neither the mouse nor his child is aware of the tramp at all. Indeed, from the depths of the muddy pond, the child mouse, gazing finally beyond infinity, sees there is "nothing but us."

That we must struggle for meaning and identity and place against the random element of loss in the attempt to gain "self-winding" underlies the most powerful of Hoban's books for children as well as his work for adults. For example, in *The Dancing Tigers*, a pride of tigers is resigned to being hunted by a rajah riding on a jeweled elephant furnished with a television, a telephone, and a stereo cassette recorder. It is what the rajah chooses to play on the recorder one day that rallies the tigers to a subtle defense: they beguile the rajah to death with fabulous dancing. The oldest tiger explains, "It's one thing to accept one's fate, but it's quite another to perish with the light classics shattering the stillness. It's insulting. It's degrading."

In *Turtle Diary* (1975), the first of Hoban's adult books to be made into a motion picture, two directionless adults conspire in a mad escapade to liberate the giant turtles from the London Zoo. They do this because the turtles' purpose in life is to be where they belong; unlike their rescuers, the turtles know where home is. And for the anthropomorphic creatures in *The Sea-Thing Child* (1972), a book mythic in its meaning and beautifully written, finding the place to be what they are is the major preoccupation. This book, illustrated by Hoban's son Abrom, concerns an undefined whatever-it-is washed up onshore by a storm. The child-thing, though it has wings, feels drawn to the sea but fears it as well. Staying on the beach where the winds brought it, the sea-thing child befriends a fiddler crab who constantly harps, so to speak, upon his lack of a bow. Eventually an old albatross, a sea-captain character, gruffly reminds the crab and the child who they are and where they belong. Leaving the wiser crab on its shore, the sea-thing child spreads its wings and departs across the waves.

Hoban has said that it "is the task laid upon me by life—to be equally present." Hoban strives always to be "equally present," from carefully observing boxers and machines and mechanical toys to attending to the domestic situations that were transformed into his early books for children, to transfiguring his own losses and pain into his later books, to witnessing the births of the three children of his second family—Hoban is a great writer because he makes unsentimental reality into art.

Even so simply funny a children's book as *Dinner at Alberta's* becomes a little gem of a tale. Called "superb" by *School Library Journal,* the thirty-six-page book contains some of Hoban's most hilarious writing. Father Crocodile, speaking to his son, Arthur, says, "Don't talk when your mouth is full. . . . Little bits of ravioli are landing on your sister. . . ." Arthur, an incorrigible feeler of saltshakers and diddler with spoons, is cured of his distressing slobbiness only when smitten by his sister's friend, Alberta. Arthur not only showers for Alberta, learns table manners for Alberta, creates a song on his electric guitar for Alberta but also trounces her sarcastic brother, Sidney.

Hoban is again surrounded by children less than three feet high; he is continually producing children's books, such as *Flat Cat,* a cartoon picture book written in monosyllables, while at the same time writing for adults. He himself has best summed up his career in "Thoughts on Being and Writing": "Life is a continuous presentation of sensation and event. Faced with that presentation and faced with himself facing it, the artist represents it. Why? He can't help it. . . . Art, like babies, is one of the things life makes us make."

References:

A. Alvarez, "Past, Present, and Future," *New York Times Book Review,* 19 November 1981, pp. 16-17;

Barbara Bannon, "Russell Hoban," *Publishers Weekly* (15 May 1981): 10-11;

Ian Mackillop, "Russell Hoban: Returning to the Sunlight," in *Good Writers for Young Readers,* edited by Dennis Butts (Hertfordshire, U.K.: Hart-Davis Educational, 1977), pp. 57-65;

Frederic Whitaker, "Unusual Career of an Illustrator-Artist," *American Artist* (1 October 1961): 48, 53, 73-75.

Irene Hunt
(18 May 1907-   )

Philip A. Sadler
Central Missouri State University

BOOKS: *Across Five Aprils* (Chicago: Follett, 1964; London: Bodley Head, 1965);

Up a Road Slowly (Chicago: Follett, 1966; London: Macdonald, 1967);

Trail of Apple Blossoms, illustrated by Don Bolognese (Chicago: Follett, 1968; London: Blackie, 1970);

No Promises in the Wind (Chicago: Follett, 1970);

The Lottery Rose (New York: Scribners, 1976);

William (New York: Scribners, 1977);

Claws of a Young Century (New York: Scribners, 1980);

The Everlasting Hills (New York: Scribners, 1985).

OTHER: "Writing for Children," in *The Writer's Handbook,* edited by A. S. Burack (Boston: The Writer, Inc., 1973), pp. 427-433.

PERIODICAL PUBLICATION: "Books and the Learning Process," *Horn Book,* 43 (August 1967): 424-429.

Irene Hunt says, "Words have always held a fascination for me, causing me to be teased often as a child when I used them lavishly without having the slightest idea of their meaning. The wish to write pages full of words, to make them tell the stories that I dreamed about, haunted me from childhood on." Writing, however, was not easy for her. She devoted thirty years of her life to teaching before she found it possible to put those words on paper and produce one of the finest books in the field of children's literature, *Across Five Aprils* (1964).

Hunt's books have received much critical acclaim. *Across Five Aprils* was the sole runner-up for the highly coveted Newbery Medal in 1965; *Up a Road Slowly* (1966) won the award in 1967. In 1966 *Across Five Aprils* was recognized with the Lewis Carroll Shelf Award, which is given to books considered "worthy to sit on a shelf with *Alice in Wonderland*" by a committee representing librar-

Irene Hunt (Gale Portrait Gallery)

ians, teachers, parents, and writers. *Across Five Aprils* was given the Charles W. Follett Award in 1964, an award provided by the Follett Publishing Company for the best book published by the company in the previous year. *Up a Road Slowly* was chosen as part of the International Board on Books for Young People (IBBY) Honor List in 1970. Because her books have continued to uphold high literary standards, Hunt has also been honored with the Certificate in Recognition of Contribution to Children's Literature at the Twelfth Annual Children's Literature Festival at Central Missouri State University in 1980.

Irene Hunt was born 18 May 1907, in Pontiac, Illinois. At the age of six weeks, she moved with her parents, Franklin P. and Sarah Land Hunt, to Newton, Illinois. Her father died when she was seven, and she and her mother moved to the nearby farm home of her grandparents. Her lonely childhood was brightened by her kindly grandfather's stories, which later influenced her writing. The stories she enjoyed most were those of his childhood during the Civil War, and these provided the framework for her first novel. Her own experiences later became the basis for her second book.

In 1939 Hunt graduated with an A.B. degree from the University of Illinois in Urbana. She earned an M.A. degree at the University of Minnesota, Minneapolis, in 1946 and did additional graduate work at the University of Colorado, Boulder. From 1930 to 1945 she was a teacher of English and French in the Oak Park, Illinois, public schools. Between 1946 and 1950 she was an instructor in psychology at the University of South Dakota, Vermillion. In 1950 she returned to elementary and junior high school teaching in Cicero, Illinois, becoming the director of language arts in that school system in 1965. She retired from that position in 1969 and devoted herself to her writing.

"During the early sixties," says Hunt, "while teaching social studies to junior high school students, I felt that teaching history through literature was a happier, more effective process." She found that her grandfather's old stories which she remembered well, could be used effectively. Her books were written to fit the needs of her students. Hunt now lives in Clearwater, Florida.

Across Five Aprils was recognized by its publishers as a worthy book and was given the Charles W. Follett Award that year. It was the sole Newbery Honor Book in 1965 and winner of the Clara Ingram Judson Award in 1965. *Across Five Aprils* is also Hunt's favorite of all her books because of its strong emotional impact and the fond memories it evokes.

Reviewers also recognized the merit of the book. The *New York Times Book Review* cited it as a "beautifully written book—a prize to those who take the time to read it, whatever their ages." In *Horn Book*, the reviewer remarked that the novel "gives the reader an intense experience because of the reality of the characters; . . . readers . . . will not be quite the same again." *Booklist* called it "a memorable story of the tragic years of the Civil War." Zena Sutherland said in her review for the *Bulletin of the Center for Children's Books* that *Across Five Aprils* was "historically authenticated" and the characters "completely convincing."

The book spans the five Aprils of the Civil War, 1861 to 1865. Set in southern Illinois away from most of the conflict, it is like a Greek tragedy in that most of the violence is talked about or reported in letters. In the first April, the protagonist, Jethro Creighton, is only nine, so the reader follows his growth into his early teens, though he emerges as a young man in the fifth April. Jethro experiences the war through his relationships with his parents; his sisters, Jenny and Mary; his brothers, John and Bill; and his schoolmaster, Shadrach

Dust jacket for a later edition of Hunt's first novel, which is set in southern Illinois during the Civil War and concerns a young boy's perception of his family's divided loyalties (Follett)

Yale. All of these characters and their differing opinions about the conflict are fully developed; the reader gets to know them almost as well as Jethro does.

After his father has a heart attack, Jethro must assume many of the adult chores around the family farm. He experiences the rift in the Union through his brothers' divided opinions: John joins the Union Army; Bill enlists in the Confederate forces. The family respects their rights to act on their beliefs, but because Bill's sympathies are with the Confederacy, the family is labeled "Copperheads" and slated for retribution. In the book, Jethro meets deserters from the Union Army, including his cousin Eb, for whom he has the greatest respect. Eb writes to Abraham Lincoln to plead for mercy. Lincoln answers with general clemency for the deserters. At the end of the war, Jethro, who has come to a knowledgeable understanding of it through letters and conversations, is taken east to school by Shadrach and Jenny, who are now married. He is wiser in the ways of life and aware of war's horrors.

Up a Road Slowly (1966) is based upon Hunt's own childhood and adolescent experiences. The book proved that the phenomenon of *Across Five Aprils* was no accident. *Up a Road Slowly*, the Newbery Medal winner for 1967, also confirms that an author writes best from vivid experience. Just as Hunt had been lonely, bewildered, and frightened upon the loss of her father, another little girl—her protagonist in *Up a Road Slowly*—might, in her loneliness, wander into the woods quoting verses from Edna St. Vincent Millay or Shakespeare.

Like *Across Five Aprils, Up a Road Slowly* is a story of growing up. Julie, at age seven, experiences the death of her mother and leaves her home, her father, and a beloved older sister to live with her Aunt Cordelia, a country schoolteacher with definite ideas about the way things should be. Treating the story with a detached realism tempered with love, Hunt introduces themes of jealousy, first love, parent-child and sibling relationships, foster-family relationships, and snobbishness and handles them

Dust jacket for Hunt's Newbery Medal-winning novel about a seven-year-old girl who, when her mother dies, must adjust to a new life with her aunt, "a country schoolteacher with definite ideas about the way things should be" (Follett)

in fresh new ways. Death, the remarriage of a parent, and alcoholism in a sympathetic character, Julie's Uncle Haskell, are profoundly probed. Emotional disturbance in an adult, the wife of a beloved family friend, is handled deftly by Hunt. She breaks new ground, shattering old taboos in children's literature, to produce a book devoid of the artificiality and superficiality of many of the teenage novels of the time.

Dorothy Broderick said in the *New York Times Book Review* that Hunt, with this book, demonstrates that she is a writer of the first rank, and a daring one as well, since she brings off a difficult tour de force and turns personal reminiscence into art. With *Up a Road Slowly* the teenage novel began to reach maturity.

The story of John Chapman in *Trail of Apple Blossoms* (1968) is for younger readers, unlike the previous two books, but it also has a maturity and an almost poetic quality that surpasses most other

books about the American folk hero known as Johnny Appleseed. There is a graceful wedding of Hunt's poetic prose and the delicate illustrations by Don Bolognese, especially in the shimmering paintings of the fragile apple blossoms which symbolize the life and accomplishments of the frontier hero.

The legendary hero is made believable in this story of his visit with a frontier family and of how that visit changes the family members' lives. With his powers of healing, Chapman treats two-year-old Rachel Bryant, who refuses to eat and is "dwindling" as her parents and brother Hoke attempt to travel to the Ohio Valley country from Boston. Using his knowledge of wholesome foods and herbs, he entices little Rachel to eat and play in the sunshine. As she recovers her strength, Chapman makes fast friends with the Bryants and spends days with young Hoke, gaining great respect from the boy. When little Rachel is fully recovered, the Bryants continue their westward journey, taking with them much more than the appleseeds supplied by Chapman. Young Hoke takes also the memory of his newfound hero, which serves as a model for his life.

The story emphasizes Chapman's philosophy and his personality more than the traditional role which gave him his nickname. Hunt recounts his experiences with the Indians and his love for animals. She tells of his travels through the pioneer country, including subsequent visits with the Bryants. He shares his stories and his love for the Indians and the animals and expresses his unwillingness to kill man or beast. He is interested in providing for the safety and well-being of all, so he is willing to warn and to aid where he can.

It is probable that young Hoke grows up to become a minister as a result of Chapman's stories and his influence. This is intimated by Hunt when a mature Rachel writes to her brother to tell him of Chapman's death. She is happily reminded of the man by a glimpse of apple blossoms on trees grown from seed given to Hoke many years before.

Trail of Apple Blossoms is not a biography; it is a mixture of truth and folklore. Hunt reveals the beauty of the life of a man who seemed to forget self for the good of all living things, a man with great love for all men and all beasts. In language of almost lyric quality, Hunt presents a passionate plea for a world devoid of bigotry, hate, and other human evils.

Hunt's fourth novel, *No Promises in the Wind* (1970), is an understandably bleak book, which deals honestly and realistically with the lives of two boys during the Depression years. That bleakness, however, is relieved by the kindness of those who help the boys through these difficult times.

Fifteen-year-old Josh Grodowski leaves home to make his way when he feels that his father no longer loves him and can no longer support the family. Josh, accompanied by his younger brother, Joey, and a friend, hops a freight at the beginning of his travels. The friend is killed when he falls beneath the wheels of the moving railroad car, an omen of things to come. The dirty gray storm clouds pictured on the book's jacket seem to hover over the two remaining boys through their travels, but though they experience cold and deprivation, they are befriended by a kindly truck driver who treats them as his own sons. When Josh recovers from a serious illness, the boys leave their benefactor and continue on their wanderings. Joining a carnival group, they again find others who will share with them their meager substance as well as their love.

The characters, major and minor, are sensitively realized. The bleakness of the Depression background is tempered by the kindness of some of the people Josh and Joe encounter. Howie, the friend who runs away with the boys at the beginning of the story, is quite tolerant of Joey, sharing his meager supply of food and encouraging the young boy to sing on the sidewalks to secure money. Hunt finds more good than bad in most people. Even the hungry hoboes offer assistance to the boys.

Lonnie, the truck driver who had lost a son, provides Josh with more understanding of what a father could be. The characterization of Josh and Joey's own father reveals the ravaging Depression's influence upon many good men who became desperate. The portrait of Josh, however, is the best realized. The boy's growth in his understanding of himself and the ways of the world culminates in his discovery that he was wrong in thinking that his father did not love him, that circumstances can color one's attitudes and actions to the point that one may not seem to be what he is. The experiences of the boys are quite grim, but Josh and Joey survive and grow, giving the reader an honest look at the times as well as faith in humanity.

The Lottery Rose, Hunt's fifth book, was published in 1976 and received mixed reviews. This story of a victimized child leans heavily toward sentimentality and is marred a bit by Hunt's use of coincidence. Seven-year-old Georgie is terrorized and beaten by his alcoholic mother and her boyfriend until he is rescued by neighbors, taken to a

hospital to heal, and sent to a boys' home supervised by kindly nuns.

Georgie, emotionally scarred and withdrawn, takes with him his most prized possession, a rosebush won in a grocery store lottery. Obsessed with the idea of finding the best place to plant it, he decides on a beautiful garden on an estate he sees from his window. The garden, however, is the property of a woman named Mollie who lives with her father and a mentally retarded son, Robin. She is mourning the tragic deaths of her husband and older son and has planted her garden as a memorial to them.

Under cover of night, Georgie secretly plants his bush in the garden, but the woman angrily uproots it and forbids Georgie to return. In the passage of time, Georgie emerges from his withdrawn state and makes friends with Robin and his grandfather, but he continues to distrust and hate Mollie. However, when Mollie sees the scarred back of the abused boy, her acceptance of him begins to grow. Finally, when Robin tragically drowns, Georgie plants his rose on the grave of the boy, and Mollie accepts him and his rosebush. As usual, Hunt is idealistic, but she does show a logical progression in the slow change from withdrawal to acceptance of love and protection.

The *School Library Journal* reviewer termed this book "disappointing and lifeless," a story that becomes "more of a case study than a novel," but the *Booklist* reviewer called it "a deeply affecting, affirmative story in which Hunt manages to lift a battered-child case into a convincingly developed character." Though the book may not be as strong a novel as her earlier ones, Hunt does provide a touching treatment of a theme out of the ordinary at the time of the book's creation—the abuse of a small child—in a manner suitable for young readers.

Hunt made a strong comeback with her next novel, *William* (1977). As a participant and an observer, William, a young, fatherless black boy who lives in Florida, tells the story of his family and the impact of the arrival of Sarah, a young, pregnant white girl who moves in next door. William's mother dies of cancer and Sarah, bringing her fatherless baby, steps in to help the family of parentless children consisting of William and his sisters, Carla and Amy, because she loves them and because William's mother had been so helpful during her pregnancy and childbirth. Sarah stays with the children for three years, helping them cope with their deprived condition. William takes a job gardening, and Sarah sells her paintings and works in town in order to support the group. The teenage Amy, only three years younger than Sarah, rebels and runs away. She returns, however, and is reconciled with Sarah when her younger sister Carla, who is nearly blind, undergoes surgery and recovers her sight. The "family" is further threatened when Sarah decides to attend art school away from Florida. William recognizes that the situation and the home he has grown up in will never be the same again, but he realizes that he must assume responsibility for the family.

Hunt, through her emotional prose and limited use of black dialect as well as her powerful ability of description of characters and action, creates characters with distinct personalities, depicting them as convincing, unstereotypical individuals. The book, with its study of the varying relationships between the characters, is completely believable in its portrayal of love and understanding without regard for racial differences and diverse backgrounds. Hunt achieves this in spite of the southern setting, where such a story might be improbable but not impossible. This is a memorable novel about typical children who squabble about differences but stick together in times of adversity, a different approach to the time-honored theme of Louisa May Alcott's *Little Women* (1868-1869) and Margaret Sidney's *Five Little Peppers and How They Grew* (1880), realistic novels about real-life situations, which have long appealed to readers. *William* is another of Hunt's stories for all ages.

Hunt has said, "I write when I have something to say, and I hope to say it as well and as gracefully as I can." She has also said that a writer "must care greatly" for his material. Although she has written about what she cares greatly for in all her books, *Claws of a Young Century* (1980) may exhibit this feeling more than the rest. She has pursued two careers, teaching and writing, and has been successful in each. She believes in every individual's right to realize himself or herself, so it seems natural that she should employ the theme of woman's rights and the suffrage movement in one of her novels. To do this, she draws a very convincing portrait of seventeen-year-old Ellen Archer, at the turn of the century, who decides to dedicate her life to the cause of woman's rights. She escapes her narrow-minded father, who derides her desire for an education. Keeping house for her brother, she meets and falls in love with her brother's friend Philip. They have an affair, she becomes pregnant, and they marry. Before their daughter is born, Philip goes off to Europe as a foreign correspondent. Ellen becomes immersed in the woman suf-

frage movement, using much of her inheritance from a cruel, domineering father for the cause. She goes to college and brings up her child alone. Philip stays in Europe, and they are divorced.

Ellen is arrested for picketing, and the brutal treatment she receives and the hunger strike she engages in to achieve her goal eventually result in her death. When Philip returns after sixteen years abroad to find Ellen dying, they realize their love and that pride has kept them apart. He promises to continue her work for the ratification of the suffrage amendment.

Hunt states that she did extensive research on the woman suffrage movement for this, her longest and most mature book. She read widely and interviewed women who had actually been persecuted for their beliefs and crusading. *Claws of a Young Century* offers accurate historical information as well as reading pleasure to its young adult audience. *Horn Book* reviewer A. A. Flowers stated that the book "sharply conveys the long struggle for women's rights." The *School Library Journal* reviewer said that it is "an exciting segment of women's history" with the "backdrop of an unusual love story."

The Everlasting Hills (1985) once again utilizes the theme of a father-son relationship such as Hunt presented earlier in *No Promises in the Wind*. Again set in the 1930s Depression era, this book tells the story of a harsh, apparently unloving father who causes unhappiness and anguish in his son before both characters gain a better understanding of themselves and their relationship to each other.

In this historical Colorado setting, Hunt creates the character of Jeremy Tydings, a twelve-year-old, mentally retarded boy who experiences speech difficulties and the inability to learn to read. Mr. Tydings resents the boy, who, he feels, was the cause of his wife's death. Tydings also compares the "weak" younger son with his stronger and older dead brother. Bethany, Jeremy's older sister, loves the boy dearly and often shelters and defends him to the consternation of the father, giving of herself almost to the point of total sacrifice.

When Jeremy realizes that Bethany is likely to devote her entire life to him, he runs away to live with Ishmael, an elderly man who teaches him to read and to overcome his speech problems. Jeremy, away from his cruel father, matures and acquires a great measure of self-esteem. Guided by the precepts taught to him by Ishmael, Jeremy returns to his home for a reconciliation with his father and finds Bethany in love with a young novelist who has come to live in the area.

Booklist reviewer Hazel Rochman found the characters "overidealized," but she also stated that the emotions portrayed "have authentic power." The characters generally act and react to each other in a convincing manner throughout the story. Barbara Chatton, reviewing in *School Library Journal*, thought the characters were "believable and strong." She also commented on the way Hunt utilized the Rockies, "the everlasting hills," to play a significant role in the book. The characters "feel at times both their peace and their foreboding power." Karen Jameyson, reviewing in *Horn Book*, also recognized Hunt's ability to develop "completely believable, unique individuals" as characters. Jeremy is a boy who "happens to be retarded"; he is not "a character who is first and foremost mentally handicapped," though Jameyson does feel that Bethany is "a bit too sweet and patient."

Zena Sutherland said, "This is not Hunt's strongest novel" because the characters are not as convincing as they might be. Bethany may be too good and the father may be too "vitriolic to a retarded child." Sutherland, however, did praise and recommend the novel by saying in her *Bulletin of the Center for Children's Books* review that "Hunt has both a fine sense of story and a command of the flow of her narrative."

Hunt established herself as one of America's finest historical novelists with *Across Five Aprils*. She

has proven that she can write good books for children that please adults as well, and she has established an international audience. *Across Five Aprils* has also been published in Canada, England, Italy, and South Africa; while *Up a Road Slowly* has appeared in South Africa, Germany, France, Denmark, Norway, Finland, Canada, and England; and *No Promises in the Wind* has been published in Italy, France, and Czechoslovakia. *William* has appeared in France.

Irene Hunt has a strong faith in the enduring qualities of courage, love, and mercy. It is to reiterate this faith that she writes her books. She shares with young people her excitement about books and the understanding that can be gained from them.

References:

Wendell Bruce Beem, "Aunt Irene," *Horn Book*, 43 (August 1967): 429-433;

Lee Bennett Hopkins, Interview with Irene Hunt, in his *More Books by More People* (New York: Citation Press, 1974), pp. 221-224.

Papers:

Manuscripts of Irene Hunt's books are housed in the Kerlan Collection, University of Minnesota, Minneapolis.

Randall Jarrell

(6 May 1914-14 October 1965)

Barbara Lovell

See also the Jarrell entry in *DLB 48, Modern American Poets, 1880-1945: Second Series.*

BOOKS: *The Rage for the Lost Penny,* in *Five Young American Poets,* edited by James Laughlin (New York: New Directions, 1940), pp. 81-123;

Blood for a Stranger (New York: Harcourt, Brace, 1942);

Little Friend, Little Friend (New York: Dial Press, 1945);

Losses (New York: Harcourt, Brace, 1948);

Randall Jarrell (courtesy of Mary Jarrell)

The Seven-League Crutches (New York: Harcourt, Brace, 1951);

Poetry and the Age (New York: Knopf, 1953; London: Faber & Faber, 1955);

Pictures from an Institution (New York: Knopf, 1954; London: Faber & Faber, 1954);

Selected Poems (New York: Knopf, 1955; London: Faber & Faber, 1956);

The Woman at the Washington Zoo: Poems and Translations (New York: Atheneum, 1960);

A Sad Heart at the Supermarket: Essays and Fables (New York: Atheneum, 1962; London: Eyre & Spottiswoode, 1965);

The Gingerbread Rabbit, illustrated by Garth Williams (New York: Macmillan/London: Collier-Macmillan, 1964);

Selected Poems Including the Woman at the Washington Zoo (New York: Atheneum, 1964);

The Bat-Poet, illustrated by Maurice Sendak (New York: Macmillan/London: Collier-Macmillan, 1964);

The Animal Family, illustrated by Sendak (New York: Pantheon, 1965; London: Hart-Davis, 1967);

The Lost World (New York: Macmillan/London: Collier-Macmillan, 1965; London: Eyre & Spottiswoode, 1966);

The Complete Poems (New York: Farrar, Straus & Giroux, 1969; London: Faber & Faber, 1971);

The Third Book of Criticism (New York: Farrar, Straus & Giroux, 1969);

Jerome: The Biography of a Poem, edited by Mary von Schrader Jarrell (New York: Grossman, 1971);

Fly By Night, illustrated by Sendak (New York: Farrar, Straus & Giroux, 1976);

A Bat is Born, illustrated by J. Schoenherr (Garden City: Doubleday, 1978);

Kipling, Auden & Company: Essays and Reviews 1935-1964 (New York: Farrar, Straus & Giroux, 1980).

RECORDINGS: *Randall Jarrell Reads and Discusses His Poems Against War* (Caedmon, TC 1363,

1972);

The Bat-Poet (Caedmon, TC 1364, 1972);

The Gingerbread Rabbit (Caedmon, TC 1381, 1972).

TRANSLATIONS: Ludwig Bechstein, *The Rabbit Catcher And Other Fairy Tales* (New York & London: Macmillan, 1962);

Brothers Grimm, *The Golden Bird And Other Fairy Tales* (New York & London: Macmillan, 1962);

Anton Chekhov, *The Three Sisters* (New York: Macmillan/London: Collier-Macmillan, 1969);

Brothers Grimm, *Snow-White and the Seven Dwarfs* (New York: Farrar, Straus & Giroux, 1972; Harmondsworth, U.K.: Kestrel, 1974);

Brothers Grimm, *The Juniper Tree and Other Tales from Grimm*, 2 volumes, translated by Lore Segal with four translations by Jarrell (New York: Farrar, Straus & Giroux, 1973; London: Bodley Head, 1974);

Goethe's Faust: Part I (New York: Farrar, Straus & Giroux, 1976);

The Fisherman and His Wife (New York: Farrar, Straus & Giroux, 1980).

Randall Jarrell emerged after World War II as a leading American poet and critic. By the time he began writing children's books in 1962, he had published seven volumes of poetry (one of which had won a National Book Award), two highly significant books of criticism, and a satirical novel. Though he died only three years later, he made an impressive contribution to children's literature, with books such as *The Bat-Poet* (1964) and *The Animal Family* (1965) almost certainly destined to become classics.

Born in Nashville, Tennessee, Jarrell was educated at Vanderbilt University, receiving a B.A. degree in 1936 and an M.A. in 1939. Except for service in the U.S. Army Air Corps as a celestial-navigation instructor and tower operator (1942-1946), he spent his adult life teaching as brilliantly as he wrote. Many of his students, some of them now writers of note themselves, remember his frequent remark that were he a rich man he would pay to teach. Many also recall Jarrell's looking up cheerfully from Kenneth Grahame's *The Wind in the Willows* (1908) to sign their cards at registration. Jarrell served on the faculties of Kenyon College (1937-1939), the University of Texas (1939-1942), Sarah Lawrence College (1946-1947), and, from 1947 until his untimely death in 1965, at the University of North Carolina at Greensboro. In addition to teaching summer school and lecturing at

various universities, Jarrell spent the 1951-1952 academic year at Princeton University and taught at the University of Illinois in spring 1953. From 1956 to 1958 he was Consultant in Poetry at the Library of Congress. Jarrell's marriage to Mackie Langham on 1 June 1940 ended in divorce, and on 8 November 1952 he married Mary von Schrader, who had two young daughters by a previous marriage. Much of Jarrell's poetry, as well as his children's books, reflects the richness of his family life. Three of his books for young readers are dedicated to Mary Jarrell while *The Animal Family* is dedicated to Elfi (their cat who appears, sometimes disguised, in his work) "From Randall and Mary." Their home in the woods in Greensboro often served as the basis for settings in his stories.

In 1962 Jarrell became ill with hepatitis, which left him with the neurological and intestinal disorders from which he suffered for the rest of his life. While he was still hospitalized, his friend Michael di Capua, who later became his editor, suggested that Jarrell, whose translations of German poetry had been widely acclaimed, contribute to a series of well-known writers' translations of Grimms' fairy tales. Impressed by Jarrell's renditions of "Snow White" and "The Fisherman's Wife," di Capua encouraged the poet to write his own children's stories. By the end of that year Jarrell had completed *The Gingerbread Rabbit* and *The Bat-Poet* (both were published in 1964).

The Gingerbread Rabbit, illustrated by Garth Williams, is a new version of the Johnny Cake or Gingerbread Man tales common in English and American folk literature. In Jarrell's book a mother is inspired by the sight of a large brown rabbit on her lawn to make one just like it from bread dough for her little daughter Mary. Like his literary ancestor the Gingerbread Man, the rabbit runs away—in this case before he has been placed in the oven—after having been severely frightened by ominous talk about his probable future from the kitchen utensils. Unlike the Gingerbread Man, who is eaten by a clever fox, the Gingerbread Rabbit is rescued from a smooth-talking fox by the same brown rabbit that Mary's mother saw earlier in the day and adopted by this rabbit and his wife. Things end well in the frame tale too, for Mary's mother makes her a brown felt rabbit that cannot run away. The book received mixed reviews, but it has proved popular and has been translated into French and Japanese.

The first of Jarrell's children's books to be illustrated by Maurice Sendak, *The Bat-Poet* is more autobiographical than *The Gingerbread Rabbit*, draw-

Title page spread for Jarrell's first children's book, a new treatment of the Johnny Cake or Gingerbread Man tales common in English and American folk literature (Macmillan/Collier-Macmillan)

ing on the poet's sense of himself as having been a gifted child estranged from other more ordinary people. In *The Bat-Poet* a small brown bat, whose curiosity prevents him from sleeping during the day like normal bats, discovers and delights in the colors, sounds, and creatures of the daylight world, particularly the song of the mockingbird. In his attempt to imitate that song, he begins making up poems about the mockingbird and other forest creatures. The story is clearly a parable about the poet's role and his relationship with his audience. Some reviewers felt that this dimension of the story would hold little interest for children; yet both the book—which has been translated into Hebrew, French, Japanese, and German—and Jarrell's expressive reading of it for Caedmon records continue to be popular. The importance the book held for Jarrell is suggested by the fact that he included several of the poems from *The Bat-Poet* in *The Lost World*, his 1965 collection of poetry for adults. The final poem in *The Bat-Poet*, "A Bat Is Born," was published separately as a picture book in 1978.

The Animal Family (1965), again illustrated by Maurice Sendak, also has autobiographical ele-

ments. The idea for the story of an orphaned hunter who charms a mermaid out of the sea and marries her is said to have come to Jarrell in 1951, not long after he met Mary von Schrader, and there are some similarities between the furnishings of the house in the book and those in the Jarrells' house in Greensboro. Along with a bear cub, the hunter and his wife adopt a lynx (whose prototype the Jarrells liked to visit in the Washington Zoo) and a shipwrecked boy. They become a family in the fire-lit cabin that the hunter has built and equipped from the offerings of the forest and the sea. Like Jarrell's other children's books, the story's magic lies in part in a captured sense of the freshness and the strangeness of the world, here made vivid as the hunter introduces a creature from an alien "land," the mermaid, to his language and to his rustic way of life. Jarrell's choice of details—a cap of bluejay feathers for the boy, the lynx's dinner-table antics with a partridge, the mermaid's delight in the sound and power of a word—is masterful, and the tone of his story is leisurely, poetic, and often humorous. Beneath this lovely texture lie the more serious issues of love and death; the hunter's

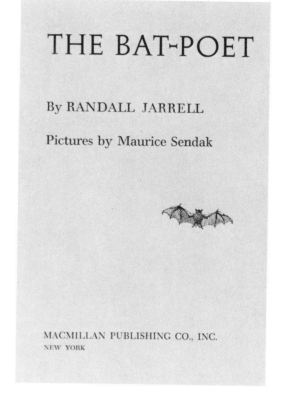

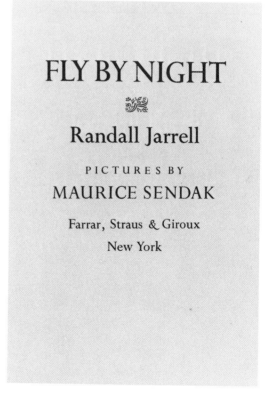

Frontispieces and title pages for two of Jarrell's three books illustrated by Maurice Sendak

cabin is filled with love, but with that love comes the potential for grief. Yet the book ends on a positive note: the boy has become so much a part of the family that it seems to him, as well as to the hunter and the mermaid, that he has been there "always." Critical reception for this book was understandably enthusiastic.

While Jarrell was working on *The Animal Family,* he was suffering from depression and intestinal problems, and in February 1965 he was admitted to a hospital in Chapel Hill, North Carolina, and diagnosed as a manic-depressive. That April, still in the hospital, he attempted suicide by cutting his left wrist and arm, but by July he was well enough to return home to Greensboro. In October he returned to the hospital for physical therapy and possible therapy on his wrist, and on 14 October, while he was on an evening walk along a country road about a mile from the hospital, he was hit by a car and killed. The people who had been in the car said that he "appeared to lunge" toward them, but the evidence was inconclusive, and his death was ruled accidental.

Fly By Night, published posthumously in 1976 and once again illustrated by Sendak, is the story of David, who—though he has no daytime memory of it—flies at night, floating above his parents and the animals outside, examining their dreams. Here Jarrell has captured the eerie dream state, sometimes called the lucid dream, in which the dreamer *feels* awake, aware of actual waking-world surroundings. As David floats over the landscape, the animals speak to him in verse. Toward the end of the book, an owl takes him to its home, where he hears the owl tell two little owlets "The Owl's Bedtime Story," a fine narrative poem that creates a story-within-the-story effect paralleling the common "I'm dreaming that I'm dreaming" experience. Well received by reviewers, *Fly By Night* is an amazingly convincing, somewhat frightening excursion into the unconscious with a totally satisfying ending: the next morning, when David goes into the kitchen for breakfast—almost, but not quite able to remember his experiences of the night before—"his mother looks at him like his mother," and begins to prepare the pancakes that David has seen her making in his dream the night before.

Jarrell was fortunate to have had Sendak as the illustrator for three of his four children's books. Sendak's sensitivity to Jarrell's nuances is acute; the exactitude of his drawings directly reflects the poet's precise details. Sendak himself has said that Jarrell "broke categories and bridged the gap between children's literature and classical literature," and John Updike has praised "the tact of his language and the depth at which his imagery [in his children's books] seeks to touch . . . the forbidden actual." In these stories Jarrell achieves the goal he sought in all his writing: "To see things as they are, to make them what they might be—."

Dust jacket for Jarrell's story of an orphaned hunter who charms a mermaid out of the sea (Pantheon)

Letters:

Randall Jarrell's Letters: An Autobiographical and Literary Selection, edited by Mary Jarrell, assisted by Stuart Wright (Boston: Houghton Mifflin, 1985).

Papers:

There are major collections of Jarrell's manuscripts and papers in the Berg Collection at the New York Public Library and at the Jackson Library, the University of North Carolina at Greensboro.

E. L. Konigsburg

Perry Nodelman
University of Winnipeg

BOOKS: *Jennifer, Hecate, Macbeth, William McKinley, and Me, Elizabeth* (New York: Atheneum, 1967; London: Macmillan, 1968);

From the Mixed-Up Files of Mrs. Basil E. Frankweiler (New York: Atheneum, 1967; London: Macmillan, 1969);

About the B'nai Bagels (New York: Atheneum, 1969);

(George) (New York: Atheneum, 1970); republished as *Benjamin Dickinson Carr and His (George)* (Harmondsworth, U.K.: Penguin, 1974);

Altogether, One at a Time, illustrated by Gail E. Haley and others (New York: Atheneum, 1971);

A Proud Taste for Scarlet and Miniver (New York: Atheneum, 1973);

The Dragon in the Ghetto Caper (New York: Atheneum, 1974);

The Second Mrs. Giaconda (New York: Atheneum, 1975; London: Macmillan, 1976);

Father's Arcane Daughter (New York: Atheneum, 1976; London: Macmillan, 1977);

Throwing Shadows (New York: Atheneum, 1979);

Journey to an 800 Number (New York: Atheneum, 1982);

Up From Jericho Tel (New York: Atheneum, 1986).

PERIODICAL PUBLICATIONS: "The Double Image: Language as the Perimeter of Culture," *Library Journal* (15 February 1970): 731-734;

"Sprezzatura: A Kind of Excellence," *Horn Book,* 52 (June 1976): 253-261.

E. L. Konigsburg

As a chemistry student in graduate school, E. L. Konigsburg twice blew up the laboratory sink, "losing my eyebrows and bangs in the flash." She claims it was her fault that "the University of Pittsburgh moved their Graduate School of Chemistry the year after I left." Since then, Konigsburg has regrown her eyebrows and written twelve excellent, sometimes annoying, but always interesting children's books. "I shall probably not return to the lab," she says, "but all those years in chemistry were not wasted; I learned useful things: to use the ma-

terials at hand, to have a point of view, to distill. And I obviously learned how to handle messy sinks—move."

These useful things are the essence of Konigsburg's writing. Her books have grown out of the material closest to hand, the events of her own life. Her writing is a witty distillation of complex experience, and she always tells her stories from an interesting point of view. Above all, Konigsburg is in her writing as in her chemistry a creator of interesting messes. A constant experimenter, she has invented more different kinds of children's fiction than any two or three other writers. When her experiments work, they do something unusually well; when they fail, they are messy. But she knows how to handle messes; she moves on, usually to something just as unusual and just as interesting.

The middle of three daughters, Elaine Lobl Konigsburg was born in New York City on 10 February 1930 to Adolph Lobl, a businessman, and Beulah Klein Lobl. She spent her childhood in various small towns in Pennsylvania, where she read books like P. L. Travers's *Mary Poppins* (1934) and Frances Hodgson Burnett's *The Secret Garden* (1911) and "thought that they were the norm and that the way I lived was subnormal waiting for normal. . . . Where were the stories that made having a class full of Radasevitches and Gabellas and Zaharious normal?" As a teenager she was a bookkeeper at the Shenango Valley Provision Company, and there she met David Konigsburg, a brother of one of the owners. After graduating from high school in Farrell, Pennsylvania, she attended Carnegie-Mellon University in Pittsburgh, where she supported herself by working as manager of a dormitory laundry, playground instructor, waitress, and library page. She received a B.S. from Carnegie in 1952 and married David Konigsburg on 6 July of that year.

While David Konigsburg studied psychology at the University of Pittsburgh, his wife was "determined to push back the frontiers of science" at the same university. She was a research assistant in the tissue culture lab and pursued her own explosive studies in chemistry. Two years later, when her husband began his career as an industrial psychologist in Jacksonville, Florida, Konigsburg found "that the only thing I had succeeded in pushing back was my hairline," and gave up chemistry.

In Jacksonville she taught science at Bartram, a private girls' school, until her first child, Paul, was born in 1955. In 1956 she gave birth to a daughter, Laurie, and in 1959 to a son, Ross. She devoted herself to getting her children through their childhoods and, unwittingly, preparing herself for her future career. "As the children grew older," says David Konigsburg, "and we became more involved with suburban living, Elaine was intrigued with the various forces exerting an influence on us." She herself says that "chemistry was my larval stage, and those nine years at home doing diaper service was my cocoon." She first thought of writing for children at this time but turned to art instead. When her husband was transferred to New York in 1962, Elaine Konigsburg took lessons at the Art Students League on Saturdays. The rest of the week she experienced what she has called "the dailiness of living. . . . I am involved in the everyday, corn-flakes, worn-out sneakers way of life of my children; yet I am detached from it by several decades."

Konigsburg had found a subject. She began her first novel in response to actual events in her daughter's life. Laurie had a hard time making friends when her family moved from New Jersey to Port Chester, New York. After many weeks she finally found one, and her mother was pleased to learn that Laurie's new friend was black: "two outsiders had found each other, and a friendship had begun."

Konigsburg told her first editor, Jean Karl, that she wrote in the morning, then read what she had written to the children when they came home for lunch: "their reaction determined what happened next: 'They laugh or they don't,' she said, 'which means I revise or I don't.' " Konigsburg brought her finished manuscript to Karl in July 1966, and Atheneum published it the following spring.

A superficial description of *Jennifer, Hecate, Macbeth, William McKinley, and Me, Elizabeth* (1967) makes it sound like a typical wish-fulfillment novel, a fantasy of power told from a child's uncritical point of view. New in town, friendless, and small for her age, Elizabeth feels inferior to the perfect Cynthia, who is "pretty and neat and smart. I guess that makes her perfect to almost any grownup." Elizabeth knows that Cynthia is a cruel hypocrite; but adults, who have all the power and none of the brains, cannot see through her. In fact, most adults are as inadequate as Great Aunt Drusilla and Great Uncle Frank, who "thought that kids were pets that talked."

Fortunately Elizabeth meets Jennifer, another outsider, who claims that she is "a witch, disguised as a perfectly normal girl." Like Superman, Jennifer is not the friendless outsider that a conventional observer might assume her to be; she actually has superheroic qualities, "nerves of steel and the heart of a witch." Armed with her wonderful secret, Jennifer defies mere circumstance. She never lets Elizabeth win an argument and never mentions where she lives or who her family is. For Elizabeth, this unbending defiance of the ordinary is wonderful; she says that even if she "discovered that Jennifer lived in an ordinary house and did ordinary things, I would know it was a disguise." Elizabeth becomes Jennifer's apprentice witch. The two enjoy feeling superior to "nor-

Dust jacket for Konigsburg's first novel (Atheneum)

mal" children, and they even plan a superheroic feat: flying.

So far, the story appears rather typical, but as its title suggests this is no ordinary novel. It is too witty; Konigsburg has given Elizabeth her own acerbic sense of humor and wonderful timing: "My mother was not always too patient about my food habits. . . . But I had this reputation for being a fussy eater. Besides, I was an only child; besides, I was a nag." Konigsburg also provides her young humorist with richly comic situations, including an outrageous school play about the cloying magic of love, and the manufacturing of a witch's flying ointment based on a three-pound can of Crisco. The novel transcends typicality in another way also; its adults are not all bad. When Elizabeth's mother displays enough real loving concern to worry about her daughter's "abnormal" lack of friends, her surprisingly sensible husband straightens her out: "my father told her that a usual body temperature was

98.6 degrees, but some people were healthy with a body temperature of only 98.4 degrees. That was normal for them. 'So who's to say exactly what *normal* is?' my father said. My mother seemed to understand." Most adults in children's novels would not understand.

The idea that it is better to be yourself than to be "normal" and accepted by others transcends the cheap egocentricity of most wish-fulfillment fantasies, in which one gets to be both triumphantly oneself and unconditionally accepted by others. Elizabeth is not accepted by anyone except Jennifer, but she learns that it is possible "to enjoy being odd. And I did." Jennifer has dealt successfully with her loneliness in much the same way, by turning to her secret fantasy of witchcraft. But Konigsburg is not content even with that; she makes both girls see that reveling in one's oddness is no easy choice. Elizabeth starts her career as a witch by learning the ugly truth about the Salem witches: "Some of them were little kids. Just like Jennifer; just like me. Some of them were hanged." As she pursues her apprenticeship she must face the discomfort of Jennifer's rituals, all of which keep her apart from normalcy and "normal" children; they allow her next to no fun at Cynthia's birthday party.

The flirtation with witchcraft culminates when Elizabeth falls in love with the toad that is to be boiled as part of the flying ointment. Jennifer tries to warn Elizabeth about giving the toad the humanity of a name; but she does it anyway. When the time comes for the toad to be thrown into the melted Crisco, Elizabeth cannot do it. If witchcraft represents the girls' retreat from society into self-sufficient oddness, then they should be hard-hearted enough, self-sufficient enough, odd enough, to kill a mere toad. The interesting thing is not that Elizabeth turns out to have more loving concern for others that she thought or hoped; it is not even that she is sensitive enough to see that Jennifer actually wanted her to save the toad: "She had purposely kept him until last. She had purposely dangled him over the pot so long. She always found a way not to get mad at herself but to get mad at me instead." What is really interesting is that Konigsburg allowed this confrontation to happen at all; suddenly a pleasurable game becomes a painful reality. The strong demands Konigsburg makes of her characters and the fine moral intelligence she gives them imply much respect for children, a respect she has continued to express in all of her books.

The novel's ending, however, is disappointing. Jennifer, who has been an enticingly mysterious, decidedly self-reliant, and resolutely eccentric character throughout the book, suddenly seems to turn into a nice, normal girl; Elizabeth admits to being the nice normal girl she seems to think she always really was: "Neither of us pretends to be a witch any more. Now we mostly enjoy being what we really are . . . just Jennifer and just me . . . just good friends." This is too succinct; it doesn't make clear how being "just Jennifer and just me" does not mean that the girls are just conventional. Whether or not Konigsburg intended it, both girls seem to lose their personalities for the sake of a message.

Earlier in the novel, Elizabeth noticed how Jennifer made her life more interesting: "each trip to and from school had become an adventure." *From the Mixed-Up Files of Mrs. Basil E. Frankweiler,* published in the fall of 1967, is a more thorough investigation of the possibilities of adventure in the lives of protected suburban children. Konigsburg

Dust jacket for a later edition of Konigsburg's Newbery Medal-winning novel about a young brother and sister who run away from home and hide in the Metropolitan Museum of Art in New York City (Atheneum)

has said the book originated at a family picnic in Yellowstone National Park, during which her children complained about everything they could think of: "I realized that if my children ever left home, they would never revert to barbarism. They would carry with them all the fussiness and tidiness of suburban life. Where could they go. . . ? Maybe they could find some way to live with caution and compulsiveness and still satisfy their need for adventure."

Adventure stories usually take a paradoxical attitude toward home life; one leaves the boredom of security in order to have the excitement of adventure but, in facing the danger of adventure, learns to value security. In *From the Mixed-Up Files of Mrs. Basil E. Frankweiler,* Claudia's adventure starts typically, with boredom: "She was bored with simply being straight-A's Claudia Kincaid. She was tired of arguing about whose turn it was to choose the Sunday night seven-thirty television show, of injustice, and of the monotony of everything." But ironically, Claudia "didn't like discomfort," including the untidiness of picnics; so the only adventure she is capable of choosing for herself offers her no real escape. She and her brother Jamie hide out comfortably in the Metropolitan Museum of Art in New York City, which is only a safe imitation of truly different and dangerous places.

At the museum, Claudia insists on fresh underwear every day and scolds Jamie for not eating properly. Jamie realizes what this means: "Claudia simply did not know how to escape." Nevertheless, both children find that even a safe adventure can be uncomfortable—and that they do not like or want discomfort. The Elizabethan bed Claudia chooses as "the most elegant place in the world to hide" smells musty, and she longs for the comforting odor of detergent; Jamie feels a thrill of horror when he realizes he has gone to bed without brushing his teeth.

Even so, things go surprisingly well, and the children begin to understand that they have not actually run away at all. The situation they have carefully placed themselves in allows nothing to happen different enough to make them homesick, and they plan so well that no one ever realizes they are staying in the museum. As Claudia says herself, "heaven knows, we're well trained. Just look how nicely we've managed. It's really their fault if we're not homesick."

Konigsburg might have left it at that and written a charming, safe novel about the safe fun of hiding in the museum. But she will not allow Claudia and Jamie to believe their safe adventure is just fun any more than she let Elizabeth and Jennifer believe that their witchcraft was just fun. Claudia especially realizes she is not satisfied by it. When she says, "I didn't run away to come home the same," she admits that she actually ran away to escape, not home, but herself, the safe values she inevitably carried with her.

Rather than do the obvious and actually provide her heroine with an exciting adventure, an escape from herself, Konigsburg does something much more subtle and meaningful: she puts Claudia in a situation which forces her to become different only in her acceptance of the fact that she *cannot* be different—at least not in the way she imagines. She develops a painful, and therefore, truly adventurous, understanding of who she is, why she cannot escape it, and what can be done about it.

Claudia reaches that understanding through a rich widow, Mrs. Basil E. Frankweiler. Claudia and Jamie leave the safety of the museum to find Mrs. Frankweiler, in hopes that she knows who made Angel, the mysterious statue she has donated to the museum. She does know the secret, and she shares it with them; and she is the person who tells us the children's story. John Rowe Townsend says, "The fact that Mrs. Frankweiler narrates the whole story, which she herself does not enter until near the end, seems to me to be a major flaw"; indeed, the biggest question about this novel is why Mrs. Frankweiler is in it at all.

But it is Mrs. Frankweiler's presence in the book that allows it to be more than lightweight. Konigsburg could not let Claudia realize the inadequacy of her museum adventure unless there was a way for her to move past it; that way is Mrs. Frankweiler, and not just because she knows the secret of Angel. Mrs. Frankweiler understands Claudia because she is herself much like Claudia. She reveals her Claudia-like dislike of discomfort as the children stare at her: "it was uncomfortable. I put a stop to that." Mrs. Frankweiler's home is filled with baths and the odors of cleanliness, and she has herself kept the secret of the statue because, like Claudia, she needs an escape from the comfortable safety her character demands: "I need having the secret more than I need the money." In fact, what Mrs. Frankweiler offers Claudia is a share in her own solution to the problem they both have: "Returning with a secret is what she really wants. . . . Claudia doesn't want adventure. She likes baths and feeling comfortable too much for that kind of thing. Secrets are the kind of adventure she needs. Secrets are safe, and they do much to

make you different. On the inside, where it counts."

That is a very explicit statement of theme. Mrs. Frankweiler has an excellent understanding of what Elaine Konigsburg wants this novel to be about, and sometimes she is an annoyingly blatant narrator. Konigsburg once admonished people who make such statements: "For goodness' sake, say all that very softly." Mrs. Frankweiler shouts it from the rooftops, but there is a good reason for it. What Mrs. Frankweiler says is not simple. If it were not said explicitly, few readers of any age would understand it. Even a child as intelligent as Claudia, who might well understand it, could not convincingly find the words to say it. So it is necessary that it be said loudly by someone other than Claudia or Jamie, and appropriate that Mrs. Frankweiler be the one to say it. She is enough like Claudia to see what Claudia would see, enough a mature observer to understand its implications. Furthermore, her telling makes for a better story; if Claudia or Jamie had told it, they would not have had the distance, the maturity, or the wit to point out its comic ironies: "She found Jamie standing on that corner, probably one of the most civilized street corners in the whole world, consulting a compass and announcing that when they turned left, they would be heading 'due northwest.' "

From the Mixed-Up Files of Mrs. Basil E. Frankweiler was published just a few months after *Jennifer, Hecate, Macbeth, William McKinley, and Me, Elizabeth;* both books were critical successes. Meanwhile, the Konigsburgs moved back to Jacksonville, where they have lived since. In the midst of moving, Elaine Konigsburg learned of her astonishing coup: her first novel was a runner-up for the 1968 Newbery Medal; her second novel had actually won the medal. The Newbery list has not included two books by the same author before or since.

Not surprisingly, critics found Konigsburg's next novel disappointing; and *About the B'nai Bagels* (1969) is certainly not as strong as the two books that precede it. David Konigsburg tells how *About the B'nai Bagels* grew out of his son Paul's involvement in Little League sports: "not satisfied with superficial knowledge, Elaine studied the official rule books. . . . We even got her to Shea and Yankee Stadiums where she let her opinions about the managers' decisions be known." In fact, the novel finally fails because Konigsburg lets her opinions about her characters' decisions be known, and not softly at all.

The first half of *About the B'nai Bagels* reads like many of the "contemporary junior problem novels" that followed it throughout the 1970s. Mark is a typical child of typical Jewish parents who tells his own typical story of his problems with interfering parents as it unfolds, with no apparent knowledge of what will occur beyond the end of each chapter; and he feels an apparently uncriticized self-pity: "You can't win with parents. They always have reasons. Even if you, their own flesh and blood child, have reasons as logical as theirs, they have more of them." Mark's mother, who seems to have sprung full grown from the untidy graves of countless Jewish-mother jokes, becomes the coach of his Little League baseball team; Mark has to put up with leftovers, the loss of friends, and his mother's interference everywhere.

But unlike the writers of most books of this type, Konigsburg does not let her protagonist enjoy his delicious self-pity for long. Mark learns that his original understanding of things is simpleminded; his mother is more than a caricature and does understand his problems. She has humbly and sensitively chosen to leave him alone to find his own way. Forced eventually to decide whether he should gain points for himself by interfering in the relationships of his teammates, Mark finds he has enough character to admire and follow his mother's high standards: "I never told Hersch about Barry then or ever. It was a decision to do the right thing."

As in her earlier novels, Konigsburg has taken easy clichés and turned them inside out. She has provided her protagonist with an easy way to understand a problem and then forced him to see its inadequacy. Unfortunately, in *About the B'nai Bagels* she seems to know what she is doing too well. Having found her theme by exploring the implications of what happens to Elizabeth and Jennifer, and to Claudia and Jamie, she states it blatantly again and again in *About the B'nai Bagels*. Like an academic essay, the book starts with a thesis statement, as Mark tells how his mother "invaded my privacy and might have declared practically the last little piece of my life as occupied territory," and closes with a priggishly sententious summary: "But I figure you don't become a man overnight. Because it is a becoming; becoming more yourself. . . . And only some of it happens on official time plus family time. A lot of it happens being alone."

Having somewhere to be alone, a secret space beyond the occupied territory of secure but numbing comfort, is as important for Mark as it was for Claudia. Mark's mother says, "every boy needs to have a little something to hide from his mother." In *(George)* (1970), Konigsburg's next novel, Ben Carr has a lot more than a little something to hide.

George, his "concentric twin" and "the funniest little man in the whole world," lives inside him. George is Ben's "unoccupied territory"; Konigsburg's idea of turning that pop-psychology commonplace into a separate personality led her to write her most unusual, messiest, and most interesting book. Not inappropriately, she provides Ben with some of her own messy background and makes him a student of chemistry.

(George) is the first of Konigsburg's novels not narrated by one of the characters involved in the story, and for good reasons. No one but Ben (or George) could accurately understand George's existence as a real, separate being. The adults in the novel are convinced he is a figment of Ben's disturbed imagination. On the other hand, Ben (or George) would believe too firmly in George's reality to tell the story accurately, for Konigsburg would like for readers to see that George is not merely real, but symbolic. While her omniscient narration never once says or even implies that George is actually not a real being, she constantly works at making his symbolic meaning clear in a way no character involved in the story could.

George is a rich symbol. He provides Ben with the sense that he is special: "If I'm peculiar, it's you who makes me so." What makes Ben peculiar might more positively be called his sense of self, for to be oneself is to be different from other people. Consequently, George acts as Ben's memory, the repository of his personal experience, and possesses his intelligence: "It was always George who understood things that didn't make sense." But, gloriously vulgar, satirically cynical, and egocentric, George also represents Ben's antisocial tendencies—his need to say to himself the things he would rarely dare to say to others, his honest perceptions of things he would rather not publically admit to perceiving. So when Ben wants to be like other people, and liked by them, George becomes Ben's conscience. George has high moral standards; he "hated people who were more concerned with appearing different than with being different. More concerned with appearing smart than being smart." In this way, too, George represents antisocial tendencies, but this time they are positive ones; he stands for Ben's need to be himself as opposed to his desire to conform, and therefore, misrepresent himself. Ben has an understandable streak of weakness; he "didn't like having George tell him things he didn't want to hear and that were correct." When Ben is weak enough to tell lies for his morally weak but attractive friend William, George refuses to talk to him anymore; Ben has made himself less than he actually is, blotted out a part of himself in order to be socially successful.

As a little *man*, George represents Ben's maturity. Ben is a child facing the usual blandishments of adolescence, the need to be "normal," to be liked, to be anything but oneself: "I never thought much about what other kids might think of me before this year. I was so busy listening to George." George represents both Ben's childish egocentricity, his vulgar lack of concern for others, and also his mature self-respect. As a child and a man, George is everything that is not adolescent.

The division of one character into two personalities allows Konigsburg to describe emotions with a subtlety unusual in children's fiction. Ben and George's arguments imply the complex confusion of Ben's self-perception; at one point, Ben even wonders "if George was jealous of William," a decidedly complex thought to have about a part of your own character. Given this psychological complexity, the number of direct theme statements in *(George)* is understandable. As in *From the Mixed-Up Files of Mrs. Basil E. Frankweiler*, the ideas are complex and probably need to be stated directly: "George realized that it would take a quiet revolution to keep Ben from making a sand castle of his life, building turrets of science surrounded by moats of silence and from wanting praise and friendship instead of growth for his skills." Since George is Ben's moral conscience, Konigsburg frequently gives him her own truths to tell. He says, among other things, "I intend to see that you are not a neat, prepackaged chemist who fits things into neat, labelled jars.... I, I, me, vulgar George, intend to keep you slightly out of bounds so that you can move, swing. In short, Benjamin Body, I intend to make a man of you, a man I'll be proud to live in."

These obvious statements of values are still perceptive enough, clever enough, to be worth saying. In fact, cleverness is the defining quality of *(George)*. The idea of the book is itself clever, and it is executed with a clever and deliciously wicked wit. Nasty-minded George calls Ben's undomestic mother every name he can think of: Betty Anti-Crocker, Queen of the Maytag, The Pillsbury Princess, Chef Burn-ar-dee, Queen Frozen Pot Pie. Konigsburg also presents a thoroughly wicked picture of Ben's father's second wife: "Marilyn was a home economics major and regularly waged anti-germ warfare. In Marilyn's house the milk cartons were put away so promptly that they never sweated, and the mayonnaise was treated like some hopelessly insane relative that was never allowed out."

This latter image is clearly related to George, whom Marilyn would never allow out either. Marilyn is like one of George's "prepackaged" people; when she uses her knowledge of children gained "from my minor in psych and all" to baldly announce to Ben that he is a paranoid schizophrenic, readers can see the comparative virtues of messiness: "I want you to know, Ben, that it wasn't easy convincing your father that you're crazy."

In a novel which makes messiness a virtue, messiness abounds. The plot complicates itself endlessly and Konigsburg allows herself every sort of verbal excess; but she is always most interesting when she seems to be least sure of her material and has least control of it. Like Claudia and Mrs. Frankweiler, she needs to escape from her own stultifying competence. In *(George)* she shows little control and accomplishes much—perhaps more than she ever did before or has since. David Rees suggested in *Horn Book* that *(George)* "is probably Elaine Konigsburg's finest achievement so far.... a light-hearted, genuinely comic novel."

Konigsburg has said, "Had I not won the Newbery, I don't know if I would have had the courage to experiment." *(George)* was the first of a series of experiments. While the innovative stories which constitute her next book, *Altogether, One at a Time* (1971), are all about children facing their limitations, they are quite different from each other, from her earlier work, and from most children's fiction.

The narrator of "Inviting Jason" never gets past his flawed perception of himself. Perceptive readers will see how fitting it is that Dick, the most popular boy in school, likes the dyslexic outsider Jason more than he likes Stanley; Stanley did not want to invite Jason to his party for fear of offending Dick. But Stanley, who tells the story with a blindness rare in children's fiction, feels too sorry for himself to see the irony. The boy in "Night of the Leonids" is more perceptive; he understands why his sixty-three-year-old grandmother slaps him when he complains about the clouds that cover the star shower which will not occur again for another third of a century: "I added it up. Sixty-three and thirty-three don't add up to another chance.... I held the hand that hit me." What is unusual here is that a child comes to understand and offer solace for an adult's pain, instead of the other way around. "Camp Fat" is a contrived allegory quite unlike anything else by Konigsburg. The annoyingly profound ghost of a dead counselor offers symbolic jewelry to help a girl find "what is inside all that fat of yours"; it turns out to be just what the girl claimed earlier (although not in the joking way she meant it): "a skinny little girl screaming 'I'm hungry!' " She was unwittingly hungry for self-perception; while the theme is typically Konigsburg's, the story seems to be trying to find a tidy way of presenting complex ideas. It fails because it takes its pretentious symbolism too seriously. "Momma at the Pearly Gates" is also too serious. It describes a confrontation between a "dirty nigger" and a "Ding Dong Dago." The "dirty nigger," who is the narrator's mother as a child, is actually the self-sufficient superchild that Jennifer only pretended to be. There is no real conflict in this story, only growing satisfaction at Momma's inevitable triumph; apparently, Konigsburg felt too strongly about the issues here to present them subtly.

Altogether, One at a Time is the only one of Konigsburg's books illustrated by someone other than herself. Each story has pictures by a different artist, and the techniques of illustration are themselves unusual. Some of Laurel Schindelman's pictures for "Night of the Leonids" communicate part of the plot; for instance, a picture rather than words show it is cloudy. But since that does not happen consistently, these pictures demand a close attention that is not always repaid; and the illustrator tries much too hard to be as witty as Konigsburg is in her prose. Gary Parker's pictures for "Camp Fat" are blurry and mostly pointless, and Gail E. Haley's folk-oriented pictures for "Momma at the Pearly Gates" do not suit the sociologically precise feeling of the story. Only Mercer Mayer's straightforward sketches for "Inviting Jason" work as well as Konigsburg's own dramatic and engagingly clumsy pictures usually do. They have something like her own mixture of careful line and sparseness of detail, an effect that beautifully balances the richly detailed comedy of her prose.

Konigsburg's next book was another surprise. An exploration of the life and times of Eleanor of Aquitaine, *A Proud Taste for Scarlet and Miniver* (1973) is filled with facts about the Middle Ages and framed by an ingenious depiction of Eleanor and her friends in a delightfully absurd version of heaven. Konigsburg says the book emerged from her consideration of the term "middle-aged child," used by publishers to define an audience for children's books, which she first thought silly: "But my acceptance of the term has come about as a result of establishing a relationship between the child, aged eight through twelve, and the Middle Ages. The Middle Ages of Western civilization." She believes that both are literal-minded, superstitious, and filled with contradictions. She also believes that Eleanor is both representative of that childlike age and "in essence everything that woman's liberation is in slogans." And for all her independence, Konigsburg's Eleanor is indeed a little childish. Like many middle-aged children, she is pleasure-loving, restriction-hating, and self-centered; above all, she has a childlike vitality, an exuberance that mesmerizes everyone in the book: "she knew what she wanted, and she had the energy to do it all."

But the book itself is not so energetic. Four narrators describe their involvement with Eleanor as they sit with each other in heaven after the event; they all know how their various stories come out and can create no suspense for each other or for us. Furthermore, they tell us what people felt rather than showing it; even Eleanor tells her part of the story in this uninvolved way. The result is like a bad historical movie: lots of lavish local color, lots of grandiose passion described grandiosely, little sense of real people engaged in real human activities; too much glamor, too little "dailiness."

Even worse, Eleanor is not allowed the humanity of being seen differently by different people. The use of four narrators cries out for four different interpretations of Eleanor, and we get only one. They all adore her. As Eleanor says herself, "No one who matters questions that I have turned out anything but right." While the novel provides evidence of much to criticize in Eleanor, Konigsburg uncritically lets her get away with attitudes and behavior that she would make her more youthful protagonists question.

In *The Dragon in the Ghetto Caper* (1974), Konigsburg returns to more familiar territory as she tells of Andrew J. Chronister's search "for something uncertain" in her most certain, most confident book. Konigsburg strides with the mastery of ownership through the territory she tentatively explored earlier, never stumbling, hardly even stopping to admire the scenery she knows so well. The book is like the ghetto it describes—like Andy's wealthy suburban home in Foxmeadow, "the whole world to the people who lived there," with "a fence circled all around it, and a security guard . . . posted at the only gate."

Andy does not understand how Foxmeadow is a ghetto, so he misses the irony when he says to a black woman about her own neighborhood, "Nice ghetto you've got here," and she replies, "It's home t'me." But while he does not know that his home is as much his prison (and his protection) as the black woman's is hers, he still feels hemmed in by it. Like Claudia, he is discomfited by too much

36 Janson Slideup until   Chapter 1 *catch line only throughout*   *16 Janson X 22 picas*   *1 em indent new ¶*

⟵ One of the things that Andrew J. Chronister never did was to attend music class. They could not make him, and they knew it. He could not
carry a tune, and he knew it. <u>They</u> was Emerson Country Day School.

Andy had gone to Emerson C.D.S. (Country. Day. School.) **for almost**
seven years, counting kindergarten. The policy there was not to <u>make</u> Andrew
go to music, but to make him <u>want</u> to go. They never succeeded. So when
the other students went to singing, Andy went to the art room where he drew
dragons. Sometimes he painted dragons. One was made out of papier-mâché,
and two were made out of construction paper, burlap and Elmer's glue; those
took four music lessons each and were the largest.

Dragons, however, were not *Andy's* true passion; crime was.
~~Dragons were one of Andy's passions and crime was the other.~~ He
was determined to be a detective when he grew up. Not an ordinary police
detective. A famous one. Famous, tough and cool. Like Ellery Queen, for
God's sake.

Immediately after he *had* decided that he would be a (famous) (tough)
(cool) detective, Andy had put himself into training. He would be ready
to solve the crime of the century the minute it occurred in Foxmeadow. Foxmeadow was where Andy lived, and it met the logical requirements <u>of being</u>
the scene of a puzzling murder. That is, when a famous, cool, tough detective like Ellery or Sherlock solved a crime, it always involved a closed
group of people. Like guests in a hotel. Or movie stars working on a film.
Or travellers on an ocean liner. Foxmeadow met that requirement. It certainly was closed.

Foxmeadow was part of the town of Gainesboro. It was
~~It was part of the town of Gainesboro.~~ a ring of houses built
around acres and acres (eighteen holes) of a championship golf course. Plus
four tennis courts and one swimming pool, Olympic-sized. There were only

Revised typescript page for The Dragon in the Ghetto Caper *(by permission of the author)*

comfort and can imagine only unsatisfying escapes from it. Also like Claudia, he meets a woman older than himself who shares his situation and leads him to self-understanding.

Edie Yakots is a young, attractive married woman who is so different from the orderly norms of Foxmeadow that she even talks confusingly. Andy finds her fascinating: "The other kids ... were all so much alike that they could have interchangeable parts. Edie was different, bordering on strange." As Andy's "sidekick" in his safe game of tough detective, Edie unwittingly leads him into the middle of a *real* game, a numbers racket in a black ghetto that forces him to face the actual implications of his imagined adventure. Furthermore, she is "better at making sense than at making sentences," as outrageous a speaker of theme statements as Mrs. Frankweiler or George. Edie sees that the dragons Andy always draws represent his difference from other people, that thing which is negatively egocentric but positively self-understanding; and she often speaks oracularly of dragons. The essence of her wisdom is, "You've got to know your dragon, but you've also got to keep him under control." Konigsburg herself makes the meaning of dragons crystal clear in a statement about Andy's sister: "Mary Jane had no room for dragons in her life. Her whole life was predictable. She would always be cool. She would never do anything foolish. . . . She would always be a nerd. Dragons were what made life hard to live, yet no fun to live without."

This is all familiar, as dragons are another version of what George stands for or of the secret Mrs. Frankweiler gives Claudia. Konigsburg is at her most confident in *The Dragon in the Ghetto Caper.* There are few moments in her writing funnier than the one in which Andy displays his ignorance of slang by saying, "I see nothing wrong with calling a spade a spade or a ghetto a ghetto." She had absolute control of her material, to the extent of giving Andy the ultimately Foxmeadowian weapon to fend off what he thinks are thieves, a can of spray deodorant: "Move, Edie. I don't have enough deodorant to hold these stinkers all day." The only problem with this novel is that it has no problems. It is as predictable as Foxmeadow, and as Edie says, "You can't get lost in Foxmeadow. All the dragons are locked out."

Given the strange failing of *The Dragon in the Ghetto Caper* to be messy enough to mirror its message, *The Second Mrs. Giaconda* (1975) might be understood as a competent person's sour grapes about competence. In her second historical novel,

Konigsburg depicts Leonardo da Vinci as a competent person who lacks the courage to express the dragons within him. In her *Horn Book* article about this book, Konigsburg says, "Leonardo lacked the ability to make a giant leap; he was too inhibited. He was too much the experimenter. . . ." She might almost be talking about herself, an experimenter whose best experiments are glorious messes and who loses her brilliance when she stops experimenting. In fact, she says that Leonardo's last painting failed because "he had written a book of rules, his famous *Treatise on Painting,* and was conscientiously following these rules." Something like that could be said of *The Dragon in the Ghetto Caper.*

That Konigsburg might be accused of seeing herself in the universally admired Leonardo quite unfairly implies a glorious conceit; but it does have the advantage of explaining her need to criticize him. For the Leonardo of *The Second Mrs. Giaconda* is not particularly lovable; a *New York Times* reviewer called him "curiously stunted." He is utterly self-centered; even worse, he is afraid of feelings: "Salai recognized the look, frozen and withdrawn, on his master's face. It was the look he always wore when human emotions became too intense or too raw."

Feeling that Leonardo clearly lacks a dragon, Konigsburg provides him with one in the person of the boy Salai. According to Leonardo's notebooks, Salai was a thief and a liar; *The Second Mrs. Giaconda* is an attempt to explain why Leonardo kept him with him for more than thirty years. The usual explanation is that Leonardo was homosexual; "but," says Konigsburg, "I am glad that I write for children. For that explanation of his use of a young boy will never do. It is simply not enough; it is not deep enough." Her deeper answer is that Salai had the human vitality Leonardo lacked. Konigsburg's Salai combines the vulgarity of George and the vitality of Eleanor of Aquitaine. As his friend Beatrice tells Salai, "Your master needs something from you. He needs your rudeness and irresponsibility. . . . He needs a wild element. . . . All great art needs it; something that leaps and flickers. Some artists can put that wild element into the treatment itself, but Leonardo cannot." Unfortunately, neither can Konigsburg, at least not in this book. Despite its breezy style, *The Second Mrs. Giaconda* is no less flat than *A Proud Taste for Scarlet and Miniver,* and for the same ironic reason: it presents Konigsburg's interpretations of character too clearly and carefully to partake itself of the wildness it praises.

Father's Arcane Daughter (1976) is another matter altogether. This novel may be Konigsburg's most daring experiment. The difference is not in meaning, for as David Rees rightly said in *Horn Book,* "This novel makes more explicit the themes that were explored in the earlier books." Here, Konigsburg develops those themes in a volatile, new mixture of highly melodramatic plotting and bald, matter-of-fact style.

Like so many of Konigsburg's other young characters, Winston Carmichael and his handicapped sister Heidi are imprisoned by their protective environment. Their parents protect Heidi because of her handicap, and both children for fear of another kidnapping like the one years earlier that led to the presumed death of their half sister Caroline. The children respond to imprisonment by imprisoning themselves even further. Uncoordinated and hard of hearing, Heidi has disappeared into a protective shell of childishness, "cutesy, clinging and cuddling." Winston is over-

Dust jacket for Konigsburg's 1976 novel about a young boy and his handicapped sister burdened by their overprotective parents (Atheneum)

careful and friendless; he has sacrificed his freedom to his concern for (and embarrassment about) Heidi. Not surprisingly in a novel by Konigsburg, Winston and Heidi escape their safe prison with the help of an unusual woman older than themselves, who understands their situation because she shares it. Martha, who pretends to be Caroline, tells Winston, "If we stretch the bars of the cage very wide—very, very wide indeed—even a cripple can walk through." Martha is, as Winston says, "unguarded" herself and gradually helps both children through the bars of their emotional handicaps.

But despite the familiarity of this situation, Konigsburg explores its ironies and ambiguities far more deeply than she explored similar situations in earlier novels. Winston and Heidi are imprisoned not by an ordinary life but by a highly unusual one. While George was afraid that Ben would imprison himself in a castle of science, Heidi's wealthy mother "was able to hide her daughter in Carmichael castle and pull up the drawbridge." Wealthy, cossetted, and victimized by undesirable celebrity, Winston and Heidi first think their half sister will free them to be normal. But Martha knows better and tells Heidi, when she says she wants to be normal, "If Heidi wants to be 'normal,' she can just go on home and continue the pretending." Ironically, Heidi's life as a handicapped person becomes a perverse but interesting image of normalcy; she is protected from her own real self because she is weak enough to need and accept protection. When she discovers the "fine mind" she has kept secret even from herself, she turns out to be the "arcane daughter" of the title.

Even more ironically, Martha, the presumed arcane daughter, wants the children to see the truth about themselves, but she herself "continues the pretending" and lets people go on believing she is actually Caroline. She lets herself be imprisoned by this lie so that she can help the children live truthfully. She does so in order to free Winston from a prison of self-sacrifice, his need to protect Heidi, and his guilt over his secret wish that she remain handicapped and inferior. But in doing so, she herself sacrifices her love for Winston's father, and pretends to be his child in order to save Heidi and Winston from the prison of their childhood and to allow them to be their own real selves. At one point, the reader is told that "it was her love for Winston and her increased recognition of and, eventually, love for Heidi that kept her bound to the role of Caroline Carmichael." But love or not, she is indeed bound, and Konigsburg insists we notice that and see the ambiguity of her entire situation.

She also has much to say about the passing of time. Winston says, "There was no history more strange to me than the immediate past history of my family." Parental horror at that lurid history has built Winston and Heidi's prison; because of history, they are protected from actually having a history—having anything happen to them interesting enough to be noteworthy. Their lives are always the same, and Winston wearily describes the comforting sameness of their "usual" Saturdays. They are imprisoned by the "comfortable" past, "where everything was known and unfinished and required no action." Martha, as Caroline emerging from the past and living in the present, hides under the "known and finished" shadow of Caroline and saves the children from what Winston calls the "shadow" of the past. She saves them from history so that they can have a history of their own—the excitingly melodramatic story Winston is in the process of telling Heidi as the novel unfolds, in which "time passes so easily."

Father's Arcane Daughter carefully balances that which is safe but stultifying with that which is dangerous but filled with potential. Konigsburg can explore her characteristic concern with security and its effect on freedom subtly here, because *Father's Arcane Daughter* reads like a well-made play. The exploration is more in the complexities of the events the books describes than in complex statements of their meaning. The meaning *is* the action; by choosing to tell of these complex events matter-of-factly, Konigsburg allows them to speak for themselves. While she does allow her characters to make statements about what it all means, they do not in fact entirely account for the novel's complexity. Winston says that his telling of the story "will be a string of incidents. Like the separate frames of a comic strip." Like a comic strip, the book is clearly drawn, succinctly detailed, episodic, filled with action, highly melodramatic—showing only the high points but doing it in a way that makes them seem like parables and implies the complexity of everything in between. In her review of this book in the *New York Times*, Natalie Babbitt suggested that "there is a great potential in what it almost says," and adds that Konigsburg should have actually written "the big adult novel it wants to be." But *Father's Arcane Daughter* is interesting exactly because it does *almost* say, because it is not that complicated, detailed adult novel. Konigsburg has found a way of communicating her rich perception of the subtleties in human relationships in a book that is surprisingly easy to read and to understand.

The same might be said of at least two of the five stories in *Throwing Shadows* (1979), which was nominated for an American Book Award. In all these stories, Konigsburg confidently describes children coming to hard terms with the difficulty of being themselves and with their ability to influence others. Avery of "The Catchee" must accept that he *is* a "catchee" and that he will never get away with anything. A lesser writer would have merely sympathized with his comic plight, but Konigsburg characteristically turns it into a source of moral strength: "It can make you very honest. . . . It can make you very brave." Ampara, the young Ecuadorian guide who tells the story "In the Village of the Weavers," guides her friend Antonio into being very brave, very honest—and very humble. Like most of Konigsburg's youngsters, Antonio has "a fine fire in his brain" and must face the dangers of arrogance. Conversely, young William in "With Bert and Ray" is surprised to learn that he and his mother are better at selling antiques than the self-styled experts who started them in the business; he also learns that he is a mature enough child to be understanding and generous about Bert and Ray's adult childishness about "being beat out by Ma."

The other two stories in the collection impressively explore the subtler implications of similar situations. In both "At the Home" and "On Shark's Tooth Beach," children confront the inadequacies of childish adults and learn how to cope with them both humbly and humanely. President Bob of "On Shark's Tooth Beach" is a retired university president incapable of seeing young Ned or his Oriental mother as anything but a child and an Oriental. Ned hates President Bob's arrogance enough to compete with him in finding shark's teeth, but when Ned finds part of a shark's jaw, the ultimate trophy, he realizes he has himself become what he despised in the very act of combatting it; "if his face was a movie called *Jealousy and Greed*, I didn't like the words I could put to mine." Ned's real triumph is an act of humility; he gives President Bob the trophy, and Bob childishly gloats over "the jawbone with which he had been smitten." Ned wins by being willing to lose; but he does clearly win. In "At the Home," Phillip wins too. The old woman whose life story he tape-records is not anything like President Bob. In fact, Phillip finds her fascinating and quickly gets past his original idea that old people are all alike and all boring. But ironically, each of the old people in the home assumes that all of the other old people are all alike and all boring; Phillip realizes he must show them they are wrong. Once again a child transcends childish egocentricity and, in doing so, discovers that he knows better and can act with more maturity than childishly egocentric adults.

Journey to an 800 Number (1982) is an accomplished variation on Konigsburg's familiar themes. A novel about a boy from a ritzy private school who spends a summer with his post-hippie father escorting a camel to shopping malls and conventions and who has strange encounters along the way with a wild assortment of eccentrics, this book might well seem strange to those who have read nothing else by Konigsburg; but those who know her work will easily recognize her distinctive style and her usual thematic concerns. Like the central characters in all of Konigsburg's later work, Maximilian R. Stubbs wittily tells his own story. Also like many of Konigsburg's protagonists, Max is a victim of an overprotected life, but he is more like Ben of (*George*) or Winston of *Father's Arcane Daughter* than like Claudia of *From the Mixed-Up Files of Mrs. Basil E. Frankweiler* or Andy of *The Dragon in the Ghetto Caper;* rather than feel constrained and seek escape from the confines of his safe life, Max actively seeks safety and confinement. As he finally admits to himself late in the novel, "I had never thought of myself as strange; I can honestly say that I have spent all my time that I can remember trying not to be strange. Trying to be as normal as everyone else at Fortnum Preparatory School for Boys."

Of course, Max is not normal; one of the underlying themes of Konigsburg's fiction is that nobody is normal—that we are all different from each other, and that wise people enjoy the differences. *Journey to an 800 Number* is the story of Max's voyage into a perception and acceptance of his own strangeness and, along with that, his acceptance and enjoyment of the strangeness of others.

Max learns from the best teacher; simply having the experience of meeting new and unusual people and liking them for what they are. Indeed, what most distinguishes this novel from Konigsburg's other books is the rich feast of weird people she offers the reader: former and current hippies, trailer-park dwellers, sexy school librarians, midgets, taco-stand operators, and even a world famous Las Vegas star.

Max comes to understand what he has learned—and as a result, Konigsburg makes it explicit for her readers—through conversations with Sabrina, a young girl he meets along the way. Max is attracted to Sabrina even though, as he says, "she was as skinny as a ball point pen and as straight"; so he is both confused and delighted when she and

her mother keep showing up at different conventions with different names on their name tags. Max finally learns the truth—that, unable to afford a holiday, Sabrina's mother Lily has managed to arrange one by sneaking into conventions without paying. Lily works for most of the year as an operator at an 800 number, accepting telephone orders: "It is the most anonymous job in the world, speaking to people you'll never know and who will never know you. Always available. Always a polite voice. Never a face. Never a personality. Never a before. Never an after." Lily's job has trained her to be the perfect conventioneer; perfectly anonymous, in no way different, she blends in equally well with groups of travel agents or members of a sorority. In fact, Lily and her 800 number anonymity represent the essence of what Max aspires to—she is exactly "as normal as everyone else."

Max comes to realize the negative implications of that as he talks to Sabrina about "freaks." Sabrina collects information about people with unique problems; they fascinate her because of their inability ever to be anonymous. As Sabrina says, "Maximilian, what you don't seem to understand is that once you're a freak, a born one or a man-made one, anything you do that's normal becomes freakish." Max's response is, "By your logic, then, anything freakish that a freak does is normal." To be a freak is directly antithetical to being an 800 number. At work, Lily has no choice but to be anonymous, and, as Sabrina says, freaks have no choice but to be freakish: "Everyone wants to pretend sometime. Needs to. But freaks like David who lives in a bubble or the Crisco Kid or Renee cannot. They cannot live with disguises. . . . I'm telling you, Max, only freaks have to live without disguises." In other words, everyone but freaks and "800 numbers" has a choice—to try to be anonymous and normal, or to accept one's own particular difference from others, one's tendency to freakishness, and not disguise it in anonymity: "Only normal people like you and me and Lily and Woody have any choice about whether or not we want to present ourselves or present a disguise."

Max only hears this at the end of the novel—after he has begun to realize how it might relate to his own situation. At the beginning he has made a choice; by the end, he has come to see what is wrong with it. Throughout, however, Konigsburg has cleverly implied what is wrong with Max's choice by paradoxically suggesting that it is his desire to be "normal" that makes him a freak. His desperate attempt to deny anything about himself that might be considered strange is a symbolic form of amputation; since he sees Woody, his father, as representing everything his school does not stand for, he tries to detest him. He accepts only those aspects of himself that he associates with his mother, who left his father and the camel because, she said, "I want a dog and a house. And meals from china plates instead of from Styrofoam containers. I don't want a life that is tied to a camel." Because his mother gave him the name Maximilian, he insists on it, and refuses to accept his father's name for him: Bo, short for Rainbow.

Having tried to cut off anything interesting and unusual about himself, Max is like the talented flute player Renee, whose hand was cut off by a subway train and who has had it sewn on again. Sabrina's comment about Renee early in the novel is good advice for Max: "No one knows if she can ever play the flute again. But you should always remember to put any part that's cut off—even if it's just a finger—into a plastic bag and take it to the hospital with you." As the novel progresses, Max rediscovers his amputated part; finally, he learns to live with the horrifying fact that he loves his father and can "just enjoy being his son"—even after he finds out that Woody is not in fact his biological father.

While it is brilliantly witty and enjoyably eccentric, there is nothing particularly new in *Journey to an 800 Number;* it has the same qualities as the best of Konigsburg's writing. It is humorously told by its young central character with Konigsburg's fine ear for the way people talk. The narrator starts out misunderstanding something, so that he is blind to various ironies in his situation; someone wiser (and female) shows him the way to better understanding by knowing what to value. Like many previous Konigsburg protagonists, Max leaves the safety of childhood for the tougher insecurity of maturity. He grows into a deeper consciousness of human individuality, his own and others, that makes him humble but that does not allow him to deny his own personality. And here as in all of Konigsburg's writing, the ironies only go so far; her characters typically grow beyond their original flawed understanding into a clear, unironic perception of the truth. Her stories typically start as satiric comedies and end as serious moral parables; like Benjamin Dickinson Carr of *(George)*, they hide the essence of their meaning under a safe veneer of cleverness, until circumstances force it to emerge. As a result, Konigsburg's biggest strength is also her most damaging weakness; her subtle perception of moral truths sometimes makes her overstate those truths.

Elaine Konigsburg continues to live in Jacksonville, where she moved in 1968. Her family has grown up; her youngest child, Ross, graduated from college in the spring of 1981. She spends her time, she says, drawing, painting, and gardening: "I have a small garden of wild things, plants that I've dug up from the fields around my house. I like to walk along the beach, and I like to think, and I like to read." Above all, she keeps writing; Atheneum published her twelfth book, *Up From Jericho Tel*, in the spring of 1986. The story of an encounter between some eccentric children and the ghost of a dead actress named Tallulah, it shares many of the best characteristics of her earlier work. It is messy and intriguing, filled with clearly etched characters, subtle moral dilemmas, and sharp wit.

References:

Carol Billman, "Young and Old Alike: The Place of Old Women in Two Recent Novels for Children," *Children's Literature Association Quarterly*, 8 (Spring 1983): 6-8, 31;

Jean Karl, "Elaine L. Konigsburg," *Library Journal* (15 March 1968);

E. A. Kimmel, "Jewish Identity in Juvenile Fiction: A Look at Three Recommended Books," in *Crosscurrents of Criticism: Horn Book Essays 1968-1977*, edited by Paul Heins (Boston: Horn Book, 1977);

Lee Kingman, ed., *Newbery and Caldecott Medal Books 1966-75* (Boston: Horn Book, 1975);

David Rees, "Your Arcane Novelist—E. L. Konigsburg: An English Viewpoint," *Horn Book*, 54 (February 1978): 79-85.

Ruth Krauss

(25 July 1911-   )

Prabha Gupta Sharma

BOOKS: *A Good Man and His Good Wife,* illustrated by Ad Reinhardt (New York & London: Harper, 1944);

The Carrot Seed, illustrated by Crockett Johnson (New York & London: Harper, 1945);

The Great Duffy, illustrated by Richter (New York & London: Harper, 1946);

The Growing Story, illustrated by Phyllis Rowand (New York: Harper, 1947);

Bears, illustrated by Rowand (New York: Harper, 1948);

The Happy Day, illustrated by Marc Simont (New York: Harper, 1949);

The Big World and the Little House, illustrated by Simont (New York: Schuman, 1949);

The Backward Day, illustrated by Simont (New York: Harper, 1950; London: Hamilton, 1950);

I Can Fly, illustrated by Mary Blair (New York: Simon & Schuster, 1950);

The Bundle Book, illustrated by Helen Stone (New York: Harper, 1951);

A Hole is to Dig: A First Book of First Definitions, illustrated by Maurice Sendak (New York: Harper, 1952; London: Hamilton, 1963);

A Very Special House, illustrated by Sendak (New York: Harper, 1953);

I'll Be You and You Be Me, illustrated by Sendak (New York: Harper, 1954);

How To Make An Earthquake, illustrated by Johnson (New York: Harper, 1954);

Charlotte and the White Horse, illustrated by Sendak (New York: Harper, 1955; London: Bodley Head, 1977);

Is This You?—How to Write an Autobiography, by Krauss and Johnson (New York: Scott, 1955; London: Initial Teaching, 1965);

I Want to Paint My Bathroom Blue, illustrated by Sendak (New York: Harper, 1956);

Monkey Day, illustrated by Rowand (New York: Harper, 1957);

The Birthday Party, illustrated by Sendak (New York: Harper, 1957);

Somebody Else's Nut Tree, and Other Tales from Children, illustrated by Sendak (New York: Harper, 1958);

A Moon or a Button: A Collection of First Picture Ideas, illustrated by Remy Charlip (New York: Harper, 1959);

Open House for Butterflies, illustrated by Sendak (New York: Harper, 1960; London: Hamilton, 1960);

Mama, I Wish I Was Snow; Child You'd Be Very Cold, illustrated by Ellen Raskin (New York: Atheneum, 1962);

A Bouquet of Littles, illustrated by Jane Flora (New York: Harper & Row, 1963);

Eyes, Nose, Fingers, Toes, illustrated by Elizabeth Schneider (New York: Harper & Row, 1964);

Ruth Krauss

228

The Cantilever Rainbow, illustrated by Antonio Frasconi (New York: Pantheon, 1965);

What a Fine Day for . . . , illustrated by Charlip; music by Carmines (New York: Parents' Magazine Press, 1967);

The Happy Egg, illustrated by Johnson (New York: Scholastic, 1967);

Everything Under a Mushroom, illustrated by Margot Tomes (New York: Four Winds, 1967);

This Thumbprint: Words and Thumbprints (New York: Harper & Row, 1967);

The Little King, the Little Queen, the Little Monster and Other Stories You Can Make Up Yourself (Chicago: Whitman, 1968);

There's A Little Ambiguity Among the Bluebells and Other Theater Poems (New York: Something Else Press, 1968);

If Only (Eugene, Oreg.: Toad Press, 1969);

I Write It, illustrated by Mary Chalmers (New York: Harper & Row, 1970);

Under Twenty (Eugene, Oreg.: Toad Press, 1970);

This Breast Gothic (Lenox, Mass.: Bookstore Press, 1973);

Love and the Invention of Punctuation (Lenox, Mass.: Bookstore Press, 1973);

Little Boat Lighter Than a Cork, illustrated by Ester Gilman (Weston, Conn.: Magic Circle, 1976);

Under Thirteen (Lenox, Mass.: Bookstore Press, 1976);

When I Walk I Change the Earth (Providence, R.I.: Burning Deck Press, 1978);

Somebody Spilled the Sky, illustrated by Eleanor Hazard (New York: Greenwillow, 1979);

Minnestrone (New York: Greenwillow, 1981);

Re-examination of Freedom (West Branch, Iowa: Toothpaste Press, 1981).

Ruth Krauss, an outstanding and prolific writer of children's stories, was born in Baltimore, Maryland, in 1911, the daughter of Julius and Blanche Rosenfeld Krauss. She was educated in public elementary schools and graduated from the Parsons School of Fine and Applied Art in New York City. She has also attended the Peabody Institute of Music in Baltimore where she studied art and music; she plays both the violin and the piano. She has participated in poetry workshops at the New School of Social Research in New York and has taken classes at the Maryland Institute of Art in Baltimore. Krauss has also studied anthropology at Columbia University, though she has noted that much of her writing "is tied in with the graphic arts." Krauss has undergone psychoanalysis and attended group and individual therapy sessions,

which together with her study of art, music, and anthropology have helped to make her an insightful writer.

In 1941 Ruth Krauss married David Johnson Leisk, who died in 1975. Under the pseudonym Crockett Johnson, he was the well-known comic strip artist who created "Barnaby," and the writer-illustrator of the famous "Harold" series, beginning with *Harold and the Purple Crayon* (1958). Crockett Johnson began his career by illustrating his wife's children's book *The Carrot Seed* (1945) and also collaborated with her on three other works. The work habits of husband and wife varied; Crockett Johnson declared that he could "work any hour of the day," whereas Ruth Krauss described herself as "haphazard, flighty and eccentric. I'm fresher in the morning and like to work on the kitchen table."

Since the early 1940s Ruth Krauss has written steadily and profusely. She has to her credit more than thirty books for children and almost as many plays in verse. She has explored the world of chil-

Dust jacket for a later edition of Krauss's second picture book, which her husband David Leisk (Crockett Johnson) illustrated (Harper & Row)

dren creatively and sensitively, trying to find expression for their whimsical, wonderful world. A measure of the appeal of her books lies in the fact that they are in great demand from children's collections in libraries. Krauss has devoted much of her later career to poetry.

Ruth Krauss persistently and carefully looks into the elusive world of children. She draws inspiration from children's fantasies, desires, word play, and sense of humor. In her books the text interacts with the illustrations; Krauss's messages may be cryptic, but intelligible, creative, and refreshing. She is credited with having "probably gone further than any other author in experimenting with the form and content of picture books," resulting in a near perfect blending of words and illustrations.

Ruth Krauss's first work, *A Good Man and His Good Wife* (1944), illustrated by Ad Reinhardt, is a folktale about a married couple and their domestic life. The story of a child's confidence in the planting and growing of a carrot, her second book, *The Carrot Seed,* has a brief text, though each sentence or line carries an image, perfect for picture books. *The*

Dust jacket for Krauss's picture book of a child's observations of his own growth and his comparisons of it to the growth of plants and animals (Harper)

Growing Story (1947) follows a child's observations of his own growth and his comparisons of it to the growth of plants and animals. At first disappointed that he is not growing, he tries on his winter clothes from the year before and realizes that they no longer fit.

Bears (1948) has fewer words than *The Carrot Seed,* but its rhymes, illustrations, and plot, concerning bears in extraordinary situations, are delightfully entertaining, appealing, and intelligible to a child. *The Happy Day* (1949), a spontaneous book about animals sleeping, awaking, sniffing, running, laughing, and dancing, and sometimes stopping to see a flower growing in the snow, subtly shows the influence of Ruth Krauss's musical training: as the reviewer for the *Chicago Sun* noted, it contains "a rhythm . . . beginning softly, wakening to swift movement, swelling to a crescendo, then pausing to a note of gasping laughter." In *The Backward Day* (1950) a small boy decides to do everything backward—dress backward, walk backward—until he decides "Backward day is gone." In letting her characters indulge in such fantasies as the "backward day" and the "secret" lives of bears and other animals, Ruth Krauss demonstrates her intuitive understanding of the games children play.

From this initial stage of writing mainly for entertainment, Krauss progressed to more inward-looking books in the 1950s. In 1952 she published *A Hole is to Dig: A First Book of First Definitions,* based on the humorous, unexpected definitions children often give things and actions they do not understand. With illustrations by Maurice Sendak this was a landmark book. The observations that "a face is so you can make faces," "a dream is to look at the night and see things," "dogs are to kiss people," or "mud is to jump in and slide in and yell doodlee doodlee doo" make reading the book a funny and touching experience.

A Very Special House (1953) depicts a child's dream world. In it Krauss includes the fantastic things a small boy would want to do in a house; some that most adults would disapprove of—writing on walls, climbing on chairs, swinging on doors, and jumping on beds. In the mad confusion which follows, one knows that the boy was fooling anyway, and the "child readers can gain a harmless release of his disapproved desires on the verbal imaginative scale." *I'll Be You and You Be Me* (1954) contains themes of loving, liking, dreaming, wishing, and wanting happiness which give the book a sense of release, reinforced by Sendak's illustrations. All these books show a close collaboration between author and illustrator. Freedom of ideas is suggested in the freedom of action conveyed in the characters' smiles, scowls, and antics.

Charlotte and the White Horse (1955), the emotional story of a poetic girl and her horse, Milky Way, profits from Sendak's imaginative illustrations, which give it a fairy-tale quality. In this story Ruth Krauss demonstrates her sensitivity to the sorrow and happiness of children, who should find special pleasure in watching Milky Way grow from a colt to a young horse.

In later works Krauss continued to experiment with the ideas and thoughts of children: *Is This You?—How to Write an Autobiography* (1955) is a different how-to book, especially suited to preschoolers and a book that parents would find perfect for a rainy day. *I Want to Paint My Bathroom Blue* (1956) presents the fantasy of a little boy about how he would make a perfect house. *The Birthday Party* (1957) is the story of a boy who has been everywhere except to a party. One day he comes home and finds the house deserted except for the dining room, where there is a birthday party awaiting him.

Whereas her early books had been well received by readers and critics, the late 1950s was a transition period for Krauss, and her works received mixed reviews. *Monkey Day* (1957), a rollicking tale with various types of monkeys "monkeying" around, was criticized for repetitiousness. *Somebody Else's Nut Tree, and Other Tales from Children* (1958), consisting of eighteen short stories reworked from the words of children, was considered uneven in quality and Sendak's illustrations were also deemed unsatisfying. *A Moon or a Button: A Collection of First Picture Ideas* (1959) is a collection of pictorial jokes and fancies inspired in part by a group of school children, including such amusingly titled pictures as "A Witch's Valentine"—a heart with a jack-o-lantern face—and "Kisses drying"—a row of Xs hanging from a clothesline. It was a new idea, but Krauss was criticized for not having used children themselves as illustrators.

After this period Ruth Krauss's work began to reflect more of her poetic talent. *Open House for Butterflies* (1960), written in childlike, descriptive sentences and illustrated by Sendak, was praised more for its amusing miniature line drawings than for its text. *Mama, I Wish I Was Snow; Child You'd Be Very Cold* (1962) is a translation of a Spanish poem in which a mother and child converse, the child wishing impossible things and the mother providing sensible reasons why such desires might not be as pleasant as anticipated. The woodcut il-

lustrations by Ellen Raskin complement the text, though some critics thought the book was not relevant for most American children. In *Everything Under a Mushroom* (1967), a big beige mushroom stands at the center of each two-page spread, and above it runs a line of rhyming words, such as "little one little two little cow little moo," while below it a group of children are drawn acting out and commenting on the illustrations above. A world of whimsy is created, but according to the *New York Times Book Review*, "the pages were laid out confusingly and there was no path for the eye to follow with ease."

With *I Write It* (1970), an illustrated poem about writing one's name in likely, unlikely, and impossible places, Ruth Krauss created a poetic text which conveys a child's fresh delight and pride in being able to write his name. Mary Chalmers's illustrations of small, gay, endearing creatures produce a wonderfully visual poem for children and adults.

In recent years Ruth Krauss has written less for children; though two works, *Little Boat Lighter Than a Cork* (1976) and *Minnestrone* (1981), have appeared within the past ten years. *Little Boat Lighter Than a Cork* is the story of a walnut-shell craft in which a baby sails on a fantasy voyage. The infant passenger says to the boat, "I will rock you for the small streams and big rivers and for dolphins . . . ," a litany which is interrupted by the observation of "a red apple popping out of the water or is it the sun." Such unique insights have continued to make Krauss enjoyable to her many readers. *Minnestrone* is a collection of short plays, adult-interest verse, "thumbprint" characters, and excerpts from previous children's books. *Minnestrone* was called "facile and shallow" by the reviewer in *School Library Journal*, who considered it to be "childish" and "filled with forced whimsey."

At present Ruth Krauss devotes her talent largely to "poem-plays." She has long been a serious student of poetry and comments that her plays are approached from the words themselves, rather than from ideas or plot. Many of these plays have been performed in the New York area and by university drama departments. Performances by the Hardware Poets in Manhattan have been characterized as "little exploding comic pellets which appeared, exploded and disappeared in dazzling succession for many long minutes," as "delightful charmers" and as "comic energy organisms, dramatic meteorites which lasted long enough to be retained forever in the spirit."

Dust jacket for Krauss's 1979 collection of poetry in picture-book format (Greenwillow)

As an interpreter of children's thoughts and ideas, Ruth Krauss has explored the whimsical, the comical, and the fantastic. Her mission in the field of children's literature has been to look into the thoughts and minds of children and then express their experiences in a delicate and sophisticated manner that makes the fragile and imaginary world of children real and acceptable. Throughout her career, Krauss has provided introspective entertainment and poetry for children. Her writing is a rewarding experience—subtle, sensitive, dynamic, and a significant influence in children's literature.

References:

Barbara Bader, ed., *American Picture Books: From Noah's Ark to the Beast Within* (New York: Macmillan, 1976), pp. 416-433;

Books Are By People: Interviews with 104 Authors and Illustrators of Books for Youngsters (New York: Citation Press, 1969), pp. 121-124.

Ursula K. Le Guin

(21 October 1929-   )

Andrew Gordon
University of Florida

See also the Le Guin entry in *DLB 8: Twentieth Century American Science Fiction Writers.*

BOOKS: *Rocannon's World* (New York: Ace, 1966; London: Tandem, 1972);

Planet of Exile (New York: Ace, 1966; London: Tandem, 1972);

City of Illusions (New York: Ace, 1967; London: Gollancz, 1971);

A Wizard of Earthsea (Berkeley: Parnassus, 1968; London: Gollancz, 1971);

The Left Hand of Darkness (New York: Ace, 1969; London: Macdonald, 1969);

Ursula K. Le Guin (photo by Lisa Kroeber)

The Tombs of Atuan (New York: Atheneum, 1971; London: Gollancz, 1972);

The Lathe of Heaven (New York: Scribners, 1971; London: Gollancz, 1972);

The Farthest Shore (New York: Atheneum, 1972; London: Gollancz, 1973);

From Elfland to Poughkeepsie (Portland, Oreg.: Pendragon, 1973);

The Dispossessed (New York: Harper & Row, 1974; London: Gollancz, 1974);

The Wind's Twelve Quarters (New York: Harper & Row, 1975; London: Gollancz, 1976);

Wild Angels (Santa Barbara, Cal.: Capra Press, 1975);

The Word for World is Forest (New York: Berkley, 1976; London: Gollancz, 1977);

Very Far Away from Anywhere Else (New York: Atheneum, 1976); republished as *A Very Long Way from Anywhere Else* (London: Gollancz, 1976);

Orsinian Tales (New York: Harper & Row, 1976; London: Gollancz, 1977);

The Language of the Night: Essays on Fantasy and Science Fiction, edited by Susan Wood (New York: Berkley/Putnam's, 1979);

Malafrena (New York: Putnam's, 1979);

Leese Webster (New York: Atheneum, 1979);

The Beginning Place (New York: Harper & Row, 1980); republished as *Threshold* (London: Gollancz, 1980);

Hard Words, and Other Poems (New York: Harper, 1981);

Compass Rose (New York: Harper, 1982);

Always Coming Home (New York: Harper, 1985).

OTHER: "Solomon Leviathan's Nine Hundred and Thirty-First Trip Around the World," in *Puffin's Pleasures*, edited by Kuye Webb and Treld Bicknell (Harmondsworth, U.K.: Puffin, 1976);

Nebula Award Stories Eleven, edited by Le Guin (New York: Harper, 1977);

Interfaces: An Anthology of Speculative Fiction, edited by Le Guin and Virginia Kidd (New York: Ace, 1980);

Edges: Thirteen New Tales from the Borderlands of the Imagination, edited by Le Guin and Kidd (New York: Pocket Books, 1980).

Ursula K. Le Guin is a writer of great versatility and power, acclaimed for her science fiction, fantasy, and children's literature. All her fiction is distinguished by careful craftsmanship, a limpid prose style, realistic detail in the creation of imaginary worlds, profound ethical concerns, and mythical reverberations created through the use of symbolic and archetypal patterns. Her typical story involves a hero's quest for maturity and psychological integration, and her major theme is the need for balance and wholeness. She is best known for the Earthsea trilogy (*A Wizard of Earthsea,* 1968; *The Tombs of Atuan,* 1971; *The Farthest Shore,* 1972), three novels concerning the career of the Wizard Ged in an imaginary land called Earthsea. The award-winning fantasy trilogy has been frequently and favorably compared with Tolkien's *Lord of the Rings* and C. S. Lewis's *Narnia* series. In her critical essays, collected in *The Language of the Night* (1979), Le Guin champions the humanizing power of the imagination and asserts that fantasy can be a moral force for both children and adults.

Ursula K. Le Guin was born in Berkeley, California, in 1929, the youngest of four children and the only daughter of Alfred and Theodora Kroeber. Her father was a renowned professor of anthropology, an expert on California Indians; her mother was an author in her own right, with several children's books published by Parnassus Press, but best known for *Ishi in Two Worlds* (1961), the biography of the last "wild" Indian in North America. Le Guin grew up in Berkeley in a secure and intellectually stimulating environment. Her parents were progressive and nonsexist in childrearing. The house was filled with books, and her father was frequently visited by major figures in anthropology and other fields. She claims that her parents' careers in anthropology strongly influenced her writing: "My father studied real cultures and I make them up—in a way, it's the same thing."

As a child, Le Guin wanted to be a biologist and a poet. She read widely as a youngster, preferring Frazer's *Golden Bough,* Norse myths, and science fiction magazines, though she temporarily lost interest in science fiction as she matured. As she explained in *The Language of the Night,* "it seemed to be all about hardware and soldiers." Lord Dunsany's *A Dreamer's Tales,* which she encountered at age twelve, was a revelation to her, making her realize that grownups were still creating myths. It opened up to her "the Inner Lands" which she calls "my native country."

Le Guin wrote her first fantasy story at nine, about a man persecuted by evil elves, and submitted her first science fiction, a story about time travel that she wrote when she was ten or eleven, to *Amazing Stories.* It was rejected, but *Amazing Stories* was to publish her first science fiction over twenty years later. She received a B.A., Phi Beta Kappa, from Radcliffe in 1951 and an M.A. in French and Italian Renaissance literature from Columbia in 1952. On a Fulbright to France in 1953, she met and married a fellow Fulbrighter, history professor Charles A. Le Guin. She abandoned graduate studies to raise a family: the Le Guins have three children and reside in Portland, Oregon.

By the early 1960s, Le Guin had published a few poems and one story in little magazines, but she also had five unpublished novels, written over ten years, mostly set in the imaginary central European country of Orsinia. She turned to science fiction at that point out of a desire to be published, and she says that her early work in that genre was beginner's writing. Nevertheless, her work quickly grew in power. She is now recognized as one of the most significant living science fiction writers and has won the highest accolades of that field, including several Hugo and Nebula awards, and a great deal of critical attention. At first, she used little science and so wrote "fairy tales decked out in space suits," redeemed, however, by her "long apprenticeship in poetry and in the psychologically realistic kind of novel." The writers she most admires are Dickens, Tolstoy, Tolkien, Virginia Woolf, and the Brontës. With *The Wizard of Earthsea,* she began to separate her pure fantasy (the "Inner Lands") from her science fiction ("Outer Space") and has continued to write in both genres ever since.

Le Guin's philosophy of writing fantasy for children is also explained in *The Language of the Night.* She believes that Americans have a moral disapproval of fantasy "which comes from fear" and is related to "our Puritanism, our work ethic, our profit-mindedness, and even our sexual mores." As a result, Americans are taught "to repress their imagination, to reject it as something childish or effeminate, unprofitable, and probably sinful." Le Guin's credo is just the opposite: "I believe that maturity is not an outgrowing, but a growing up: that an adult is not a dead child, but a child who survived. I believe that all the best faculties of a mature human being exist in the child, and that if these faculties are encouraged in youth they will act well and wisely in the adult, but if they are

Dust jackets for the first and final volumes in Le Guin's Earthsea trilogy. The first part of the trilogy was published by Parnassus, the second and third by Atheneum.

repressed and denied in the child they will stunt and cripple the adult personality." For that reason, she believes it is the "pleasant duty" of librarians, teachers, parents, and writers to stimulate and encourage the humanizing power of the imagination "by giving it the best, absolutely the best and purest, nourishment that it can absorb."

In her National Book Award Acceptance Speech (given for *The Farthest Shore*), Le Guin praised fantasy as the best means of communicating in fiction with both children and adults: "At this point, realism is perhaps the least adequate means of understanding or portraying the incredible realities of our existence. . . . The fantasist, whether he uses the ancient archetypes of myth and legend or the younger ones of science and technology, may be talking as seriously as any sociologist—and a good deal more directly—about human life as it is lived, and as it might be lived, and as it ought to be lived. For, after all, as great scientists have said and as all children know, it is above all by the imag-

ination that we achieve perception, compassion, and hope."

Le Guin claims that she doesn't plan her works but must discover them in her subconscious. The discovery of Earthsea began with a story about a wizard, "The Word of Unbinding," published in *Fantastic* in 1964. A later story, "The Rule of Names," developed both the islands of Earthsea and the rules of its magic and introduced a dragon. In 1967 Herman Schein, publisher of Parnassus Press in Berkeley, California, wanted to branch out from the young juvenile market and asked Le Guin to write a book for older children. Schein gave her complete freedom of subject and approach. Le Guin returned to the imaginary islands of Earthsea she had discovered and wrote *A Wizard of Earthsea*, which was published in 1968. The second volume of the Earthsea trilogy, *The Tombs of Atuan*, followed three years later. *The Farthest Shore* completed the series in 1972. Although each novel can be read independently, the same themes and images reverberate through all three, and they form a unit which is greater than the mere sum of the parts.

The trilogy covers the youth, young manhood, and old age of the Wizard Ged, who rises from goatherd to become Archmage of all Earthsea. We are told at the beginning of *A Wizard of Earthsea* that the hero will become famous in song and legend. He is a mythic hero, and the trilogy follows many of the traditional patterns of myth: the orphan hero of obscure origins, the early evidence of his great powers, the wizard who guides him, his struggle with inner demons, the quest, and the initiation whereby he is made whole and comes into full possession of his powers. Aside from the borrowings from standard myth, the trilogy shows a decided Jungian influence, which many critics have noted, though the author denies having read Jung at that time. Eleanor Cameron, in *Horn Book*, labeled *A Wizard of Earthsea* "high fantasy," the kind which deals with cosmic issues, and mentioned that Ged's pursuit by his "shadow," or repressed dark side of his character, is related to Jungian thought. Le Guin wrote at length about her admiration of Jung's wisdom several years later.

Other critics have mentioned the possible influences on the trilogy of Tolkien, George MacDonald, M. R. James, and C. S. Lewis's fantasies, although Le Guin has been praised for her "original allegory" which, Naomi Lewis said in the *Times Literary Supplement*, has none of the "theological quiddities of C. S. Lewis." In fact, Le Guin creates a world without a deity, although magic exists, along with tremendous powers for good and evil. Hers is a modern, existential, humanistic universe where the weight of responsibility rests on the individual to act wisely, for by acting otherwise he can imperil the balance of the world. As Ged is taught at the school for wizards on Roke Island, " 'you must not change one thing, one pebble, one grain of sand, until you know what good and evil will follow on that act. The world is in balance, in Equilibrium. A wizard's power of Changing and Summoning can shake the balance of the world. It is dangerous, that power. It is most perilous. It must follow knowledge, and serve need. To light a candle is to cast a shadow. . . . ' " In the emphasis in the trilogy on balance—of good and evil, light and dark, life and death—many critics have seen the influence of Taoist notions of dynamic equilibrium, of the necessity for a balance of yin and yang.

The plot of *A Wizard of Earthsea* concerns the disastrous consequences of power used unwisely, disturbing the Equilibrium. Like the classic "sorcerer's apprentice," young Ged overreaches himself through pride and anger. While summoning up the spirits of the dead, he unleashes his own formless "shadow" and nearly dies from the encounter. Chastened, he completes his training; but once he leaves the protection of Roke, he is pursued across the world by the evil shadow. He is tempted twice to gain power over the shadow (that is, to learn its name) by allying himself with the forces of evil, but both times he refuses the temptation. Then his old mentor, the wizard Ogion, advises him to turn from hunted to hunter and seek out the shadow. After many adventures, he finally confronts the shadow on the open sea and calls it by its name: *Ged*, his own name. By accepting and embracing his dark side as part of himself, Ged is made whole and becomes a man.

What the child needs to grow up, Le Guin asserted in *The Language of the Night*, "is reality, the wholeness which exceeds all our virtue and all our vice. He needs knowledge; he needs self-knowledge. He needs to see himself and the shadow he casts. That is something he can face, his own shadow, and he can learn to control it and to be guided by it." Le Guin sees fantasy as a psychic and a moral journey "to self-knowledge, to adulthood, to the light." The goal of that journey is psychic wholeness. *A Wizard of Earthsea* succeeds as myth, as moral allegory, and as vivid adventure story. It received the Boston Globe-Horn Book Award and was named an American Library Association Notable Book.

The Tombs of Atuan concerns a feminine coming of age to match the masculine one of *A Wizard of Earthsea;* it focuses on the rite of passage of the adolescent Tenar. Tenar had the misfortune to be born the same day the old Priestess of the Tombs of Atuan died and so was hailed as her reincarnation. She is taken away from her parents, given the new name of "Arha," or "The Eaten One," and raised to become the next Priestess. The place of the Tombs is an unchanging, sterile, desert environment where no men are allowed, only females and eunuchs. Everything is consecrated to the perverse worship of death and the "Nameless Ones," the dark powers who inhabit the Tombs and the immense underground Labyrinth. The first third of the novel deals with the childhood apprenticeship of Tenar in this gloomy place, where her natural humanity is suppressed.

The adventure begins when Tenar, now an adolescent Priestess, discovers a light in the Labyrinth. It is Ged, seeking the lost half of the ancient Ring of the wizard Erreth-Akbe. The Ring contained a lost Rune of Wholeness; once the two halves of the broken Ring are brought together, wholeness and good government can be restored to Earthsea, and the wars may cease. But Ged has defiled the holy place. As Priestess, it is Tenar's duty to have him put to death. Nevertheless, she becomes fascinated by this man and keeps him imprisoned instead, thereby earning the enmity of Kossil, the Priestess of the Godking, who has the power to destroy Tenar. Eventually, Ged wins Tenar over. He tells her her original name, so that she can be reborn as a whole human being, and entrusts her with the restored Ring (which serves as a symbolic wedding ring for the two). Finally they escape from the Labyrinth with the Ring. An earthquake swallows the Tombs and the Labyrinth, and the worship of death and evil is ended.

The novel resonates with image patterns of silence versus sound, dark versus light, and death versus life. For example, Ged tells Tenar, "You were never made for cruelty and darkness; you were made to hold light, as a lamp burning holds and gives its light." Once again, Le Guin emphasizes the need for balance: darkness must be recognized and accepted as a part of the whole, but it must not be allowed to overwhelm the balance. The dark powers " 'should not be denied nor forgotten, but neither should they be worshiped. The Earth is beautiful, and bright, and dark, and cruel. . . . There are sharks in the sea, and there is cruelty in men's eyes. And where men worship these things and abase themselves before them, there evil breeds. . . . They exist. But they are not your Masters.' "

The Tombs of Atuan was a Newbery Honor Book and was nominated for the National Book Award for Children's Literature. Nevertheless, while beautifully written, it is the least entertaining novel of the trilogy, perhaps because Ged does not appear until the story is a third over and also because the unpleasant fairy-tale world of the Tombs is established with a gloomy, detailed realism that the upbeat ending cannot dissipate. Finally, Tenar is a less sympathetic character than Ged.

The Farthest Shore, a novel of epic scope, brings the trilogy to an exciting conclusion. It won the National Book Award for Children's Literature. If *A Wizard of Earthsea* concerns balance and wholeness on the individual level and *The Tombs of Atuan* concerns the union of two people, then *The Farthest Shore* extends the concern with Equilibrium to the entire cosmos. *The Tombs of Atuan* deals with the imbalance caused by worshiping death over life; *The Farthest Shore* shows the imbalance created by worshipping life over death.

As the novel opens, there is trouble in Earthsea, signified by ominous signs such as wizards forgetting their craft. Prince Arren of Enlad is sent by his father as a messenger to the Archmage Ged on Roke Island to inform him of the trouble in their region. Ged decides to go on a quest to find the source of the rapidly spreading decline, and he invites young Arren to accompany him. They sail first to Hort, a town with no laws or rulers. There Arren is sold into slavery and rescued by Ged. Next they travel to Lorbanery, an island of weavers who no longer weave. After Ged is wounded in a savage attack by the islanders of Obehol, he and Arren drift in their boat until they are saved by "the children of the open sea," a tribe of gentle raft people. Yet the decline reaches even there; the singers forget the words to their songs.

Finally, the dragon Orm Embar leads Ged and Arren to the deserted island of Selidor, "the westernmost cape of all the lands, the end of the earth." There Ged meets the anti-King, the Unmaker, the cause of all the trouble: the renegade wizard Cob. Cob made a spell to open the gate between life and death, so that no one will ever die. But in defeating death, he destroyed the Equilibrium and also defeated life, causing it to lose its savor and reality, lack a center, and become a hollow void. To defeat Cob, Ged and Arren must descend into the kingdom of death itself. There Ged shuts the door between the worlds of life and death. Arren guides and carries the exhausted Ged over the Mountains of Pain back into life. A dragon returns them to Roke. Ged then disappears on the dragon's back, his great task of restoring the Equilibrium done and his wizardry ended. Arren is acclaimed King of all Earthsea, having fulfilled the prophecies about a ruler who would return from the land of death.

The relationship between Arren and Ged is reminiscent of that between young Arthur and Merlin; and Arren, like Arthur, wields a magic sword, fulfills the prophecies, and unites the land. Ged has come full circle in the trilogy, from the young apprentice to the master who must pass his wisdom on to the next generation. In Ged's training of Arren, Le Guin gives us the fullest exposition of the necessity to learn to keep the balance of contraries and to do only what is necessary: " 'On every act the balance of the whole depends. . . . we must *learn* to do what the leaf and the whale and the wind do of their own nature. We must learn to keep the balance. Having intelligence, we must not act in ignorance. Having choice, we must not act without responsibility.' " Only man, of all creatures on earth, is capable of evil. But " 'in our shame is our glory. Only our spirit, which is capable of evil, is capable of overcoming it.' "

The *Earthsea* trilogy is the sort of fantasy which teaches about reality and is appropriate for all ages. Because it draws on the powerful, archetypal patterns of myth, the stories have an inevitability and an ethical and psychological truth. Le Guin's only failing is an occasional preachiness; not content to let the action speak for itself, she must elucidate the moral. Nevertheless, the trilogy works both as high fantasy and realistic epic adventure. It establishes the patterns of initiation, fine style, and ethical concern that can be seen in all of Le Guin's books for children, which, while not on the scale of the trilogy, are nonetheless worthy achievements.

Very Far Away from Anywhere Else (1976) is a rare Le Guin try at straight realism. It was named an American Library Association Notable Book for Young Adults. This contemporary love story about two adolescents is Le Guin's first attempt to deal in

fiction with the problems of adolescent sexuality. Central characters Owen Griffin and Natalie Field are teenagers in their senior year of high school, both extremely bright—he wants to be a scientist, she a composer—and consequently both misfits and loners in the local school, although Natalie is more self-confident and better adjusted than Owen. They are drawn together out of loneliness. Natalie has the confident assertiveness Owen lacks, and Owen has a sense of humor that brightens Natalie's severe, disciplined existence. They become best friends because they can understand and talk to each other. Problems arise when sex intrudes on their relationship, because neither is ready for it yet. Natalie kindly but firmly rejects Owen's blunt sexual aggression. Distraught, Owen drives recklessly and his car turns over on a curve. After he recovers from the accident, he finally stops being childishly angry at Natalie and they are reunited. In the end, as they go off to separate colleges, it seems likely they will remain friends and may one day mature into lovers. Meanwhile, both

Dust jacket for Le Guin's realistic love story about two adolescents drawn together by loneliness (Atheneum)

have grown and learned about life and themselves from the relationship. Owen learns to stop being scared of life, to accept himself as he is and thereby to accept others. Like all Le Guin's fiction, *Very Far Away from Anywhere Else* concerns the painful effort involved in becoming a whole human being.

Charlotte Spivack says that "Owen's voice is convincing, for what he discovers about himself is never filtered through an adult consciousness." Nevertheless, Owen is not as naive and funny as Holden Caulfield in J. D. Salinger's *The Catcher in the Rye*, and his problems seem minor compared to Holden's agony.

Leese Webster (1979), Le Guin's only fiction for young juveniles that is available in America, is a charming, wise little story about a spider. The delicate line drawings by illustrator James Brunsman, in black against a gold background, are appropriate for the intricate spiderwebs Leese weaves. Le Guin uses images of spiders, webs, and weaving throughout her works, with both positive and negative connotations, so this story is a logical extension of the concerns of the rest of her fiction. Moreover, little children can often identify with spiders, who are like children in certain positive ways: small, persistent, industrious, creative, and beneficial. Spiders are celebrated in nursery rhymes and in E. B. White's *Charlotte's Web*, which attests to the fascination they hold for children.

Leese Webster is a spider born in a deserted palace. She grows up alone, in the bedroom of a princess. At first, Leese spins her family's traditional webs, but then she begins to experiment with new patterns. Not all her experiments succeed, but she tries copying the patterns she sees around her in the paintings and carpets. The other spiders either ignore her webs or dismiss them as a waste of time. Nevertheless, Leese persists and begins creating successful original designs. But no matter how hard she tries, her webs are grey and cannot approach the beauty she remembers of the jewels on the throne, which had light inside them.

When the palace is cleaned to be made into a museum, Leese's webs amaze the authorities, who preserve them behind glass. Leese is saved by a cleaning lady, who says, " 'Never kill a spider. . . . It's bad luck,' " and drops Leese out the window. Leese's long plunge into the garden outside is traumatic, and she imagines herself to be dead. But it proves instead to be a rebirth into a marvelous new world. The stars appear to her like the jewels in the throne room. Flies are plentiful, so Leese no longer goes hungry. Best of all, Leese achieves her highest goal as an artist, for the light of sunrise on

the dewdrops clinging to her webs makes them shine "brighter than the jewels of the throne, brighter even than the stars." While the tourists admire her weavings inside the palace, Leese is happy with her "wild webs" outdoors, "shining with the jewels of the sun."

The story shows Le Guin's style, with its clarity and natural patterns of imagery, at its best. And though Le Guin omits the usual moralizing, the message of the story is nevertheless clear: it is a parable about the artist and her craft. It implies that the artist may suffer loneliness, neglect, and even ridicule, but it is worth persevering. The artist must constantly experiment to grow, even if those experiments do not always work. Leese triumphs through talent, hard work, and persistence. The final message of the story is that nature itself is the greatest work of art and that our own creations will shine brightest not as they copy other man-made things but as they approach the status of natural artifacts. Though the child reader may not register all these messages consciously, she will be encouraged by the story of Leese to persist in her own creative efforts, knowing that, although the rewards may be slow in coming, the effort is worthwhile in terms of self-fulfillment.

In addition to *Leese Webster*, Le Guin also wrote a story for young juveniles, "Solomon Leviathan's Nine Hundred and Thirty-First Trip Around the World" (1976), but it is only available in an English anthology, *Puffin's Pleasures*.

The Beginning Place (1980), Le Guin's most recent novel suitable for younger readers, demonstrates that, like her character Leese, she continues to experiment and weave totally original webs. While it was not marketed as children's literature, *The Beginning Place* is another Le Guin story of adolescent maturation and love, almost a companion piece (although far superior) to *Very Far Away from Anywhere Else*. Once again, we have male and female adolescent misfits who find companionship, love, and maturity together. Here, however, Le Guin creates a unique blending of realism and romantic fantasy. Her teenage hero and heroine escape from homes which are not real homes and families which are not real families into a fantasy world, "a good place." She returns to the mythic quest mode of the Earthsea trilogy but goes further in showing the complementary relationship between the fantasy world and our so-called real world.

The central characters of *The Beginning Place* are Hugh Rogers and Irene Pannis. Hugh wants to attend college and become a librarian, but he has stayed at home because of his possessive mother and worked as a supermarket checker. He lives in a development named Kensington Heights. "To get to Oak Valley Road, he crossed Loma Linda Drive, Raleigh Drive, Pine View Place, turned onto Kensington Avenue, crossed Chelsea Oaks Road. There were no heights, no valleys, no Raleighs, no oaks." Finally, Hugh runs away from home and discovers in the woods at the outskirts of the city a gateway into a land of perpetual twilight. In that land he finds a town called Tembreabrezi, which exemplifies a pastoral, ordered, medieval form of existence.

Irene has left home because of a stepfather who makes sexual advances toward her and has been living with a couple who are in the process of breaking up. She has vowed never to fall in love, associating it only with the power to inflict pain. Years before Hugh does, she has discovered Tembreabrezi and made an alternate home there with a tranquil, totally accepting substitute family. She idolizes the master of the town; he is both father and lover to her, for he seems to offer "desire without terror . . . love without effect, without penalty or pain. The only price was silence." But as she grows up, she finds it increasingly difficult to pass through the gateway.

When Irene discovers Hugh in Tembreabrezi, she resents him as an intruder on her secret land. However, the villagers hail Hugh as their long-awaited savior. The town has fallen under a curse: no one visits and the roads are closed. It all seems to be caused by some unnamed menace in the mountains. The Master tries to leave with Irene but cannot pass the borders of the town. Seeing his fear, Irene loses faith in him. Hugh accepts the sword of the Lord of the region and agrees to slay the menace because he wants to help the people and he has fallen in love—ironically, not with Irene, but with Allia, the Lord's daughter.

Hugh and Irene go into the mountains together to face the menace, just as Ged and Tenar threaded the Labyrinth hand in hand to restore wholeness to Earthsea. When Hugh finally slays the dragon, the act is vividly described in terms that suggest sexual intercourse and matricide. In a symbolic rebirth, the wounded Hugh is dragged out from under the dead creature by Irene. Together they find their way back to the city, where Hugh recovers from his wounds in a hospital.

In a rather abrupt ending, Hugh's mother refuses to let him come home, so Hugh and Irene take an apartment and decide to make a life together. Tenar in *The Tombs of Atuan* was also a child

without a home, and she ends up holding Ged's hand, "like a child coming home." In *The Beginning Place* Le Guin is extending the concerns of *The Tombs of Atuan*—coming of age, finding oneself, becoming whole, and coming home—and taking her characters the next step, into romantic love. As she does in all her fiction, Le Guin emphasizes in *The Beginning Place* the need to accept the pain and suffering involved in growing up and falling in love. By slaying the dragon, Hugh is symbolically slaying his mother and cutting the umbilical cord, readying himself for a painful rebirth. Arren in *The Farthest Shore* also had to cross the "Mountains of Pain" to return to life and win his kingship.

The achievement of *The Beginning Place* is its vivid, detailed realism, which brings alive both the plastic suburb and the haunting twilight land and makes us believe in the possibility of crossing the threshold between the two. The "real" world and the "fantastic" one are coexisting and complementary: the people of Tembreabrezi need Hugh and Irene to save them, and the young couple in turn need Tembreabrezi so that they may find themselves and grow up. Le Guin's writing in *The Beginning Place* has her characteristic purity and clarity and is frequently lyrical. She shows an admirable new restraint in not spelling out her moral for the reader but allowing the story to speak for itself.

The critic Peter Nicholls has praised Le Guin for bringing to the field of science fiction "an intelligent and feeling use of image structures, in the manner of a poet" and "the interest of the traditional novelist in questions of character and moral growth." She brings these same talents to the fields of fantasy and children's literature. Le Guin has great gifts as a writer; she has been lauded by many critics for her style, her adaptation of mythic structures, her psychological insight, and her moral wisdom.

Having mastered high fantasy, Le Guin has moved on to straight realism, fantasy for juveniles, and a unique blend of realism and romantic fantasy. The Earthsea trilogy is her finest work thus far, but as her later works indicate, she is continuing to experiment with different modes of writing and to grow in artistic range.

References:

James W. Bittner, *Approaches to the Fiction of Ursula K. Le Guin* (Ann Arbor: University of Michigan Research Press, 1984);

Barbara J. Bucknall, *Ursula K. Le Guin* (New York: Ungar, 1981);

Eleanor Cameron, "High Fantasy: *A Wizard of Earthsea*," *Horn Book*, 47 (April 1971): 129-138;

Thomas D. Clareson, ed., *Extrapolation*, Special Ursula K. Le Guin Issue, 21 (Fall 1980);

Joe De Bolt, ed., *Ursula K. Le Guin: Voyager to Inner Lands and to Outer Space* (Port Washington, N.Y.: Kennikat Press, 1979);

Geoff Fox, "Notes on 'Teaching' *A Wizard of Earthsea*," *Children's Literature in Education* (May 1973): 58-67;

Wendy Jago, "*A Wizard of Earthsea* and the Charge of Escapism," *Children's Literature in Education*, 8 (July 1972): 21-29;

Naomi Lewis, "Earthsea Revisited," *Times Literary Supplement*, 28 April 1972, p. 284;

Lewis, "A Hole in the World," *Times Literary Supplement*, 6 April 1973, p. 379;

Lewis, "The Making of a Mage," *Times Literary Supplement*, 6 April 1971, p. 383;

R. D. Mullen and Darko Suvin, eds., *Science Fiction Studies: Selected Articles on Science Fiction 1973-1975* (Boston: Gregg, 1976), pp. 146-155, 223-231, 233-304;

Peter Nicholls, "Showing Children the Value of Death," *Foundation*, 5 (January 1974): 71-80;

Joseph D. Olander and Martin Harry Greenberg, eds., *Writers of the 21st Century Series: Ursula K. Le Guin* (New York: Taplinger, 1979);

T. A. Shippey, "The Magic Art and the Evolution of Works: Ursula Le Guin's Earthsea Trilogy," *Mosaic*, 10 (Winter 1970): 147-163;

George Edgar Slusser, *The Farthest Shore of Ursula K. Le Guin* (San Bernardino, Cal.: Borgo Press, 1976);

Charlotte Spivack, *Ursula K. Le Guin* (Boston: Twayne, 1984).

Madeleine L'Engle
(29 November 1918-   )

Marygail G. Parker

BOOKS: *18 Washington Square, South: A Comedy in One Act* (Boston & Los Angeles: Baker's Plays, 1944);

The Small Rain (New York: Vanguard, 1945; London: Secker & Warburg, 1955); republished as *Prelude* (New York: Vanguard, 1968);

Ilsa (New York: Vanguard, 1946);

And Both Were Young (New York: Lothrop, Lee & Shepard, 1949);

Camilla Dickinson (New York: Simon & Schuster, 1951; London: Secker & Warburg, 1952); republished as *Camilla* (New York: Crowell, 1965);

A Winter's Love (Philadelphia: Lippincott, 1957);

Meet the Austins (New York: Vanguard, 1960; London: Collins, 1966);

A Wrinkle in Time (New York: Farrar, Straus & Giroux, 1962; London: Constable, 1963);

The Moon by Night (New York: Farrar, Straus & Giroux, 1963);

The Twenty-Four Days Before Christmas, illustrated by Inga (New York: Farrar, Straus & Giroux, 1964);

The Arm of the Starfish (New York: Farrar, Straus & Giroux, 1965);

The Love Letters (New York: Farrar, Straus & Giroux, 1966);

The Journey with Jonah (New York: Farrar, Straus & Giroux, 1967);

The Young Unicorns (New York: Farrar, Straus & Giroux, 1968; London: Gollancz, 1969);

Dance in the Desert, illustrated by Symeon Shimin (New York: Farrar, Straus & Giroux, 1969; London: Longman, 1969);

Lines Scribbled on an Envelope, and Other Poems (New York: Farrar, Straus & Giroux, 1969);

The Other Side of the Sun (New York: Farrar, Straus & Giroux, 1971; London: Eyre Metheun, 1972);

A Circle of Quiet (New York: Farrar, Straus & Giroux, 1972);

A Wind in the Door (New York: Farrar, Straus & Giroux, 1973; London: Metheun, 1975);

The Summer of the Great-Grandmother (New York: Farrar, Straus & Giroux, 1974);

Prayers for Sunday (New York: Morehouse-Barlow, 1974);

Everyday Prayers, illustrated by Lucile Butel (New York: Morehouse-Barlow, 1974);

Dragons in the Waters (New York: Farrar, Straus & Giroux, 1976);

The Irrational Season (New York: Seabury, 1977);

A Swiftly Tilting Planet (New York: Farrar, Straus & Giroux, 1978; London: Souvenir, 1980);

The Weather of the Heart (Wheaton, Ill.: Shaw, 1978);

Ladder of Angels (New York: Seabury, 1979);

A Ring of Endless Light (New York: Farrar, Straus & Giroux, 1980);

The Anti-Muffins, illustrated by Gloria Ortiz (New York: Petgrin, 1980);

Walking on Water (Wheaton, Ill.: Shaw, 1980);

A Severed Wasp (New York: Farrar, Straus & Giroux, 1982);

And Both Were Young (New York: Delacorte, 1983);

And It Was Good: Reflections on Beginnings (Wheaton, Ill.: Shaw, 1983);

Dare To Be Creative (Washington, D.C.: Library of Congress, 1984);

A House Like a Lotus (New York: Farrar, Straus & Giroux, 1984);

The Twenty-Four Days of Christmas (Wheaton, Ill.: Shaw, 1984);

Trailing Clouds of Glory: Spiritual Values in Children's Books (Philadelphia: Westminster, 1985).

OTHER: "The Expanding Universe," in *Newbery and Caldecott Medal Books: 1956-1965,* edited by Lee Kingman (Boston: Horn Book, 1965);

Spirit and Light: Essays in Historical Theology, edited by L'Engle and William B. Green (New York: Seabury, 1976).

Madeleine L'Engle's writings reflect her passionate concern with major aspects of life: a happy family life, the right and responsibility of the individual to make choices, the art of writing, death, and God. Because L'Engle writes about such topics in so many different genres—science fiction, suspense, young adult novels, poetry, playwriting, and nonfiction—she defies convenient classification as a writer. Yet because approximately half her works are written for children, she is primarily known as a children's writer.

There are paradoxes in L'Engle's writing. Although she is a Christian, some of L'Engle's most

Madeleine L'Engle (©Nancy Crampton)

theological works have been written as a reaction against what is thought of in some circles as Christian piety. Her constant grappling with the idea of God and her all-encompassing theology might well offend readers with a very traditional view of Christianity, while her obviously Christian philosophy might antagonize those who tend toward atheism or agnosticism. She writes her most difficult works for children since she believes that children's minds are open to the excitement of new ideas and that they are able to understand what their parents have rejected or forgotten. Yet no matter how difficult a theme L'Engle writes of, or what personal or universal crisis her characters face, there is an underlying joy in her books, a feeling that her characters will eventually make the best choices.

L'Engle's life has paralleled her books in many ways. She was born in New York City in 1918. Her father, Charles Wadsworth Camp, was a foreign correspondent. Her mother, Madeleine Barnett Camp, was a southern gentlewoman who had studied music extensively and was talented enough to have been a concert pianist had she so desired. The southern background and love of classical music exerted a strong influence on L'Engle's writing. Several of her works portray the staunch tradition of southern gentility and characters imbued with its ideals. Throughout her works, L'Engle's characters exhibit a great fondness for classical music—for example, Mrs. Austin vacuuming to it, Katherine Forrester studying it, and Adam Eddington whistling it as a code. In her science fiction works, L'Engle's extraterrestrial beings often speak in voices compared to musical instruments: English horn, woodwind, harp.

L'Engle was an only child (her only brother died as an infant) brought up in the formal English tradition her father wished, with a nanny and governess. Because of the rather solitary childhood, she developed a great love of reading, writing stories, and drawing. Her father had been gassed in World War I; as his physical health deteriorated, his professional work also suffered. His lungs became so afflicted that he could no longer live in New York or any of the other cosmopolitan cities he loved. The family moved to Switzerland, and L'Engle went to the first of a series of boarding schools both in Europe and in the United States. L'Engle graduated from Smith College with honors in 1941 and pursued a career in the theater for the next five years, because she thought it would be good schooling for a writer. Both the boarding schools and theatrical experience provide the dramatic backdrop for L'Engle's first book, *The Small Rain* (1945).

The Small Rain deals with one of L'Engle's predominant themes: that an artist must constantly discipline herself; otherwise her talent will become dissipated and she will never achieve her greatest potential. It also deals with the theme of the individual making her own choices and the importance those choices will have in her life. L'Engle demonstrates in her first novel the ability to portray strong, believable characters that engage the reader's interest deeply.

The protagonist of *The Small Rain*, Katherine Forrester, has the talent to become a great concert pianist. She has studied with her mother, a renowned artist who dies in an automobile accident. She has also studied with a brilliant young teacher, Justin Vigneras, at her boarding school in Switzerland. Her music lessons are one of the few aspects of school life that she really enjoys. The only other part of school that is bearable is her friendship with Sarah Courtmont, which is halted when a narrow-minded teacher hints that it may be a lesbian re-

lationship. Katherine also loses her beloved music teacher, who has found a much better position, but she hopes that she may be able to study with him again someday.

When Katherine finally graduates from school, she returns to New York and is able to persuade her mother's former teacher, now a very old man, to become her teacher. Katherine becomes engaged to a rising young actor named Pete Burns. Her friendship with Sarah is also renewed since Sarah is studying acting in New York. As her life becomes more involved with Pete's career, and socializing with Sarah and her crowd, Katherine's time for practicing her music becomes more constricted. She exhausts herself trying to find enough time and energy for both her music and Pete. Finally the old teacher becomes enraged and plays some of Katherine's mother's recordings, which Katherine has not heard before. She begins to devote herself utterly to her music and to spend less time with Pete and Sarah.

At the time Katherine makes her decision to dedicate her time to her art, she naively believes she can also have a loving marriage with Pete; as the weeks wear on, she begins to sense that Pete might not understand or allow this. It comes almost as a relief when Pete and Sarah announce they have fallen in love. Although Katherine is hurt, she realizes that this is the best thing that could have happened; she makes plans to return to France to continue her studies with Justin Vigneras. The reader knows long before the novel *A Severed Wasp* (1982), which continues Katherine's story many years later, that she will have a brilliant career.

L'Engle again looks to the past for the settings of her next three books: *Ilsa* (1946) takes place in the South and provides a memorable portrait of southern family life; *And Both Were Young* (1949), L'Engle's first "junior" novel, takes place in a Swiss boarding school; and *Camilla Dickinson* (1951) is the story of a sheltered young girl growing up in New York. Although each of these novels introduces enjoyable, unique characters and *Camilla Dickinson* was seen by some critics as the female counterpart to *The Catcher in the Rye*, it is *Ilsa* which portrays the most haunting characters, especially the independent title character. This characterization and L'Engle's insight into a society based on a rigid set of mores (and the effect of that society on individuals who cannot or will not subscribe to its mores) render it one of L'Engle's finest works. *Ilsa* is the story of a southern girl growing up in the early decades of the twentieth century. The narrator is Henry Porcher, a shadowy, ineffectual man who has loved Ilsa from childhood. Ilsa, an outcast as far as most of Porcher's family is concerned, lives a happy and relatively unstructured existence in a cabin on the beach with her father, a distinguished naturalist. Their life-style and attitudes are in direct contrast to the rigid traditions and views observed by the proper Porcher family.

Again, choice is an important theme; unfortunately, Henry is too weak a character to make choices. Ilsa's choices are not wise; she marries Montgomery Woolf, Henry's handsome but spoiled cousin. Monty becomes a churlish man who takes pleasure only in their daughter, Brand, and in his hunting trips and hounds. Ilsa realizes the mistake she has made but remains in the marriage. She must also cope with the problems of her rapidly failing eyesight and her strong attraction to Franz Werner, the handsome leading actor in a summer touring company. When Monty is killed in a hunting accident, he does not leave Ilsa well off financially and she is forced to take in boarders. Brand is growing up to be a strange, bitter young woman. Given the opportunity to leave town with Franz Werner, Ilsa finally makes a right choice. Her experience has given her wisdom, and she knows that although Werner loves her, she would become an insupportable burden to him and their love would not withstand it. In the end, even Henry Porcher has the gumption to make a choice: knowing he will always be under Ilsa's spell if he stays in town, he resolves to take a job elsewhere and try to make a new life for himself.

The characters in this novel, especially Ilsa, exemplify the joy that underlies L'Engle's philosophy. Although they are confronted with difficult problems, they do not become permanently embittered; rather, they learn from experience. L'Engle's strongest characters are neither martyrs nor saints, but human beings who are willing to try new things and laugh at their foibles along the way.

While she was writing these three novels, changes were taking place in L'Engle's life. During a run of *The Cherry Orchard* she met a young actor named Hugh Franklin; on 26 January 1946 they were married. When Franklin decided to leave the theater "forever" (a time span which lasted nine years), the family moved from New York to Connecticut. In these years L'Engle was busy coping with the disadvantages and delights of a 200-year-old house, helping her husband in the general store they purchased, and mothering their three children, Josephine, Maria, and Bion.

As always, L'Engle devoted as much time as she could to reading and writing. This decade was a time of professional discouragement to her; she could not seem to get anything published. Publishers rejected *A Winter's Love*, an adult novel, for being "too moral"; they rejected *Meet the Austins*, a children's book, because it opened with a death; they rejected *A Wrinkle in Time* because it was a "difficult" book—it failed to fit into either their adult or juvenile marketing slots.

All these rejections are chronicled in L'Engle's first nonfiction book, *A Circle of Quiet* (1972). An inveterate journal keeper, L'Engle has written this and three other nonfiction works (*The Summer of the Great-Grandmother*, 1974; *The Irrational Season*, 1977; and *Walking on Water*, 1980) largely from journal entries. These books not only give insight into the oeuvre of Madeleine L'Engle, but also into the discipline involved in being a writer. The most recent of these, *Walking on Water*, discusses at length the interplay between her writing and her Christianity. L'Engle's journals also trace the close parallel of her actual experiences and her writing.

Although the journals provide settings and plots for some of L'Engle's work, it is her reading and constant quest for a theology which provide the themes that dominate her most cosmic works, including the Time trilogy (*A Wrinkle in Time*, 1962; *A Wind in the Door*, 1973; and *A Swiftly Tilting Planet*, 1978) as well as *The Arm of the Starfish* (1965) and *A Ring of Endless Light* (1980). In these works L'Engle deals with profound themes in a positive way: the constant battle of good versus evil, and the importance of an individual knowing the differences between the two and from that knowledge making choices that will not only enhance his existence in the cosmos but also affect the entire universe. Once he makes his choices, he must remain committed to them whether it is easy or not.

Meg and Charles Wallace Murry and Calvin O'Keefe have many opportunities to make such choices and commitments in the 1963 Newbery Medal winner *A Wrinkle in Time*. This book was written while L'Engle was reading Albert Einstein and Max Planck. It was also written as her rebellion against Christian piety; she was trying to discover a theology by which she could live. The fictional character Meg Murry who rails against the ridiculous things she has to learn in school and the Madeleine L'Engle who rails against the narrowness of some forms of Christianity have more similarities than are at first apparent.

The Murry family is suspect in the small New England village where they live. A mother who reputedly makes stew over a Bunsen burner might not know which end of the mop is used to scrub

Dust jacket for the first book in L'Engle's Time trilogy. A Wrinkle in Time won the Newbery Medal in 1963 (Farrar, Straus & Giroux)

the floor, no matter how many Nobel Prizes she has. Prickly, weird Meg is quite homely and does not fit in with any group at school. The twins, Sandy and Dennys, give a semblance of being normal since they are good at sports and gardening; but the youngest boy, Charles Wallace, never speaks and is considered to be not quite right in the head. The father has been away for several years, and no one has heard from him for over a year.

Things begin to change for the Murrys, especially Meg and Charles Wallace, when the outlandish character of Mrs. Whatsit shows up at their house one night. Although Mrs. Whatsit has the appearance of an eccentric tramp, she is able to read Meg's thoughts. She startles Mrs. Murry by reassuring her that there *is* such a thing as a tesseract (a wrinkle in time). Because Mr. Murry is on a highly classified mission to explore the possible existence of such a thing, Mrs. Murry is taken aback when the strange old lady mentions this. The next afternoon Meg and Charles Wallace are on their

way to visit Mrs. Whatsit's cabin when they meet Calvin O'Keefe, a popular boy in Meg's high school. Although Calvin is a star athlete, he feels very much alone since he comes from a family where no one cares about him. Charles Wallace recognizes Calvin as a kindred being and allows him to come along with them. It is Calvin, Meg, and Charles Wallace along with Mrs. Whatsit and her friends, Mrs. Which and Mrs. Who—really celestial beings—who make the arduous journey to the planet of Camazotz, where Mr. Murry is held captive. On the way the children learn of the battle which is taking place throughout the universe against the dark, shadowy Thing. They do not quite understand what it is, but they sense it is a great evil. They also know that certain planets are totally within its powers, while certain others have been fighting it off. The list of opponents of the Thing is impressive: it includes Leonardo da Vinci, Michelangelo, Shakespeare, Beethoven, Einstein, and Jesus.

The planet of Camazotz proves to be the antithesis of the names mentioned above—strong, creative individuals. It is L'Engle's symbol for the ills of the world caused by a lack of creativity and individuality. Everything on Camazotz is exactly alike: every house is the same shape, same size, and same color. Children bounce their balls in the same rhythm; all the mothers open and shut their doors at the same time. The children make their way to CENTRAL intelligence, where they learn that the evil force is named IT. Charles Wallace tries to fight IT with his exceptional intelligence, but not even he can withstand its force. He becomes a robotlike creature, mouthing all the thoughts IT wishes him to say.

The children finally find Mr. Murry and together they face IT. IT is a disembodied brain, curiously more awful than any monster imaginable. IT is a masterful symbol for L'Engle's belief that the human intellect untempered by emotions is a destructive, dangerous force. Without emotions and experiences, the brain is not part of an individual at all; there is no such thing as individuality.

It is only when Meg realizes she has one thing IT does not have that she is able to rescue Charles Wallace and bring them all safely home: she is able to love. By concentrating on her love for Charles Wallace, Meg is able to bring him back to his true identity. At certain points in the novel, choices must be made by these young people, some seemingly small decisions which affect not only their own lives but lives throughout the universe because they are able to defeat IT. Charles Wallace's invitation to Calvin to visit Mrs. Whatsit, the children's decision to make the journey, and Meg's return visit to Camazotz are all small but important decisions which ultimately ensure the right and privilege of each individual in the universe to make choices. Yet all the symbolism and thematic weight of *A Wrinkle in Time* would amount to nothing more than a philosophical tract were the characters not so realistically portrayed. Meg's worries about school and her "awful" looks, Calvin's longing for honest affection rather than mere popularity, and Mrs. Murry's loving concern for her husband greatly affect the reader. L'Engle also depicts vivid scenes on each planet the children visit, and her extraterrestrial beings are strong, unusual characters who contribute to the charm and warmth of the novel. Aunt Beast, the Happy Medium, Mrs. Who, Mrs. Whatsit, and Mrs. Which delight the imagination.

In the second book of the trilogy, *A Wind in the Door*, L'Engle expands the theme of love as a powerful opponent against evil by developing the concept of love according to theological guidelines. In the first book, Meg concentrated on her love for Charles Wallace to conquer evil; now she must expand that love to include Mr. Jenkins, the stodgy, unimaginative school principal with whom she has fought many battles. Her decision to love Mr. Jenkins has cosmic implications, because she, Calvin, and Mr. Jenkins embark on a journey to save Charles Wallace, who is a very important being in the order of the cosmos. This journey is traveled not through outer space but through inner space. Meg, Calvin, Mr. Jenkins, and an irascible cherubim named Proginoskes, who resembles a drive of dragons, must convince Sporos, one of Charles Wallace's fora, to "deepen" (mature) so that Charles Wallace will live. Throughout the journey the children must avoid the Echthroi or un-namers of the universe who are behind the attempted destruction of Charles Wallace. In the end, the Echthroi almost destroy them also, and only the sacrifice of Proginoskes saves them. The cherubim shows the ultimate love for his friends by *Xing* himself to insure their safety.

In this book the theme tends to overpower the characters, weakening the overall effect. The shadowy Blajeny, the teacher of Proginoskes, remains too much of an enigma; Mr. Jenkins is never quite sure why he is asked to come on the journey; and Sporos is such an irritatingly silly little creature that his decision to "deepen," a process requiring some measure of sacrifice, is not quite convincing.

The third book in the Time trilogy, *A Swiftly Tilting Planet,* won the American Book Award in 1980 for Best Children's Paperback. It is even more universal in scope than the first of the books. In it, Charles Wallace and a unicorn named Gaudior are on a quest to avert a nuclear war. L'Engle draws heavily on Welsh mythology to weave the strands of her plot together. Charles Wallace must journey through space and time, still eluding the Echthroi, in order to change the Might-Have-Been. He must determine which branch of the family the South American leader "Mad Dog" Branzillo is descended from. Depending on whether his origins are from the good or the evil ancestors, there may well be a nuclear war within twenty-four hours. Again, the universe will not only survive but thrive because of choices made by individuals: Charles chooses to make the journey on Gaudior, knowing he may lose his life; Meg "kythes" (a form of intuitive, unspoken communication) knowledge from a reference book and from Mrs. O'Keefe to Charles Wallace to help him on his journey; Mrs. O'Keefe gives Charles Wallace the rune to begin with. All these small steps converge to change what may have been a nuclear disaster. The most difficult choices in this book are made by Mrs. O'Keefe, Calvin's strange, disheartened mother, a woman made old before her time by the hard life she has endured. She has suppressed her feelings for years so that she would never again have to endure the pain of losing someone she loves. Now she must use the rune her grandmother gave her and find the letter she and her beloved brother Chuck used to read. This letter provides the necessary connection between the South American leader and the Welsh mythology to insure the proper course of history.

Although the structure of *A Swiftly Tilting Planet* is a bit difficult to follow because of Charles Wallace's nonchronological jumps in time, the writing here is of a quality consistent with that of *A Wrinkle in Time*. L'Engle uses her gift of spinning a story that quickly involves the reader in the action. The characters encountered throughout time are skillfully drawn. The character of Mrs. O'Keefe, who up until this time has been no more than a frowsy complainer, is fully and sympathetically developed. She becomes, in a sense, a character like Ilsa; the difference is that her background and temperament lead her to entirely different reactions from the ones Ilsa has. L'Engle repeats her theme that the most expedient choices are not necessarily the most creative ones.

Although L'Engle uses some broad Christian symbolism in the Time trilogy, such as the unicorn in *A Swiftly Tilting Planet* or the cherubim in *A Wind in the Door,* her most extensive use of Christian symbolism occurs in the suspense novel *The Arm of the*

Dust jacket for the final volume in the Time trilogy, which won the American Book Award in 1980 for Best Children's Paperback (Farrar, Straus & Giroux)

Starfish (1965). The young protagonist's name is Adam, and he is going to spend his summer working on the island of Gaea, a paradise which is just now beginning to feel the encroachment of civilization. When Adam finally arrives at this idyllic setting, he is thoroughly confused by the information the young, seductive Kali Cutter has given him. Not only does Adam have to decide whom he should work for in his regenerative starfish experiments; he must also decide who is good and who is evil. Once Adam decides Dr. O'Keefe is representing good, it is not enough for him to remain neutral; he must commit himself to an important mission: to deliver Dr. O'Keefe's papers to the proper people in Lisbon. Joshua, a young man from the American embassy and a dear friend of the O'Keefes, tries to help him accomplish this, but because Adam has withheld a small bit of information from Dr. O'Keefe, Joshua is killed.

There are several Christian and cosmic ironies in the book: Canon Tallis, a devoted, honorable ecclesiastic, is pointed out to Adam as being evil; corrupt Dr. Ball (a name similar to the degenerate deity Baal) is introduced as a caring, benevolent clergyman. Joshua, the Christ figure, is really a nonbeliever. In the end, Tyrone Cutter must get from Dr. O'Keefe the knowledge he has planned to use for his own evil purposes. Cutter's daughter Kali has been attacked by a shark, and only Dr. O'Keefe's knowledge of the regeneration process can save her arm.

Although L'Engle has been criticized for making her characters too good here, they are consistent with her theme of love conquering evil, and with her character development up to this point. Calvin O'Keefe has made choices throughout the Time trilogy which are consistent with his decision at the book's conclusion—although it is of interest to note that *The Arm of the Starfish* was written before the final two books of the Time trilogy. The reader cannot imagine Calvin making a decision other than that of helping Kali, any more than he can imagine this book without Joshua, who becomes a focal character even though he was not in the outline of the manuscript. When Adam woke up in the Ritz Hotel and saw Joshua sitting in his room, there was no one more surprised than Madeleine L'Engle. Her development of Joshua's character is a tribute to her discipline as a writer, since it caused her to rethink the entire book.

If Adam seems somewhat naive in the beginning, he at least learns from his mistakes. He returns as an important character in *A Ring of Endless Light,* in which he is able to use some of the wisdom he learned from his short experience with Joshua to give comfort to the Austin family. The Austins were introduced in *Meet the Austins* (1960). In *The Moon by Night* (1963) they were involved with an unhappy, confused rich boy on their cross-country camping trip before moving to New York for a year. *The Young Unicorns* (1968) catapulted them into an international plot which included a young blind girl and a fake Episcopalian bishop. *A Ring of Endless Light,* a Newbery Honor Book, is L'Engle's latest and most profound book about the Austins. Its theme is much more universal than those of the earlier books; it deals with death. L'Engle again affirms her faith in God through the images of resurrection that abound in the novel: butterflies, water, the constant association of Vicky and Adam with light. Zachary, the troubled boy Vicky and her family met the previous summer, is associated with darkness.

But not only does the novel deal with death, it deals with the theme of coming of age. Vicky, who has felt rather inferior and insecure up until now, begins to have a sense of self-worth. She starts to show real maturity through her poetry, her acceptance of responsibilities people thrust on her, and her participation in a special experiment Adam is conducting with dolphins.

The theme of choice is again important. The family chooses to spend the entire summer with the dying grandfather; Zachary chooses to leave the hospital emergency room in the face of so much suffering. Vicky makes the most dramatic choice of all, choosing the light of hope over the darkness of cynicism in a world where little girls die in hospital emergency rooms and dolphins are clubbed to death capriciously. Again, as in all of L'Engle's books, the most creative choice is not necessarily the easiest or safest. And each act may have unforeseen implications; Zachary, for example, willfully sailing in bad conditions, does not realize until too late that his selfishness will cause the death of a good man. As Grandfather says, "If someone kills a butterfly, it could cause an earthquake in a galaxy a trillion light years away."

L'Engle's last three novels are concerned with the religious theme of redemption through love and forgiveness. In her two latest, *A Severed Wasp* and *A House Like a Lotus* (1984), she concentrates on this theme in very different ways.

A Severed Wasp, which takes its title from a George Orwell quote concerning modern man's spirituality, is perhaps L'Engle's most complex novel for adults. In the hands of a less gifted storyteller the convoluted plot might approach melodrama. Yet L'Engle weaves all the threads of human faults and foibles together both pleasingly and realistically. Although the characters achieve the redemptive love of forgiveness and enjoy a fuller, more creative life because of it, they have each suffered mightily because of their failures.

Katherine Forrester Vigneras, the protagonist of L'Engle's first novel, *The Small Rain*, is the character around whom most of the action coalesces in *A Severed Wasp*. Madame Vigneras has come home to her brownstone on 10th Street in New York's Greenwich Village to live a quiet life after a long and successful career as a concert pianist. Although she is an artist whose music has been of primary importance in her life, she is also a compassionate and understanding human being who becomes embroiled—although sometimes reluctantly—in other people's problems. The cast of characters in her present life includes a retired bishop, Felix Bodeway, whom she knew many years ago; Allie Undercroft, the present Episcopal bishop; Undercroft's wife, Yolande; Dave and Suzy (Austin) Davidson; and other ecclesiastics from the community centered around the great cathedral of St. John the Divine in upper Manhattan. Other characters are Dorcas, a young, pregnant ballet dancer who is deserted by her husband; Llew, a brilliant organist whose wife and baby recently died during the birthing process; Emily Davidson, the young daughter of Suzy and Dave, whose bright talent as a ballet dancer was ended by a hit-and-run accident; and Dr. Mimi Oppenheimer, who evolves from a tenant into a close friend.

Interwoven with Katherine's present life are the memories of her past, the part of her life she feels she must come to terms with. Present incidents trigger flashbacks of relationships which were an integral part of her life: her difficult but loving marriage to composer Justin Vigneras; their healing friendship with the great Roman Catholic Bishop Wolfgang von Stromberg; her relationship with Likas von Hilpert, a former Nazi *kommandant*. Each of these relationships, although filled with pain as well as love, has taught Katherine wisdom and compassion. She is now able to impart the message of forgiveness and love to some of the souls tortured by guilt and sadness. Felix, Yolande, and Allie realize through their encounters with Katherine that they must seek forgiveness not only from God and others; they must also be able to forgive themselves. It is only when one is able to risk rejection in order to seek absolution that one is free to continue a creative and rich existence, unshackled by guilt and enhanced by the wisdom gained from experience.

This is the theme examined in L'Engle's novel *A House Like a Lotus*, but from a different perspective: Polly O'Keefe must learn to forgive and love again. The story line focuses mainly on Polly's relationship with the artist Maximiliana Sebastiane Horne. Max (as her friends call her) has come to her home on Benne Seed Island off the Carolina coast to die, although Polly learns that only by accident. Polly's favorite uncle, Sandy, is a great friend of Max's, and he introduces the two. Polly becomes the daughter Max never had; Max becomes the mentor Polly needs. Max, with her artist's eye and soul, gives Polly a new way to view other people and also herself. Through Max's insight, Polly discovers a respect and compassion for her high school English teacher, a heightened admiration for her mother, and a recognition of her own writing and acting talents.

One night, however, Polly is left alone with Max, who has drunk excessive amounts of alcohol in order to cope with the pain of her disease. Max, a lesbian who has lived with her lover, Ursula, for over thirty years, makes a sexual advance toward Polly. Polly considers this the ultimate betrayal and refuses to see or forgive Max.

It is only when Polly journeys to Cyprus for a conference on writing and related arts that she is able to forgive Max. Through her meetings with the irresponsible Zachary, who has appeared in several of the books about the Austins, Polly begins to comprehend that a lapse made by someone who genuinely loves is not a betrayal; it is an honest human failure. Zachary rents a kayak and rows Polly and himself out beyond the safety zone, where they are nearly drowned. It is a willful, careless action; Zachary is too self-centered to love. Polly realizes that flawed though Max is, she cannot wish that Max had never become part of her life. To wish that would diminish part of herself; Max has helped her discover some of the wondrous knowledge she now has.

Although occasionally criticized for being pedantic, L'Engle's books have generally been favorably reviewed. *A Wind in the Door* and two Austin family books, *The Young Unicorns* and *The Moon by Night,* have received mixed comments. Perhaps John Rowe Townsend sums up the critiques best in *A Sense of Story* as he calls her "a curiously-gifted, curiously-learned, curiously-imperfect writer." In 1984 L'Engle received the Catholic Library Association's Regina Award, given for consistent, sustained quality of work.

The fact that readers appreciate L'Engle's work is apparent through her book sales. In February 1981 *American Bookseller* ran an article on children's books which included a list of the fifty most popular authors and illustrators. Madeleine L'Engle was in the top ten. The 24 July 1981 issue of *Publishers Weekly* carried an article on children's bookstores. In a poll conducted with the owners of these nationwide stores, L'Engle was listed as one of the top six best-selling authors.

L'Engle's writing could well be called timeless rather than timely. Her warm portraits of caring families, her fervent belief in the dignity and creativity of each individual, and her sense of the universal importance of particular acts give her work a peculiar splendor. Her victories are bittersweet; in accordance with her great respect for the laws of thermodynamics, her characters do not get something for nothing. But each of her books leaves the reader with joy and hope, and, as L'Engle herself so ably states it, "a vision which includes angels and dragons and unicorns, and all the lovely creatures which our world would put in a box marked 'Children.' "

References:
Hugh Franklin, "Biographical Note," in *Newbery and Caldecott Medal Books: 1956-1965*, edited by Lee Kingman (Boston: Horn Book, 1965), pp. 124-128;
John Rowe Townsend, *A Sense of Story: Essays on Contemporary Writing for Children* (Philadelphia: Lippincott, 1971), pp. 120-129.

Lois Lowry
(20 March 1937-)

Laura M. Zaidman
University of South Carolina, Sumter

BOOKS: *Black American Literature* (Portland, Maine: Walsh, 1973);

Literature of the American Revolution (Portland, Maine: Walsh, 1974);

Values and the Family (Portland, Maine: Walsh, 1977);

A Summer to Die, illustrated by Jenni Oliver (Boston: Houghton Mifflin, 1977);

Find a Stranger, Say Goodbye (Boston: Houghton Mifflin, 1978);

Here in Kennebunkport, photographs by Lowry with text by Frederick H. Lewis (Kennebunkport,

Maine: Durrell, 1978);

Anastasia Krupnik (Boston: Houghton Mifflin, 1979);

Autumn Street (Boston: Houghton Mifflin, 1980);

Anastasia Again!, decorations by Diane de Groat (Boston: Houghton Mifflin, 1981);

Anastasia at Your Service, decorations by de Groat (Boston: Houghton Mifflin, 1982);

Taking Care of Terrific (Boston: Houghton Mifflin, 1983);

The One Hundredth Thing About Caroline (Boston: Houghton Mifflin, 1983);

Anastasia, Ask Your Analyst (Boston: Houghton Mifflin, 1984);

Us and Uncle Fraud (Boston: Houghton Mifflin, 1984),

Anastasia on Her Own (Boston: Houghton Mifflin, 1985);

Switcharound (Boston: Houghton Mifflin, 1985);

Anastasia Has the Answers (Boston: Houghton Mifflin, 1986).

Lois Lowry, best known for her six Anastasia Krupnik adventures, has enjoyed popularity with readers and critics alike. Her thirteen books for children, featuring realistic themes and delightful characters, help them answer their own questions about life, self-identity, and human relationships.

The daughter of Robert E. Hammersberg, an army dentist, and Katharine Landis Hammersberg, Lowry was born in Honolulu, lived in Pennsylvania during World War II and in Japan after the war, attended private school in Brooklyn, and then completed two years at Brown University. In 1956, at nineteen, she quit college to marry Donald Grey Lowry. Working part-time so her husband could finish his law degree at Harvard, she had four children by the time she was twenty-five. Lowry later completed her B.A. degree in writing at the University of Maine in 1972. In the 1970s she wrote two textbooks, *Black American Literature* and *Literature of the American Revolution,* and a booklet entitled *Values and the Family* and had various articles and stories published in magazines and newspapers; a professional photographer, she also produced a book of photographs, *Here in Kennebunkport* (1978), with a text by Frederick H. Lewis. She began her career as an author for young adults when a Houghton Mifflin editor read one of Lowry's published short stories about her childhood and asked if she would be interested in writing books for children. Her first novel, *A Summer to Die* (1977), was inspired by her sister's death from cancer in her twenties. The publication of the book

photo by Robert Jones

marked a period of auspicious beginnings and endings for Lowry. The novel was well received, and she was divorced in 1977 after twenty-one years of marriage.

Lowry now has an apartment on Beacon Hill in Boston and a 150-year-old farmhouse in rural New Hampshire. Her realistic novels, replete with vivid remembrances of her own childhood, reflect a love for the feelings of the past as well as an enthusiasm for the here-and-now drawn from observations of her children.

Although she postponed her childhood aspiration to be a novelist as long as "there were children to raise, education to complete, experience to learn from, and losses to mourn," her varied experiences contribute a rich diversity of themes to her fiction. She believes teenagers must be prepared to live in a complicated world and must not be overprotected from life's realities. Considering them too "sophisticated nowadays to enjoy a completely idealized view of human existence," she does not worry about limiting her humor unnecessarily because she thinks "kids are tasteless and irreverent." Consequently, her novels contain lively humor and serious universal themes as well. She has a fascination with "the general continuity of life, the beginnings and ends, transitions, people's adjustments to change." What she cares about most is the ability of humanity to laugh at itself.

A Summer to Die (1977), a remarkable first novel, is narrated by Meg Chalmers, age thirteen, who experiences two dramatic events one summer: her fifteen-year-old sister Molly dies of leukemia and her friends Ben and Maria invite her to photograph the birth of their baby. When Meg and Molly's father, a university English professor, takes a sabbatical to write a book on irony in literature, they move to the country for a year. Meg, in adjusting to the new environment, must also face the uncertainties, fears, restlessness, and impatience of growing up. She is jealous of her sister's easy-going, self-confident nature, her beauty, and her popu-

Dust jacket for Lowry's first novel, about a thirteen-year-old girl's adjustment to her older sister's death from leukemia (Houghton Mifflin)

larity as a cheerleader. After Molly begins to suffer sudden nosebleeds, which turn out to be the first symptoms of leukemia, the Chalmers' lives change dramatically. Meg begins to mature, discovering her own strengths and beauty, as well as her deep love for Molly. The warmth of a close family and good friends sustains Meg through this traumatic time, allowing her to understand that her world must change and those she loves will not always be with her.

Juxtaposing universal themes of birth and death, Lowry superbly portrays the effects of a child's serious illness and eventual death on the entire family. Meg reflects on the bittersweet truth about death: "Time goes on, and your life is still there, and you have to live it. After a while you remember the good things more often than the bad. Then, gradually, the empty silent parts of you fill up with sounds of talking and laughter again, and the jagged edges of sadness are softened by memories."

In addition, the insights derived from minor characters result in Meg's increasing maturity. For instance, seventy-year-old Will Banks, who befriends Meg, shares her love of photography and makes her see her own beauty. Having once lived in the 140-year-old house that Meg's family rents, he left his name carved in the closet floor, just as he has etched an impression on Meg's life forever. Another friendship that changes Meg's perspective is with Ben and Maria, a married couple who have been unfairly stereotyped by the townspeople as hippies who grow marijuana and walk around nude. Meg's photographing of the birth of Ben and Maria's child helps her come to terms with Molly's death. Lowry shows how appearances seldom mirror reality and provides a good lesson in judging others' moral values.

In Lowry's skillful conclusion to the novel Meg's mother makes a lovely patchwork quilt using material from her daughters' clothes; its orderly, geometric patterns rekindle her memories of her children's past—the pale pinks and yellows of baby dresses, the flowery prints and bright plaids of little girls' dresses, and the faded denims and corduroys of the clothes they wore later. The quilt reminds the reader that endings may bring new beginnings. Just as her husband finishes his book manuscript by the end of the summer that Molly dies, Lydia Chalmers completes her quilt as a loving tribute to her daughters' childhoods, hoping, no doubt, that Meg will cherish it and be able to pass it on to her daughter. Lowry's ability to bring the story full circle after the agony of death and the ecstasy of birth makes *A Summer to Die* a memorable novel. Besides receiving the International Reading Association's Children's Book Award, it was also named to *Horn Book*'s Honor List of 1977.

Find a Stranger, Say Goodbye (1978) presents another variation on the theme of growing up. Natalie Armstrong, an adopted seventeen-year-old, upsets her parents by announcing her desire to find her natural parents. Her uncertainty about her identity surfaces when she responds to a college application's questions about what makes her different and how that quality will affect her life. In an essay, which she later decides not to submit, she explains that she has to find her natural mother and discover why she was given away. This search for identity takes her many miles; yet after she discovers the answers, she realizes she already knows who she is—a girl with a loving family and a bright future.

The theme of the novel is clearly foreshadowed in the commencement address given at Natalie's graduation. Commencement is a time of beginning, but some doors are not ready to be opened, and, if certain paths are chosen, the consequences may result in unhappy surprises. Free-spirited Tallie (Natalie's grandmother, for whom she is named) tells her story of running away at twenty from her boring New York stockbroker husband to live with the incredibly exciting painter with whom she found a lifetime of happiness. Yet, Tallie tells Natalie, "I hurt people, by trying to save myself."

Tallie also gives Natalie the letters Natalie's adoptive mother, Kay, wrote about her adoption in 1960; Natalie is assured by these letters that she is very much loved and that Kay wants her to be her own person. In reading the letters Natalie recalls from her childhood her grandfather's drawings of Red Riding Hood and of the dangers Red Riding Hood confronts, similar to the uncertainties Natalie now faces. She begins her search with the letters and the adoption documents, which her parents give her, fully supporting her quest. She first tries to contact the lawyer who arranged the adoption but learns he has been dead for ten years. The doctor who delivered her, now dying of cancer, gives her the needed information: her mother, Julie, was fifteen and unmarried. The pieces begin to fit together as she learns more. She gets an eerie feeling seeing a lovely blue-eyed, brown-haired Julie Jeffries in a high school yearbook, for she sees herself. The clues lead her to a phone conversation with Julie's mother and, finally, to a luncheon meeting with the woman who gave her up five days after birth.

Her *real mother*, Natalie soon realizes, is the woman who raised her; however, the fascinating diary Julie kept in 1959-1960, which she shows to Natalie, completes the story Natalie is so anxious to know: her father was the doctor's son, who was killed in an accident soon after Julie became pregnant. She later tells her adoptive father that Julie Jeffries, now a rich, beautiful wife and mother, is no longer part of her life; she has said goodbye. As she packs her clothes at the end of August and prepares to leave for college, where she plans to major in pre-med, she sorts out the past, but she knows the memories will remain forever.

The theme of emerging into adulthood is reinforced throughout the novel with effective imagery; for instance, Tallie gives Natalie an abstract bronze sculpture—it could be a motionless gull at sunrise, its head bent in a folded wing, or perhaps the thick, unopened leaves of a deep-forest plant in early spring. Whatever it is, it represents the young adult, ready to open up and grow.

Anastasia Krupnik (1979), named an American Library Association Notable Book, begins the Anastasia series. Ten-year-old Anastasia keeps track of her pleasant and unpleasant experiences on lists of "Things I Love!" and "Things I Hate!" Most of the despised things, such as her teacher, boys, babies, her parents, and her name, eventually get crossed off the "Things I Hate!" list and are transferred to the list of adored things. Anastasia loves her ninety-two-year-old grandmother but hates that she is senile. Her understanding parents, Harvard English professor Myron Krupnik and freelance artist Katherine, help her understand her ambivalent feelings. They also sympathize with her anxieties about their expected baby; consequently, they give her the honor of choosing the baby's name. She soon realizes that her parents' love for her will never change because of the baby, so she chooses "Sam" in her grandfather's memory, rather than the horribly obscene name she devilishly selected in her moments of greatest resentment: "One-Ball Reilley."

Perhaps the strongest qualities of this book as well as of the five sequels are the lively, funny dialogue, the intelligent plot, and the superbly drawn characters. The sensitive observations about family life are skillfully woven into the fabric of the novel. An illustration of the high quality of the writing is the description of Anastasia's visit to her father's class, where he futilely tries to teach William Wordsworth's "I Wandered Lonely as a Cloud." Dr. Krupnik's students' laughably unperceptive com-

Dust jacket for the first Anastasia novel, in which Lowry's young heroine keeps track of her pleasant and unpleasant experiences on lists of "Things I Love!" and "Things I Hate!" (Houghton Mifflin)

ments drive him to dismiss the class. Ironically, Anastasia, not the college students, has the greatest insight into the poem when she figures out that memory ("the inward eye") will help to ease the pain of her grandmother's old age. Anastasia is a budding poet: she treasures her father's poetry, especially the book dedicated to her; she writes her favorite words in her notebook; and she creates a lovely poem describing the sounds of tidepool organisms moving in the dark. When her teacher, Mrs. Westvessel, gives her an F because the poem has neither capital letters nor rhyme, the teacher's name promptly gets added to the "Things I Hate!" list. These lists are the way in which Anastasia deals with her strong, rapidly changing emotions about antagonistic people and humiliating events.

The ambivalence Anastasia feels toward her often-puzzling world is tied in beautifully with her parents' compassion toward her problems. When Anastasia tells her mother she hates the way her grandmother cannot remember Anastasia's name, or that her children are grown, or that her husband

Sam died years before, her mother empathizes with her. Her parents also understand her anger about her name. She complains she is practically an outcast in the fourth grade because her name is too long to fit on a T-shirt, because no one can spell it to vote for her as Class Secretary, and because she cannot join the "i Club" without a nickname ending in *i* like all the other girls. Only when her father intrigues her with the story of the murdered Anastasia, youngest daughter of Czar Nicholas II, does she decide she likes her unusual name.

Anastasia's parents are indeed exceptional, always there to rebuild her self-confidence and to help her make decisions when she asks them. Lowry has explained that the father is a professor for a very pragmatic reason—it enables him to be home more than usual to have the needed interaction between father and child. Her mother, Katherine, works at home, so she too is easily accessible. Dr. and Mrs. Krupnik are perhaps too good to be true, being so compassionate, loving, humorous, and intelligent; however, they are important to the success of each Anastasia book.

Autumn Street (1980), Lowry's darkest vision of childhood, is narrated by Elizabeth Jane Lorimer, recalling traumatic events she faced as a six-year-old child. The book is autobiographical in content, for Elizabeth's family (as did Lowry's) moves to her grandfather's home in Pennsylvania after America's entrance into World War II takes her father away to war. Elizabeth encounters unfamiliar situations, strange people, and cruel realities of the adult world in her new environment. In the end, though, the family is reunited, and Elizabeth has grown wise beyond her years.

The novel's central metaphor is the seasonal cycle of life, focusing on autumn, when the death of nature makes life seem so bleak. Though she is precocious like most of Lowry's heroines, Elizabeth faces horrifying events that other characters do not have to contend with. In fact, the cruelties Elizabeth hears about and sees make this novel unique among Lowry's work in its exploration of painful memories and unknown terrors. For example, the little boy Elizabeth plays with, Noah Hoffman, is seeing a psychiatrist because he is so sadistic, evidenced by his burning his twin's arm with a cigarette lighter, causing him to be stung by yellow jackets, and murdering a cat by twisting its neck. Because the child is so diabolical, she ignores his anguished cries when, wracked by a 106° fever, he calls for help. He dies the next day, and, consequently, Elizabeth tries to absolve her guilt by praying, not to "Our Father who art in heaven," but to *her* father, because she had promised Mrs. Hoffman she would listen out for Noah's calling. Still other shocking realities force an end to Elizabeth's childhood innocence, such as her cousin's suffering from shell shock and the stories she hears about Nazi and Japanese war atrocities. Moreover, she discovers the secret of a great-aunt's dream of marrying her grandfather years ago, she sees the dramatic contrast between her grandparents' austere, quiet, luxurious home and a friend's noisy, cluttered home, and she realizes the sadness of her grandfather's recent stroke. Most terrifying is the tragic death of housekeeper Tatie's grandson, Charles, Elizabeth's favorite playmate. At the end of *Autumn Street*, in the ominous dark forest, Charles is brutally murdered. Elizabeth subsequently catches a serious case of pneumonia and lapses into a coma. It is no wonder that the bleakness of autumn fits the events of this novel set in wartime.

Lowry, however, does not let tragedy carry the theme of *Autumn Street,* for with spring comes rebirth and renewal. On the first day of spring—on her birthday, in fact—Elizabeth miraculously recovers consciousness. Too contrived perhaps, this bittersweet resolution brings her father home. Leaning on a cane, having lost a leg in the war, he assures her that bad things won't happen any more; however, Elizabeth knows differently, for she has already been initiated into the terrifying world of experience and taken away from her safe world of innocence. She learns that people need to pretend to overcome feelings of powerlessness against those things that cannot be controlled.

Elizabeth's narration, distanced by time, reveals such dramatic memories that the book is more appropriate for mature readers. The typical ten-to-twelve-year-old reader may not fathom the poignancy as suggested in the epigraph, a quotation from E. E. Cummings: "along the brittle treacherous bright streets/of memory comes my heart." An outstanding book for young adults, it was named an American Library Association Notable Book for 1980.

Anastasia Again! (1981), Lowry's next book, provides a pleasant contrast to the grimness of *Autumn Street*. In it, Lowry's young heroine contemplates one of life's great puzzles—"The Mystery of Why Some People Make Decisions Without Consulting Their Twelve-Year-Old Children"—as she faces moving from the family's Cambridge apartment to a house in the suburbs. She tries to convince her parents not to move; however, seeing the beautiful Victorian house and her dreamed-of tower bedroom, with its panoramic view of Boston and Cambridge, makes Anastasia reconsider. She quickly recuperates from the trauma of moving and makes new friends, including their elderly neighbor Gertrude Stein (not *the* Gertrude Stein), and Anastasia makes plans to introduce her to a lively group of senior citizens as well as to enhance her own social life during an afternoon party, a celebration of new beginnings.

Anastasia's adventures realistically portray her need to assert independence and to be involved in important family decisions. Her anxieties about moving are overcome with her parents' help. They understand their daughter all too well; for example, they ignore her threat to kill herself by jumping out the window—as soon as she finishes her chocolate pudding—but take seriously her plea to have a special type of house.

One of the reasons why the author's anecdotal style works so perfectly is that the episodic plot is cleverly connected by incorporating Anastasia's attempts at writing a mystery novel. The creative writing of this twelve-year-old aspiring writer is delightful. Moreover, the humor is always on target, and the characterization is credible, even if not always completely realistic. Most readers, and especially children, allow some suspension of disbelief once they get absorbed in the fictional world; however, some adult critics might not agree. One reviewer calls the Krupnik family as portrayed in the book "just another briefly entertaining, warm and flippant TV sitcom family." Most will agree though that this Anastasia book is a marvelous blend of the humor and the anxieties of being twelve. It was nominated for an American Book Award in the juvenile paperback category for 1983.

Anastasia at Your Service (1982) covers Anastasia's twelfth summer. To alleviate her boredom, financial dependence, and depression, she advertises for a job; however, instead of becoming a companion to a rich old lady, Willa Bellingham, she ends up as her maid. She would quit this humiliating job except she must work out restitution for a $35 silver spoon which she mangled in the garbage disposal. She befriends her employer's outrageously spoiled granddaughter, Daphne Bellingham, and together they plot to seek vengeance on the grandmother. A benefit party which the wealthy matron hosts becomes the target of their carefully laid plans that go awry with several cases of mistaken identity. They invite street derelicts, hoping to disrupt the party and discredit the grandmother; however, when they try to get someone they think is a bum to leave, they find out he is actually the mayor. Both girls learn about responsibility and compassion from their mistakes, but it is Anastasia's brother Sam's tragic fall from a second-story window which results in a skull fracture that shocks Anastasia into realizing her love for her pesky, precocious sibling.

In the Anastasia tradition, many funny scenes are integrated with serious commentary about growing up. One nice thing about Lowry's humor is that it includes literary allusions; for example, to combat her boredom and to feel sorry for herself, Anastasia acts out how Beth of *Little Women* says farewell to her dear sisters, how Juliet bids adieu to Romeo, and how Charlotte the spider writhes before her legs go straight up in the air. Would her mother care if she dies, wonders Anastasia. No, she imagines she would just say, upon finding Anastasia dead on the floor, " 'For Pete's sake, I just cleaned this room yesterday, and now look at it.' " Another hilarious scene has Anastasia disguised as a forty-year-old maid so no one would recognize her serving at a party; however, she is less than inconspic-

uous when her pantyhose bosom spills over into the hors d'oeuvres. Also very funny (maybe funnier to older readers) are the notes Anastasia is tempted to inscribe in Mrs. Bellingham's magnificent leather-bound, gold-lettered classics she is dusting in the study. For instance, inside *The Turn of the Screw:* "To my dear Willa, with fond memories of the passionate night we spent together. Henry James." Other witty temptations strike her: "Willa, dearest: I will never forget the week in the hotel room in Paris. Fondly, Scott Fitzgerald"; and "Willa, my love, you are the inspiration for all of my work. Charles Dickens."

This genuinely funny and skillfully crafted book dramatizes how adolescents cope with adults and vice versa. After all, as Daphne says in confessing her misbehavior, growing up is not easy, because life gets very complicated at thirteen. Lowry continues to help her readers understand that others have suffered some of the same problems they are undergoing and survived.

Taking Care of Terrific (1983) is narrated by Enid Irene Crowley, a fourteen-year-old who, like Anastasia, is independent, clever, and precocious and also hates her name because *Enid* sounds like other repulsive words: horrid, putrid, sordid, acrid, viscid, squalid, fetid, and stupid; so she calls herself Cynthia. She has many exciting adventures taking care of Tom Terrific, as four-year-old Joshua Warwick Cameron IV has renamed himself in honor of the television cartoon hero. Enid's daily trips to Boston's Public Garden lead to interesting friendships with a jazz saxophonist named Hawk and a bag lady, both of whom have surprising identities. After successfully organizing twenty-four bag ladies to picket for root beer Popsicles, Enid and classmate Seth Sandroff attempt the bold project of taking their friends on a daring midnight swan-boat ride. The profoundly moving scene with the bag ladies singing softly to Hawk's haunting "Star Dust" melody is superb, as is the following chaotic scene when they are blinded by police spotlights as a loudspeaker blares "You are all under arrest," and then are grabbed, handcuffed, and threatened with jail. After these exciting events, Enid realizes that while her friends did break the law, they provided treasured moments of happiness, and consequently she sees herself more positively. Indeed, *Enid* now sounds more like SPLENDID.

Besides Enid's strong presence, Lowry has created other intriguing characters and a wonderfully varied cast. The divorced Mrs. Cameron over-protects Joshua, warning babysitter Enid not to let him pet dogs, eat sweets, pick flowers, take off his sweater, or talk to strangers; of course, Enid completely disregards her wishes. She has the perfect opportunity to show Tom Terrific a world he has never known—the joys of all-the-way pizza, bubble baths, prank phone calls, and life after 8:00 P.M.—when Mrs. Cameron goes out of town "on business" with a man, although Enid knows Mrs. Cameron does not work. Another vividly evoked character is Enid's live-in housekeeper Mrs. Kolodny, whom she calls a "space cadet." One of her flakiest antics is mistaking a box of instant mashed potatoes for a box of detergent, ruining both the laundry and the chowder in the process. Yet Enid interacts more with Mrs. Kolodny than with Dr. Crowley, her radiologist mother who hired Mrs. Kolodny fourteen years ago, or with her father, a lawyer who hides behind his *Wall Street Journal*. Since the parents generally ignore Enid, they are not described in much detail. However, Mrs. Kolodny is depicted as the "Technicolor Lady" with blue hair, yellow-gray skin, purple veins, red nose, and bloodshot eyes—"an honest-to-goodness human rainbow." A third memorable character, one who never appears in person, is Mrs. Sandroff, a well-known child psychologist, author of the best-seller *Get in Touch: Living with Adolescents*, based on the theory that most parents do not like living with adolescents but need to know how to do so without committing suicide. Her own twin daughters, caught shoplifting, have been shipped off to "fat camp" for the summer. All these minor characters reflect family values gone awry.

Indeed Lowry shows that her adolescent characters inhabit a privileged world of private schools and material affluence. They are not delinquents; rather, they are worldly. Seth jokes that Enid will get hooked on heroin and become a prostitute; Enid retorts that she does not have needle tracks from mainlining yet. Enid and Seth get into minor trouble because of their boredom and lack of attention from their parents; thus Lowry humorously portrays what happens when adolescents do not have strong parental guidance and support.

The One Hundredth Thing About Caroline (1983) presents another Anastasia-like character in a different family setting. Like Anastasia, Caroline Tate is independent and bright; she has a close relationship with her mother, Joanna, and her brother J. P. often annoys her. But eleven-year-old Caroline lives in a different type of family than Anastasia does because Joanna Tate is a single parent. The two baffling mysteries Caroline and her best friend Stacy try to solve lead to their zany adventures.

They first investigate the Pulitzer Prize-winning poet who lives in Stacy's building. Despite their diligent spying (even searching through his garbage), they fail to learn the identity of his mystery woman until Stacy's mother tells them the woman is his wife, not paramour. An even more serious challenge to their detective work is to foil the murder plot of the enigmatic Frederick Fiske, the new occupant in Caroline's building, and the man now dating her mother. Not until a wild dinner party at the end of the book is the truth revealed about Fiske's plan to eliminate the children.

The characterization is excellent, especially in portraying Caroline. She has a strong sense of who she is and who she wants to be—a vertebrate paleontologist specializing in Mesozoic Era dinosaurs. Caroline, who sleeps with her stuffed Stegosaurus, believes that some people are little more than barely evolved dinosaurs; in fact, she often categorizes people according to her Tate Theory of Evolution. She visits New York City's Museum of Natural History and reads *National Geographic* to prepare for her career. Her relationships with her mother, her thirteen-year-old brother James Priestly (nicknamed "Beastly" because even her mother agrees thirteen is a beastly age), her friend Stacy, and her mentor Gregor Keretsky, the museum paleontologist, are all realistically portrayed. The fights she has with her brother and the hostility she feels toward her father in Des Moines define relationships that are developed further in the 1985 sequel, *Switcharound*.

The theme of family life in *The One Hundredth Thing About Caroline* is well presented. Caroline's mother, a bank teller who wants to be a poet, often upsets the children by making inexpensive meals such as eggplant when her paycheck must stretch to cover too many bills; however, Mrs. Tate maintains an affectionate rapport with her adolescents. She frequently tells Caroline what she loves about her, including her perpetual ability to wake up cheerful on Saturdays, her expertise in doing the family laundry, and (the one hundredth thing about Caroline) her being "completely incomprehensible." Maybe that is what makes this strong family portrait so charming.

Anastasia, Ask Your Analyst (1984) focuses on Anastasia's seventh-grade science project, which is to mate her gerbils, Romeo and Juliet, and then study the pregnancy for the twenty-five-day gestation period and observe the babies. Her first major scientific "discovery" is that she has two females; five days later nine baby gerbils appear. Soon, eleven gerbils are on the loose. More havoc is crea rock.

"It's a chip of ~~a Mastodon~~ *a mastodon* bone," Gregor Keretsky explained.
"Radiocarbon dates it about ~~11,500~~ *one and a half million* years ago."

"~~Late~~ *Early* Pleistocene," breathed Caroline, in awe. She turned

it over and over in her hand.

"A glacial period," Gregor Keretsky explained. "New York

was probably covered with ice, when this mastodon lived."

"Even the Empire State Building?" asked Stacy, reaching

for some more string beans.

Everyone laughed, even Stacy, after she had thought for a

moment. "Someday we'll all be extinct," said Frederick Fiske.

"Someday I suppose scientists will be digging up <u>our</u> bones."

His voice, and what he had said, brought Caroline back

to reality from the ~~Late~~ *Early* Pleistocene Age. You first, she thought;

you're going to be extinct before I am, Frederick Fiske. J.P.

and I are going to see to that as soon as we finish the dessert.

"Well," said Joanna Tate, "this leg of lamb is extinct.

I guess it's time for chocolate cake."

"Mom," said Caroline, "you stay right in your seat. J.P.

and I can clear the table and serve the cake." Carefully she *put*

~~rewrapped her chip of~~ *the* mastodon bone, ~~and put it~~ into the pocket

of her skirt. "Thank you, Mr. Keretsky. It's the best gift anyone

ever gave me, ~~even better than my membership in the Museum of Natural~~

~~History."~~

She and her brother conferred in the kitchen as they scraped

the bits of food from the plates into the garbage disposal. Lightning

streaked across the sky outside, and was followed by heavy, shuddering

thunder.

Revised typescript page for The One Hundredth Thing About Caroline *(by permission of the author)*

ated by her brother Sam's nursery-school nemesis named Nicky, who comes over with her equally obnoxious mother. Sam, a three-year-old genius, plots a wonderful revenge against them both and solves the gerbil dilemma simultaneously by sending all of them to Nicky as a "gift" after she breaks both her legs.

This sequel depicts in Lowry's typical fashion the problems children face at home and at school. Anastasia, convinced she needs a psychiatrist to cure her of all the "different personalities seething inside," must settle for a $4.50 bust of Freud bought at a garage sale and a book of Freud's essays because her parents decide a psychiatrist is not the answer. The problem, they say, is hormones, which are causing these emotional and physical changes. Thus, her plaster analyst must suffice in consoling her. Another way Anastasia endures life's unfairness and humiliation is by writing her science project journal entries, delightful notes at the end of each chapter which document her less-than-scientific experiment.

Not only is this end-of-the-chapter writing something to look forward to in each Anastasia novel, but also intriguing are Sam's growth and the portrayal of the parents. Sam, with "an IQ of about a billion," types incredible notes; Dr. Krupnik keeps his unfinished poetry manuscripts in the refrigerator crisper drawer in case of a fire; and Mrs. Krupnik stores oatmeal boxes for three years to make creative toys for Sam. Even though Sam is sometimes a "huge humongous humiliation" and her parents do crazy things, the adventures of the Krupnik family make for thoroughly entertaining reading. This sequel was selected for *Booklist*'s "Editor's Choice" of the Best Books for Children in 1984.

Us and Uncle Fraud (1984) describes the excitement surrounding eleven-year-old Louise Cunningham's Uncle Claude and his very brief stay with her family. Louise's mother recalls that her brother, now thirty-five, was always different as a child, living in his own fantasy world, preferring dreams to responsibility. Her father, a newspaper editor dedicated to his work, says Claude is a lush, a con artist. Her fourteen-year-old brother Tom agrees; Claude's dream-weaving disillusioned him three years ago, though Lowry does not specify how. Just as magically as Claude appears, he disappears—and so does five thousand dollars' worth of silver from a wealthy family. Coincidentally, Louise and her younger brother Marcus had shown him where the mansion's key was kept, a secret they knew because their playmate's father was the se-

curity guard. Louise and Marcus are at first charmed by Claude, for he makes their imagination soar, makes them laugh, and promises them a valuable Easter egg treasure he has hidden for them: a Fabergé egg he smuggled out of Russia; however, she is soon convinced he is a liar and a thief. Perhaps the most exciting drama in any of Lowry's books occurs amid a violent storm that brings Louise and her two brothers near death. Swirling, explosive river currents flood the cemetery where Marcus has gone to look for bones floating out of graves. Tom, trying to save Marcus and Louise, who had jumped in to save Marcus, is swept away. They are rescued, but Tom is seriously injured. In addition to this exhilarating subplot, the clever "whodunit" mystery of the theft and the meaning of Claude's esoteric farewell message, which turns out to be Russian for "I love you," provide even more exciting suspense.

Lowry again focuses on family values. Louise's father, gruff and short-tempered, changes when his oldest son lies near death in a coma. Realizing his family has priority over his work, he finally shows the affection that binds family members closer after a tragedy. Claude remains an intriguing character, though never as fully developed as is his effect on the children, who discover their genuine love for one another.

Anastasia on Her Own (1985), the fifth in the series, shows Anastasia taking charge of the household while her mother goes to California for a ten-day consulting job. "Organized housekeeping is ridiculously easy, once you have a schedule," boasts Anastasia confidently. However, contrary to believing that "any moron could do it," she learns it takes more than a schedule to confront the subsequent reigning chaos. Her carefully made plans are wrecked when she must deal with Sam's chicken pox, telephone soliciting, and an unexpected visit from her father's old girlfriend. Things fall apart when she gets ready for her first date with Steve, her classmate. She plans a romantic gourmet dinner, complete with candlelight and a tablecloth she had dyed passionate purple, unwittingly dying her arms as well.

The humor is marvelous, as always. Anastasia tries to cover up the purple dye which covers her arms, and she gives Sam baths in baking powder, instead of baking soda. Furthermore, the wordplay with the hilarious nicknames Steve teases her with, "Anapestic," "Anaconda," "Analgesia," "Anachronism," is very clever. Similar to lists of "Things I Hate!" and "Things I Love!" or science project notes are this book's continually abridged, sad-but-true "nonsexist housekeeping schedules" at the end of each chapter to show Anastasia's desperate attempt to achieve some semblance of order to a rapidly disintegrating situation.

Beyond the humor, Anastasia learns to have more compassion for her mother, who just cannot seem to organize household tasks, due to unexpected events like the furnace exploding, the carpool driver having a flat tire, or Sam shoplifting gum. Running a home gets very complicated; in fact, being in charge takes on new meaning as she unwittingly uses her father's credit card to order unnecessary merchandise. Sam, as usual, is incredible; who else would carefully draw green and purple Magic Marker lines from one chicken pox to another to play "follow the dots"? And Annie, her father's former girlfriend, is outrageous as well, as she curses, bellows, and makes obnoxious remarks. Witty, realistic characterization makes this a fine addition to the Anastasia stories.

Switcharound (1985) presents the continuing saga of Caroline Tate and her brother J. P., who are not pleased about having to visit their father, whom they have not seen in years, in Des Moines, where he lives with his new wife and family. Caroline resents having to spend a summer away from home, especially so far away; moreover, she does not trust a city that does not pronounce its final consonants. She discovers upon their arrival that she is expected to babysit for her father's six-month-old twins and share a room with them, and J. P. has to coach an awful baseball team of six-year-olds. The usually feuding brother and sister join forces to plot their revenge on their father, agreeing to call a truce to their sibling war because of these threats to their mutual well-being.

Lowry again constructs a clever, humorous, and swiftly moving plot. The strong relationship between sister and brother is exceptionally well portrayed, demonstrating the same fun and mutual affection (observable between arguments) seen in their earlier banding together to get revenge against Frederick Fiske, the man they think may be a child murderer. Again their annoyance with each other changes to cooperation; in helping each other survive the summer, they become even closer. The hilarious descriptions of baseball games, J. P.'s distaste for sports, Caroline's satiric commentary on babies, and their observations of their father all make for another fine book about the joys and traumas of growing up.

Anastasia Has the Answers (1986) recounts Anastasia's humiliating experience as the only seventh-grade girl who cannot climb the rope in gym

Dust jacket for the latest installment in the Anastasia series (Houghton Mifflin)

class. Determined to master this skill, she enlists her father's help in hanging a rope from the top ceiling beam in the garage, and her mother shows her that even an old lady of thirty-eight can climb up effortlessly like a monkey. When Ms. Willoughby, her perfectly dressed, beautiful, sensitive PE teacher picks her to be the whistle blower to save Anastasia from embarrassment in front of foreign visitors, Anastasia becomes even more determined to prove herself, diligently practicing her rope climbing and memorizing her poem in order to impress the school visitors. Unfortunately, her moment of glory, when classmates, teacher, and international educators will watch with pride and delight, has an unexpected ending.

Each Anastasia sequel seems to be better than the previous one. Lowry maintains her high standards for plot, characterization, and dialogue to reinforce the central theme of understanding adolescence. Besides struggling to conquer rope climbing, Anastasia also answers these questions: Should she overcome her fear of flying? Does she have a serious psychological problem, having a crush on Ms. Willoughby? Why did Daphne's parents divorce? Will Uncle George find a wife to replace the late Aunt Rose? Now an aspiring journalist, Anastasia asks the "who, what, when, where, why" questions of situations. *Anastasia Has the Answers* has these five questions as headings for her news stories' leads after each chapter. They show Anastasia's composing, in her typical melodramatic, witty fashion, variations of fantasized news articles about events covered in the chapter. Lowry astutely demonstrates both the creative process of writing and Anastasia's reactions to events.

Still another fine touch that adds to the novel's richness is the use of literary allusions to show children's responses to reading, perhaps even encouraging adolescent readers to explore literature beyond her books (consider the bumper sticker on the book jacket: I'D RATHER BE READING). While Anastasia's classmates memorize Robert Frost's "Stopping By Woods on a Snowy Evening" and Matthew Arnold's "Dover Beach," she has mastered Edna St. Vincent Millay's "God's World." Anastasia's recitation of the poem at the top of the rope provides a tragicomic ending when she dramatically adds hand gestures to the first line—"O world! I cannot hold thee close enough!"—and naturally falls to the floor. She wakens in the hospital.

Anastasia's love of words illustrates Lowry's keen wit. Anastasia plays linguistic games; for instance, when Aunt Rose dies of food poisoning in an elegant California restaurant, Anastasia says she's "grossed out" by "salmonella": "A mobster, a hitman, my Aunt Rose was killed by Sal Monella." Lowry captures a typical thirteen-year-old's mutilation of the English language—*nerd, gross, yuck, barf*—and skillfully mixes the comic with the serious. Katherine Krupnik also has quite a sense of humor—necessary to put up with her children's antics. Her sweatshirt says: GOD ISN'T DEAD—SHE'S COOKING DINNER—a typical example of Lowry's irrepressible, irreverent humor and her feminist touches. Beyond the humor, which is always witty and gentle, she has a subtle way of reinforcing the changing views of women, such as presenting a woman doctor who treats Anastasia in the hospital. In these ways Lowry provides superior role models for girls who need to be assured that they can do anything they strive to do—within reason.

Her Anastasia books have given Lowry the reputation of "the Beverly Cleary for the middle grades," for they offer adolescents the solid, charming writing that Cleary's Ramona stories give younger readers. According to *Horn Book* reviewer Ann A. Flowers, the Anastasia stories resemble the Ramona series in having realistic but not overpowering family problems, a likable central character, and sensible, affectionate parents. Dr. and Mrs. Myron Krupnik are often hailed as among the most understanding, sympathetic, cheerful, and amusing parents in recent children's fiction. This Harvard English professor and free-lance artist have created not only poetry and paintings but also two articulate, bright, genuinely funny children. While Anastasia's intriguing character has also been compared to Louise Fitzhugh's Harriet the spy, one can readily see that the Krupniks are a more loving, close-knit family than the emotionally distant Welsches in Fitzhugh's book.

As the professional photographer she is, Lowry presents through many "snapshots" a marvelous montage of all stages of childhood, focusing on Anastasia, ages ten to thirteen, for a realistic portrait of early adolescence. These novels all have snappy, humorous dialogue and plenty of action, skillfully handled from the third person point of view. Anastasia's clever lists and notebook entries allow a more intimate voice to express her inner thoughts and to organize the confusion in her life. The books can be read independently and out of sequence, for Lowry integrates all the necessary information to make each one easily accessible. For Anastasia fans, picking up the latest book in the series is like flipping the pages of a family photograph album, seeing friendly faces that are all so familiar.

Lowry's children's books realistically depict problems of growing up in a confusing adult world, and though they are usually recommended for readers ages eight to twelve, one is intended for more mature readers (*Find a Stranger, Say Goodbye*). Lowry has presented characters in much the same way she herself has been described by several interviewers: conversational, friendly, good-humored, and lively. After reading Lowry's canon, one senses certain patterns emerging, particularly within the Anastasia books. Her protagonists tend to be bright, high-spirited, independent, somewhat mischievous in their searching for adventures to alleviate their boredom or to get revenge on adults. The main characters, all females, often team up with boys in their wacky, entertaining, and exciting antics; consider Enid and Seth, Louise and Marcus, Caroline and J. P., Anastasia and Sam. However, Lowry presents a more serious side of adolescence, for example, in depicting the way Meg faces not only sibling rivalry but also the trauma of her sister's death and the wonder of childbirth. Lowry's youngest protagonist is six-year-old Elizabeth, but her story is actually revealed from the sophisticated perspective of an adult, turning back the clock to a painful remembrance of things past. For this reason, *Autumn Street* is Lowry's most poignant human tragedy. Lowry's oldest protagonist is seventeen-year-old Natalie, who searches into the past in *Find a Stranger, Say Goodbye;* while this story contains adult themes that are too quickly becoming adolescent concerns, the resolution is a celebration of life's bright promises. Perhaps it is difficult to write realistic fiction for teenagers today without referring to premarital sex, drug abuse, peer pressure, parental conflict, and the like. Lowry's honesty about these contemporary problems of adolescence—and humor, when the situation allows—contributes to her popularity.

Most critics agree that Lowry's strength as a writer is in her ability to create strong central characters whose determination, intelligence, and humor surmount the difficulties they face; however, not every reviewer has unqualified praise for Lowry's work. One might find fault with her creating humorous situations with stereotypes of racial and ethnic groups or the elderly, but never does this rich diversity of characterization hold a group up to ridicule; on the contrary, Lowry clearly shows the often tragic results of discrimination against minorities and the underprivileged. She produces clever surprises, such as when a supposedly indigent bag lady is quite wealthy or a supposedly disreputable man is a Harvard professor. Her lively and diverse characters reflect the multiplicity that makes America the great melting pot but they appear to be stereotypes. Another possible source of

criticism is that Lowry's plots are too neatly rounded off, too tidily resolved, with no loose threads left hanging. It might also be a criticism if this were not done, for most readers of children's books expect some degree of contrivance to wrap up the plot's action. Furthermore, some may find Lowry's characters too likable and too attractive. For instance, Sam the Boy Wonder may be too delightful, precocious, and articulate to be believable, and it may seem unrealistic for Natalie to have it all: beauty and brains, the perfect family life, and even the most attractive, affluent biological mother and father. Based on Lowry's popularity, one can conclude that readers like these admirable adolescent characters and the way they confront their problems.

Lowry's success is well deserved, based on her clear writing, delightful humor, intriguing characters, and memorable stories with universal values. She portrays a variety of family situations and skillfully incorporates almost all of the varied contemporary life-styles into her fiction. A fluent storyteller, she has portrayed these generally warm, loving families in well-crafted stories, each one a meaningful whole. Separately, these books have a touching significance all their own; together, they form a truly remarkable canon. The high quality of her children's books has earned Lois Lowry a distinct place in contemporary children's literature.

Interviews:

A Visit with Lois Lowry (videotape) (Boston: Houghton Mifflin, 1985);

Amanda Smith, "PW Interviews: Lois Lowry," *Publishers Weekly,* 229 (21 February 1986): 152-153.

Robin McKinley

(16 November 1952-   )

Marilyn H. Karrenbrock
University of Tennessee

BOOKS: *Beauty: A Retelling of the Story of Beauty and the Beast* (New York: Harper & Row, 1978);
The Door in the Hedge (New York: Greenwillow, 1981);
The Blue Sword (New York: Greenwillow, 1982);
The Hero and the Crown (New York: Greenwillow, 1984).

OTHER: *Imaginary Lands,* edited by McKinley (New York: Ace Fantasy Books, 1985); published in hardcover with new introduction (New York: Greenwillow, 1986);
Rudyard Kipling, *Jungle Book,* adapted by McKinley as *Tales from the Jungle Book* (New York: Random House, 1985);
Anna Sewell, *Black Beauty,* adapted by McKinley (New York: Random House, forthcoming 1986).

PERIODICAL PUBLICATION: "Newbery Medal Acceptance," *Horn Book,* 61 (July/August 1985): 395-405.

Robin McKinley achieved renown in the field of children's literature with her first novel, *Beauty: A Retelling of the Story of Beauty and the Beast* (1978), and her reputation has continued to grow. Her fourth book, *The Hero and the Crown* (1984), won the Newbery Medal in 1985. McKinley has said that she writes about "girls who do things." Her books depict strong female characters whose feats are heroic enough to satisfy any lover of adventurous fantasy. They are equally noted for their romances. McKinley's females do not simper; they do not betray their own nature to win a man's approval. But neither do they take love lightly or put their own desires before anything else. In McKinley's books, the romance, like the adventure, is based upon ideals of faithfulness, duty, and honor.

Jennifer Carolyn Robin McKinley was born in her mother's hometown of Warren, Ohio, on 16 November 1952. She was the only child of William McKinley, an officer in the United States Navy, and Jeanne Turrell McKinley, a teacher. She grew up

all over the world, following her father from one naval post to another. Her favorite activity was reading, and she associates the various places she has lived with the books which she first read there: the *Blue Fairy Book* in California, the *Chronicles of Narnia* in New York, *Lord of the Rings* in Japan, *The Once and Future King* in Maine. She also loved horses: "I played the same sort of wild-horse games—I was always big on anything that involved whinnying and jumping over things—on the rocky shores of Lake Ontario and under palm trees in Japan." She was a solitary child who found it hard to make friends, especially with her family moving so frequently. She was absent-minded and awkward, reticent and restless; as an adolescent, she had none of the expected social graces. "I didn't discover boys because boys didn't discover me, and because their standards of discovery seemed to me too odd to be aspired to." Boys, in fact, were the enemy: "They were the ones who got to have adventures, while we got to—well, not have adventures." It is not surprising that McKinley's peripatetic childhood, constant reading, and desire for adventure should lead to the creation of a world where real and unreal meet. Most of her favorite fantasies extolled exploits almost exclusively male, but the stories she told herself were concerned with girls who stumbled and bumbled their way to triumphant conclusions.

McKinley was educated at Gould Academy, a preparatory school in Bethel, Maine. In 1970-1972, she attended Dickinson College in Carlisle, Pennsylvania. She then spent some time in Washington, D.C., working as an editor and transcriber for Ward & Paul, a stenographic reporting firm, and "living the Bohemian life." She completed her education at Bowdoin College in Brunswick, Maine, graduating summa cum laude in 1975. She remained in Maine for several years, working as a research assistant and later in a bookstore. It was during this period that her first book was written.

McKinley had always told herself stories, and she began to write them down while she was still a child. Her stories of "girls who do things" gradually

Dust jacket for McKinley's first book (Harper & Row)

crystallized into stories of a land she was to call Damar. She had begun to record the Damarian cycle when, "terrified of how much of it there seemed to be," she set it aside to write *Beauty* instead. *Beauty: A Retelling of the Story of Beauty and the Beast* was snatched up by the first publisher who saw it and immediately catapulted its author to prominence. It was named by the American Library Association as both a Notable Children's Book and a Best Book for Young Adults. It appeared on virtually every other "Best Books of the Year" list as well.

Beauty is an excellent example of a relatively rare but by no means unknown genre, the expanded and personalized version of an old fairy tale. Sometimes the author attempts to modernize the stories or to make them realistic. McKinley does not do either of these. She retains the magic; indeed she adds to it in the description of the enchanted castle and especially in the charming portrait of Bessie and Lydia, the determined maids

who dress and care for Beauty but who appear to her as a little chattering breeze. Beauty's first person narration presents her world vividly and lyrically. The setting is a might-have-been world where witches and magicians live but where students study Sophocles and Euripides, houses have Oriental rugs, and ships sail to China. The book is the finest and most noble of love stories. Beauty is the nickname of a merchant's youngest daughter. Her real name is Honour, and that is what the story is about. Because she is honorable, she goes to live with the Beast to save her father's life. Gradually her fear and horror turn to pity, then to friendship, and finally to love. As for the Beast, he cannot live without her; she personifies the qualities, beauty and honor, which make life bearable.

In 1978-1979 McKinley was a teacher and counselor at a private school in Natick, Massachusetts. She then moved to Boston and took a job as an editorial assistant in the Children's Book Department of Little, Brown. While in Boston, she wrote *The Door in the Hedge* (1981), a collection of four fairy tales. Two of the stories are retellings of old tales: "The Princess and the Frog" and "The Twelve Dancing Princesses." McKinley's version of the former story is a new and unusual interpretation in which the frog and the princess are allied against an evil enchanter. "The Twelve Dancing Princesses" follows the plot of the original tale more faithfully. In an unusual departure for McKinley, the story concentrates on a male character, the soldier who discovers the princesses' secret. The other two stories in the collection are original. The title story is a romance based on legends about children who are stolen by the fairies. On her seventeenth birthday, a human princess awakens in fairyland, where she is destined to marry the fairy prince. Although she loves him, her sense of duty and honor calls her back to her human kingdom because she is the only heir to the throne. "The Hunting of the Hind" tells of sacrifice and transformation. It has two heroines, a lady who is forced to assume the shape of a Golden Hind and lure hunters to their death and a Princess who risks her life to save her brother. Although the four stories are more personal and therefore less archetypal than most fairy tales, they seem formal in style, like the set patterns of a court dance. They are cool, well-bred stories which lack the compassionate warmth of *Beauty* or the surging vitality of the Damar stories which were to follow.

Although McKinley's books were well received, she still needed to hold another job in order to support herself. In 1981 she took a job living and working on a horse farm in Massachusetts. This allowed her to indulge her passion for horses while she continued to write. Unfortunately, shortly before she was due to finish *The Blue Sword* (1982), a horse fell on her and broke her hand, which delayed the completion of the book by about six weeks.

The Blue Sword was McKinley's first published book about the land she called Damar. Harry Crewe is sent out to join her brother who is serving with the Homelander army in The Royal Province of Daria, once the ancient Kingdom of Damar. Almost immediately, Harry feels drawn to the harsh desert and the distant hills of her new home. The feeling is only intensified when she is stolen by Corlath, the native Damarian king, who sees her when he comes to the Homelander fort to seek help against the evil, inhuman forces of the North who after many years of quiet are threatening to invade

Dust jacket for McKinley's novel inspired by John Huston's 1975 film, The Man Who Would Be King, *based on Rudyard Kipling's short story (Greenwillow)*

Damar. Corlath is not happy with his reception by the Homelanders, and his followers are equally unhappy with his decision to steal the Outlander girl, but his *kelar*, his Gift, tells him that she is important to his cause. His presentiment is soon proved right. Harry adjusts easily to life in the hills; sees visions of the Lady Aerin, the heroic queen who lived more than five hundred years before; becomes laprunminta, the winner of the trials for young, previously untested warriors; and is named one of the elite band of King's Riders. Bearing Gonturan, the Blue Sword of Lady Aerin, she proves to be the key to Damarian victory during the Northerners' invasion.

According to its author, *The Blue Sword* has "its roots in Rudyard Kipling and Rider Haggard and P. C. Wren—and, for that matter, in E. M. Hull's *The Sheik*, though I suppose I should blush to admit it." The specific inspiration for the story was John Huston's film *The Man Who Would Be King*, which was based on Kipling's story of the same name. Intrigued by the story of friendship, idealism, and loyalty, McKinley set out to write a story of a woman motivated by the same qualities, "perhaps even as grand and as improbable." In *The Blue Sword*, the government of Damar, in which a small military force armed with guns imposes Homelander rule on fiercely independent but less well-equipped native tribes, is definitely reminiscent of Kipling's India, but the desert scenes seem more indebted to romantic fantasies about Bedouin life. It is a fresh and interesting setting for a novel of high fantasy. Like the desert air, the tone is open and bright and brilliant. The emphasis is less on the struggle with evil than on Harry's development into a Damulur-sol, a Lady Hero. Although she does not consider herself marriageable by Homelander standards, once in the desert she seems to have few self-doubts. The growing love between Harry and Corlath is entirely believable.

The Blue Sword was a Newbery Honor Book and was listed on many "Best Books of the Year" lists. McKinley, who had moved to New York City, was soon involved in writing another Damarian novel, the story of Lady Aerin. She again suffered an accident shortly before the book was scheduled for completion. She fell and broke her ankle, which was "very good for the book because there was for nine weeks very little I could do but type, but I do now suffer from an interesting new paranoia and am planning to withdraw into a padded room with my typewriter when the next book gets close to its end."

The Hero and the Crown (1984) was the winner of the 1985 John Newbery Medal for the best children's book published in the United States. Aerin is the daughter of Arlbeth, the Damarian King, but she is not his heir; his marriage to Aerin's mother, who many of his people think was a witch from the North, was morganatic. Aerin is pale and redhaired among cinnamon-skinned brunettes; she seems to have no Gift, no *kelar*, as other members of the royal family do. Her only friends are Tor, her cousin and heir to the throne, and Talat, her father's old warhorse, who had been retired to a pasture when he was lamed in battle. While the kingdom prepares for battle with the evil forces of the North, Aerin finds a way to make herself useful by killing the little dragons who infest the countryside. When the Black Dragon Maur, a Great Dragon whose like has not been seen for many years, appears, Aerin sets out alone to meet him. Although she is successful in killing Maur, she is badly burned in the struggle. Her only hope of being restored to health lies with the immortal wizard Luthe, who had befriended Harry Crewe in *The Blue Sword*. It is from Luthe that Aerin learns of her heritage. Armed with Luthe's gift, the magic sword Gonturan, she sets out to meet the evil mage Agsded, who has stolen the hero's Crown which holds Damar's power.

The story takes place approximately five hundred years before the previous novel, and the portrait of Damar is radically different. This book is based not on the works of Kipling, but on those of Tolkien. It was inspired by the scene in *The Return of the King* in which the warrior Dernhelm, preparing to defend his fallen king, is revealed to be the maiden Eowyn. McKinley says, "It's not that I am tall and light-skinned myself that has made my subconscious carry around all these years a picture of a tall, pale woman carrying a sword and defying something undefiable. . . ." However, McKinley's background suggests that she identifies strongly with Aerin. Aerin is very different from Harry Crewe; she is far more shy, awkward, and unsure of herself. Harry learned her lessons in warfare easily; Aerin puts in several years of struggle before she is able to face her first dragon. She is much less confident of her own powers, though much of Harry's assurance may be due to the visions in which Aerin gives her advice. Harry emerges almost unscathed from her adventures, but Aerin is hurt badly several times. Aerin's story makes a strong emotional impact upon the reader because she feels her shortcomings so intensely and because the presence of evil as a potent force in

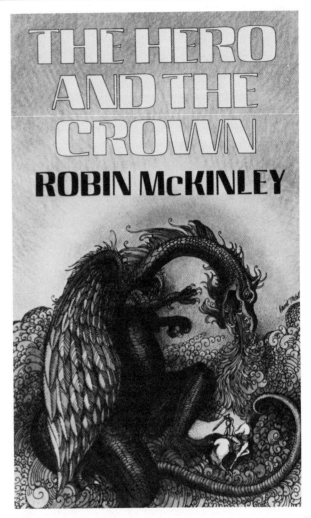

Dust jacket for McKinley's 1985 Newbery Medal-winning fantasy (Greenwillow)

Damar is vividly depicted.

The book is most effective in the characterization of Aerin, the description of the setting, the excitement of the plot, and the suspenseful tone. It is probable that the plot of this tale was worked out before *The Blue Sword* was written. Many of Harry's visions in that story are scenes from Aerin's life which appear in the later book. Also, McKinley's command of her plot is less sure in *The Hero and the Crown*, which might be expected if the story were developed early but may simply be due to the fact that the plot is more complex. In *The Blue Sword*, it is clear from the first pages that Harry's fate lies in the mountains, and the shape of the adventure is revealed with Harry's first vision given by the Meeldtar, the Water of Sight, which occurs less than a third of the way through the book. In *The Hero and the Crown*, however, the reader's understanding of the problem would have been increased if several clues to the solution, including the significance of the Hero's Crown and of the dragon's bloodstone, had been provided earlier. The existence of Agsded, the chief threat to Damar, is not even revealed until halfway through the book, and the prophecy that he can only be defeated by a member of his family is not emphasized until Aerin's battle with the wizard. Since Agsded holds the Hero's Crown, this episode should be the high point of the book, but it becomes almost anticlimactic to the final battle with Maur's spirit. Nevertheless, *The Hero and the Crown* is a rousing story which convincingly makes McKinley's point: girls can be heroes, too.

Since the publication of *The Hero and the Crown*, McKinley has had short stories published in fantasy anthologies and has herself edited an anthology, *Imaginary Lands*, which first appeared in paperback by Ace Fantasy Books in 1985 and was published in hardback by Greenwillow, with a new introduction, in 1986. It is a fine collection from noted authors. McKinley's own story, which closes the collection, is "The Stone Fey." It is laid in Damar and tells of Maddy, who "has Hillrock for bones" and who must choose between the inhuman stone fey whom she loves and the man to whom she is betrothed. McKinley first wrote about a human's love for a nonhuman creature in *Beauty*, and several of her short stories also explore this situation. It is always treated with compassion. Another recurrent motif in McKinley's work is her loving portrait of horses. Beauty, Harry Crewe, and Aerin all have a horse whom they love, but it is Aerin's Talat who is so well developed that he is a definite character in the book.

McKinley has also adapted the texts of two classic books, which will be published as picture books for young children. In each case, she capitalizes on one of her particular interests: Kipling and horses. In *Tales from the Jungle Book* (1985), she has adapted three of Kipling's Mowgli adventures. Her adaptation of *Black Beauty* is scheduled for publication in 1986.

McKinley has many interests besides her writing. Now that she is better established as a writer, she keeps an apartment in New York City but spends most of her time in a house which she has purchased in a small town in Maine. She is eclectic in her musical tastes, which range from grand opera to heavy metal rock. She reads constantly and haunts used-book stores. Fantasy is her first love, but she also likes nineteenth-century novels, murder mysteries ("not too gore-spattered"), old-fashioned adventure, and British history. She would like someday to write realistic novels and perhaps mysteries but does not expect ever to abandon the field of fantasy.

There are many tales of Damar left to tell. In *The Hero and the Crown*, Aerin has several visions of persons who will undoubtedly be characters in future books—one of them is Harry Crewe. McKinley feels that her stories are given to her; she is simply the historian of Damar who writes them down. Her books are popular with adult fantasy readers as well as children. She will undoubtedly produce more exciting, original stories about heroic girls and perhaps about male characters as well; as she says, "both sides of our gender-specific event horizon need to be extended." Her stories should continue to improve. Her minor characters, especially the males, are not always fully developed. Her short stories show a tenderness which is sometimes obscured by the exciting adventures in the longer Damarian books. But to fantasy readers, these are minor matters. They are eagerly looking forward to the next story from the Damarian cycle.

Reference:

Terri Windling and Mark Alan Arnold, "Robin McKinley," *Horn Book*, 61 (July/August 1985): 406-409.

Andre Norton
(Alice Mary Norton)
(17 February 1912-)

Francis J. Molson
Central Michigan University

See also the Norton entry in *DLB 8: Twentieth-Century American Science Fiction Writers.*

BOOKS: *The Prince Commands,* illustrated by Kate Seredy (New York & London: Appleton-Century, 1934);

Ralestone Luck, illustrated by James Reid (New York & London: Appleton-Century, 1938);

Follow the Drum (New York: Penn, 1942);

The Sword is Drawn, illustrated by Duncan Coburn (Cambridge, Mass.: Houghton Mifflin, 1944; London: Oxford University Press, 1946);

Rogue Reynard, illustrated by Laura Bannon (Boston: Houghton Mifflin, 1947);

Scarface, illustrated by Lorence Bjorklund (New York: Harcourt, Brace, 1948; London: Methuen, 1950);

Sword in Sheath, illustrated by Bjorklund (New York: Harcourt, Brace, 1949); republished as *Island of the Lost* (London: Staples, 1953);

Huon of the Horn, illustrated by Joe Krush (New York: Harcourt, Brace, 1951);

Star Man's Son, 2250 A.D., illustrated by Nicholas Morduinoff (New York: Harcourt, Brace, 1952; London: Staples, 1953); republished as *Daybreak, 2250 A.D.* (New York: Ace, 1954);

Star Rangers (New York: Harcourt, Brace, 1953; London: Gollancz, 1968); republished as *The Last Planet* (New York: Ace, 1953);

At Swords' Points (New York: Harcourt, Brace, 1954);

Murder for Sale, by Norton and Grace Allen Hogarth as Allen Weston (London: Hammond-Hammond, 1954);

The Stars are Ours! (Cleveland: World, 1954);

Sargasso of Space, as Andrew North (New York: Gnome Press, 1955); as Andre Norton (London: Gollancz, 1970);

Star Guard (New York: Harcourt, Brace, 1955; London: Gollancz, 1969);

Yankee Privateer, illustrated by Leonard Vosburgh (Cleveland: World, 1955);

The Crossroads of Time (New York: Ace, 1956);

Andre Norton

Plague Ship, as Andrew North (New York: Gnome Press, 1956); as Andre Norton (London: Gollancz, 1971);

Stand to Horse (New York: Harcourt, Brace, 1956);

Sea Siege (New York: Harcourt, Brace, 1957);

Star Born (Cleveland: World, 1957; London: Gollancz, 1973);

Star Gate (New York: Harcourt, Brace, 1958; London: Gollancz, 1970; revised edition, New York: Ace, 1963);

The Time Traders (Cleveland: World, 1958);

Secret of the Lost Race (New York: Ace, 1959; London: Hale, 1977);

Voodoo Planet, as Andrew North (New York: Ace, 1959);

The Beast Master (New York: Harcourt, Brace, 1959; London: Gollancz, 1966);

Galactic Derelict (Cleveland: World, 1959);

Shadow Hawk (New York: Harcourt, Brace, 1960; London: Gollancz, 1971);

The Sioux Spaceman (New York: Ace, 1960; London: Hale, 1976);

Storm over Warlock (Cleveland: World, 1960);

Catseye (New York: Harcourt, Brace & World, 1961; London: Gollancz, 1962);

Ride Proud, Rebel! (Cleveland: World, 1961);

Star Hunter (New York: Ace, 1961);

The Defiant Agents (Cleveland: World, 1962);

Eye of the Monster (New York: Ace, 1962);

Lord of Thunder (New York: Harcourt, Brace & World, 1962; London: Gollancz, 1966);

Rebel Spurs (Cleveland: World, 1962);

Judgment on Janus (New York: Harcourt, Brace & World, 1963; London: Gollancz, 1964);

Key Out of Time (Cleveland: World, 1963);

Witch World (New York: Ace, 1963; London: Tandem, 1970);

Night of Masks (New York: Harcourt, Brace & World, 1964; London: Gollancz, 1965);

Ordeal in Otherwhere (Cleveland: World, 1964);

Web of the Witch World (New York: Ace, 1964; London: Tandem, 1970);

Three Against the Witch World (New York: Ace, 1965; London: Tandem, 1970);

Year of the Unicorn (New York: Ace, 1965; London: Tandem, 1970);

The X Factor (New York: Harcourt, Brace & World, 1965; London: Gollancz, 1967);

Quest Crosstime (New York: Viking, 1965); republished as *Crosstime Agent* (London: Gollancz, 1975);

Steel Magic, illustrated by Robin Jacques (Cleveland: World, 1965; London: Tandem, 1970); revised as *Grey Magic* (New York: Scholastic, 1967);

Moon of Three Rings (New York: Viking, 1966; London: Longman, 1969);

Victory on Janus (New York: Harcourt, Brace & World, 1966; London: Gollancz, 1967);

Octagon Magic, illustrated by Mac Conner (Cleveland: World, 1967; London: Hamish Hamilton, 1968);

Operation Time Search (New York: Harcourt, Brace & World, 1967);

Warlock of the Witch World (New York: Ace, 1967; London: Tandem, 1970);

Dark Piper (New York: Harcourt, Brace & World, 1968; London: Gollancz, 1969);

Fur Magic, illustrated by John Kaufman (Cleveland: World, 1968; London: Hamish Hamilton, 1969);

Sorceress of the Witch World (New York: Ace, 1968; London: Tandem, 1970);

The Zero Stone (New York: Viking, 1968; London: Gollancz, 1974);

Bertie and May, with Bertha Stemm Norton, illustrated by Fermin Rocker (New York: World, 1969; London: Hamish Hamilton, 1971);

Postmarked the Stars (New York: Harcourt, Brace & World, 1969; London: Gollancz, 1971);

Uncharted Stars (New York: Viking, 1969; London: Gollancz, 1974);

Dread Companion (New York: Harcourt Brace Jovanovich, 1970; London: Gollancz, 1972);

High Sorcery (New York: Ace, 1970);

Ice Crown (New York: Viking, 1970; London: Longman, 1971);

Android at Arms (New York: Harcourt Brace Jovanovich, 1971; London: Gollancz, 1972);

Exiles of the Stars (New York: Viking, 1971; London: Longman, 1972);

Breed to Come (New York: Viking, 1972; London: Longman, 1973);

The Crystal Gryphon (New York: Atheneum, 1972; London: Gollancz, 1973);

Dragon Magic, illustrated by Jacques (New York: Crowell, 1972);

Garan the Eternal (Alhambra, Cal.: Fantasy, 1972);

Spell of the Witch World (New York: DAW, 1972);

Forerunner Foray (New York: Viking, 1973; London: Longman, 1974);

Here Abide Monsters (New York: Atheneum, 1973);

Iron Cage (New York: Viking, 1974; London: Penguin, 1975);

The Jargoon Pard (New York: Atheneum, 1974; London: Gollancz, 1975);

Lavender-Green Magic, illustrated by Judith Gwyn Brown (New York: Crowell, 1974);

The Many Worlds of André Norton, edited by Roger Elwood (Radnor, Pa.: Chilton, 1974); republished as *The Book of André Norton* (New York: DAW, 1975);

Outside, illustrated by Bernard Colonna (New York: Walker, 1974; London: Blackie, 1976);

The Day of the Ness, with Michael Gilbert, illustrated by Gilbert (New York: Walker, 1975);

Knave of Dreams (New York: Viking, 1975; London: Penguin, 1976);

Merlin's Mirror (New York: DAW, 1975; London: Sidgwick & Jackson, 1976);

No Night Without Stars (New York: Atheneum, 1975; London: Gollancz, 1976);

The White Jade Fox (New York: Dutton, 1975; London: Allen, 1976);

Perilous Dreams (New York: DAW, 1976);

Red Hart Magic, illustrated by Donna Diamond (New York: Crowell, 1976; London: Hamish Hamilton, 1977);

Star Ka'at, with Dorothy Madlee, illustrated by Colonna (New York: Walker, 1976; London: Blackie, 1977);

Wraiths of Time (New York: Atheneum, 1976; London: Gollancz, 1977);

The Opal-Eyed Fan (New York: Dutton, 1977);

Trey of Swords (New York: Grosset & Dunlap, 1977; London: Star, 1969);

Quag Keep (New York: Atheneum, 1978);

Star Ka'at World, with Madlee, illustrated by Jean Jenkins (New York: Walker, 1978);

Velvet Shadows (New York: Fawcett, 1978);

Yurth Burden (New York: DAW, 1978);

Seven Spells To Sunday, by Norton and Phyllis Miller (New York: Atheneum, 1979);

Snow Shadow (New York: Fawcett, 1979);

Star Ka'ats and the Plant People, with Madlee, illustrated by Jenkins (New York: Walker, 1979);

Iron Butterflies (New York: Fawcett, 1980);

Lore of Witch World (New York: DAW, 1980);

Voor Loper (New York: Ace, 1980);

Forerunner (New York: Tor, 1981);

Gryphon in Glory (New York: Atheneum, 1981);

Horn Crown (New York: DAW, 1981);

Star Ka'ats and the Winged Warriors, by Norton and Madlee, illustrated by Jenkins (New York: Walker, 1981);

Ten Mile Treasure (New York: Archway, 1981);

Moon Called (New York: Simon & Schuster, 1982);

Ware Hawk (New York: Atheneum, 1983);

Wheel of Stars (New York: Simon & Schuster, 1983);

Gryphon's Eyrie, by Norton and A. C. Crispin (New York: Tor, 1984);

House of Shadows, by Norton and Miller (New York: Atheneum, 1984);

Stand and Deliver (New York: Dell, 1984);

Were-Wrath (New Castle, Va.: Cheap Street, 1984);

Forerunner: The Second Venture (New York: Tor, 1985);

Ride the Green Dragon, by Norton and Miller (New York: Atheneum, 1985).

OTHER: Malcolm Jameson, *Bullard of the Space Patrol*, edited by Norton (Cleveland: World, 1951);

Space Service, edited with an introduction by Norton (Cleveland: World, 1953);

Space Pioneers, edited with an introduction by Norton (Cleveland: World, 1954);

Space Police, edited with an introduction by Norton (Cleveland: World, 1956);

Gates to Tomorrow: An Introduction to Science Fiction, edited by Norton and Ernestine Donaldy (New York: Atheneum, 1973);

Small Shadows Creep: Ghost Children, edited by Norton (New York: Dutton, 1974);

Magic in Ithkar, edited by Norton and Robert Adams (New York: Tor, 1985).

Andre Norton ranks among the top best-selling authors published by Ace, the leading paperback publisher of science fiction and fantasy. Her novels, which have sold in the millions, stay in print longer than those of most other science fiction authors, and her works have been translated and made available in thirteen foreign countries.

Critical approval too has accompanied popular approval, as Norton has been honored by receiving a variety of awards. She is the first woman elected to Lin Carter's Swordsmen and Sorcerers Guild, a select company of writers of fantasy. In 1964 and 1968 she was nominated for the Hugo, the award given by the general readership of science fiction and fantasy to the author of the best work in those genres the preceding year. In 1977 she was presented with the Gandalf, a special Hugo for overall excellence in science fiction and fantasy—only the fourth time such an award has been bestowed.

It is surprising, however, that specialists in children's literature have been hesitant in acknowledging her importance, for Norton does have impressive credentials as an author of children's fiction. Having written many "juvenile" science fiction and fantasy novels, she enjoys a wide following among young readers, and along with Robert Heinlein she played a major role during the 1950s in establishing science fiction as a viable category of mainstream children's literature. Yet, in spite of these credentials Norton has never been the recipient of any of the awards that single out for special praise writers of children's books.

There are two explanations why specialists in children's literature hesitate to endorse the praise Norton has received elsewhere. One is the uneasiness some specialists feel in the presence of science fiction or space fantasy. Apparently they still think of the latter as escapist reading in the manner of the Tom Swift books, consisting of quick-moving, incident-packed, poorly written stories which contain pasteboard, stereotypic characters and featuring implausible futuristic technology and gadgetry. Frankly, there is little chance of Norton's ever being universally acclaimed an important author of children's fiction as long as there are those who cling to a bias against science fiction and refuse to consider it a valid subgenre of children's literature.

A second explanation for the reluctance of some specialists in children's literature to acknowledge Norton's importance has to do with two problems that have vexed children's literature from its origins: the difficulty of distinguishing books truly intended for children from those aimed at least partially at adults and the relatively low prestige writing children's fiction enjoys when measured against that of writing adult fiction. In Norton's case, these problems give rise to two key questions. Is Norton to be approached as an author primarily of adult fiction or of children's fiction? Has Norton's artistic reputation been enhanced or diminished by association with children's books?

Finding satisfactory answers to these questions is not easy. When Norton first wrote science fiction in the early 1950s she was perceived by many as a children's author because her novels, upon initial publication in hardcover, were marketed as juveniles. In the eyes of reviewers and critics of adult science fiction, this marketing strategy had a deleterious effect upon Norton's reputation despite the fact that these same novels, when reprinted in paper as adult books by Ace, sold in the hundreds of thousands. In 1966 Lin Carter, the well-known fantasy writer and editor, pointed out that when he sought information about Norton, he was urged to stop wasting his time "on the work of a writer of minor or peripheral value, at best." That is, presumably, a writer primarily of juvenile fiction. At the same time, Norton was likewise receiving minimal recognition from spokespersons for children's literature in spite of her well-crafted and entertaining novels that did so much to make children's science fiction "respectable."

Today, however, Norton's reputation has undergone a marked change. Her stature as a writer of science fiction and fantasy is much higher now than in the 1950s, as indicated by the various awards she has received and by the Gregg Press hardcover republications of several of her early novels. It now seems that any Norton novel, regardless of its original market or putative audience, should be categorized as "adult" if it is deemed to have any adult appeal. Accordingly, in the introduction to his bibliography of Norton, Roger Schlo-

bin explains his method of classification in these words: "It is often not clear whether Ms. Norton's works are specifically adult or juvenile. Those titles with adult appeal have been listed as such, and only those that are clearly identifiable as children's books have been listed as juvenile."

Schlobin's reclassification would require a drastic pruning of the list of Norton's publications for children. For example, *Star Man's Son, 2250 A.D.* (1952), her first science fiction novel, and one marketed as a juvenile book, would no longer be a children's book; presumably, it would have to be shifted from the children's section of the library, where it has been since its publication, to the adult section. Yet, just as it was almost thirty years ago, the novel today is clearly appropriate for young readers as it speaks directly and forcefully to them through its convincing story of a boy's passage from a questioning, unsure adolescence to confident, assured young manhood.

Dust jacket for Norton's 1970 science-fiction/mystery novel (Harcourt Brace Jovanovich)

In addition, the important contribution of *Star Man's Son, 2250 A.D.* to the development of modern children's science fiction cannot be ignored. As a children's librarian at Cleveland Public Library from 1932 to 1950 Norton must have been aware of the success Robert Heinlein scored in 1947 with the publication of *Rocket Ship Galileo* and then repeated in succeeding years with other juveniles—all science fiction clearly designed for young readers and all dramatizing in different ways the importance of passage or initiation in the lives of young people. Perhaps influenced by Heinlein, Norton might very well have been prompted not only to put aside historical fiction, the genre she had been working in, and begin writing children's science fiction but also to incorporate into her first science fiction subject matter and focus similar to those of Heinlein's juveniles. Fortunately for Norton and children's science fiction, *Star Man's Son, 2250 A.D.* was successful; and she went on to write more children's science fiction which, along with her initial foray, showed, as did Heinlein's juveniles, that children's science fiction could be not only entertaining but also well written.

According to Schlobin, moreover, what he now classifies as Norton's children's books are only those narratives "clearly identifiable as such." Unfortunately, he does not explain what he means by "clearly identifiable." An examination of Schlobin's proposed list of children's books, however, indicates that they are the relatively brief stories, like *Outside* (1974) or the Star Ka'at trilogy, which depict the exploits and concerns of "small children," age ten or younger, and often contain explicit didacticism. Interestingly, Norton seems to approve of Schlobin's reclassifications, since he states that she read the introduction and raised no objections. Hence, it would appear, Norton now thinks of herself as a writer primarily of adult science fiction and fantasy.

Whether Norton is an author of children's fiction or of adult may seem to some observers a matter of little moment. What matters, they say, is that fiction should be read and enjoyed. Regardless, it should prove very useful to indicate the several ways much of Norton's science fiction and fantasy has spoken to and attracted young readers for nearly three decades.

Viewed in retrospect, the early years of Norton's life can be said to have prepared her in a special way to become an author of children's books evocative of history and rich in the portrayal of young characters attaining maturity despite adversity. She was born Alice Mary Norton in Cleveland, Ohio, on 17 February 1912. As a child of parents Adalbert and Bertha Stemm Norton, who could trace their roots to the original settlers of the midwest, including a grandfather who married a Wyandot Indian, Elk Eyes, and became the first person legally to marry an Indian in what was to become the state of Ohio, Norton soon grew aware of history as more than an assemblage of lifeless facts and dusty dates. This awareness, nurtured by a habit of reading also established early in childhood, eventually became a lifelong interest in history. To her family's awareness of its pioneer roots and its tradition of amicable relations with native American Indians, Norton may owe the beginnings of that sympathetic insight much of her fiction manifests into individuals or small groups living precariously on the margins of society and forced either to conform or strike out on their own to find liberty or a new home. Incidentally, as a child Norton was fond of playing with toy miniature animals, perhaps the origin of her fascination with animals, especially cats.

Norton began to write as early as high school, actually completing a first version of *Ralestone Luck* (1938). Later she rewrote and published it as an adventure novel, a genre she felt comfortable with and initially favored as she set about mastering the writer's craft. When her plan to graduate from Western Reserve University (1930-1932) was halted by the Great Depression, she found employment in the Cleveland Public Library, where she was eventually assigned to the children's book section. There Norton had ample opportunity to grow familiar with the range of children's literature and the various ways it meets the needs and wants of children. One of her responsibilities was the children's hour, for which she had to find or create suitable material. She subsequently wrote and published several of her first children's books: *Rogue Reynard* (1947), a retelling of the beast fable about Reynard the Fox; *Huon of the Horn* (1951), a prose adaptation of the medieval romance of Huon of Bordeaux, part of the Charlemagne saga; and *Steel Magic* (1965), a fantasy incorporating some Arthurian material. All three books bespeak their author's familiarity with what goes into the making of the type of children's fiction which is grounded in historical material, as all three narratives feature an entertaining mix of history, legend, adventure, and didacticism—a mix as long lived as children's literature itself.

During her years in the Cleveland Public Library system Norton wrote nine novels and two short stories. Considered as a whole, they clearly reveal that the young author, successfully completing her apprenticeship, had learned to fashion quick-moving fiction that emphasized adventure, mystery, and intrigue—all characteristics she would incorporate into the science fiction and fantasy she would write next. In these first novels can also be detected the beginnings of Norton's fascination with jewels, talismans, and their historic or occult associations, a fascination, later on, especially manifest in her gothic novels and the Witch World series. Interestingly, for the first of her early novels, *The Prince Commands* (1934), Norton used the pseudonym Andre Norton. She did so because she had been informed that a masculine-sounding name for its author might make the novel attractive to male readers, its primary audience, whereas her given name, she was afraid, might have the opposite effect. She must have been satisfied with the pseudonym and its usefulness because she later made Andre Norton her legal name. This name change must have, again, seemed fortunate when she turned eventually to science fiction, whose predominantly male readership had, it was believed, the same reservations concerning female authors as did the audience for historical mystery and adventure.

In 1950 Norton resigned from the Cleveland Public Library in part because of health problems and in part because of her belief that she was being exploited. She thought that her years of professional experience, including a year spent during World War II in the Library of Congress working as a researcher for the government, and her accomplishments as an author were not adequately appreciated by her supervisors. Fortunately, she was able to find an editorial position at Gnome Press more suited to her experience and skill. At Gnome she found ample time to continue her writing. She turned to a new genre, science fiction, and began to publish extensively. Unfortunately, in 1958 ill health forced an early retirement, and in 1966 Norton moved to Florida where she hoped the climate would be salubrious. She has lived there ever since in the company of her many beloved cats.

To the casual observer Norton's life must seem unexciting and uneventful in the conventional sense. The excitement and zest of great deeds or intrepid voyaging across galactic distances readers sense in Norton's science fiction and fantasy originate within her creative and prolific imagination, especially as it draws inspiration from and refashions material she has discovered in her extensive reading and research in history and related fields.

Norton has underscored the importance of history to the fantasy writer in her essay "On Writing Fantasy."

> For my own books (unless I am dealing with some specific period of history when research becomes highly concentrated) I read anthropology, folklore, history, travel, natural history, archeology, legends, studies in magic, and similar material, taking notes throughout.
>
> But the first requirement for writing heroic or sword and sorcery fantasy must be a deep interest in and love for history itself. Not the history of dates, of sweeps and empires—but the kind of history which deals with daily life, the beliefs and aspirations of people long since dust.

Thus, details of setting and background, although never the paramount elements in Norton's science fiction, are as accurate as history indicates or as speculative as research justifies. Oddly, her love for history has come to include a fascination with the pseudoscience of psychohistory: that is "the detection by a sensitive of the residue that exists in an artifact that has been handled by man through the ages. This residue contains events, human emotions and experiences, and, in the case of religious or mystical objects, psychic powers."

Norton acknowledges reading and enjoying authors as diverse as Susan Cooper, E. R. Burroughs, Alan Garner, A. Merritt, H. Rider Haggard, J. R. R. Tolkien, Ruth Plumly Thompson, William Hope Hodgson, and Anne McCaffrey. She also admits to probable influences from some of these authors; perhaps what she gained above all is the priority of "an aesthetic commitment to the value of a clear, fast-moving plot." More direct evidence of Norton's research and reading can be found in some of her novels: *The Time Traders* (1958) is indebted to the discussion of Bronze Age traders in Paul Herrmann's *Conquest by Man* (1954); *Year of the Unicorn* (1965) is loosely modeled upon the popular fairy tale "Beauty and the Beast"; *Lord of Thunder* (1962) contains Navaho phrases and customs; and *Dark Piper* (1968) echoes "The Pied Piper of Hamlin." In brief, Norton's fiction testifies, once more, that a conventional, quiet, and unassuming exterior sometimes masks an interior that is richly imaginative and creative—qualities necessary to the gifted storyteller.

Indeed Norton is a skilled teller of stories, and this is the prime reason why young readers find her fiction interesting and attractive. Characteristically, her stories, either science fiction or fantasy, are replete with incident; take place in the near or far future; feature alien or bizarre life forms, futuristic technology or exotic settings; and involve a youthful protagonist that young readers can readily identify with.

Sea Siege (1957) aptly illustrates Norton's story-telling skill. Set in a near future when nuclear proliferation and experimentation have advanced to the point that worldwide war appears inevitable and radiation has altered various species in unexpected ways, the narrative focuses on the adventures of young Griff Gunston. Unhappy to be on the Caribbean island San Isadore with his scientist father who finds his research more important than building a warm relationship with his son, Griff involves himself in the underwater exploration the U.S. Navy is secretly carrying out in order to assess the effects of radiation on sea life. The island natives, many of whom believe in voodoo, resent the Navy's research, which they associate with the Devil. The island is soon wracked with fire and destruction, first from the frightened natives who object violently to the scientists' meddling and then by the effects of nuclear explosions when the outside world finally goes to war.

> And it was in that moment that light came in a burst—not the lightning of the sky, but a pillar of flame out at sea, hurtling skyward, bathing them all in a bloody glare.
>
> Griff crouched without knowing that he was sobbing. He watched while weatherworn houses collapsed—some in a sudden flattening, some slowly stone by stone....
>
> The blazing torch at sea had not been quenched. And the land was still moving. . . . This was the end of the world; why try to escape? . . . The red fires of hell blazed to light them on—on where? There was nothing left for man—no hole to hide in.

Only after the inhabitants withstand the shock waves and fallout and beat off attacks by hostile mutated sea animals, in particular, octopuses who begin to exhibit a high degree of intelligence and leadership, do the survivors, both native and white, agree to work together in building whatever future is left them. Although there is mention of Griff's unhappiness over his father's neglect, and some attention is paid to the rival claims of science and magic, the disastrous effects of misapplied technology, and the importance of cooperation, the novel is primarily crisply narrated adventure and

Dust jacket for the British edition of Norton's novel set on the darkened world of the planet Dis (Gollancz)

graphic description. Typical is the passage in which Griff must simultaneously confront two horrors: the oncoming wave of nuclear fallout and the spawning of sea monsters that begin laying siege to the island: "This wasn't true, Griff assured himself. Nightmare! It had to be a nightmare! That—that *thing* wallowing down the streaming road, the water curling before it as it came—was nothing for any sane world to spawn. Lightning ripped across the sky, a jagged purple sword. And a monstrous head swung; fanged jaws opened and—closed! A ragged scarecrow thing mewled and squirmed and then hung limp between those jaws, as the dark came down once more."

Young readers, like their older counterparts, can take delight in another strength of Norton's storytelling—the ability to create imaginary worlds that are both fascinating in their strangeness and yet plausible in their structure and operating laws. Probably her most widely known imaginary world is the medieval-like one of magic and mystery Norton fashioned for her adult fantasy series concerning Witch World. Perhaps the most striking world she has created is Dis, the darkened world of *Night of Masks* (1964), whose protagonist, Nik, is a young adventurer with a horribly disfigured face.

On Dis the rays of the sun are infrared and dangerous to the unprotected human eye; hence humans can see only by means of Cin, specially devised goggles. Long ago a massive sun flare had steamed the planet, wiping out the indigenous people and accounting for the frequent torrential rainfall that sustains or destroys haphazardly. Norton's description of being caught out in the rain of Dis is highly suggestive: "This was like drowning while one walked on land. Nik flung his arm across his nose and mouth, trying to make a sheltered pocket in which to breath. He staggered under the weight of water. At least the wind was not as great here as it had been back in the city ruins. He brought up against a rock and clung to it with the same frenzy as a man would embrace an anchor when being borne along in a wild current. . . . "

Humans can survive only in carefully built and maintained structures under the surface of Dis; for above ground virtually every step in the seemingly omnipresent mud and slime is precarious and often fatal. Also found above ground are plants with reptilian roots, lizards of all sizes, fungoid vegetation emitting a strange, often poisonous phosphorus, and "naked, thin ghostly creatures," all that is left of the humanlike and civilized species that originally peopled the planet.

The plot revolves around Nik's attempt to guide to safety a rich alien boy named Vandy, who is programmed to kill anyone seeking to pry into his memory. If Nik is successful in carrying out his part in a plan to hold Vandy for ransom by retaining the boy's confidence, his reward will be a new face to replace the repulsively disfigured one he suffers from. The plot, when baldly paraphrased, may seem melodramatic. But, in actuality, *Night of Masks* is not only suspenseful adventure but a plausible study of a youth's passage into manhood as Nik, displaying physical and moral courage, comes to place honor and integrity above sensual gratification and wealth.

Because children readily identify with youthful protagonists, enter enthusiastically into fantasy situations where youths are often more competent than adults and always succeed, and find reassurance in similarity of plot and cast of characters,

series fiction is popular with young readers. Although Norton has written no series fiction as such, she does have a fondness for writing sequels and sequences. For instance: the Ross Murdock series, *The Time Traders* (1958) and *Key Out of Time* (1963); the Krip Vorlund series, *Moon of Three Rings* (1966) and *Exiles of the Stars* (1971); the Hosteen Storm series, *The Beast Master* (1959) and *Lord of Thunder* (1962); the Travis Fox series, *Galactic Derelict* (1959) and *The Defiant Agents* (1962); the Shann Lantee series, *Storm over Warlock* (1960) and *Ordeal in Otherwhere* (1964); the Ayyar series, *Judgment on Janus* (1963) and *Victory on Janus* (1966); and the Star Ka'at books, coauthored with Dorothy Madlee, *Star Ka'at* (1976), *Star Ka'at World* (1978), and *Star Ka'ats and the Plant People* (1979).

There are also Norton novels which, although not linked by reappearing characters, are related in subject matter or approach because of similarity in title. There are, for example, the Star books—*Star Man's Son, 2250 A.D., Star Rangers* (1953), *Star Guard* (1955), *Star Born* (1957), *Star Gate* (1958), and *Star Hunter* (1961); or the "Magic" group—*Steel Magic* (1965), *Octagon Magic* (1967), *Fur Magic* (1968), *Dragon Magic* (1972), *Lavender-Green Magic* (1974), and *Red Hart Magic* (1976). It is both a mark of Norton's skill at storytelling and a tribute to her genuine popularity that her publishers have acquiesced in the writing of the many sequels and sequences she has produced despite the claims that reviewers normally frown upon sequels and in light of the high percentage of such books that do not sell well.

It is possible that the pace and suspense of Norton's storytelling may so ensnare some readers that they may overlook the themes or concerns her narratives embody. In the eyes of these readers Norton's science fiction is definitely fast moving and entertaining but lacking in thematic seriousness. Hence, her novels may seem serieslike in the pejorative sense: fiction that makes little demands upon its readers and does not require ethical sophistication or sensitivity. Such a reputation would be unfair, for Norton's science fiction is actually serious on the whole—sometimes even explicitly earnest and didactic—as it dramatizes several themes and concerns. In fact, one theme, above all others, is pervasive in Norton's science fiction and fantasy: the centrality of passage or initiation in the lives of many of her protagonists.

There are those, reflecting the position that Norton's fiction addresses the general reader, who claim that passage appears in her novels as the protagonist's struggle to overcome politically repressive and intellectually stifling societies. Schlobin, for example, describes this theme as "the success and elevation of the innocent. In this process, bondages and wastelands are overthrown, new and generative orders are established, and the protagonists are ennobled."

On the other hand, those who contend that Norton does speak to young readers in a special way point out that she has taken pains to dramatize the rite of passage in ways that youth finds especially relevant, appealing, and, if it so wishes, even supportive. The central concern of much of Norton's science fiction is the young protagonist's struggle to overcome a variety of obstacles, physical, psychological, and moral, and in doing so successfully, demonstrating that the immaturity, frustration, and uncertainty of childhood and adolescence have been outgrown. The protagonist, as a further consequence of successful passage, earns acceptance as an equal by adults.

This central concern is already present in Norton's very first science fiction novel, *Star Man's Son, 2250 A.D.* A young, white-haired boy, Fors, who is a mutant born from the unconventional marriage of a Star Man, one of the Puma Clan, the mountain people living in the Eyrie, and of a woman, one of the Plains people who live in a shaky truce with the Puma Clan, suspects that his parentage and obvious physical differences will always set him off from the people of the Eyrie. Accompanied only by a big cat, Lura, that is also a mutant and with whom the boy can communicate telepathically, Fors secretly leaves the Eyrie to test "his strength and the ability to use it, his knowledge and his wits." Before the test is passed successfully, the boy must undergo several perilous adventures: a journey through a land ravaged and still burning in places from the radiation of the Blow Up, a nuclear war that had occurred sometime in the past; violent encounters with the Beast Things, a degenerate and savage offspring of human beings who had been massively exposed to radiation; and meeting and befriending Arskane, the dark-complected prince of a previously unknown people.

Fors's ordeal tests more than his physical strength, mental agility, or instinct for survival. At several key moments in the story Norton shows the boy's having to choose, even at the risk of being branded disloyal and cowardly, between the claims of the Puma Clan and those of Arskane, between his own interests and those of the mountain people, between his own survival and that of the several clans. By making these choices integral to the plot, Norton underscores the point that passage into adulthood involves an ethical maturing as well as physical and mental maturation and demands another kind of courage—accepting responsibility for one's own actions and their consequences.

Young protagonists in other Norton novels undergo similar ordeals and emerge successfully, often as individuals who have at last discovered meaning and purpose in their lives. Kana Karr of *Star Guard,* having proven his worth, is invited to join the Terran Combatants who, finally besting Central Control, can work realistically at achieving humanity's dream of galactic colonization, a goal long denied Earth. Murdoc Jern of *The Zero Stone* (1968) works his way free of the Thieves' Guild and their oppressive control, becoming in the process an independent trader with his own ship. In *Star Gate* Kincar s'Rud, by his mother one of the Star Lords, willingly accepts a destiny of seeking and questing rather than finding and settling down after victory. Dard Nordis in *The Stars are Ours!* (1954) realizes that escaping the intellectual and political repression of Pax and finding liberty on another planet are not enough. People must carefully and zealously protect liberty if they want to continue enjoying it.

Sometimes Norton dramatizes passage as a choice between right and wrong in a struggle between Good and Evil. In *Steel Magic* three children, Greg, Eric, and Sara, are drawn magically into Avalon, where they are informed by Merlin that their coming into that legendary country had been foretold long ago. The children learn that their destiny involves assisting King Arthur's forces as he contends against the Dark, but there is nothing automatic about their participation, nor can they be coerced. Rather, they must choose deliberately and freely to embark on quests to track down magical objects, the sword Excalibur and Huon's horn, essential to Arthur's chances for victory. The youngsters do choose rightly, as might be expected, but Norton shows the children's hesitation and reluctance, making their choice believable:

> "Then I choose to do as you wish," Greg answered. "It's for Dad, in a way." He looked questioningly at Sara and Eric.
>
> "All right." Eric's agreement was reluctant. He looked as scared and unhappy as Sara felt inside.
>
> She held to the basket which was the only real thing now in this mixed-up dream. And her voice was very small and thin as she said, "Me, I'll help too," though she did not want to at all.

Central to the other fantasies in the Magic series is the importance of making ethical choices without actually having to display physical courage or acumen. The young protagonists differ in racial, socioeconomic, and cultural backgrounds—some are white; others, black or Chinese; some are well-to-do; others, relatively poor. But they are all alike in that they have maneuvered themselves into situations which demand a choice between feeling sorry for themselves and caring for others and between passive, sullen introspection and invigorating, outgoing action.

Although each protagonist eventually does choose life and the claims of community, circumstances always vary; hence, the stories, because they are different, can be enjoyed without readers becoming bored on account of the plot similarity or resenting the didactic purpose behind the plot. Occasionally, Norton is unsuccessful in controlling her didactic intent, and readers sense that they are being "preached at" or asked to consider the "social relevance" of plot complications. *Seven Spells To Sunday* (1979), written in collaboration with Phyllis Miller, is one such occasion. The notion of a mail box unexpectedly and magically providing two unhappy orphans advice and the means of acting upon it may be novel and potentially interesting; but the earnest, almost explicit psychologizing with which the plot is unfolded renders the narrative heavy-handed bibliotherapy, rather than entertaining storytelling.

Sandra Miesel, in the 1978 Gregg Press reissue of *Sargasso of Space* (1955), has suggested that employment, or, to be precise, either the lack of it or the fear of losing it, is sometimes a key point in Norton's characterization: "the issue of employment . . . is a matter of desperate importance to each hero. It is the motive and the reward for their deeds." Norton's making the finding of suitable employment part of the success her protagonists often achieve is one more of the special ways her fiction speaks to young readers. What other age group among her readers is already aware, or soon will be, that the particular job, occupation or position the individual attains often defines the worth of that person and measures the degree of society's approbation? Finding satisfying and productive work is a key step, even if it is sometimes resented or feared, in the passage into adulthood.

Obviously, Norton's science fiction and space fantasy uses terminology and plot situations pointing to or implying an advanced, extrapolated, or futuristic technology or scientific breakthrough.

Almost any novel picked at random will allude to alien beings, ESP, galactic explorations, newly discovered planets and star systems, space colonies, atomically energized powerpacks, spaceports, star ships, identity disks, stunners, and other such fantastic gadgets and situations. Yet as a rule Norton does not devote much space to lengthy descriptions or explanations of technical processes or procedures. Instead, she is content to allow the immediate context to suggest either the meaning or function of many of these terms. Also, since a good number of her novels are sequels or part of a sequence, attentive readers sense behind these novels a background or a "future history" that functions as a kind of context, although loose and not always internally consistent, which shapes or clarifies plot or story complications.

Further, Norton spends little time explicitly speculating about science and its importance, its contribution to human welfare and progress, or its abuses—all concerns that are hallmarks of "hard" science fiction. What she does have to say about these concerns is usually implied through action and dialogue. Some adult readers, it is true, may point to this as evidence that her science fiction is relatively thin and fails to challenge or provoke. However, it must be kept in mind that young readers, unlike adults, are not likely to be troubled by Norton's emphasis on characterization and action; actually they prefer her science fiction's "softness" to the "hard" type.

The prominence of animals, especially cats, is another feature of Norton's fiction that attracts and intrigues young readers. In her very first science fiction novel, it will be remembered, a cat, Lura, plays a major role. Not only is there a special relationship between Lura and Fors—they communicate telepathically—but this special relationship is one of the reasons why Fors feels he is alien. In some novels the relationship between humans and animals is depicted as that of friends, allies, and even members of a military team.

In *Catseye* (1961), for example, Troy Horan befriends a mixed group of animals—two cats, a fox, a kinkajou, and a fussel hawk—and together they plan to find liberty for themselves. In *The Zero Stone* Murdoc Jern joins with a feline mutant, Eet, and the two seek the source of a powerful stone. Travis Fox and mutant coyotes in *The Defiant Agents* make up a team that scouts and fights. In *The Beast Master* Hosten Storm is the human member of a scouting team in which the animals, Baku, an African eagle; Hing, a meerkat; and Surra, a dune cat, are equals of human beings in skill and sensi-

Dust jacket for Norton's first gothic tale, set in nineteenth-century America (Dutton)

tivity. Mallen the Moon Singer in *Moon of Three Rings* telepathically communicates with her animals so that together they can form a traveling show.

In other novels animals are portrayed as superior to human beings in moral sensitivity and rectitude. In *Breed to Come* (1972), for instance, cats, dogs, and cattle, survivors of a nuclear war on Earth that forced human immigration to another world, band together to head off a possible second devastation. A team of human explorers returns to Earth to determine whether human settling is possible. The team becomes divided over the morality of using animals for experiments and the possibility that Earth and its resources will be exploited again. One group, opting for "progress," finds allies among rats; the other group, fearful of the damage humans are capable of, agrees to abandon Earth, once the first group is captured or killed, and leave it to other species that know how to husband the planet's resources.

The bears of *Iron Cage* (1974) are afraid that humans, who have returned to scout Earth for possible colonization, once more seek to dominate and exploit. Eventually the bears succeed in resisting

an attempt to restore humanity's dominance on Earth through the caging of animals and forcing them to undergo experimentation. Finally, in *Star Ka'at*, first of the Star Ka'at stories, Ka'ats come to Earth to save as many cats as possible from a nuclear devastation. Cats, it turns out, are actually descendants of a colony of Ka'ats established long before. On account of their kindness to one of the Ka'ats, two children, Jim and Elly Mae, are invited to come along with the Ka'ats, who have retrieved those cats left from the colonization attempt which ultimately failed because of abuse by the human species.

Whether viewed as an author of adult science fiction or of children's, Andre Norton is an important writer. How important is, admittedly, debatable. There are those who argue that when all of Norton's science fiction and fantasy is examined, little growth, thematic and otherwise, is detected. That is to say, she began as a writer of one kind of science fiction and for nearly three decades has produced only minor variations of that kind.

Thus, if literary significance is defined in terms of plot complexity, stylistic experimentation, or sensitive probing of moral, ethical problems, then Norton's importance is problematic. On the other hand, there are those who suggest that literary significance can be measured by other standards—long-lasting popularity with a broad range of readers; a commitment to craftsmanship which does not tolerate hack work or slipshod performance; or a professionalism that does not patronize or play to readers' biases or prejudices.

By these measurements Norton is a significant author. Put another way, Norton's significance is that she is, above all else, a creator of stories that can remind readers, once they open their imaginations to her storytelling, of the wonder that can be found around and within them.

Bibliography:

Roger C. Schlobin, *Andre Norton: A Primary and Secondary Bibliography* (Boston: G. K. Hall, 1980).

References:

Rick Brooks, "Andre Norton: Loss of Faith," in *The*

Book of André Norton (New York: DAW, 1975), pp. 187-210;

Lin Carter, "Andre Norton: A Profile," in *The Sioux Spaceman* (New York: Ace, 1966);

Sandra Miesel, Introduction to *Sargasso of Space* (New York: Gregg Press, 1978), pp. vi-xix;

Gary Alan Ruse, "*Algol* Profile: Andre Norton," *Algol,* 14 (Summer-Fall 1977): 15-17;

John Rowe Townsend, "Andre Norton," in his *A Sense of Story: Essays on Contemporary Writers for Children* (Philadelphia: Lippincott, 1971), pp. 143-151;

Donald Wollheim, Introduction to *The Book of André Norton,* pp. 7-10.

Papers:

Andre Norton's manuscript collection is located at the George Arents Research Library, Syracuse University, New York.

Scott O'Dell

(23 May 1903-   )

Malcolm Usrey
Clemson University

BOOKS: *Representative Photoplays Analyzed* by Scott O'Dell (Hollywood, Cal.: Palmer Institute of Authorship, 1924);

Woman of Spain: A Story of Old California (Boston & New York: Houghton Mifflin, 1934);

Hill of the Hawk (Indianapolis: Bobbs-Merrill, 1947);

Man Alone, by O'Dell and William Doyle (Indianapolis: Bobbs-Merrill, 1953);

Country of the Sun: Southern California, an Informal History and Guide (New York: Crowell, 1957);

The Sea is Red: A Novel (New York: Holt, 1958);

Island of the Blue Dolphins (Boston: Houghton Mifflin, 1960; London: Constable, 1961);

The King's Fifth, decorations and maps by Samuel Bryant (Boston: Houghton Mifflin, 1966; London: Constable, 1967);

The Black Pearl, illustrated by Milton Johnson (Boston: Houghton Mifflin, 1967; London: Longmans, Green, 1968);

The Psychology of Children's Art, by O'Dell and Rheda Kellogg (San Diego: Communications Research Machines, 1967);

The Dark Canoe, illustrated by Johnson (Boston: Houghton Mifflin, 1968; London: Longman, 1969);

Journey to Jericho, illustrated by Leonard Weisgard (Boston: Houghton Mifflin, 1969);

Sing Down the Moon (Boston: Houghton Mifflin, 1970; London: Hamish Hamilton, 1972);

The Treasure of Topo-el-Bampo, illustrated by Lynd Ward (Boston: Houghton Mifflin, 1972);

The Cruise of the Arctic Star, maps by Bryant (Boston: Houghton Mifflin, 1973);

Child of Fire (Boston: Houghton Mifflin, 1974);

The Hawk that Dare not Hunt by Day (Boston: Houghton Mifflin, 1975);

The 290 (Boston: Houghton Mifflin, 1976; London: Oxford University Press, 1977);

Scott O'Dell (photo by R. J. Gomber)

Zia (Boston: Houghton Mifflin, 1976; London: Oxford University Press, 1977);

Carlota (Boston: Houghton Mifflin, 1977);

Kathleen, Please Come Home (Boston: Houghton Mifflin, 1978);

The Captive (Boston: Houghton Mifflin, 1979);

Sarah Bishop (Boston: Houghton Mifflin, 1980);

The Feathered Serpent (Boston: Houghton Mifflin, 1981);

The Spanish Smile (Boston: Houghton Mifflin, 1982);

The Amethyst Ring (Boston: Houghton Mifflin, 1983);

The Castle in the Sea (Boston: Houghton Mifflin, 1983);

Alexandra (Boston: Houghton Mifflin, 1984);

The Road to Damietta (Boston: Houghton Mifflin, 1985);

Streams to the River, River to the Sea (Boston: Houghton Mifflin, 1986).

OTHER: "Newbery Award Acceptance," in *Newbery and Caldecott Medal Books: 1956-1965*, ed-

ited by Lee Kingman (Boston: Horn Book, 1965), pp. 99-104.

PERIODICAL PUBLICATIONS: "David, an Adventure with Memory and Words," *Psychology Today*, 1 (January 1968): 40-43;

"Acceptance Speech: Hans Christian Andersen Award," *Horn Book*, 48 (October 1972): 441-443.

Scott O'Dell is one of the best-known writers of historical fiction for children from eight to ten through adolescence. His contributions to literature for children would be significant if he had written no other books besides *Island of the Blue Dolphins* (1960) and *The King's Fifth* (1966). O'Dell has won many awards for his children's books, including the Newbery Medal in 1961 for *Island of the Blue Dolphins*, and three of his works have been Newbery Honor books. In 1972 he won the Hans Christian Andersen Award for lifetime achievement, the second American writer to win that award. He was also presented the University of Southern Mississippi medallion in 1976, the Regina Medal in 1978, and the *Focal* Award from the Los Angeles Public Library in 1981.

O'Dell, the son of Bennett Mason and May Elizabeth Gabriel O'Dell, has spent much of his life in the region where he was born, Los Angeles and southern California; he has often lived near the sea, which figures predominantly in several of his novels. *The Cruise of the* Arctic Star, published in 1973, reflects his love of the sea and the land, as well as California history; an autobiographical book, it is an account of a voyage up the California and Oregon coasts. O'Dell attended Occidental College in 1919, the University of Wisconsin in 1920, Stanford University in 1920-1921, and the University of Rome in 1925, but he did not take a degree. A motion-picture cameraman and a book editor for a Los Angeles newspaper, O'Dell became a full-time writer in 1934, and between then and 1967 he wrote three novels for adults: *Woman of Spain: A Story of Old California* (1934), *Hill of the Hawk* (1947), and *The Sea is Red: A Novel* (1958). During the same period, he wrote two nonfiction books for adults. It was not until the late fifties that he began writing for children.

In 1981, O'Dell established the Scott O'Dell Award for Historical Fiction, an annual award of $5,000 for a book of historical fiction set in the New World and written in English by a citizen of the United States. The book must be for children or young adults and must have been published in the year preceding the award. If a book of sufficient merit is not found, the award is not given.

Scott O'Dell's first book for children won him almost immediate acclaim and established him firmly as a first-rate writer of historical fiction. *Island of the Blue Dolphins* is the story of Karana's eighteen years alone on the Island of the Blue Dolphins, how she came to be there, and what she did during much of her long period of isolation. She existed by providing herself with food from the sea and the island, by taming Rontu, one of the wild dogs that had killed her brother after the other members of her decimated tribe had been taken away, by taming other animals and birds, and by learning to make weapons.

As a Robinsonade, or survival story, *Island of the Blue Dolphins* has few equals in children's literature. Based on the life of the "lost woman of San Nicolas," the book was created from the few facts known about her, and O'Dell turned them into a remarkable story. The woman lived by herself on

Dust jacket for a later edition of O'Dell's best-known novel, based on a true story of an Indian girl who survives alone for eighteen years on an island off the coast of southern California (Houghton Mifflin)

San Nicolas Island off the coast of southern California from 1835 to 1853, when she was discovered living with "a dog in a crude house on the headland, dressed in a skirt of cormorant feathers." Little else is known about her because she could not speak any of the languages of the Indians living at Santa Barbara Mission where she was taken after her rescue.

The novel attests to the skills and talents of O'Dell as a writer of historical fiction. He has woven a suspenseful tale around one of the most appealing of all subjects, survival of a man or woman against the odds of nature in an extremely primitive environment. Karana, as O'Dell names her, has few implements and is even forbidden by the traditions of her tribe to make weapons for her survival. The winters are cold and the summers are hot. Karana has to think about where and when and how she can get food and shelter and the best places on and around the island that provide them. O'Dell shows Karana carefully thinking about the location of her house, the fence she constructed of whale ribs and kelp rope to keep out the wild dogs and foxes, and her fear in making weapons. He describes how afraid she was the first time she used a weapon, recalling her "father's warning that a bow in the hands of a woman would always break in a time of danger. . . ." Against all the odds, however, Karana proves resourceful, a somewhat hollow word in the light of O'Dell's masterful descriptions of and details about her years alone. But the book is more than one of survival; it is the story of great courage, endurance, perseverance, ingenuity, and, perhaps most important of all, it is a story of a woman's surviving great loneliness and an even greater sense of isolation. It is Karana's loneliness and isolation that give the book one of its most powerful and universal themes, that all people need to be with others, to love and to be loved. As O'Dell himself said in his Newbery Award acceptance speech, "The human heart, lonely and in need of love, is a vessel which needs replenishing."

After her brother's death, Karana feels more acutely the absence of the other members of her tribe. "I had never noticed before how silent the village was. Fog crept in and out of the empty huts. It made shapes as it drifted and they reminded me of all the people who were dead and those who were gone. The noise of the surf seemed to be their voices speaking." The presence of the village, empty of her people, is so painful to Karana that she burns it. Her sense of isolation and loneliness is made greater when, after several years, the Aleuts, the enemies of Karana's tribe, come to hunt otter, bringing with them Tutok, a young woman about Karana's age, with whom she becomes friends. On the morning after Tutok and the Aleuts leave, Karana realizes how much she misses Tutok: "as I stood there on the high rock looking down at the deserted harbor and the empty sea, I began to think of Tutok. I thought of all the times we had sat in the sun together. I could feel her voice and see her black eyes squinted closed when she laughed." Her dog, Rontu, was barking, gulls were screaming, pelicans were chattering, and sea elephants were bellowing, "But suddenly, as I thought of Tutok, the island seemed very quiet."

Another significant theme of the novel is the interdependency of human beings and other life. In her taming of Rontu, the leader of the wild dogs that killed her brother, the theme is exemplified. Karana resolves to avenge her brother's death by killing Rontu, but she succeeds only in wounding him. She rescues him and, though she cannot understand why, nurses him back to health and later wonders how she could ever have thought of killing him. Rontu is Karana's companion and, in a sense, her savior. After she makes pets of a pair of birds, a fox, and a young otter, Karana says, "animals and birds are like people, too, though they do not talk the same or do the same things. Without them the earth would be an unhappy place." Though Karana never kills another animal for shelter, weaponry, or clothing, she does have to kill fish for food.

Critics have often commended O'Dell for his style in *Island of the Blue Dolphins*. Linda Peterson and Marilyn Solt, in *Newbery and Caldecott Medal and Honor Books, an Annotated Bibliography*, write, "In this as in his other books, Scott O'Dell's style adds distinction to the narrative. Since Karana is telling the story, it reads much like a diary or journal. The sentence structure is basically short and simple. She tells her story with stoicism, dignity, and a certain restraint. The natural world provides the subject for the metaphorical language throughout: 'The sea . . . is a flat stone without any scratches'; the sea elephants 'like gray boulders. . . . ' The style is particularly suitable to the concept of the book considering the setting and Karana's cultural background."

Island of the Blue Dolphins is surely O'Dell's masterpiece and one of a half dozen or so great historical novels for children by an American writer in the past two or three decades. In addition to the Newbery Medal, the book won the Rupert Hughes Award, the Southern California Council on Literature for Children and Young People Notable Book Award, the Hans Christian Andersen Award of Merit, the William Allen White Award, the German Juvenile International Award, the Nene Award, and the OMAR Award.

Told by seventeen-year-old Esteban de Sandoval, *The King's Fifth*, O'Dell's second novel for young readers, ranges over much of Mexico and what is now the southwestern part of the United States during 1540 and 1541. Esteban is a mapmaker sailing with the fleet to supply Coronado until Captain Mendoza, by appealing to Esteban's desire to be the first to map the unknown lands north of Mexico, lures him away. Mendoza's one aim is to find the fabled cities of Cibola and their gold. Mendoza, three soldiers, Father Francisco, Zia—a young Indian girl who serves as their guide and interpreter—and Esteban do find gold, but it brings them nothing but grief. Mendoza is killed by his own dog; the soldiers either die or abandon the group; Zia, seeing Esteban become infected with the fever for gold, abandons him and Father Francisco, leaving them to take the gold back to Mexico. Father Francisco begs Esteban to leave the gold, but Esteban will not. After Father Francisco dies in the Inferno (Death Valley), Esteban throws the gold into a bubbling sulphur pit and is put into prison in Vera Cruz for not giving the king his fifth of the treasure as required by law. Esteban's trial lasts for several weeks, during which time he recounts the search for gold with Mendoza. He is sentenced to three years for withholding the king's fifth.

The King's Fifth is O'Dell's most complex novel, not only in technique but also in substance. O'Dell uses flashbacks about the search interspersed with accounts of Esteban's trial. Esteban writes all of the incidents down in his cell at night, paralleling parts of the trial with the appropriate parts of the search; thus, both parts of the story unfold simultaneously. Esteban de Sandoval is perhaps O'Dell's most dynamic character. At first he is interested only in mapmaking; he is more or less indifferent to Mendoza's and the others' desire for gold. However, after he finds a good-sized nugget in a stream that flows through the Abyss (the Grand Canyon), he too is infected with the lust, becoming an accessory to the crimes that Mendoza and his men subsequently commit. It is only after he realizes he is responsible for Father Francisco's death in the Inferno that Esteban abandons the gold. Esteban no longer is interested only in maps, no longer is indifferent to men's lust for gold, and no longer desires gold himself. Having been baptized by the fire of the Inferno and by his experiences, he is no longer a seventeen-year-old boy; he is a man. The shifts in the growth and development of Esteban's insight and understanding make him a dynamic character who changes for worse, then for better; these shifts also make *The King's Fifth* a Bildungs-roman.

One of the major themes of *The King's Fifth* is couched in a thought Esteban records after he first realizes how mendacious Mendoza truly is: "the dream of gold can bend the soul and even destroy it.... " With the exception of Zia and Father Francisco, all the principal characters in the novel are adversely affected by the quest. Mendoza and his men kill sheep, which are sacred to the Indians of Nexpan who live in the Abyss; they set fire to Nexpanians' grasslands and burn their corn crops. Mendoza's greed causes him to wreck the City of Clouds by flooding it to get the gold at the bottom of the pool the Indians had built for worship. After Esteban is infected with gold fever, he becomes deceitful and fearful. It is Esteban who shows Mendoza how the dam in Cloud City can be breached. Zia recognizes the change in him and tells him he is like Mendoza, and after a few days she leaves him and Father Francisco.

The Spaniards are mercilessly cruel, and O'Dell does not spare them for their mistreatment of the Indians they encounter. Though they go in the name of Christianity and to convert the Indians, their true motives are made clear. With the exception of Father Francisco, none of the Spaniards respect the Indians, their attitudes, or their way of life. They attack first and ask questions later—if there's anyone left of which to ask questions. In this respect, O'Dell reflects a fairly recent trend in fiction for children; that is not to slight or bend the truth in favor of the European conquerors.

There are, however, some flaws in the book. One cannot but wonder how Zia, a young Indian girl, could travel with a group of men who are generally criminal toward the Indians and yet never be harmed by them. And Zia is all good; she is by far the most intelligent—or most sensible—character in the novel. The only thing she does in the novel that might be considered negative is to ride horses, a privilege denied the other Indians by the Spaniards. Furthermore, nearly all the Indians are honorable while most of the Spaniards are oppressive. Only Esteban is a mixture of both good and bad. He is, of course, the central figure, and the other characters represent foils to show his character and growth; for O'Dell to imply, however, that the Europeans are generally evil and that the American Indians are generally good is to deny

the realities of human nature. Nonetheless, *The King's Fifth,* a Newbery Honor Book, the winner of the German Juvenile International Award and the Nene Award, is a fine historical novel for any age. In 1971, after O'Dell had published six novels for youngsters, John Rowe Townsend wrote in *A Sense of Story,* "*The King's Fifth*—a sombre, almost stately novel—is his best of all."

O'Dell's second Newbery Honor Book, *The Black Pearl* (1967), is set in La Paz in Baja California before boats were powered by coal or oil. Ramón Salazar, who is sixteen during the time of the story, finds a large black pearl in a lagoon believed to be the home of the Manta Diablo, a huge manta about which there are numerous legends and superstitions, especially among the Indians. Ramón's father, Blas Salazar, a pearl dealer with a fleet of five ships, gives the pearl to the church when four pearl dealers refuse to pay his asking price. Even though Father Gallardos blesses Salazar's fleet before it leaves La Paz, the fleet and all the crew members, except Gaspar Ruiz, are lost in a storm. Thinking the Manta Diablo has brought the death of his father and the loss of the fleet, Ramón steals the black pearl to throw it back into the lagoon where he found it, but Gaspar stops him, forcing him to go with him by sea to Guaymas to help him sell the pearl. On the way, followed by the giant manta for many hours, Gaspar finally harpoons it, and later tries to kill it by climbing on its back and stabbing it. He drowns, and Ramón returns the pearl to La Paz and gives the pearl back to the Madonna, as a gift of adoration and love.

The plot of *The Black Pearl* is one of the most exciting and suspenseful of all O'Dell's novels. The characterization is adequate, though as with many of O'Dell's characters, not a great many facets of their personalities are revealed. The most important theme of the novel is that a gift of great price must be made out of love, not out of selfishness. Blas Salazar gives the pearl to the church out of spite and anger, and he believes that his fleet will be protected from harm because of his gift.

The novel may be seen as another Bildungs-roman, for it essentially shows a major step of Ramón's development toward manhood. Ramón had thought that his sixteenth birthday, the day he was brought into his father's business as a full partner, made him a man. Being made a partner and learning how to dive for pearls does not make Ramón mature. Though it may be accompanied by outward manifestations, his maturation occurs within, as O'Dell demonstrates. Ramón's returning the pearl as a gift of adoration and of love is both an inward and outward expression of his maturing. Ramón returns the pearl at dawn, climbs to the belfry, and rings the bells, both acts visible and outward. But inside, Ramón's heart rings with the bells. He says, "Outside, the sun now lay golden on the roof tops and the big bells were still ringing over the town. They rang in my heart, also, for this new day was the beginning day of manhood. It was not the day I became a partner in the House of Salazar nor the day I found the Pearl of Heaven. It was this day."

Related by sixteen-year-old Nathan Clegg, *The Dark Canoe* (1968) recounts the story of the *Alert*, a small barquentine from Nantucket, in search of the sunken whaler the *Amy Foster*, in Magdalena Bay in Baja California, sometime during the latter part of the nineteenth century. The ostensible purpose of the voyage is to recover casks of ambergris and whale oil, but the real purpose is for Caleb Clegg to locate the logbook of the ship so that he can prove to himself—and to others— that he as captain of the *Amy Foster* had given orders

Dust jacket for O'Dell's novel about a sixteen-year-old boy on board a ship in search of a sunken whaler
(Houghton Mifflin)

to take her out of Magdalena Bay so that she would be in less danger of sinking during a chubasco, a storm of great force. At the trial, his brother Jeremy had testified Caleb had not given such an order, and Caleb had been divested of his captain's license. When the men of the *Alert* finally find the *Amy Foster*, they discover that there is little ambergris aboard and the oil is not fit for salvaging, but Caleb does find the logbook that exonerates him.

The *Alert* has sailed from Nantucket under the command of Jeremy Clegg, the idol of young Nathan. After arriving in Magdalena Bay, Jeremy mysteriously disappears and is thought to be dead. Later, Nathan and Old Man Judd, the ship's carpenter, find Jeremy's body on Isla Ballena, and the Indians there explain how he died.

The Dark Canoe is an enigmatic story, made more so by its repeated allusions to Herman Melville's *Moby-Dick.* O'Dell makes Caleb Clegg resemble Captain Ahab (as does Gaspar Ruiz); and he has Nathan discover a coffin that appears to be the one that Queequeg had had made for himself on the *Pequod.* The physical and mental or psychological similarities between Ahab and Caleb are numerous but are mainly superficial and unimportant. Caleb is not the madman that Ahab is nor is the *Amy Foster* the *Pequod.* O'Dell has Nathan to say early in the story, "It was my *brother* Caleb Clegg I feared, whom I had feared since first I could remember and through all the years of my childhood. I suppose it was his scarred face, his hobbling walk, his curious way of speaking that repelled me and was the reason for my fear. I could have feared him because he hated Jeremy, or because he chose his own grim path and asked nothing of anyone. I don't know." However, there is not much to indicate that Nathan has any real reason to fear Caleb, as he does to be wary of Jeremy, who lied about Caleb's not giving the order to sail the *Amy Foster* out of Magdalena Bay; and, as we later learn, Jeremy lost his life apparently going to take gold from the Indians on Isla Ballena, whatever the cost to the Indians or to Jeremy himself.

Queequeg's coffin, or the "dark canoe," figures prominently in the story, but its function remains obscure in spite of O'Dell's devoting considerable time and space to it and his naming the novel for the coffin. It is Nathan who discovers the coffin, and it is he and Old Man Judd who conceal it on the shore. Caleb has little to do with the canoe until Nathan tells him about it. At the end of the story, Caleb sets the coffin adrift in the Pacific, the *Alert* sails for Nantucket, and Caleb says, "The dark canoe moveth with the wind and the waves and the moon's constant tides. It moveth at its own pace, slower by far than this stout bark which bears us homeward. Yet in time it will outpace our many sails and make ports we shall never see." Caleb's statement seems to suggest that he and the dark canoe—and many human beings—are pulled by forces beyond their control and that many do make their voyages alone; but the novel does not wholly support this theme because the *Alert* and her crew are in Magdalena Bay because Caleb has brought them there, aided by forces over which he and others have some control.

Finally, *The Dark Canoe* is no more than an exciting adventure story reflecting O'Dell's love of *Moby-Dick*. Its nebulous theme is never imaginatively reflected in the action nor is the character of Caleb Clegg ever dramatically realized.

Set in Big Loop, West Virginia, in 1965, *Journey to Jericho* (1969) is O'Dell's first book for children in the middle grades. After David Moore's father leaves his family behind in West Virginia to go to

Dust jacket for O'Dell's novel about a boy who guards a jar of his grandmother's pickles on a long journey from a mining camp in West Virginia to a California lumber camp (Houghton Mifflin)

work in California, David, his mother, and sister follow in a few weeks—with a jar of Grandma's famous watermelon pickles. David carefully takes care of the jar all the way to Jericho, California, by wagon, train, plane, bus, and logging truck, only to drop them when his father holds out his arms to hug him. The jar breaks and pickles scatter, but David and his father just laugh.

Journey to Jericho is a charming and delightful story suggesting that some things, pickles or whatever, are not nearly as important as being with those one loves. David is a well-delineated little boy who loves fishing and going secretly into coal mines (where once he is nearly run over by the coal train), and he is determined, as his devotion to Grandma's pickles shows. O'Dell has not created a more appealing and genuine male character in all his books than David Moore.

Sing Down the Moon (1970), another Newbery Honor Book, is based on the infamous Long Walk that American soldiers forced about 10,000 Navaho Indians to make in 1864 from their homes in Utah, Arizona, Colorado, and New Mexico to Fort Sumner, New Mexico. Of the 8,491 Navahos that reached the fort, 1,500 died during their imprisonment, which lasted until 1868.

O'Dell's fictional account is told by Bright Morning, a young Navaho woman from Canyon de Chelly, who made the Long Walk with her family and tribe. Weaving the fictional narrative and the historical facts of the Long Walk, O'Dell has created a powerful and moving story, made poignant by his restraint and simplicity, reflecting the stoic, proud, and quiet or passive strength of Bright Morning.

Sing Down the Moon is one of several novels in the O'Dell canon reflecting the ill treatment of native Americans by white Americans. As in his other novels dealing with the relationship of Indians and Americans, O'Dell strikes at the indifference of the whites toward the suffering caused the Indians by monstrous cruelty and by not understanding the Indians' attitudes, religion, or way of life.

A realistic historical picture book, *The Treasure of Topo-el-Bampo* (1972) is set during the late eighteenth century in the little mountain village of Topo-el-Bampo, the poorest city in all of Mexico, which, ironically, sits near the richest silver mine in the country. Poverty and near-starvation are ever-present in the little village. Unable to feed his burros (Leandro and Tiger) the mayor sells them to the Vargas brothers, of the Three Brothers Mine. They are needed to carry silver to the coast for shipment to Spain. The villagers never share in any of the profits from the mines; the only thing they realize from the great wealth beneath them is a fiesta each time silver goes down to the sea, a pot of beans each day, and a hut to live in. When the largest load of silver leaves, the train is attacked by robbers, and Tiger and Leandro return to the little village with the silver bars strapped to their backs, saving the villagers from starvation.

After the fiesta in honor of the shipment, the Vargas brothers go into the church, praying that the silver will remain safe until it reaches the King of Spain. One of the prayers they offer professes the hope that the King will "use it wisely in the holy service of God." When Tiger and Leandro return to their home village laden with the silver bars, O'Dell wryly comments that "one of the six prayers the Vargas brothers prayed was answered." O'Dell is suggesting thematically that sometimes the exploited poor will be helped even when the exploiters do not intend it or realize it.

Child of Fire (1974), about gang wars among Chicano youths in the area of Del Mar, California, is one of two contemporary problem novels for young adults O'Dell has written. Though seen through the eyes of parole officer Delaney, the story is essentially about Manuel Castillo, a sixteen-year-old Chicano descended from an old California Spanish family who has lost or sold through the years all but a few acres of their original 47,000-acre grant from the King of Spain. For a while, Manuel is the leader of a gang known as the Conquistadors; his rival, Ernesto de la Sierra, is the leader of the Owls. Though Manuel, a bright and appealing youngster despite his strong sense of machismo, is not one of Delaney's parolees, he wants to help him.

The plot is essentially about the rivalry between the two young Chicanos, with emphasis on Manuel. When Ernie Sierra is finally sent to prison for smuggling heroin from Mexico with homing pigeons, Manuel loses interest in the gang fights and signs on a Panamanian fishing boat, where he leads a mutiny against the captain and receives a prison sentence of five years in Ecuador. Escaping and working his way back to San Diego, Manuel immediately joins a group of Chicano grape pickers protesting the use of a mechanical grape picker. The day the picker begins harvesting, Manuel kneels in front of it as a dramatic gesture of protest and is killed.

Child of Fire is a story of the conflict between two cultures, American and Chicano. As a problem novel, it does not directly confront the causes of many of the young Chicanos' problems, why they go "wrong," except to show that they are generally poor, lack interest in school, and adhere to an ancient code of machismo dimly related to chivalry. Delaney thinks that "The machista fights for a woman against another man. But in this fight the woman is only an excuse. She is not important. It is the defeat of the rival that's important."

The restless young Chicano gangs take out their lust for blood in periodic, illegal gamecock fighting in Mexico, where the authorities are easier to bribe than those in California. O'Dell, through Delaney, describes the cockfights with authority and detail, and he presents a strong resemblance between the cocks in the pit and the young Chicano gang fighters. The cocks are bred to kill each other; O'Dell consciously or unconsciously is suggesting that the young Chicanos seem to have bred in them the same kind of desire. A possible theme of *Child of Fire*, then, is that violence and romantic notions of a chivalric code have degenerated into machismo, which produces young men insensitive to violence—whether it results in the deaths of roosters, where one cock viciously kills another or is killed, or in the deaths of young men in gang wars.

Closely related to this theme is another which suggests that a lack of parental guidance and direction often makes for irresponsible and immature behavior in young people, an idea fairly well borne out in the novel. When Delaney talks to his wife Alice about Manuel, he says that Manuel "needs a little direction. . . . He's not getting much at home." Earlier in the conversation, Alice, a high school history teacher, had suggested to Delaney that children are kept children too long. "In the old days, . . . in the sixteen hundreds and long before that, children were adults by the age of nine or ten. They took their places alongside their fathers and mothers. They worked at the looms and in the fields. If their parents carried stones to build a road or a bridge or a cathedral, they carried stones too. . . . The family was a working unit." Delaney asks Alice if she thinks we should "go back to the Middle Ages?" Alice's reply is significant: "No, . . . we could quit treating children exclusively as children and give them a few adult responsibilities."

Much of Manuel's behavior in the story reflects his impetuosity, lack of maturity, and undeveloped sense of responsibility. Delaney first comes into contact with Manuel in Tijuana after Manuel rashly jumps into the bullring and places himself in front of the tunnel from which the bull enters, the most dangerous place in the ring. Manuel offers to marry Yvonne, the Anglo girl for whom he and Ernie Sierra are rivals, just because she says she is pregnant with his child; he does not attempt to learn for sure that she is pregnant nor does he know for sure that the child is his or Ernie's. He signs on the Panamanian fishing boat because there is no longer excitement at home. After Manuel is imprisoned and after Delaney says he cannot help him, Alice observes, "That's good. . . . Before this, there's always been someone around to bail him out." The implication is that now he may have to act responsibly and maturely, but Manuel's kneeling in front of the grape harvester is a rash and dramatically romantic act which costs him his life. The novel is aptly and symbolically named; Manuel Castillo is a "child of fire," a fire of the machista that is hot and quick and uncontrolled.

Set in England and in western Europe between 1524 and 1536, *The Hawk that Dare not Hunt by Day* (1975) is narrated by Tom Barton, who is sixteen when the story opens. Tom sails aboard his Uncle Jack's ship, the *Black Pearl*, engaged in legitimate commerce as well as in smuggling, which is more profitable. Tom smuggles contraband tracts written by Martin Luther into England. Trying to find a buyer for them, he looks up William Tyndale, who cannot buy the tracts but does confess to Tom that he must leave England to work on his translation of the New Testament from the Greek into English.

Tom and Uncle Jack take Tyndale to Hamburg, Germany, and they agree to smuggle his translations of the New Testament into England when he has finished them. Nearly two years later, Tom and Jack are able to smuggle into England a few thousand copies of Tyndale's translation. Even from the beginning of their association with Tyndale, Tom and Uncle Jack realize the dangers inherent in smuggling and the greater danger of smuggling the translation into England. Tom also soon comes to realize how much danger Tyndale is in, how many powerful people want to be rid of him, including Charles V, Emperor of the Holy Roman Empire. Within a few years, Uncle Jack is caught, accused of smuggling, and dies of the black plague in the Clink, one of England's worst prisons. Tom continues to ship both legitimate goods and contraband and to help Tyndale all he can. Over the years, Tom and Tyndale become close friends, and Tyndale teaches Tom how to read. Tom is with Tyndale when Henry Phillips betrays him and he stays for much of his trial and sees him strangled at the stake and his body burned.

The Hawk that Dare not Hunt by Day is as good as any historical novel O'Dell has written. It has a gripping plot, the characterization is well done, especially that of Tom Barton, and it is a highly accurate recounting of the political and religious turmoil and strife surrounding the beginnings of the Reformation in England, at least as far as the beginnings were related to Tyndale's translation of the New Testament into the English vernacular. It is also very likely to be as accurate and detailed an account of the shipping industry in England in the early sixteenth century as can be found in a book for young readers. To his credit as a historical novelist, O'Dell has not slighted the greed, the violence, and the cruelty of men in all walks of life, be they politicians, tradesman, clergymen, or royalty.

As he had in *Island of the Blue Dolphins* and in *The King's Fifth*, O'Dell has a theme worthy of his talents, one that inspired him to write one of his best novels for young adolescents and which strongly reflects the idea that the noblest and greatest achievements of mankind are or have been born out of strife, chaos, and struggle and that they are often nurtured by evil, cruelty, disdain for truth,

Dust jacket for O'Dell's novel about a boy and his uncle, who help William Tyndale smuggle his English translation of the Bible into England (Houghton Mifflin)

and love of money. The epigraph O'Dell chose for the novel, written by George Steiner, quotes Tyndale's translation of a part of Christ's "Sermon on the Mount," which includes, "No man can serve two masters. For either he shall hate the one and love the other: or else he shall lean to the one and despise the other: ye cannot serve God and mammon." Henry Phillips, acting as an agent of Charles V or of the English forces wanting to kill Tyndale, or both, befriends Tyndale so that he can betray him. O'Dell implies, but does not make clear, that Phillips betrays Tyndale more for gain than out of his own religious beliefs and convictions. Nor does O'Dell make clear whether Jack Barton smuggles religious tracts and later Tyndale's New Testament for a love of truth and Christianity or for the profit smuggling such articles brings. It is unimportant that he does not make these details clear; what is important is O'Dell's point that the English Bible did not come to England simply through the goodness and generosity of noble and righteous men.

Set in 1853 at the Mission Santa Barbara in California, *Zia* (1976), a sequel to *Island of the Blue Dolphins*, is an episodic story told by Zia Sandoval, a mountain girl, about her and her brother Mando's aborted trip to the island where she thinks Karana, her aunt, may still be living. The reader learns how the whalers of the *Boston Boy* capture Zia and Mando on their way to the island to look for Karana and put them to work, how they escape, how Captain Cordova imprisons her when she will not help him find the Indians who have runaways from the Mission, how Karana and she have a few weeks of happiness before Karana dies of a mysterious sickness, and how Zia takes Karana's dog and returns to the mountains and her own people.

Zia is an entertaining story, but it lacks the verve and force of *Island of the Blue Dolphins* and *The King's Fifth*. O'Dell's main interest is to relate the mistreatment of the Indians at the hands of the missionaries, the Spaniards, and the Americans, typified by the callous and indifferent attitude directed toward Karana while she is in the mission. The Indians have been made homeless by the whites and are at the mercy of the poverty-stricken missions—forced to live and work at the mission, they even have their freedom taken from them. When Karana first comes to Santa Barbara, she is treated with compassion and understanding by Father Vicente; after he is transferred to another mission, his successors are interested only in making her fit their concept of what they think an Indian should be. They force Karana to stop sleeping on the floor with her dog, then force him to sleep apart from Karana. She takes the dog and hides in a cave, where she soon dies, but not before Zia tries to get help for her. None of the authorities at the mission will help Karana unless she returns.

Zia is a stoic, fourteen-year-old young woman; she philosophically takes all that the missionaries, that Captain Cordova (who represents the remnants of the Mexican government and the ranchers), and that the men on the whaler put her through. She relies on her own wits and good sense, recognizing that none of the white people understand her or her people. O'Dell's understanding of and sympathies for the American Indians of the Southwest are clearly apparent in all his novels set in the West, and *Zia* is no exception.

The 290 (1976) is a historical novel about the Confederate raider the *Alabama*, also known as the *290*. Captain Raphael Semmes used her to sink sixty-nine northern ships, without any enemy deaths, during the nearly two years she roved the seas between July 1862 and June 1864, before she was sunk by the U.S. *Kearsarge* just out of the harbor of Cherbourg, France. The main character, sixteen-year-old James (Jim) Lynne, who signs on the *290* as a seaman the day she is launched, is purely fictional, and the book is centered around two nonhistorical incidents, one involving the *290* and the other involving one of the captured ships, the *Dauphine*. Jim helps to quell a mutiny on the *290* by knocking the leader unconscious. In the other episode, Jim ships on board the *Dauphine*, a vessel the *290* has seized and upon which the captured passengers are being taken to Port-au-Prince, Haiti, to pick up coal and provisions for the *290*. Meanwhile, Jim's father and his father's partner have bought slaves from Haitian officials and plan to sell them in Cuba. Instead of picking up the supplies, Jim and two other crewmen put the slaves on the *Dauphine*, leave the man Semmes put in charge of the ship in Port-au-Prince, and set the slaves free on an uninhabited island before meeting Captain Semmes and the *290*.

O'Dell's main objective in writing *The 290* seems to have been to relate the story of Captain Semmes and his exploits with the *290*, for as he says in the foreword, "The name of Raphael Semmes is known to very few. The reason is not hard to find: history, as often noted, is written by the victors." One of the main themes O'Dell explores through the thoughts of Jim Lynne is accepting life as it comes. At the end of the novel Jim says he did not search for the answers to the questions of how long it would take him or what would happen to him before he reached New Orleans or Port-au-Prince, where his father had owned property and business which he has left to him. During his two years on the *290*, Jim thinks he "had gained some confidence . . . to meet things as they came and a belief that surprise was a part of life best not anticipated."

Both the fictional and factual parts of *The 290* reflect this central concern of the novel somewhat superficially. Captain Semmes, his crew, and his ship take "things as they come" and do not anticipate surprise either in their two-year voyage in search of Yankee ships. Jim Lynne also meets things as they come, but the things that come to or happen to Jim are most often tempered by Jim's desires. He does *not* have to sign on the *290* but chooses to. He does *not* have to knock the leader of the mutineers unconscious with a spanner but chooses to. He does *not* have to free the slaves his father and his father's partner are planning to sell in Cuba, but he does.

Scott O'Dell's weakness as a historical novelist is most apparent in *The 290*. Jim Lynne's encounter with the slaves in the barracoon in Port-au-Prince is not as graphic or as real as the accounts that Elizabeth Yates gives in *Amos Fortune, Free Man* (1950) or that Paula Fox gives in *The Slave Dancer* (1973). Another apparent weakness in the book is Jim's lack of motivation in freeing the slaves; readers do not know enough about him or why he has such an aversion to slavery to make us believe he would take the risks he does to free the slaves. Furthermore, his punishment for freeing the slaves and for taking command of the *Dauphine* and using it to transport the slaves to freedom is rather unrealistic, considering the fact that Captain Semmes is a southerner fighting for the Confederacy. To punish Jim, Captain Semmes confines him to his quarters for a week and sets him to scraping the deck during his free time. It is unlikely that a captain of a Confederate raider would take lightly the freeing of slaves or the seizure of the vessel.

In writing *The 290*, O'Dell was apparently more interested in the story of the ship than he was in developing the fictional plot and the main character. As a result, the principal theme of the story is not soundly and dramatically realized. O'Dell does not do justice to the factual, historical story of the *290* or to the fictional parts involving Jim Lynne.

Set in southern California in 1847, *Carlota* (1977) is a novel whose principal historical episode is the Battle of San Pasqual. The last battle fought in California during the Mexican War, it pitted a

dozen or so Spanish ranchers and vaqueros against a hundred or so soldiers of the "American Army of the West," a grand name for a pitiful remnant. Against all odds the Spanish win the battle, though the war was already lost. The novel is primarily about the effect the change from Mexican to American rule had on the old Spanish families of California, especially represented by the proud de Zubaráns.

That change is constant and those who cannot adapt to or accept it will fall is one of the book's main themes, reflected strongly in the three main characters: Doña Dolores de Zubarán; her son, Don Saturnino; and her granddaughter, Carlota de Zubarán. In spite of Doña Dolores's adamant, conservative, proud, and opinionated attitudes, she can adapt to and accept change, if grudgingly. Don Saturnino, however, cannot; he dislikes the present Mexican government but prefers the status quo to the unknown, represented by the Americans—the "gringos." To preserve the old, Don Saturnino organizes a few ranch owners and their vaqueros against the Americans. Winning the battle of San Pasqual, though, does not preserve the status quo; it only hastens to bring about the greatest change of all for Don Saturnino. During the battle, Don Saturnino, the only Spaniard injured, is mortally wounded.

Carlota de Zubarán not only accepts and adapts to change; she also initiates it. Don Saturnino has reared her to take the place of his dead son, Carlos, and Carlota has always acquiesced to her father's wishes and desires, ignoring those of her grandmother, Doña Dolores. When the Spaniards go to fight the Americans at San Pasqual, Carlota goes along and during the battle guards the extra horses. After the battle, an American soldier, John F. Fleming, tries to take one of the horses, and Carlota, intending to kill him, severely wounds him with an iron-tipped lance. As she prepares to take Don Saturnino back to their ranch, she decides to take Fleming, too. Don Saturnino is unconscious and cannot protest or forbid Carlota's decision though Don Saturnino's friend does protest. When Don Saturnino recovers enough from his wound to move about, he confronts both Fleming and Carlota and demands that Fleming leave immediately though he is not physically able to do so. Carlota defies her father for the first time in her life, causing Don Saturnino to faint, and, soon after, he dies.

Even before the battle, Carlota recognizes the futility of her father's action against the Americans but goes along with the plan to placate him. Carlota seems to realize better than even her grandmother the necessity of not aggravating the Americans. It is not until the confrontation with her father that Carlota sees that her wounding of Fleming had been an unnecessarily cruel and vicious act. In thinking for herself about the coming of the Americans and the battle, Carlota accepts the inevitability of change and seeks to adapt to it. In defying her father, Carlota precipitates change, by indirectly contributing to the causes of her father's death and thereby becoming mistress of the 47,000-acre Rancho de los Dos Hermanos. And though she dislikes many of the Americans, she does deal with them fairly and is strongly attracted to a young American physician, John Brett. Both Carlota and Doña Dolores accept the changes that the war brings and the severe drought that follows Don Saturnino's death. They survive mainly because of their adaptability and pliability.

Plot is secondary to characterization in *Carlota*. All three of the main characters are well delineated, but Doña Dolores is the most memorable. She is not only cold and haughty; she is also commanding, regal, and insensitive, best exemplified in her attitdue toward Rosario, a small Piute boy Don Saturnino had captured in a raid when Rosario was two, who serves as Doña Dolores's footstool and personal servant. Doña Dolores, like her son, is forcefully direct in all her dealings with everyone—family, friends, Yankees, and Indians.

As a historical novel, *Carlota* gives some glimpses into the daily lives of the Californians, though O'Dell only superficially pictures for his readers the huge adobe and tile ranch headquarters. He is somewhat better in telling about their diet, their love of horses, and their clothes, but it is as if he himself, so steeped in the details of nineteenth-century Californian life, assumes that his readers will be satisfied with his somewhat lean and sketchy attention to the kinds of details that make good historical fiction come alive.

Kathleen, Please Come Home (1978) is O'Dell's second contemporary problem novel. Set in southern California and in Baja California, it is a painful tracing of Kathleen's descent into drug addiction and alienation from her mother which result in her running away. Written in diary form in three parts, parts one and three are Kathleen's diary and part two is her mother's, giving two points of view and a greater understanding of how Kathleen became an addict and why her mother's misguided but well-intended efforts to help her are often misunderstood by Kathleen.

Dust jacket for O'Dell's contemporary problem novel about a young girl's descent into drug addiction and alienation (Houghton Mifflin)

Though the novel ends on a slight note of hope, it has a depressing and hopeless tone that the small degree of optimism does not easily erase from a reader's mind. After all her efforts to find her daughter, Kathleen's mother sells her home and goes east to look for her. When Kathleen returns home, she learns her mother has gone, and she and her friend wander to the bay into which they throw a package of heroin. Afterwards, Kathleen quotes the four-line stanza from "The Rime of the Ancient Mariner" that begins, "He prayeth best, who loveth best. . . . " The ambiguities of this quotation are several, including the possibilities that Kathleen will overcome her addiction, that the trouble between her and her mother stemmed from a lack of love and understanding, and that they may eventually come together through a new understanding of and a new kind of love for each other.

Based on the life of a real person, *Sarah Bishop* (1980) is set on Long Island during the early part of the American Revolution. Sarah Bishop's father is a Loyalist, and her brother Chad is a Patriot. A group of rebels brutally tar and feather Mr. Bishop, causing his death. Chad, who has joined the American army, has been taken prisoner and Sarah sets out to find him only to learn that he has died on board a prison ship. Accused by the British of setting a fire in New York City, Sarah escapes and flees to a wilderness area that lies to the north of the city to hide from the British and to heal her deep and bitter spiritual wounds. Just as she is about ready to rejoin society, she is accused of being a witch.

Sarah Bishop has a strong conflict, and Sarah is a well-delineated character; for the most part, she is consistent and believable. Thematically, O'Dell is suggesting that life is often paradoxical. When Sarah works for the Pennywells, owners of the Lion & Lamb Tavern, she notices that a pane of glass has been broken. A bird broke the glass, Mrs. Pennywell explains: "thought it was flying through air. . . . The world is full of surprises, my dear, things that seem what they ain't." She hopes Chad will be taken prisoner and be safe from bullets and danger, but the prison is far more dangerous than the battlefield. During the raging fire, she innocently picks up a knife dropped by a man who has cut the leather firebuckets and is falsely accused of cutting the buckets as well as starting the fire. Furthermore, a leading Quaker in Ridgeford accuses Sarah of being a witch, though one would expect no such act from a Quaker.

The Captive (1979), *The Feathered Serpent* (1981), and *The Amethyst Ring* (1983) comprise a trilogy set in Central and South America in the 1520s. It centers on Julián Escobar, a sixteen-year-old seminarian, who in *The Captive* is drafted as the religious representative for a voyage from Spain under a young nobleman, Don Luis. Landing on the wrong island, Don Luis and his men exploit the natives and their gold; their ship later wrecks near a Mayan island with Julián apparently the only survivor. A Spanish dwarf, an earlier castaway on the island, introduces Julián as the legendary Mayan god Kukulcán, under whose impersonation Julián sets out to restore the ancient and once fabulous City of Seven Serpents.

In *The Feathered Serpent,* Julián goes to Tenochtitlán (Mexico City) on the pretext of learning how Moctezuma rules and controls his vast Aztecan empire so that Julián can do the same with the Mayans of the City of Seven Serpents. His trip happens to coincide with Hernán Cortés's conquest, giving Julián the opportunity to witness first hand Cortés's cruel devastation of the magnificent Aztec

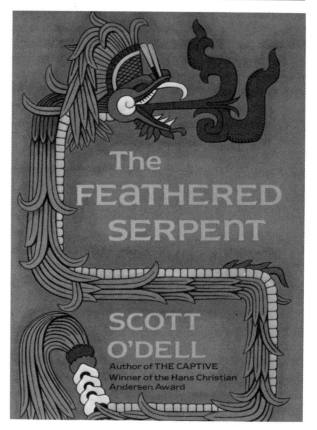

Dust jacket for O'Dell's novel about a sixteen-year-old Spanish boy caught in the tragic encounter between Hernán Cortés and Moctezuma (Houghton Mifflin)

empire.

Escaping Cortés, Julián returns, in *The Amethyst Ring,* to the City of Seven Serpents just a few months before Cortés overruns it. Julián then becomes a wanderer until he joins Francisco Pizarro to witness the early and decisive stage of the Spaniards' conquering of the Incas in South America. The trilogy concludes with Julián in Spain, apparently about to enter the order of the Brothers of the Poor.

O'Dell's trilogy is historically accurate as far as the conquest of the Aztecs and Incas is concerned; the rest is fiction. In the fictional parts, however, O'Dell disregards credibility by having Julián taking the role of Kukulcán, making him a witness to the downfalls of the Aztecs and the Incas, making him privy to both Cortés and Pizarro, and stretching the story over a period of ten to fifteen years and over great distances. Furthermore, Julián's dozens of adventures and escapes, some from sure death, make the trilogy even more incredible and tax the reader's sense of reality and probability.

The trilogy does not succeed as good historical fiction, not only because the story lacks credibility but also because O'Dell fails to make his historical epic real and alive for readers. The books move so rapidly from event to event that neither character nor action can generate real conflict.

Julián Escobar is never convincing in the various roles he plays—god, soldier, or lover to name only three; he remains essentially an underdeveloped character because O'Dell does not involve his readers emotionally with Julián. He lacks the convincingness of Esteban de Sandoval in *The King's Fifth* and of Karana in *Island of the Blue Dolphins,* because O'Dell is more interested in recreating a panorama of the Europeans' conquest of the Aztecs and Incas than in the creation of a fully developed character to carry the story.

Thematically, the trilogy is related to O'Dell's earlier historical novels that deal with the confrontations of Euro-Hispanics and the natives of the New World, in which the Europeans are portrayed as malicious and greedy and the natives are pictured as naive and peace-loving—no match for the cruel and rapacious Europeans. A major theme in the trilogy is similar to one of the main themes in *The King's Fifth;* the trilogy points up the idea that the lust for gold leads men to incomprehensible acts of shameful cruelty and evil. This theme, however, is not as strongly defined in the trilogy as in *The King's Fifth.*

As historical fiction, the trilogy is a failure; its main appeal lies in its dramatic and sensational presentation of the downfall of two great civilizations. Ultimately, the reader knows the civilizations will fall, and how and why. But, from O'Dell's trilogy, the reader does not know how it felt to be either the conquerors or the conquered.

The Spanish Smile (1982) and its sequel, *The Castle in the Sea* (1983), both set in recent times, tell the strange story of Lucinda de Cabrillo y Benivides and her father, who has kept her a prisoner nearly all her life on Isla del Oro, off the coast of southern California, to protect her from the evils of the twentieth century. Don Enrique de Cabrillo y Benivides is an emotionally sick man whose "protection" of Lucinda is only one of his aberrations. Isla del Oro is literally an island of gold, and Don Enrique is a wealthy and powerful man, able to carry out many of his sick and insane schemes, such as murdering and mummifying eighteen beautiful, blonde women, brought to the island as companions or prospective brides but in whom he always finds

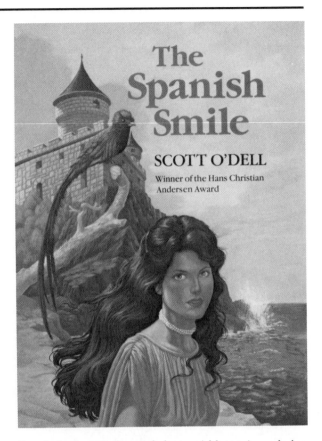

Dust jacket for O'Dell's novel about a girl kept prisoner by her overprotective father on his island off the coast of southern California (Houghton Mifflin)

some serious flaw. Near the end of the novel, in the black marble-lined, incense-perfumed, and candle-lighted crypt deep beneath the castle, a bushmaster, a deadly tropical snake guarding the crypt, strikes Don Enrique and kills him. This leaves his daughter the heiress of Isla del Oro; however, Lucinda, who knows nothing about the twentieth century and its customs and mores, also inherits all the problems Don Enrique has created for her.

The Castle in the Sea deals with the determination of who the true guardian of Lucinda will be: her fiancé, Porfirio de Puertoblanco, a spoiled young Spanish nobleman to whom Lucinda was betrothed as a young child, or señor Ricardo Villaverde, Don Enrique's longtime servant and loyal friend. In the end, neither man wins because señor Villaverde blows up Castillo Santiago, Don Enrique's magnificent castle, "built with pride, in defiance and hatred," with both Porfirio and Villaverde in the honeycomb of tunnels lying beneath it.

In spite of the preposterous plotting and characterization, the two novels are entertaining because of the mystery, intrigue, and multiplicity of farfetched episodes, motives, and effects. In these two stories, O'Dell suggests that wealth brings not only power but also corruption. This theme, however, is so overwrought with the mazes of the plot, subplots, and bizarre characters and incidents that it is lost.

Alexandra (1984) features a contemporary setting—Tarpon Springs, Florida, home to generations of Grecian sponge divers. After her father's death, Alexandra Papadimitrios, under her Grecian grandfather's tutelage, learns to dive for sponges. Not until a bidder at the Sponge Exchange offers Alexandra and her grandfather unheard-of prices for a few loads of sponges, some of which are of poor quality, does Alexandra begin to understand the scheme; she and her grandfather are unwittingly helping the wealthy Spyros Stavaronas, fiancé of Alexandra's sister Daphne and the owner of the Stavaronas Shrimp Company, to smuggle cocaine into Florida. Two men, whom Grandfather Papadimitrios has hired, are actually in the secret employ of Spyros and have tucked cocaine into the sponges. When Alexandra discovers proof, she does some moral searching but decides that, regardless of the consequences to Daphne and others, she will turn Spyros in.

In *Alexandra*, O'Dell again uses the theme that lust for money corrupts, reflected in the handsome and appealing young Spyros Stavaronas. This theme is not strongly realized because it is reflected through a secondary character, not a main one, as it is in Esteban de Sandoval in *The King's Fifth*. A primary theme of the story indicates that making a moral decision may result in hardship and suffering for all involved, including the person who must make the right decision, but, because Alexandra is always an upright and honest young woman, her dilemma does not engage a reader to the degree that Esteban's does when he determines in *The King's Fifth* to throw the gold into a sulphur pit and put behind the evil person it has made him.

Alexandra's reasons for turning Spyros in are many and complex, which O'Dell presents with dexterity and convincingness, making Alexandra more richly conceived and believable than Julián Escobar and Lucinda de Cabrillo y Benivides. However, Alexandra, though dramatically and emotionally well drawn, lacks the appeal and strength of character with which O'Dell embues his best-realized characters such as Karana of *Island of the Blue Dolphins* and Bright Morning of *Sing Down the Moon.*

The Road to Damietta (1985) tells the story of Saint Francis of Assisi through the eyes of Ricca di Montanaro, who is sixteen when the story opens. She is the daughter of Davino di Montanaro, a wealthy merchant, farmer, and landowner of Assisi and a member of its governing body, the podestà. Impulsive and headstrong, Ricca loves Francis Bernardone, a vain and impetuous young man.

In her pursuit of Francis, Ricca disgraces her family. When the elder Bernardone brings Francis to trial for stealing money and cloth from his shop to give to the poor, Bishop Guido, presiding at the trial in Santa Maria Maggiore Square, asks Francis to make restitution. Francis undresses and, standing naked before the Bishop and the huge crowd, returns the money and his clothing to his father. In a trancelike state, seeing Francis as Adam and

Dust jacket for O'Dell's novel about an adolescent girl who is forced to make adult decisions when she discovers that her grandfather's sponge-fishing operation is being used to smuggle cocaine into Florida (Houghton Mifflin)

Dust jacket for O'Dell's 1985 novel about the life of Saint Francis of Assisi (Houghton Mifflin)

herself as Eve, Ricca also disrobes amid the crowd.

When Ricca learns that Francis has taken vows of chastity and poverty, she too takes a holy vow to win Francis "away from the new life he had thoughtlessly chosen." Later, Ricca brings more humiliation to her family when she helps her friend, Clare di Scifi, escape her family and join Francis and his followers, the Friars Minors, at Porziuncola, out of Assisi where Francis and his followers live and work.

These as well as other acts cause Ricca's parents to send her to the monastery of San Andreas in Venice where Ricca's Aunt Sofia is the prioress. For more than a year, Ricca works as a copyist, helping the monastery to rebuild its burned library. Though her parents hope that she will forget Francis, she does not. Learning that Francis is in Venice with thousands of others to go to Jerusalem by way of Damietta in Egypt for the Fifth Crusade, Ricca leaves the monastery and finds passage on a ship for Damietta.

At Damietta, Francis decides to go to Malik-al-Kamil, the Sultan of Egypt, to plead for peace

and to convert him to Christianity. Acting as translator, Ricca goes with Francis and Brother Illuminato, a devoted follower. The Sultan regards them as prisoners and, learning that Ricca loves Francis, has Ricca taught to dance seductively to test Francis.

For the Sultan, Francis, and Illuminato, but mainly for Francis, Ricca dances, gradually removing her costume until she stands naked before the men. Francis is unmoved; he simply and kindly asks Ricca to repent. The Sultan releases them and they return to Damietta, which falls to the Christians. The crusaders pursue the Sultan and his army, who later defeat the Christians. After several months in Damietta, Ricca returns to Assisi. After his return to Assisi, Francis dies a few years later (1226) with Ricca still loving him.

O'Dell's story gives the bare outlines of St. Francis's life with the exceptions of a few dramatic events detailed from it. He focuses on the appeal that Francis had for people; his charisma was more than spiritual according to the fiction of *The Road to Damietta*. Ricca di Montanaro's attraction for Francis seems to have stemmed from his physical and spiritual qualities, for, from the beginning of her infatuation, both his courage and ethereality appealed to her. As the story develops, however, O'Dell plays down the spiritual, emphasizing more the physical attraction Ricca felt.

The Road to Damietta is somewhat disappointing. Ricca di Montanaro seems to be a young girl with twentieth-century feelings and attitudes put down in the Middle Ages. Though she is more colorful, she somehow remains a pallid creation in comparison with Karana of *Island of the Blue Dolphins* and Bright Morning of *Sing Down the Moon*. Her purpose to win Francis from his vows seems inconsistent with the time and with her careful upbringing and religious training. When nearly all women of Ricca's class were learning the fine art of stitching, it is strange that Ricca would be learning writing, astronomy, numbers, and languages of the world, including Arabic, especially during the Middle Ages, before the emphasis on learning that characterized the Renaissance had begun.

Furthermore, her determination to win Francis away from his vows seems a rather ignoble goal. That such an infatuation might develop is probable, but that it lasts for twenty years in the face of opposition from family, friends, churchmen, reason, and Francis himself is improbable. For its shortcomings, though, *The Road to Damietta* reaffirms that Saint Francis was one of the most lovable and strongest of men.

Chapter 18 -- 178

When we approached the Roman wall, a band of horsemen burst forth from San Rufino Square. They rode at a gallop and carried the blue and gold penons of the house of Davino di Montanaro. Without a word, without so much as a smile, I passed them by, nor did I move faster when they turned about and followed us at a distance.

The family was not at home. Where they had gone, a servant who had not gone with them would not none of the servants would chance a guess, but from her their uneasy looks, I knew that they were abroad in the city, everyone was abroad; searching for their daughter. me, in the Streets.

The family They came at supper time and sat down at the table and began to talk in a cheerful way. But they talked among themselves, not to me, as though I were not there, at the table, as though nothing at all had happened. I did notice, however, that my father's hands shook when he washed them, that my mother's eyes were red from weeping, and Rinaldo's voice had an angry edge to it. Only Raul spoke to me that evening and then not in their family's presence.

After I had eaten alone, from all appearances, I went to the scriptorium and began a letter to Francis Bernardone. This one was symbolic like the others, dealing again with the unhappy love between Abelard and Heloise, which continued to disturb me.

Raul came in cautiously, afraid, I presumed, that I might fly at him. He spoke about the flowers that were

Revised typescript page for The Road to Damietta *(by permission of the author)*

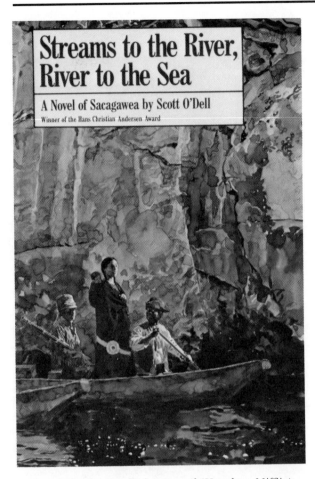

Dust jacket for O'Dell's latest novel (Houghton Mifflin)

Scott O'Dell is one of two or three major American novelists of the past two decades who has written historical fiction for children. His rank as one of the foremost historical novelists is attested to by the number of prestigious awards he has won, by the thousands and thousands of young readers he has claimed since the publication of *Island of the Blue Dolphins* in 1960, and by the critical acclaim he has received for several of his books.

Any good historical novel should speak not only of the past but also to the present, and *Island of the Blue Dolphins, The King's Fifth, Sing Down the Moon,* and *The Hawk that Dare not Hunt by Day* succeed in their expression of timeless truths. Scott O'Dell writes for children to make them aware of man's inhumanity but also of the possibilities for endurance, resourcefulness, and moral courage.

References:

Maud Hart Lovelace, "Scott O'Dell," in *Newbery and Caldecott Medal Books: 1956-1965,* edited by Lee Kingman (Boston: Horn Book, 1965);

Edith McCormick, "Scott O'Dell: Immortal Writer," *American Libraries,* 4 (June 1973): 356-357;

Perry Nodelman, "A Second Look: Sing Down the Moon," *Horn Book,* 60 (February 1984): 94-98;

Linda Kauffman Peterson and Marilyn Leathers Solt, *Newbery and Caldecott Medal and Honor Books, an Annotated Bibliography* (Boston: G. K. Hall, 1982);

"Scott O'Dell," in *The Pied Pipers,* edited by Justin Wintle and Emma Fisher (New York: Paddington Press, 1975);

"Scott O'Dell Founds $5000 Children's Book Award," *Publishers Weekly,* 220 (11 September 1981): 29;

John Rowe Townsend, "Scott O'Dell," in *A Sense of Story* (Philadelphia: Lippincott, 1971).

Katherine Paterson

(31 October 1932-   )

M. Sarah Smedman
University of North Carolina at Charlotte

SELECTED BOOKS: *The Sign of the Chrysanthemum*, illustrated by Peter Landa (New York: Crowell, 1973; Harmondsworth, U.K.: Penguin, 1975);

Of Nightingales That Weep, illustrated by Haru Wells (New York: Crowell, 1974; Harmondsworth, U.K.: Penguin, 1976);

The Master Puppeteer, illustrated by Wells (New York: Crowell, 1975);

Bridge to Terabithia, illustrated by Donna Diamond (New York: Crowell, 1977; London: Gollancz, 1978);

The Great Gilly Hopkins (New York: Crowell, 1978; London: Gollancz, 1979);

Angels & Other Strangers: Family Christmas Stories (New York: Crowell, 1979); republished as *Star of Night* (London: Gollancz, 1980);

Jacob Have I Loved (New York: Crowell, 1980; London: Gollancz, 1981);

Gates of Excellence: On Reading and Writing for Children (New York: Elsevier/Nelson, 1981);

Rebels of the Heavenly Kingdom (New York: Dutton, 1983);

Come Sing, Jimmy Jo (New York: Dutton, 1985);

Consider The Lilies: Plants of The Bible, by Paterson and John B. Paterson, illustrated by Anne Ophelia Dowden (New York: Crowell, 1986).

OTHER: Sumiko Yagawa, *The Crane Wife,* translated by Paterson, illustrated by Suekichi Akaba (New York: Morrow, 1981).

PERIODICAL PUBLICATIONS: "Newbery Award Acceptance," *Horn Book,* 54 (August 1978): 361-367;

"National Book Award Acceptance," *Horn Book,* 55 (August 1979): 402-403;

"Newbery Award Acceptance," *Horn Book,* 57 (August 1981): 385-393;

"Sounds in the Heart," *Horn Book,* 57 (December 1981): 694-702;

"Do I Dare Disturb the Universe?," *Horn Book,* 60 (September/October 1984): 640-651;

Katherine Paterson

"Where Is Terabithia?," *Children's Literature Association Quarterly,* 9 (Winter 1984-1985): 153-157;

"Wednesday's Children," *Horn Book,* 63 (May/June 1986): 287-294.

Katherine Paterson's reverence for words coupled with her respect for the power of story prompted her to keep writing for years when, not ready to publish, she was learning her craft. Her reluctance overcome, her apprenticeship served, the stories and essays Paterson has published establish her as a major artist, skilled, discerning, and compassionate. What she has written achieves excellence because her artistic vision embraces all that is human and because she is a master craftsman.

What Paterson has said about her work in *Gates of Excellence: On Reading and Writing for Children* (1981) makes explicit basic convictions about life and literature which infuse her eight novels and one collection of Christmas stories. Three principles, embodied in her fiction, might be said to comprise the heart of her literary creed: her belief, first, that children have an inalienable right to stirring stories; second, that these stories must be told in beautiful, vibrant language worthy of the intellectual and imaginative power of their young readers; and third, that stories for young readers must deal honestly with ultimate issues. She believes that adults who write for children bear a two-edged responsibility. They must set before their readers solid fare, books with serious, moral themes. At the same time, they must keep feeding the fragile flame of hope that life, despite its crushing accoutrements, is exhilarating, is rich, is joyous.

Katherine Paterson was born of American missionary parents, George Raymond and Mary Goetchius Womeldorf, in Tsing-Tsiang Pu, China, on 31 October 1932, the third of five children. Twice the family was forced by the exigencies of war to return to the United States, the second time permanently.

Moving about between China and various locations in Virginia, North Carolina, and West Virginia, the young Paterson experienced a variety of cultures and almost continual change. Before she graduated summa cum laude from King College in Bristol, Tennessee, in 1954, she had attended thirteen schools. In 1957 she received an M.A. in English Bible from the Presbyterian School of Christian Education in Richmond, Virginia. Though as a child living in China she had hated and feared the Japanese, as an adult she wished to go back there to live. In 1957 she enrolled at the Naganuma School of Japanese Language in Kobe, then served as a Christian Education Assistant for eleven pastors in rural areas of Shikoku Island. During the four years she spent in Japan, she came to love the country and its people, returning later to do research for *The Master Puppeteer* (1975), the third of her novels set in Japan. She returned to New York City where, on a fellowship to the Union Theological Seminary, she earned an M.R.E. in 1962 and met and married John Barstow Paterson, a Presbyterian minister. Within a few years Paterson had become the mother of four, two natural sons, John and David, and two adopted daughters, one Chinese, Elizabeth Polin, and one Apache Kiowa, Mary Katherine. As she told Linda T. Jones

in a *Language Arts* interview, "Needing something . . . that wasn't either eaten up, dirtied or torn apart by the end of the day," she began writing in "what little scraps of time" she could find for herself. Paterson's books grow from the fiber of her being. Conversely, wrestling with literary problems has helped the author through wrenching situations in her personal life: surgery for and recovery from cancer, which brought her face-to-face with her own mortality; the death of her mother; the sudden death of her eight-year-old son's closest friend. As to the question of whether her own children have influenced her writing, Paterson, in *Gates of Excellence*, answers in the affirmative: "the very persons who have taken away my time and space are those who have given me something to say." Besides her fiction Paterson has written educational materials for the Presbyterian Church, U.S.A. and the National Council of Churches. After thirteen years in Takoma Park, Maryland, the family moved to Norfolk, Virginia, where John Paterson served as pastor of Lafayette Presbyterian Church until August 1986.

Each of Paterson's characters begins as a dimension of herself, then becomes an independent entity. Until a book is completed Paterson is conscious of the story, not of the audience. She guards her work jealously, talking about it to no one until it is written. Its first reader is her husband, of whose astute but encouraging criticism, along with that of her editor, Virginia Buckley, she speaks with affectionate appreciation.

The distinctive quality of Paterson's art is her colorful concision. Whether she is narrating or describing, her mode is understatement, her style pithy. She dramatizes, never exhorts, creating powerful scenes in which action subtly elicits and restrains emotional response. Gestures and dialogue are natural and real. Metaphors derive from the novel's setting and come alive through strong verbs and the often unnoticed but perfectly apt detail. The effect is twofold: image after sharp, memorable image is engraved in readers' minds while at the same time they are ensured "the great open spaces they need to set their own imaginations soaring." Paterson weaves plot strands and symbols seamlessly into tightly meshed stories in which each character, each episode, each image, each bit of dialogue helps to incarnate what the author is imagining.

Paterson writes of Japanese and American youngsters, who, despite their cultural differences, are in many ways alike. Entangled in chaotic childhoods, her sensitive but tough young protagonists, each a social or a spiritual outsider, set out to achieve self-determined goals. During the course of each story, the child, caught in potentially tragic circumstances, must come to grips with the limitations with which reality circumscribes one's dreams. In each Paterson story, the protagonist turns tragedy to triumph by bravely choosing a way which is not selfishly determined. In relinquishing vainglorious dreams and opening themselves to tenacious love, Paterson's protagonists gain dignity and happiness. They embody the theme of redemption through the sacrifice of oneself and one's ambitions, a theme that resounds convincingly, never clichéd, never preached, always with the force of fresh discovery.

Inspired by an affinity for the Japanese, their history and culture, Paterson turned to that setting for her first three novels. In *The Sign of the Chrysanthemum* (1973) and *Of Nightingales That Weep* (1974) the twelfth-century civil wars between the rival Heike and Genji clans provide a finely detailed background and create the circumstances which incite the protagonists' dreams and quests.

The Sign of the Chrysanthemum opens with thirteen-year-old Muna burying his mother, dead of "the lung disease." Christened Muna ("No Name" in Chinese) by a pretentious daimyo, the boy had been born of the impoverished peasant woman after her romantic encounter with a transient samurai. Mourning his mother, Muna nonetheless accepts her death as her release from privation and his freedom to search for his warrior father, to find his true name. Fortified by his mother's stories of the grandeur of his noble sire, to be identified by a small chrysanthemum tattooed on his left shoulder, Muna stows away on a river boat, leaving his native Awa for the capital, appropriately and ironically named Heiankyo, the City of Eternal Peace.

Lonely and sick, Muna is befriended by the rascal ronin Takanobu, a samurai in want of both a lord and a moral code. Once in the city, evoked in the indigence and stench of its wretches at Rashomon Gate as well as in the shimmer and delicacy of its white palace and cherry blossoms, Muna's romantic yearnings are tempered as his awareness of human misery and treachery increases. Shocked by the knowledge that Takanobu is a thief, Muna nevertheless is grateful that the ronin does not despise him, a gratitude that becomes rueful when Takanobu ridicules and abandons him. After Muna collapses at a saloon fire in which he believes Takanobu has died, he is picked up unconscious from the street by a swordmaker, Fukuji. Recovered, he chafes under the tedious tasks of a house-and-errand boy to a master who repeatedly

Dust jacket for Paterson's first novel (Crowell)

exposes his inadequacies.

Despite his resentment, Muna stays with Fukuji, held by intangible bonds: the swordmaker's music which manifests a prophetic wisdom; his acceptance of a boy whose background he does not know but whose discontent he recognizes; and, finally, the boy's own hope that the master will take him as his apprentice. When Takanobu reappears to demand that Muna get him a sword from Fukuji to replace the one he had gambled away, the boy, "like an animal caught between two opposing lines of bowmen—all of the arrows flying towards him," is torn between his loyalty to the opportunist and his admiration of the steely artisan's refusal to make weapons for men who dishonor them. Takanobu's insinuation that he is Muna's father disabuses the boy of his grandiose fantasies and precipitates his climactic internal conflict. Realizing that, if not Takanobu, someone like him may be his father, the tortured Muna asks Fukuji whether he intends to apprentice him. Misinterpreting as rejection Fukuji's aphoristic reply—"The proper question must be, What do you think of yourself?"—Muna rages through an inner storm, emerging coldly determined to steal a Fukuji sword for Takanobu in exchange for the latter's promise to give him his name.

Furious at the ronin's refusal, Muna slashes Takanobu's hand with the fierce weapon, then takes to the hills to bury it. Fleeing from Fukuji, not knowing whether he more fears getting caught or going unpunished, the anguished Muna sentences himself to the hell of the Rashomon Gate, living there with the penurious and the profligate through the summer, fall, and winter. "He now belonged fully to that class of people who expect to be bullied by the rest of the world, who think that by objecting they will only bring further misery upon themselves. He had no dreams of personal worth left to smash." In the winter, as the clash between the Heike and Genji climaxes, Muna's memory of the shining blade held aloft by the tempered, polished Fukuji overcomes his self-loathing and he resolves to return the sword, henceforward to accept his destiny as an outcast.

Fukuji, however, forgives the boy, and Muna, "with a fierce joy known only to those who have escaped the jaws of Hell," returns to his household chores. Nursing the city's homeless wounded, victims of the civil war, Muna quietly passes the New Year and his fifteenth birthday, that of his majority, with Fukuji. With the spring come the ends of both the war and of Muna's personal battle. Having let go of his phantom of a glorious father, Muna rejoices in the truth and beauty of the swordsmith's song: "The Great Creator, in the variety of his works/Blesses as well the lowly and the small." As he enters his manhood, he chooses to keep the name Muna. When he tells Fukuji, the master, in a ritual acceptance of the boy as his apprentice, cuts his long hair with a sword. More important, the "powerful, cleansing joyful fire" which sears through Muna at his decision signals his recognition of himself as worthy. Muna has learned what Fukuji has known, that a man, like a mountain, is more beautiful for the scar at the summit, which attests "to the tumult that had once raged within."

Typical of the hero in a Paterson novel, Muna does not attain what as a callow youth he dreamed of. His egocentric, romanticized quest is both thwarted and extended by his encounter with the destructive forces of evil. When the beautiful, gentle Akiko, whom he loves, is orphaned and sold into prostitution by a wanton uncle, Muna rails at the brutality, at his own powerlessness, and simultaneously glimpses something of the universal extent of suffering and sorrow. He begins his figurative descent into hell. Like subsequent Paterson protagonists, Muna believes himself to be irreligious. Yet the realization that he is not the sole troubled occupant of the world precipitates his fall from innocence to an awareness of a cosmic providence, whether it be the gods whom he had long forgotten or the Great Creator of Fukuji's song. Once aware of himself, not as the center of creation, but as part of a universal whole, Muna has the courage to surrender his dreams and to love, even in their imperfections, himself and others.

The world Muna lives in yields the major images and symbols of the novel, both the cyclical imagery of the seasons and the dialectical symbols for good and evil. Cherry blossoms, summer rains, fiery maples, and freezing storms provide both natural setting and objective correlatives for Muna's disillusionment and joy. The filth and gleaming splendor at opposite ends of Suzaki Oji, Heiankyo's central avenue, constitute both a background for Muna's movements and the symbols of the choices open to him. With its motto, "Through fire is the spirit forged," the sword, fashioned by Fukuji as carefully and ceremoniously as a ritual is performed by a high priest, becomes the central symbol, a symbol both for the boy and the relationship between him and his mentor. The motto, revealed only at the end of the book, encapsulates the novel's binding symbol—fire—which burns, flashes, and sears everywhere in Muna's physical and spiritual worlds, destroying dross and dreams alike, purifying painfully, and enlightening gloriously.

Paterson creates vivid, believable characters through clear, clean portrayal of the complex intercourse of endearing, admirable, and despicable qualities within each. Takanobu epitomizes the lawlessness Muna repudiates; his intentions and actions are discrepant; yet his self-confidence and flamboyance are alluring. Fukuji embodies the disciplined wisdom that Muna ultimately embraces, but he agonizes over his own hypocrisy, and his forbidding manner is chilling. Consistent with Japanese custom, Paterson's characters frequently mask their fiercest emotions in conventional gestures of courtesy. The tension between internal disposition and external manifestation conveys and controls feelings almost ineffable.

Paterson's images and symbols overlap, intertwine with characters and events so that each fictional element gradually, subtly takes on the ambience of the others. When, at the end of *The Sign of the Chrysanthemum,* the seasons, the dreams, death and life, the great and the small fuse in Fukuji's song, the story is resolved in Muna's decision to embrace his "No Name." Having experienced the beauty of life, as well as its suffering, Muna is renewed in hope.

Of Nightingales That Weep is a historical romance, an inverted Cinderella story in which the beautiful, gifted Takiko has neither a fairy godmother to waive the harsh realities of life in wartorn Japan of the 1180s nor a handsome prince to whisk her into wonderland. In relinquishing her fantasies, raising another's well-being above her own, and accepting the tribulation which surrounds her, she discovers a true prince and a happiness deeper than she had known she desired.

In an unpublished 1982 interview, Paterson outlined the composition of the book. Asked by a close friend and ardent feminist to write her second novel about "a girl, a strong person who overcomes many odds," Paterson, listening to the story she had begun in response to that request, realized that her "strong girl was also selfish and vain, and she would

Dust jacket for Paterson's historical romance set in war-torn Japan in the 1180s (Crowell)

be brought low by her flaws as well as exalted by her strengths. She turned, you see, in the course of the story into a human being in a specific time of history and in an actual geographical location, both of which conspired against her budding feminism." Although *Of Nightingales That Weep* may displease those feminists who believe a successful woman must attain worldly power and wealth, the story holds true to the tenet that feminism is radically concerned with the wholeness of all human beings. The novel depicts the feminine as healer, peacemaker, creator from chaos of order and harmony. If, in its affirmation of life, it also asserts the indispensability of self-sacrifice and humility in the achievement of wholeness and beauty, it portrays those virtues honestly as dynamic and hard-won and enfleshes them in the male character, Goro, as well as in Takiko and other less fully developed women characters.

Takiko is a passionate but disciplined child, intolerant of hypocrisy and, at the beginning, unaware of her own. She is as sensitive an instrument as the koto she plays; her quest is for beauty and romance, in art and in life. Orphaned by a Heike war hero, the haughty eleven-year-old moves to the farm of Goro, a potter and distant relative of noble blood whom her widowed mother Chieko marries. Raised in the city house of a wealthy maternal aunt, Takiko had never known men other than dignified but dissolute nobles and contemptuous but fawning servants, so she looks forward to meeting an artisan and dreams of learning his craft. Shocked by the deformed Goro's resemblance to a huge monkey, Takiko rejects him as a father and thereby cuts herself off from her mother. In her loneliness, she plays a lovely old koto that had belonged to Goro's mother. Gradually the music heals her, strengthening her will to ask forgiveness of Goro and her mother to take her place in the family. Takiko's story begins in, recapitulates, and augments that first incident. In a series of ensuing episodes, she goes eagerly into new situations, at first clinging willfully to her fantasies. Gradually, through her own and others' weakness, she is disabused of her romantic dreams and discovers beauty beneath the coarsest exterior.

Of Nightingales That Weep proclaims the possibility of rich, creative life even amid the appalling destruction of nature and of "men who did not remember the acts of mercy of their enemies. They only remembered obligations of vengeance." Takiko's gradual recognition and appreciation of Goro's veiled, steadfast love and her wholehearted response are rendered strong and unsentimental

62

been ~~shut up in the dark~~ shuttered house like a bear in ~~its~~ a winter cave. How to leave the shadowy shell

pale and sickly life seemed here in comparison to ~~Mieko's~~ Gori's farm where ~~summer and~~ even in the winter the great house

winter shutters were thrown open in the day time for ~~warmth~~ warmth and light ~~How she longed~~

from the sun, ~~where~~ where ~~they~~ one continued to go outside even in the ~~for the smell of green growth In the~~

bitterest weather for there was work to be done and no one was permitted to ~~spring air~~ even there

hibernate. ~~seemed more~~

She and Mieko climbed into the carriage and snuggled in among the friendly to her nostrils ~~the rains would be early this year. There was an oppressive feeling in the air.~~

~~furs and~~ quilts. Each of them put a hand on the koto to keep it from bumping than the heavy perfumes

about during the ride. It had been ~~Mieko's~~ Gori's mother's and Takiko could not bear of the court.

to think of it being scratched, much less broken.

"Have you been to court before, Mieko?"

"What, me? No, never," she laughed.

Princess Aoi had given her some instructions in etiquette--how to

how to refuse refreshments,
kowtow, how to address the Emperor, a few questions which might be

considered appropriate conversation before she began to play. She rehearsed

these now with Mieko, at first anxiously, then collapsing into nervous giggles.

"I'm so nervous."

"Ohh, madaam, with your charm?" And as usual, Mieko's flattery had

a soothing effect on her and she was able to sit a little striaghter in the

bumpy carriage.

Revised typescript page for Of Nightingales That Weep *(by permission of the author)*

through the Japanese setting with its indigenous religious and social rituals, folklore and superstitions; through energizing contextual imagery; and through gentle irony—all integrally fused in the structure of the novel. The Gempei Wars of twelfth-century Japan provide the distancing conducive to the aura of romance as well as the wellspring of oriental customs and traditions from which so much of the texture and tension of the novel derives. That setting serves, too, to intensify the mythic dimensions of Takiko, Goro, and other less fully developed characters.

The binding images of this novel, the potter's clay and the koto, also become symbols of the main characters. Goro, "one man of peace in a nation gone mad with War," when his world is destroyed, turns "himself to the molding of clay like a god starting creation all over again." Though this "little god" is a cocreator, he is also crippled in body and spirit, a creature in need of healing. Takiko, a born "maker of music," learns pottery making from Goro, which gives her "the same feeling of power that her music gave her. She was inside the clay, yet master and creator of it." A passage at the end of the novel giving ecstatic voice to the interdependence of Takiko and Goro, of human and physical nature, of creature and creator is representative of Paterson's talent for drawing together disparate symbols and themes in a final, consummate image and of her exquisite use of language:

> The daughter of a samurai does not cry out in childbirth. Within her head Takiko laughed at the injunction. It was as though her very body was the koto of a god whose powerful hand struck a chord so fierce that for the wild moment she became the storm music of the sea. Then throbbing, ebbing, the great wave would pass over her, and she would drift on the surface of the water, the sun warm upon her face until another stroke upon the strings.
> *I am mixing it all up.* She smiled. *I am music and storm and strings. I am Izanami as She brooded over Creation.*

Of Nightingales That Weep celebrates the transformation of "This fragile dream of joy/Into lasting love," of which the book's epigraph sings.

Paterson's mystery novel, *The Master Puppeteer* (1975), is set in eighteenth-century Osaka, when the famine of 1783-1787 has reduced the populace to bestial scavengers who plunder and burn their city. The hero of the poor and the center of the story's suspense is the cunning Saburo, elusive leader of a band of sworn secret followers who rob the rich to feed the hungry. In contrast with the chaos of the streets is the disciplined world of the Hanaza, the theater compound ruled by master puppeteer Yoshida and the blind reciter Okada. Jiro, the son of Hanji, the puppet maker, and Kinshi, Yoshida's son, bridge the two worlds. Thirteen-year-old Jiro, who was born unwanted in the year of the plague, and who survives three older siblings, has become the target of his mother Isako's bitter anger. Guilty and hurt by her reproaches and his family's penury, clumsy at his father's craft because his empty belly diverts his attention, Jiro runs away to the Hanaza to become a puppeteer. Unlike Takiko's, Jiro's motives are basically altruistic and simple. He wants to succeed at something, to earn money to alleviate his parents' suffering, and to bring honor to his father's name. Because his mother cannot understand what she misconstrues as unadulterated selfishness and abandonment, the breach between them widens. Once inside the Hanaza, the spirited Jiro respectfully requests Okada, the senior chanter, to intercede for him with Yoshida, once a student, now founder and master of his own theater. Jiro immediately likes and respects Kinshi, Yoshida's son, for the ironic banter under which he masks both his kindness and his pain at his failure to meet his father's expectations. Jiro loves Kinshi's steely courage though he fears the consequences of his friend's lack of judgment. Kinshi reciprocates the affection, helping Jiro to find his place in the company, to learn puppeteering, and to assist his mother. In this strange new world where it is hard for an outsider to understand the ways of the theater, the reader learns with Jiro that "All of the Hanaza was a play—not just what they did upon the stage, but off it as well. Each person had a part," and to step out of the bounds of one's role was to disturb the whole drama.

While it sustains a provocative mystery and a fascinating account of bunraku, the art of the Japanese puppet theater, *The Master Puppeteer* delicately handles the serious, intricate moral questions it raises. Many of the social and political issues of eighteenth-century Japan are contemporary, world-wide problems as well: the conflict between the upper and lower classes, the rights of the poor, and the degree to which the young are bound to conform to the values of their parents as they struggle to understand their world and to develop personal moral codes. The novel proposes no simple answers but depicts graphically, never sensationally, the icy revulsion and terror of life in a society

Dust jacket for Paterson's mystery novel set in eighteenth-century Osaka (Crowell)

that proffers no viable solutions.

A story foremost about friendship and love of life, the novel poignantly embodies cosmic issues in the personal relationships among the characters, centrally that between Jiro and Kinshi. Although the younger boy does not share Kinshi's empathy with bestial humanity, he comes to know that his love for his friend, tangled as it is with his ambitions, filial responsibilities, and fear of reprisals, is the highest law. The esteem Kinshi has for Yoshida gives him strength to accept with stoical courage and witticisms the abuse of a father he does not understand and whose values he cannot accept. His affection for his father and Jiro, added to his innate kindness, spills over to such concern for Isako, who has become one of the night rovers who pound the Hanaza gates demanding food, that he automatically plunges to her aid without any thought of the consequences to himself. Paterson's third novel challenges the validity in desperate situations of

ritual manners and customs, particularly that of honorable suicide. Direct and hasty, Jiro tends to bypass conventional courtesy, finding straightforwardness more effectual. The ceremonial bow serves him chiefly as a convenience when out of shyness or shame he would rather avoid his elder's eyes. Jiro smarts under the embarrassment he causes his father when he breaks the rules and accepts Yoshida's invitation to a meal, but his hunger is greater than his training. Yoshida excuses him: "Ah—manners—they can be taught, but spirit— that is a gift of the gods." In a paean to life, even amid misery and pain, the novel attests that "Jiro had never been completely convinced by the samurai tradition which held it to be a noble thing to throw one's life away for the sake of those to whom one is bound by the ties of duty or affection. He was very attached to his scraggly body and the somewhat less than grand spirit that animated it."

The movement back and forth, in and out from the streets of Osaka and the Hanaza provides the novel a structural framework, creates and controls the dramatic and emotional tension, and incorporates another major theme: that life and art are parallels that reflect each other. The author selectively narrates the stories of plays performed in the Hanaza, commenting judiciously on their relevance to the reality of the novel. Insights into the plays suggest to Jiro alternatives in his personal dilemma. The interweaving of drama and actuality raises the question, "What is real?," provides clues to the mystery of Saburo and his role as defender of the poor, and adds to the store of information about bunraku smoothly integrated into the book. Succinct and historically precise details about making and operating the large puppets, about staging the shows, and about the hierarchy among puppeteers, samisen players, and reciters and their life within the theater compel the reader's interest, which, with the suspense that builds up as the narrative progresses, tempers the raw horror of brutal street scenes. The tension between suspense and horror, attraction and revulsion, life inside the theater and out, stage plays and human history propels the narrative action and equilibrates the reader's response.

The two heroes of *The Master Puppeteer*—Jiro, the initiate, and Kinshi, the scapegoat—incarnate that hope for which, Paterson said in her acceptance of the National Book Award, she wanted to be a spy. An ordinary boy, "stubborn and unwise, but always kind," Kinshi is splendid in the unflinching sacrifice of his hand and with it his ambition to become a puppeteer great enough to satisfy his father's perfectionist standards. *The Master Puppeteer* suggests that hope for redemption of debased worlds, like eighteenth-century Osaka, may well lie in people like Kinshi, self-possessed and altruistic, who will give of themselves until it hurts.

Bridge to Terabithia (1977) is different from the earlier books in notable ways: it is more closely focused on foreground characters, blurring the background of universal suffering; it is set in rural America; although it is more immediately about place, the places in the novel are not as fully depicted as are, for example, the Rashomon Gate or the Hanaza Theater. Rather, places are evocatively outlined, inviting readers to paint in details from their own experiences. Paterson's analogy for *Bridge to Terabithia* is apt, "a simple melody in tune with questions children ask," "a flute solo," this time without full orchestral accompaniment. The novel is about special places that entice children into imaginative realms where they become kings and

KATHERINE PATERSON

BRIDGE TO TERABITHIA

Illustrated by Donna Diamond

Dust jacket for a later edition of Paterson's 1978 Newbery Medal-winning novel about childhood friendship (Crowell)

queens and heroic defenders against the giants of evil. It is about the sudden and senseless death of a child. Above all, it is about friendship, the friendship between two lonely children who find each other.

Ten-year-old Jesse Aarons is a middle child, an only boy with four sisters—two clothes- and boy-crazy teenagers, a first grader who adores him, and a whining toddler. An artist in the philistine stronghold of rural Virginia, he knows enough to do his drawing away from the eyes of contemptuous classmates, teachers who screech about wasted time and talent, and his father who scorns artists as unmasculine. Determined to make his father proud and to earn acclaim as the fastest runner at Lark Creek Elementary, Jesse has practiced running in the cow pasture in the early summer mornings. On the first day of school, surprisingly, he is beaten by Leslie Burke, a new girl who has come to live at the Perkins place down the road from the Aarons home. Despite himself Jesse feels sorry for, then likes, this odd newcomer who wears tacky clothes on the first day of school, who does not have sense enough not to tell the whole class that her family has no television, and who writes beautifully. Scintillating and straightforward, well-read and wildly imaginative, Leslie evokes first the taunts and then the disregard of everyone in the fifth grade except Loud-Mouth Myers, the teacher, and Jesse, for whom she and the Friday-afternoon half hours of music with Miss Edmunds are the only bright spots in the colorless world of school. After school Jesse follows Leslie's lead in Terabithia, their secret land across a creek into which they swing on a rope tied to a crab apple limb. In Terabithia they build a castle from scrap boards and stock it against siege. "Like God in the Bible, they looked at what they had made and found it very good." Venturing deeper into the woods they discover a pine grove, a sanctuary which they visit to offer ritual petitions or thanksgiving when the kingdom is particularly threatened or blessed. Having grown up in a conventional family where need keeps the father alternately working or tired from work and the mother incessantly peevish, Jesse is "taller and stronger and wiser in that mysterious land," where Leslie introduces him to the world of story and the wonders of language.

Although it takes him time, Jesse becomes comfortable in Leslie's actual world too, where parents and daughter are friends, where together they discuss world affairs, listen to classical music, and read poetry aloud. When Christmas comes, Jesse, because "Sometimes . . . you need to give people something that's for them, not just something that makes you feel good giving it," spends most of his pittance on a Barbie doll for May Bell, his pesky six-year-old sister for whom he has a special affection. Penniless and troubled, he chances upon a free puppy as the perfect gift for Leslie, who delightedly christens him Prince Terrien (P.T.) and dubs him guardian—and fool—of Terabithia. Leslie gives Jesse paints and brushes for she perceives that someday he will capture on paper "the poetry of the trees." While Leslie is initiating Jesse into the pleasures and possibilities of the imagination and its expressions, Jesse teaches her practical matters of country life and sensitizes her to the feelings of others.

During Easter week the eternal rains swell the creek which borders on Terabithia into a roaring sea, "hungry waters licking and sometimes leaping the banks, daring them to try to confine it." Afraid and ashamed, Jesse reluctantly swings after the daring Leslie, P. T. tucked in the front of her raincoat, into Terabithia where they make a pilgrimage to the pine grove to beseech the spirits for "the wisdom to discern this evil and the power to overcome it." In the middle of that night Jesse decides that he must tell Leslie he is afraid to go back to Terabithia until the creek goes down. Doing the morning milking, he reflects that she will not make fun of him and smiles in anticipation of her reaction to his nonsensical notion that he will have to go to the Medical College for a gut transplant. All thought of his gutlessness and Terabithia are driven from his head by a phone call from Miss Edmunds inviting him on a visit to Washington.

Duly but deviously extracting permission from his mother without really waking her, Jesse does not think of asking Miss Edmunds to take Leslie too. When he does sometime later, he cannot "suppress a secret pleasure at being alone in this small cozy car with Miss Edmunds." Intoxicated by his nearness to the teacher he idolizes and the sacred wonders of the National Gallery and the Smithsonian Institution, Jesse returns dazzled to a world of sunshine fortified to face his mother's anger. "This one perfect day of his life was worth anything he had to pay."

Jesse returns to the horrifying news that Leslie is dead and to a family terrified by the uncertainty that he may be too. Unlike Jesse, for whom their secret kingdom held no magic when he was alone, Leslie had gone to Terabithia. The frayed rope had broken, and she had hit her head on a stone as she fell. It is analytically accurate but unjust to the power of the novel to say that Jesse's reaction to the news follows predictable psychological paths.

From the moment he races frantically down the road believing that as long as he runs he can keep Leslie alive, through his numbness, his guilt, his fury, his hatred, to the moment when his father speaks to him like a man—"Hell ain't it?"—and cradles him in his lap as a baby, Jesse suffers excruciating incomprehension and emptiness. The reader feels the sobbing boy's relief when the common sense voice of the father assures his child, "Lord, boy, don't be a fool. God ain't gonna send any little girls to hell."

By the next morning Jesse is anxious to get back to the normalcy of routine chores and to retrieve the paints he had hurled into the turbulent creek. Driven by the need to do something fitting for Leslie, he goes to Terabithia, where he is momentarily overcome by a sense of his own helplessness and anger at Leslie for opening doors, then not being there to show him where to go. In the days that follow, wonderful, ingenuous Jesse realizes that it is time for him to move on from Terabithia, "to pay back to the world in beauty and caring what Leslie had loaned him in vision and strength." He builds a plank bridge into Terabithia, across which he leads May Bell crowned with a wreath of flowers.

Typical of a Paterson novel, *Bridge to Terabithia* insightfully penetrates the thoughts and feelings of children and adults, like Jesse, tenderly infatuated with Miss Edmunds and surprised and touched that even his tyrant teacher, Mrs. Myers, grieves and needs comfort, and Mr. Aarons, habitually preoccupied with the material needs of his family and his son's manliness but ready in extremities with gestures of paternal understanding and love. The novel is wrought with the artistry characteristic of its author: the right word in the right place; the restraint of sentiment with wit; light ironic foreshadowing; the creation of a world through antithetical balance, such as the contrast of the poor, earthy, inarticulate Aarons family with the well-off, intellectual Burkes; imagery engendered by the setting and woven seamlessly into the fabric of the novel—metaphors from country cooking, from popular culture, from nature, and from the Bible. The story against which the children's is set, of which it is a variation in a minor key, is the birth, death, and resurrection of Jesus. Less explicitly, more subtly than Japanese history, the Christian story adds levels of meaning to *Bridge to Terabithia*'s "simple melody." Although the religious backdrop has shifted to Christian beliefs and practices in this novel, the values embodied are consistent with Paterson's belief that "through fire is the spirit forged," as she put it in *The Sign of the Chrysanthemum*. Once having glimpsed beauty through suffering and grace, the spirit will not be self-contained.

The Great Gilly Hopkins (1978), according to Paterson, is a book for which the writing came easily and joyously. Because it grew out of what she deems her failure as a foster mother, in *Gates of Excellence* Paterson calls the novel "a confession of sin," the sin of not dealing with problems because the Cambodian children placed in her home would be with her for only two months. The realization that she had been "regarding two human beings as Kleenex, disposable," impelled her "to think, what must it be like for those thousands . . . of children . . . who find themselves rated disposable?"

The result of Paterson's reflections is sassy, sensitive, sagacious Gilly, an eleven-year-old orphan in search of her mother. Determined to bra-

Dust jacket for a later edition of Paterson's novel which explores the relationship between an antagonistic orphan and her slovenly foster mother (Crowell)

zen out her stay with Maime Trotter as the latest in a succession of stopovers, Gilly discovers too late that the slovenly, large-souled woman "with the huge lap smelling of baby powder" is both "God" and "home." Abandoned to the care of the state of Maryland by her mother, Courtney, a flower child of the 1960s, Gilly, short for Galadriel, has bounced through nearly a half-dozen foster homes. Bright, with a need to be singled out, she shields her vulnerability behind a sharp tongue and a strategy designed to manage the "craziness" in her world: she pegs people, anticipates their reactions, then attempts to outwit them. Distrusting affection, bothered by muddle, Gilly responds antagonistically to Maime Trotter and her shrinking, near-sighted foster son William Ernest Teague, as well as their blind neighbor, Mr. Randolph. However, as long as Gilly stays "in charge," she can tolerate "a house run by a fat, fluff-brained religious fanatic with a mentally retarded seven-year-old" and "a blind black man who came to eat."

Gilly's method of staying in charge is dichotomous. First, from memories and a glamorous photograph of her mother, she constructs a fantasy in which the immortal goddess-queen Courtney will sweep "gruesome Gilly" home as the long lost princess, after which she will be transformed into "gorgeous, gracious, good, glorious Galadriel. And grateful." Second, Gilly uses people and disposes of them when they have served her purpose. If the story of Jesus is the allusive framework for *Bridge to Terabithia*, the fairy tale is the evident archetype for *Gilly Hopkins*. Gilly's aspirations have been nourished not only by traditional tales—Rumpelstiltskin, the Frog Prince, and Bluebeard among them—but also by fantasies fed her by contemporary culture—Hallmark cards, the comics, Walter Cronkite, laxative commercials, and Humphrey Bogart reruns on TV. In the course of her story, the plucky little know-it-all has got to learn what Paterson jotted to herself on the back of a used envelope when the story was germinating: "Life is tough. They don't never tell you that when you're growing up. They tell you happy ever after. . . . you had to leave me & find out on your own—It's like a bad secret we think we can keep from children & they always find out—Life's tough. It ain't bad—unless you make it that way yourself—but it's tough. . . . But somehow we're scared to tell our children that. I don't know why."

Gilly knows from the beginning that life is tough; what she must learn is "That all that stuff about happy ending is lies," a fact she can accept when finally she can acknowledge that her biological mother does not want her but that she loves Trotter and Trotter loves her. Unfortunately, Gilly only learns this after she sends Courtney a letter which misrepresents the situation at Trotter's and asks Courtney to come get her, a letter which her irresponsible mother forwards to her own mother, who does take action. Gilly—and the reader—understands what Trotter tries to explain to her: "doing good on a tough job" makes a person happy. Gilly's "tough job" will be to see through her disillusionment over Courtney's lack of love for her and come to accept life with her grandmother and without Trotter. For the first time Gilly can say to Trotter, "I love you," though she cannot "keep the squeak out." Disillusioned, but staunch, Gilly is ready to go peacefully home with her grandmother; "No clouds of glory, perhaps, but Trotter would be proud."

These closing words allude to Wordsworth's "Ode: Intimations of Immortality," which Gilly reads to Mr. Randolph, and which provides the novel with a unifying motif. When Mr. Randolph gives Gilly the cherished book which contains the ode as a farewell gift, she reads the poem again. Her inability to understand it all does not inhibit her glory in the "sounds that turned and fell in kaleidoscopic wonder" nor her reflections about God and home. The final dexterous reference to the ode ties together several strands of the novel. Paradoxically, Gilly's hostility toward the world diminishes as her belief in happy endings fades.

The Great Gilly Hopkins is set in a suburban community very like the "wildly heterogeneous" Takoma Park, Maryland, where the Patersons lived for thirteen years and which, according to Paterson, reflects "every sociological configuration and problem in our country." Fun and funny, the book relies for its humor on the author's perception of the comic in the ordinary, the bizarre, and the potentially tragic, a perception that permeates the stand-off scenes between Gilly and Maime Trotter—some slapstick, many sparkling with verbal wit, others augmented by William Ernest's literal-mindedness. Much of the comedy derives from the novel's irreverence toward cultural phenomena, from commercial television to Sunday sermons. Gently, kindly, Paterson exposes stereotypical thinking and behavior of righteous but ineffectual social workers, school principals, teachers, and preachers, usually through estimable characters like Miss Ellis, Miss Harris, Mr. Randolph, and Maime Trotter herself, who, transcending the type, frustrate Gilly's prejudices. The only unlikable character, perhaps the only one in the Paterson canon who has no redeeming qualities, is the thoroughly selfish Courtney Hopkins, with her "gorgeous shattering smile," who indeed shatters those lives she touches. Manifestly delighting in language, Paterson gleefully, lavishly plays with alliteration, puns, and "creative curses," but never randomly, so the sound does seem the echo of the sense. Gilly's crude metaphors for the other characters, particularly for Trotter, are at once exaggerated and apt; they evoke sympathetic laughter, in part because her volubility when she is angry is clever and enviable.

The Great Gilly Hopkins is Paterson's funniest book, but heartbreak is never far beneath the humor. Though the novel's major thesis may be, in Gilly's words, that "the world is woefully short on frog smoochers," its ending is characteristically hopeful.

The nine short stories in *Angels & Other Strangers: Family Christmas Stories* (1979) were orig-

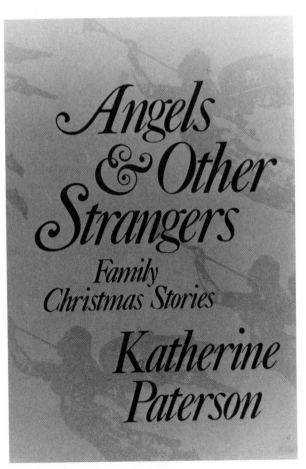

Dust jacket for Paterson's collection of Christmas stories, originally designed to be read aloud in lieu of a Christmas Eve sermon by Paterson's husband, a minister (Crowell)

inally written at the suggestion of John Paterson for reading aloud in lieu of a sermon at Christmas Eve services in his Takoma Park Church. Because of the hearty response of the congregation and because Paterson, having herself looked for Christmas stories to supplement the Gospels, had been "underwhelmed by the frosty flakes character of most of the stuff in print," she published the collection, believing many people "would welcome something with flesh and backbone which still is a story." More explicitly Christian than her novels, the stories reflect the author's concern for the modern world's lost and lonely. Economically told, tempered to oral reading, their metaphors inherent in the season and the urban and suburban settings, the stories blend pathos and humor. Young children have prominent roles in each story, though the majority focus on adults who, in their isolation and fear, recognize and reach out to the suffering of others. Although realistic, the stories are not grim. They are filled with joyous Christmas motifs.

Jacob Have I Loved (1980), the most complex of Paterson's novels, is a provocative and powerful story of an adolescent's submergence by and victory over her bitter jealousy of her twin sister, which blinds her to her own worth and to others' appreciation of it. Speaking, as she frequently has, of how hard it is for her to get a bookworthy idea, Paterson claims that she "cursed that book," which was three years in the writing, and would have thrown it away, but it "was the only book I had to write and I was condemned to write it."

Discovering where the story would take place proved a puzzle, which, once solved, resulted in one of the book's indelible attributes, its sense of place. Rass, an isolated island in the Chesapeake Bay, is itself a dominant character, palpable in the sounds, smells, and feel of its salt marshes, its white frame village, its aging boats, and in the stark rhythms of a people in tune with the sea. Careful research stands behind precise details of ferocious storms, of ferry transportation, of crabs and oysters and the science of fishing for them.

The language and ethos of the island, of a plain, hard-working waterfolk committed to a strict biblical ethic, has formed the consciousness and conscience of Sara Louise Bradshaw, intensifying the hatred and the guilt which press upon her. This firstborn, healthy, and diligent daughter at thirteen rankles with envy of her twin sister Caroline's frailty, which has always caused the family so much worry, and of her beauty and musical talent, which have endowed her with a sense of purpose and a constant place in the limelight. In her envy Louise

colors herself graceless, "all gray and shadow"; her sister, "so sure, so present, so easy, so light and gold." Twisting lack of worry into lack of parental love, Louise relies for friendship on Call Purnell, a steady, unimaginative boy, and on crabbing for the money she needs to enter a song lyrics contest secretly and to contribute to household expenses. Two events occur to disrupt the tenor of life on Rass: the Japanese attack on Pearl Harbor and the return of old Captain Hiram Wallace. Louise's fertile imagination transforms Captain Wallace into a German spy, and she enlists Call's help in capturing him. When the scheme backfires, the three become fast friends; however, through ensuing incidents Louise's jealousy is exacerbated by loneliness and self-condemnation until it consumes her.

One of the novel's elusive themes is that one is paradoxically freest when one has elected one's limitations. Unlike her grandmother, who lived and died on the island, waiting, hating, and hurling curses, Louise leaves Rass, having grown beyond her circumscribing jealousy, and chooses to live and work as a midwife among the poor and deprived in the Appalachian village of Truitt.

Jacob Have I Loved is the only one of Paterson's novels written in the first person, a point of view the author would have eschewed as too narrow had not the story itself seemed to force it upon her. She had considered telling the story from three points of view in order to make clear the inability of Call and Caroline to understand Louise as well as her shocked surprise when what she thought was her complete understanding of them crumbles; after both have left the island, they announce their marriage.

An artist who listens to her stories to discover what they have to teach her, Paterson ultimately limited the story to what can be revealed through Louise's eyes. In so doing, she has not only structured a cohesive novel but has illuminated the terrifying force of jealousy, which restricts vision to a hateful singleness. She avoids the pitfalls of the first person by providing, first, clues to Caroline's and the mother's admiration and affection for Louise, which Louise reports but misconstrues, and, second, glimpses, as Louise grows, of Call, her grandmother, and her parents that she had not previously perceived. With Louise the reader becomes aware that Call is not stupid, that he perceives and responds to Caroline's need for love and support out of his own similar needs; that the grandmother is pitiably vulnerable as well as a viperous termagant; that the mother's love for her lonely daughter is deep enough that she will never

Dust jacket for Paterson's 1981 Newbery Medal-winning novel about a young girl's bitter jealousy of her twin sister (Crowell)

attempt to force her child's will nor make her over in her own image. What appears to Louise as lack of love is a natural unobtrusiveness combined with a respect for both her daughters' individuality. The first person, in Paterson's sensitive hands, simultaneously brings to life sympathetic characters, rounded rather than caricatured even in their eccentricities, and the disposition of jealousy to poison an adolescent's ability to see straight.

Each of Paterson's novels integrates action with character development; *Jacob Have I Loved,* however, concentrates more on the protagonist's feelings. The account of Louise's virgin love for the old Captain embodies the poignant experience common to schoolgirls, whose first crush on an older man is too mysterious, too sacred, and perhaps suffused with too much shame to talk about. As in the earlier books, several story levels are intertwined: first, the story which the unhappy adolescent contrives in her attempt to cope with life on a day-to-day basis; second, the story the older, more perceptive Sara Louise tells through the con-

figuration of people and events she remembers from her tumultuous teen years, enlarged by the incidents and insights she adds from a maturer perspective; and third, the Bible stories of Jacob and Esau, from which the book's title is derived, and the story of the birth of Christ, which is an allusive touchstone for the first two stories and deepens the meaning of Louise's personal narrative.

The final two chapters, which take Louise rapidly from her late teens to her late twenties, structurally and thematically complete her awareness and reconciliation. Their condensation complements the immediacy of Louise's realization. *Jacob Have I Loved* is a tender and serious book, in which the potentially comic yields to compassion. Characteristically, irony is operative, but this is a darker irony than in earlier novels, perhaps because no humor is inherent in the cruel jealousy at the book's core. The title contains a dry humor. Read against all three story levels, it goes beyond the irony of Louise's misunderstanding of her grandmother's taunt, that she, like Esau, was hated, to imply that God himself, who if he is omniscient providence must have spoken the words "Jacob have I loved" in an ironic tone.

With *Rebels of the Heavenly Kingdom* (1983), Paterson turns again to historical fiction, this time to the 1850-1853 revolt of the Taiping Tienkuo (the Heavenly Kingdom of Great Peace) against the corrupt Manchu rulers, re-creating mid-nine-teenth-century China with cartographic precision and tangible earthiness. Magnificent and momen-tous, this starkly realistic adventure-romance re-wards discriminating readers with the poignant stories of Wang Lee and Mei Lin, two young people caught in the devastation wrought by fanatic war-lords whose religious ideals are shot through with political ambitions. The author, extraordinarily able to adapt her style to the needs of her story, writes with searing restraint that characterizes the Chinese.

A superficial reader may mistake the book's dispassionate tone as indicative of the author's lack of emotional involvement. On the contrary, in de-picting a people and events remote in time, she reveals painful contemporary issues. Zealotry, eas-ily tainted though its sources may be pure, too soon turns to the spiritual blindness, arrogance, and in-tolerance which drive people to prey upon each other and upon the land. War, always heinous, be-comes inconceivably monstrous when waged in the name of the High God of Heaven.

In the dramatic opening of the novel, fifteen-year-old Wang Lee is kidnapped from his ancestral home by bandits in the wake of battle and cata-pulted into slavery. Freed by seventeen-year-old Mei Lin, a member of the Taiping, that curious cultural hybrid of Christianity and Chinese nation-alism, Wang Lee is at first skeptical of a sect which promotes women with unbound feet to high mili-tary rank. The daughter of a patriarch and a slave, Mei Lin had been taught to read with her brothers, and her feet had never been bound because she was useless to her father as a woman but had worth as "a beast of burden."

Dust jacket for Paterson's historical novel about a teenage boy and girl caught in the 1850 revolt of the Taiping Tienkuo (the Heavenly Kingdom of Great Peace) against corrupt Manchu rulers (Dutton)

In recalling that part of her past in which she had been sold into prostitution, Mei Lin discloses ineffable suffering, physical and psychic: "What right did this raw boy have to know? How could he begin to understand her suffering—her deep shame that even yet, after all that had happened had the power to darken her spirit and drag it down.... There were still some ghosts that even the Heavenly Kingdom had not put to rest." By the time Wang Lee is rescued by Mei Lin, she is a captain in the Heavenly Army and when "the Heavenly Kingdom is established on earth, she will receive property in accordance with her high position and great valor."

Mei Lin teaches Wang Lee to read and instructs him in her faith, thus opening for him the doors to peace. Gradually his doubt gives way to admiration, then love, for his mentor and her cause. Baptized, half against his judgment and will when he is carried forward by mass enthusiasm, Wang Lee subsequently surrenders to dogmatic propaganda. "He no longer fought just to save his life. He fought for the Heavenly Kingdom. It was like wrapping his body in metal armor and filling his heart and liver with the spirit of God."

The inexorable progress of war alternately separates then reunites Wang Lee and Mei Lin. The doubt, the conviction, the despair, and the exultation of the military struggle parallel and symbolize the spiritual odysseys of the protagonists. Much of the action of *Rebels of the Heavenly Kingdom* takes place on the Yangtze River or in the mountains, which serve as traditional symbols for the journey of life and of spiritual transcendence.

A major theme of the book is the equality of women with men in the Heavenly Kingdom of Great Peace. Imbedded in this is the more personal concept that to be whole, individuals must integrate the feminine and masculine aspects of their personalities. The novel is certainly too complex to be read as allegory, yet there is much in the story, paradoxically, to associate Mei Lin with the masculine principle and Wang Lee with the feminine, and to interpret their wedding as the integration of the two. Frequently the young woman Mei Lin and the boy Wang Lee are disguised as members of the opposite sex. Wang Lee's ancestors are farmers; he comes from the fields, which at the opening of the novel stand "nearly bare, a great angry wound upon the flesh of the earth," a wound healed finally when the woman and man cultivate it together.

Mei Lin is educated and she is a soldier. Three times Wang Lee, in the company of men, refuses, as Peter does Christ, to recognize Mei Lin: "It would not look good for him if he appeared to be talking to a woman." Because Paterson, through allusion, associates both Mei Lin and San-niang, the leader of the women horseguards, with Christ, she hallows the redemptive power of those qualities conventionally regarded as feminine: patience, sensitivity, gentleness, and self-sacrificial love. However, both women also possess traditionally masculine traits, like aggressiveness, decisiveness, courage, and strength.

The epilogue celebrates the marriage of Mei Lin and Wang Lee. But the celebration is subdued. Mei Lin and Wang Lee have learned to live quietly with the ambivalence consequent upon the knowledge that they, and society, have betrayed the high principles they profess in their acts of war. In the light of their understanding, they will do what lies in their power to redress the ravages of wrongheaded zealotry. They will till and conserve the land, beginning with the seed rice Wang Lee's father had left sealed in the wall of the house, behind the fifth brick. They will raise their children, not binding their daughters' feet but teaching them, with their sons, to read. They will make of their own little world a peaceable kingdom.

Neither her most provocative nor most profound novel, *Come Sing, Jimmy Jo* (1985) is, however, vintage Paterson. The story of a shy, gifted mountain boy, James Johnson, who within six months becomes a country-music star, resonates with variations on themes from earlier books. Paterson again probes relationships between child and parents. As are the protagonists from her earlier works, especially Muna, Kinshi and Jiro, and Gilly Hopkins, Jimmy Jo Johnson is engaged in a search for himself, allied with his quest for his father, his mother, and home. The book's leitmotif, a corollary of that of *The Great Gilly Hopkins*, is articulated by James's Grandma: " 'Nothin's ever pure, James. Joy and pain always show up in the same wrapper.' "

Paterson inverts the conventional pattern of the quest for a father in *Come Sing, Jimmy Jo*. Again she enriches a major theme by making it operative on several levels of the story. The theme, the biblical one of sharing rather than hiding one's gifts, applies not only to James's musical talent but also to the blessings of a father and grandmother whose seasoned love envelops and sustains James, but is not centered on him. James Johnson has always had a father, Jerry Lee Johnson. Only when Flem Keeser appears, claiming to be his real father, does the boy learn that the man who has always been there for him is not his parent and, consequently,

Dust jacket for Paterson's latest novel, the story of a shy, gifted, mountain boy who becomes a country-music star (Dutton)

that Grandma, his nurturer, mentor, and ballast, is not his grandparent. Finally, after great pain, the eleven-year-old in a sense becomes his own father, integrating James and Jimmy Jo, his stage persona, through an act of disciplined choice. He advisedly acknowledges Jerry Lee as his father and his own good fortune in having a daddy who "don't run off and leave my momma no matter how tough things get." Then, realizing "I done it. I growed up," he is able to recognize that the fans are not crass exploiters, as he first thought, but people "full of love, looking up at him . . . like little children on Christmas morning—waiting all full of hope for a present. And he had the gift." He has not only the gift of song, but also the more important gifts of the selflessness, strength, and wisdom required to help his father keep the "circle" that is his family.

James Johnson is the scion of a family of country and gospel singers. Until James's mother Olive came along, the Johnson Family had consisted of Grandpa, Grandma, Jerry Lee, and his younger brother Earl. Olive, who could "tear up a song"

even when, at fifteen and pregnant, she married Jerry Lee, replaced Grandma, who chose to step aside because her voice was gone.

Until he was eleven, James was raised by Grandma on the Appalachian farm. As he grew, he assumed more and more of the chores to spare Grandma's arthritic joints, simultaneously assimilating all she could teach him about singing and playing "except how to want to sing and pick a guitar in front of people." When the Family comes home between road trips, James joins their music making, singing for the first time for someone other than Grandma. Eddie Switten, the about-to-be-hired manager of the Johnson Family, arrives in time to hear James's high sweet harmony, is impressed, and arranges an appearance for the Family on a *Countrytime* television special.

Persuaded by Grandma that he has the Gift, even though he is "scairt," James joins the Family. Pushed on to a stage of "blinding brightness" which blurs the audience, he begins to sing purely and joyously, enchanting not only the fans but also Norman Wallace, the manager of the show, who agrees with Switten that the youngest Johnson is "the sweetest little thing to come along in country music since little Anita Carter yodeled at the Old Dominion Barn Dance in 1947." Consequently, Wallace offers the Johnsons a six-month contract as the only regulars on the WQVR-*Countrytime* home show in Tidewater, Virginia.

Olive changes her name to Keri Su and finds a house for the Family in Tidewater. With trepidation James becomes Jimmy Jo, leaves Grandma alone on the mountain, and goes to live with Keri Su, Jerry Lee, Uncle Earl, and Grandpa.

Characteristic of Paterson's perceptiveness, *Come Sing, Jimmy Jo* is peopled with marvelous minor characters, whose personalities match their technicolor vibrations: "The world comes in different colors. The farm was a deep green. The stage was electric orange. When he [James] was with Jerry Lee, the house was blue like a bright October sky; with Keri Su, it was a throbbing pink—too strong to leave your eyes on for very long. Grandpa made everything a pale green. And Earl, well, what did Earl make? Sometimes no color at all, sometimes flashes of that same disturbing, throbbing pink."

The staunchest of these characters, and the most important to James, are the gentle Jerry Lee, "almost as wise and good as Grandma," and feisty Grandma herself, who bakes bread that smells "like the love of Heaven," smokes a pipe, can "tease a taillight off a lightning bug," is addicted to soap operas, and loves comfort songs and James too much to hide him and his gift under her "own private little bushel." Olive/Keri Su—tiny, blond, beautiful, with "a voice that could blow the colored glass out of the back of a church"—and contentious Uncle Earl—"with a voice that *boom-boomed* all over the scale"—are thoroughly self-centered, much like Courtney in *The Great Gilly Hopkins*. Resentful and ambitious, they are determined to scratch their way to the top of the charts, willing to cheat and hurt those who love them best. For Keri Su and Earl, however, the author communicates a compassion she did not feel for Gilly's mother. From loving hearts, Grandma and Jerry Lee share insights with James and with the reader which elicit sympathy for the pair. James comes to understand that he had "never known where Keri Su was at. Maybe Grandma was right. Maybe Keri Su herself didn't know. Twenty-five isn't very old. She'd been hardly older than he was now when she'd had him. There wasn't anybody like Grandma to take care of her when she was little."

Theme is seamlessly woven into story in *Come Sing, Jimmy Jo*. The book is structured of scenes in rural West Virginia; in the local country-music capital, Tidewater; and on the road back and forth. The roads, particularly the tunnel under the Chesapeake Bay, are indigenous emblems of James/Jimmy Jo's journey to wholeness. Fearful of the "hole under the water" which "was forever going to be between him and home," James sometimes panics because "every inch of his life" seems to be "pinched in a new direction" and sometimes he feels "like one of those possums that didn't make it across the road." He does, however, conquer his fears and bridge his worlds. Allusions to biblical characters unite James's quest with those of Moses, Jonah, Noah, and even Judas.

People, places, and events come alive through a wealth of imagery rooted in nature, country living, and popular culture, omnipresent but inobtrusive in the novel. Music is, naturally, the novel's unifying image. Also a significant symbol, James's glasses correct both his physical and spiritual myopia. Grandma insists upon buying them so he can see straight. Eddie Switten forbids Jimmy Jo to wear them during performances, for they mar his angelic childlikeness, making him "look more like a Baptist deacon." In the final episode, in his rush to get on stage, Jimmy Jo forgets to take his glasses off and sees clearly for the first time what it means to share his gift, in gratitude and humility, with a world which needs it. The novel is alternately or simultaneously suspenseful, relaxed, comic, and

ironic, and the homespun regional and ethnic dialects and the trade jargon are authentically captured.

Paterson's work has won international popular and critical acclaim. Collectively, her books have swept every conceivable award for children's literature. Six have been named ALA Notable Books. *Bridge to Terabithia* won a Lewis Carroll Shelf Award in 1978; *The Great Gilly Hopkins*, the Christopher Award that same year. Two novels, *The Master Puppeteer* in 1977 and *The Great Gilly Hopkins* in 1978, received National Book Awards. *The Master Puppeteer* also received a special award from the Mystery Writers of America. *Gilly Hopkins* was named a Newbery Honor Book in 1979, and two novels, *Bridge to Terabithia* in 1978 and *Jacob Have I Loved* in 1981, have been awarded the Newbery Medal. In 1980 Katherine Paterson was the United States' nominee for the international Hans Christian Andersen award, and her work was nominated for the 1986 Laura Ingalls Wilder Award.

Because Paterson perceives the grandeur with which the world is charged and because she writes from the heart of themes which haunt her, her books have the enduring value that will help tomorrow's children, as well as today's, make the connections she outlines in *Gates of Excellence*, the connections "in the living of this life that will reveal the little truths . . . that point to the awesome, unknowable unity, the Truth, which holds us together and makes us members of one another."

References:

Anthea Bell, "A Case of Commitment," *Signal*, 35 (May 1982): 73-81;

Virginia Buckley, "Katherine Paterson," *Horn Book*, 54 (August 1978): 368-371;

Caroline Goforth, "The Role of the Island in *Jacob Have I Loved*," *Children's Literature Association Quarterly*, 9 (Winter 1984-1985): 176-178;

John Gough, "*Bridge to Terabithia*: the Subtlety of Plain Language," *Idiom*, 18 (Summer 1983): 19-22;

Ann Haskell, "Talk with a Winner," *New York Times Book Review*, 26 April 1981, pp. 52, 67-68;

Nancy Huse, "Katherine Paterson's Ultimate Realism," *Children's Literature Association Quarterly*, 9 (Fall 1984): 99-101;

Linda T. Jones, "Profile Katherine Paterson," *Language Arts*, 58 (February 1981): 189-196;

James H. McGavran, Jr., "Bathrobes and Bibles, Waves and Words in Katherine Paterson's *Jacob Have I Loved*," *Children's Literature in Education*, 17 (Spring 1986): 3-15;

Gene Inyart Namovicz, "Katherine Paterson," *Horn Book*, 57 (August 1981): 394-399;

Douglas Powers, "Of Time, Place, and Person: *The Great Gilly Hopkins* and Problems of Story for Adopted Children," *Children's Literature in Education*, 15 (Winter 1984): 211-219;

David Rees, "Medals and Awards," in *Painted Desert, Green Shade* (Boston: Horn Book, 1984), pp. 89-101;

M. Sarah Smedman, " 'A Good Oyster': Story and Meaning in *Jacob Have I Loved*," *Children's Literature in Education*, 14 (Autumn 1983): 180-187.

Papers:

The Kerlan Collection, University of Minnesota, Minneapolis, contains Katherine Paterson's manuscripts.

Ellen Raskin
(13 March 1928-8 August 1984)

Marilyn H. Karrenbrock
University of Tennessee

BOOKS: *Nothing Ever Happens on My Block* (New York: Atheneum, 1966);

Silly Songs and Sad (New York: Crowell, 1967);

Spectacles (New York: Atheneum, 1968);

Ghost in a Four-Room Apartment (New York: Atheneum, 1969);

And It Rained (New York: Atheneum, 1969);

A & THE or William T. C. Baumgarten Comes to Town (New York: Atheneum, 1970);

The World's Greatest Freak Show (New York: Atheneum, 1971);

The Mysterious Disappearance of Leon (I Mean Noel) (New York: Dutton, 1971);

Franklin Stein (New York: Atheneum, 1972);

Who, Said Sue, Said Whoo? (New York: Atheneum, 1973);

Moe Q. McGlutch, He Smoked Too Much (New York: Parents' Magazine Press, 1973);

Figgs & Phantoms (New York: Dutton, 1974);

Moose, Goose and Little Nobody (New York: Parents' Magazine Press, 1974);

The Tattooed Potato and other clues (New York: Dutton, 1975);

Twenty-two, Twenty-three (New York: Atheneum, 1976);

The Westing Game (New York: Dutton, 1978).

BOOKS ILLUSTRATED: Claire H. Bishop, ed., *Happy Christmas: Tales for Boys and Girls* (New York: Stephen Daye, 1956);

Dylan Thomas, *A Child's Christmas in Wales* (New York: New Directions, 1959);

Ruth Krauss, *Mama, I Wish I Was Snow; Child You'd Be Very Cold* (New York: Atheneum, 1962);

Arthur G. Razzell and K. G. Watts, *This is 4: the Idea of a Number* (Garden City: Doubleday, 1964);

Edgar Allan Poe, *Poems of Edgar Allen Poe*, selected by Dwight Macdonald (New York: Crowell, 1965);

Aileen Fisher and Olive Rabe, *We Dickinsons* (New York: Atheneum, 1965);

Louis Untermeyer, ed., *The Paths of Poetry: Twenty-five Poets and Their Poems* (New York: Delacorte, 1966);

Molly Cone, *The Jewish Sabbath* (New York: Crowell, 1966);

Razzell and Watts, *Probability: The Science of Chance* (Garden City: Doubleday, 1967);

Robert Herrick, *Poems of Robert Herrick*, edited by Winfield T. Scott (New York: Crowell, 1967);

D. H. Lawrence, *D. H. Lawrence: Poems Selected for Young People*, edited by William Cole (New York: Viking, 1967);

Vera Cleaver and Bill Cleaver, *Ellen Grae* (Philadelphia: Lippincott, 1967);

Nancy Larrick, ed., *Piping Down the Valleys Wild: Poetry for the Young of All Ages* (New York: Delacorte, 1968);

Fisher and Rabe, *We Alcotts* (New York: Atheneum, 1968);

Ellen Raskin

Razzell and Watts, *Symmetry* (Garden City: Doubleday, 1968);

Susan Bartlett, *Books* (New York: Holt, Rinehart & Wilson, 1968);

Suzanne Stark Morrow, *Inatak's Friend* (Boston: Atlantic/Little, Brown, 1968);

Renee K. Weiss, ed., *A Paper Zoo: A Collection of Animal Poems by Modern American Poets* (New York: Macmillan, 1968);

Rebecca Caudill, *Come Along!* (New York: Holt, Rinehart & Wilson, 1969);

Razzell and Watts, *Circles and Curves* (Garden City: Doubleday, 1969);

Razzell and Watts, *A Question of Accuracy* (Garden City: Doubleday, 1969);

Sara Brewton and John E. Brewton, eds., *Shrieks at Midnight: Macabre Poems, Eerie and Humorous* (New York: Crowell, 1969);

Razzell and Watts, *Three and the Shape of Three* (Garden City: Doubleday, 1969);

Alan Gardner, *Elidor* (New York: Walck, 1970);

Christina Rossetti, *Goblin Market* (New York: Dutton, 1970).

OTHER: William Blake, *Songs of Innocence*, two volumes, with music and illustrations by Raskin (Garden City: Doubleday, 1966).

PERIODICAL PUBLICATIONS: "Picture Books for Today's Child," *Texas Library Journal*, 47 (Summer 1971): 60-63;

"The Creative Spirit and Children's Literature: A Symposium," by Raskin and others, *Wilson Library Bulletin*, 53 (October 1978): 152-154;

"Characters and Other Clues," *Horn Book*, 54 (December 1978): 620-625;

"Newbery Medal Acceptance," *Horn Book*, 55 (August 1979): 385-391.

Ellen Raskin's life was a series of paradoxes. She was trained in the fine arts but became a commercial artist who took great care and pride not only with her artwork but with every phase of its production. She was an extraordinarily creative artist who attributed her success to training which had emphasized technical mastery and discipline. She first won fame as a children's book illustrator for her visual ingeniousness, but she was equally capable of delightful verbal jokes. She used many differing media in her illustrations (in six months she produced the serenely beautiful woodcuts of *Songs of Innocence* and the hilarious cartoons of *Nothing Ever Happens on My Block*), yet her works are instantly recognizable. She was a well-known author and illustrator of picture books for preschoolers who won her greatest fame as an author of books for older children. She wrote tightly plotted mysteries filled with wildly improbable flights of fancy. Her first book was her best picture book, and her last book was her most praised novel. She wrote about art and drew pictures about books. She is known as a humorist, but her books are often deeply serious in tone. She was a highly acclaimed artist who dreamed of winning the Caldecott Award (although her books were never named even as Honor Books), but she won the Newbery Medal for a book totally unlike any other which won that award. She was a creative artist who would have made a great financier. She survived a miserable childhood and lived a life often filled with pain, but she left a legacy of beauty, wit, and cheer in her books.

Ellen Raskin, whose early years were somber ones, was born in Milwaukee, Wisconsin, on 13

March 1928. At age four, she recalled, she decided to become a musician and practiced hours every day until the piano was repossessed by the finance company. When she was seven, her parents, Sol and Margaret Goldfisch Raskin, headed with Ellen and her sister, Lila Ruth, for the golden streets of California; three months later the family returned to Milwaukee. Raskin said, "Those were hard times, the Depression years; they made me a humorist. Just about anything is funny after that." There *were* happy things about those years: the joys of reading ("I . . . developed a disgusting nose problem. 'Get your nose out of that book, Ellen,' my mother would say six dozen times a day."); inventing her own characters to act out with her sister ("We were the Pie family: I was Peachy Pie, and my sister was Porky Pie, among others. We were the Baum family: I was Pinky Baum, and my sister was Stink Baum. Needless to say, I am the older sister."); holidays and Saturday night poker games with her mother's family, where Raskin and her cousins entertained the family until the night her cousin Zelda, the "ballet dancer" ("Zelda danced all right, but not ballet."), taught her a very special routine involving three chiffon scarves, a "provocative smile," and "a bump and a grind."

Raskin apparently wrote and drew throughout childhood, but her stories about the process are contradictory. In 1972, in her autobiographical sketch in *Third Book of Junior Authors*, she said, "determined to become a writer, I filled composition book after book with a labored hand. During this time I was drawing, but that was too much fun to take seriously." About the same time, in an interview published in *Top of the News*, she recalled, "I drew objects and portraits from life and hounded my mother with 'What shall I draw next?' . . . My mother didn't tell me what to write, my teachers did. Everything I wrote and drew during my childhood and youth was on assignment. . . . Creativity came late to me."

Raskin attended college from 1945 to 1949 at the University of Wisconsin at Madison. When she entered college, she intended to become a writer; she "desperately wanted a career, and journalism seemed terribly romantic to a 17-year-old." The direction of her work turned in the summer of 1946, when she visited the Chicago Art Institute and saw the first major exhibit of nonobjective art. Raskin later said, "For the first time in my life I understood what an artist was; and I knew that was what I had always wanted to be." Raskin changed her major to fine arts, studying the fundamentals of painting and sculpture: anatomy, perspective,

light and shade, color and techniques.

A brief first marriage occurred during this period, which ended in divorce about the time Raskin moved with her young daughter, Susan Kuhlman, to New York. A practical person who realized that few people made a living in fine arts, Raskin turned to commercial art, and, in order to learn the mechanical processes used in reproduction, she took a job in a commercial art studio where she prepared other people's work for the printer. While she was learning about pasteups and color separations on the job, she was learning about type at home at night; she had acquired her own printing press and ten fonts of type. After two years at the art studio, she quit her job, put together a sample book combining woodcuts and type, and showed it to art directors in advertising agencies and publishing houses. At the time, she had only two hundred dollars in the bank, but she received over one thousand dollars worth of commissions in her first week as a free-lance artist. In the next fifteen years, she drew thousands of pictures: magazine illustrations, pharmaceutical ads, calendars, posters, and book jackets.

Raskin herself, as well as most persons writing about her, seems to suggest that she had not illustrated any books until she began writing her own. However, during her free-lance period she illustrated several children's books. The first was Claire H. Bishop's *Happy Christmas: Tales for Boys and Girls* (1956). Other books which she illustrated early in her career include Dylan Thomas's *A Child's Christmas in Wales* (1959); *Mama, I Wish I Was Snow; Child You'd Be Very Cold* (1962) by Ruth Krauss; *Poems of Edgar Allan Poe* (1965), selected by Dwight Macdonald; and *We Dickinsons* (1965) by Aileen Fisher and Olive Rabe.

Raskin credited the change in her career to the realization that she had designed 1,000 book jackets. She was tired of always interpreting someone else's ideas, never her own, so she decided to take some time off and try to write her own book. It would be a children's book because "they have pictures, children are able to learn and be impressed, and because I'm still a child!" She prepared a dummy book of eighteen pages to show to Jean Karl at Atheneum. "I was so dumb then. She explained to me that a book had to be either twenty-four or thirty-two pages. She had to *tell* me that. But she sent me a contract anyway." The book was *Nothing Ever Happens on My Block* (1966).

Raskin immediately received a contract for a second book. She had never forgotten her early desire to be a musician. Several years before, she had bought a harpsichord and taken up the study of baroque music. She had long been an admirer of William Blake, and when she learned that Blake's music for *Songs of Innocence* had been lost, she began to write her own melodies for the poems. Alex Gotfryd, art director at Doubleday, heard that she was writing music and asked to see it. Raskin submitted several songs, adding a few illustrations, and Doubleday promptly offered her a contract for both the artwork and music. Raskin took six months off to do *Nothing Ever Happens on My Block* and *Songs of Innocence*, both of which appeared in 1966.

Later Raskin was to say that all her energies had gone into *Songs of Innocence*, and that it was "very arty." Her woodcuts for the book are bold, colorful, stylized, and surprisingly intricate. Simple piano and guitar accompaniments are given for Raskin's pleasant melodies, though there is also a companion volume without the music. The book was placed on the *School Library Journal* list of best books of the year, and it appeared in the American Institute of Graphic Arts (AIGA) show for books which exhibit excellence in design and manufacture.

Nothing Ever Happens on My Block, on the other hand, is a charming and hilarious cartoon story. Chester Filbert, a very bored and boring boy, sits on the curb saying, "Nothing ever happens on my block." Around him, witches appear at windows; part of a house burns, is repaired, is struck by lightning, and is repaired again; a thief is chased by a policeman; the postman gets a bucket of water emptied on his head by mistake; a parachutist lands on the sidewalk; a girl breaks her leg jumping rope and is taken away on a stretcher; a man planting a tree finds all kinds of buried treasure; a cat has kittens; a weathercock flies from one house to another during a rainstorm; and a collision between a car and an armored truck releases fifty-dollar bills over the neighborhood; but Chester never sees any of these things—he is too busy feeling sorry for himself. Raskin uses all kinds of visual tricks to make the reader take notice of her story. The Victorian houses on Chester's block are finely detailed in black ink, but the action going on all around is highlighted by bold color overlays. The text gives Chester's complaints in simple unadorned type, but the cartoon balloons in which the other characters speak are filled with many varying type styles, each carefully selected to fit the particular situation.

Nothing Ever Happens on My Block did not have an auspicious debut. The first review said that it was a boring book in which nothing happened—it

had been read by one person to a library review committee, and no one had seen the illustrations. Almost immediately, the book was selected by the *New York Herald Tribune* as the best picture book of the year; unfortunately the review was never published because the *Herald Tribune* workers went on strike. However, *Nothing Ever Happens on My Block* was chosen as a Notable Children's Book by the American Library Association (ALA) and as one of the ten best illustrated children's books of the year by the *New York Times,* and it was on the Library of Congress list of children's books of the year.

Raskin's first book epitomizes one of her principal themes, the need to see truly and clearly. She often said that she was the original Chester Filbert, probably referring to the fact that until she began to wear eyeglasses, she had visual problems which kept her from seeing all the details of her environment. She also, however, seemed to suggest obliquely that people, including herself, are wrapped up in their own concerns, seeing what is of interest to them but often missing many things upon which others might focus. Art, Raskin believed, was "the sharing of a visual experience." Because a child can control a book, looking at the pictures in any order and for as long as he or she desires, a picture book becomes a personal experience unique to an individual child. The job of a picture book is to help a child learn to see.

Raskin was an inveterate puzzlemaker, a trickster, a razzle-dazzle-sleight-of-hand artist. In her picture books, she played with both words and images, emphasizing sometimes one, sometimes the other. In *Nothing Ever Happens on My Block,* her visual high jinks produce just the right effect; however, few of her subsequent books are equally successful. Her second book, *Silly Songs and Sad* (1967), is a collection of verses which are often labored in style and perplexing in subject matter. The illustrations, which feature many differing styles, are usually superior to the rhymes they accompany.

In the perennially popular *Spectacles* (1968), which Raskin wrote "for all the little poor-seers all over the country," Chester Filbert's friend, Iris Fogel, steps front and center. She is another of Raskin's alter egos, but her problem is the opposite of Chester's; she sees things that are not there. Not until she gets spectacles does she realize that a fire-breathing dragon is actually her Great Aunt Fanny, and the giant pygmy nuthatch on the lawn is Chester. Raskin is successful in teaching a gentle lesson about eyeglasses in a humorous way. The fuzzy images which Iris sees contrast nicely with the real scenes which are sharply delineated, but the merriment cannot compare to the joyous exuberance of *Nothing Ever Happens on My Block. Spectacles* was, however, chosen as an ALA Notable Book, appeared in the AIGA Book Show, and was listed in several best-books-of-the-year lists.

Like many of Raskin's stories, *Ghost in a Four-Room Apartment* (1969) is based on her childhood experiences. Her family had once lived in an apartment which was often crowded with relatives. A poltergeist's monologue alternates with a cumulative rhyme which cleverly introduces a child to family relationships. The bright four-color pictures suggest how crowded a small apartment can be, but the story is disappointing because nothing really happens. Horace and Doris, the children in the book, appear again, along with their friends Chester and Iris, in *A & THE or William T. C. Baumgarten Comes to Town* (1970). This book has the same fascinating background detail of neighborhood houses that was found in *Nothing Ever Happens on My Block,* but the words "a" and "the" are always written in boldface type, which makes the text dif-

ficult to read smoothly. The book starts out as a straightforward tale about making new friends, but takes a bizarre turn, becoming a teacher's description of the Battle of Hastings, complete with scenes redrawn from the Bayeux Tapestry. It is difficult to know for whom the book was written, presumably for Raskin herself.

Much more successful in execution, *And It Rained* (1969) is a highly stylized cartoon story in green, yellow, and blue about a pig, a parrot, and a potto whose four o'clock tea was ruined every afternoon because it always rained at five past four. Raskin said that she had intended the book as a lesson in elementary logic, and she was delighted when she received a letter from a psychology professor at Rutgers who had read the book to his child and had found the solution—to have hard biscuits and strong tea which the rain would soften and weaken—"elegant—a fine example of recentering in problem solving." Said Raskin, "Needless to say, that was a great boost to my ego. Suddenly I was an expert in problem solving; and I had never even

Title page spread for Raskin's 1970 book which features two children, Horace and Doris, introduced in Ghost in a Four-Room Apartment, *published in 1969 (Atheneum)*

heard the term 'recentering' before. For the next few days I figured I could solve any problem set before me (especially if I chose the problem to begin with)." She also remarked that it was really a book about how she made a book, because making a book was really an exercise in problem solving. *And It Rained* was chosen as an ALA Notable Book and for the annual lists of the Library of Congress and *School Library Journal.*

Raskin began her picture books with the story; the pictures came next. Then she rewrote the book, eliminating most of the text because it could be seen in her pictures. Finally she did the finished artwork. She was personally responsible for every aspect of her books, from the first conception of the idea to the first pressrun. She once said, "Writing comes much easier for me than illustrating, for writing is just ideas; after a character has been delineated, all that's necessary is the name. In illustration, after the idea comes consistency in drawing. The same characters have to appear page after page, and tons of research has to be done for every book." This, however, was before she wrote a book for older readers. Perhaps she changed her mind later about the relative difficulty of writing and illustrating.

During this period, Raskin continued to illustrate books by other authors. *Books* (1968), by Susan Bartlett, was chosen for the AIGA Book Show. Her illustrations were exhibited in the AIGA Fifty Years of Graphic Arts in America show in 1966 and at the Biennale of Illustration in Bratislava, Czechoslovakia, in 1969.

At the urging of an editor for whom she had worked, Ann Durell of E. P. Dutton, Raskin began to write for older children. Durell suggested that she write a novel about her childhood, about growing up in Milwaukee during the Depression. This was the heyday of the "problem novel" for children, but when the book appeared, in 1971, it certainly was no slice of gritty realism. *The Mysterious Disappearance of Leon (I Mean Noel)* begins with a can of soup, Mrs. Carillon's Pomato Soup, and ends with a racehorse named Christmas Bells. In between it blossoms into a riotous, slapstick adventure, and a first-rate mystery as well.

Caroline Fish and Leon Carillon, joint heirs to a soup fortune, are married at the tender ages of five and seven respectively, then separated for fourteen years. In their one brief meeting at the end of this time, Leon (who has changed his name to Noel, which is Leon written backwards) is seemingly drowned, leaving one brief message as he goes: "Noel *glub* C *blub* all . . . I *glub* new. . . ." Car-

oline Carillon is convinced that he is not dead and sets out on a twenty-year search for her missing husband. Along the way she adopts a pair of orphan twins, Tina and Tony; always wears purple because that is what she was wearing when Leon last saw her; looks for Leon in cowboy movies because he likes horses; is arrested when she starts a riot in Bloomingdale's; and generally leads the wackiest life an enthralled reader can imagine.

Like any good mystery writer, Raskin provided a set of clues and challenged the reader to find the answer. As with her picture books, she determined the book's format, using headings, illustrations, lists, and footnotes as devices to make the book attractive and to break up the text into units easily accessible to young readers. At the same time, these devices provide clues to the mystery. The book is filled with outrageous puns, wordplay, and visual and verbal twists. Although she meticulously supplies all the information needed to solve the mystery, Raskin is such an expert at misdirection that it takes several rereadings to locate all the clues, skillfully integrated into the plot so that they are often skipped over even when a footnote calls attention to them. Although the book bewildered some readers, it was selected for the ALA Notable Books list and for those of the Library of Congress and *School Library Journal.* It was also named a Children's Book Council (CBC) Showcase book for its design.

In the early 1970s Raskin continued to produce picture books. *The World's Greatest Freak Show* (1971) and *Moe Q. McGlutch, He Smoked Too Much* (1973) were both praised for their full-color illustrations but criticized for their content. In the first book, several reviewers feared that a book about physical disability would offend readers, despite the clear message: freakishness is in the eye of the beholder; those who look down upon others are likely to be treated the same way. *Moe Q. McGlutch, He Smoked Too Much* was castigated both because its antismoking campaign was too didactic and because it did not clearly make the point that smoking is dangerous to one's health. Although it won no awards, *Franklin Stein* (1972), a gentle satire on the fickleness of public opinion as well as a statement about the need for friendship, has proven popular with children, but the book's appeal is undoubtedly the humorous allusion, both verbally and visually (in the person of Franklin's monster Fred), to the Frankenstein horror fantasy.

Who, Said Sue, Said Whoo? (1973) was the most successfully executed of Raskin's picture books of this period. In a bouncing cumulative rhyme more

Dust jacket for Raskin's mystery about the disappearance of a young heir to a soup fortune (Dutton)

and more animals pile into Sue's tiny car. The cartoonish pictures are delightful and the ending, in which a skunk frightens off all the animals except the ape, who has a cold and cannot smell, is an amusing surprise. It was a Boston Globe-Horn Book Honor Book, was named an ALA Notable Book, appeared on the Library of Congress annual list, and was chosen for the CBC Showcase. *Moose, Goose and Little Nobody* (1974) is not as humorous, but its simple plot about a little lost mouse who searches for his identity is appealing to children. It was listed by the Library of Congress and appeared on the International Reading Association Children's Choice list, which is compiled from books chosen by children as their favorites for the year. In 1972 Raskin's work was exhibited at the Biennale of Applied Graphic Art, Brno, Czechoslovakia.

Raskin's second novel was *Figgs & Phantoms* (1974), which, like all of her books for older children, has been called a mystery, though it is the least like a conventional mystery of the four she produced. It begins as a highly improbable but

nevertheless realistic story, but in the latter third of the book the story changes into a surrealistic dream sequence that bears little resemblance to any of Raskin's other books.

The characters in *Figgs & Phantoms* are surely some of the most amazing to be found in children's fiction. The Fabulous Figgs were once vaudeville performers: Florence Italy ("Baby Flo"), now a rare book dealer; Romulus the Walking Encyclopedia and his twin brother Remus the Talking Adding Machine ("Ask Them Anything"); Truman the Human Pretzel, a sign painter who cannot spell; and Kadota ("Kadota and his Performing Kanines") who has a son named Fido. The baby of the family, Sister Figg, was too young to join the act before the family settled in the town of Pineapple, but she tap-dances through life, to the delight of her husband Newton "Newt" Newton, the best high school quarterback and the worst used car salesman Pineapple ever knew. Mona Newton, only child of Sister and Newt, feels totally estranged from her eccentric family, feeling affection only for her Uncle Florence. In spite of her embarrassment at her family's

Dust jacket for Raskin's gentle satire on the fickleness of public opinion (Atheneum)

antics, she herself (balanced on Uncle Flo's shoulders) is part of the family's most astonishing act—the Figg-Newton Giant who once a month raids Ebenezer Bargain's bookstore for the rare books he keeps on the top shelf. To Mona, books are objects important for their value, but, to her uncle's sorrow, she is oblivious to their contents. Flo's worry about Mona's increasing alienation from her family is paralleled by Mona's fears for his poor health. She is aware that Flo is searching for the way to Capri, the Figg's own private paradise (which they celebrate in a ceremony called Caprification), and the thought of losing him drives her almost to frenzy. When Flo dies, Mona follows him into a nightmare fantasy which nearly costs her her life; she is saved only when she realizes that she must find her own dream, one in which she can be herself.

In spite of its preposterous characters and surface humor, *Figgs & Phantoms* is a profoundly serious book in its exploration of the loneliness and pain of a sensitive and alienated child. Many of

Raskin's books portray elements of her own life, but autobiographical content is particularly significant in this book. Raskin once said of her own childhood, "I was very shy, sheltered, and doted on, and I was so unhappy." This description applies equally well to Mona. Indeed, writing about her characters in *Horn Book* in 1978, Raskin said, "most of all I am Mona." She also identified other characters who were rooted in her past. Her mother, who was only sixteen when Raskin was born and who "came from the era of the flapper," was the model for happy, flapping, tapping Sister Figg, and lovable, gullible, ineffectual Newt Newton was Raskin's father, a pharmacist "who even after the Depression managed to go broke." Uncle Flo is her Grandpa Hersh, her father's stepfather (her own grandfather died young) whom she loved very much. After his death, her grandmother was briefly married to a handsome, much younger Spaniard. Raskin saw him only once, at her grandmother's funeral, but "on rereading *Figgs & Phantoms*, I found him again: The Spanish pirate lives forever in a castle on Capri." Other facets of Raskin's life are part of the story: her love for books and the book trade ("All man has ever known or dreamed of can be found in books," said Uncle Flo), her interest in the works of Joseph Conrad (several of his first editions, which Raskin owned, are mentioned in the book), her enjoyment of tap dancing and of the music of Gilbert and Sullivan. Some of the deeper meanings found in the book, especially Raskin's use of typographical and pictorial clues to reveal Mona's character, and the influence of Conrad's writings upon the work, have been pointed out by Constance Hieatt in "The Mystery of *Figgs & Phantoms*." The novel was a Newbery Honor Book, an ALA Notable Book, and a CBC Showcase book, and it was listed by Library of Congress and *School Library Journal* as one of the best books of the year.

In 1975 Raskin's third novel, *The Tattooed Potato and other clues,* was published. She often used stories involving disguises, stories which reiterated the need for seeing beneath the surface, but nowhere did she examine this theme as deeply as in this book. Dickory Dock, an art student, is hired as an assistant by Garson, who paints sleek and slippery portraits of society people. Garson has another side, however, and it is he who teaches Dickory to see the real persons beneath the disguises which most people wear. Dickory's curiosity is aroused by the strange characters who inhabit the neighborhood: Garson's gangster tenant, Manny Mallomar, and his partner, Shrimps Mar-

Frontispiece and title page for Raskin's book which explores the loneliness of a sensitive and alienated child (Dutton)

inara; the blind beggar who haunts the street and the derelict who sleeps on doorsteps; the mysterious sailor who wears the word "potato" tattooed upside down on his arm. Most of all, she probes beneath the disguises worn by Garson—is he a phony, a talented artist, a sensitive and caring friend, a clever detective, a blackmailer, a murderer?

The book includes a neat parody of Sherlock Holmes; Garson, as Inspector Noserag, and Dickory, as his assistant Sergeant Kod, are asked by Joseph P. Quinn, Chief of Detectives of the New York Police Department, to help solve several cases. The book is arranged in a series of chapters which are treated as if they were the individual cases often found in collections of mystery stories. Although the book is much more like a conventional mystery than was *Figgs & Phantoms,* not all clues necessary to solve the puzzle are provided in a timely manner. In fact, it is almost the end of the book before the reader, like Dickory, realizes that the real case which Chief Quinn is investigating is the disappearance of two young artists, Edgar Sonneborg

and Frederick Schmaltz, fifteen years before. Their fate is linked to the mystery of Garson's identity and to his protection of his monstrous but childlike companion, Isaac Bickerstaffe.

In this book, Raskin directly confronts a topic for which she had earlier been criticized: deformity. Isaac Bickerstaffe is a huge, scarred, one-eyed, brain-damaged deaf-mute. In addition, both the main characters have their own disabilities: Dickory's withdrawal and pain caused by her parents' murder and Garson's unexplained tremor.

Raskin reveals the essential value of every human being, however different they may be, but she does not gloss over the suffering and rejection caused by disability, a topic which she was well qualified to explore. From the age of fifteen, she suffered from a connective-tissue disease, which ultimately resulted in her death in 1984. Afterwards, her friend Alice Bach explained the disease. "In the simplest terms, her body was allergic to itself. Her immune system made antibodies against her own tissues. Variously diagnosed as lupus erythematosus and scleroderma, it is a condition sim-

Dust jacket for Raskin's novel which includes a parody of Sherlock Holmes (Dutton)

In 1974-1975 Raskin's work was included in a touring exhibit of Contemporary American Illustrators of Children's Books. Her last picture book, published in 1976, is entitled *Twenty-two, Twenty-three* and is another of her books about books. The story makes little sense; it is about a lot of animals wearing unusual clothing who are going to Twenty-two, Twenty-three, which turns out to be pages twenty-two and twenty-three of the book. Raskin labels the parts of the book with road signs and reveals a sly humor in her borrowing of animals from such other writers as Fritz Eichenberg (ape in a cape, pig in wig) and Dr. Seuss (cat in the hat, fox in socks), but overall, *Twenty-two, Twenty-three*, an ALA Notable Book, is disappointing.

However, Raskin's last book, *The Westing Game* (1978), is her best known and most highly praised work. It appeared on the Library of Congress, *School Library Journal, Horn Book* Fanfare, and ALA Notable Books lists, was a finalist for the American Book Award, won the Boston Globe-Horn Book Award for fiction, and brought a glowing close to

Dust jacket for Raskin's most highly praised novel which won the Newbery Medal in 1979 (Dutton)

ilar in etiology to multiple sclerosis and rheumatoid arthritis. When she experienced an acute flare-up of her illness, her tissues became inflamed, and she suffered great pain." Bach suggests that Raskin's frequent use of disguises in her books was related to her attempts to hide her own suffering.

The Tattooed Potato and other clues, like *Figgs & Phantoms*, describes the essential isolation of the human condition. In the previous book, this isolation could be countered by sharing others' dreams in books; here it is shared through art and by reaching out to the human being beneath the disguise. The humor is restrained, with fewer extravagances than the two previous novels; the tone is deeply compassionate. The plot is stronger and more unified than that of *Figgs & Phantoms* and has an equally worthwhile theme, but it lacks the emotional intensity of the earlier book. It was an ALA Notable Book, and a Library of Congress and *School Library Journal* choice. The year it was published, Raskin received an Edgar Allan Poe Special Award from the Mystery Writers of America.

a fine career by winning the Newbery Medal in 1979. Sixteen characters, of assorted ages, races, occupations, characters, and circumstances, are brought together through the machinations of Samuel W. Westing, mysterious and reclusive millionaire industrialist. By the terms of his will, they are heirs to his fortune, but they must first "dare to play the Westing game." The players are divided into eight pairs; each pair receives $10,000 and a different set of clues, but no other information. The game's purpose, rules, and rewards are a mystery which the players must solve; at the end, only the winner succeeds in doing so.

In her Newbery award acceptance speech, Raskin described how the book came to be written. It was begun in 1976, the Bicentennial year, which prompted the use of the words of "America the Beautiful" as clues. The death of Howard Hughes was much in the news at the time, which inspired the strange will and multiple heirs. She intended the book to have a historical background and set it on the shores of Lake Michigan, where she grew up. Wisconsin had a history of labor disputes (perhaps she remembered the career of her Grandfather Raskin, a member of the Industrial Workers of the World who was murdered at age thirty-four), so she chose to write about a slain industrialist. Raskin said, though, that as she wrote, "My tribute to American labor history ended up a comedy in praise of capitalism." It was a true Bicentennial book.

The Westing Game is a "puzzle-mystery," and here Raskin is in complete control. The book is tightly plotted and swiftly paced, with every relevant, cleverly disguised clue in place. The characters, too, and even the corpse(s), are not what they seem. Seeing beneath the surface is as important as in the previous books, but here the characters are searching for their own hidden identities; each is struggling to become what he or she is meant to be. The characters are not as well developed as in the two previous books, for there are simply too many of them; but they are human; they are dynamic; they matter. Child readers will, of course, identify with Turtle Wexler, the junior high student and stock market wizard who wins the Westing game. Surprisingly, Raskin identifies herself not with the plain, brilliant Turtle, but with her beautiful older sister Angela, who feels trapped by the life her parents expect of her—a perfect marriage to a promising young doctor. Her frustration leads her to become the "mad bomber"; when she sets off an explosion at her wedding shower, her perfect beauty is destroyed but a whole new life opens up for her.

Raskin started her novels with an idea and a list of characters. She said that the first few words were the most important, because they had to catch the reader, but she did not plot her books out beforehand. She simply started writing, and as the characters developed, they shaped the action. As with her picture books, she wrote much more than she needed and then cut most of it out. She usually wrote four or five drafts of a book. She never knew the ending when she started to write: "If I do know the ending by the second draft, I don't want to write the book. The ending is my reward for doing that book."

In one way, Raskin was certainly Turtle Wexler, and *The Westing Game* as a tribute to capitalism is not surprising because she was a capitalist herself. She maintained a portfolio of stocks and played the market successfully. She was very proud that she was once asked to manage a mutual fund but felt it would take too much time.

Raskin had such a variety of interests that it is difficult to see how she found the time to write. She was a proud mother and a housewife who lived in a Greenwich Village home with her husband, Dennis Flanagan (editor of *Scientific American*), whom she married on 17 October 1966, and her daughter and son-in-law, Susan and Jim Metcalfe. She was a gardener during the summers at her house on Long Island, a sports fan, a collector of first editions of Henry James and Joseph Conrad, and a lover of chess, word games, and bullfights.

Ellen Raskin died on 8 August 1984 of complications of her disease. Her individual and unusual work is of the type that does not date easily. Her picture books continue to amuse, and her illustrations retain their remarkable beauty, but it is her novels which reveal the depth and discipline of which she was capable. Her unique, well-plotted mysteries with their preposterous situations are popular, but they have much more to offer. They are much like Garson's portraits. At first glance they are slick, shiny, and shallow, but for the perceptive reader the faces of real, suffering, struggling people are laid bare. Her characters are not always nice, not always noble or strong or good, but they try; they strive to be true to themselves, to be better than they are. They are sometimes freakish or deformed, but they are always recognizable; they are human.

Interviews:
"Profile of an Author—Ellen Raskin," *Top of the News* (June 1972): 394-398;

Jim Roginski, *Behind the Covers: Interviews with Authors and Illustrators of Books for Children and Young Adults* (Littleton, Colo.: Libraries Unlimited, 1985).

References:

Alice Bach, "Ellen Raskin: Some Clues about Her Life," *Horn Book*, 61 (March/April 1985): 162-167;

Dennis Flanagan, "The Raskin Conglomerate," *Horn Book*, 55 (August 1979): 392-395;

Constance B. Hieatt, "The Mystery of *Figgs & Phantoms*," in *Children's Literature*, volume 13 (New Haven: Yale University Press, 1985);

Lee Bennett Hopkins, *Books Are by People* (New York: Citation Press, 1969);

Linda Kauffman Peterson and Marilyn Leathers Solt, *Newbery and Caldecott Medal and Honor Books: An Annotated Bibliography* (Boston: G. K. Hall, 1982);

Jim Roginski, ed., *Newbery and Caldecott Medalists and Honor Books Winners* (Littleton, Colo.: Libraries Unlimited, 1982).

Papers:

Collections of Ellen Raskin's papers are at the Milwaukee Public Library, Wisconsin; in the Kerlan Collection, University of Minnesota, Minneapolis; and at the Children's Cooperative Book Center, University of Wisconsin, Madison.

George Selden
(George Selden Thompson)
(14 May 1929-   )

Lesley S. Potts

BOOKS: *The Dog That Could Swim Underwater: Memoirs of a Springer Spaniel*, illustrated by Morgan Dennis (New York: Viking, 1956):

The Garden Under the Sea, illustrated by Garry MacKenzie (New York: Viking, 1957); republished as *Oscar Lobster's Fair Exchange*, illustrated by Peter Lippman (New York: Harper & Row, 1966);

The Cricket in Times Square, illustrated by Garth Williams (New York: Ariel/Farrar, Straus, 1960; London: Dent, 1961);

I See What I See!, illustrated by Robert Galster (New York: Ariel/Farrar, Straus, 1962);

The Mice, the Monks and the Christmas Tree, illustrated by Jan Balet (New York: Macmillan, 1963; London: Collier-Macmillan, 1963);

Heinrich Schliemann, Discoverer of Buried Treasure, illustrated by Lorence Bjorklund (New York: Macmillan, 1964; London: Collier-Macmillan, 1964);

Sir Arthur Evans, Discoverer of Knossos, illustrated by Lee Ames (New York: Macmillan, 1964; London: Collier-Macmillan, 1964);

Sparrow Socks, illustrated by Lippman (New York: Harper & Row, 1965);

The Dunkard, illustrated by Lippman (New York: Harper & Row, 1968);

Tucker's Countryside, illustrated by Williams (New York: Ariel/Farrar, Straus & Giroux, 1969; London: Dent, 1971);

The Genie of Sutton Place (New York: Farrar, Straus & Giroux, 1973);

Harry Cat's Pet Puppy, illustrated by Williams (New York: Farrar, Straus & Giroux, 1974; London: Dent, 1978);

Chester Cricket's Pigeon Ride, illustrated by Williams (New York: Farrar, Straus & Giroux, 1981);

Irma and Jerry, illustrated by Leslie H. Morrill (New York: Avon, 1982);

Chester Cricket's New Home, illustrated by Williams (New York: Farrar, Straus & Giroux, 1983);

Harry Kitten and Tucker Mouse, illustrated by Williams (New York: Farrar, Straus & Giroux, 1985).

photo by Alex Gotfryd

OTHER: James Clavell, *The Children's Story*, play adaptation by Selden (New York: Dramatists Play Service, 1966).

Author of sixteen books to date for children of varying ages, George Selden's modern classic, *The Cricket in Times Square* (1960), has assured him a lasting place in children's literature. The creation of the memorable trio, Tucker Mouse, Harry Cat, and Chester Cricket, and their reappearances in five critically acclaimed sequels to *The Cricket in Times Square* have demonstrated Selden's ability to write effective animal fantasies which have been linked to the works of E. B. White and Kenneth Grahame. By placing his stories in an urban setting, Selden has made a unique contribution to anthropomorphic fantasy, while his frequently recurring theme of the importance of loyalty and friendship echoes similar concerns in White's *Charlotte's Web* (1952), Robert Lawson's *Rabbit Hill* (1944), and Grahame's *The Wind in the Willows* (1908). Gentle, humorous satire on the human condition pervades Selden's stories, and the New York City locale of such books as *The Cricket in Times Square* and *Harry Cat's Pet Puppy* (1974) offers a particularly rich opportunity for his satiric comments on modern life.

George Selden Thompson, who writes under the abbreviated name of George Selden, was born on 14 May 1929, in Hartford, Connecticut, the son of Dr. Hartwell Green and Sigrid Johnson Thompson. Growing up in the Connecticut countryside that was to become the setting for *Tucker's Countryside* (1969) and *Chester Cricket's New Home* (1983), Selden developed a variety of interests, which were to figure prominently in his writings, among them conservation, music, and archaeology. He comments, "I didn't have a particularly artistic home, but I realized early that I wanted to be a writer. Both my brother and I had plenty of exposure to music, especially opera, through my mother. And it was my father, a doctor, who read a lot. I never had any idea that one day I'd write for children. I always liked children's literature, even as an adult."

Selden received his B.A. degree from Yale University in 1951 and that same year was awarded a Fulbright Fellowship to the University of Rome. Settling in New York City as a free-lance writer, Selden presently lives in Greenwich Village. Besides writing fiction and nonfiction for children, Selden has also been both a playwright and a screenwriter.

He began writing for children as an experiment at the suggestion of a friend. His first book, *The Dog That Could Swim Underwater: Memoirs of a Springer Spaniel,* was published in 1956. An animal fantasy told from the point of view of a springer spaniel named Flossy, the book shows the attention to details of characterization and setting that was to mark Selden's later, more mature writing. Flossy's discovery of her peculiar talent, an ability to swim underwater, enables her to come to the aid of a friend in need. This theme of friends helping friends was to become a familiar one, more fully developed, in Selden's subsequent books. The story itself is slight and is one which Selden admits he no longer likes himself, but it shows the beginnings of a breezy, warm, and humorous style of writing.

A more successful undertaking was *The Garden Under the Sea*, first published in 1957 and later republished with new illustrations as *Oscar Lobster's Fair Exchange*. In this book Selden laid the groundwork for later books by spinning an original and fanciful yarn about a group of undersea creatures living in Long Island Sound. There are definite parallels with *The Wind in the Willows* in the adventures of Oscar Lobster, Peter Starfish, Hector Crab, and James Fish. To revenge himself on the summer vacationers for "stealing" rocks and shells along the shore, Oscar persuades his three friends to help him "salvage" items belonging to the humans. The book is not a single unified story but a series of episodes chronicling the animals' salvaging adventures over the course of the summer. It is a slow-moving tale, but Selden's knowledge of marine life and of Long Island Sound add authenticity, and he effectively satirizes well-meaning human blundering through the animals' eyes. Each character is a distinct and engaging personality. Oscar is stubborn and shrewd, a forerunner of Tucker Mouse, the streetwise protagonist of *The Cricket in Times Square*, whereas Hector is a fearful, nervous soul. One of the book's finest comic scenes is that in which Oscar and Hector "haunt" an old shack to frighten away two children and carry off their lunch boxes as loot, an operation that terrifies Hector as much as the children. In every scene the deep affection and spirit of self-sacrifice of the animals toward one another convey Selden's familiar theme of the importance of friendship. A second theme in *The Garden Under the Sea* is respect for the sea and the creatures that live there, as well as respect for property; Oscar's "salvaging" is really looting, and he gradually learns this. *The Garden Under the Sea*, though lacking the brisk pace of Selden's later work, is characterized by fine touches of humor, suspense, and warmth, and in many ways it served as a prototype for his better-known works to come.

The Cricket in Times Square (1960) is a minor modern classic which fulfilled the promise of Selden's first two books. Tightly structured and briskly paced, it is a happy blend of engaging characterization, whimsical situations, and lively, witty dialogue. For the first time, also, an animal fantasy was located entirely in the big city, in this case New York City's Times Square. The theme of friendship and loyalty suggested in *The Garden Under the Sea* emerges full-blown in the persons of the book's three incongruous protagonists, Tucker Mouse, Harry Cat, and Chester Cricket. An unlikely trio to strike up a fast friendship, they nevertheless do so when Chester, a country cricket from Connecticut, finds himself accidentally transported to Times Square via a picnic basket. Stranded and alone, Chester is first "adopted" by a boy named Mario Bellini and then befriended by Tucker and Harry. The Bellini family's newsstand is on the verge of bankruptcy, and the well-meaning efforts of the three animals to help them only make matters worse—until they inadvertently discover Chester's musical abilities. Quickly acquiring a repertoire of hymns, popular tunes, and arias, learned from listening to the radio, Chester saves the Bellinis' fortunes and acquires fame for himself by staging concerts in the newsstand. Chester is a country cricket, however, and ultimately fame is no antidote for homesickness. With the help of Tucker

and Harry, Chester returns to Connecticut, knowing that Mario and his family are secure.

The inspiration for *The Cricket in Times Square* came when Selden heard a cricket singing in the subway, and the story equally incorporates Selden's love for music, for his Connecticut home, and for New York City. Critics have stated that the book is an "urban counterpart" of *Charlotte's Web*, and the similarities of theme and situation are striking. Just as Charlotte the spider spins webs with writing in them, so Chester Cricket chirps beautiful music, helping his friend Mario just as Charlotte saves Wilbur the pig. Chester, a mere insect, is, like Wilbur, an unlikely hero, but with the coaching and encouragement of his friends Tucker and Harry he brings fame and fortune to himself and the Bellinis. The whole book, like *Charlotte's Web*, is thus a grand celebration of the power of faith and friendship.

The theme is advanced by means of Selden's characterization of the three animals. Their all-too-human concerns and the give-and-take of their relationships lend complete credibility to the whimsical notion that a cat, a mouse, and a cricket could be the truest of friends. Selden's ability to create animal characters that are as diverse as the soft-spoken Harry, the slangy, money-loving Tucker, and the gentle, naive Chester, yet who evince a genuine regard and respect for one another despite their differences, reaches its peak in *The Cricket in Times Square*. Tucker's dialogue, straight from a Damon Runyon short story, particularly reveals his character: "So say hello! Hello, Harry, Hello, Chester. So, the greetings being over, let us get on with the practicing." The animals' personalities are further extended through the adept pen-and-ink illustrations of Garth Williams, which impart life and warmth to the animals without sentimentalizing them. Similarly, Selden's clear and simple writing style provides insight into human frailties such as snobbery, greed, possessiveness, prejudice, ignorance, and vanity in a gently probing, yet affectionate, manner, without resorting to sentimentality.

Finally, the friendship theme is given further dimension by the book's human characters, particularly Mario, Sai Fong, and Mr. Smedley. Sai Fong, an elderly Chinese, gives Mario a cricket cage for Chester, similar to the ornate ones used in China for centuries, and he instructs Mario on what to feed Chester, providing him with leaves from his own tree. His interpretation of Chester's chirping is that it is ancient wisdom. Mr. Smedley is a music lover with a deep regard for all in nature that pro-

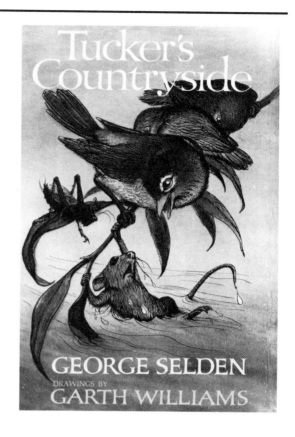

Dust jackets for Selden's most popular book, The Cricket in Times Square, *and three of its five sequels (Farrar, Straus & Giroux)*

vides music. He views Chester not as a lowly insect but a true natural musician. Therefore both Sai Fong and Mr. Smedley provide Chester with a sense of self-worth, Sai Fong through veneration of Chester's wisdom and Mr. Smedley through his appreciation of the cricket's musical abilities.

As diverse a trio as Chester, Tucker, and Harry are, they are drawn together by their mutual goal, and it is the stories told to Mario by Mr. Smedley and Sai Fong—the Greek legend of Orpheus and the Chinese legend of the first cricket—that give the plot its focus and serve to prepare the reader for the moving climax of the book: Chester's final concert in New York, when all of Times Square is entranced by his music.

The Cricket in Times Square is Selden's most successfully plotted and structured book, drawing upon his own background and interests to create a completely convincing, original fantasy. Named a Newbery Honor Book in 1961, it was also chosen to receive a Lewis Carroll Shelf Award in 1963 as a book "worthy enough to sit on the shelf with *Alice in Wonderland*." It was also made into a dramatized recording by Miller Brody Productions in 1972 and an animated television special by the American Broadcasting Company in 1973.

None of Selden's subsequent animal fantasies have quite come up to *The Cricket in Times Square*'s standard of excellence. In *I See What I See!* (1962) Selden temporarily departed from animal fantasy to tell the story of a group of creative children who teach a "practical" friend to see things through more imaginative eyes. When he fails to join in their games of imagining New York as an exotic fantasyland, Jerry is ostracized by his friends. Finally he is converted and describes the New York skyline as a cobweb of lights. The theme is the importance of fanciful thinking, but the point is driven home too forcefully to be effective; Jerry's treatment by the other children is harsh and the reader sympathizes with him rather than with his friends. Despite natural dialogue and a generally engaging style of writing, *I See What I See!* lacks the gentle charm and tolerance of Selden's animal fantasies and is his least successful book.

Following *I See What I See!* Selden ventured into nonfiction writing. In 1964 he produced two titles which utilized his knowledge of archaeology: *Heinrich Schliemann, Discoverer of Buried Treasure* and *Sir Arthur Evans, Discoverer of Knossos*. The story of Heinrich Schliemann, the self-taught archaeologist who discovered the ancient city of Troy, provides details of Schliemann's background, digging techniques, and finds. Similarly, *Sir Arthur Evans,*

Discoverer of Knossos tells a fascinating story of Evans and the capital of the all-but-forgotten Minoan civilization. While the primary intent of these books is to inform young readers, Selden brings to them the same attention to detail and the same simplicity and clarity of style that characterize his fiction. Both books convey the personalities of two men who set out to prove the truth behind legend, and Selden's enthusiasm for his subject plainly shows.

Happily, Selden turned again to animal fantasy with one of his most engaging books for younger readers, *Sparrow Socks*. Published in 1965, the book tells the delightfully absurd story of a "wonderful sock machine that clicked and that clacked, and that purred and that whirred," illustrated Rube Goldberg-fashion by Peter Lippman in black-and-white line drawings with red accents. The McFee sock factory in Scotland is slowly going bankrupt because the townspeople are buying their socks at the big new stores. When a boy named Angus McFee uses the machine to make tiny socks for sparrows whose feet are cold, the strange sight piques the townspeople's curiosity and makes them clamor for "sparrow socks" of their own, "a beauteous new, warm and woolly winter sock with stripes and a bright red toe."

Selden has a fine time with words in this tale; the humans and the sparrows all speak in Scottish accents and the repetition of certain words and phrases gives lilt and bounce to the narrative. The humorous story is well integrated with equally humorous pictures of the mammoth sock machine and the tiny, sock-clad sparrows: the words "sparrow socks" in the text are printed in red, just as the tiny socks themselves are embellished with bright red stripes and toes. The theme of friendship is again at the heart of the story. Angus's thoughtful deed causes the sparrows to reciprocate by returning their socks to help him so he can reuse the cloth, and ultimately the McFee sock factory is saved. Though not a major work, *Sparrow Socks* is a warmhearted tale, a gentle satire on the power of advertising, and an effective animal fantasy for a younger audience.

Sparrow Socks was followed by *The Dunkard* (1968), another departure from animal fantasy. In this picture book Selden spoofs special event days at school. The protagonist, young George, searches for "the most interesting grownup that anyone had ever seen" to bring to Grown-Up Day at his school. He discovers a happy, middle-aged man who has devoted his life to perfecting the fine art of dunking his food in his drink, singing as he dunks, "Oh, dunking is a joyous thing,/A genuine delight./It makes you want to laugh and sing./I dunk both day and night." George brings the Dunkard to Grown-Up Day and, after some initial skepticism, his teacher and friends enter wholeheartedly into the joys of dunking. *The Dunkard,* though its premise is pleasantly whimsical, does not rank with Selden's better work, and, surprisingly, it lacks the enlivening illustrations of *Sparrow Socks,* even though Peter Lippman provided the pen-and-ink drawings for both works.

In 1969, nine years after the publication of *The Cricket in Times Square,* its first sequel appeared. Selden explained the reason for his delay in writing *Tucker's Countryside* when he said, "Although I had hundreds of requests for a sequel, I put it off until I thought I had an equally good idea, for the conservation theme is dear to me. I used my own childhood home and the meadow across the street as the book's setting." Transporting Tucker Mouse and Harry Cat to the Connecticut countryside, Selden introduces the theme when Chester Cricket asks his old friends' help in saving his meadow home from a building project. Tucker is baffled both by the difficulty of his task and the inconveniences of country living; Harry fares better, much to Tucker's annoyance, when he is "adopted" and pampered by Ellen, the little girl who loves the Old Meadow as much as Chester and his friends do and who works valiantly but ineffectually to save it from the bulldozers. The Old Meadow seems doomed until Tucker concocts the brilliant scheme of turning it into what he terms a "benign deception"; that is, a trumped-up historic site complete with bogus "relics" which supposedly belonged to Joseph Hedley, the town's founder.

Though *Tucker's Countryside* has been called a less original book than *The Cricket in Times Square,* the country setting provides the city-bred Tucker and Harry with fresh opportunities for satire on the strangeness of human behavior, particularly the human penchant for questionable "progress" as well as the naive reverence for historic relics. Removing the pair from their familiar Times Square setting also places Tucker and Harry in the amusing dilemma of coping with the simplicity and ruggedness of country living. "Oh, the countryside, the countryside!," rhapsodizes Tucker, just prior to a violent attack of hay fever. Carried over from the earlier book, though, are the intertwined concerns of humans and animals. The children of Hedley want to save the Old Meadow because they love it, and the animals want to because it is their home; through this situation Selden stresses the importance of conservation for both of these rea-

sons. As in *The Cricket in Times Square,* he pokes gentle fun at human gullibility. His characters always mean well but often suffer from skewed priorities. The Hedleyites are concerned about what is happening to the Old Meadow but vaguely feel it is wrong to stand in the way of "progress." Later on, they are completely taken in by the animals' faked "historic" site and dutifully call a halt to the meadow's destruction. Much of the fun of the story derives from the humans' ignorance of the animals' work behind the scenes; only Ellen dimly suspects the truth.

Tucker, Harry, and Chester are once again engagingly characterized. Tucker retains his snappy dialogue and slightly devious tendencies, even while he is floundering hilariously to survive outside his urban element. "Subways I can sleep through," he complains; "Commuters I can sleep through. But that brook just goes on . . . and on . . . and on!" Once again Garth Williams's illustrations complement the story's mood well, capturing the three creatures' affection for one another and the humor of Tucker's frustration at "camping out."

Selden's handling of his human characters is not as effective; Ellen lacks the life and dimension of Mario Bellini and his family. Her sweetness and earnestness are overdrawn; also, the structure of the plot is weakened by the constant shifting of viewpoint between Ellen and the animals. *Tucker's Countryside* lacks the brisk pace and tight structure of *The Cricket in Times Square,* but it succeeds in conveying its conservation message as well as Selden's favorite theme of friends helping friends. Selden has called *Tucker's Countryside* his favorite book. It won a Christopher Award in 1969 as well as general critical acclaim as a worthy sequel to *The Cricket in Times Square.*

In *The Genie of Sutton Place* (1973) Selden created his first full-length fantasy about humans. After his father's death, twelve-year-old Tim Farr is left in the care of his rich, fussy Aunt Lucy and moves into her stately home. After a life of complete freedom, Tim and his adoring dog Sam are uncomfortable in Sutton Place, particularly when Aunt Lucy decrees that Sam must go. In desperation Tim retrieves an ancient spell from his archaeologist father's notes and summons a genie, who proceeds to transform Sam into a man. Magic seems, at first, to be the answer to all of Tim's problems, but it has serious and unforeseen consequences when the genie, Abdullah (Dooley for short), falls in love and begins to lose his magic powers.

The original, warm, and gently humorous story deals with the themes of free choice and growth and change, symbolized by Tim's thirteenth birthday and the decisions finally made by Dooley and Sam to become, and remain, mortal men. While the character of Abdullah is vigorously drawn, and Selden's knowledge of archaeology, music, and, of course, animals is woven into the story, adding interest and credibility, *The Genie of Sutton Place* strives for a sophistication that is never quite achieved; it lacks the quiet, ingenuous charm of his animal fantasies, and most of the human characters never quite come to life. The affection shared among Tim, Sam, and Dooley does have echoes of Tucker Mouse and friends, however. Selden later rewrote *The Genie of Sutton Place* as a television play for Westinghouse "Studio One."

With *Harry Cat's Pet Puppy* (1974) Selden continued the adventures of Harry Cat and Tucker Mouse in New York. Once again the theme is loyalty among friends despite differences, as Tucker and Harry rise to the challenge of helping a friend in need. Harry's "pet puppy" is a bedraggled orphan rescued from an alley and lodged in the Times Square drainpipe, over Tucker's protests. The puppy, who names himself Huppy, soon outgrows his new home, and Tucker and Harry are faced with the problem of finding a home for a mongrel dog in a city already overrun with them. Mr. Smedley, the piano teacher introduced in *The Cricket in Times Square,* becomes their target, but Mr. Smedley is singly devoted to Miss Catherine, a severely blue-blooded Siamese cat who dislikes dogs. Miss Catherine is won over after Huppy defends her against a tough dog named Max, and Mr. Smedley is won over in turn when Huppy "rescues" Miss Catherine from a staged plunge into the river.

The cast of *Harry Cat's Pet Puppy* is a potpourri of urban types, ranging from the hard-boiled gang leader Max to the bohemian Lulu Pigeon and the aristocratic Miss Catherine. Selden's characterization is generally strong and convincing, and the story liberally laced with humor, pathos, and suspense. Tucker is his usual volatile self, displaying a particularly human weakness for his hoarded "life savings." When Huppy innocently carries the money away, Tucker is the picture of incredulous horror: he "clutched his chest and fought off a heart attack."

Similarly, Huppy's clumsy appeal and Miss Catherine's hauteur are convincingly portrayed, although Huppy lacks Chester Cricket's depth as a character. The plot structure of *Harry Cat's Pet*

Puppy is uneven; the pace becomes breathless as Tucker and Harry labor to find Huppy a home before he becomes just another delinquent stray, and the introduction of new characters and twists of plot are jarringly abrupt. Perhaps the most serious weakness is that the happy ending evolves less from a natural unfolding of events than from a series of fortunate accidents. The vigorous writing style, vivid settings, and warmheartedness of the story mitigate, but do not entirely overcome, these weaknesses. However, Garth Williams's illustrations capture each animal's personality and appeal and effectively convey the humorous spirit of the story, which was the winner of the William Allen White Children's Book Award in 1978.

Chester Cricket's Pigeon Ride (1981) is an unusual third sequel to *The Cricket in Times Square* and totally different from Selden's preceding or subsequent books. It is an adventure in picture book format, a panoramic vignette of New York City. The story goes back into the past, beginning when Chester Cricket meets Lulu Pigeon in the park about two weeks after Chester's arrival in Times Square. Lulu takes her new friend on an aerial tour of New York, and Selden's lively, lucid prose in this bird's-eye-view narrative clearly pays homage to the city. Garth Williams's illustrations include several double-page spreads, and text and pictures are nicely integrated throughout the book. The breathlessness of Chester's perch atop the Empire State Building and the glitter of lights in New York Harbor are described equally by the author's spirited prose and the illustrator's use of perspective to convey height and distance. Tucker and Harry have minimal but typically entertaining roles, and a double-page illustration of the three friends chatting together is one of Williams's best.

Chester Cricket's Pigeon Ride has been criticized for its departure from full-length storytelling and for the slightness of the story line, but in this book Selden is trying something new, creating a mood rather than telling a tale. He allows Williams to explore the picture possibilities of his animal characters, and together Selden and Williams convey the essence of the city through the medium of flight. *Chester Cricket's Pigeon Ride* offers younger readers the chance to meet Harry, Tucker, and Chester, and, within its limitations as a pictorial essay, it succeeds very well.

Some of Selden's later animal fantasies retained elements of whimsy and charm but showed less plot development and more sentimentality. *Irma and Jerry,* published in 1982, is a story involving a cultured but naive springer spaniel and a

Dust jacket for Selden's third sequel to The Cricket in Times Square *(Farrar, Straus & Giroux)*

streetwise cat. Jerry and his master, a Yale professor, have moved to Greenwich Village, where Jerry meets the slangy, bohemian Irma. The story of their adventures together has many of the familiar elements of earlier books: the theme of friendship between animals of differing backgrounds and personalities, a lively writing style, a mixture of humor and pathos, and a skillfully imparted sense of the atmosphere of New York. Vivid descriptions and humor arise naturally from Irma's induction of Jerry into the New Yorker's way of life. Though a vigorous narrative in the spirit of *Harry Cat's Pet Puppy, Irma and Jerry* is a disjointed tale; the author's touch is less sure in the handling of situation and dialogue, and the tone is at times uncomfortably sentimental.

Chester Cricket's New Home (1983) returns the reader to the rural setting established in *Tucker's Countryside*. In this quietly humorous story, Chester's tree stump is destroyed, and his various animal friends offer him a place in their homes. In each dwelling, however, Chester is miserable; he needs a home all his own and finally takes up residence in an old log his two friends, Simon Turtle and Walter Water Snake, have provided for him. The story is slight, but its witty, sometimes poignant

glimpses into human behavior disguised as animal ways lend it a quiet distinction. The theme, as always, is friendship, as well as the individual's need for a place of his own in the world. In this book, with its more introspective tone, simple plot, and return to a character well delineated in past stories, Selden again achieves a subtle and warmhearted storytelling effect.

While the scope of Selden's writing has been broad, encompassing juvenile fiction, nonfiction, and picture books about a wide variety of characters and situations, his books have a number of characteristics in common. Like all good fantasy, Selden's plots are grounded in reality, based upon his own background and experiences. *The Dog That Could Swim Underwater* was his own pet; the meadow setting of *Tucker's Countryside* was a part of his boyhood home in Hartford; and the Long Island Sound setting for *The Garden Under the Sea* as well as the New York setting for several novels including *The Cricket in Times Square* are locales which Selden knew intimately. Extensive research into archaeology, Selden's hobby, is reflected in his two nonfiction works about Heinrich Schliemann and Sir Arthur Evans. About selecting the material for his books, Selden has said, "My stories have to first please me, . . . I search for new ideas, am gratified when I find one, am nervous at the thought of putting even one down in words, and feel happiness when I think I've succeeded." He incorporates into his stories everything which is of interest to or has meaning for him, whether it is grand opera, cats, or conservationism. Concerning the creation of his animal characters, he states: "You become the character. Grow fur, claws, antennae—and it's all difficult!"

Selden's fiction is invariably characterized by his favorite theme, a deep regard for human friendship shown through anthropomorphic fantasy. While this theme is most perfectly realized in *The Cricket in Times Square*, it appears in virtually all of his stories. The birds in *Sparrow Socks* loyally return the socks Angus gave them in order to help their friend; Oscar Lobster and his friends risk their lives to help one another and the odd trio of companions in *The Genie of Sutton Place* share a close, sacrificial bond of friendship. Even stories which contain few or no animal characters, such as *The Dunkard*, treat friendship based on a common pleasure, such as dunking, in a warm and whimsical manner.

Coupled with his treatment of friendship is his use of humor to poke gentle fun at human eccentricities. In Selden's fictional world, people are basically kind and well meaning, even if they do suffer (as cats, lobsters, and mice) from lapses into vanity, stubbornness, and materialism. Self-interest always gives way to concern for others.

A clear and lively writing style predominates in most of Selden's work, a style which adapts itself well to his simple themes and satiric commentaries on humanity. It ranges from the lightly humorous rhymes of *The Dunkard* and cheerful word pictures of *Sparrow Socks* to the poignant climax of *The Cricket in Times Square*. As Chester sang his last song for the city, "Traffic came to a standstill. The bus-

ses, the cars, men and women walking—everything stopped. And what was strangest of all, no one minded. Just this once, in the very heart of the busiest of cities, everyone was perfectly content not to move and hardly to breathe. And for those few minutes, while the song lasted, Times Square was as still as a meadow at evening, with the sun streaming in on the people there and the wind moving among them as if they were only tall blades of grass."

Implicit in Selden's friendship theme is the importance of understanding and caring between people of different backgrounds, beliefs, and temperaments. Whether the characters involved in a story are as incongruous as a cat, a mouse, and a cricket or a boy, a dog-turned-man, and an Arabian genie, their differences are minimized and their common bond of humanity is stressed. Selden makes each of his characters unique, a personality possessed of strengths and weaknesses; for him, the individual is important, and individuality is precious, but equally important is how each person relates to others and to the world around him.

Without doubt Selden's greatest contribution to children's literature was the creation of Harry Cat, Tucker Mouse, and Chester Cricket in *The Cricket in Times Square*, his most critically acclaimed and popular book. While his later works have been of uneven quality, they still retain Selden's characteristic humor and brisk style. He has tended more toward the urban setting for his novels, apparently realizing his gift for conveying the atmosphere of New York. Like O. Henry, Selden celebrates New York, just as he extolls human warmth and kindness and even human failings. Despite some lapses into oversentimentality and lightweight plotting, Selden's vision of basic human goodness and his ability to convey this vision in his convincing and entertaining animal fantasies remain intact.

Isaac Bashevis Singer

(21 November 1904?-   )

Sylvia W. Iskander
University of Southwestern Louisiana

See also the Singer entries in *DLB 6, American Novelists Since World War II, Second Series,* and *DLB 28, Twentieth-Century American-Jewish Fiction Writers.*

SELECTED BOOKS: *The Family Moskat,* translated by A. H. Gross (New York: Knopf, 1950; London: Secker & Warburg, 1966);

Satan in Goray, translated by Jacob Sloan (New York: Noonday, 1955; London: Owen, 1958);

Gimpel the Fool and Other Stories, translated by Saul Bellow and others (New York: Noonday, 1957; London: Owen, 1958);

The Magician of Lublin, translated by Elaine Gottlieb and Joseph Singer (New York: Noonday, 1960; London: Secker & Warburg, 1961);

The Spinoza of Market Street, translated by Martha Glicklich, Cecil Hemley, and others (New York: Farrar, Straus & Cudahy, 1961; London: Secker & Warburg, 1962);

The Slave, translated by Isaac Bashevis Singer and Cecil Hemley (New York: Farrar, Straus & Cudahy, 1962; London: Secker & Warburg, 1963);

Short Friday and Other Stories, translated by Joseph Singer and others (New York: Farrar, Straus & Giroux, 1964; London: Secker & Warburg, 1967);

In My Father's Court, translated by Channah Kleinerman-Goldstein, Elaine Gottlieb, and Joseph Singer (New York: Farrar, Straus & Giroux, 1966; London: Secker & Warburg, 1967);

Zlateh the Goat and Other Stories, translated by Elizabeth Shub and Isaac Bashevis Singer, illustrated by Maurice Sendak (New York: Harper & Row, 1966; Harmondsworth, U.K.: Longman, Young, 1970);

Selected Short Stories of Isaac Bashevis Singer, edited by Irving Howe (New York: Modern Library, 1966);

Mazel and Shlimazel; or, The Milk of A Lioness, translated by Elizabeth Shub and Isaac Bashevis Singer, illustrated by Margot Zemach (New York: Farrar, Straus & Giroux, 1967; Lon-

Isaac Bashevis Singer

don: Cape, 1979);

The Manor, translated by Joseph Singer and Elaine Gottlieb (New York: Farrar, Straus & Giroux, 1967; London: Secker & Warburg, 1968);

The Fearsome Inn, translated by Elizabeth Shub and Isaac Bashevis Singer, illustrated by Nonny Hogrogian (New York: Scribners, 1967; London: Collins, 1970);

When Shlemiel Went to Warsaw and Other Stories, translated by Isaac Bashevis Singer and Elizabeth Shub, illustrated by Margot Zemach (New York: Farrar, Straus & Giroux, 1968; Harmondsworth, U.K.: Longman, Young, 1974);

The Séance and Other Stories, translated by Roger H. Klein, Cecil Hemley, and others (New York: Farrar, Straus & Giroux, 1968; London: Cape, 1970);

A Day of Pleasure: Stories of a Boy Growing Up in Warsaw, translated by Channah Kleinerman-Goldstein and others, illustrated with contemporary photographs by Roman Vishniac (New York: Farrar, Straus & Giroux, 1969; London: MacRae, 1980);

The Estate, translated by Joseph Singer, Elaine Gottlieb, and Elizabeth Shub (New York: Farrar, Straus & Giroux, 1969; London: Cape, 1970);

Joseph and Koza; or, The Sacrifice to the Vistula, translated by Isaac Bashevis Singer and Elizabeth Shub, illustrated by Symeon Shimin (New York: Farrar, Straus & Giroux, 1970);

Elijah the Slave, translated by Isaac Bashevis Singer and Elizabeth Shub, illustrated by Antonio Frasconi (New York: Farrar, Straus & Giroux, 1970);

A Friend of Kafka and Other Stories, translated by Isaac Bashevis Singer, Elizabeth Shub, and others (New York: Farrar, Straus & Giroux, 1970; London: Cape, 1972);

An Isaac Bashevis Singer Reader (New York: Farrar, Straus & Giroux, 1971);

Alone in the Wild Forest, translated by Isaac Bashevis Singer and Elizabeth Shub, illustrated by Margot Zemach (New York: Farrar, Straus & Giroux, 1971);

The Topsy-Turvy Emperor of China, translated by Isaac Bashevis Singer and Elizabeth Shub, illustrated by William Pène du Bois (New York & London: Harper & Row, 1971);

Enemies, A Love Story, translated by Aliza Shevrin and Elizabeth Shub (New York: Farrar, Straus & Giroux, 1972; London: Cape, 1972);

The Wicked City, translated by Isaac Bashevis Singer and Elizabeth Shub, illustrated by Leonard Everett Fisher (New York: Farrar, Straus & Giroux, 1972);

A Crown of Feathers and Other Stories, translated by Isaac Bashevis Singer, Lauru Colwin, and others (New York: Farrar, Straus & Giroux, 1973; London: Cape, 1974);

The Hasidim (New York: Crown, 1973);

The Fools of Chelm and Their History, translated by Isaac Bashevis Singer and Elizabeth Shub, illustrated by Uri Shulevitz (New York: Farrar, Straus & Giroux, 1973);

Why Noah Chose the Dove, translated by Elizabeth Shub, illustrated by Eric Carle (New York: Farrar, Straus & Giroux, 1974);

Passions and Other Stories, translated by Isaac Bashevis Singer and others (New York: Farrar, Straus & Giroux, 1975; London: Cape, 1976);

A Tale of Three Wishes, illustrated by Irene Lieblich (New York: Farrar, Straus & Giroux, 1975);

A Little Boy in Search of God: Mysticism in a Personal Light, translated by Joseph Singer (Garden City: Doubleday, 1976);

Naftali the Storyteller and His Horse, Sus, and Other Stories, translated by Joseph Singer, Isaac Bashevis Singer, and others, illustrated by Margot Zemach (New York: Farrar, Straus & Giroux, 1976; Oxford: Oxford University Press, 1977);

A Young Man in Search of Love, translated by Joseph Singer (Garden City: Doubleday, 1978);

Shosha, translated by Joseph Singer and Isaac Bashevis Singer (New York: Farrar, Straus & Giroux, 1978; London: Cape, 1979);

Old Love, translated by Joseph Singer, Isaac Bashevis Singer, and others (New York: Farrar, Straus & Giroux, 1979; London: Cape, 1980);

Nobel Lecture (New York: Farrar, Straus & Giroux, 1979; London: Cape, 1979);

Reaches of Heaven: A Story of Baal Shem Tov (New York: Farrar, Straus & Giroux, 1980);

The Power of Light: Eight Stories for Hanukkah, illustrated by Irene Lieblich (New York: Farrar, Straus & Giroux, 1980);

Lost in America (Garden City: Doubleday, 1981);

The Collected Stories of Isaac Bashevis Singer (New York: Farrar, Straus & Giroux, 1982; London: Cape, 1982);

The Golem, illustrated by Uri Shulevitz (New York: Farrar, Straus & Giroux, 1982; London: Deutsch, 1983);

Yentl the Yeshiva Boy, translated by Marion Magid and Elizabeth Pollet (New York: Farrar, Straus & Giroux, 1983);

The Penitent (New York: Farrar, Straus & Giroux, 1983);

Love & Exile: A Memoir (Garden City: Doubleday, 1984);

Stories for Children (New York: Farrar, Straus & Giroux, 1984);

The Image and Other Stories (New York: Farrar, Straus & Giroux, 1985).

Isaac Bashevis Singer, winner of the Nobel Prize for Literature in 1978, first began to write for children in 1966. Three of his first four books were Newbery Honor Books; his fifth, *A Day of Pleasure*, was the winner of the National Book Award in 1970. His other books for children have continued to win prizes, as have his works for adults, and Singer has had many honorary degrees conferred upon him. A popular lecturer, Singer captures live audiences as well as an ever-expanding reading public.

A modest, soft-spoken man with a keen sense of humor, Isaac Singer weaves a spell as storytellers of old have done and good storytellers of today continue to do. The prizes, the long-awaited recognition, the adoration of fans seem to have had little impact on this most accommodating author who autographs books without complaint, who grants interviews to help young writers and scholars, and who is, according to a book reviewer for *Time* (16 October 1978), "perhaps the only Nobel prizewinner with no pretensions whatever." Singer certainly recognizes the fact that many of the readers of his children's books are adults, but he feels, as do most scholars in the field of children's literature, that a good children's book is a good book for readers of all ages.

The world Singer's stories depict, with a few exceptions, is that of the Jewish ghetto during or prior to World War II. In the enclosed world of the *shtetl* (small Jewish village) religion and custom dominate life and a rich folktale tradition abounds. The tenement houses, the muddy streets, the dark alleyways, the hard-working, poverty-stricken people who turn to their rabbi for solutions to problems—this is the world Singer knew intimately and describes vividly for children and for adults. For Singer the supernatural is omnipresent whether it be in the form of God, angels, demons, witches, goblins, hobgoblins, or imps.

Even though the Yiddish-speaking audience was decreasing in number when he began writing, Singer chose to write in Yiddish since it is his mother language. He would succeed or fail in it, since it is the language of the people about whom he wanted to write. By translating many of his works himself and working in close collaboration with his assistants, he keeps as close as possible to the exact meaning and spirit of the original. He continuously revises even while translating and calls his translators his "most constructive critics."

Since Singer's first books were for adults and were about a world no longer in existence, a world filled with the supernatural in multiple forms, he had never thought about writing for children. He credits his friend Elizabeth Shub, then a children's editor at Harper's, with suggesting that children would love that bygone world filled with devils and demons. Singer was sixty-two years old when he entered this new phase of his writing career, a

phase which has been, and continues to be, successful.

Singer has developed what might be called a philosophy of writing for children. He never patronizes, for he believes that children are "the best readers." He says in his introduction to *When Shlemiel Went to Warsaw* (1968) that "there is no basic difference between tales for adults and for young people. The same spirit, the same interest in the supernatural is in all of them." It does seem that the supernatural is the universalizing agent in Singer's writing, crossing cultural lines by bringing the foreign world of a past time to present-day America and to other countries as well, for his works have been translated into approximately fifteen languages.

What might be called the cardinal rules for Singer are to write about the world he knows, to have a plot and the passion to write, and to put his seal upon his work; that is, to write a story no one else could write. A study of Singer's writings for children shows that he abides by these rules, making his stories uniquely his own.

Singer was born Icek-Hersz Zynger in Leoncin, Poland, about 21 November 1904, the second son and third child of Pinchos-Mendel and Bathsheba Zylberman Zynger. Later he would assume the name Bashevis after his mother, Bathsheba, and change the spelling of his last name to Singer. His birthdate is somewhat confusing, for he states it is 21 November, but he frequently celebrates it on 14 July; the *New York Times* (3 September 1984) published an account of a recent attempt to convert his birthday "in Cheshvan [a month in the Jewish calendar], on a Wednesday during the third week" to the standard Western calendar for 1904; the result was a birthdate of 26 October, a date which he has not heretofore used. Singer is the son and grandson of rabbis, of the Hasidic Judaic tradition on the paternal side and the *misnagdim* (Orthodox Jews who did not agree with the Hasidic) on the maternal side. His mother, the daughter of the rabbi of Bilgoray, received more education than was usual for women at that time. Her practical and skeptical nature often seemed in contrast to Singer's father's Hasidic approach, which caused him to turn to God, to the Torah, and to other holy books for answers.

Young Singer's reaction to these two opposing traditions is seen most vividly in "Why the Geese Shrieked," an episode from *A Day of Pleasure* (1969) in which a woman brings her slaughtered geese which she wants to prepare for the Sabbath dinner to Singer's father with the terrifying problem that when they are thrown against one another, they shriek with an eerie, high-pitched sound. While the rabbi ponders whether this event is an omen from heaven or a sign from the devil, Singer's mother asks to hear the sound again. While Isaac's father speaks about blasphemy and truth, his mother asks if the windpipes have been removed. When she receives a negative answer, she removes them. Singer writes:

> Everything hung in the balance. If the geese shrieked, Mother would have lost all: her rationalist's daring, her skepticism, which she had inherited from her intellectual father. And I? Although I was afraid, I prayed inwardly that the geese would shriek, shriek so loud that people in the street would hear and come running.
>
> But, alas, the geese were silent, silent as only two dead geese without windpipes can be.

Singer's education came from three primary sources: first, his family, whose storytelling gave him a lifelong interest and vocation and whose intellectual pursuits provided a vital stimulus to his eager young mind; second, his own voracious reading; and third, his study at religious primary schools.

Storytelling was quite popular in the Singer household; Singer describes both his parents as excellent storytellers. The rabbi told his children stories of miracles, imps, devils, and good and evil powers; young Isaac preferred the less didactic ones. On the other hand, his mother told stories of Bilgoray, her hometown in Poland, and of their relatives there. Singer has described her stories as "beautiful" and less moralizing. "Fool's Paradise" in the *Zlateh the Goat* collection is an example which Singer states was told to him, with some variations, by his mother. Its ending carries a message, which is the logical outgrowth of the action, not an attached moral. Consequently whenever he writes for children today, he tries not to be didactic. Isaac's

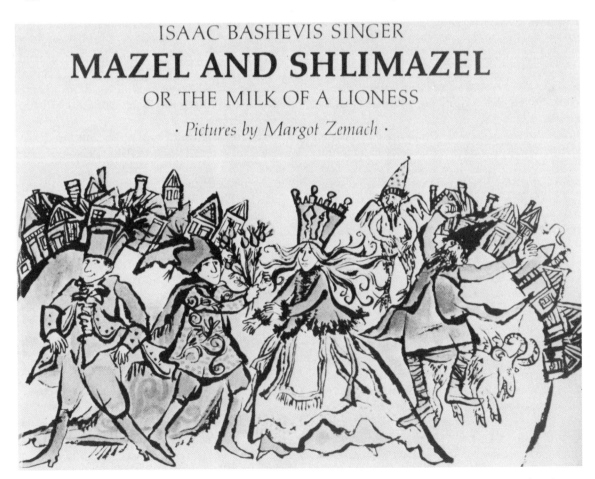

Cover for one of Singer's best-selling children's books which includes recreated folktales and three original stories
(Farrar, Straus & Giroux)

brother Israel Joshua (eleven years older) told him stories about other countries, races, and cultures in the vivid manner that was later to characterize Joshua's writing, for he was the first of the Singer children to become a well-known novelist. Indeed for many years Isaac Singer was known as "Singer's brother." Isaac's sister, Hinde Esther (thirteen years older), also told him stories, mostly about romantic love, a subject which Singer often writes about today in his adult novels.

In addition to the stories the family wanted him to hear, Singer heard ones not intended for his ears. He eavesdropped on his father's court of *Beth Din.* In the introduction to one of his books of memoirs, *In My Father's Court* (1966), Singer defines the *Beth Din* as "a kind of blend of a court of law, synagogue, house of study, and, if you will, psychoanalyst's office where people of troubled spirit could come to unburden themselves." The impetus for many of the short stories of the adult writer was to come from information gleaned by the youthful listener outside his father's study. Young Singer also listened to family discussions involving his older brother.

Israel Joshua Singer was an artist, a journalist, a philosopher, and a man much interested in politics, people, and the world. A devotee of the Jewish Enlightenment, he broke away from the enclosed world of the Polish Jewish ghetto. Joshua's discussions with his mother included such subjects as Buddha and Confucius and other religious figures, his friends, and his bohemian life-style. As an adult, Isaac Singer writes in "A Boy Philosopher": "Although later in my life I read a great deal of philosophy, I never found more compelling arguments than those that came up in my own kitchen."

As soon as Singer learned to read, he read with an appetite for all kinds of books. He has said that he found religious books like the Bible and the Talmud "wonderful." He borrowed books that his father had forbidden him to read. He read in the Cabala, which is based upon a mystical interpretation of the Scriptures and traditionally not given to a young man until he is thirty years old.

The nonreligious books Singer read included little storybooks in Yiddish which he purchased for a small amount whenever he could. There were a few score of them, and one he recalls today was about a golden hair. A king found the strand of hair and was so enchanted by it that he searched for its owner. He traveled extensively until he came to Madagascar, and there he found the owner, a beautiful blonde-haired woman who became his

queen. This type of tale was of great interest to young Singer because of its contrast with the serious religious books which comprised most of his reading and because there were very few storybooks for children in Yiddish at that time.

At about age twelve he discovered the Brothers Grimm, whose stories were, of course, written in German. Since Yiddish has affinities with German, Singer was able to read this collection, and he loved it. When he was about sixteen, he discovered the stories of Hans Christian Andersen, which he recalls as "even more wonderful." These were the only books written specifically for children that he can remember reading before he began to write his own stories.

Other nonreligious books which he read were to have an impact on his later writing for adults just as the writings of the Brothers Grimm and Andersen were to have on his children's stories. He read *Sherlock Holmes* in Yiddish, afterwards fancying himself a detective. Then his brother Joshua gave him a copy of Fyodor Dostoyevski's *Crime and Punishment* to read when he was about eleven. He did not completely understand it at that time, but it gave him new insights, made him want to read more of the Russian realists, and encouraged his interest in philosophy. Among the other classics he read Edgar Allan Poe in Polish, Charles Dickens's *The Pickwick Papers* in Hebrew, and Shakespeare in Yiddish.

Singer's formal education consisted of attendance at a number of *cheders* (religious primary schools). At the age of three he began to attend *cheder* in Radzymin, where he lived for about a year; then, after the family moved to Warsaw in 1908, he went to a series of *cheders* in that city. Here Singer learned to read religious books and to write Yiddish.

From 1914 to 1917 Singer was under his father's tutelage. He read religious texts to prepare for the more extensive study necessary to become a rabbi, a profession that both his parents desired for him but which he later rejected because he felt he was not suited for it since he had serious doubts about religious dogma. This part of his education ended when various external problems caused the family to separate for a period of time.

Singer, his mother, and his younger brother Moishe moved to Bilgoray, where they lived in the home of his maternal grandfather. The reasons for the move were many: Singer's mother was concerned about her father, from whom she had not heard for some time; typhus and typhoid fever raged in Warsaw; food was rationed; Tsar Nicholas was under house arrest (Poland was torn and divided by German, Austrian, and Russian factions); and suddenly and inexplicably visas to Bilgoray were obtainable. Singer's father remained behind to continue as rabbi of Krochmalna Street (where the Singers' three-room apartment was located in a tenement building in a very poor neighborhood), and Joshua stayed in Warsaw to continue his newspaper work and to see the girl he would later marry. The years at Bilgoray proved to be fruitful ones for the imaginative, impressionable thirteen-year-old, who had recently been *bar mitzvahed.*

Bilgoray, an authentic *shtetl,* was as it had been for hundreds of years, virtually untouched by the modern world. Here Singer came in contact with the older Jewish ways and traditions. He drew from these experiences when he wrote his first novel, *Satan in Goray* (1955). In Bilgoray also he first began to doubt orthodox dogma. He discovered Hillel Zeitlin's *The Problem of Good and Evil* (1898), which synthesized mystical writings with intellectual ones like those of Baruch Spinoza, Arthur Schopenhauer, and Friedrich Nietzsche. He read Anton Chekhov, Leo Tolstoy, and others. At the Turisk study house, he learned German, Polish, and modern Hebrew to add to his command of languages, having already learned ancient Hebrew in the *cheder* and Yiddish at home. He read more secular literature, fell in love, taught conversational Hebrew, and began to write in Hebrew, first poetry and then fiction.

After about four years in Bilgoray, Singer returned to Warsaw, where he enrolled at his father's request in Tachkemoni Rabbinical Seminary. Remaining there only one year, he left, he has said, because he already knew much of the religious subject matter taught there, although he was behind in the secular subjects. He has also remarked that he could not become a rabbi because of serious doubts he had, not about God but about tradition and dogma. He returned to Bilgoray. At this time he discovered the writings of Rabbi Nachman of Bratzlav, a saintly man, a scholar, a poet, and an extraordinary storyteller, who was also a great grandson of Baal Shem Tov, the Jewish teacher and healer in Poland who founded Hasidism in 1750. Singer would later credit Rabbi Nachman with influencing his work immensely.

In the meantime his brother Joshua had returned to Warsaw from Russia, and in 1923, unable to support himself giving Hebrew lessons, Isaac moved to Warsaw to join Joshua and his free-thinking friends. Isaac wanted to become a writer, much to the regret of his father and the dismay of his mother. His father was never able to accept the fact that two of his sons were secular writers. A religious writer himself, Rabbi Singer considered secular Yiddish writers heretics; thus he preferred to say that his sons sold newspapers rather than say they wrote for them. Isaac was to remain in Warsaw for the next twelve years, in which his career as a writer began to take shape.

At nineteen years old, Singer took a job as a proofreader for the Yiddish journal *Literarishe Bletter,* coedited by Joshua Singer. Two years later, in 1925, he won third prize in the journal's literary contest. He published several other stories in this journal and continued to work for it in some capacity for ten years. During this time he began to use the name Isaac Bashevis for his stories, the name he uses today when he publishes in Yiddish. When he writes for a deadline, or writes things he does not have time to polish, he uses the name Isaac Warshawsky (Isaac of Warsaw). Occasionally a work such as *In My Father's Court* is published under the name Isaac Warshawsky and later suitably revised to be published under the name Isaac Bashevis.

Dust jacket for Singer's story about three young girls held prisoner and forced to serve a wicked witch and her half-man, half-devil husband (Scribners)

In the difficult Warsaw years, Singer also supported himself by translating. During the period from 1927 to 1932, he translated into Yiddish Knut Hamsun's *Die Volger* (1927), *Victoria* (1898), and *Pan* (1894); Erich Maria Remarque's *All Quiet on the Western Front* (1929) and *The Road Back* (1931); Thomas Mann's *The Magic Mountain* (1924); and Stefan Zweig's *Romain Rolland* (1920). Later in New York, in 1938, he would translate Leon S. Glaser's *From Moscow to Jerusalem*. He also translated some popular German novels, a job which paid poorly but helped to support him.

During the first years of his return to Warsaw, he felt isolated, for he had few friends and little money, spoke broken Polish, and was bashful. The idea of suicide as a protest against an unjust world first crossed his mind at this painful time in his life. He filled long hours reading philosophy and psychology, science, and works about the occult. He went out with Gentile girls, attended the Yiddish Writers' Club, and met Aaron Zeitlin, the son of author Hillel Zeitlin. Aaron Zeitlin was also a published author, recognized for his writings in Yiddish about Yiddish culture. Zeitlin's encouragement and his example were just what Singer needed at the time to give him confidence to write in Yiddish. Then, too, Singer's work as a journalist was boring him, and he recognized his preference for creating his own stories about his own culture.

Around 1925 Singer met Runya (her full name remains unknown), who was to become the mother of his only child, Israel Zamir, born in 1929. Runya reared the child in Palestine after taking him first to Russia and then Turkey when she and Singer parted in 1935 and he left for America. Today Israel Zamir lives in Israel and has four children, a daughter and three sons. He is a journalist who has translated some of Singer's children's stories into Hebrew.

Two years prior to Singer's leaving for America, he began writing his first novel. *Satan in Goray* was published in 1934, in book form in 1935 by the Polish Yiddish Chapter of the P.E.N. Club, and in English in 1955. Even before its acceptance, another publisher wanted a collection of Singer's short stories. With the proofs in hand, Singer decided that he was not ready to have them published, and he withdrew them, promising the publisher a translation in exchange. He destroyed many of these stories because he considered them immature. His first collection of short stories was not published until some twenty-eight years later. Singer appears to be his most critical judge; his criticism is reflected in the pen names he uses today.

When Singer arrived in America on 1 May 1935, his brother having preceded him by two years, he settled in New York and took a job, which he held for about ten years, as a free-lance writer for the Yiddish newspaper the *Jewish Daily Forward*. A period of five or six years followed his arrival in America when he could not write; he says he suffered from "literary amnesia." During this period he met Alma Haimann Wasserman, from Munich, Germany, and they were married in 1940. Two years later they moved to Upper West Side Manhattan, where they still live when they are not traveling or spending the winter months in Miami. Mrs. Singer's work in Manhattan stores helped support them during the leaner years, for Singer's recognition was slow in coming.

In 1943 Singer became a naturalized citizen of the United States and began to publish stories in *Zukunft* and *Svivah*, the latter a literary magazine which he helped start. The next year his brother Joshua died at age fifty-one. Long Isaac's literary mentor, Joshua was the author of a number of works including *The Brothers Ashkenazi* (1936) and *The Family Carnovsky* (1943), both social novels and family chronicles which influenced the structure of some of Isaac Singer's novels. Singer has said that he learned much from his brother about construction and literary mannerisms, such things as not mixing essay with fiction or not discussing or analyzing his characters. His beloved older brother was not his only loss during World War II, for his mother and younger brother Moishe both died during that time in a Russian camp.

From 1950 on Singer published many novels and short stories. A pattern for publication of the novels emerged. *The Family Moskat, The Magician of Lublin,* and *The Slave* were first published serially in the *Forward*, then in book form in Yiddish, and then translated into English and published in 1950, 1960, and 1962 respectively. *The Manor* also appeared serially between 1953 and 1955 but followed a somewhat different publication course in that it was amplified and then published in English in two volumes: *The Manor* (1967) and *The Estate* (1969).

It was Saul Bellow's translation of a short story, "Gimpel the Fool," however, that brought Singer to the attention of an English-speaking audience. Translated in 1953 for the *Partisan Review*, "Gimpel the Fool" is considered by many critics to be one of the best, if not the best, of Singer's short stories. Singer's English-speaking audience continued to increase in number as *Satan in Goray* came out in English in 1955.

In 1966 *In My Father's Court,* Singer's combination of memoirs and belles lettres, was published; sections of this book would be used later to produce an award-winning children's book. While Singer was a writer in residence at Oberlin, he became interested in writing for children. Singer's publisher—Farrar, Straus and Giroux—was convinced that he could not be a successful writer for children, so Harper and Row published his first venture into this new genre, *Zlateh the Goat and Other Stories* (1966). Illustrated by Caldecott Award-winner Maurice Sendak, it was awarded Newbery Honor Book status, included in the American Library Association's list of Notable Children's Books, and also included in "Fanfare," *Horn Book*'s annual list of noteworthy books.

This collection of seven stories is quite diversified and includes those kinds of tales most representative of Singer's canon: humorous stories about Chelm, stories having supernatural creatures as characters, and animal stories. Chelm is a Polish city that the Yiddish people singled out as a place of fools and is, consequently, the source of much humor. The three Chelm stories are "The Snow in Chelm," "The Mixed-Up Feet and the Silly Bridegroom," and "The First Shlemiel."

"The Snow in Chelm" introduces the seven elders, the oldest and greatest fools, who are called upon to preserve the snow, which they consider a treasure, from being trampled by the residents of Chelm. A decision to send a messenger to each house informing the people not to walk on the snow is vetoed by Dopey Lekisch because he realizes that the messenger himself will trample the snow. The solution is obvious: have the messenger carried on a table. While some of the elders admit to making a mistake the next morning when they see the snow trampled by the table carriers, others reason that the four table carriers should themselves have been carried. In all the Chelm stories, the humor is based upon this type of seemingly logical reasoning. Singer deserves praise for introducing to children the elders of Chelm, known previously only to adults.

The *Zlateh the Goat* collection also introduces Singer's readers to the first *shlemiel* character, who is, naturally, a resident of Chelm. (*Shlemiel* is a Yiddish world meaning the eternal loser.) He is a fool, but a delightful one. "The First Shlemiel" is a tale about Mr. Shlemiel, who has been asked by his wife not to do three things while she is at the market: not to let the baby fall out of the cradle, not to let the rooster out of the window, and not to eat the potful of poison on the shelf (which is not really

poison but is jam prepared especially for the Hanukkah pancakes). Shlemiel, of course, does all three and prepares to die. The story ends happily, however, as do almost all of Singer's children's stories, for he recognizes the sensitivity of children and does not want them to conclude at too early an age that there is a lack of justice in the world.

The happy ending is one of the few differences Singer sees between writing for children and adults. Another difference is that in writing for children he omits material unsuitable for a young audience. He shows them demons, devils, and witches; but while a child or young adult may be held hostage by one of these creatures of darkness for a period of time, he is always rescued. Singer's children's works never show a person possessed by a devil as he describes in *Satan in Goray,* his first novel for adults. The explicit and frank treatment of sexual matters present in the adult novels does not appear in the children's stories. However, the vocabulary is not deliberately simplified for children because Singer believes that an unknown word will not stop a child reader, but a boring story will. Singer also believes in combining the serious with the humorous in his short-story collections.

"Fool's Paradise," the opening story of the *Zlateh the Goat* collection, is quite serious; it is a variation of a tale told to Singer by his mother. Reprinted in *Reader's Digest* in April 1979, the tale tells of a young boy, Atzel, who has heard so many delightful stories about paradise that he wishes he were dead so he could be there. Atzel's parents are so desperate when the boy refuses to eat or speak that they call in a specialist, who urges them to create a facsimile of Atzel's vision of paradise; after a short stay in "paradise," Atzel is so bored that he is willing to work, study, and eat plain foods—all of which he had refused to do before he "died." Miraculously, he thinks, a mistake was made, and he learns that he is not truly dead. The Atzel returned from "paradise" is no longer the same idle boy he was. There is a message inherent in "Fool's Paradise," but the message is an integral part of the action and not a didactic moral attached to the end.

The *Zlateh* collection also includes three other stories: "Grandmother's Tale" and "The Devil's Trick," both having a devil for the antagonist, and the title story, "Zlateh the Goat." Reprinted in *McCall's* in December 1977, "Zlateh the Goat" tells of a boy and his goat who provide for one another physically while lost in a snowstorm and who build a relationship of mutual respect and love. This beautifully simple story shows the attitude of the author toward both children and animals. He clearly loves and respects children. His attitude toward animals is reverent and led him to become a vegetarian some years ago. He sees in the animal world a dignity that he respects. "Zlateh the Goat" is the only one of Singer's children's stories to date to be made into a movie. Singer does not like the film; he feels that those who filmed it in Czechoslovakia did not understand him and that the movie was not successful.

The next year, 1967, when Singer was writer in residence at the University of California, *The Manor* was published in English translation from the Yiddish; at this time he also published two books for children: *The Fearsome Inn* and *Mazel and Shlimazel. The Fearsome Inn*, published by Scribners (where Elizabeth Shub had moved by this time), is a longer short story about three young girls held prisoner and forced to serve a wicked witch, Doboshova, and her half-man, half-devil husband, Lapitut. Illustrated by Caldecott Award-winner Nonny Hogrogian, this Newbery Honor Book is filled with supernatural creatures like the witch and her husband and magical items like chalk and herbs. Ultimately the three girls are rescued by three young men, whom they marry, and the fearsome inn is no longer a frightful place.

The Jewish weddings of the three couples under a canopy at the no-longer fearful inn are described; Passover is mentioned. For the non-Jewish child reader these traditional Jewish events are not a hindrance to comprehension because they are only secondary to the action. If anything they add a somewhat exotic ambience, appropriate to the faraway (for American children) setting in Poland.

What is not foreign to children is the interest in the supernatural. A hierarchy among the evil creatures of Singer's fictive world places Asmodeus as king of the devils over other devils, witches, spirits, imps, goblins, and hobgoblins. Somewhat less obvious are the creatures of good: God, angels, good spirits, and playful imps called "lantuches."

A good spirit controls much of the action of *Mazel and Shlimazel; or, The Milk of A Lioness*, also published in 1967. Mazel, whose name is Yiddish for good luck, and his counterpart Shlimazel (bad luck) make a wager. Mazel bets that he can make the poorest boy in the village, Tam, happy; and Shlimazel says that in one minute he can undo what may take Mazel a year to accomplish. Here Singer uses the traditional fairy-tale motif of a young man going through a series of trials and, upon their successful completion, being rewarded with the hand of the princess in marriage, but it is the Yid-

dish folktale elements of the spirit of good luck and bad luck that make the story unusual. (The name Tam in this tale does not mean fool as it does in Yiddish, however, for Tam is not a fool; Singer has said that he used the name Tam here as a variation of *Thomas* in Polish.)

Margot Zemach illustrated this book, as she did three of Singer's later books. Although *Mazel and Shlimazel* was not a Newbery Honor Book, it was chosen as an American Library Association Notable Book of 1967, as was *The Fearsome Inn* for that year. *Mazel and Shlimazel* received a starred review in the *School Library Journal*, denoting that the periodical considered it "excellent in relation to others of its kind." Later the editors of *School Library Journal* selected it as one of their Best Books of the Year.

Further recognition was forthcoming for Singer. In 1968 the first book-length analysis of his work was published—*Isaac Bashevis Singer and the Eternal Past* by Irving H. Buchen. *The Séance and Other Stories* was published in the same year, and Singer was writer in residence at the University of Wisconsin. His fourth children's book, *When Shlemiel Went to Warsaw and Other Stories*, was included in the prestigious Newbery Honor list and the American Library Association's Notable Book List. One of his best-sellers, it is illustrated by Margot Zemach and includes recreated folktales told to Singer by his mother, who had heard them from her mother and grandmother. Three of the stories in the collection are original: "Tsirtsur and Peziza," "Rabbi Leib and the Witch Cunegunde," and "Menaseh's Dream." The collection also contains three Chelm stories—"The Elders of Chelm and Genendel's Key," "Shlemiel the Businessman," and "When Shlemiel Went to Warsaw"—and two others—"Utzel and His Daughter Poverty" and "Shrewd Todie and Lyzer the Miser."

The opening story of the collection, "Shrewd Todie and Lyzer the Miser," is a marvelous combination of folk motifs, imagination, and rabbinical wisdom. Todie, a poor man with a family to support, goes to Lyzer to borrow a silver tablespoon. The only valuable objects that Todie owns are three silver teaspoons. When Todie returns the tablespoon, he also gives Lyzer one of his three silver teaspoons, explaining that the tablespoon gave birth to the teaspoon at his house. Lyzer is shocked but so pleased to be increasing his wealth that he lets Todie borrow the tablespoon two more times, each time with the same result. Todie then asks to borrow silver candlesticks, and Lyzer agrees thinking they too will give birth; but Todie sells them to feed and clothe his poor family. When he tells Lyzer that the candlesticks died, Lyzer is outraged. The rabbi is called in, and he decides that, if one accepts nonsense that brings profit, one must accept nonsense that brings loss.

The three teaspoons are but one example of Singer's use of the mystical or magical numbers three and seven. He says he does so unconsciously but would rather choose numbers with magical associations. He repeats them in most of the stories: three things that Shlemiel's wife says not to do, three wishes that the children have in the story by that name, three nights that Aaron spends in the haystack with his goat Zlateh; seventh heaven that is God's home, seven days and nights that the seven elders of Chelm need to make decisions, and many others.

The preference for mystical or magical numbers is not surprising given Singer's background, which he describes vividly in the children's book *A Day of Pleasure: Stories of a Boy Growing Up in Warsaw*, published in 1969, the same year that *The Estate* was published. Fourteen of the nineteen episodes in *A Day of Pleasure* were taken from *In My Father's Court*, appropriately revised, and then photographs by Roman Vishniac were added. Only three are pictures of the Singers: Isaac, his brother Joshua, and his grandfather from Bilgoray. The others, scenes of daily life in Poland, were taken in the 1930s, although the stories described took place a generation earlier. The combination of Vishniac's visual images and Singer's descriptions is particularly apt and forceful in giving the reader a comprehensive picture of Jewish ghetto life in the Poland of an earlier time.

The five stories added to *A Day of Pleasure* are "Who I Am," "The Trip From Radzymin to Warsaw," "Reb Itchele and Shprintza," "The Mysteries of the Cabala," and "Shosha." "The Mysteries of the Cabala," the story awarded the highest praise by *Horn Book* in their February 1970 review, tells of young Isaac and his good friend Mendel, who try to outdo one another telling imaginative tales. Isaac takes liberties with the Cabala in order to impress Mendel and then is frightened by his own audacity.

"Shosha" is another especially delightful addition in its description of the childhood friendship between Isaac, age eight, and Shosha, age nine. The imaginary world they created in their stories was filled with excitement. A second section of "Shosha" takes place some years later. Isaac, grown to manhood and a father himself, decides to visit the street where he grew up before he leaves for

Dust jacket for Singer's 1976 collection of children's stories which includes three tales set in Chelm, a Polish city that the Jewish people singled out as a place of fools and which Singer frequently satirizes in his children's fiction (Farrar, Straus & Giroux)

the United States. He finds there a child who looks just like the Shosha he left behind; the child, Basha, turns out to be Shosha's daughter. Basha knows all the stories that Shosha and Itchele (Isaac's family nickname for him) shared. The story has sentiment but not sentimentality, and the reminiscences of the author about the stories he told Shosha as a youth are a fitting conclusion to *A Day of Pleasure*, the story of a young boy who grew up to become a writer.

This story predates Singer's adult novel by the same name which was published in 1978. *Shosha* the novel is closer to the truth. Singer did make a return visit to his neighborhood and did find his childhood friend, but she did not have a daughter, nor was she in fact married or even engaged.

"Shosha" provided a magazine title as well, for there is a cricket behind the stove in Shosha's kitchen that Singer imagined "was telling a story that would never end." Publisher Marianne Carus took the title for *Cricket* magazine from this story, feeling that the magazine had the same goal: to tell stories that never end.

A Day of Pleasure was an American Library Association's Notable Children's Book in 1969 and won in 1970 the second National Book Award ever given for children's literature. In accepting the National Book Award, Singer made his well-known speech about why he writes for children. It is worth quoting because it shows a fundamental understanding of the child reader and because Singer himself chose to read it when he was awarded the Nobel Prize in 1978 for his adult literature. It was enthusiastically received in Sweden, as it has been elsewhere:

> 1. Children read books, not reviews. They don't give a hoot about the critics. 2. They don't read to find their identity. 3. They don't read to free themselves of guilt, to quench the thirst for rebellion, or to get rid of alienation. 4. They have no use for psychology. 5. They detest sociology. 6. They don't try to understand Kafka or *Finnegans Wake.* 7. They still believe in God, the family, devils, angels, witches, goblins, logic, clarity, punctuation, and other such obsolete stuff. 8. They love interesting stories, not commentary, guides or footnotes. 9. When a book is boring, they yawn openly, without any shame or fear of authority. 10. They don't expect their beloved writer to redeem humanity. Young as they are, they know that it is not in his power. Only the adults have such childish illusions.

Singer published two books for children the year that he first made that speech—*Joseph and Koza* and *Elijah the Slave*—and only one book for adults—*A Friend of Kafka and Other Stories* (1970). *Joseph and Koza; or, The Sacrifice to the Vistula,* illustrated by Symeon Shimin, is a myth of Singer's own creation. Set in pagan times when the Polish people worshipped idols of clay and stone and sacrificed humans and animals, this story is basically one of conflict between good and evil.

While traveling from Jerusalem, a young man named Joseph comes upon Mazovia, a land near the Vistula River. Koza, the daughter of Chieftain Wilk, is to be sacrificed to the river to pacify the evil spirits who live there. Chosen by the witch Zla for the annual sacrifice because she is the most beautiful maiden, Koza is ultimately rescued by Joseph; the two marry and live happily ever after.

This mythical tale is more outstanding for its redemption theme than for its love theme. The

people of Mazovia learn about God's commandments and give up their pagan ways. The forces of evil are defeated, but not before the evil Zla has called upon Topiel (King of the Vistula), Baba Yaga (an evil witch flying in a mortar, carrying a pestle in one hand and a broom in the other), lesser *babas*, little imps called *dziads*, and various other creatures such as goblins, hobgoblins, and sprites.

The other children's book published in 1970, *Elijah the Slave*, illustrated by Antonio Frasconi, is a retelling of a Hebrew legend taken from a very old story in the Midrash. Set "in ancient times, in a distant land," *Elijah the Slave* tells of a miraculous occurrence which happens to Tobias, a scribe and a holy man, who strongly believes that God will help those who are in need. When Tobias injures his hand and thus can no longer earn his living, his poor family is soon destitute. Tobias's wife offers the practical suggestion that her husband should do something even while waiting for a miracle. As Tobias sets out for the city, following his wife's advice, a stranger greets him and shakes his hand. Tobias's hand is miraculously cured, and Tobias learns that the stranger is Elijah, the messenger of God.

In an earlier, anonymous version of this tale, Tobias is out of work, but there is not so tangible a cause as an injured hand which is later miraculously cured, an action foreshadowing for both Tobias and the reader the greater miracle to happen in the story. This added detail of the injured hand shows the deft craftsmanship of a master storyteller who understands that children will ask why Tobias did not go to work when his family was poor and hungry. In the latter part of the tale, Elijah becomes the central figure. This tale is somewhat unusual for Singer in its ending, for all are rewarded and happy; there are no evil people or creatures to punish, the only enemies being poverty and hunger.

Miracles and supernatural events of all kinds appear in Singer's next work for children, *Alone in the Wild Forest* (1971). Also illustrated by Margot Zemach, it is Singer's longest story for children. The combination of folktale motifs, fairy-tale qualities, and religious elements, such as reincarnation and transmigration, makes it a most interesting tale. Miracles and biblical references, souls of the dead, angels, witches, magical amulets, and apples all enable a young couple, alive and in love in a previous life but prevented from marriage, to find each other and marry in this life. Further, an evil minister of the king learns to correct his ways and is redeemed through love, Singer's final message

XIV

my possessions I carried in this sack. As I told you I still car-

ry the prayer book that the soldier gave me some-sixty-odd years

ago, as well as my parents Chanukah lamp . Sometimes when I,m

on the road and I feel especially downhearted, I hide in a forest

and light Chanukah candles even though it is not Chanukah. At

night, the moment I close my eyes, Zeldele is with me. She is

young and she wears the white silken bridal gown which her parents

had pepared in her trousseau. She pours oil into a magnificent

Chanukah lamp and I light the candles with a long torch. Sometimes

the sky turns into an otherworldly Chanukah lamp with the stars

as its lights. I told my dreams to a rabbi and he said, "Love

comes from the soul and souls radiate light. I know that when

my time comes, Zeldele soul will wait for me in Heaven. Well,

it's time to go to sleep. Good night, a happy Chanukah

Revised typescript page, with an initialed self-portrait, of the conclusion to "Hanukkah in the Poorhouse," the final tale in Singer's
The Power of Light: Eight Stories for Hanukkah *(by permission of the author)*

being that all are redeemed and cleansed before God even if it takes several lifetimes.

The title *Alone in the Wild Forest* refers to young Joseph, who has to find his way in the world, but there are several references to such a title in earlier works by Singer. Menaseh, a character in *When Shlemiel Went to Warsaw*, carries a book entitled *Alone in the Wild Forest.* Singer's publishing venture as a boy, described in "Growing Up," from *Naftali the Storyteller and His Horse, Sus, and Other Stories,* was to be entitled "Into the Wild Forest." Singer apparently uses this expression at times to indicate literally a wild forest, and at other times to indicate figuratively the world into which all people are thrown, alone and without definite knowledge of who they are, where they are going, and what they should do.

This story, typical of Singer's others in its Judaic ambience, is set in the time of Baal Shem (a saintly rabbi). A no-longer young husband, whose marriage has remained childless, wants a son to recite the Kaddish prayers for him after his death. He visits Baal Shem, who tells him he shall have his wish, but he should name his son Joseph because the boy will have many trials and temptations as did his namesake, the son of Jacob the patriarch. The child is born, named, attends *cheder* as a youth, but never quite fits in. His parents die, and he must seek his own living. At this point the traditional Jewish aspects of the story are dropped, and Joseph emerges as a fairy-tale hero. His adventures take him on the back of an eagle to his final destination, the kingdom of Good King Maltuch.

The story is somewhat episodic in that it leaves its central character and the traditional fairy-tale motif of a young man successfully completing a task and being awarded the king's daughter as a bride, in order to focus on the redemption of Bal Makane, the jealous first minister of the king. His punishment for trying to drown Joseph and for robbing and killing merchants in the forest during a former life is banishment to the wild forest where the wicked witch Zlichah lives. Approximately one-third of the book is devoted to Bal Makane's adventures in the forest and his transformation from the man of envy to the repentant one, a change symbolized by his new name, Bal Tshuvah. The theme of reincarnation and transmigration is seen in reference to other characters in the story as well, such as Tarnegol, who is a rooster in this life, and Zeivah, a wolflike human; both have animal characteristics to atone for bad deeds in a past life.

When questioned about his belief in reincarnation and transmigration, Singer hastens to say that he is not a believer, but a skeptic. He feels that one's genes are millions of years old and that there is more to life than birth, death, and disappearance forever. He admits there is no scientific evidence for such a feeling. He does not use the word *believe*, nor does he say others should believe. On the other hand, he writes about reincarnation and transmigration in a positive, nonskeptical way.

Published the same year as *Alone in the Wild Forest*, 1971, was *The Topsy-Turvy Emperor of China*, with illustrations by William Pène du Bois. This book has not been very successful in America, although Singer feels that it is a good book. Set in China (for no particular reason, according to the author), the tale centers around the coarse and mean Emperor Cho Cho Shang, his Empress, and their counterparts, the handsome, intelligent Prince Ling Ling and his lovely bride-to-be, Min Lu. In his desire to be handsome, the ugly Emperor declares that everything just and beautiful will be unjust and ugly and all mean and hideous things will be fair and lovely. Everything is topsy-turvy: table manners, clothing, knowledge, schoolwork, love, taxes, religion, justice, music, and art. When friends meet, they do not politely bow to one another, but each tweaks the other's nose and exclaims how unpleasant it is to have met and hopes they shall not meet again.

The turning back of life in China to right-side-up is, of course, expected and desired by the child reader. Singer provides a satisfying resolution at the close with the marriage of Ling Ling and Min Lu and the death of the ugly parents of Ling Ling.

In 1972 *Enemies, A Love Story* was published for adults and *The Wicked City* for children. The latter was named a Notable Children's Book for 1972 by the American Library Association. Illustrated by Leonard Everett Fisher, it is a retelling of the biblical tale from the book of Genesis about the destruction of Sodom, the story of Abraham's attempt to save his nephew Lot and Lot's wife and daughters. Fire, smoke, and flame engulfing the city of evil and Lot's wife being changed into a pillar of salt give the tale its color and drama, but at the same time a quiet sense of justice and goodness is seen in the character of Abraham, whose wife Sarah gives birth in her old age to a son from whom will be born the future generations of Israel. The retelling is didactic but dramatic.

Not at all didactic but satiric and witty, *The Fools of Chelm and Their History* (1973), with illustrations by Caldecott Award-winner Uri Shulevitz, tells the story of how Chelm came to be; the war the Chelmites fought with Mazelborsht instead of Gorshkov because Haskel turned left instead of right; the defeat followed by revolt and the overthrow of Gronam Ox; the establishment of the regime of Bunem Pokraka, who abolished all money in favor of a barter system; the overthrow of Bunem Pokraka by Feitel Thief and the issuance of paper money; the conquering of neighboring towns, which inspired revenge in the form of a siege; and finally the restoration of order and Gronam Ox to command.

The decision-making process by Gronam and his Council of Sages—Dopey Lekisch, Zeinvel Ninny, Treitel Fool, Sender Donkey, Shmendrick Numskull and Shlemiel, their secretary—with its bungling manner and ineptitude—can be considered a parody of government as well as a source of humor. Another humorous element is the marital fighting between the Supersage, Gronam Ox,

Dust jacket for Singer's 1982 children's book about a pious rabbi who creates and brings to life a giant clay creature, the Golem, to help a friend accused of murder, but who then abuses the Golem's power with disastrous results
(Farrar, Straus & Giroux)

and his wife, Yente Pesha; these spats seem frequently to end with Yente Pesha pouring the slops over the feet of the super-wise leader.

The humor of Shlemiel is timeless. He opens his mouth and sticks out his tongue whenever he wants to speak; however, in some ways, he is one of the wiser ones, for he asks several pertinent questions about the war that the Chelmites intend waging, questions so significant and difficult to answer that the other members of the Council of Sages want to imprison him or hang him. Even more indicative of his wisdom is his refusal to marry Yente Pesha if she divorces Gronam Ox when he has fallen from power.

In addition to *The Fools of Chelm and Their History*, Singer had two more books published in 1973, both for adults: *A Crown of Feathers and Other Stories* and *The Hasidim*. The next year he published *Why Noah Chose the Dove*. Beautifully illustrated by Eric Carle, *Why Noah Chose the Dove* is generally considered a picture book for young readers, ages five to seven, whereas most of Singer's children's books are for ages eight through thirteen (*Elijah the Slave* being an exception in that it is aimed at an audience somewhere in between). When asked if he liked to write for a very young audience, Singer replied that he is delighted to if he has the right kind of story, for he believes that the story is the most essential ingredient; he does not begin with a character or with a theme.

Why Noah Chose the Dove has been translated into several languages; most recently it came out in Israel in Hebrew. The story of Noah and the animals on the ark has long been a fascinating one for children. Singer makes the story his own by having each animal boast of his own virtues and belittle the others in order to ensure his place on the ark—all except the dove who, in his modesty and silence, never brags or argues. And so it is that Noah chooses the dove to bring back the message at the conclusion of the flood. The dove, symbol of peace, lives today happily without fighting.

A similarly happy ending is reserved for the three characters in Singer's next book for children, *A Tale of Three Wishes* (1975). Illustrated by Irene Lieblich, it is set in Frampol, where a brother and sister, Shlomah and Esther, ages seven and six respectively, play with a mutual friend, Moshe, also seven. The boys heard a story at *cheder* that on Hoshanah Rabbah, the last day of the Feast of Tabernacles, the sky opens for one minute and those who witness it may have a wish granted. Singer is at his best in evoking an atmosphere appropriate to the big event. Just the right amount of the irrational elements of fright and awe are comingled with the rational elements of hunger and a lack of sleep so that when the children witness the opening of the sky, they wish for all the wrong things and not what they intended to wish for. Esther wants to be as beautiful as Queen Esther, but instead she wishes for a blintz to eat. Shlomah, disgusted with his sister's wasted wish, requests that she become a blintz herself and thus neglects to wish to be as wise as Solomon, his namesake. Moshe, in despair over Esther, now a blintz, wishes she would be a little girl again instead of asking to be as learned as Rabbi Moshe Maimonides. However, all is not lost, for one of Singer's God-figures, The Watcher in the Night, explains that those who wish for too much receive nothing, but he does not forget them or their wishes. When they are old enough to understand and when they are deserving, then the three real wishes are granted.

Beautifully written and illustrated in a somewhat primitive fashion, the story rises above its Jewish Polish locale to speak to any child anywhere who makes a wish. It is perhaps didactic, yet not in an offensive way; the lessons to be learned are integral to the action. The story is enriched by the inclusion of superstitions and traditions, such as the idea that corpses pray after midnight in synagogues and that Esther should wear two aprons, one forward and one backward; according to the author, the wearing of the aprons was thought to be a prevention against demons.

Not all the reviews of *A Tale of Three Wishes* were favorable; however, the unfavorable criticism was clearly in the minority. Allene Stuart Phy in *School Library Journal*, April 1976, called it "a thin fable" and felt that the child reader would be disappointed.

Singer next published for adults *Passions and Other Stories* (1975) and a book of memoirs, *A Little Boy in Search of God: Mysticism in a Personal Light* (1976). For children he wrote *Naftali the Storyteller and His Horse, Sus, and Other Stories* (1976), which was illustrated by Margot Zemach. Critic Norma Rosen in the *New York Times Book Review* (14 November 1976) faulted the editor of *Naftali* with allowing "a bit of comic dialogue that appeared almost word-for-word in . . . *Zlateh the Goat*." She said, "No child wants to come upon a character who speaks in borrowed words." Other reviewers, such as *Horn Book*'s praised *Naftali the Storyteller*, and *School Library Journal* gave it a starred review. It is listed as an American Library Association Notable Book for 1976.

This collection, like the two others for children which preceded it, contains three Chelm stories: "Dalfunka, Where the Rich Live Forever," "The Fools of Chelm and the Stupid Carp," and "Lemel and Tzipa." There are two autobiographical stories: "A Hanukkah Eve in Warsaw" and "Growing Up"; the title story contains some autobiographical elements, as does "The Lantuch." Rounding out the group is an animal story, "The Cat Who Thought She Was a Dog and the Dog Who Thought He Was a Cat." Taken collectively these stories paint a picture of a way of life no longer in existence but rich with variety and with the supernatural.

The title story of the collection is a moving one in which the main character, who loves books and stories, decides as a young man to become a storyteller. Both Naftali and Reb Zebulum, the bookseller, on occasion speak for Singer. Reb Zebulum, for example, says, "At times I read a story that seems to me completely unbelievable, but I come to some place and I hear that such a thing actually happened." He says also, "If stories weren't told or books weren't written, man would live like the beasts, only for the day."

This story is notable also for the relationship between Naftali and Sus, Naftali's beloved horse. Sus lives some forty years, unusually long for a horse, because he has been well cared for and loved by Naftali. When Sus dies, Naftali places the horsewhip, which he never used, over Sus's grave as a marker. The whip begins to grow and an oak tree sprouts, taking its sustenance from Sus's body. Years later Naftali is buried under that same oak, and on his tombstone the following words are carved: "LOVELY AND PLEASANT IN THEIR LIVES, AND IN THEIR DEATH THEY WERE NOT DIVIDED." The respect which the author has for Sus is shown throughout the story and in the way that Sus dies, in a sunny place, quietly and with dignity.

The two autobiographical stories also give the reader insights about Singer's desire to be a writer, from age seven in "A Hanukkah Eve in Warsaw" and at eleven in "Growing Up." In *cheder* Singer hoped he would grow up quickly since he felt self-conscious about looking different from other boys because of his old-fashioned clothes and fiery red hair and because he pronounced some Yiddish words differently. He learned, however, that he could be accepted as a storyteller, and he loved to tell stories. On the Hanukkah eve in the story of that name, young Isaac gets lost in a snowstorm on his way home from *cheder*. When he finally arrives at his gate at 10 Krochmalna Street, instead of going into his house he goes to the neighboring home of his friend Shosha; in that way he will not have to face his anxious parents nor tell them that the assistant teacher has failed to walk him home. Besides, he wants to run away with Shosha, for he loves her. They will marry; he will study and become a professor. As soon as he suggests that they run away to Berlin, Shosha calmly asks what they will eat. With good humor, Singer recalled in an interview the event on which the story is based and said that he had forgotten about eating.

"Growing Up," the final story in the collection, describes Singer's first experiences with publishing. Black Feivel, a friend who was a year older, has purchased a printing set and he plans to print Isaac's first book, "Into the Wild Forest"—all sixteen pages of it. The publishing venture poignantly fails, however, for Feivel loses several parts to his printing set; Isaac cannot find the right kind of paper to use in his father's study, nor can he decide on the proper ending for the story. Finally they are unable to find a suitable place to print their masterpiece, for which they estimate some fifty thousand boys and girls in Warsaw would be willing to give two kopecks each. As doomed to failure as this venture was, it was successful in another way: the child Isaac retained the dream and goal of becoming a writer.

"The Lantuch," another story in the collection, is named for its central figure; a lantuch is a helpful imp in contrast to other malicious imps. While many storytellers have acquainted children with fairies and elves, "The Lantuch" presents more fully than Singer's previous ones this delightful creature who is usually invisible, living in a cellar, in a woodshed, or behind a stove. Attached to the family of the household where he lives, a lantuch is also friendly with crickets. (A cricket and his imp friend are the title characters in "Tsirtsur and Peziza" in *When Shlemiel Went to Warsaw*.) The lantuch in the story of the same name, however, is more serious-minded; devoted to his "family"—a bedridden widow with a blind daughter—he brings food, chops wood, draws water from the well, and does other good deeds for them.

This excellent collection was followed two years later by the publication of *Shosha* and a book of fictionalized memoirs, *A Young Man in Search of Love;* but perhaps the most important event of 1978 for Singer was the winning of the Nobel Prize for Literature. Singer's reaction to the news, as quoted in *Time* (16 October 1978), was "Are you sure?" Singer's lifetime achievement was recognized, ac-

cording to the spokesman for the Swedish Academy, for his "impassioned narrative art which, with roots in a Polish Jewish cultural tradition, brings universal human conditions to life." In accepting the award for his adult literature, Singer mentioned his writing for children, citing the reasons previously quoted for writing children's books. The entire acceptance speech has been published by Farrar, Straus and Giroux and is entitled *Nobel Lecture* (1979).

Also published in 1979 was another collection of stories, *Old Love*. In 1980 *Reaches of Heaven: A Story of Baal Shem Tov* was published as was *The Power of Light: Eight Stories for Hanukkah*. *Lost in America*, another volume of the fictionalized memoirs, was published in 1981. Singer regularly contributes fiction to the *Jewish Daily Forward*, and his stories are published in such magazines as the *New Yorker, Saturday Evening Post, Esquire, Harper's, Commentary, Mademoiselle, Playboy*, and *Atlantic Monthly*. He teaches for the winter months each year at the University of Miami, where he is a distinguished professor, and he lectures by invitation around the country.

This work load may account for Singer's delay in writing *The Power of Light*, which Irene Lieblich asked him to write for her to illustrate. The frame for the first story in this collection, "A Hanukkah Evening in My Parents' House," is autobiographical; in it Singer's father tells his children a story involving a miracle. Each of the eight stories in the collection tells of some type of miracle. In "The Extinguished Lights" the spirit of a young girl who died before Hanukkah keeps putting out the Hanukkah candles and later stops the wind so the candles can remain lighted. In "The Parakeet Named Dreidel," the first of Singer's children's stories to be set in America, a Yiddish-speaking parakeet is found by its original owners some nine years after being lost on a Hanukkah night. In "Menashe and Rachel" a young blind boy and girl sit by the Hanukkah lamp to tell stories to each other, and they learn that they can see, from the inside, from the heart. In "The Squire" a wealthy man attracted by an antique Hanukkah lamp gives 500 gulden as an advance payment on the lamp to the poor hungry family who owns it; upon his departure, the ailing father of the family is miraculously recovered.

The entire collection is more unified than the three preceding collections because of the many traditions of Hanukkah: the lighting of the candles, one a night for eight nights; the giving of gifts to the children; the serving of potato pancakes; and the playing of the dreidel by the children. This last, a game of chance, has a religious significance in that each of the four sides of the dreidel has a Hebrew letter—*nun, gimel, he,* and *shin;* these are the initials of words signifying the great miracle, referring to the victory of the Maccabees over the Greeks in 170 B.C. and the purification of the Holy Temple in Jerusalem from idols. To the children involved in the game Singer says in "A Hanukkah Evening," "*Gimel* meant winning, *nun* losing, *he* half winning, and *shin* another chance for the player."

The Power of Light, like Singer's other books, gives insight into many traditions and customs. In particular this book mentions traditional medical treatments: applying "leeches, cups, and bleeding" ("The Squire") or "cups or leeches or rub[bing] the patient with turpentine" ("Hershele and Hanukkah"). While many of Singer's books refer to leeches and bleeding, the application of cups is not an often-mentioned treatment. Singer, who had cups applied to him as a child, describes the process as heating a little glass in a fire and putting it immediately on the fleshy parts of the body, especially the back. The vacuum created pulls the skin up for a while. It is supposed to be good for the prevention of colds and is actually not unpleasant.

These eight Hanukkah stories show a departure in format from the previous short-story collections in that there are no Chelm stories. There are two which might be called animal stories—"The Parakeet Named Dreidel" and "Hershele and Hanukkah"—but the role of the human characters is as significant as, if not more so than, that of the parakeet and the fawn.

Structurally this collection is closer to *Naftali the Storyteller and His Horse, Sus* in its use of interpolated stories or frame stories. For example, the rabbi tells his children the story of a miracle within the context of a Hanukkah evening in the Singer home. Old Reb Berish from Bilgoray narrates "The Extinguished Lights," "The Squire," and "Hershele and Hanukkah." Yankele, as an old man, narrates the story of his youth in "Hanukkah in the Poorhouse." In the first two collections, Singer employs the frame device only once, in "Grandmother's Tale" from *Zlateh the Goat. Naftali the Storyteller and His Horse, Sus* makes use of both techniques more extensively. Zelig in the title story tells an interpolated tale as does Singer himself in the autobiographical "Growing Up." Frame stories include "The Lantuch" narrated by Aunt Yentl, and Singer himself introduces "Lemel and Tzipa" as a story told to him by his mother.

The Power of Light has received mostly favorable reviews. The most valid negative criticism, made by Marjorie Lewis in *School Library Journal* for December 1980, seems to be against the stories' excessive moralization and didacticism. However, this charge should not be directed at all eight stories, and her comments should be compared with others like those of Saul Maloff, whose review in the *New York Times Book Review* (18 January 1981) calls these tales a "small miracle of delight." The book received the Kenneth B. Smilen/Present Tense Literary Award for 1981. The illustrator also has been highly praised in most reviews for her ability to capture in visual form the essence of wonder and mystery of the cold but bright Hanukkah nights in Poland long ago.

Also set in Poland, probably in the sixteenth century, is *The Golem,* Singer's next book for children. Illustrated by Uri Shulevitz, it was published in 1982, the same year as *The Collected Stories of Isaac Bashevis Singer.* The golem, with its biblical antecedent in a verse from Psalms, is a huge creature of clay, created to help the Jews during a period of extreme danger. That danger occurs when a leading Jewish banker in Prague is jailed after being accused of killing the child of a wealthy count in order to have blood to make Passover matzohs. The pious Rabbi Lieb is visited by a mysterious stranger who gives him instructions for creating the golem, called Joseph, and for imbuing it with life by means of holy letters inscribed on its forehead. The golem comes to life, completes his assignment of finding the count's child, and the banker is freed.

Singer does not end his story here, however, but depicts the rabbi tempted by his wife to let Joseph live in order to move a huge stone and free a treasure with which she plans to help the poor and needy. Deciding to use Joseph for his own purposes, no matter how charitable, is clearly a mistake. The rabbi can no longer control Joseph, who causes many problems before he is finally returned to the earth from which he came. The rabbi's servant girl, Miriam, who had loved Joseph, disappears, never to be heard from again, after she helps the rabbi to subdue Joseph. This ending is most unusual for Singer, whose children's stories ordinarily have a happy close.

In an article for the *New York Times* (12 August 1984), Singer has compared the creation of a monster who later turned on his master with modern-day computers and robots. He links the legend of the golem with artistic creativity and says, "The artist must love the matter which he forms. He must believe in it, grant it life, bewitch it and be bewitched by it." The golem of his story is one who follows directions literally. When asked to carry well water to the house of the rabbi, he continues to do so until the house floods, for no one asked him to stop. The problems of a creator are clearly addressed here, as is the mystery of life. The conflict between good and evil and the power of love are also prevalent themes.

The Golem has received favorable reviews: *School Library Journal* praised both the tale and the illustrations; *Horn Book* commented on the "strange and powerful conclusion," the "understated humor," and "the ultimate sadness of the story" and included it on their Honor List for 1982. The American Library Association added it to their Notable Children's Books list for 1982.

Between *The Golem* in 1982 and *Stories for Children* in 1984, Singer published for adults *Yentl the Yeshiva Boy*, *The Penitent*, and *Love & Exile: A Memoir*. Since *Stories for Children*, he has published for adults *The Image and Other Stories* (1985).

Many of Singer's most delightful protagonists appear in *Stories for Children* (1984), a collection of thirty-six tales, which includes all tales previously published in *Naftali the Storyteller and His Horse, Sus*, *When Shlemiel Went to Warsaw*, *The Power of Light*, and others published individually; the following four are the only ones published for the first time for children: "The Day I Got Lost," "Ole and Trufa," "Topiel and Tekla," and "Tashlik." "The Day I Got Lost" introduces Professor Shlemiel, an American version of the Shlemiels of Chelm. The personification of the absent-minded professor, Shlemiel forgets his own address and cannot return to his home in New York City on the evening a birthday party is being given in his honor. He tries to telephone friends to help him but learns that they are at his house for the party. He meets a lost dog and befriends him. Just by chance, a friend on his way to the Shlemiels' party, sees the professor and the dog standing in the rain, and offers them a ride. The dog is given a home with the Shlemiels, and everything ends happily in spite of the professor's forgetfulness. Although one of the story's themes is kindness to animals, its main purpose seems to be humorous, satirizing professors who forget the obvious.

The humorous tone contrasts with the seriousness of "Ole and Trufa," which appeared earlier in the *Atlantic* and has been reprinted elsewhere. Originally published for adults, this story is for all ages. Its characters are two leaves, all that remain on a tree. They love one another and cling to the twig to be near each other. When the wind blows Ole down, a grief-stricken Trufa hangs on as long as she can through the bitter cold. In her loneliness she questions the meaning of life, looking upon the tree from which she hangs as a god. During the night she too is blown off and awakens, no longer alone, but a part of the universe, next to her beloved Ole. The power of love is the main theme in this simple, beautiful story, which could easily assume allegorical significance.

The inclusion of "Topiel and Tekla" in a children's volume is somewhat questionable for Singer, who usually advocates happy endings. While this story is a typical one for the author in its setting along the Vistula River where the devil Topiel lives and rules, the story is not a typical children's story in plot. A sixteen-year-old girl, Tekla, pregnant by a tramp, suffers the indignity of having her father plan to sacrifice the forthcoming child for a hog. The child will be given to Topiel to appease him, and the grateful community will donate the hog to Tekla's family. As time passes, Tekla, growing more and more isolated from society and her family, has no one to confide in. The pathetic child decides that her only recourse is to join Topiel at the bottom of the Vistula and plead for the life of her baby. She dreams that he will show her the kindness that she did not receive from anyone else. After her death, her parents are accused of hiding her somewhere and reneging on their agreement about sacrificing the child. They are reported to the Russians, who had warned these villagers earlier about sacrifices to the river. The Russians arrest Tekla's parents and others and send them to Siberia without a trial. The village suffers fires, storms, fogs, locusts, hunger, and sickness. In spite of the poetic justice, certain aspects of the story seem inappropriate for a young audience of the age for whom Singer usually writes, such as the girl pregnant out of wedlock, her wish for the devil to fondle her, the theme of revenge, and the criticism of Russian rule. The themes in this story of sacrifice, revenge, and even love (Tekla's for her unborn child) make it more appropriate for an adult or a young-adult reader.

"Tashlik," a story of a first love, would be especially interesting for young adults. The "I" narrator tells of his desire to meet Feigele, the watchmaker's daughter, but shyness prevents his approaching her. The young man, betrothed to the daughter of a rabbi, has a rich fantasy built up about Feigele living with him in exile, much as Singer felt exiled as a young man. The narrator also inexplicably believes that he will meet Feigele at the reading of the tashlik prayer on Rosh Hashanah. Feigele not only appears there but also asks him for help in finding the tashlik prayer in her prayer book. Knowing that they are the object of curiosity and that he will be rebuked for unseemly behavior when he gets home, the young man delights in his power and success at attracting Feigele. Youthful rebellion and first love make this story universal.

This volume concludes with the essay "Are Children the Ultimate Literary Critics?," first published in the *Chicago Sun Times*. Recounting Singer's beliefs about writing stories, it begins by reiterating his reasons for writing for children, and his three conditions for writing (a story to tell, the passion to write, and the conviction that only he could tell or write this story). He advocates that children read the Bible and question the world about them and that writers root their stories in their own environments and tell a good story, not just present a good message.

Singer seems to follow his own advice. His stories are uniquely his own. This collection, however, is different from the others, for it has no illustrations. Singer explains in the "Author's Note" that "the power of the word is the best medium to inform and entertain the minds of our youngsters" and that the biblical stories that he read so often as a child had no illustrations. The collection has been reviewed favorably, including a starred review for this "superb collection" by *School Library Journal*, and the comment "God's plenty" by Ethel Heins of *Horn Book*. The book has been included among the American Library Association's Notable Books for 1984.

Singer's fondness for children and his sensitivity to them can be seen in his desire to apologize publicly for not being able to answer all the letters he receives from them. He has said, "I love to write for children." Certainly the union of stories by a Nobel laureate storyteller with illustrations by some of the finest artists in the field of children's literature has produced outstanding books. But it is the content of the stories—the combination of folklore, fairy tale, religion, and imagination—that makes Singer's books unique and inimitable.

Interviews:

Joel Blocker and Richard Elman, "An Interview

with Isaac Bashevis Singer," *Commentary*, 36 (November 1963): 364-372;

Marshall Breger and Bob Barnhart, "A Conversation with Isaac Bashevis Singer," in *Isaac Bashevis Singer and the Eternal Past*, edited by Irving Buchen (New York: New York University Press, 1968), pp. 27-43;

Cyrene N. Pondrom, "Isaac Bashevis Singer: An Interview and a Biographical Sketch, Part I," *Contemporary Literature*, 10 (Winter 1969): 1-38; Part II (Summer 1969): 332-351;

David M. Anderson, "Isaac Bashevis Singer: Conversations in California," *Modern Fiction Studies*, 16 (Winter 1970-1971): 423-439;

Students from the University of Connecticut, "Isaac Bashevis Singer on Writing for Children," *Children's Literature*, 6 (1977): 9-16;

Katha Pollitt, "Creators on Creating: Isaac Bashevis Singer," *Saturday Review*, 7 (July 1980): 46-50;

Richard Burgin, *Conversations with Isaac Bashevis Singer* (Garden City: Doubleday, 1985).

Biographies:

Paul Kresh, *Isaac Bashevis Singer: The Magician of West 86th Street* (New York: Dial, 1979);

Edward Alexander, *Isaac Bashevis Singer* (Boston: Twayne, 1980).

References:

Marcia Allentuck, *The Achievement of Isaac Bashevis Singer* (Carbondale: Southern Illinois University Press, 1969);

David Bird and Maurice Carroll, "Turning 80 Three Times," *New York Times*, 3 September 1984, I: 29;

Irving Malin, *Isaac Bashevis Singer* (New York: Ungar, 1972);

Lance Morrow, "The Spirited World of I. B. Singer," *Atlantic Monthly*, 243 (January 1979): 39-43;

"Nobel Prize for I. B. Singer," *Time*, 112 (16 October 1978): 129;

Roy Eugene Toothaker, "Profile—Isaac Bashevis Singer: Good Luck for Children," *Language Arts*, 55 (April 1978): 527-533.

Doris Buchanan Smith

(1 June 1934-)

Hugh T. Keenan
Georgia State University

BOOKS: *A Taste of Blackberries,* illustrated by
Charles Robinson (New York: Crowell, 1973;
London: Heinemann, 1975);
Kick a Stone Home (New York: Crowell, 1974);
Tough Chauncey, illustrated by Michael Eagle (New
York: Morrow, 1974);
Kelly's Creek, illustrated by Alan Tiegreen (New
York: Crowell, 1975);
Up and Over (New York: Morrow, 1976);
Dreams & Drummers (New York: Crowell, 1978);
Salted Lemons (New York: Four Winds, 1980);
Last Was Lloyd (New York: Viking, 1981);
Moonshadow of Cherry Mountain (New York: Four
Winds, 1982);
The First Hard Times (New York: Viking, 1983);
Laura Upside-Down (New York: Viking Kestrel,
1984);
Return to Bitter Creek (New York: Viking Kestrel,
1986).

Doris Buchanan Smith (photo by Tim Brantley)

PERIODICAL PUBLICATION: "Honey in the
Heart of a Turtle," *Advocate* (University of
Georgia), 1 (Fall 1981): 10-18.

Though her books deal realistically with contemporary problems, Doris Buchanan Smith resists
being typecast as an "issues author." When an Atlanta friend remarked that her previous books had
dealt with "death, divorce, drugs, delinquency, and
dyslexia," she dropped the notion that the protagonist of *Last Was Lloyd* would have diabetes. Neither
would the next hero/heroine have epilepsy as one
teacher had suggested. Smith explains that her
books begin with a character and then the character
has problems, because people do in real life. She
does not invent a character because she wants to
write about a problem. In fact, she came to be a
children's writer by accident (or gentle coercion).
As she says, "I came to write for children as innocent as a virgin, not even knowing that children's
literature was a field. I sort of stumbled into it, or
was pushed, in one of those lucky accidents we have
sometimes, when someone suggested that an adult
short story that I had written about a child should
be a story for a child. Child freak that I was, I was
amazed it hadn't occurred to me to write for children."

Smith had wanted to be a writer since age
eleven, and after her five children and over a score
of foster children were in school, she began being
serious about a career. After she had tried writing
poetry and adult short stories, she audited a course
in writing children's literature at an annual writers'
conference at St. Simon's Island, Georgia; the
teacher, Helen Diehl Olds, requested she write a
children's story like everyone else in the class. Her
mild protests were ineffective, so she wrote the
story, and the experience determined her profession.

Her first book, which remains unpublished,
is an adventure story; her second, *A Taste of Blackberries* (1973), brought her success and established
her reputation as a sensitive and skilled delineator
of character. Though she did not know it, she had

broken a taboo in the field of children's literature at that time in writing about the death of a child's playmate. The book details a young boy's feelings when his friend suddenly dies and does so without providing easy, simplistic, pious, or contrived consolations. Critics and the public at large praised its honesty and sensitivity.

Her other eleven books have dealt directly with other serious topics usually excluded from juvenile fiction at the time they were written. Sex, death, drugs, runaways, handicaps, abused children, divorce—her books explore the gamut of contemporary issues. Smith presents a world in which individuals come to assume responsibility for their own actions and to realize that there are not always happy endings in life, though there are choices to be made.

Doris Smith was born in Washington, D.C. She spent her earliest years in a Maryland suburb but moved at age nine to Atlanta, Georgia. Because her family lived in a house one-half block over the county line, she attended the county school, unlike the neighborhood children who went to the city school. Immediately she was labeled an outsider by the other children, both in her neighborhood and at school. This setting and part of the author's experience were used in *Up and Over* (1976) and *Salted Lemons* (1980). Atlanta and Brunswick, Georgia, have been the principal locales for her other stories about city or small-town children.

Both her parents, Charles A. and Flora Robinson Buchanan, followed business careers. She grew up with two brothers, one older and the other younger. She attended South Georgia College in Douglas, Georgia, and took courses in journalism. When she married R. Carroll Smith on 18 December 1954, they planned to have a large family. Subsequently, they had five children, four of their own and one they reared from age twelve, in addition to more than a score of foster children. Smith, who was divorced from her husband in 1977, now laughs that she had an overactive maternal gland.

Though her various children kept her in touch with contemporary issues, her characters come more from what she calls the essences of her own childhood. She recalls that *A Taste of Blackberries* took shape only when she set it in her own Maryland neighborhood. She is generally successful at verbalizing internal feelings and conflicts: as one of her publishers has claimed, she is able "to slide inside the skins of her characters, whether it is a nine-year-old boy who has a learning disability and whose classmates consider him dumb [*Kelly's Creek*] or whether it is a fifteen-year-old girl who is

shy and a little reluctant to grow up [*Kick a Stone Home*]."

When critics infrequently fault her books, it is for their issue-orientation and lack of well-made plots, but perhaps the episodic structure of her novels is simply a reflection of the apparent plotlessness of life itself, which she vividly captures in the lives of her central characters. There is not always a "why" for what happens in life.

Because she played basketball in high school, hiked, rode a bicycle, and continues to enjoy outdoor activities such as canoeing, walking, and bicycling, she writes convincingly about the sports and play of active children. She divides her time now between the south Georgia beach and the north Georgia mountains, living during the fall and winter at her large family home in Brunswick and spending summers alone in a simple A-frame cabin just four miles over the Georgia line in North Carolina.

A Taste of Blackberries (1973) was an ALA Notable Book and winner of the Child Study Association Award in 1973. It won the Georgia Children's Book Award in 1974, the Sue Hefley Award of the Louisiana Association of School Librarians in 1978, as well as the Children's Best Book Award in Holland. The book focuses on the guilt and loss suffered by the unnamed narrator when his best friend, Jamie, "a show-off and a clown," dies from an allergic reaction after being stung by bees. The sensitive, introspective character of the narrator emerges as he recalls the daring, mugging, fun-loving nature of his friend.

Doris Smith says she discovered the importance of setting when she wrote the book, which takes place in a Maryland neighborhood. In subsequent stories, settings have played even stronger roles. The second thing she discovered was that events in a story sometimes determine themselves. The death of Jamie was one of those accidents that pop into an author's mind. The book was originally going to be about friendship, and the incident of Jamie stirring up the bees' nest was intended to be only amusing, one of those childish pranks which backfires. Instead, it occurred to her that Jamie would die from the stings, but she resisted this tragic turn of events and put the story aside. Later, as she completed it, she enhanced the story with a realistic and honest account of how children and parents view death in different ways.

The narrator at first denies Jamie's death, then grieves alone, feels isolated, and refuses to eat, while the adults go through the familiar rituals, visiting the family, bringing food, caring for the

Frontispiece and title page for Smith's first novel, which broke a taboo in children's literature by focusing on the effect a child's death has on his playmate (Crowell)

younger children, and attending the funeral service and burial. At the conclusion of the story, the narrator establishes a bond with Jamie's mother by bringing her a basket of the blackberries the two boys had intended to pick when they were ripe. In turn Jamie's mother asks him to visit now and then and to slam the screen door as the two boys used to do, despite her chidings. The brief story ends with the protagonist challenging his dead companion: " 'Race you,' I called to him and I ran up the hill." The memory of his friend has become part of his present life, not a suppressed incident of the past.

The telling of the story is natural, unforced, and sympathetic to the young boy's point of view. He learns to accept death as a fact, without relying on the clichés society offers. The black-and-white ink-and-charcoal drawings by Charles Robinson are as simple and honest as the story.

In two books published in 1974, Doris Smith deals with the alienation experienced by two quite different characters. In *Kick a Stone Home*, the protagonist is a fifteen-year-old Atlanta girl named

Sara Jane Chambers, who feels alienated and shy because she has not adjusted to her parents' divorce and her move three years ago to a different neighborhood. To shield herself, she has invented a game with elaborate rules for kicking a stone home each day after school. She lives in a Tarleton Terrace apartment with her mother, who works in a real estate office, two brothers, Donnie and Lowe, and her dog Tally.

The story unfolds in the final months of the school year. Sara's best female friend, Kay, is quite unlike her. Sara is sports minded and enjoys playing baseball, football, and basketball with the neighborhood boys; Kay is feminine and flirts with them instead. Sara's male chum is Sammy Carlisle, the leader of the group Sara has played sports with for three years. At school she has to deal with an unpleasant teacher, Miss Parmalee Dickerson, "known for her bleach blonde hair and her too-fancy-for-school-teaching-clothes," who has assigned her the whole history book to outline.

Thus at the critical period of adolescence, Sara, who wants to become a veterinarian, is torn between her desire to remain one of the boys or to follow her mother's wishes and the example of Kay by becoming more feminine and dating. As the story progresses, Sara comes out of her shell, learning that Kay's parents are also divorced, and comes to accept her father's second wife, whom Sara calls F. W. (Father's Wife). She also begins to date, initiated by a friendly outing with Sammy to a movie. She soon receives the flattering attentions of John Dutton, a football player, but when he persists in touching her breast at school, she slaps him and becomes the talk of her classmates. A formal date with Bill Sluker, the son of a friend of Sara's mother, goes little better, as Bill is imperceptive, forward, pushy, and too sexually aggressive. Finally she finds a more relaxed friendship with Francis Farnesworth, a classmate.

The episodic plot includes a thwarted burglary of Sara's apartment and her suspicion that Dave Kellerman, a friendly neighbor who is a married college student, is guilty; her becoming an assistant to Dr. Montini, a veterinarian; and her training of a new dog after her old one was hit by a car. At the end of the story, Sara has become both more mature and more feminine and less self-absorbed. She is comfortable with her athletic abilities, her vocational interests, and with her life as a normal teenaged girl.

Tough Chauncey (1974) has a male protagonist, also deeply affected by divorce, but, unlike Sara, Chauncey is a poor white who is much less admirable on the surface and in his relations with others. He is scrappy, delinquent, belligerent, and failing in school because he cannot read, will not obey or pay attention to adults or get along with his classmates. He is physically abused by his grandfather and neglected by his divorced mother as he alternates between his grandparents' house and her temporary apartments. The book's opening provides a terse description of Chauncey, his physical appearance as well as his mental outlook: "Chauncey Childs was small for thirteen and as thin and tight as a guy wire. He walked with the confidence of a boy who knew he could whip anyone twice his size."

Chauncey's only friend is Jack Levitt, a black boy also from a broken home and now living with a married sister. Together they are the "two toughest guys at school," but their friendship is a wary and cautious one, especially after Jack, known as "Black Jack," sets Chauncey up to be blamed for stealing a bike.

Chauncey's grandparents work at the freezer plant in Rambleton, a small town in middle Georgia. The grandfather is especially harsh, beating the boy and locking him in his room. His mother is constantly on the move, changing apartments, telephone numbers, husbands, and boyfriends, but she is repeatedly drawn back by her immature emotional dependence on her parents. The men in her life, Chauncey's father and most of the others, have been drunkards. Chauncey muses wryly that if one "used all of her names, she was Frances Elizabeth Sellers Childs Daniels Allegiano." She has had two other children, but one has died and the other was taken by the father.

Though externally Chauncey is tough, inside he is sensitive and in search of loving, responsible adults to parent him, something he cannot find in a rigid grandfather, an overly pious grandmother, and a weak, unstable mother. His sensitivity is shown in his continuing protection of a kitten, "Little Orange," when the rest of the litter is shot by his grandfather.

Another central character is a neighbor of his mother's, whom he calls "Fat Lady" and who later calls herself "Aunt Ann," claiming to be a legal relative when she, instead of his grandparents or mother, takes Chauncey to the hospital after he injures his leg trying to hop a freight train. From playing hooky, shoplifting, stealing money from his mother's purse for cigarettes, quarreling and fighting with other children, and setting a field on fire while smoking, Chauncey eventually elevates to the ill-fated attempt to catch a ride on the train; but the serious leg injury finally jars him into taking responsibility for his own fate, as he realizes the adults in his life are undependable.

Chauncey wishes to model himself after Johnny Cash, but he cannot read the story about his hero in a popular magazine. With the aid of Jack Levitt, he hides out in an empty garage for three days and then takes a taxi to a social service agency, which may place him in a foster home. He takes his parting line from the story about Johnny Cash, which Jack has read to him, declaring "You haven't seen the complete me yet!" The inconclusive ending shows that Chauncey has become more whole and that there is hope that he will get both an education and a proper home.

Kelly's Creek (1975), dedicated by the author to the men in her life, "my father, my husband, my sons," deals with the social and educational problems of nine-year-old Kelly O'Brian. Handicapped by dyslexia, Kelly had to repeat first grade. Now in the third grade, not only is he considered slow and stupid by regular classmates, but he is also behind the others in the special class he is attending.

Kelly finds school to be uncongenial, and his stern parents are disappointed. His father, who would like a son who could play ball and be a scout, is especially frustrated because Kelly prefers to dabble in the creek in their backyard in Brunswick, Georgia.

Kelly's interest in the tidal creek and his unlikely friendship with Phillip, a junior college student who is doing marine research, do provide him an educational outlet, though. Phillip teaches Kelly to identify the wildlife, especially various kinds of fiddler crabs. When he reports successfully on this subject to his regular class, they recognize that he is not really slow, and he regains briefly the friendship of Zack, with whom he used to play.

Both the biological description of the fertile marsh life and the sterile therapeutic exercises that Kelly must repeat to overcome dyslexia are authentically detailed. As the story ends, Kelly's interest in the marsh life has opened his mind to formal learning and to overcoming his visual problems. The descriptions of his thoughts, which often focus on fantasy, are well done, and the simple black-and-white pen-and-ink illustrations by Alan Tiegreen reflect the realism of the story and the isolation of Kelly.

Up and Over (1976), a rite-of-passage book of the type popular in the 1970s, is set in Atlanta in 1974, the year that streaking was popular and that Hank Aaron hit his record-breaking home run. Drug addiction, racial tension, teenage marriage and pregnancy, overrigorous parents, and the problems of an athletic but slightly retarded high school student are some of the things which frame the simpler struggle of Kim Kalambach, a high school senior and track runner, as he chooses whether to go to college or to become a professional photographer.

The book covers three weeks, the climax of Kim's senior year, through the end of track season and the regional and state meets, the Special Olympics, and finally graduation itself. The five friends of seventeen-year-old Kim are Robert Earl Sapp, who has quit the track team for drugs and a freer life; and teammates Bryon "Waxy" Baker, a transfer from Waxahachie, Texas, who has to marry his pregnant girlfriend secretly there; Devo Justice, a born-again Christian; Willie Demott, a black who has recently joined the team; and Mitchell Mullins, who is the slightly retarded and overprotected equipment manager. There are several outstanding minor characters in the novel, especially Miss Treadwell, the senior English teacher, an old maid

who is in love with words and has the class repeatedly practice vocabulary drills.

The episodic plot includes scenes of Kim shaving his head for spring pledge week, Robert Earl, high on drugs, eating a snake's eyes, Mitchell running away from home and his victory at a Special Olympics meet, Bryon announcing his marriage, and Robert Earl streaking the graduation dance. The reader also gets a real sense of the details of running track and how the runners feel about the sport. Kim's avocation of photography reveals itself as one way he keeps life, family, and friends at a distance.

By the end of the book, all the problems raised, such as drug abuse and teenage pregnancy, have not been solved, but Kim has decided not to plod through the college education that his parents want for him but to pursue photography instead. Also, he has decided to engage himself with life rather than just take pictures of it.

The descriptions of the Special Olympics, which Kim helps coach, and its participants and spectators are very good, but the culminating and concerted protest action by the student body over the principal's initial refusal to let Robert Earl receive a diploma due to the streaking episode is not convincing. Mainly, the story reveals Kim's consciousness of his changing relationships with his family and friends as graduation approaches and his awareness, due to his involvement in the Special Olympics, that he must help himself.

Dreams & Drummers (1978), dedicated to Doris Smith's "sundelightful" daughter Susan, is a charming departure from her previous novels, though the book *is* about growing up. Its protagonist, Stephanie Stone, a fourteen-year-old ninth grader and the lead drummer in the junior high school band, finds herself at the beginning of the story four paces ahead of the rest in the practice drill. Actually, the other drummers are off count and she is really in step. Stephanie's "problem" is that she does not have the normal problems of teenagers.

Instead the characters around her have problems. Mr. Brewster, the band director, is a male chauvinist who would like to see her lose the first chair. Otis Wentzel, the third best drummer and a rude pest, wants to win her chair, despite the fact that her only real rival is her friend "Way-Tall" Paul Roberts, who is a keen, flashy, black drummer. Her best friend is Easter, a black flutist in the band, but another friend, Mary Bennett, is a bland, overprotected, conventional ninth grader who is jealous of Stephanie's awards in the science fair.

Stephanie's adventures and misadventures at school and at home take second place to the actions of others. Mary Bennett rebels against her mother, runs away, and then wins the grand prize at the science fair. Sixteen-year-old Seth, Stephanie's brother, runs away too but returns home. Her younger brother, Simon, age thirteen, is jealous of her privileges, especially her learner's driving permit.

Because she is mature, interested in science, playing the drums, studying nature, writing poetry, and riding bikes, Stephanie finds herself "out of step" with both boys and girls her age. She tries being normal by acting up in class, doing her work late, and by flirting with the boys. Her note writing to James Marbury gains her a boyfriend, but she then decides that she is not yet ready for dating.

The unfolding of these events in the small coastal town of Brunswick, from the fall through Christmas and New Year's holidays, does not have much suspense. The events happen around and not to Stephanie. Unlike parents in other books, Stephanie's are liberated and understanding, so there is no conflict there, but the story reveals much about the process of growing up: maturity, individualism, and parenting roles. The conflicts the book does explore are the mild ones of upper-middle-class, suburban families everywhere. Some of the chapter titles, such as "Eagles are Great, but They Can't Swim" and "The Queen of Hearts is a Card," reveal the light and ironic tone of the book.

Salted Lemons (1980), dedicated to "Roy Rogers, with whom I fell in love at the Sylvan Theater in 1943," is a partially autobiographical story which recounts the author's experiences upon moving to Atlanta as a child. Ten-year-old Darby Bannister finds herself simultaneously ridiculed as a Yankee, because she has recently moved from Washington, D.C., and a country bumpkin, because her family lives in a house just outside the city limits. Having moved from a progressive school in the nation's capital, she finds it hard to accept a traditional school system and small-town prejudices.

More grievous prejudices affect other characters in the story, which takes place during World War II. Yoko, Darby's newly made Japanese-American friend who lives across the street, is forced to resettle with her parents in Florida. The neighborhood grocer, Mr. Kaigler, is accused by children and some adults of being a spy because he is German. Gordon, the leader of the neighborhood gang of kids, keeps Darby, an "outsider," from participating in group activities.

Darby is bright, proud, sure of herself, even arrogant at times. She secretly refers to herself as "Queen of the World," but gradually she learns how to make friends and become accepted by the neighborhood and its people. The story shows how people can coexist by exercising tolerance. Darby's mother is a Methodist who promptly joins the choir of her new church, but her father is an agnostic who stays home on Sundays. One of Darby's best friends is Fancy Potter, a poor white of fundamentalist religion, and another is Jeannine, the daughter of millenarians who rent Yoko's house.

This novel about prejudice, alienation, and friendship is nicely symbolized by the salted lemons shared first by Yoko and Darby and then by Darby and Jeannine. Darby at first thought the lemons a strange fruit but quickly learns to enjoy the experience of communal sharing as much as the taste. Eventually, Darby comes to realize "There were bad times as well as good, but she was glad to be there." As the *Kirkus Reviews* critic said, the book gives a "sense of how it was to be ten in the Forties, how it is to be ten and new in town, and how the pervasive in-group prejudices guide playground society."

Last Was Lloyd (1981) is about another bright outsider, but twelve-year-old Lloyd Albert, a pampered, overweight sixth grader, is last in everything, especially sports. The butt of classroom jokes, he retaliates by letting the team down, tripping and hitting other children, barely getting by in school assignments, and by being a glutton in the cafeteria. At home, his divorced mother, who works in a shrimp plant, caters to his every whim, calling him "Baby," tying his shoes, and letting him skip school, determine the dinner menus, and lounge in his bath watching television while she prepares his meals. But at softball practice with his mother's team, Lloyd is an expert batter, something he keeps hidden at school.

At first Lloyd joins the class in jeering at Ancil, a new girl in school who has a freckled face and spaghetti hair, but her sharp tongue and keen insight into Lloyd's weaknesses not only humble him but soon they are friends. Gradually Lloyd comes out of his shell of isolation and fantasy which is symbolized by the olive shell from the beach which he carries in his pocket. He loses weight by running laps with his mother's softball team; he even hits a home run at a class birthday party. He insists on more independence from his mother, and at the same time he is more thoughtful of her. Finally he gives his most precious possession, the olive shell, to Ancil. In Lloyd, the author shows the twin values

(Crowell)

(Four Winds)

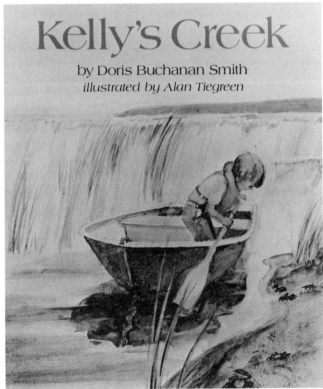

(Viking)

Dust jackets for three of Smith's novels which treat a particular problem which children and adolescents often have to confront, such as obesity, adjustment to a new neighborhood or school, and dyslexia

of being independent and also being part of a group.

Moonshadow of Cherry Mountain (1982), a dog story set in the North Carolina mountains, marks some significant shifts in the author's usual material and point of view. It is more a theme book than one based on character. The point of view is principally that of Moonshadow, a Labrador retriever, though it does shift to that of two children, Greg and Clara. As the theme is one of the establishment and adjustment of animal and human territorial boundaries, the mountain setting is highly detailed.

As the story opens, Greg, the adopted fifteen-year-old son of schoolteachers Grant and Peg Riley, has had with his dog Moonshadow free range of Cherry Mountain for six years. They have accustomed paths and rituals, including chasing a wild fox, which perhaps preys on the chickens of their only neighbor, Mr. Cherry, after whose grandfather the mountain is named. This free life is increasingly circumscribed for both boy and dog when the Rileys adopt nine-year-old Clara, who does not feel comfortable in the country and is afraid of and allergic to Moonshadow. As a consequence, the dog is banished outside.

More constraints arise when other people buy adjoining property, build houses, bring in their families and pets, and establish their boundaries. One family consists of a hippie couple, Theo and Karen, who are potters and have a female shelty named Gally. Though the dog is friendly, Moonshadow treats her as an enemy. The Rileys take exception to the couple's counterculture dress and primitive house, a modified A-frame without electricity or indoor toilet. To make matters worse, Theo and Karen refrigerate their food in a running brook on their property, from which Moonshadow steals it as a game.

The second family to move onto the mountain consists of the five Katzes: mother, father, two girls, and a boy, who bring with them several cats which Moonshadow terrorizes, except for McTeer, a large red tabby. The Katzes are not friendly people and they threaten Moonshadow if he should continue to bother their cats; as a consequence, he is temporarily locked up.

A third family builds a house right in the middle of the shortcut Moonshadow uses to overtake the Rileys' car. For a while he persists despite the construction, but the owner's black German shepherd soon bluffs him away. Out of frustration, Moonshadow attacks a skunk with the predictable result. This incident provides the turning point of the novel, for Theo shampoos the dog and treats

the odor with tomato juice. As a consequence, Moonshadow accepts Theo and Karen and their shelty.

Other conflicts between the humans are resolved by neighborly help, and at the end of the story, animals and humans have established their territorial lines and rights and have learned to respect, if not to like, each other.

As territory is so important to the theme, this novel is filled with concise nature descriptions of land and animals, including an old mica mine, a fox, and a hawk. The characterization of the people, however, seems somewhat sketchy. For example, we never learn what the Rileys teach or how the Katzes make a living, but the author's thematic approach is successful. The *Horn Book* stated that "while utilizing strong action and types, rather than stereotypes, the narrative evades the sentimentality which often plagues stories of both animals and adoption and develops the themes of tolerance and accommodation with evenhandedness and insight."

The First Hard Times (1983), a companion book to *Last Was Lloyd*, focuses on the adjustment problems of Ancil Witherspoon. This twelve-year-old girl resists accepting her mother's new husband, Harvey Hutton, and the family's move to the Georgia coastal town of Hanover. She clings instead to a desire to return to Juniper, Georgia, forty miles inland, and the home of her paternal grandparents where she used to live. Ancil also retains the futile hope that her real father, Alexander, missing in action in Vietnam for eleven years, will return.

The story covers a few tense, climactic summer weeks. Ancil's mother and her three sisters, Zan, Margaret, and Lyddy, have adjusted to the move and blandishments of affection by Harvey after only six weeks. Ancil stubbornly resists and lashes out at Harvey's overearnest attempts to win her affection. Silently she makes fun of the local paper, the *Hanover Historian*, which he owns and runs.

Both the Hutton and the grandparent Witherspoon establishments are liberated, upper-middle-class homes. Her mother, Laura, works as a commercial artist in her home studio. Grandfather Witherspoon is an architect, and his wife, Gran, is a potter who also has a home studio. Both groups rotate responsibility for meal preparation or each fixes his own. Margaret works at Harvey's paper. Lyddy, who loves animals, is happily employed at the Humane Society. Ancil becomes progressively estranged from these happily involved individuals, and only Lloyd remains her friend, able to communicate with her despite her silence and hostility.

region / sphere / realm / area / orb / circuit / domain /
bailiwick / dominion /

7/21

MOONSHADOW OF CHERRY MOUNTAIN -- Running down the mountain   ①

On weekday.
~~In the~~ mornings, ~~also~~   going east
~~then~~ the family car pulled away from the house, ~~it headed~~
for a quarter of a mile before it   moved   The black labrador
~~east~~ then hairpin ~~turned~~ and ~~drove~~ west. ~~Moonshadow~~ galloped
through the woods   hed
~~straight~~ down the north ridge and ran ~~was running~~ ~~down the road~~ ahead   (over) The car overtook
along   dog,
of the car ~~by the time it was on~~ the westward road. ∧ Near the bottom
of the mountain the dog, ~~who was by~~ now ~~trailing the car~~, cut ~~off~~
and again came   ahead of
across woods and field ~~to come~~ out ~~alongside~~ the car after it had
the final   R "Goodbye, Moonshadow," the boy
followed the road around ~~one more~~ turn.   "yeah, over
~~Greg pounded the side of the car + shouted encouragement~~   Moonshad
~~At the edge of the paved road, she stopped.~~ ② As a puppy,   he called
the dog ∧   on the
when she had first learned to escort the family's daily descent,

the edge of   there had been much scolding and naysaying before she learned that
this was her / The run to here was just over a mile ① Standing   between the pavement +
~~boundary limit~~ ~~she must not go any further.~~ ∧ ~~she stood~~ on ~~the~~ knoll, ~~and~~ watched   the gra
territory. familiar   La   Moonsh
the ∧ blue car wind its way across ~~the~~ Cherry Valley + diminish~~ing~~ in the

distance. ~~Then, as though filling herself with the view, she~~ ~~XXXX~~   stood a whil
~~longer at this~~   northwestern
~~continued standing a while~~ perimeter of her territory.
        In front
~~ahead~~ of her was ~~Cherry Valley~~, a geometric patchwork of greens +
browns.   were dots of yellow on the ~~green~~ corn ~~newly plan~~
                                grass + red clay
~~fields~~ Huge rolled bales of hay ~~dotting the~~ hillside. and the green-
                And all around ~~It in the background was~~
blue-purple ~~humps mountains~~ of the southern ~~Blue Ridge mountains~~
                                        Appalachidant –
~~beyond~~   mountains.

                was her own particular domain
        Behind her ~~were the several hundred acres of her own~~ ~~per~~
particular ~~pres~~   Nearby, on the approach to the
~~small mountain~~, (Cherry Mountain) ~~and behind them was~~ was Mr.   mountain,
        and his
Cherry ~~whose grandfather had once owned it all.~~ ~~when the family~~
                                                        It was Mr.
~~left for the day, Mr. Cherry~~ and attendant cows and chickens. ~~were~~
Cherry's grandfather for whom the mountain was named + only he
~~the only domestic things that moved on the mountain.~~ The Riley's .
knew more about the mountain than Moonshadow.
~~owned nearly twenty-five acres near the top of the~~ gentle mountain,
the ~~most~~   then Moonshadow
~~[the dog~~ had roamed
~~But~~ for six years ∧ ~~Moonshadow had roved the~~ ~~entire~~ mountain ~~as~~, nothing
∧   had changed except the seasons, + the
~~though she were the queen~~   weather and the population of the woodland
Beginning   creatures.
sentence.

(left margin, vertical) With the family gone, Moonshadow the dog was the only domestic being on the entire mountain.

Revised typescript page for Moonshadow of Cherry Mountain *(by permission of the author)*

The plot is framed by two family outings to the beach. In the first, Ancil shows her hostility toward Harvey; in the second she evidences her acceptance of him as her father. Overall, the book's characters are well drawn and individualized. Lloyd's growth in skills and independence counterpoint Ancil's self-restricted life, and his wistful memories of his own less attractive stepfathers are in opposition to Ancil's resistance to accepting Harvey. The book's descriptive details are as colorful and exact as the expensive stained glass parrot, a present from Harvey, that hangs in the window of Ancil's newly painted room. The psychological description of Ancil's struggle, including her reaction to the redecoration of her father's former bedroom in her grandparents' house and to Harvey's showing her the picture of his wife and two daughters, who were all killed in an automobile accident, is accurate without being clinical.

By the end of the novel, such details as Gran's making a ceramic totem pole topped with the life mask of each member of the family and Ancil's elaborate and cooperatively built sand castle at the beach have contributed to the resolution of the theme of alienation and unity. Overall, the psychological portrait of Ancil's grief, anger, and adjustment gives strength to the book. As the *School Library Journal* reviewer said, "Smith's handling of this difficult subject is neither sentimental nor oversimplified." As a result of her achievement, the book has been named an ALA Notable Book.

Laura Upside-Down (1984), a rather complex, episodic novel set in a south Georgia town, also explores the theme of tolerance and the resolution of conflicts within the family and the neighborhood. The central character, Laura Catherine Frazier, known as Cat, is most happy seeing the world upside down, by hanging in a large tree. Her close friends are her same age, ten years old, but they are quite different in their beliefs. Zipporah Greengold comes from an orthodox Jewish family, Anna Banner's family is fundamentalist Christian, and Laura's family is agnostic. Needless to say, the values of the girls clash despite their close friendship.

The novel is built around a series of parties (Halloween, Thanksgiving, Hanukkah, and Christmas) that the girls give at each other's house. Learning about the origin of each holiday helps them to understand their differences better. Along the way, they come to realize that Daurice, an elderly neighbor woman, is not a witch, as they have assumed, but she is mildly disturbed.

The novel is filled with minor characters and subplots, some of more interest than the main char-

acters and plot. For example, Gi Gi, Zipporah's grandmother who is intolerant of Christians, has a very good scene in which she plays, and wins, a hopscotch game with the girls, despite the fact that she is in a wheelchair. Though she will compete with non-Jews, she continues to refuse to be at the table with them. The pathetic story of Daurice and her lasting guilt over the death of her twin Maurice in childhood overshadows the guilt that Laura feels when her own seven-year-old brother Mark and Anna's brother Haim are kidnapped, though they are released.

The messages and didacticism of the novel reduce the three girls to researchers rather than doers. They are continually busy looking up information in the library about how to do things, how to plan games for the parties, and how to understand the meanings of the holidays they celebrate, but though the novel is loosely structured, it has been praised for handling "deeply troubling problems—of sin and guilt—with verve and uncommon understanding." The most honest thing about the novel is that characters retain their prejudices and differences to the end. There is no false conversion on anyone's part.

Return to Bitter Creek (1986) is the story of a twelve-year-old girl who was born in the mountains but was taken away when she was two years old. In the novel she returns with her family and faces the problems of adjustment to the conservative mores of that society.

Doris Smith continues to work on other projects. One is finalizing the manuscript of "Karate Dancer," in which the protagonist, a fourteen-year-old male practitioner of the martial arts, falls in love with a dancer at school. A new novel in progress represents a shift away from Doris Smith's realistic stories of contemporary teenagers. In "Voyager," a part-fantasy, a girl who has been traumatized by being held hostage is recovering in a hospital. A teacher introduces her to Norse mythology and the stories of Freyr and his marvelous boat Skidbladnir. Suddenly she is wafted into the violent Norse world. Her adventures there help her to cope with the violence she has experienced in the real world.

Smith is also pursuing projects outside the realm of children's literature, writing occasional feature articles and developing a couple of ideas for adult novels, though she says she will never stop writing for children. As a writer, Smith's greatest asset is her effectiveness at portraying the inner life of her protagonists; whether they are nine or seventeen, boy or girl, she writes assuredly and hon-

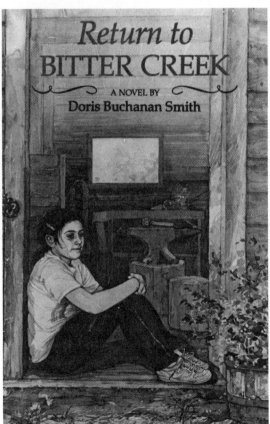

Dust jackets for Smith's two most recent novels (Viking Kestrel)

estly from that character's point of view, and, consequently, critics and ordinary readers have responded well to the integrity of her novels for children.

Reference:
"They Write the Books," *Atlanta Journal and Constitution*, 5 April 1981, pp. 52-53.

Mildred D. Taylor

(1943-)

David A. Wright
Bryan College

BOOKS: *Song of the Trees,* illustrated by Jerry Pinkney (New York: Dial, 1975);
Roll of Thunder, Hear My Cry (New York: Dial, 1976; London: Gollancz, 1976);
Let the Circle Be Unbroken (New York: Dial, 1981; London: Gollancz, 1982).

PERIODICAL PUBLICATION: "Newbery Award Acceptance Speech," *Horn Book,* 53 (August 1977): 401-409.

Mildred Taylor rose to prominence as an author of children's books in the mid 1970s. With the publication of her novel *Roll of Thunder, Hear My Cry* (1976) and its subsequent winning of the Newbery Medal, Taylor achieved recognition as a writer able to portray an accurate and believable picture of a southern, rural black family in the 1930s by addressing her readers with honesty and integrity and by presenting them fully realized characters. Much of Taylor's inspiration for her writing comes from her father's stories about his family and their experiences in rural Mississippi, and though the settings of her novels may suggest writings of a regional nature, her themes are, in fact, universal and timeless.

The second daughter of Wilbert Lee and Deletha M. Taylor, Mildred Taylor was born in Jackson, Mississippi, in 1943. Taylor's childhood years were spent in Toledo, Ohio, where her father moved his wife and two daughters, Wilma and Mildred, a few months after Mildred was born. Taylor's early experiences listening to her father's stories of aunts, uncles, and grandparents, told at home as well as on the front porches of relatives' homes on summer trips of the Taylor family to

Mildred Taylor

Mississippi, had a profound effect upon her: when her father spoke, she imagined that she was the storyteller. Taylor realized that the stories were about people who had courage, dignity, and self-respect, in spite of the efforts of the white society around them to strip them of their self-worth.

Listening attentively to her father's and others' stories made Taylor critically aware of the discrepancies between what she had read about blacks in history books and what she had heard in the stories told in her family. Taylor states that she does not remember when her daydreams about being a storyteller became more than daydreams, but she says, "By the time I entered high school, I had a driving compulsion to paint a truer picture of Black people. . . . I wanted to show a Black family united in love and pride, of which the reader would like to be a part."

Although the Toledo schools she attended were integrated city-wide, Taylor often found herself the only black student in college preparatory courses. She was intensely competitive, especially in her major area of English. Her senior yearbook prophecy read: "The well-known journalist Mildred Taylor is displaying her Nobel Prize-winning novel. . . ." Mildred Taylor's early aspiration to be a writer was but one of the goals she set for herself. She set her mind specifically on a Peace Corps assignment in Ethiopia, and after graduation from the University of Toledo, she received an assignment to teach English and history to Ethiopian children.

Upon returning to the United States, Taylor pursued further studies in the School of Journalism at the University of Colorado. During this time she became a member of the Black Student Alliance, helped create a black studies program, and continued to work in the program for two years after receiving her master's degree. During the years of studying and traveling, Taylor said she found herself "turning again and again to the stories I heard in my childhood. I was deeply drawn to the roots of that inner world which I knew so well, yet I could never capture in writing the warmth of it, the deep emotions and strength of those people who were so vivid in my mind."

As Taylor struggled with writing a story that her father told her about the cutting of some trees on the family land in Mississippi, a character in the form of eight-year-old Cassie Logan emerged. The story, Taylor realized, could be successfully told from Cassie's point of view. Cassie is a composite of several people, including Taylor's aunt, and her uncles are based on Taylor's uncles and also her father. Taylor finished the manuscript and submitted the story to the Council on Interracial Books for Children in a competition for new writers. Taylor's first story about Cassie, "Song of the Trees," won first prize in the African-American category. When Taylor was in New York for the awards ceremony, she discussed the publication of her manuscript with several potential publishers, eventually signing with Dial, whose editors suggested some minor revisions for her manuscript. Phyllis Fogelman, editor of Dial Books for Young Readers, recalls that her first impression of Mildred Taylor was of someone who cared deeply about communicating her material and who had an intense desire to do it right.

Song of the Trees (1975) is a novella which concentrates on an incident related by Taylor's father. While David "Papa" Logan is in Louisiana laying railroad track during the Depression, a white neighbor offers Big Ma, the grandmother, money for a large number of trees on the Logan land—trees which the neighbor has already marked as his own and sold. Cassie and her brothers, as well as Mary "Mama" Logan, are determined to help save the trees.

The book's theme concerns family unity, and Taylor shows in this brief incident the intense pride, dignity, and self-respect that are an integral part of the close-knit Logans. The love of the land which the family owned—an uncommon occurrence for a black family in Mississippi in the early 1930s—is a repeated theme throughout Taylor's novels. The rural setting and the major characters which Taylor has used in all her published work originated in *Song of the Trees*, a short, intense glimpse into a family who believes strongly in their principles. Taylor's first publication, the novella was named an Outstanding Book of the Year by the *New York Times* in 1975.

Roll of Thunder, Hear My Cry (1976) is Mildred Taylor's second volume about the Logan family. Characters from her earlier work are developed in more careful detail in this full-length novel. As Taylor stated in her Newbery Medal acceptance speech, the characters she had created for *Song of the Trees* would not leave her. She had to write another book, "one in which I could detail the teachings of my own childhood as well as incorporate many of the stories I had heard about my family and others. Through artistic prerogative I could weave into those stories factual incidents about which I had read or heard, as well as my own childhood feelings to produce a significant tapestry which would portray rural Black southern life in the 1930s."

Taylor creates a remarkable family portrait in *Roll of Thunder, Hear My Cry*. The events take place during one year, between 1933 and 1934. Cassie, the nine-year-old narrator, relates incidents which involve her parents and her three brothers, Stacey, Christopher-John, and Little Man. Although Papa Logan is in another state working on the railroad,

Dust jacket for Taylor's first book. The novella portrays the struggle of the Logan family, who live in Mississippi during the Depression, to preserve the timber on their land that a neighbor has marked to be sold (Dial).

his presence is felt in the book through frequent references to him and to the family's loneliness without him. Because it is a priority to maintain their 400 acres of land, the family must make sacrifices to see that the land is not lost.

Mama Logan teaches at the black grammar school and is later fired because she teaches the truth about slavery instead of the textbook account. In this novel, Cassie's reaction to the cruelties, the inequities, and the injustices of a racist society is one of anger. Her parents counsel her that resentment cannot change what is wrong in her world. Cassie's most significant growth in this novel comes as she understands her parents' advice, realizing that they have kept their independent spirits and pride despite the social inequality forced upon them. The influence of Taylor's father upon her and her work is prominent at this point. She states that "Throughout my childhood he impressed upon my sister and me that we were somebody, that we were important and could do or be anything we set our minds to do or be. . . . Through him my growing awareness of discriminatory society was accompanied by a wisdom that taught me

that anger in itself was futile, that to fight discrimination I needed a stronger weapon." For Mildred Taylor, that weapon was her writing.

Racial prejudice emerges as a theme in *Roll of Thunder, Hear My Cry* in a natural way through the incidents involving the Logan children. The children fear the burnings and lynchings that were frequent happenings in the South during those years. They feel outrage when whites are waited on in stores before they have a chance to state their requests. Taylor intends for the reader to sense the anger and desperation of the characters while remaining aware of the strength and love provided by the family to help overcome societal evils. Taylor provides deft touches of humor to lighten the mood and to show the mischievous side of the characters, as in the incident where Cassie, her brothers, and their friends dig an enormous pothole in the dirt road to stop the bus from the white school. Some days earlier the driver had hit a puddle and splashed them with mud while they walked beside the road.

The reception to Taylor's *Roll of Thunder, Hear My Cry* was overwhelmingly positive. An ALA

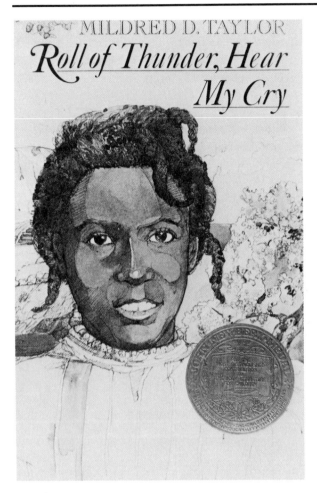

Dust jacket for a later edition of Taylor's Newbery Medal-winning novel which continues the saga of the Logan family, focusing on eight-year-old Cassie and her attempts to understand the inequities and injustices of the Depression-era South (Dial)

Notable Book in 1976, it received the Newbery Medal for 1977 and was a finalist for the National Book Award in the same year. The *School Librarian* reviewer declared that Mildred Taylor had done for Depression-era black southerners what Laura Ingalls Wilder did for the pioneers. The book has been published in eleven countries, and in 1985 Mildred Taylor was awarded the Buxtehuder Bulle, a German award for excellence in children's literature. *Roll of Thunder, Hear My Cry* has been cited by many as a book that deserves to become a classic. The memorable characters and controlled power that are part of Taylor's novel make it thoroughly deserving of the awards it has won. A few critics feel that the characters have been manipulated to fit certain situations and that the book could have been more appropriately written as a family

memoir. Taylor deliberately chose the form of a novel to communicate ideas that would not have had as great an impact in another form.

In Taylor's third book about the Logan family, *Let the Circle Be Unbroken* (1981), the ill-fated trial of T. J. Avery, a minor character from the previous book, opens the action. The trial is a mockery of justice, and the Logan children realize that because T. J. is black he cannot have a fair trial, despite the efforts of the white lawyer, Mr. Jamison, a family friend. Other racial incidents occur, and Stacey, the eldest Logan child, runs away to work in the cane fields of Louisiana in order to help support the family and their effort to keep their land. As Cassie and her brothers mature, their spirits are tested, but they remain true to the family and appreciate in new ways the strong bonds of family ties. Cassie takes careful notice of the blatant racism around her, and the family is subjected to grief and pain in Stacey's absence, yet they survive as a stable unit.

A cast of colorful minor characters adds a new dimension to Taylor's third accounting of the Logan family's struggles. Suzella, a city cousin sent to stay with the Logans, gives Cassie an opportunity to understand herself in relation to others unlike her. Mrs. Lee Annie memorizes the entire state constitution under Cassie's tutelage only to be humiliated and threatened when she attempts to register to vote on her sixty-fifth birthday.

Taylor's recurrent theme of family unity has its strongest appearance in *Let the Circle Be Unbroken*. The Logan family suffers when Stacey runs away, and an all-out effort is made to find him. Papa comes back from his railroad work and Cassie's Uncle Hammer leaves his job in the North and comes home to help. Papa Logan says, "We all part of one body in this family, and with Stacey gone, we just ain't whole."

Attitudes of bigotry and the evils of a racist white society are also part of Taylor's scenario in *Let the Circle Be Unbroken*. Although she presents in sometimes harrowing detail the atrocities committed against blacks, she lets the facts speak for themselves. Her book might have been nothing more than a strident social tract in an unskilled writer's hands, but Taylor involves the reader in the action and transcends the anger and bitterness that might have been the novel's dominant theme.

Let the Circle Be Unbroken has been compared to Harper Lee's *To Kill a Mockingbird* (1960). It has been praised for its power and forcefulness and was nominated for the American Book Award in the hardcover fiction category in 1982. *Let the Circle*

Be Unbroken also won the Coretta Scott King award. In this book Taylor's style seems to be more natural and unaffected than in her earlier works, especially in the novel's finely crafted dialogue, and she is more open and unguarded, particularly with regard to racial issues.

At present Taylor is working on two novels which will bring the story of Cassie Logan and her family to the outbreak of World War II, then through the war. She lives in Colorado and is devoted to writing full time. Other writing projects are planned after the Logan series is complete.

References:

Sharon L. Dussell, "Profile: Mildred D. Taylor," *Language Arts*, 58 (May 1981): 599-604;

Phyllis J. Fogelman, "Mildred D. Taylor," *Horn Book*, 53 (August 1977): 410-414;

David Rees, "The Color of Skin. Mildred Taylor," in his *The Marble in the Water: Essays on Contemporary Writers of Fiction for Children and Young Adults* (Boston: Horn Book, 1980), pp. 104-113.

Judith Viorst

(2 February?-)

Douglas Street
Texas A&M University

BOOKS: *Projects: Space* (New York: Washington Square Press, 1962);

150 Science Experiments Step-by-Step, illustrated by Dennis Telesford (New York: Bantam, 1963);

The Natural World: A Guide to North American Wildlife (New York: Bantam, 1965);

The Village Square, illustrated by Tom Ballenger (New York: Coward-McCann, 1966);

The Changing Earth, illustrated by Feodor Rimsky (New York: Bantam, 1967);

Sunday Morning, illustrated by Hilary Knight (New York: Harper & Row, 1968);

It's Hard to Be Hip Over Thirty, and Other Tragedies of Married Life (New York: World, 1968);

I'll Fix Anthony, illustrated by Arnold Lobel (New York: Harper & Row, 1969);

Try It Again, Sam: Safety When You Walk (New York: Lothrop, Lee & Shepard, 1970);

The Washington, D.C. Underground Gourmet, by Viorst and Milton Viorst (New York: Simon & Schuster, 1970);

People & Other Aggravations (New York: World, 1971);

The Tenth Good Thing About Barney, illustrated by Erik Blegvad (New York: Atheneum, 1971; London: Collins, 1972);

Alexander and the Terrible, Horrible, No Good, Very Bad Day, illustrated by Ray Cruz (New York: Atheneum, 1972; London: Angus & Robertson, 1973);

Yes, Married; A Saga of Love and Complaint (New York: Saturday Review Press, 1972);

My Mama Says There Aren't Any Zombies, Ghosts, Vampires, Creatures, Demons, Monsters, Fiends, Goblins, or Things, illustrated by Kay Chorao (New York: Atheneum, 1973);

Rosie and Michael, illustrated by Lorna Tomei (New York: Atheneum, 1974);

How Did I Get to Be Forty . . . and Other Atrocities (New York: Simon & Schuster, 1976);

A Visit From St. Nicholas (To a Liberated Household) (New York: Simon & Schuster, 1977);

Alexander, Who Used To Be Rich Last Sunday, illustrated by Cruz (New York: Atheneum, 1978);

Love & Guilt & the Meaning of Life, etc., illustrated by John Alcorn (New York: Simon & Schuster, 1979);

If I Were in Charge of the World and Other Worries: Poems for Children and Their Parents (New York: Atheneum, 1981).

SCREENPLAY: "Annie, The Women in the Life of a Man," CBS-TV, 1970.

PERIODICAL PUBLICATION: "Books Children Love Most," *Writer*, 89 (April 1976): 20-22.

Judith Viorst (photo by Milton Viorst)

The 1960s spawned a number of innovative and provocative writers for children, who, owing to the intellectual frenzy of the time and to their willingness to explore characters, situations, and topics thought taboo but a few years earlier, expanded the long-established boundaries and extended the lines of communication of the traditional domain of American children's literature. Of these practitioners, only a select few have garnered the critical acclaim and audience popularity to generate their continued longevity into the 1970s and 1980s. One of the best is Judith Viorst, whose stories of her young sons, Anthony, Nicholas, and Alexander, show the sensitivity, humor, and timeliness readily accessible to American children today. From her first children's novel, *Sunday Morning* (1968), through her widely praised *The Tenth Good Thing About Barney* (1971) and *Alexander and the Terrible, Horrible, No Good, Very Bad Day* (1972) to her *Alexander, Who Used To Be Rich Last Sunday* (1978), Viorst has shown herself to be a writer of talent and insight who has successfully

combined entertainment and enrichment in her creations for the child audience.

Judith Viorst, her husband, Milton Viorst, also a writer, and their three boys have resided in Washington, D.C., since 1960. Viorst was born and raised in New Jersey. After graduation from Rutgers University (she was an honors graduate and a member of Phi Beta Kappa) she journeyed to New York City. Tenures as a children's book editor with a New York publishing concern and as a science book editor in Washington laid the foundation for her own initial publications. *Projects: Space*, published in 1962, her first of four teen science nonfiction books preceding her better-known children's stories, finally established her as a "published author." The book detailed the development of American space technology to 1961, sang obligatory praises of the glories of U.S. space exploration, and offered the teenage reader projects and resources to better acquaint and inform the reader firsthand of the problems, particulars, and potential of space exploration. Though now outdated, it is quite readable and, as a historic document of prelunar space technology, it is quite revealing.

Projects: Space was followed by *150 Science Experiments Step-by-Step* (1963), *The Natural World: A Guide to North American Wildlife* (1965), and *The Changing Earth* (1967). In each of these informative publications, Viorst follows the same pattern established in her first effort—each details its specific scientific matter in clear, concise terms to enhance the knowledge of the teen reader. Each book contains a historical overview of the discipline, a delineation of its more specific branches, and a bank of informational resources and projects to allow the reader to delve further into the subject. These works are functional and readable, yet they are undistinguished efforts. With *Sunday Morning*, released by Harper and Row the year following *The Changing Earth*, Viorst's career as a children's writer properly began.

Sunday Morning, as are the majority of her following works, is inspired by the antics of her own young children. It is a wonderful, true-to-life comedy about Anthony and Nick and their efforts on a Sunday morning to abide by their father's dictum: "We do not want to hear anything until after 9:45 A.M.—and *we'll* tell you when *that* is." The older brother awakens at 5:00 A.M. and the fun begins. The silhouette illustrations further strengthen the comedic qualities of this tale, beginning a trend in characterization which becomes a trademark of Viorst books—these children are not juvenile paragons; some adults have labeled them obstreperous and unsuitable role models for the already energetic juvenile reading public. The parental characterizations likewise break tradition; the strict adult disciplinarian recoils at Viorst's seeming disdain for punishment. Yet the story is effective—the boys' adventures are so preposterous that, even with the pandemonium which ensues, it is difficult for the reader not to join in the laughter at the end.

Following close on the heels of the success of *Sunday Morning* came *I'll Fix Anthony* (1969), also published by Harper and Row. The stylized silhouettes by Hilary Knight are here replaced by the bold, colorful caricatures by Arnold Lobel. This story, printed in quarter-inch type, appears geared to a bit younger audience than *Sunday Morning*, yet it contains characters and attitudes similar to those evidenced in the earlier volume. The book portrays the same two boys but each is a year older, though here it is the younger, Nick, who takes focus as he plots ways to get even with his older brother for all the mean things done to him. The younger brother fantasizes, "When I'm six I'll fix Anthony," and the

book explores the various ways in which the younger brother, when six, will finally gain the upper hand over Anthony. This is at once a humorous and probing examination of the attitudes and emotions expressed in sibling rivalry. The characters and language, in their realistic portrayal of such situations, are not to the liking of all (mainly adult) readers, but they nevertheless are real and effective. The retreating cry which brings the story to a close is that of all five-year-olds ever tormented by an older sibling—"Anthony is chasing me out of the playroom. He says I stink. He says he is going to clobber me. I have to run now, but I won't have to run when I'm six. When I'm six I'll fix Anthony."

By 1970 Judith Viorst had firmly established herself as a writer to be reckoned with. In addition to her two juvenile successes, she had gained popularity with her humorous collection of adult poems, *The Village Square* (1966); the paean to approaching middle age, *It's Hard to Be Hip Over Thirty, and Other Tragedies of Married Life* (1968); her newly syndicated column for the *Washington Star Syndicate* (a column she wrote for two years);

Dust jacket for Viorst's book about a young boy who fantasizes about "fixing" his brother for all the wrongs which he perceives the older boy has committed against him (Harper & Row)

and her Emmy Award-winning writing for the CBS-TV special, "Annie, The Women in the Life of a Man." The year 1970 also produced her third children's work, *Try It Again, Sam: Safety When You Walk.*

Try It Again, Sam centers around Sam's first walk to David's house all by himself. Mother's warning, "If you get into any trouble on your way to David's, I expect you to turn right around and come back home," throws a damper of sorts on the adventure while triggering some interesting, though highly improbable, situations. The story is the most verbose effort by Viorst to date, and though "Safety When You Walk" is emphasized throughout (a separate list of rules is appended to the story for those, it is presumed, unable to get the message through the text), the message drowns in a rather awkward tale. Sam must return home four times before finally reaching David's house error-free.

The year 1971 marked the release of the poetic *People & Other Aggravations* for the adult market and the haunting *The Tenth Good Thing About Barney* for the juvenile. "My cat Barney died last Friday. I was very sad. I cried, and I didn't watch television.

Cover for Viorst's 1971 book which explains death to children through the portrayal of a young boy whose parents tell him to think of "ten good things" to say about his cat at the pet's funeral (Atheneum)

I cried, and I didn't eat my chicken or even the chocolate pudding. I went to bed, and cried. My mother sat down on my bed, and she gave me a hug. She said we could have a funeral for Barney in the morning. She said I should think of ten good things about Barney so I could tell them at the funeral." This is an intelligently written work about a difficult subject. The reader sees the young boy dealing with death in quite a frank way. There is a discussion of whether Barney is "in heaven" or "in the ground," a discussion not to the liking of many less liberal Christians. The boy's emotions are complicated further by his inability to find that tenth "good thing" (he can easily produce nine). His father explains to him in the course of the story that Barney, buried in the yard, will eventually "change until he's part of the ground in the garden. . . . He'll help grow the flowers. . . ." An unorthodox solution to some, it nevertheless satisfies this child (and numerous readers) as the book ends with this "tenth good thing about Barney."

Alexander and the Terrible, Horrible, No Good, Very Bad Day is without a doubt Viorst's most successful book. Since its appearance in 1972 it has enjoyed continuous popularity, in this country and in England. Though other Viorst works have appeared in Britain, *Alexander and the Terrible, Horrible, No Good, Very Bad Day* is the sole offering currently available into the 1980s—a significant barometer of the universal appeal of this fine story. Herein the author reverts to the successful pattern of the earlier tales; the characters are again based on her own children, and the situations are those of the child who wakes up on the one day when nothing goes right. Ray Cruz's illustrations add to the charm and humor of Alexander and his brothers. This is a fun tale; the moroseness of *The Tenth Good Thing About Barney* is nowhere here in evidence. It seems Viorst too was happy with this "Alexander" format for she quickly and effectively followed it with one similar in *My Mama Says There Aren't Any Zombies, Ghosts, Vampires, Creatures, Demons, Monsters, Fiends, Goblins, or Things* (1973), a book that, happily, is not as long-winded as its title.

The book deals with the childhood fears experienced at one time or another by all children and the appropriate parental response, "There are no such things." Here, however, the author has dared to call the parent's credibility into question by supplying the young boy with reasons why she should not be considered totally trustworthy. Each realization of parent error is accompanied by the child rationale, "So . . . sometimes even mamas make mistakes." Viorst's propensity for truthful

Dust jacket for Viorst's most popular children's book which describes a day in the life of a child when nothing seems to go right (Atheneum)

child/adult portrayals at the risk of diluting the traditionally angelic facade of either, as evidenced from her initial children's plots, is at once her most important and most controversial trait. She illuminates real issues by conceiving them within the context of real children and real adults—in so doing she is able to put characters and ideas in a framework and on a plane tangible to today's child. As with all of her plots, though the infallibility of the adult is challenged here, at the end the respect and love of the child for that imperfect parent are shown stronger and more emphatic than before. This idea of mutual understanding and love is important to Viorst as she carries it from story to story.

The 1974 *Rosie and Michael* (illustrated by Lorna Tomei) diverts from the pattern of utilizing Alexander and company as prototypes, though the two children of the title are cut from similar cloth. The book is a forty-page homage to childhood friendship, flip-flopping between the two young children and their convictions for the loyalty of the other. The author's conviction that a good friend is a treasure is readily understood within the first half of the book—though amusing, the overall

story is weak due to its overreliance on this one element.

After *Rosie and Michael,* the book-a-year string begun in 1967 came to an end as Judith Viorst seemingly concentrated more on her continuing column for *Redbook* magazine, her poetry for adults, and the raising of children into adolescents. She published *How Did I Get to Be Forty . . . and Other Atrocities* in 1976 and *A Visit From St. Nicholas (To a Liberated Household)* in 1977 (both from Simon and Schuster). Her next (and it is hoped not last) children's novel appeared in 1978 from Atheneum.

In *Alexander, Who Used To Be Rich Last Sunday* (wherein she is happily reunited with illustrator Ray Cruz) the pattern so successful in *Alexander and the Terrible, Horrible, No Good, Very Bad Day* is once again given life in the further antics of the author's impish third child. The lesson behind this book is the judicious spending of one's money—if you throw your money away on foolish things you will end up like Alexander, stuck with nothing but bus tokens. The story is well drawn and in time may be seen to rank with the other "Alexander" story as the best of Judith Viorst's output for children.

Three years passed and though Viorst's column and humorous poetry for adults continued, a new book exclusively for children seemed not in the immediate offing. With her children no longer young, her stories, much inspired by their youthful antics, transformed to keep pace with adolescence. Viorst herself has been heard to speculate: "I notice that my books aren't growing any older, even though my children certainly are. Perhaps I'll go on to write for that mid-aged child but I suspect that an important piece of myself is arrested at that golden age of picture books."

A possible attempt to arrest at once "that golden age" while addressing herself to the "mid-aged" child and his family came to fruition with the fall 1981 appearance of *If I Were in Charge of the World and Other Worries: Poems for Children and Their Parents*. Published by Atheneum, the volume features forty-one poems on a variety of subjects, enhanced by a series of black-and-white illustrations capably executed by Lynne Cherry. It is a slight volume, difficult to pigeonhole. As the subtitle suggests, while the bulk of the work is child-inspired, several share a decidedly adult sensitivity. The quality of the work is uneven but the overall effect achieved is more than satisfying. The reader encounters such humorous child pieces as the over-titled "Thoughts on Getting Out of a Nice Warm Bed in an Ice Cold House to Go to the Bathroom at Three O'Clock in The Morning." The entire poem reads subsequently: "Maybe life was better/ When I used to be a wetter." Another in traditional Viorst fashion begins: "I can't get enoughsky/of Lizzie Pitofsky," and continues to inform us that, "I want her so terrible/I'd give her my gerbil." This sort of nonsensical style is compatible with a real sensibility—real for both the parent and the child. It is made plain in the title poem which begins: "If I were in charge of the world/You wouldn't have lonely." Adding to the several pieces of this sort are some of Viorst's fairy-tale reworkings. Always with a twist or charming play on words or theme, she captures feelings inherent in the most sensitive child. In her twist on the traditional ending for *Cinderella*, when she sees the Prince is not so charming in the daylight, Cinderella decides she will "just pretend that this glass slipper feels too tight." Though concise, this first of the author's 1980s children's work sets solid standards to, we hope, be surpassed by decade's end.

Whether we have indeed seen the last of her novels for children, whether she will devote her attention to poetry, whether she will fade out of the children's book scene completely all remain to be seen. Those fans of Alexander, Anthony, Rosie, and the rest have nevertheless clearly voiced their satisfaction with the child worlds of Judith Viorst. If, Heaven forbid, she ended her career tomorrow, her place in the annals of postwar American children's fiction is justifiably assured.

Barbara Wersba

(19 August 1932-   )

Kay E. Vandergrift
Rutgers University

BOOKS: *The Boy Who Loved the Sea*, illustrated by
Margot Tomes (New York: Coward-McCann,
1961);

The Brave Balloon of Benjamin Buckley, illustrated by
Tomes (New York: Atheneum, 1963);

The Land of Forgotten Beasts, illustrated by Tomes
(New York: Atheneum, 1964);

A Song for Clowns, illustrated by Mario Rivoli (New
York: Atheneum, 1965);

Do Tigers Ever Bite Kings?, illustrated by Rivoli (New
York: Atheneum, 1966);

The Dream Watcher (New York: Atheneum, 1968);

Run Softly, Go Fast (New York: Atheneum, 1970);

Let Me Fall Before I Fly (New York: Atheneum,
1971);

Amanda, Dreaming, illustrated by Mercer Mayer
(New York: Atheneum, 1973);

The Country of the Heart (New York: Atheneum,
1975);

Tunes for a Small Harmonica (New York: Harper &
Row, 1976);

Twenty-Six Starlings Will Fly Through Your Mind, illustrated by David Palladini (New York: Harper & Row, 1980);

The Carnival in My Mind (New York: Harper & Row,
1982);

The Crystal Child, illustrated by Donna Diamond
(New York: Harper & Row, 1982);

Crazy Vanilla (New York: Harper & Row, 1986).

Barbara Wersba

Although more than half of her published
works are for younger children, Barbara Wersba
is best known as the author of young adult novels
in which sensitive and artistic teen protagonists,
alienated from their rather traditional middle-class
parents, find consolation in friendships with somewhat eccentric, often much older characters. Her
novels are more likely to employ quiet reflection
and introspection than lively action, but they record
episodes which are turning points in the characters'
lives and capture a flavor of contemporary teen
culture. Wersba has an eye for and a sympathy with
people and events which are slightly off-center; car-
nivals, circuses, and other more common city and
suburban habitats of teenage misfits and dreamers
are the settings for her works.

Her books for younger readers are more lighthearted and more fanciful than those for young
adults, but her work consistently displays a sophisticated humor which is frequently bittersweet or
poignant. Wersba's lyrical language and vivid imagery not only give a mystical, dreamlike quality to
many of her stories, but these elements also contribute to an overall romantic vision of the world
in spite of its harsh realities.

Barbara Wersba was born 19 August 1932 in
Chicago, Illinois, the only child of Robert and Lucy
Jo Quarles Wersba. Her parents were divorced
during her childhood, and Wersba has said that

this had a marked influence on her young life. She grew up in California and New York, and although she wrote stories and poems from a very early age, she wanted to be an actress. She began acting in a community theater at age twelve and continued her stage career until 1960, when she decided to write full-time. She took acting classes in high school and majored in drama at Bard College, from which she graduated with a B.A. in 1954, and which awarded her a doctorate of humane letters, honoris causa, in 1977. In addition, Wersba studied acting at the Neighborhood Playhouse and the Paul Mann Actors Workshop and dance with Martha Graham. From 1944 to 1959, while acting on radio and television, in summer stock, Off-Broadway, and with touring companies, she continued to be a "closet writer" of poems, stories, and fairy tales. It was only in 1960, when a theater company of which she was a member folded, and after she caught hepatitis, that she began writing for publication. Wersba wrote her first book for children when a friend urged her to write something to pass the long months spent recuperating from the illness. Within a year, *The Boy Who Loved the Sea* (1961), the first work Wersba had been able to finish, was published, and she began a new career as a writer. Since then she has been a summer lecturer at New York University, a writing instructor at the Rockland Center for the Arts, and a reviewer of children's books for the *New York Times* as well as a full-time writer.

Immediately after the acceptance of her first book, Wersba began writing *The Brave Balloon of Benjamin Buckley* (1963), the lighthearted story of a young boy who is the only person in Peaceful Valley who welcomes the balloon which descends there. Soon Benjamin is aloft on a series of adventures which reach legendary proportions. This story is probably best read aloud because its lyrical language, sophisticated humor, and quiet satire could easily be lost on young readers attracted to its simple format and illustrations. As is true of many of Wersba's stories, however, the book can be read on several levels, with younger children enjoying its sense of adventure while the more accomplished reader will appreciate its underlying ideas.

Those first years of writing were, as Wersba has described them, like a religious conversion. She published four books in four years, all for young readers. *The Land of Forgotten Beasts* (1964) is perhaps her most obvious statement of a theme that is evident throughout her work: the importance of the imagination. In this story, Andrew Peterson Smith, a boy scientist who has no time for fantasy,

discovers a Latin bestiary and reluctantly goes off to the land of the unicorn and other forgotten beasts. The episodic plot, although charmingly told, does not come together powerfully enough to raise this work above the level of a slight but very enjoyable story. *A Song for Clowns* (1965) is an allegorical tale that makes a strong statement about the power of love. Written and illustrated in medieval style, the book tells of a wicked king, who, in grief at the loss of his son, has abolished all imperfect and human things from his kingdom. A minstrel wandering through the land singing of the king's tyranny discovers that the king is really just a lonely old man who does not want to harm his people. *Do Tigers Ever Bite Kings?* (1966) combines love and laughter in a rollicking rhymed tale of a gentle king and a timorous tiger who stage an elaborate drama for a militant and shrewish queen. This whimsical, often absurdly funny story is also a sophisticated message of peace, all the more powerful for its nonsensical delivery.

The Dream Watcher (1968), Wersba's sixth book and her first for adolescents, is a move to more realistic, if also somewhat romanticized, fiction. In a publicity pamphlet entitled "Notes on *The Dream Watcher*," Wersba tells of being in a struggle to finish a long novel about eighteenth-century London when the character Albert Scully forced his way into her mind with what were to become the opening words of *The Dream Watcher*: "I'd better begin this story by telling you that until a month ago I was quite a mess." Unlike her previous works, which had been carefully planned and plotted, *The Dream Watcher* seemed to grow, almost as if the author were taking dictation from the character.

The book was greeted with a flurry of positive reviews, though J. A. Morrison, in the September-October 1969 *Children's Book News*, found Albert to be an "excruciating bore. In addition to marking the change in Wersba's career from books for children to the young adult novel, *The Dream Watcher* was the first representation in her work of a concern which was to be a major theme in the author's subsequent stories. Albert was the first of her sensitive, thoughtful young men of contemporary society who do not fit the expectations for the modern male and who must find the courage to express their own individuality.

Diane Gersoni-Staun, in her January 1971 *School Library Journal* article entitled "The Skirts in Fiction about Boys: A Maxi Mess," criticized Wersba's portrayal of Albert's mother from a feminist's perspective, viewing it as a stereotypical representation of the most unhealthy pressures of modern suburban society. On the other hand, the destitute, elderly, eccentric, and perhaps even self-deceptive Orpha Woodfin, who shares a touching friendship with Albert, is always treated with kindness, concern, and sympathy. Even after her death, when Albert discovers that the past she had shared with him is a fiction rather than a reality, he is grateful for the relationship and for her valuing of him and his dreams. This kind of understanding of and sensitivity to adults is uncommon in young adult fiction.

Run Softly, Go Fast (1970), which was awarded the Deutscher Jugend Buchpreis in 1973, has as its theme, according to Wersba, "the fact that children who are 'given everything' quite often do not want it." She has said that in writing the story she wanted to probe her own life more deeply than she had done in *The Dream Watcher* and to understand certain things about her own parents. *Run Softly, Go Fast* is written as the diary of nineteen-year-old

Dust jacket for Wersba's fictional diary of a nineteen-year-old male that explores the deterioration of his relationship with his materially successful father (Atheneum)

David Marks as he explores the deterioration of his relationship with his materially successful father, Leo, who only wants what he considers to be best for Davy. Davy has other ideas; and his story details the late 1960s counterculture, with its artiness, acid trips, free love, and other accoutrements of that alternative life-style then called "hippiedom." The mother in *Run Softly, Go Fast* is realistically and sympathetically portrayed as she attempts to bring about a reconciliation between her husband and son before Leo's impending death.

The story is told mainly through flashbacks, after Leo's death, as Davy reflects on his relationship with his father. In this process of reflection, the son does come to some understanding of his father. The complex literary techniques and introspective narrative of this work seem at times to be in contrast with Wersba's conventional portrayal of Davy as an alienated, middle-class youth. The story, however, overcomes these limitations to help young readers see beyond the character types to the underlying concern with personal values in a time of social upheaval.

Wersba has described the young, nameless character who discovers a two-inch circus that performs in his garden in *Let Me Fall Before I Fly* (1971) as "simply the essence of childhood loneliness." As the child becomes more absorbed with the circus, he is less in touch with his parents and with reality. This mystical atmosphere is shattered when a storm washes away the circus while the child is vacationing with his parents. Withdrawn and despondent, the child is coaxed back to this world through the efforts of his family and a doctor who "did not wish to examine his body, but his mind."

Let Me Fall Before I Fly, a complex and difficult allegorical tale in spite of its apparent simplicity, has received widely divergent reviews from Wersba's fellow author-critics. Doris Orgel, in the *New York Times Book Review,* describes the child as "functioning neither as individual nor as symbol. He remains, in the author's own words, 'distant, peculiar, vague' throughout. So does the book." The opposite point of view was expressed by Julia Cunningham, whose *Horn Book* report stated that "As a writer, I must rejoice in this nearly perfect book."

Let Me Fall Before I Fly is an enchanting story for those special readers who can suspend their sense of disbelief and accept this work on its own, highly unusual terms. For Wersba, this book clarifies her "philosophy of what it means to be young" in representing "the young person as an anarchist, a dreamer, an outcast." In Wersba's opinion the book "states that visions are as real as—if not realer than—the daily world we can touch."

Amanda, Dreaming (1973), a prose poem about the romantic images that float through a child's dreams, does not share the mix of fantasy and reality in *Let Me Fall Before I Fly*. Here the fancies are clearly the details of a young girl's dreams. This makes the work more accessible to many youngsters and less disturbing to their parents, but it also may reduce its power to engage and to enthrall its audience. This quiet mood piece, with its loosely connected images, might best be shared with children and adults who can appreciate its beautifully crafted language.

In *The Country of the Heart* (1975) Wersba returns to some of the themes identified in her earlier young adult novels. Stephen, an adolescent would-be poet, idolizes and finally has a brief affair with forty-year-old Hadley, an accomplished poet who is dying. The intensity of Stephen's feelings for Hadley and of his literary aspirations could be the makings of melodrama, but the author manages to create a touchingly sincere, rather than a maudlin, relationship. Once again, the hero is a sensitive

young man, alienated from his parents, whose move toward maturity is enhanced by his friendship with an eccentric and literary older woman.

Tunes for a Small Harmonica (1976) was on the ALA Best Books for Young Adults and Notable Children's Book lists for 1976 and was nominated for a National Book Award in 1977. It was also selected as a favorite reading choice of sixteen to nineteen year olds in *English Journal*'s Young Adult Book Poll of 1977. Wersba considers this "a funny book, and in many ways, a joyous book." This first-person narrative of an offbeat Park Avenue teenager is indeed told with bolder humor than the author's previous young adult novels. Some of its characters and events are outrageously funny. The "tunes" of the title are played by J. F. McAllister, a rebellious, chain-smoking tomboy who attends a prestigious girls school in Manhattan. The harmonica was given to her by her long-suffering best friend, Mary Lou, who encourages her to play it rather than to smoke her usual three packs of cigarettes a day. The story revolves around J. F.'s crush on Harold, her vapid poetry teacher, who

Dust jacket for Wersba's novel about an aspiring adolescent poet and his relationship with an accomplished middle-aged female poet with a terminal illness (Atheneum)

may be one of the more unlikely romantic figures in fiction. J. F. attempts to raise money to send him to England to complete his Ph.D. by enlisting Mary Lou's little brother, "the Hubert Humphrey of the first grade," to join her in street corner concerts only to discover that the object of her affections is already wealthy—and married. Nonetheless, in the process, J. F. has learned not only to play the harmonica but to accept herself for who she is; and readers have met, and laughed with, a whole gallery of zany characters. *Tunes for a Small Harmonica* probably has the greatest popular appeal of all of Wersba's books; and J. F., the only female protagonist of her young adult novels, is one of the author's most endearing and delightful characters.

Twenty-Six Starlings Will Fly Through Your Mind (1980) is one of Wersba's books for which it is difficult to identify a specific audience. This unconventional alphabet book, with its anthropomorphic letters, complex language and concepts, and elaborately intricate illustrations, will be appreciated by

Dust jacket for Wersba's novel about a rebellious, chain-smoking tomboy who attends a prestigious girls school in Manhattan (Harper & Row)

readers who value imagination, beauty of language, and a sense of mystery.

Another of Wersba's books which appeals to special readers is *The Crystal Child* (1982), a mystical modern fairy tale in which a boy's love brings a statue to life. The statue is of a young girl, Alison, whose mother was killed in a fire. Alison cried so much that her tears turned her whole body to crystal, and she has stood as a statue for eighty years. Wersba's writing is delicately poetic, in keeping with the sensitive tale. An elderly gardener is one more in the cast of superior senior citizens found in Wersba's books for young people.

The Carnival in My Mind (1982), Wersba's second ALA Best Book for Young Adults, is a return to the realistic young adult novel in which a young boy from a middle-class, urban neighborhood has a relationship with an eccentric older woman, in this case an out-of-work actress. Fourteen-year-old, five-feet-tall Harvey meets and falls in love with twenty-year-old, six-feet-tall Chandler. When Harvey leaves home and his mother is too busy raising Irish setters to notice that he is gone, he moves into Chan's apartment, where they share a humorous, touching, and platonic personal arrangement, even though they share the same bed. The *Washington Post Book World* described this novel as "the literary equivalent of a *New Yorker* cartoon" and Wersba as a writer with "a knack for setting her scenes, and delivering the punch lines in a manner worthy of Woody Allen." Thus, this work combines the humor of J. F.'s story with some of the quiet sensitivity of Wersba's earlier young adult novels. The slightly bizarre but glamorous Chandler is a believable target for lonely Harvey's affections; and from their first shared afternoon of champagne cocktails in the hotel, it is clear that her brand of optimism would have a profound effect on the depressed young man. His subsequent discovery that she is a prostitute and an alcoholic, and that she has a child who lives with her parents, in no way lessens or cheapens their relationship or the value that each gains from it. The confidence and self-understanding they draw from each other results in their parting to return to their own worlds and families. The carnival of the title refers to Harvey's fantasies of a happy childhood, and Chan's parting gift to him is a visit to a carnival after he admits he has always dreamed of one. Again there is a minor adult character on the fringes of the story, Harvey's family's butler, named Holmes, who, prior to Chan, seems to be the only positive and stable influence in the young protagonist's life. As Harvey returns home and begins to come to terms with his preoccupied mother and absent father, Holmes's comforting influence is essential to the novel's resolution.

Crazy Vanilla (1986) is another story of a fourteen-year-old boy who learns to accept himself and his family through his relationship with a somewhat unconventional young lady. In this book, the "older woman" is only fifteen, but Mitzi Gerrard is much older than Tyler Woodruff in the ways of the world. Both are interested in wildlife photography on Long Island; but the Hamptons, where the wealthy Woodruffs live, is a different place from the Long Island Mitzi knows; and their approaches to photography, and to life, are also worlds apart. Cameron, Woodruff's older brother and former hero who has been "the star" of the family, has been banished because he is gay, but he remains a pivotal character in the story, though Woodruff is not quite sure how he feels about his brother now that he knows Cameron is a homosexual. To make matters worse, Cameron's sexual preference has made his father suspicious of Woodruff's preoccupation with photographing birds, and he has refused to buy the elaborate camera Woodruff believes he needs. The camera that he does have, however, is an expensive one and certainly far better than the beaten-up relic Mitzi uses, although she takes the more interesting photographs because she is more willing to take chances to get what she wants. These two very different young people learn to care for each other and their respective families in the short time they share together; and then, they part and lose touch with each other. This interlude in their lives, however, has brought them more in touch with themselves and with others close to them.

Wersba's readers will recognize the adult characters in *Crazy Vanilla*, from Woodruff's hyperactive upper-middle-class society mother who drinks too much and her distant and reserved husband to Mitzi's bizarre hippie mother who haphazardly runs a kind of health food store and has a series of relationships with less-than-appealing live-in men. Cameron and his companion Vincent are more sympathetically and realistically portrayed; in fact, they present one of the most positive images of a homosexual couple in young adult literature. This book seems to bring together many of the best and most powerful aspects of Wersba's work—strong and fascinating, somewhat zany characters; a gentle, bittersweet humor with touches of bold laughter; and a believable relationship captured in a language and style that is both engrossing and delightful.

Barbara Wersba is an established writer who seems to have three different, but complementary, strands in her works. She writes fanciful stories for young readers, mood pieces that appeal to the special reader of any age, and her own unique version of the young adult coming-of-age story. All share a keen eye for the idiosyncrasies of characterization, a melodic and imaginative use of language, a reflective view of human society, and a delightful, if sometimes dark, sense of humor. In her realistic young adult novels, she presents a painfully accurate look at middle- and upper-class life-styles with some of their less public and less pleasant undercurrents. The precocious teenagers who people these stories frequently encounter characters who live on the other side of that society. *Crazy Vanilla*'s Cameron and Vincent are developed just enough to distill the prejudice that many young adults have for homosexuals and to demonstrate that their gayness is just one facet of their overall healthy and productive lives. Wersba's ability to bring to life such minor characters and make them memorable is one of the major achievements of her work.

Another characteristic of Wersba's fiction is her uncommon ability to portray adults realistically to her young readers. Even in the usual "parent as antagonist" mode of story for the teen reader, she gives young protagonists glimpses of adult concerns, motivations, and uncertainties.

There is a sense of truth in much of Wersba's writing. Her characters are forced to face life as an ongoing process in which significant events and encounters with special human beings may not alter life in any outward way even if they lead to personal growth. Many young adult problem novels present the reader with extreme problems which are resolved in the course of the story. Wersba is more likely to present close-up views of everyday life incidents which may be of major importance in the characters' lives only for that moment in time. Wersba's background in the theater may contribute to the acute sense of timing evident in her stories, and her delivery of a humorous line at the most dramatic moment contributes to the sense of a heightened reality which is prominent in her work.

Interviews:

"Sexuality in Books for Children: An Exchange by Barbara Wersba and Josette Frank," *Library Journal,* 98 (15 February 1973): 620-623;

"Barbara Wersba—As a Writer," *Top of the News,* 35 (June 1975): 427-428;

Paul Janeczko, "An Interview with Barbara Wersba," *English Journal,* 65 (November 1976): 20-21.

Ester Wier
(17 October 1910-   )

Marilyn H. Karrenbrock
University of Tennessee

BOOKS: *The Answer Book on Naval Social Customs,* by Wier and Dorothy C. Hickey, illustrated by Grace W. Harrison (Harrisburg, Pa.: Military Service Publishing, 1956);

The Answer Book on Air Force Social Customs, by Wier and Hickey, illustrated by Harrison (Harris-

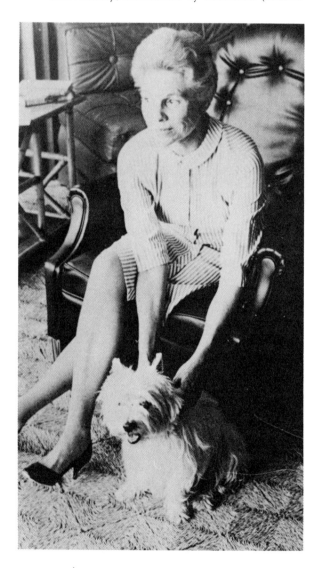

burg, Pa.: Military Service Publishing, 1957);

Army Social Customs, illustrated by J. Franklin Whitman, Jr. (Harrisburg, Pa.: Military Service Publishing, 1958);

What Every Air Force Wife Should Know (Harrisburg, Pa.: Military Service Publishing, 1958);

The Loner, illustrated by Christine Price (New York: McKay, 1963); illustrated by Anthony Maitland (London: Constable, 1966);

Gift of the Mountains, illustrated by Richard W. Lewis (New York: McKay, 1963);

The Rumptydoolers, illustrated by W. T. Mars (New York: Vanguard, 1964);

Easy Does It, illustrated by Mars (New York: Vanguard, 1965);

The Barrel, illustrated by Carl Kidwell (New York: McKay, 1966);

The Wind Chasers, illustrated by Kurt Werth (New York: McKay, 1967); illustrated by A. R. Whitear (London: Constable, 1968);

The Space Hut, illustrated by Leon Summers (Harrisburg, Pa.: Stackpole, 1967);

The Winners, illustrated by Ursula Koering (New York: McKay, 1968);

Action at Paradise Marsh, illustrated by Earl R. Blust (Harrisburg, Pa.: Stackpole, 1968);

The Long Year, illustrated by Koering (New York: McKay, 1969);

The Straggler: Adventures of a Sea Bird, illustrated by Leonard Vosburgh (New York: McKay, 1970);

The White Oak, illustrated by Anne Marie Jauss (New York: McKay, 1971);

The Partners, illustrated by Anna Maria Ahl (New York: McKay, 1972);

The Hunting Trail, illustrated by Richard Cuffari (New York: Walck, 1974);

King of the Mountain (New York: Walck, 1975).

Ester Wier's first book for children, *The Loner* (1963), was a highly acclaimed Newbery Honor Book of 1964. Her fourteen subsequent books exhibit a surprising variation in quality directly linked to her choice of settings. Wier's best works have

380

exceptionally strong regional backgrounds, while her poorer ones are usually placed in unspecified and undifferentiated locations. Wier is particularly noted for stories of western North America and the Everglades of Florida.

Except for three nature narratives, each of Wier's children's books is a highly consistent example of contemporary realism. The setting is fully described and often specific in location. Not only is there unity of plot and setting, but the paramount focus of the book is often either the place itself or an action inherent to that place. The chief character is a young male, ten to fifteen years old, who is without family or friends and has usually been left, due to circumstances, in an unfamiliar environment. From the setting and the people who inhabit it, he learns important lessons which serve as markers on the road to maturity. There is often another character who serves as mentor, role model, or nurturer for the boy. This character is usually an adult, middle-aged or older, male or female, who is always strong, independent, and at home in the environment. Animals are important in the plot, conflicts with nature are common, and contrast is an important element in many of the books. Thematically Wier emphasizes adaptation to the environment, and much of the impact of her books comes from the tension between the character and the place.

Ester Alberti Wier was born on 17 October 1910, the daughter of Robert Armenio Alberti, a broker, and his wife Lydea Harshhbarger Alberti. Wier was born in Seattle, Washington, but grew up in California. She began writing very early, "producing reams of poetry" by age seven, and was only ten when some of her poems were published. She continued to write all during her schooldays, "dreaming of becoming another Millay or Dickinson." She attended Southeastern Teachers College in Durant, Oklahoma, in 1929-1930, and the University of California at Los Angeles in 1931-1932. Her dreams of a writing career were postponed upon her marriage to Henry Robert Wier, a lieutenant in the United States Navy. They were married on 29 October 1934, in Hankow, China, and spent their first year in Shanghai and various ports along the Yangtze River. For the next twenty years, she followed her husband as he was transferred from one military post to another; they lived in such varied places as California, Massachusetts, New York, and Florida. She raised two children, David Anthony and Susan, and took part in the many activities expected of a military wife.

In the 1950s, the family settled in Washington, D.C., where Captain Wier was stationed at the Pentagon. With her children now in high school, Wier was able to resume writing. Her first books were written for service wives like herself and concerned military social customs. *The Answer Book on Naval Social Customs* (1956) and *The Answer Book on Air Force Social Customs* (1957) were written with Dorothy Hickey. In 1958, Wier published *Army Social Customs* and *What Every Air Force Wife Should Know*.

It was in a workshop at George Washington University that Wier discovered the field of juvenile literature. She published several stories, then decided to try writing a book. Nearly ten years before, while visiting a sheep ranch, Wier had conceived the idea of a story about a boy in such an environment. Later, while observing shepherds at work in Italy, Spain, and Israel, she had stored up facts which she could now put to use. By this time her husband had retired from the Navy and was working on a master's degree at Purdue University. Wier found that "Indiana was a fine place for research on farm animals," and it was there that *The Loner* was written.

The book tells of a nameless boy, a migrant farm worker, who travels from Alabama to Montana, where he is found by Boss, a lonely sheepherder who has recently lost her only son. She adopts the boy, names him David after the Biblical shepherd-king, and teaches him the shepherd's art. The plot focuses on David's changing perceptions of himself and on the activity of sheepherding. The setting is Montana's winter sheep range, and its stern beauty strongly influences David's developing character, though the setting is not the central focus of this book, as it would be in later ones. Already present, however, is the tension produced when an inexperienced boy is confronted with a formidable environment which cannot be conquered but in which he must learn to live.

Many other elements common to Wier's subsequent books can also be found. A lonely boy is placed in an unfamiliar environment. From Boss, his role model, he learns to give and accept affection and trust, and animals—in this case dogs and sheep—must be loved, nurtured, and protected from the dangers of a severe environment. Contrasts abound, although they are not as important to the overall plot as in later books. Obstinate Boss is contrasted with her more moderate daughter-in-law Angie; the protective dogs with the helpless sheep; David sees himself in contrast to Boss's dead son Ben. The inhospitable environment imposes enormous hardship upon the characters; they meet its challenge with strength and courage, molding their behavior to it rather than pitting themselves against it.

Wier's faults are already present, too. She is not a strong plotter and relies heavily on coincidence. The most effective climax in the book, as one reviewer remarked, comes in the first chapter, when Raidy, the boy's new friend, is killed when her long hair catches in a crop-picking machine. The characters often survive unbelievable hardships through coincidence, luck, and seemingly superhuman capabilities. David falls in a water-filled mineshaft; lands on a piece of timber; by light of a match, he finds a rotten ladder and climbs out; he then stumbles home through a blizzard and does not even catch cold. Tex, the ranch hand, survives three days buried under the snow with his arm in a bear trap but is hardly hurt. Despite its flaws, *The Loner* was named a Newbery Honor Book in 1964 and was made into a two-part television production, *The Young Loners,* by Walt Disney in 1968. A British edition was published by Constable in 1966.

Wier's second children's book, *Gift of the Mountains,* was also published in 1963. Like *The Loner,* it was a selection of the Junior Literary Guild. Indito, a young Mexican peasant, finds a hoard of gold hidden beneath a rock in the mountains. He takes one coin, intending to return, dig up the rest of the treasure, and rebury it in his own yard where he can conveniently "find" the coins on the nameday of his little blind sister Teco. After he spends the coin at a fiesta in the nearby town of Saint Inez, his father says that disturbing a buried treasure will anger the evil spirit which guards it. Indito realizes that this is an ignorant superstition, something which his priest, Father Luis, has warned him against, but he nevertheless fears what he has done. When his father is injured at work, he half-believes the curse, and he is convinced of it when he returns to the treasure and finds a yellow beard (a fer-de-lance), the most deadly of Mexican snakes, occupying the hole where the gold is hidden. He determines to leave the gold undisturbed. Only later, after meeting the good ranchero, Don Roberto, and learning how the gold was hidden during a revolution, does he go back to recover the treasure so that Don Roberto, who has sought it all his life, may die in peace. Because Indito's action brings great good to the village, he will have a chance to get an education and Teco will receive medical treatment.

Gift of the Mountains is Wier's only book which is set outside the United States. It is laid in the tierra caliente, the hot lands of Mexico's central plain, just east of the Sierra Madre Mountains. The countryside, towns, and local customs are lovingly described. Spanish words and expressions are frequently used and explained naturally in context. The plot lacks the tension often found in Wier's books, however, because Indito is native to his environment and has a loving family to whom he can turn. The source of the conflict is not the setting, but superstition, the ancient Indian beliefs which persist among the uneducated Mexican peons even today. Indito must struggle with these beliefs internally; only the priest can help him become free of them. The story is weakened because the misfortunes which can result from ignorance and superstition are not made clear. The plot complications are few, and the resolution is weak and coincidental. Although Indito is thirteen, the book seems to be written for younger children, unlike most of Wier's books.

When *The Loner* was named a Newbery Honor Book, Wier and her family were living in Arizona, which was to be the setting of her third children's book, *The Rumptydoolers* (1964). Fifteen-year-old Whit Stewart is the classic rich boy who has never suffered hardship until he spends several months on his uncle's ranch, where he accompanies the sheep herd on a two-hundred-mile trek to pasture on the summer range. The book is a nice complement to *The Loner,* which describes life on a winter sheep range. The setting is not only carefully described; it is specific to the extent that the reader can follow the herd's progress on a map of the state. The primary focus of the book is the activity of sheepherding, which is discussed in fascinating detail, but there is also plenty of adventure and even a mystery. After Ramon, the assistant herder, is bitten by a rattlesnake and an Apache named Juh is hired in his place, bad things begin to happen: a poisoned dog, a dead burro, stampeding sheep. Eventually Juh is revealed as the villain who is sabotaging the drive because he had earlier been fired for fighting. During the course of the book, Whit gradually comes to understand that a good shepherd always puts his sheep first. The lesson is reinforced in the book's climax, when Chihu, an Apache boy who befriends and influences Whit, kills his beloved dog Zuma because the dog has become a sheep killer.

Whit is less well drawn than many of Wier's protagonists. At first he is vehement in rejecting friendly overtures and help from Chihu and from his adult mentor, an Australian herder named Digger. Whit's change from a spoiled child to a rumptydooler (an Australian slang term for a champion) is abrupt, but nevertheless his complete surrender to the Arizona desert and to the sheep makes a satisfying ending. Wier uses Native American characters in several of her books, but Juh is the only one who is a villain. The portrayal is balanced by that of Chihu, who earns Whit's respect and friendship. In the end, the two boys become blood brothers.

Wier's next book, *Easy Does It,* was published in 1965. It is a typical "integration novel," a type of story which was popular at that time when racial integration in the United States was a major concern. Chip Woodman, who has just moved into the neighborhood, is accepted by the other boys, but A. L. Reese, his next-door neighbor, who is black, is not so lucky. Many of the people in the neighborhood, led by the bigoted Mr. Hacker, plan to boycott the Reese family, and the Woodman family is ostracized when they do not take part. Later Mr. Woodman accidentally hits Fritz, Mr. Hacker's half-blind dog, with his car. Hacker accuses Mr. Reese of the killing, and Reese takes the blame because the Woodmans had been supportive of his family. Chip finally reveals the truth, and the Reeses are accepted by the neighborhood. The acceptance is furthered when it is learned that Terrible Thomas, "the Blackest and Best," a famous major league pitcher and hero of all the neighborhood boys, is Mr. Reese's cousin. The plot is predictable and the ending unbelievably coincidental. Very few of Wier's books are set in a town, and this is her only book which has no connection with nature and the outdoors. The book has none of the hallmarks of her regional novels; nevertheless, *Easy Does It* and *The Rumptydoolers,* Wier's two books published by Vanguard, are her only books in print in 1986.

The Loner is generally considered Wier's best book. Of all her works, it probably creates the most emotional impact upon the reader, and it is outstanding in its character portrayal. Two other books, however, epitomize Wier's prototypical plot and her extraordinary ability to convey regional settings. In both *The Barrel* (1966) and *The Wind Chasers* (1967), the locale is itself a main focus of the book. It is more than a background or a setting for an activity; it is a real presence, brooding, menacing and dangerous, but always oblivious to the puny humans who inhabit it. Each of these books also has a second focus, an idea or abstract quality which the characters, influenced by the setting, either embrace or reject. In *The Barrel* this quality is bravery; in *The Wind Chasers* it is hope.

The Barrel concerns twelve-year-old Chance Reedy, who was left by his father with a child welfare agency many years before and is reunited with his grandmother and brother who live in the Everglades of Florida. Chance finds it a lush and beautiful setting, filled with "water oak and gumbo-limbo, magnolia and wild orange, paradise and palm, satinwood and Indian almond." His older brother Turpem, however, sees the Everglades as threatening. "The wild back country is a hostile land. Here walks the panther stealthily at night. Here the black bear in a surly mood roars like a hurricane through the dense stillness of the swamp. Here the bull alligator bellows hideously, the cottonmouth slips beneath the sluggish waters, the wild hog roots and scavenges throughout the jungle." The book is full of contrasts. Chance is level-headed, even-tempered, but still unsure of himself. Turpem is rash, intemperate, and obsessed with the need to prove his bravery. Chance has two nurturing role models who teach him about his new home. Granny, who has lived in the Everglades all her life, represents custom and superstition, while Mr. Fairday, a naturalist who studies the swamp, is the voice of knowledge and reason. The tension which Chance feels comes not only from the environment but from his relationships with people very different from those he has known. His adaptation to the area is soon more acute than that of Turpem, who has lived there all his life but who thinks that prudence in the face of danger is an admission of cowardice. The brothers are reconciled when Chance demonstrates his bravery by saving his puppy, Angus, from Old One-Ear, a vicious wild hog. Ever since Chance had come to the Everglades, Turpem had threatened to put Angus in a barrel with a raccoon in order to test the young dog's courage. Chance himself insists on the test, and the two animals are found curled up together in the barrel. This coincidental ending is even less credible than Wier's usual contrived conclusions, and it seriously mars what is otherwise an exciting and well-handled plot.

The Wind Chasers proved less popular than *The Loner* and *The Barrel,* perhaps because it is more complex. It is set in the Strip of Arizona, the northwest corner cut off from the rest of the state by the Grand Canyon, an area as dry and stark as the Everglades are dank and luxuriant. People who live in the Strip can survive only by dreaming: of a rose bush that will bloom someday, of wild horses that come at one's call, of making enough money to get away. Although Nate Klink is new to this land, he is not really a loner. He has his father, Job; his older twin brothers, Matt and Mark; and his younger brother, Benjy. The brothers contrast in several ways: Matt and Nate are realists, Mark and Benjy dreamers; Matt and Benjy hate the Strip, Nate and Mark like it; Matt and Mark are independent, though inseparable, while Nate must spend his time with Benjy, for whom he is responsible. Job, who considers dreaming to be "wind chasing," is worn down by hatred of the Strip's harsh reality; as such, he contrasts with Ma Hernandez, who holds on to hope. She is the role model who teaches practical Nate to dream. The book is slow-paced and more introspective than Wier's other works. Although the dangers of the Strip are real, the book's tone reflects Benjy's dream of wild horses: it may all be a mirage on the hot desert air. *The Wind Chasers* was published in Britain by Constable in 1968.

In *The Winners* (1968), Wier returns to the Everglades, as the book's protagonist, Scrub Nolan, escapes from a pair of evil brothers with whom he is traveling only to find himself lost in the swamp. Unlike *The Barrel*'s Chance Reedy, who embraced the area, Scrub fights his new environment and is therefore more easily hurt by it. Although he finds two mentors in Cap Revere, a transplanted New Englander who loves the swamps, and Johnny Cloud, a Muccosukee Indian boy who is native to the land, Scrub has difficulty earning their trust because he does not respect the life of the region. He has always seen life as competitive but lacks self-confidence in this strange and dangerous land where Cap and Johnny live successfully. Gradually Scrub comes to realize that through cooperation, everyone can be a winner. When he accepts the Everglades he does so wholeheartedly, hoping to return someday as a park ranger. Except for its setting, *The Winners* most closely parallels *The Rumptydoolers*. Both books feature a protagonist who finds it hard to adapt to new surroundings; two mentors, an older man not native to the region and an Indian boy; conflict with other men as well as with nature; and a long journey with a specific setting that can be followed on a map.

Wier's next two books were published by Stackpole and were unusual because they were connected by a common character, the friendly but slightly mysterious Mr. Moon. Both books involve conflict between a boy who is concerned about the natural world and bureaucrats who permit and promote urban values. *The Space Hut* (1967) was a selection of the Weekly Reader Book Club and is shorter and simpler than any of Wier's other books. Mike McAllister fights to keep his treehouse, his

"space hut," which City Hall considers an eyesore, with the help of his pet skunk Beetlejuice and his friend Mr. Moon. The situation is resolved in Mike's favor when the unfriendly city manager conveniently changes his mind because he once owned a pet skunk. The book is set in an unknown city, and the only evidence of Wier's interest in nature is the presence of the skunk.

In *Action at Paradise Marsh* (1968), Wier returned to a book with a rural setting and a strong emphasis on the environment, though the exact locale is not stated. Radish Johannsen lives in town, but most of the novel's action takes place in a nearby marsh. There Radish meets Mr. Moon, who is better developed and more realistically portrayed than in the earlier book. Radish and his brother Nels, a fish hatchery manager, are fighting to protect the marsh from an urban developer who wishes to drain it. The book is a strong plea for preservation, but the climax is strangely at variance with the theme. Radish sacrifices Big Gold, his enormous pet brown trout that lives in a pool in the marsh, and Nels takes the fish to the legislature to show the members what the marsh can produce if it is protected. Killing the giant fish seems a poor way to promote wildlife conservation. Nevertheless the book was a Junior Literary Guild selection.

Jesse Kingman, the protagonist of *The Long Year* (1969), is a well-developed character who lives on a remote Arizona ranch. During a long and worrisome year, he learns to take responsibility, wins his father's approval by making mature decisions, and realizes that all things change. Although Jesse has many adventures, the tension created in Wier's earlier books when the central character is forced to adapt to an unfamiliar environment is missing here, as Jesse is a native to the region.

In 1970, Wier published the first of three nature books. *The Straggler: Adventures of a Sea Bird* describes a year in the life of a gannet, or sea goose. The setting ranges from the North Atlantic to the Gulf of Mexico as the bird migrates. As a fledgling, the bird learned to fear people when two fishermen invaded the nesting area, killing birds for bait. Later the bird is swept up in a hurricane, caught in an oil slick, and trapped for banding, though in each case he was befriended by humans. *The White Oak* (1971) describes the history of a white oak tree, covering more than four hundred years, during which the tree survives a forest fire and a blast of lightning. However, most of the book describes the animals who live in and near the tree during one of its last years. *The Hunting Trail* (1974) describes several years in the life of an Arizona coyote. Wier, at home in the familiar setting, invests the daily life of the animal with drama as he learns to deal with floods and quicksand, contend with other animals for food, and escape from men's snares, traps, poisons, and guns. The tension between coyote and environment is similar to that experienced by so many of Wier's human characters, and *The Hunting Trail* is her best nature book.

The Partners (1972) is Wier's only book which features a girl as one of the protagonists. A migrant, Wilhelmina Katerina Margarita Eyck, known as Willy, is taken as a partner by Frank Martin, who wants to be called Fearless, as he is trying to prove his independence by raising earthworms for fishbait. They befriend a stray dog, Spook, who leads them to a cave where they almost get lost. Later in the summer, Fearless is trapped there when he takes refuge from a tornado. He breaks his ankle and spends three days in the cave before Willy and Spook lead rescuers to him. The story is told alternately from the points of view of Fearless and Willy, and the characterization, especially that of Willy, is well done. The story takes place in the great heartland of America (perhaps in Illinois or Indiana), though regionalism is less important in this book than in Wier's stories of the West and Florida. The story's conflict does not arise from the need to adapt to an alien environment but from the real physical dangers which Fearless and Willy undergo in the cave and from their desires to earn the approval of their families.

However, Wier's last book, *King of the Mountain* (1975), again makes use of her successful formula of adaptation. The setting is not specifically named, but the desert and the salt and borax beds of the area suggest that it may take place in Utah. Weedy Hastings and his son Orph return to the valley where Weedy grew up, and Orph is sent to live with his great-aunt Em, who teaches him to value and protect the endangered bighorn sheep. Orph soon has a dilemma; he is afraid that his father may be one of the poachers who are destroying the animals. Although the book is didactic in its emphasis on conservation, it is also the most violent and exciting of Wier's books. Smiling, friendly Guvner, who makes a fortune poaching bighorn sheep while pretending to protect them, is Wier's greatest villain.

The quality of all Wier's work is closely related to the setting. Most of her books have a strong environmental orientation, and in most cases, the more important and more specific the setting, the better the book. She is outstanding in her portrayal of the West and the Florida Everglades; in these books, a happy and successful character is one who has adapted to the environment. One adapts by accepting, even embracing, the place and its people. The chief task of Wier's protagonists is to successfully complete this process of adaptation. Those who accept the area, like David, Chance Reedy, Nate Klink, and Orph Hastings, are quickly assimilated; ones who hold out against the environment, like Scrub Nolan and Whit Stewart, are not trusted by the other characters and must prove their worth before they gain acceptance. The really unhappy characters in Wier's books are the natives who find themselves at odds with their environment. They may try to escape it, as Job Klink once did, or pit themselves against it, like Turpem Reedy, but they will not be happy or successful until they surrender themselves to it, although such surrender does not indicate weakness. The most successful characters are strong enough to withstand nature, but they neither invite nor run from a confrontation with it. They are, however, quick to defend their environment from villains, men who seek to destroy rather than protect it.

Wier, who lives in retirement in Florida, has not published a book since 1975. At the time they were written, her books were well reviewed, but they were not enormously popular. She wrote in a period when urban settings were in demand and when ethnic integration was a goal. Wier preferred rural places and wrote of cultures which are different and distinctive. Not only does she focus on unusual settings, but she invites the reader to recognize the value of living in harmony with his environment.

Reference:

Bertha Gunterman et al., "Ester Wier," *Library Journal*, 89 (15 March 1964): 1381-1382.

Papers:

Ester Wier's papers are in the Kerlan Collection, University of Minnesota, Minneapolis, and in the de Grummond Collection, University of Southern Mississippi, Hattiesburg.

Nancy Willard

(26 June 1936-   )

E. Charles Vousden

and

Laura Ingram

See also the Willard entry in *DLB 5: American Poets Since World War II.*

BOOKS: *In His Country: Poems* (Ann Arbor, Mich.: Generation, 1966);

Skin of Grace: Poems (Columbia: University of Missouri Press, 1967);

The Lively Anatomy of God (New York: Eakins, 1968);

A New Herball, illustrated by Helen Siegl (Baltimore: Ferdinand Roten Galleries, 1968);

Testimony of the Invisible Man: William Carlos Williams, Francis Ponge, Rainer Maria Rilke, Pablo Neruda (Columbia: University of Missouri Press, 1970);

19 Masks for the Naked Poet, illustrated by Regina Shekerjian (Santa Cruz, Cal.: Kayak Books, 1971);

Childhood of the Magician (New York: Liveright, 1973);

Carpenter of the Sun (New York: Liveright, 1974);

Sailing to Cythera and Other Anatole Stories, illustrated by David McPhail (New York: Harcourt Brace Jovanovich, 1974);

The Merry History of a Christmas Pie: With a Delicious Description of a Christmas Soup, illustrated by Haig and Regina Shekerjian (New York: Putnam's, 1974);

The Snow Rabbit, illustrated by Laura Lydecker (New York: Putnam's, 1975);

All On a May Morning, illustrated by Haig and Regina Shekerjian (New York: Putnam's, 1975);

Shoes Without Leather, illustrated by Lydecker (New York: Putnam's, 1976);

The Well-Mannered Balloon, illustrated by Haig and Regina Shekerjian (New York: Harcourt Brace Jovanovich, 1976);

Stranger's Bread, illustrated by McPhail (New York: Harcourt Brace Jovanovich, 1977);

Simple Pictures Are Best, illustrated by Tomie de Paola (New York: Harcourt Brace Jovanovich, 1978);

The Highest Hit, illustrated by Emily McCully (New York: Harcourt Brace Jovanovich, 1978);

Papa's Panda, illustrated by Lillian Hoban (New York: Harcourt Brace Jovanovich, 1979);

The Island of the Grass King: The Further Adventures of Anatole, illustrated by McPhail (New York: Harcourt Brace Jovanovich, 1979);

The Marzipan Moon, illustrated by Marcia Sewall (New York: Harcourt Brace Jovanovich, 1981);

photo by Michael Metz

386

A Visit to William Blake's Inn: Poems For Innocent and Experienced Travelers, illustrated by Alice and Martin Provensen (New York: Harcourt Brace Jovanovich, 1981);

Uncle Terrible: More Adventures of Anatole, illustrated by McPhail (San Diego: Harcourt Brace Jovanovich, 1982);

Household Tales of Moon & Water (New York: Harcourt Brace Jovanovich, 1982);

The Nightgown of the Sullen Moon, illustrated by McPhail (New York: Harcourt Brace Jovanovich, 1983);

Angel in the Parlor: Five Stories & Eight Essays (San Diego: Harcourt Brace Jovanovich, 1983);

Things Invisible to See (New York: Knopf, 1985).

PERIODICAL PUBLICATIONS: "Angel in the Parlor: The Reading and Writing of Fantasy," *Antioch Review* (1977): 426-437;

"The Well-Tempered Falsehood: The Art of Storytelling," *Massachusetts Review* (Summer 1978): 365-378;

"The Secret Process of Story Writing," *Writer* (July 1979): 7-10;

"The Spinning Room: Symbols and Storytellers," *Horn Book* (October 1980);

"Magic and Craft in Writing Children's Books," *Writer* (April 1981): 17-19;

"Becoming a Writer," *Michigan Quarterly Review* (Winter 1982): 77-84.

Nancy Willard, a versatile and prolific writer whose works for children include picture books, short story collections, novels, and a book of poetry, was born on 26 June 1936 in Ann Arbor, Michigan, where her father, Hobart Hurd Willard, was a university chemistry professor. Her childhood penchant for artistic and literary expression was encouraged by her family, to whom she frequently gave hand-bound, illustrated storybooks as gifts. Willard's mother, Marge Sheppard Willard, noted that she "was always drawing, writing, winning prizes. . . . In high school they let her draw instead of take gym." At age seven Willard had a poem published in a Unitarian church magazine, and as a high school senior she had a booklet entitled "A Child's Star" published as an insert in *Horn Book*'s 1955 Christmas issue. Moreover, Bertha Mahony Miller, the editor of *Horn Book,* later sent Willard ten dollars and asked for permission to use one of her illustrations for a *Horn Book* Christmas card.

Though Willard has illustrated other people's texts, she does not do the artwork for her own books. She often provides a layout for her picture books, "to help the editor see the possibilities," but she tells the artists working with her "never to be bound by anything I've done."

In 1954 Willard entered the honors English program at the University of Michigan. While there, she wrote and illustrated a children's book which appeared as part of the student literary magazine. Marianne Moore, on a visit to the campus, saw the work and later sent Willard "five dollars wrapped in a pink Kleenex requesting another copy." Willard has said of the incident, a highly encouraging gesture for a prominent writer to make toward an undergraduate, that "she was very touched" and sure that she "saved the Kleenex."

Willard received a B.A. degree in 1958 and enrolled in the master's program at Stanford University. She wrote her thesis on medieval folk songs, acquired her M.A. in 1960, and returned to the University of Michigan for her Ph.D., which she was awarded in 1963. Willard then moved to Poughkeepsie, New York, to teach at Vassar, where she is now a creative writing instructor.

She married Eric Lindbloom, a photographer, in 1964. In 1966 she published her first book, a collection of adult poetry called *In His Country.* In the next five years she published two more volumes of poetry, a short story collection, and a book of literary essays. Not until after the birth of her son, James, did she begin writing for children, with her first publication in the genre consisting of a trilogy of short stories called *Sailing to Cythera and Other Anatole Stories* (1974), which won the Lewis Carroll Shelf Award in 1976.

The central figure of these stories is an imperturbable youngster named Anatole, whose adventures take him to a world that is a mixture of C. S. Lewis's Narnia, Lewis Carroll's Wonderland, and Frank L. Baum's Oz. In "Gospel Train," Anatole, accompanied by a sententious cat named Plumpet, takes a mystical train voyage to Morgentown for the christening party of Plumpet's Aunt Pitterpat. He helps a soldier recover thirty missing years of his life in "The Wise Soldier of Sellebak" and enters the wallpaper of his grandmother's house and befriends a fearful monster in "Sailing to Cythera." The stories in *Sailing to Cythera* endorse what Willard calls "the magic view of life" and are based on the same logic that pervades fairy tales and myths. They confirm "the power of the invisible" and support the notion that things unseen are as important as things seen.

Willard wrote her next book after observing a young friend snooping around in a spice cabinet and talking to the different spices as if they had personalities. *The Merry History of a Christmas Pie: With a Delicious Description of a Christmas Soup* (1974) is a short picture book with a simple poem for text. Introduced by the puppet, Punch, the particular ingredients parade one at a time across a stage reciting brief poems about themselves, an example of which is Sir Cinnamon's poem:

> Here I come, Sir Cinnamon
> Under my hat a thousand men
> and if you don't believe what I say
> here comes Miss Mace to clear the way.

Like most of Willard's later picture book texts, *The Merry History of a Christmas Pie* emphasizes simplicity and repetition.

The Snow Rabbit (1975) and *The Well-Mannered Balloon* (1976) are picture books with prose texts which concern events in the life of a young boy named James. As Willard has suggested, both were obviously inspired by her own son. *The Snow Rabbit* is about James's attempt to bring a snow sculpture into his warm house, where it naturally melts. Seeing the pool of water, he thinks the rabbit has gotten lost and then draws a house for it, hoping it will come back. The next morning the rabbit appears mysteriously sketched into the drawing wearing a smile of contentment. In *The Well-Mannered Balloon*, James gets a balloon and paints a pirate face upon it. In the middle of the night, when all the grown-ups are asleep, the balloon changes from a friendly companion to a demanding and voracious antagonist and James is forced to pop it. The stories of both books are quite simple, reflecting the author's desire to write for her young son, who was just learning to read, but neither book lacks the strain of magic that is so important to Willard.

A picture book poem, published between *The Snow Rabbit* and *The Well-Mannered Balloon*, called *All On a May Morning* (1975) begins with this rhyme:

> Primrose and poppy,
> Basil and bay,
> My gentle heart
> has flown away.

The pictures and poem continue with a little girl's search for her heart, which takes her "over and under" such things as unicorns, hunters, mayapples, horses and carts, chairs of hollyhocks, and Van Eyck's portrait of Arnolfini and his bride. Despite the brevity, the flavor of a magical, medieval world is just as evident in Willard's poetic text to

this picture book as in her longer, more complex works.

Simple Pictures Are Best (1978) is another prose picture book. It depicts a shoemaker and his wife posing for their anniversary photograph with increasing numbers of their favorite items, in spite of the photographer's warning that "Simple pictures are best." As with most of Willard's works, the author's values are clearly expressed, but she does not forget that her first intent is to entertain and amuse.

Anatole returns as the protagonist of *Stranger's Bread* (1977). In this story, Anatole is asked to deliver a loaf of bread from the corner store to Mrs. Chiba's house. Like Pinocchio, he is accosted on the way by a variety of characters, though in this case they are friendly and only ask for a slice of bread and a ride in his wagon. Of course by the time he reaches Mrs. Chiba's house, the bread has been entirely consumed and he must report that sad fact to her.

In *Stranger's Bread* Willard emphasizes the admirableness of Anatole's generosity and honesty over the placid acceptance of the strange and unusual. She leaves the reader with the following thought:

> "If you have two loaves of bread," Mrs. Chiba said, "give one to your friends."
> "And if you only have one," Anatole replied, "give it to your strangers."

The protagonist of *The Highest Hit* (1978), Willard's first novel for children, was actually modeled upon herself. Kate Carpenter is an irrepressible young girl whose exploits include teaching her mother to play baseball, writing a neighborhood newspaper (as Willard and her older sister Ann had done), getting her head stuck in a magician's guillotine, falling through a window into a priest's living room, and entering a germ in a pet contest. Although this work is not one of fantasy, like the Anatole stories, Willard does present a magical view of life in the book. Its humor and hopefulness are apparent primarily in the way Kate responds with ingeniousness and curiosity to everything that happens.

If there is one book in which Willard is openly didactic, it is the prose picture book entitled *Papa's Panda* (1979) in which a father explains to his son, who wants a pet panda, why he cannot have one. The book's moralizing tone is muted somewhat by the amusing tale, but the admonition that one should not desire anything without giving careful thought to the consequences of having it is conspicuous. When the boy's father describes how much effort would have to go into feeding, cleaning, and entertaining such a creature and that Jim, his son, would be overwhelmed by these demands, Jim is grateful to receive a toy panda instead of a live one as a birthday gift.

In her next book, *The Island of the Grass King: The Further Adventures of Anatole* (1979), Willard again draws on traditional myth and folklore to create a fantasy world peopled by improbable but engaging creatures. In this adventure, Anatole's wish to obtain some fennel to cure his grandmother's asthma propels him on a strange journey to the Island of the Grass King, which is under the spell of the unfriendly Mother Weather-Sky. His companions include his cat, Plumpet, an animated silver coffeepot, an enchanted human-sized green rabbit named Captain Lark, and a little girl who has been turned to glass.

On his quest for fennel, Anatole encounters a variety of characters, some familiar from folklore, such as a flying horse and the Four Winds, and others that are of Willard's own invention, such as

the Mender, who repairs wounded animals, the Keeper of the Roads, and a society of talking dogs whose favorite pastime is executing intruders by means of a mysterious swing which flings its victims into the sky. The company reaches the island, transported on the back of the North Wind, and, after a brief enslavement by Mother Weather-Sky, Anatole and an enchanted boar named Toby fulfill a cryptic prophecy and free the Grass King and his kingdom from Mother Weather-Sky's evil spell.

David McPhail's illustrations echo the fancy and whimsical detail of Willard's tale. *Publishers Weekly* praised the manner in which "both author and illustrator weave tapestries in which make-believe and reality blend joyfully." A reviewer for *School Library Journal* described the book as "full of details that surprise yet rub together with a kind of kaleidoscope consistency" and recommended it "for those who revel in the unexpected, in wonderful invention, in powerful and vivid and even mystical fancy."

The Island of the Grass King received the 1979 Lewis Carroll Shelf Award "for the beauty of its language." It has been criticized, however, for in-

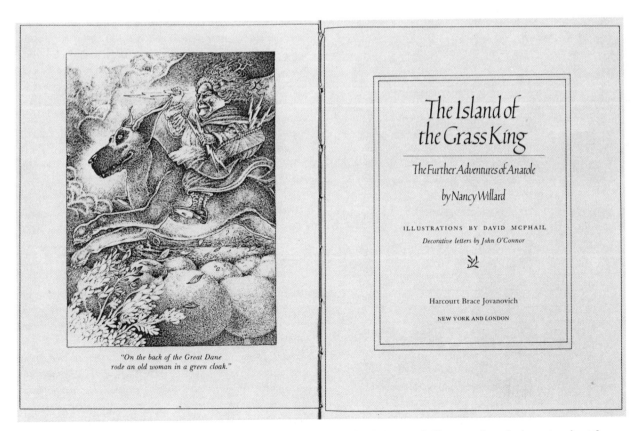

"On the back of the Great Dane
rode an old woman in a green cloak."

The Island of
the Grass King

The Further Adventures of Anatole

by Nancy Willard

ILLUSTRATIONS BY DAVID MCPHAIL
Decorative letters by John O'Connor

Harcourt Brace Jovanovich
NEW YORK AND LONDON

Frontispiece and title page for Willard's third book featuring Anatole, an imperturbable young boy who has a penchant for magical adventures

frequent uncredited references to other works, such as in the green rabbit's recitation of a fragment of Tennyson's "Crossing the Bar," but no one has argued that this work is thus a failure. Indeed most critical responses have been purely laudatory.

The Marzipan Moon (1981) is the story of a priest, who, after receiving a broken crock on his birthday, has his wish for a marzipan moon each morning granted. The "miracle" is exploited by a bishop whose greed causes the magic to stop. Here again, Willard's work carries a message. The priest is a very pious man who can be forgiven his single indulgence, but the bishop is an ostentatious, overbearing sort whose pride causes him to lose sight of his responsibility to his parishioners. Willard ends her tale with the following comment: "But the clay crock, that's the one you want to get hold of. And if you do, remember the priest's story. Wish for something sensible."

Willard's latest installment in the Anatole stories, *Uncle Terrible: More Adventures of Anatole* (1982), also illustrated by McPhail, takes the hero

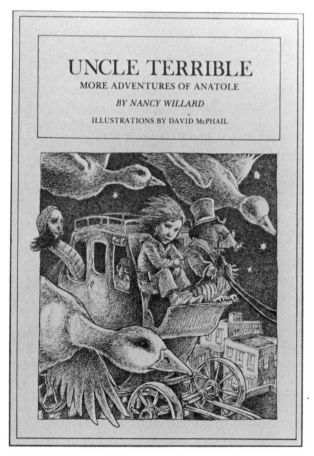

Dust jacket for Willard's latest installment in the Anatole stories (Harcourt Brace Jovanovich)

on a visit to his friend, Uncle Terrible, so named "because he's so terribly nice." Soon after Anatole's arrival, they encounter the wizard Arcimboldo the Marvelous, who gives them an advertisement in the form of a fan and, Anatole is convinced, transforms a woman into an owl. Their adventures begin when the two make themselves small enough to inhabit a dollhouse, by means of a book of magic spells, and must venture beneath the floorboards to rescue the book from a band of scavenger cockroaches who have stolen it. In the roaches' trading post, Anatole finds a magical ring which transforms Uncle Terrible into a snake and summons a miniature stagecoach which transports them to the domain of the mysterious Mother, a benevolent caretaker of nature. Their fellow travelers are the enchanted owl and a girl to whom Anatole had given the wizard's fan, now invisible as a result of an offhand wish.

Mother reveals to Anatole that he is the hero sent to recover the threads of life and death, stolen and separated by the evil magic of Arcimboldo, and thus to save the world from being taken over by the wicked magician. After winning the thread of death by beating Arcimboldo in a bizarre game of checkers, Anatole disguises himself as a cat and becomes the pet of Cicero Yin, an honest tailor who, with twelve enchanted golden needles, is unknowingly knitting the thread of life into a cloak which will give Arcimboldo power and leave Mother helpless to break his enchantments. By befriending some mice and enlisting an absentminded bat to summon his companions, Anatole is able to trick the wizard into reading the spell for making oneself small. Arcimboldo is eaten by his own helper, the enchanted owl, and his evil spells are broken, restoring the victims of his magic to their original forms and removing the threat to Mother's benevolent guardianship of the world. Once again McPhail's fanciful drawings enhance Willard's story by presenting visual renditions of the precisely drawn scenes and characters.

Though her contribution to children's literature consists primarily of several picture books and the Anatole stories, Willard received highest recognition (the 1982 Newbery Medal) for *A Visit to William Blake's Inn: Poems For Innocent and Experienced Travelers* (1981), a book that is unlike anything she had previously done for children. Ostensibly based on Blake's *Songs of Innocence and Experience*, the collection portrays the poet and artist as a keeper of an inn in which plants and animals speak, guests ride in Blake's fantastic flying car, and celestial bodies cavort for the entertainment of all.

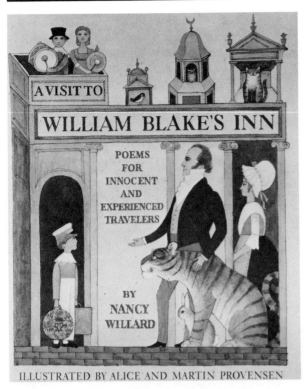

Dust jacket for Willard's Newbery Medal-winning poetry collection based on Blake's Songs of Innocence and Experience *(Harcourt Brace Jovanovich)*

Many of the fifteen poems are nonsense verses, such as "The Man in the Marmalade Hat Arrives," "The King of Cats Orders an Early Breakfast," and "The Wise Cow Enjoys a Cloud," while others express morals or messages clearly, such as "When We Come Home, Blake Calls for Fire," which praises the virtues of fire, and "The Marmalade Man Makes a Dance to Mend Us," which bids all creatures to live in peace. Willard indulges in a clever play on words and a mild satire on the idiosyncrasies of the English language in "The Wise Cow Makes *Way, Room,* and *Believe.*" "Blake Tells the Tiger the Tale of the Tailor," a verse story of a tailor who builds his house of body parts stolen from animals only to discover that his home is haunted by his victims, is the most disturbing of the collection.

The poems presented here are short and simple, making use of traditional forms. The subject matter ranges from the didactic to the purely fanciful, but the poems are always markedly nonsensical and literal-minded: breakfast served "on the house," for instance, is served on the roof of the inn.

As impressive as the poetry itself are the illustrations by Alice and Martin Provensen. The drawings, done in subdued colors and a quaint style, reflect the action of each poem, often depicting the scenes word for word. Filled with smiling animals, fantastic contraptions, and detailed cutaway views of the rooms of the inn, these illustrations provide an amusing and richly detailed complement to Willard's poetry.

Willard's most recent book for children is *The Nightgown of the Sullen Moon* (1983). This bedtime story, enhanced by David McPhail's vividly colored, humorous illustrations, offers a fanciful explanation of the phenomenon of a moonless night. The main character in Willard's modern fable is, not surprisingly, the moon herself. Portrayed as a luminous, mild-faced bulb in McPhail's drawings, the moon floats close to the earth and observes human life. The tale begins on "the billionth birthnight of the full moon," when she spies a blue flannel, star-covered nightgown flapping on a clothesline and decides that she must have an identical gown of her own. The text, aided heavily by illustrations, chronicles her search for a nightgown over the countryside and through the town, past church and tavern, until she arrives at a small store labeled "Slumber Shop."

There the salesgirl shows her an array of sleepwear ranging from animal and floral prints to plain white and lacy, beribboned black. None of these satisfies the moon, being too small, too large, too pale, and too dark respectively, and with amazing accuracy she asks if there might be "one more nightgown hidden in a drawer at the back of the shop?" The obliging salesgirl produces a blue star-covered gown which the moon buys and wears home. Happy at last with her nightgown, the moon returns to the sky, though she is now covered by the gown.

Soon, the people and animals of the earth miss the moon in the night sky. They become lost in the dark and cannot remember their songs. Without the moon overhead, the night is dark and silent, and people from all over the world begin to lament her absence and call for her. At this point the Sun steps in and tells the Moon that she must take back the nightgown, explaining that because "so many things change on earth" the people "want nothing to change in the sky." With a disappointing lack of argument, the moon agrees; however, she hides the gown in "a drawer at the back of the sky instead," and when she cannot be seen in the night sky, it is because she has once more put on the gown.

Willard remarked once that she did not choose her books but was chosen by them, and that only they knew whether they were prose or poetry, realism or fantasy, for adults or for children—her job was merely to write them. Certainly the variety of her work supports her statement. Despite the number of genres in which she seems at ease, there is a striking consistency in her literature. Everything she writes affirms her belief in the "magic view of life"; that is, a view of life that incorporates the imagination and stresses the appropriateness of things meant to be taken metaphorically.

Laurence Yep
(14 June 1948-   )

Joe Stines

BOOKS: *Sweetwater,* illustrated by Julia Noonan (New York: Harper & Row, 1973);
Dragonwings (New York: Harper & Row, 1975);
Child of the Owl (New York: Harper & Row, 1977);
Seademons: A Novel (New York: Harper & Row, 1977);
Sea Glass (New York: Harper & Row, 1979);
Kind Hearts and Gentle Monsters (New York: Harper & Row, 1982);
The Mark Twain Murders (New York: Four Winds, 1982);
Dragon of the Lost Sea (New York: Harper & Row, 1982);
Liar, Liar (New York: Morrow, 1983);
The Serpent's Children (New York: Harper & Row, 1984);
The Tom Sawyer Fires (New York: Morrow, 1984);
Dragon Steel (New York: Harper & Row, 1985);
Mountain Light (New York: Harper & Row, 1985).

Because he was raised in a black ghetto and attended a grammar school in San Francisco's Chinatown, Laurence Yep has firsthand knowledge of cultural alienation and racial conflict. A third-generation Chinese-American, Yep is a short story writer, a novelist, and an author of books for young people whose fictional characters are forever struggling to adapt, to thwart the effects of prejudice and injustice by seeking a personal identity. His works for young people have been consistently praised for their depth and lucidity and for his strong, realistic characterizations. Yep has written one adult novel, *Seademons* (1977), three excellent young adult novels about Chinese-Americans, sev-

Laurence Yep

eral moderately interesting juvenile mysteries, as well as science fiction and fantasy, though many critics agree that his success as a writer is due more to his imaginative, well-paced writing style than to his subject matter.

Yep grew up in San Francisco, where he was born on 14 June 1948, the son of Thomas Gim Yep, a postal clerk, and Franche Lee Yep. After attending Marquette University from 1966 to 1968, he received his B.A. degree from the University of California, Santa Cruz, in 1970. In 1975, Yep received his Ph.D. from the State University of New York at Buffalo. He currently lives in Sunnyvale, California.

Having been associated with both black and Chinese-American life-styles as a child, and having encountered white society first during high school, Yep feels that his roots lie entangled in several cultures. He says, "In a sense I have no one culture to call my own since I exist peripherally in several," and goes on to say, "However, in my writing I can create my own."

Many of Yep's leading characters must also deal with a complicated heritage. These individuals are typically twelve or thirteen years old, usually facing an identity crisis, and sometimes in need of establishing family relationships. His plots challenge those young people to dare to be themselves. During the course of a story, they mature gradually and naturally, displaying tolerance, strength, and understanding.

Yep's stories evolve smoothly from the interaction of his characters. In reference to style critics note that Yep's frequent use of first-person, tough-kid narration sometimes makes his dialogue appear forced. However, these critics also note that his use of metaphors and symbolism gives life and personality to his characters and story lines. Most important, Laurence Yep allows both his characters and his readers the experience of a sense of wonder.

Yep's career as a writer began with science fiction short stories contributed to such magazines as *Worlds of If* and *Galaxy*, and several of these have appeared in collections, including *World's Best Science Fiction of 1969*, edited by Donald Wollheim and Terry Carr. In 1973 Yep published his first novel, *Sweetwater*. This science fiction tale for young readers has for its setting a distant planet ironically named Harmony. It is the story of Tyree Priest, who belongs to a minority group called Silkies. From Tyree and the warm, complex relationships between his family members, the reader views a boy's growing up, his awakening to a creative ambition within himself, and the struggle and eventual destruction of his family's life-style due to the intrusion of a covetous capitalist and an immense sea dragon.

Dust jacket for Yep's first novel, a science fiction tale set on a distant planet named Harmony (Harper & Row)

The inhabitants of Harmony include the Silkies, descendants of intelligent and capable star-pilots who have adapted to life in the partially submerged city of Old Sion; the Mainlanders, colonists from Earth who built an inland city, New Sion, after disastrous sea floods inundated the original city; and the native Argans, a spiderlike people who live segregated in an ancient section of Old Sion.

The plot of this story is complex, involving racial prejudice, social jealousy, the evil influences of money, and, more subtly, the issues of patience and personal freedom. Against his father's wishes, young Tyree crosses the race line and establishes a musical bond with old Amadeus, a respected grandfather among the Argans. It is this bond which allows Tyree, his blind sister, Caley, and his parents to endure the onslaught of the bloodthirsty Argan Hydra, the shrewd manipulation of the capitalist Satin, and the violent attack of Old Sion by an embittered sea dragon.

Placing high value on patriarchal authority and on family and community loyalty, Yep explores the themes of progress versus tradition, the rights of minorities, the costliness of integrity, the necessity for courage, ecology versus destructive imbalance, and the practical purpose of art. Of major interest in the book is the father-son relationship, handled with uncommon respect and compassion.

Sometimes using American slang, the author provides a believable story with exhilarating action scenes and an imaginative story line steeped in nostalgia. This first novel by Laurence Yep was best summarized by Brian Stableford in a 1976 review for *Vector 78:* "*Sweetwater* has one powerful thing going for it, and that is the fact that its writing is, in every sense of the word, beautiful."

Although well received, *Sweetwater* did not bring immediate financial and literary success to its author. Yep's recognition and acceptance, particularly in the world of children's literature, came with the publication of *Dragonwings* (1975). Prior to this publication, Yep spent six years exploring his Chinese-American heritage. He found that the first-generation Chinese-Americans, most of whom settled in San Francisco, had important roles in the development of their new country, though they remain faceless and nameless to historians and writers alike. Through his research he discovered the story of Fung Joe Guey, who flew a biplane of his own construction over Oakland, California, in 1909, and Yep decided to use the flight of this early aviator as the basis for his second novel.

Yep was able to uncover few facts concerning the history of the early Chinese-Americans, but he successfully integrated what he did know into his novel. In "Writing Dragonwings," which Yep published in the January 1977 issue of the *Reading Teacher*, he states that most of the immigrants who began to arrive in the 1850s were men from troubled southern China who came to America in order to support their families at home. Partly due to fear of prejudice, they came alone, creating a "society of bachelors" which lasted into the 1930s, though a "small number" were able to have their wives and families join them. The early Chinese were more adept at handling discrimination than other minorities, but even so, they segregated themselves, "choosing to imitate their white counterparts within the confines of Chinatown."

The author chose to keep children in mind as the main reading audience for the first of three novels concerning Chinese-Americans. With so lit-

tle historical fact from which to draw, each action within his story line became a unique discovery for Yep, who said that when he "chose to describe things from the viewpoint of an eight-year-old Chinese boy, it was more than simply choosing a narrative device; it was close to the process of discovery I myself was experiencing in writing the story."

On the surface, *Dragonwings* is simply the story of a Chinese man, Windrider, who came to the Land of the Golden Mountain, America, to challenge the unknown in a new country. He is joined by his eight-year-old son, Moon Shadow, who arrives in San Francisco in 1903. Together they fulfill the father's dream to fly. The story is narrated with humor and detail, blending Chinese folklore, myths, and legends with historical facts, such as the great San Francisco earthquake, the Chinese bachelor community of Chinatown, and the daring biplane flight of Fung Joe Guey.

Yep provides the reader with a new way of viewing Chinese-Americans, not as yellow men living in white society but as ordinary as well as extraordinary people. In his afterword to *Dragonwings*, he states: "I wanted to show that Chinese-Americans are human beings upon whom America has had a unique effect."

The story's multidimensional characters exhibit courage, determination, and intelligence. They must contend with the harsh realities of a new land, including racism and oppression. Windrider and Moon Shadow are befriended by a white woman, Miss Whitlaw, and her niece, Robin. These ladies appear as strongly drawn feminist characters and atypical whites as they exhibit respect and belief in Windrider's dream of flying. Windrider's uncle, Bright Star, represents tradition and practicality, but he too learns to accept his nephew's dream.

The thematic structure of *Dragonwings* is developed in a more subtle manner than in *Sweetwater*. The relationship between father and son is emphasized by Moon Shadow's devotion to his father. Underlying themes such as the search for identity, the need for family relationships, and the necessity of imagination are enhanced by Yep's figurative language and skillful application of symbolic Chinese folklore.

Having been described by critics as sensitive, adventurous, and original, *Dragonwings* remains Yep's most acclaimed and successful work, chosen as an ALA Notable Children's Book in 1975 and selected as a Newbery Honor Book for 1976.

In 1977 Yep published a second Chinese-American novel for children, *Child of the Owl*. In many ways, this narrative, with its contemporary 1960s setting, made a greater contribution to ethnic literature than did *Dragonwings*. The book's setting, San Francisco's Chinatown, is vividly drawn and realistically detailed, so that *Washington Post Book World* reviewer Maxine Hong Kingston remarked, "There are scenes in *Child of the Owl* that will make every Chinese-American child gasp with recognition. 'Hey! That happened to me. I did that. I saw that.'"

The protagonist, struggling with a dual heritage, is twelve-year-old Casey Young. The Chinese girl goes to live with Paw-Paw, her maternal grandmother, after her compulsive gambler father, Barney, is beaten and hospitalized. Named for Casey Stengel by her father, who paid the hospital bill when she was born with money won on baseball bets, Casey has never thought of herself as Chinese. In the beginning, she is vulnerable and confused, but by story's end, Casey is wise and strong—an individual who is secure with her own identity. Through Paw-Paw's wisdom and sensitivity, Casey learns about her mother, Jennie, who died when Casey was very young, about her true Chinese name, and about the legend behind the family's owl charm.

The author takes an entire chapter to relate the legend of the owl, which allows Casey to realize that she may never feel completely at ease as Chinese or American, but she must hold on to her Chinese heritage. The owl tale describes how the owl Jasmine was tricked out of her feather skin and was made the wife of a human. Through Paw-Paw, Yep says, "we became a little like owls the moment we turned our backs on China and the old ways." In the afterword, Yep states, "although I have never seen an owl charm or heard a story about owls, I've presented the owl story . . . based upon stories of filial devotion once popular among the Chinese and upon Chinese folklore concerning owls and other animals."

The book reveals the dangers of Chinatown with the climactic robbery of the owl charm, during which Paw-Paw is seriously hurt. This incident and Casey's loss of her innocent belief in Barney's impossible dreams and promises are handled realistically but with sensitivity. Yep gives his readers an exciting and well-plotted story in *Child of the Owl*, creating strong and interesting characters. His portrayal of Chinatown is fascinating, and the book is worthy of the Boston Globe-Horn Book Fiction Award which it received in 1977.

Sea Glass (1979), Yep's fifth novel, deals less with history and folklore and more with the reality of growing up Chinese in a Western society. In the story, twelve-year-old Craig Chin moves from San Francisco's Chinatown to the predominantly white coastal village of Concepcion, finding himself trapped between two cultures with no identity to call his own. A major theme of this novel is the eternally present conflict between generations. "A Chinese has to try twice as hard as any Western person," says Craig's father as he constantly urges Craig to pursue excellence in sports as a means to "fit in." Craig rebels against his father's wishes and turns to his reclusive old Uncle Quail for understanding.

Craig's first-person narrative creates believable characters struggling with realistic problems. Craig is overweight, awkward, and only vaguely interested in sports. The story points out that children are too often burdened with the aspirations of their parents, without the encouragement to find their own dreams.

Craig, however, treats his father with utmost respect, displaying remarkable understanding and patience for a boy his age, and he eventually succeeds in getting his father to let go. By illuminating attitudes and portraying change within his characters Yep reveals the complex souls of seemingly ordinary people. Like Tyree Priest in *Sweetwater* and Casey Young in *Child of the Owl*, Craig Chin is able to overlook the barriers of environmental and social pressures and to search within himself for his own identity. Yep's faith that such a quality or human truth exists for every individual makes *Sea Glass* rewarding for readers young and old.

During the early 1980s, Yep wrote three mysteries, *The Mark Twain Murders* (1982), *Liar, Liar* (1983), and *The Tom Sawyer Fires* (1984), which are generally less absorbing than his other writings, largely due to the fact that the author seems detached from his work. However, *Kind Hearts and Gentle Monsters* (1982), the story of Charley Sabini, a high school sophomore who develops an unlikely romance with an antagonistic girl named Chris Pomeroy, marks an important development in Yep's work. Charley, from a large, Catholic family with strong and loving parents, is totally rational and a firm believer in a well-organized life. He is surrounded by an atmosphere of self-satisfaction, at least until he receives a poison-pen chain letter. The letter refers to Charley as "an arrogant meddler" and goes on to accuse him of being "everything from . . . teacher's pet to . . . a callous pig." The person who started the chain had stated, "To know him was to loathe him (at least secretly)." Charley discovers that Chris Pomeroy started the letter, and he goes to her home to confront her.

Chris reacts to things on a purely emotional level. At San Francisco's Lowell High School, she has developed the reputation of being the most sarcastic, outrageous, and sadistic girl in school. Even before he received the letter, Charley has remarked, "Well, she was pretty enough, but she had a regular chainsaw for a tongue." Her father is dead, and her mother, Maxine Pomeroy, has a history of mental problems.

When Charley meets Mrs. Pomeroy he begins to understand Chris. Although Mrs. Pomeroy often demonstrates erratic behavior and is a constant burden to Chris, Chris loves her mother. In coming to understand the Pomeroys Charley learns how to care about other people.

Yep vividly portrays the collision of logical thinking and pure emotion. The resulting compromise between Chris's emotional view of life and Charley's logical, reasoned viewpoint does not so much change Chris and Charley as it brings them an improved understanding of each other and themselves. With the publication of *Kind Hearts and Gentle Monsters,* Laurence Yep successfully broadened his scope as a writer.

With the publication of *Dragon of the Lost Sea* (1982), Yep returned to the fantasy he had previously written into his science fiction works. Alluding to "Old Mother of the Waters" and other Chinese myths, Yep presents a simple, easy to read, episodic adventure in the story of dragon princess Shimmer and her efforts to capture the witch Civet so as to free the inland sea that was once her home. The imprisoned Lost Sea exists inside a pebble that hangs from Civet's neck. Along the way, Shimmer befriends a homeless, thirteen-year-old boy, Thorn, and against her better judgment, she allows him to accompany her in pursuit of the witch.

Critics have noted a stiffness of style and an uneven telling of the story as the narration alternates chapter by chapter between Shimmer and Thorn. Reviewer Robin McKinley, in *Voice of Youth*

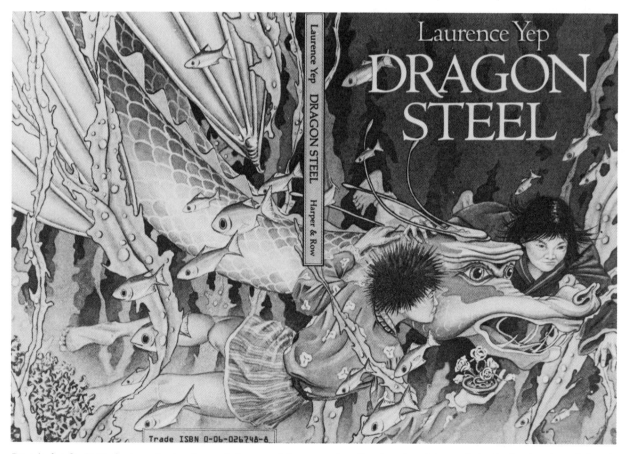

Dust jacket for Yep's fantasy about a dragon princess and her struggle to free her clan from a witch who has imprisoned them in underwater forges (Harper & Row)

Dust jacket for Yep's historical novel set in nineteenth-century China during the Taiping Rebellion (Harper & Row)

Advocates, says, "It's as though Yep couldn't quite make up his mind between the conversational style more suited to the filling-out of personalities, and the lofty distant style more suited to the retelling of old folk tales. . . ." Nevertheless, *Dragon of the Lost Sea* is fast-paced reading.

Thematically, the story is characteristic of Yep's writing in its exploration of the ideas of identity, good versus evil, friendship, and loyalty. Shimmer, who never imagined Thorn's "almost dragonish" courage, is surprised by his intense loyalty and unrelenting kindness. She comes to respect the human, feeling that "loyalty ought to count for something in the wicked world," even though her friendship with Thorn exposes her to ridicule from her own kind. Though the structure of *Dragon of the Lost Sea* is problematic, the interaction between Yep's unique and carefully drawn characters is the book's main redeeming feature. The story's incon-

clusive ending, with Shimmer, Thorn, and a captured Civet heading toward the "mighty undersea kingdoms of the dragons," points the way toward its sequel, *Dragon Steel* (1985), in which Shimmer continues her struggle to regain her home sea while freeing her clan from slavery at underwater forges. Along the way, she and Thorn, along with their new human companion, Indigo, must combat the Dragon King's envy and treachery. Indigo, a female counterpart to Thorn, develops from an orphaned slave into a personable heroine, and by the end of the story, Civet is remorseful for having stolen the Inland Sea, and she joins Shimmer's odyssey to restore it to its rightful clan.

To ensure that *Dragon Steel* can stand alone as a high adventure fantasy, Yep offers a verse prologue disguised as a "popular dragon ballad," which summarizes the adventures of Shimmer, Thorn, and Civet recorded earlier in *Dragon of the Lost Sea*. Told from Shimmer's viewpoint, *Dragon Steel* is more complex and stimulating than the earlier work, and more attention is given to developing secondary characters.

Yep's writing style settles, to use McKinley's division, to that which is "conversational, more suited to the filling-out of personalities." The continued story offers more magic, more action, and more wisdom. The climactic escape of Shimmer and her cohorts through a blue hole with the Dragon King's cauldron, which now contains the imprisoned sea, is adventure fantasy at its best.

At the tale's end, the stage is set for yet another sequel. Indigo and friends return to her beloved homeland, the Green Darkness, to find it in great despair. Indigo comes to the realization, just as each of the others had, that "you can't go home again," though Thorn assures her that "Restoring a village will be child's play next to bringing back a whole sea."

Since Yep has used his writing as a vehicle for exploring his own identity as a Chinese-American, it seems only natural that he would eventually turn to the genre of historical fiction in a broader sense. In *The Serpent's Children* (1984), he uses the nineteenth-century Chinese Taiping Rebellion as the backdrop for a first-person narration of a young girl, Cassia, as she struggles to protect her family from the threat of famine, bandits, and an ideological conflict between her brother and father.

Cassia was only eight years old, and her brother, Foxfire, was seven, when their revolutionary father left their peasant village to assist the ruling Manchus in removing the British from the Middle Kingdom. The story's specific setting is

Kwangtung Province, an area wracked by drought, poverty, political corruption, and social disintegration. After her mother dies, Cassia rebels against clan members. Her father returns home crippled both in body and spirit, and Foxfire, as did so many young men, travels to America so as to send hard-earned money back to Cassia.

As is true of Yep's earlier works, *The Serpent's Children* is well plotted and shows good characterization, as does its sequel, *Mountain Light,* published in 1985. Cassia's saga continues as she and her father meet Squeaky Lau, who narrates this novel after they have all been fighting against the tyrannical Manchus. In *Mountain Light* the setting shifts from Kwangtung Province to America. Serious and belligerent Cassia falls in love with free-spirited Squeaky, who follows Foxfire to the goldfields of California, where he encounters brutality, corrup-

tion, and danger. The hopes, fears, and dreams of the Chinese immigrants are explored with objectivity and a sense of wonder in this book, as the novel's strong characters participate in, rather than compete with, the historical background.

Laurence Yep's novels encourage the best from youthful readers with their consistent appeal for individuality. Through his frequent use of personal themes he has established his ability to speak to readers on an individual basis, and though he has maintained his lucid and evocative style, he has also exhibited growth and development in his handling of characters and themes. Having proved himself adept at science fiction, fantasy, mystery, and historical fiction, Yep promises to be an important influence on the continued development of children's literature.

Jane Yolen
(11 February 1939-   )

William E. Kreuger
Millikin University

BOOKS: *See This Little Line?,* illustrated by Kathleen Elgin (New York: McKay, 1963);

Pirates in Petticoats, illustrated by Leonard Vosburgh (New York: McKay, 1963);

The Witch Who Wasn't, illustrated by Arnold Roth (New York: Macmillan, 1964);

Gwinellen, the Princess Who Could Not Sleep, illustrated by Ed Renfro (New York: Macmillan, 1965);

Trust a City Kid, by Yolen and Anne Huston (New York: Lothrop, Lee & Shepard, 1966);

The Emperor and the Kite, illustrated by Ed Young (Cleveland: World, 1967);

Isabel's Noel, illustrated by Roth (New York: Funk & Wagnalls, 1967);

The Minstrel and the Mountain: A Tale of Peace, illustrated by Anne Rockwell (Cleveland: World, 1967);

World on a String: The Story of Kites (Cleveland: World, 1968);

Greyling, illustrated by William Stobbs (Cleveland: World, 1968);

The Longest Name on the Block, illustrated by Peter Madden (New York: Funk & Wagnalls, 1968);

The Inway Investigators; or, The Mystery at McCracken's Place, illustrated by Allan Eitzen (New York: Seabury, 1969);

The Wizard of Washington Square, illustrated by Ray Cruz (New York: World, 1969);

It All Depends, illustrated by Don Bolognese (New York: Funk & Wagnalls, 1969);

The Seventh Mandarin, illustrated by Young (New York: Seabury, 1970);

Hobo Toad and the Motorcycle Gang, illustrated by Emily McCully (New York: World, 1970);

The Bird of Time, illustrated by Mercer Mayer (New York: Crowell, 1971);

The Girl Who Loved the Wind, illustrated by Young (New York: Crowell, 1972);

Friend: The Story of George Fox and the Quakers (New York: Seabury, 1972);

The Wizard Islands, illustrated by Robert Quackenbush (New York: Crowell, 1973);

Writing Books for Children (Boston: Writer, 1973);

© Bill Burkhart

The Girl Who Cried Flowers, and Other Tales, illustrated by David Palladini (New York: Crowell, 1974);

Rainbow Rider, illustrated by Michael Foreman (New York: Crowell, 1974);

The Boy Who Had Wings, illustrated by Helga Aichinger (New York: Crowell, 1974);

The Magic Three of Solatia, illustrated by Julia Noonan (New York: Crowell, 1974);

Ring Out! A Book of Bells, illustrated by Richard Cuffari (New York: Seabury, 1974);

The Little Spotted Fish, illustrated by Friso Henstra (New York: Seabury, 1975);

The Transfigured Hart, illustrated by Donna Diamond (New York: Crowell, 1975);

An Invitation to the Butterfly Ball, illustrated by Jane Breskin Zalben (New York: Parents' Magazine Press, 1976);

The Moon Ribbon and Other Tales, illustrated by Palladini (New York: Crowell, 1976);

Milkweed Days, photographs by Gabriel Amadeus Cooney (New York: Crowell, 1976);

Simple Gifts: The Story of the Shakers, illustrated by Betty Fraser (New York: Viking, 1976);

The Sultan's Perfect Tree, illustrated by Barbara Garrison (New York: Parents' Magazine Press, 1977);

The Seeing Stick, illustrated by Remy Charlip and Demetra Marsalis (New York: Crowell, 1977);

The Hundredth Dove and Other Tales, illustrated by Palladini (New York: Crowell, 1977);

The Giants' Farm, illustrated by Tomie de Paola (New York: Seabury, 1977);

Hannah Dreaming, photographs by Alan R. Epstein (Springfield, Mass.: Museum of Fine Arts, 1977);

The Mermaid's Three Wisdoms, illustrated by Laura Rader (New York: Collins & World, 1978);

Spider Jane, illustrated by Stefen Bernath (New York: Coward, McCann & Geoghegan, 1978);

No Bath Tonight, illustrated by Nancy Winslow Parker (New York: Crowell, 1978);

The Simple Prince, illustrated by Jack Kent (New York: Parents' Magazine Press, 1978);

All in the Woodland Early: An ABC Book, illustrated by Zalben, music and lyrics by Yolen (Cleveland: Collins, 1979);

Dream Weaver, illustrated by Michael Hague (New York: Collins, 1979);

The Giants Go Camping, illustrated by de Paola (New York: Seabury, 1979);

How Beastly!: A Menagerie of Nonsense Poems, illustrated by James Marshall (New York: Collins, 1980);

Spider Jane on the Move, illustrated by Bernath (New York: Coward, McCann & Geoghegan, 1980);

Commander Toad in Space, illustrated by Bruce Degen (New York: Coward, McCann & Geoghegan, 1980);

Mice on Ice, illustrated by Lawrence Di Fiori (New York: Dutton, 1980);

The Robot and Rebecca: The Mystery of the Code-Carrying Kids, illustrated by Catherine Deeter (New York: Random House, 1980);

Dragon Night and Other Lullabies, illustrated by Demi (New York: Methuen, 1980);

Shirlick Holmes and the Case of the Wandering Wardrobe, illustrated by Anthony Rao (New York: Coward, McCann & Geoghegan, 1981);

The Gift of Sarah Baker: A Novel (New York: Viking, 1981);

The Boy Who Spoke Chimp, illustrated by David Wiesner (New York: Knopf, 1981);

The Robot and Rebecca and the Missing Owser, illustrated by Lady McCrady (New York: Knopf, 1981);

The Acorn Quest, illustrated by Susanna Natti (New York: Crowell, 1981);

Brothers of the Wind, illustrated by Barbara Berger (New York: Philomel, 1981);

Sleeping Ugly, illustrated by Diane Stanley (New York: Coward, McCann & Geoghegan, 1981);

Touch Magic: Fantasy, Faerie and Folklore in the Literature of Childhood (New York: Philomel, 1981);

Uncle Lemon's Spring, illustrated by Glen Rounds (New York: Unicorn/Dutton, 1981);

Commander Toad and the Planet of the Grapes, illustrated by Degen (New York: Coward, McCann & Geoghegan, 1982);

Dragon's Blood: A Fantasy (New York: Delacorte, 1982);

Neptune Rising: Songs and Tales of the Undersea Folk, illustrated by Wiesner (New York: Philomel, 1982);

Commander Toad and the Big Black Hole (New York: Coward-McCann, 1983);

Tales of Wonder (New York: Schocken, 1983);

Children of the Wolf (New York: Viking, 1984);

Heart's Blood (New York: Delacorte, 1984);

The Stone Silenus (New York: Philomel, 1984);

Commander Toad & the Dis-Asteroid, illustrated by Degen (New York: Coward-McCann, 1985);

Dragonfield and Other Stories (New York: Ace, 1985).

OTHER: *The Fireside Song Book of Birds and Beasts,* edited by Yolen, music arranged by Barbara Green, illustrated by Peter Parnall (New York: Simon & Schuster, 1972);

Zoo 2000: Twelve Stories of Science Fiction and Fantasy Beasts, edited with an introduction by Yolen (New York: Seabury, 1973);

Shape Shifters: Fantasy and Science Fiction Tales About Humans Who Can Change Their Shapes, edited by Yolen (New York: Seabury, 1976).

Jane Yolen is one of the most prolific contemporary writers of children's stories. Since 1963, she has written well over sixty books, including poetry collections, realistic stories, animal tales, ABC books, and fantasies. Her special talents, however, lie in the writing of literary folktales, noted for their beauty of language and imagery and their abstract, philosophic mode. These tales tend to appeal to older children; Yolen has commented that her stories "are better known to more sophisticated and romantically-inclined young people and college students."

Born in New York City on 11 February 1939, Yolen grew up in an atmosphere conducive to her becoming a writer, for, in her family, reading and writing were always considered valuable. An interest in stories and story telling seems to have been traditional, for Yolen's paternal great-grandfather was a Reb, a storyteller, in his village in Fino-Russia. Her father, Will Hyatt Yolen, besides being a champion kite flyer, was also a well-known author of books and radio scripts. Her mother, Isabelle Berlin Yolen, wrote adult stories, one of which was published, and composed crossword puzzles, many of which appeared in children's magazines. Inspired by her parents to value books and love words, Yolen knew she wanted to be a writer but at first assumed she would be a journalist, even though she was intrigued by poetry and folklore. While in college, she wrote poetry and sang folk songs professionally in order to earn money for living expenses, and she has commented that she hopes her "tales sound as if they could be sung." After receiving her B.A. degree in 1960 from Smith College, Yolen was a production assistant for *Saturday Review* magazine for half a year, after which she worked for several publishing houses, first as assistant editor for Gold Medal Books from 1960 to 1961, then as associate editor for Rutledge books from 1961 to 1962, and finally as assistant editor of juvenile books for Alfred A. Knopf from 1962 to 1965. The year she came to Knopf, Yolen married David W. Stemple, a photographer and computer expert. She also began writing children's books; *See This Little Line?,* a concept book in rhyme, appeared in 1963. By 1965, when she left Knopf, she had written three other books.

After a trip to Europe, Yolen began her freelance career with the publication of *Trust a City Kid* (1966). Written by Yolen and her friend Anne Huston, the realistic story is about a boy from Harlem named Reg, who lives one summer on a Pennsylvania farm owned by the Bradshaws, who are Quakers. The book is an interesting story of reverse prejudice, but the characters, unfortunately, are quite wooden and flat. The book reflects Yolen's association with a Quaker family, Jim and Dee Bristol, who supervised a Quaker-sponsored work project Yolen was involved with in Ohio when she was younger. The Bristols became the Bradshaws in *Trust a City Kid,* but their given names, Jim and Dee, remained the same. Later, Jane wrote that "bits and pieces of my own personal history, or my parents' or my husband's or my friends', find their way into my stories. I use these scraps the way a bird makes a nest and a mouse makes a home—snippet by snippet, leaf and bough and cotton batting and all."

Yolen's work with her father was also an inspiration. In 1961 she had been doing research with him preparatory to their writing a book on kites. In volume two of Joseph Needham's *Science and Civilization in China*, she came upon the following sentence: "Emperor Shen was rescued by his daughter from a tower prison by means of a kite." In 1966, the year her first child, Heidi Elisabet, was born, Yolen began writing a tale based upon the incident. When the book was finished it was not immediately published, though Macmillan bought rights. They chose not to proceed with publication and, eventually, the picture book *The Emperor and the Kite* was accepted and published by World Publishing Company in 1967. The story, reminiscent of old tales about the maligned youngest child, recounts the legend of Djeow Seow, youngest daughter of an emperor in ancient China; she is ignored because she is so small and apparently insignificant. But when her father is kidnapped by men who take over the kingdom, Djeow Seow saves the emperor by sailing to him in his tower prison a kite to which has been attached a strong, thick rope woven of grass, vines, and strands of her hair. The story is simply told in the folk tradition, with traditional motifs which provide an aura both of antiquity and of familiarity to the tale. The legend is efficiently and poetically handled and is not only readable but tellable. The theme, that those whom society considers deficient are capable and perhaps more proficient than others, recurs in subsequent tales; Yolen saw that many injustices were constantly occurring because of society's prejudicial attitude toward those considered inferior.

The picture book brought Yolen and her illustrator, Ed Young, immediate recognition. It was a Caldecott Honor Book in 1968 and became a Lewis Carroll Shelf winner, an American Library Association Notable Book, and one of the *New York Times* Best Books of the Year. Yolen was acclaimed for her ability to tell a good story and for her poetic rendering of the legend in the folk tradition.

In 1968 Yolen's second child, Adam Douglas, was born. Published that same year was the nonfiction work *World on a String: The Story of Kites*. This book, developed from her work with her father, is a well-organized and documented collection of facts about kites. For the older child, the book's theme concerns the development of interest in kites from aesthetic appreciation to utilitarian interest. Yolen follows the history of the kite from its origin in the East, where the kite was closely associated with the lore of the people, to its development in the West, where it was linked with man's interest in flight. Although the book deals with facts, Yolen handles them informally and delightfully. She provides anecdotes to illustrate the use of and interest in kites, and her economy of words is a noteworthy element in the book's success: like *The Emperor and the Kite*, it was selected as an ALA Notable Book. The work is well illustrated with sketches and photographs and has a two-page bibliography of kite books, primarily those on the adult level.

By the time a third child, Jason Frederic, was born in 1970, Yolen had written sixteen books, and soon to follow were other stories, including *The Bird of Time* (1971), inspired by her awareness of the intensity of her mother's illness; *The Girl Who Loved the Wind* (1972), a magical, mythical story about parental fears for a child; and *Friend: The Story of George Fox and the Quakers* (1972), a biography complete with a map of Fox's travels and a bibliography.

The latter is a sensitive account of George Fox and his indomitable character, set against the background of seventeenth-century England and the persecutions of dissenting church figures. Yolen researched her material carefully. She comments that she traveled, in her mind, the length and breadth of seventeenth-century England and tried to understand that world as Fox experienced it. With the aid of Fox's journal, Yolen uses the Quaker's own words to develop his character. She attempted to be as unbiased as she could; she wrote that she tried to balance both the good and the bad, the "sinner and saint," in her handling of the life. Thus she reveals not only Fox's intense faith but also his tendency to judge others superficially in his upholding of that faith. Fox's life of persecution was attractive to Yolen, whose own tales often stress injustice. She also saw in Fox someone that young people of today could identify with, for she believed that with his "long hair and funny clothes, with his pronouncements in favor of women, against slavery, against war—even with his funny 'thee's' and 'thou's'—he had a spirit that matched any of the young radicals of our era."

The account is effectively straightforward. Yolen has managed a quite readable biography, interesting and, in places, quite touching, without fictionalization. Yolen's enthusiasm for her subject took an interesting turn when in 1971 she became a member of the Religious Society of Friends.

In 1974, an important year for Yolen, she was living with her family at Phoenix Farm, Hatfield, Massachusetts. Her book *The Girl Who Cried Flowers*,

Dust jacket for Yolen's 1974 collection of short stories which are surrealistic and mythical in their suggestion of a close relationship between man and nature (Crowell)

and Other Tales, a collection of five stories, appeared and was quickly followed by three novels. The tales are surrealistic and mythical in their suggestion of a close relationship between man and elemental forces. All five tales are in the folk tradition and have the same complex aura of the familiar and yet the strange that Yolen's other works have. The title story was inspired by Botticelli's painting "Primavera." This story, as well as the final one, "Silent Bianca," concerns a woman who has a special gift: in the first, Olivia weeps flowers, and in the last, Bianca speaks slivers of ice which can be heard only when the ice has melted. Both are moral tales, for Olivia unselfishly weeps flowers for anyone who wishes them, despite her husband's opposition, and Bianca speaks ice slivers which "cut through lies."

In the first story, Olivia's frustration over the conflict between her love for her husband and her need to satisfy the wishes of others brings about

her transformation into an olive tree. Bianca, on the other hand, passes the test of wisdom and true nobility by tricking the king's guards who have been sent to test her. The second story in the collection, "Dawn-Strider," is a tale of cosmic dimensions: it is the story of the conflict within the giant Night-Walker, for the giant prefers darkness and shadows but he loves the child, Dawn-Strider, who brings the sun. The two remaining stories, "The Weaver of Tomorrow" and "The Lad Who Stared Everyone Down," are tales of destructive self-interest and pride. In the first of the two, Vera, a selfish young woman, wants to know everything, including the future. The tale, which has Faustian tones, concludes with Vera's being forced to assume the responsibility of being the Weaver of Tomorrow when the old weaver dies. The final story, "The Lad Who Stared Everyone Down," though it has whimsical and humorous touches, ends with sobering consequences. The boy in the tale manages to stare everyone down and is quite proud of his ability until he takes up the challenge of staring down the sun. When the sun goes down and everyone congratulates him, the boy can still see it, for he has severely damaged his eyes by staring at it so long; so he continues to stand and stare.

A bittersweet tone permeates the collection, which is haunting in its mythic implications. One critic has said about these stories that they "read as if they had first been told hundreds of years ago." The traditional motifs and themes are present, but the tone and poetic elements are Yolen's unique contributions. *The Girl Who Cried Flowers, and Other Tales* was quite successful, winning the Golden Kite Award given by the Society of Children's Book Writers in 1974 and selected as a nominee for the National Book Award and as an ALA Notable Book in 1975.

The Magic Three of Solatia, a heroic tale in the tradition of high fantasy, appeared in 1974. Told in four parts, it concerns Sianna, daughter of a button maker who lives in the land of Solatia, and three magic silver buttons that had originally been given by Dread Mary, the Seawitch, to her lover. The story concerns the traditional struggle between good, represented by Sianna, and evil, represented by Blaggard the king, both of whom have magical powers. Sianna, however, uses her powers wisely, for she has learned that magic has its consequences. The king, on the other hand, misuses his powers to satisfy his selfish desires, chief of which is Sianna, who constantly eludes him. Eventually, Sianna's son, Lann, a wandering minstrel, destroys Blaggard after an arduous quest and with the help of magical people, all of whom had been previously enchanted by the evil king. The story is beautifully told, and the magical aura is sustained by Yolen's sharp images and poetic language. Some critics have commented that her characters in this as well as in other tales are "remote," that they lack sharpness. Actually the characters are no more remote than those in other quest tales, particularly the Grail stories. The remoteness undoubtedly is due to the ethereal quality of the settings and themes.

Yolen began working on her doctorate in Children's Literature at the University of Massachusetts in 1975; eventually, she completed all of her course work but left the university without the degree. One of the most haunting collections of tales, *The Moon Ribbon and Other Tales* (1976) was published while she was at the university. It is a collection of six tales which share in common the theme of the need for familial love and devotion. "The Moon Ribbon," a Cinderella tale of plain but good Sylva, whose widowed father has married a woman with two beautiful daughters, is perhaps the most enchanting and mysterious story in the collection. Sylva has nothing but a magical ribbon woven from the gray hair of her mother and grandmothers. With this ribbon, Sylva eventually overcomes her enemies and comes to understand the importance of integrity and true love. The magical transformation of the ribbon into a silver river and then a silver road, a long dark hall which leads to a crystal door behind which stands a tall silver-haired woman, the frustration of Sylva as she tries to reach the mysterious woman—only to fall into a deep pit and then gently land on the lawn before her own house—are some of the story's elements which suggest an abstract, surrealistic world, a world of enigma. The tale's mystery and enchantment are intensified by the poetic description of the soft glow surrounding the world of the moon ribbon.

"The Honey-Stick Boy" is reminiscent of the story of the gingerbread boy but with a focus upon the need of an old couple for a child to love and to help them. "Rosechild" has a cumulative effect, as an old woman who has found a tiny child in a rose asks three different individuals how to make the child grow, until she finally learns that her love is what will cause the child to flourish. The fourth tale, "Sans Soleil," is a mythic story about a king's fear for his son, Sans Soleil, who, fate has decreed, will be destroyed by the sun. Eventually the son is destroyed through the trickery of his incredulous wife. The story is suggestive of old etiological myths in that on the site of Sans Soleil's death, a sunflower

begins to grow; this sunflower, however, turns away from rather than toward the sun. The next tale, "Somewhen," hints of an endless tale in that it appears to be starting over as it concludes. It is a quest tale of Tom, a young man who is seeking his fortune, when he comes upon an old man resting beneath a tree. The man tells Tom to look for "Somewhen" to find his fortune. After a life of adventure, Tom is now an old man resting beneath a tree confronted by a young man seeking his fortune. Tom tells the young man to look for "Somewhen." The final tale, "The Moonchild," is a melancholy tale of loneliness and rejection, for Mona, the moonchild who has been born during the night, lives with her parents in a land where the sun is worshipped and births occur only during the day. Mona, therefore, is unique, an oddity, and is shunned, even by her parents. Eventually, Mona is forced to leave the town to live in the dark forest edging the area, a forest which the villagers also fear. These wonder tales all concern the search for fulfillment: of love, of self, of destiny. The abstract, surrealistic aura provides a rather adult tone to the tales and implies a philosophic depth which is quite enticing. Ideas appear to sparkle clearly at one moment, only to fade elusively from one's grasp. The result is an intriguing, alluring set of stories. This book, like others written by Yolen, was elected an Honor Book for the Golden Kite Award in 1976.

By 1978 Yolen had written or edited well over forty books for children. She had also begun writing Beginning-to-Read books, in which she typically reveals her fascination for words. *The Giants' Farm* (1977) and *Spider Jane* (1978) are two such books. In these as well as in others of the same type, Yolen tries not to oversimplify the language and works to provide stories which will amuse and interest beginning readers. She deplores what she calls "Coffee Break Books," which she considers "simple-minded non-books" that are turned out "in short order." Yolen's own stories involve much wordplay and metaphor; they delight because of the intriguing combinations of sounds.

One of the most delightful of these books is *The Simple Prince* (1978), a humorous tale of a prince who has tired of his princely life and wants to live a simpler existence, so he, as is his custom, claps three times and orders simple clothes for his venture. He rides off and eventually enters a small simple cottage of a poor farmer and his wife. When the prince orders tea, he learns that he must work for it: chop wood, draw water, churn butter, and help make bread. Once finished, the prince falls asleep, too tired to eat or even clap his hands. He immediately retires from the simple life; it is too difficult. This delightful story is told with humorous ironies which both the adult and the child can enjoy. The whimsical tale has a moral, of course, but one which develops from the character and the plot and therefore does not override the story.

An unusually delightful book, *All in the Woodland Early: An ABC Book* (1979) includes music composed by Yolen. The song tells of animals, birds, and insects that one may find in the woods. The familiar ant, bear, and deer are included; but Yolen also introduces the king snake, newt, and shrew, and the exotically unfamiliar urbanus, vole, xyleborus, and zemmi in a work which is imaginative and colorful. The narrator tells of seeing a young man go off to the woods to hunt. He sings of what he sees, his song having the refrain "All in the woodland early" and a frequently appearing couplet "And where are you going this morning in May?/'We're going a-hunting,' was all they would say." After the last animal, the zemmi, is introduced, the young man sings that all are hunting, but "hunting for friends." A beautifully composed book, reminiscent of cumulative nursery rhymes, the song is reprinted at the end, together with music for playing and singing. This work exhibits Yolen's delightful handling of image, verse, and music.

Commander Toad in Space (1980), a Break-of-day, easy-to-read book with a hint of George Lucas's *Star Wars* in some of the characters' names, is a delightful "science fiction" work for the primary reader. Commander Toad and his crew, Mr. Hop, Lt. Lily, and Jake Skyjumper, visit a watery planet and almost become the lunch of the monster Deep Wader. For this humorous work, Yolen received, in 1983, the Garden State Children's Book Award presented by the New Jersey Library Association.

Yolen's interest in the sea is evident in the many stories and poems she has written about magical water creatures. As a child, she spent much time with her grandparents, who lived in Virginia near Chesapeake Bay. Thus, in the introduction to *Neptune Rising: Songs and Tales of the Undersea Folk*, published in 1982, she wrote, "I know a little about water. Perhaps that is why I have always been attracted to the lore and fantasy of the merfolk." *Neptune Rising* is a collection of stories and poems, many of which had been previously published, about such "merfolk": undines, mermen, selchies. Themes of love, hopeless love, and jealousy mark this collection, which, despite its humor, most often conveys the melancholy tone of the ebb and flow of the sea tide.

Dust jacket for Yolen's 1982 fantasy about a dragon that helps a young boy and girl escape from bondage on a planet called Austar IV (Delacorte)

Besides her interest in fantastic sea creatures, Yolen is also fascinated by dragons, which she sees as metaphoric: "the dragon is a symbol for the dragon inside...." In the fantasy *Dragon's Blood: A Fantasy* (1982) and its sequel *Heart's Blood* (1984), she has created a powerful figure of a dragon that not only helps her master, Jakkin, overcome his bondage on the planet Austar IV in the first book but also, in the sequel, helps Jakkin and the girl Akki escape murderous rebels after she has been slain. When Jakkin and Akki climb inside the dragon's body to keep from freezing, they are transformed; when they emerge the next day, they now have new insights and are stronger than they have ever been. Thus the dragon becomes a symbol of human potential, of inner strength necessary to overcome any adversity.

Having written books of fact and of fiction, Jane Yolen manages to bridge both kinds in *Children of the Wolf* (1984). The book is based on diary entries of the Reverend J. A. L. Singh, an Indian missionary who, in 1920, found two little girls who had been raised by wolves. From these entries, Yolen has woven a fascinating story, told by Mohandas, an Indian orphan. When the two little girls are found and are brought back to the orphanage, Mohandas tries to protect them from the other children, and he tries to teach them to speak. In a touching narrative, Yolen depicts Mohandas's frustration and sadness as first one girl dies and then the other.

Continuing to write, turning out one or more books a year, Yolen believes that constant composition prevents one from turning stale. Though she has written realistic stories and fantasies, her major interest is in the literary folktale, for she believes that a child, like an adult, "needs a mythology." She also believes that effective language is an important requisite for a good book: she has written that "an excellent book is a powerful book, an excellent writer is one who uses words powerfully." Yolen taught children's literature at Smith College and is a frequent lecturer at conferences throughout the country as well as a book reviewer. In 1981, she received an honorary Doctor of Laws degree from Our Lady of the Elms College, Chicopee, Massachusetts. She was elected president of the Science Fiction Writers of America in 1986.

Papers:

The Kerlan Collection, at the University of Minnesota, Minneapolis, has manuscripts by Jane Yolen.

Paul Zindel
(15 May 1936-   )

Theodore W. Hipple
University of Tennessee

See also the Zindel entry in *DLB 7: Twentieth Century American Dramatists.*

BOOKS: *The Pigman* (New York: Harper & Row, 1968);

My Darling, My Hamburger (New York: Harper & Row, 1969);

I Never Loved Your Mind (New York: Harper & Row, 1970);

And Miss Readon Drinks a Little (New York: Dramatists Play Service, 1971; New York: Random House, 1972);

The Effect of Gamma Rays on Man-in-the-Moon Marigolds, illustrated by Dong Kingman (New York: Harper & Row, 1971);

Let Me Hear You Whisper and The Ladies Should Be in Bed (New York: Dramatists Play Service, 1973);

The Secret Affairs of Mildred Wild (New York: Dramatists Play Service, 1973);

Let Me Hear You Whisper, illustrated by Stephen Gammell (New York: Harper & Row, 1974);

I Love My Mother, illustrated by John Melo (New York: Harper & Row, 1975);

Pardon Me, You're Stepping On My Eyeball! (New York: Harper & Row, 1976; London: Bodley Head, 1976);

Confessions of a Teenage Baboon (New York: Harper & Row, 1977);

Ladies at the Alamo (New York: Dramatists Play Service, 1977);

The Undertaker's Gone Bananas (New York: Harper & Row, 1978);

A Star for the Latecomer, by Zindel and Bonnie Zindel (New York: Harper & Row, 1980);

The Pigman's Legacy (New York: Harper & Row, 1980);

The Girl Who Wanted a Boy (New York: Harper & Row, 1981);

To Take a Dare, by Zindel and Crescent Dragonwagon (New York: Harper & Row, 1982);

Harry and Hortense at Hormone High (New York: Harper & Row, 1984);

When Darkness Falls (New York: Bantam, 1985).

Paul Zindel (©Roger Ressmeyer/Starlight)

Critics of adolescent literature generally cite three late-1960s novels as helping this subgenre break its ties with its past romanticism and move dramatically into a much more realistic mode: *The Outsiders* (1967) by S. E. Hinton, *Mr. and Mrs. Bo Jo Jones* (1967) by Ann Head, and *The Pigman* (1968) by Paul Zindel. Before these works appeared, literature for young adults seemed almost an extension of the grade school primers, with Dick and Jane as teenagers and Spot replaced by an Irish setter. But after these books came a flood of novels—which is still coming—that placed young adult novels squarely in a new realistic tradition. Much of the credit for this long overdue change must go to these authors, and especially to Zindel, who, more prolific than the others, has kept the movement flourishing with a steady stream of novels that explore teenagers' lives in realistic ways.

Zindel wrote *The Pigman*, in 1968, largely at the prodding and encouragement of Charlotte Zolotow, the senior editor of the juvenile books department of Harper and Row. Zolotow had seen a local educational production of Zindel's play *The Effect of Gamma Rays on Man-in-the-Moon Marigolds*, which, when later modified and produced for Broadway, won the Pulitzer Prize for Drama in 1971. Realizing that Zindel possessed an accurate ear for incisive dialogue and an eye for honest, even if unusual, personal relationships, and knowing that these qualities were needed but lacking in fiction for teenagers, Zolotow convinced Zindel to write an adolescent novel. Zindel felt he knew the territory for he had spent ten years as a high school chemistry teacher. Just as important to his writing, though, are the facets of his own life which Zindel included not only in *The Pigman* but in many of his later works as well: a virtually fatherless adolescence (the result of divorce); a turbulent relationship with a mother who was, Zindel later said in an interview, "a beautiful case of paranoia"; a feeling of worthlessness; and an absence of many long-term friendships, caused in part by his mother's insistence on changing residences every six months or so.

The story of *The Pigman* is essentially a tragic one. High school sophomores John Conlan and Lorraine Jensen, through a telephone hoax, meet Mr. Angelo Pignati, an aged widower with a zest for life and a passion for the assortment of model pigs he and his wife have collected. John and Lorraine become friends with Pignati, go to the zoo with him, and drink his homemade wine; theirs is a relationship that begins in sympathy but grows in affection. When Pignati is hospitalized due to a slight heart attack, John and Lorraine use his house to host a party which gets out of control, resulting in serious damage to Pignati's property and the complete destruction of his collection of glass and clay pigs. Pignati returns home at the height of the chaos, finds the devastation more than he can stand, and dies a short time later of a more severe heart attack, leaving John and Lorraine to wonder to what degree, if any, they had played a part in his death.

John and Lorraine alternate as first-person narrators, a technique which affords some insight into Zindel's skillful use of language. John swears; Lorraine does not. Her sentences are longer than his. Hers is the more sentimental voice; his, the more matter-of-fact. This first novel anticipates Zindel's later work in a number of ways. Not surprising in an author whose previous work had been in drama, the dialogue carries much of the action. In *The Pigman* lies Zindel's first treatment of teenage alienation, principally from parental authority. Rarely does Zindel feature teenagers who have solid, normal relationships with both parents. More typical are John, who labels his father "the Bore,"

Dust jackets for Zindel's most popular novel, The Pigman, *and its sequel. The books portray an adolescent couple, John Conlan and Lorraine Jensen, and their friendships with two elderly men (Harper & Row).*

and Lorraine, whose divorced mother tries to infuse her daughter with her conviction that all men are sex maniacs. Often, Zindel's novels contain autobiographical details; for instance, his mother was a practical nurse who boarded the terminally ill, as is Lorraine's; in *Confessions of a Teenage Baboon* (1977), Chris Boyd's mother works as a live-in nurse for the dying. In addition, school in a Zindel novel is more a place where teens meet than where they learn. In the opening paragraph of *The Pigman* John says, "I hate school," a message implied if not actually echoed by most later Zindel characters.

In *The Pigman's Legacy*, a sequel written twelve years and many literary successes after the first novel, John and Lorraine, now juniors in high school, happen to return to the pigman's house, only to discover that it is lived in—"squatted in"—by an old recluse, who, they later learn, is dying of cancer. They become the "colonel's" friends, accompany him to Atlantic City where John gambles away the old man's savings, and arrange a deathbed marriage for the old man with Dolly, a worker in

the school cafeteria. The feelings that Dolly and the colonel share, even at the end of his life, help John and Lorraine learn that the legacy left them by the pigman was not shame or sorrow or regret; it was love. This sequel is, in part, redundant, a common source of trouble in sequels. John's father is still "the Bore." Lorraine's mother tells her: "Don't let them touch you; boys are out for only one thing. Don't ever be alone with a boy or he'll take advantage of you. Don't let a boy get you in his car or you'll end up pregnant." Despite such frequent paranoiac admonitions, Lorraine does find a boy—John—and finds love. It has taken the deaths of the two old men, both of whom they loved and both of whom loved them, to show John and Lorraine the strength of their own love for each other.

Between *The Pigman* and *The Pigman's Legacy* Zindel wrote seven highly successful novels for teenagers. *My Darling, My Hamburger* (1969) continues the trend toward realism begun in *The Pigman.* Zindel portrays two couples, popular and confident Sean and Liz and shy and uncertain Maggie and Dennis. The book's provocative title, a Zindel trademark, points out the absurdity of a teacher's advice to Liz that she deflect Sean's sexual advances by asking him out for a hamburger. Given such inane guidance, and saddled with an overstrict stepfather, Liz succumbs to Sean's pressures and becomes pregnant. After Sean reneges on his promise to marry Liz, Maggie secretly accompanies her to an abortionist but has to tell Liz's mother when Liz almost dies from the aftereffects. The novel ends with the four teens going their separate ways, matured and embittered by their experiences.

Zindel reiterates themes established in *The Pigman* in this novel; Sean and Liz have mutually destructive relationships with their parents; school is merely tolerated. Zindel continues to break new ground for adolescent fiction in this novel. High schoolers are seen smoking and drinking. They have sex and they get pregnant and go to illegal abortionists. However, Zindel does not generalize his characters. Maggie and Dennis are precious in their self-consciousness. Dennis spends four times the required fifteen seconds gargling mouthwash and still worries about bad breath. On their first date Maggie fears that her attempt to get a share of the armrest in the movie theater may be mistaken as a signal that she really wants Dennis to move his arm and put it around her. Both miss most of the movie because of their concern about a later goodnight kiss.

In many ways *My Darling, My Hamburger* is Zindel's best novel for adolescents. Its characters, though unique, are not bizarre themselves or placed in bizarre situations. Moreover, what happens in the novel, though it ranges from first-date behavior to a butchered abortion, is well within the experience of teenagers. Although Zindel provides no definitive solutions—indeed, he properly avoids such presumptions—his insights in this novel are informative in positive ways.

In 1975 Zindel wrote his only work to date for very young children. *I Love My Mother*, a picture book illustrated by John Melo, tells in the first person how much a little boy loves his mother. The fatherless boy, about six years old, tells the reader that his mother says "Absolutely not" when he wants to drive the car and "Have a good time" when he threatens to run away to Miami and that when he says "I miss my father, she hugs me and says he misses me too."

Zindel's next three novels for adolescents portray teenagers, adults, and experiences for which

Dust jacket for Zindel's novel about the strained relationship between a seventeen-year-old high school dropout and his flower-child girlfriend (Harper & Row)

the adjective "bizarre" is most apt. In *I Never Loved Your Mind* (1970), Dewey, a seventeen-year-old dropout, meets Yvette Goethals in the autopsy room of the hospital where they both work. An eighteen-year-old flower child, she steals everything she can from the hospital, eats broccoli sandwiches for lunch, and sleeps "nonsexually" in the same bed with a drummer for a rock band, though she and Dewey do share a sexual relationship. Dewey's involvement with her ends, at least temporarily, when Yvette and the rock group have to leave their rented house because the landlord objects to their keeping horses in the living room. They go to Taos, New Mexico, where they make and sell "genuine Navaho" pot holders. At book's end Dewey wonders whether to follow Yvette, even though she had told him that their sexual adventure still did not mean that she loved his mind. "Marsh" Mallow and Edna Shinglebox share the protagonist's role in *Pardon Me, You're Stepping On My Eyeball!* (1976).

Marsh, who carries a live raccoon in his coat pocket, engages Edna in a search for his father. Through Marsh's alcoholic mother, Edna learns that Marsh's father is dead and subsequently helps Marsh accept this fact. In so doing, she assumes some independence of her own. Minor characters, such as Mr. Meizner, the school shrink whose absorption with sensitivity exercises renders him insensitive, and God Boy, a teenage "evangelist" whose exaltations about the human body turn a teen party into a Roman orgy, are also well developed.

Confessions of a Teenage Baboon is the story of fifteen-year-old Chris Boyd, who lives with his mother, a nurse, wherever she is caring for a terminally ill patient, as they have no home of their own except for the dilapidated Ritz Hotel, where they stay when she is between assignments. In the novel they are in the Dipardi household, where old Mrs. Dipardi is dying of cancer. Her son, Lloyd, takes young fatherless boys like Chris under his wing and tries to make men of them, using psychologically brutal methods. Lloyd labels Chris "a nurd," "out of it," "retarded," all, he says, in an effort to provide the hapless and passive Chris the help "your father would have given you." After receiving a thinly veiled accusation of homosexuality, Lloyd commits suicide, and Chris, with a new understanding of Lloyd's harassment, moves on with his mother to her next patient.

These three novels stretch the boundaries of adolescent realism. Throughout, there are serious implications, such as Edna Shinglebox's mother's demands that Edna be the beauty queen she clearly cannot be, and Yvette's supporting of her own brand of morality with materials she steals from the hospital. There are also moments of great humor, such as a boy wearing a T-shirt that reads "Lower the age of puberty," but one is never sure whether Zindel is laughing with or at his characters and their dilemmas. In *The Pigman, My Darling, My Hamburger,* and *The Pigman's Legacy* readers know where their sympathies are intended to lie; in these intermediate novels the goal is out of focus and less well realized.

Despite its characteristic title, *The Undertaker's Gone Bananas* (1978) represents a sharp departure from Zindel's earlier novels. The book is a mystery, in which two friends, Bobby and Lauri, accuse an undertaker in their apartment complex of murdering his wife. When she appears, the charge is dropped, and when Bobby and Lauri bring it up again, the police accuse them of crying wolf. The two teenagers do solve the mystery, discovering that the undertaker had killed his girlfriend and

Dust jacket for Zindel's novel which depicts a group of high school adolescents and their desire to find a "hero" for their school (Harper & Row)

then had killed his wife. Both Bobby and Lauri have supportive, normal parents, and, the murders aside, there are no lingering deaths from heart attacks or cancer in this novel, no nurses, and no particular hatred of school. But certain features common to Zindel's novels do appear: Bobby and Lauri are each other's best friends, a reprise of the John-Lorraine relationship in *The Pigman* and the Marsh-Edna duo of *Pardon Me, You're Stepping On My Eyeball!* Bobby, like other Zindel males, is not liked by his peers, in his case because he is too smart and too outspoken. Also apparent is Zindel's careful sense of place, his awareness that teens often define themselves by their parties and their hangouts.

Paul Zindel's wife Bonnie shared the authorship of *A Star for the Latecomer* (1980). The first Zindel novel to feature a girl as its protagonist—in the twosomes mentioned above, the boy is always the dominant figure—this story presents Brooke

Hillary, who attends a fine arts school in order to pursue a dancing career that is more her mother's goal for her than her goal for herself. Brooke loves her mother and wants to please her, but her difficulty in accepting her mother's plan for her is compounded by a growing realization that her mother is ill. Treated most sensitively and unsentimentally, the disease and ultimate death release Brooke from her goal and permit her to let her life take whatever course it will.

In *The Girl Who Wanted a Boy* (1981) Zindel again uses a female protagonist, Sibella Cametta, daughter of divorced parents, younger sister of the popular and sophisticated Maureen, and without a boyfriend. As the title indicates, Sibella can tolerate her parents and her sister (the latter barely) but not her romantic condition. She sees a picture of Dan in the newspaper, decides he is the one, finds him, falls in love that is not reciprocated, and, when Dan ultimately leaves for Florida, decides that love is really for later—at least beyond fifteen. As in all Zindel novels, the dialogue crackles with contemporary realism. Marijuana and beer replace the more common cigarettes and cokes of earlier novels, and sex is referred to as almost a given of teenage life.

Zindel wrote *To Take a Dare* (1982) with Crescent Dragonwagon. In the book, Chrysta Perretti, a thirteen-year-old runaway, takes to the road as a hitchhiker and has three years of assorted adventures before ending up in a small town in Arkansas. There she meets Luke, who becomes her lover; has a hysterectomy; and becomes a surrogate parent for Dare, a dyslexic runaway of fourteen. At the end of the novel Chrysta is wiser, more mature, able to forgive her parents, and able to view her life, now without Dare who has again run away,

with optimism for a settled future.

Zindel returns to his earlier strategy of male and female protagonists in *Harry and Hortense at Hormone High* (1984). Harry and Hortense resemble John and Lorraine of *The Pigman* novels, including the penchant for meeting unusual characters. Believing himself a reincarnation of Icarus, Jason Rohr, a classmate of Harry and Hortense at the school they nickname Hormone High, tries to become the hero they believe the school badly needs. He places circulars attacking the school and its administration on the bulletin boards and signs them "Icarus, a God." But his imagination overtakes this mentally unstable teen, and soon he believes he is indeed Icarus and can fly. His death is predictable, but he leaves a legacy of wisdom and philosophy for Harry and Hortense, making this novel, therefore, more thoughtful and provocative than most of Zindel's works.

Clearly the body of Zindel's work and its individual parts place him in the forefront of adolescent novelists. Few other writers match his awareness of teenagers' problems and attitudes. He even compensates for their dislike of reading by including in his books all manner of graphics—letters in longhand, charts, diagrams—to lessen the potential boredom of page after page of print. It is not at all surprising—indeed, it is gratifying—that he is among their most esteemed novelists.

References:

Audrey Eaglen, "An Interview with Paul Zindel," *Top of the News* (Winter 1978): 179-185;

Paul Janeczko, "An Interview with Paul Zindel," *English Journal* (October 1977): 20-21;

Jean Mercier, "Paul Zindel," *Publishers Weekly*, 64 (5 December 1976): 6-8.

Charlotte Zolotow
(26 June 1915-   )

Elizabeth Francis
University of Nevada at Reno

BOOKS: *The Park Book,* illustrated by H. A. Rey (New York & London: Harper, 1944);

But Not Billy, illustrated by Lys Cassal (New York: Harper, 1947);

The Storm Book, illustrated by Margaret Bloy Graham (New York: Harper, 1952);

The Magic Word, illustrated by Eleanor Dart (New York: Wonder Books, 1952);

Indian Indian, illustrated by Leonard Weisgard (New York: Simon & Schuster, 1952);

The City Boy and the Country Horse, as Charlotte Bookman, illustrated by William Moyers (New York: Treasure Books, 1952);

The Quiet Mother and the Noisy Little Boy, illustrated by Kurt Werth (New York: Lothrop, Lee & Shepard, 1953);

Charlotte Zolotow (Gale Portrait Gallery)

One Step, Two . . . , illustrated by Roger Duvoisin (New York: Lothrop, Lee & Shepard, 1955);

Over and Over, illustrated by Garth Williams (New York: Harper, 1957);

Not a Little Monkey, illustrated by Duvoisin (New York: Lothrop, Lee & Shepard, 1957);

Do You Know What I'll Do?, illustrated by Williams (New York: Harper, 1958);

Sleepy Book, illustrated by Vladimir Bobri (New York: Lothrop, Lee & Shepard, 1958);

The Night When Mother Was Away, illustrated by Reisie Lonette (New York: Lothrop, Lee & Shepard, 1958); republished as *The Summer Night* with new illustrations by Ben Schecter (New York: Harper & Row, 1974);

The Bunny Who Found Easter, illustrated by Betty Peterson (Berkeley: Parnassus, 1959);

Big Brother, illustrated by Mary Chalmers (New York: Harper, 1960);

In My Garden, illustrated by Duvoisin (New York: Lothrop, Lee & Shepard, 1960);

The Little Black Puppy, illustrated by Lilian Obligado (New York: Golden Press, 1960);

The Three Funny Friends, illustrated by Chalmers (New York: Harper & Row, 1961);

The Man With the Purple Eyes, illustrated by Joe Lasker (London & New York: Abelard-Schuman, 1961);

When the Wind Stops, illustrated by Lasker (London & New York: Abelard-Schuman, 1962); republished with new illustrations by Howard Knotts (New York: Harper & Row, 1975);

Mr. Rabbit and the Lovely Present, illustrated by Maurice Sendak (New York: Harper & Row, 1962; London: Bodley Head, 1968);

Aren't You Glad?, illustrated by Elaine Kurty (New York: Golden Books, 1962);

A Tiger Called Thomas, illustrated by Werth (New York: Lothrop, Lee & Shepard, 1963);

The Sky Was Blue, illustrated by Williams (New York: Harper & Row, 1963);

The Quarreling Book, illustrated by Arnold Lobel (New York: Harper & Row, 1963);

The White Marble, illustrated by Obligado (New York: Abelard-Schuman, 1963); republished with new illustrations by Deborah K. Ray (New York: Crowell, 1982);

a rose, a bridge, and a wild black horse, illustrated by Uri Shulevitz (New York: Harper & Row, 1964);

The Poodle Who Barked at the Wind, illustrated by Duvoisin (New York: Lothrop, Lee & Shepard, 1964);

I Have a Horse of My Own, illustrated by Yoko Mitsuhashi (London & New York: Abelard-Schuman, 1964);

Someday, illustrated by Lobel (New York: Harper & Row, 1965);

When I Have a Little Girl, illustrated by Hilary Knight (New York: Harper & Row, 1965);

Flocks of Birds, illustrated by Joan Berg (London: Abelard-Schuman, 1965); republished with new illustrations by Ruth Lercher Bornstein (New York: Crowell, 1981);

If It Weren't For You, illustrated by Schecter (New York: Harper & Row, 1966);

Big Sister and Little Sister, illustrated by Martha Alexander (New York: Harper & Row, 1966);

I Want to Be Little, illustrated by Tony De Luna (London & New York: Abelard-Schuman, 1967);

When I Have a Son, illustrated by Knight (New York: Harper & Row, 1967);

All That Sunlight, illustrated by Walter Stein (New York: Harper & Row, 1967);

Summer Is . . . , illustrated by Janet Archer (New York: Abelard-Schuman, 1967); republished with new illustrations by Bornstein (New York: Crowell, 1983);

My Friend John, illustrated by Schecter (New York: Harper & Row, 1968);

The New Friend, illustrated by Arvis L. Stewart (London & New York: Abelard-Schuman, 1968); republished with new illustrations by Emily A. McCully (New York: Crowell, 1981);

A Week in Yani's World: Greece, photographs by Donald Getsug (New York: Macmillan, 1969);

Some Things Go Together, illustrated by Sylvie Selig (London & New York: Abelard-Schuman, 1969); republished with new illustrations by Karen Gundersheimer (New York: Crowell, 1983);

The Hating Book, illustrated by Schecter (New York: Harper & Row, 1969);

River Winding, illustrated by Regina Shekerjian (London & New York: Abelard, 1970); republished with new illustrations by Kazue Mi-

zumura (New York: Crowell, 1978);

A Week in Latef's World: India, as Sarah Abbott, photographs by Ray Shaw (New York: Crowell-Collier, 1970);

Where I Begin, as Sarah Abbott, illustrated by Rocco Negri (New York: Coward-McCann, 1970);

You and Me, illustrated by Robert Quackenbush (New York: Macmillan, 1971); republished as *Here We Are* (New York: Macmillan, 1971);

A Father Like That, illustrated by Schecter (New York: Harper & Row, 1971);

Wake Up and Goodnight, illustrated by Weisgard (New York: Harper & Row, 1971);

The Beautiful Christmas Tree, illustrated by Ruth Robbins (Berkeley: Parnassus, 1972);

The Old Dog, as Sarah Abbott, illustrated by George Mocniak (New York: Coward-McCann, 1972);

Hold My Hand, illustrated by Thomas di Grazia (New York: Harper & Row, 1972);

William's Doll, illustrated by William Pène Du Bois (New York: Harper & Row, 1972);

Janey, illustrated by Ronald Himler (New York: Harper & Row, 1973);

My Grandson Lew, illustrated by Du Bois (New York: Harper & Row, 1974);

The Unfriendly Book, illustrated by Du Bois (New York: Harper & Row, 1975);

May I Visit?, illustrated by Erik Bleguad (New York: Harper & Row, 1976);

It's Not Fair, illustrated by Du Bois (New York: Harper & Row, 1976);

Someone New, illustrated by Bleguad (New York: Harper & Row, 1978);

Say It!, illustrated by James Stevenson (New York: Greenwillow, 1980);

If You Listen, illustrated by Marc Simont (New York: Harper & Row, 1980);

The Song, illustrated by Nancy Tafuri (New York: Greenwillow, 1982);

I Know a Lady, illustrated by Stevenson (New York: Greenwillow, 1984).

OTHER: *An Overpraised Season: Ten Stories of Youth,* edited by Zolotow (New York: Harper & Row, 1973).

Charlotte Shapiro Zolotow, born to Louis J. and Ella Bernstein Shapiro on 26 June 1915, in Norfolk, Virginia, studied literature at the University of Wisconsin from 1933 to 1936 before joining the children's book department of Harper and Brothers in 1936. She married writer Maurice Zolotow on 14 April 1938. They had two children and

Dust jacket for a later edition of Zolotow's lyrical account of the arrival and passage of a rainstorm (Harper & Row)

were divorced in 1969. Charlotte Zolotow served as senior editor in the children's division at Harper from 1938 to 1944 and again from 1962 until 1976, when she became vice-president, associate publisher of Harper Junior Books, and editorial consultant. On 29 September 1981 Zolotow resigned as vice-president and associate publisher when given her own imprint, Charlotte Zolotow Books, for the 1982 Harper Junior Books list, though she remains editorial consultant for the department she has long served. In addition to her work as editor, Zolotow is a teacher of her craft who lectures widely, often to audiences of other writers. She has participated in the University of Colorado Writer's Conference on Children's Books and the University of Indiana Writer's Conference. Since the publication of *The Park Book* in 1944 she has produced more than sixty books for children.

Recognized in the limited criticism that exists on her work as a realist writing in the lyric mode and a writer who insists on the importance of carefully plotted sound patterns to convey meaning to the attentive child, Zolotow is remarkably sensitive to changing cultural attitudes and their place in literature for children. Her most enthusiastic critics, who value her crafted style and sometimes humorous, often wistful accounts of the personal relationships in which children participate, note her ability to empathize with the child reader. Less enthusiastic critics claim that the "gentle reflective style" praised by Zolotow's admirers limits the range of her audiences, "feminizes" her subjects, and diminishes the effectiveness of her plots. But whether they like or dislike her lyrical style, few critics analyze the thematic, social, and linguistic concerns of her work. Close study reveals that Zolotow's underlying interests remain constant as the social attitudes and subjects of her books shift from decade to decade to reflect newly dominant attitudes within American culture; that Zolotow often writes brief occasional books on subjects which do not include the sum of her larger concerns; and that periodically she publishes moving and highly successful volumes which summarize and synthesize her smaller efforts.

Three of Zolotow's books from the 1950s mark out the lyric, thematic, social, and linguistic concerns she was to combine and integrate into her work in the 1960s. *The Storm Book* (1952) describes the central "event" typical of a Zolotow story; *Not a Little Monkey* (1957) places the child in a domestic value system which is a base from which later books depart; *Sleepy Book* (1958) illustrates the linguistic practices which were to be a source of elegant complexity in Zolotow's later work. *The Storm Book* takes as its event not adventure, escape, or conflict (likely subjects in a child's picture book at the time of its writing) but sensory apprehension valued for its own sake and expressed through the coming and going of a storm. The book begins with stasis and heat; the storm arrives as motion in stillness; a young boy, waiting, sees the darkness forming in the distance and recognizes the storm as a fresh and profoundly dramatic event. The first half of the book is purely experiential. Zolotow presents each phase of the storm as a unified impression built on heavily assonated, onomatopoeic lines and on an intense rhythmic lyricism which overrides concern for plot. Zolotow forces sensation upon the reader until he hears, along with the boy, "a great silver sighing stretch down the hill." Then the storm begins, "Shooting through the sky like a streak of starlight comes a flash so beautiful, so fast, that the little boy has time to see the flowers straining with the storm wind."

The boy senses, recognizes, and "thinks," making a connection between forms of light he has already seen. Finally, he shouts. In the first half of the book, Zolotow writes in the present tense, compelling the reader to live an aesthetic and emotional event with the child. At the outset, Zolotow presents knowledge gained through sensation evoked rather than exposition or plot; then her intention falters. At midpoint in the book she abruptly shifts voice, becoming a distant narrator who, unlike the child who receives and reacts to events, can observe the storm overtake distant landscapes and "tell" the reader about it. The book recovers its coherence only when Zolotow returns in conclusion to the controlling point of view of the child.

In *The Storm Book* the child is internally active, externally passive, subject to forces larger than himself; he cannot shape the natural world in which he lives. This is equally true of the domestic experience of the child in *Not a Little Monkey*. As her mother gently but authoritatively resolves conflicts over the child's perceived lack of attention, the morning passes imperceptibly away, child and mother marking out the good rituals of domestic order. The book portrays the stability and wholeness of everyday life, and the worth of an intimate but controlled relation between parent and child. It places value on cleanliness, order, discipline, calmness, and material presence—that is, domestic values as defined by dominant American cultural attitudes in the 1950s. At the same time the portrait of the close relationship between mother and child, and of the child's delicate efforts to gain attention for herself, exemplifies Zolotow's persistent effort to understand the psychological situation of the child, no matter what his or her social context. Structured on a repeated verbal pattern which constitutes a logical order, *Not a Little Monkey* is entirely coherent, as tidy as the household and day its plot celebrates. It represents the succinct, tough verbal structures Zolotow was able to make early in her career when she admitted no lyricism to her work.

Sleepy Book builds on the strict stylistic economy of *Not a Little Monkey* as Zolotow attempts to combine disciplined verbal structures with controlled lyricism. Modest as the book appears to be, it predicts strategies of coherence in Zolotow's best work and implicitly makes claims about the appropriate language system of the contemporary child's picture book. In *Sleepy Book*, Zolotow defines how various creatures sleep, though her definitions prove to be exercises in sentence formation as they build an increasingly complex system of modifiers and conditions. On the first spread "bears sleep in their dark caves the long winter through"; by the third, "fish sleep among the green water ferns with their eyes and mouths wide open." In the fourth Zolotow introduces a simile: "moths sleep with wings folded together. They look like little white leaves on walls, and windows, and screens." Maintaining the form of the initial statement with its prepositional phrases and adjectives, Zolotow gradually adds conjunctions, metaphors, and similes to her syntactic repertoire, thus making her examples increasingly precise. By the sixth spread she uses a simple declarative sentence for the sake of elegant variation, returning then to extended metaphors in spreads seven and eight and to a strongly assonantal line. The writing deliberately expands and contracts before the final pages, and the increasing complexity of syntax on the book's late pages suggests Zolotow's approach to closure and her wish to focus her book firmly on the experience of the child. The last statement is the most extensive: "but little boys and girls, when the night comes and the wind whispers gently in the trees and the stars sparkle and shine, sleep warm under their blankets in the beds." In this brief picture book Zolotow focuses on nighttime and sleep, characteristic subjects in her overall work. Without undue sentimentality she offers the comfort and security of home, claiming stability and coherence in the nature of things. But she also offers a lesson in syntactic competence, in the principles of sentence ordering and manipulation by which experience is controlled and interpreted.

The principles of language, ordering, subject, and complexity used with varying success in books from the early 1950s come to full development and combination in Zolotow's work of the early 1960s, work which sets standards from which her best writing in the last fifteen years does not depart. In *Mr. Rabbit and the Lovely Present* (1962), *The White Marble* (1963), and *The Sky Was Blue* (1963), time, language, continuity, order, relationship, and closure are all at issue beneath the overt subjects Zolotow chooses to discuss.

Mr. Rabbit and the Lovely Present represents the remarkable control of tone and emotion Zolotow achieves in her best work and the means by which she achieves it. The problem is simple enough: what to give a mother for her birthday:

> "Mr. Rabbit," said the little girl, "I want help."
>
> "Help, little girl, I'll give you help if I can," said Mr. Rabbit.

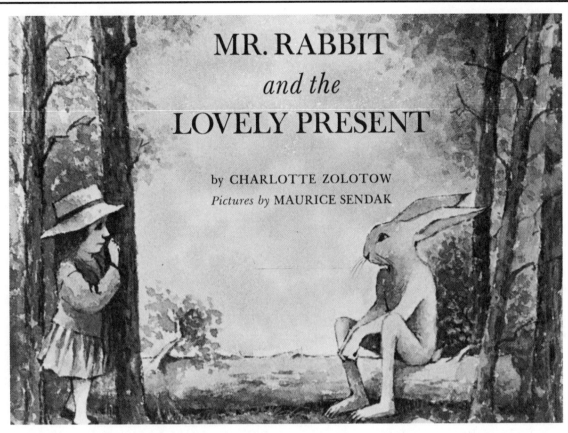

Dust jacket for Zolotow's book that offers a lesson in the use of logic as a problem-solving device in the story of a young girl's search for an appropriate birthday present for her mother (Harper & Row)

"Mr. Rabbit," said the little girl, "it's about my mother."

"Your mother?" said Mr. Rabbit.

"It's her birthday," said the little girl.

"Happy birthday to her then," said Mr. Rabbit. "What are you giving her?"

Without any external exposition Zolotow establishes respect and equality between the conversants, one of whom, Mr. Rabbit, is a gently questioning alter ego the child has imagined for herself. In a text amplified by Maurice Sendak's marvelous illustrations, Mr. Rabbit invites the girl into a landscape of choice—fields, orchards, and woodland—where he questions, states, comments, echoes, and repeats in order to guide his friend to succeeding stages of thought. *Mr. Rabbit and the Lovely Present* extends to logic and the problem of appropriate choice the lesson in syntactic complexity offered in *Sleepy Book*. As Zolotow repeats patterns of syntax with significant variation, the girl discerns categories of quality, object, and idea from which her choice of gifts can be made. Finding that her mother likes red, then yellow, green, and blue, the girl discovers, through questioning and exclusion, an appropriate object to specify each color. In *Mr. Rabbit and the Lovely Present* Zolotow simultaneously writes a color book, a friendship book, a birthday book, a conversation book—and a book about reasoning. She asks on what basis and under what conditions we reason well. She claims that we reason well when we take the trouble to discern the general categories which govern language and thought and when parties exchange ideas under conditions of respect and mutual sympathy. *Mr. Rabbit and the Lovely Present* is a balanced and completely resolved story, for when all of the categories of color have been specified, a birthday present has been chosen, an evening closed, a friendship strengthened, and a child satisfied. This is Zolotow's art at its best. The linguistic security and structural completeness of the book match Zolotow's restricted fantasy and control its psychological implications.

In *Mr. Rabbit and the Lovely Present* Zolotow combines logical toughness with a portrait of interior exchange. She tries a different synthesis in *The White Marble,* replacing logical structures with imagery and sensation reminiscent of *The Storm Book* in order to further explore the question of exchange. The time is nightfall, after the enervating heat of an urban day and before the coming of a storm. Zolotow catches the privacy of a child who finds a marble and tells no one; his silence expresses power over experience he does not have in his family by virtue of his childhood. To see "something white" coming toward him in the darkness and discover that it is only "Pamela from school" provokes a scene in which he and Pamela leave the adults and find unspoken intimacy in their common experiences of darkness. Zolotow images the scene in a simple palette of deep purple, black, and white—white dress, moths, marble, foam at the fountain, lightning. The event at the center of this book is not the coming of the storm as it is in *The Storm Book* but the gift of the marble, placed in Pamela's hand. The boy echoes the exchange Zolotow values in *Mr. Rabbit and the Lovely Present.* Using elements familiar from her earlier writing, Zolotow creates a layered narrative which is relatively complex and in which she is able to include but control lyrical elements. Zolotow's tight layering of relationship over sensation, her control of language at once descriptive and narrative, suggest that she has mastered her temptation to unalloyed lyric cry.

A third book from the 1960s, *The Sky Was Blue,* explicitly codifies the ideas about time, continuity, and relationship evident in *Mr. Rabbit and the Lovely Present* and *The White Marble.* In the book a mother and daughter look at a picture album. On each spread they see the image of a prior generation and note its characteristic dress and behavior. The child reader apprehends the material differences that mark the lives of her forebears; of each case, each grandmother, she asks:

"What was it like? How did she feel?"
"Oh," said her mother, "the way you feel."
"The sky was blue,"
"Grass was green,"
"Snow was white and cold,"
"The sun was warm and yellow,"
"Just as they all are now."

From generation to generation important events remain the same—a mother's care at bedtime, the sound of clocks ticking, grown-ups talking, stars shining, wind blowing. By her acts of "reading" and questioning, the child places herself among the

Title page for Zolotow's book about a sensitive boy's need for a doll to which he can make expressions of paternal love

generations. Zolotow thus puts her characteristic use of repetition to a new and larger end only implied in earlier books. Repetition of syntactical structures and ideas, like repetition of acts, argues for a continuity of human experience that overrides all changes and that links generations together despite external differences of circumstance. To this fundamental statement strategies of style and choice of subject in Zolotow's work both tend.

Few of Zolotow's other books from the 1960s match the standard of these three, though many address problems and circumstances real enough for the child. *My Friend John* (1968) celebrates a friendship based on common "likes"; *I Want to Be Little* (1967) gives the child permission to be what he/she is; *The Hating Book* (1969) acknowledges hostility; *Big Sister and Little Sister* (1966) recognizes the dominance of older siblings and the measures a young child takes to overcome it. Perhaps the most interesting of Zolotow's late 1960s publications is *The New Friend* (1968), which frankly states the pain of emotional betrayal. For a tense moment it appears the book will have a forced "happy ending"; however, Zolotow has her young narrator state: "I will look for that new friend and when I find her I'll remember my first friend, my dear friend with long brown hair. But maybe then I won't care."

The honesty of *The New Friend* was an apt prelude to the best of Zolotow's writing in the early 1970s, when she turned to topics of current social interest: death, sexism, single parenthood, and adolescence. Topical books alternate with Zolotow's usual subjects thereafter. In *My Grandson Lew* (1974), a moving and structurally complete book, Zolotow writes about death from the point of view of a child who suddenly and compellingly remembers his grandfather as a physical presence. Zolotow confronts her reader not with sudden death but with memory, with the mixed pain and comfort memory gives. Once again she values exchange: when the boy tells his memory to his mother both acknowledge the death and the worth of the man who has died. In *a rose, a bridge, and a wild black horse* (1964), Zolotow had differentiated the sexes by allowing a small boy to tell his sister what he would do for her when he grows up: build a castle, fight anyone on her behalf, break rocks, drive a fast car, pluck a rose. When he goes off to "explore the world," he intends to bring her a friend to keep her company. The book echoes the now infamous textbook illustrations for children which describe men as strong and women as passive and confined to domesticity. In *The Summer Night,* a 1974 revision of *The Night When Mother Was Away* (1958), Zolotow radically changes the early text, which is conditioned entirely by a mother's absence, to portray a single father caring alone for his child. Although her revision of *The Summer Night* is relatively successful, it leads us to question the sincerity of a change apparently made to meet market shifts dependent on altered social values.

Such questions do not arise about the value or integrity of *William's Doll* (1972), a book which states a boy's anticipation of fatherhood and describes the social forces that repress his nurturing instinct. William, a perfectly normal boy who enjoys playing with basketballs and trains, is honest enough to express his desire for a doll to cuddle, love, and care for. He meets the frustrations and denials familiar to sensitive children in American society, even in his own home, but he pursues his wish, encouraged by a grandmother who understands his needs. The grandmother—wise, articulate, sensitive, and kind—takes on the traditional position of truth teller in this work, explaining to

Dust jacket for the 1975 republication, with new illustrations, of Zolotow's 1962 book which explores the questions of beginnings and endings (Harper & Row)

her son the significance of the child's actions and voicing the book's peroration. *William's Doll* is a book conceived in sympathy and written with a quiet passion, a book that allows the child's voice to speak convincingly for itself and to be seconded by an adult's. In its form and use of character, its attention to family relationships and the child's need for self-knowledge and a sense of worth, in its use of the grandmother as a wise teller, it places Zolotow in a tradition of storytelling she has not often invoked before. At the end of the book the grandmother offers the child a promise of paternity which resembles the mother's promise to the little girl at the end of *The Sky Was Blue.* He, too, will rear children to share the experience of the world he knows; and unlike his father, he will be prepared for his task, having taken responsibility for it in his own childhood.

If, since the 1960s, Zolotow looked at change and continuity in the contexts of memory and death, of childbearing and child rearing, of inner growth and of adolescence, then she also recapitulates the language in which she has considered these themes earlier. *When the Wind Stops,* which was originally published in 1962 and reissued in 1975, is a summary statement, a book which illustrates Zolotow's recurrent need to return to her earliest themes and means of expression. The book, which portrays a child at bedtime, is perhaps the best testament we can find to the values that underlie her work and to her ability to discipline her lyricism when she chooses to do so. The child has questions to ask before he can sleep: "Why does the day have to end?," "Where does the sun go . . . when the day ends?," "Where does the wind go when it stops?" The statement of the book, applied to the sun, wind, road, and mountain, is that "Nothing ends. It only begins in another place or in a different way." Zolotow thus expresses the value at the center of her writing, what she balances with closure in her most realized works and what undoes closure in the less successful. In various ways she writes about the forces that subdue or reconcile us to change: memory, language at once closed and continuous, secure relationships, integrity of feeling and exchange.

To watch Zolotow's writing develop from 1944 to the present is to confront questions of sincerity as the author shifts social attitudes; problems of voice as the writer attempts to balance the child's voice she posits against her own; difficulties of propriety as she experiments with lyrical writing in the contemporary picture book. If Zolotow's style admits feeling which many (indeed most writers for young children today) avoid or find old-fashioned, her plots do not always bear the weight of the emotion she elicits. And if, in her most disciplined work, Zolotow strives for a combination of elements which reach mutual closure, she also from time to time abandons the desire for closure altogether, giving free rein to a lyrical impulse that denies ending for the sake of pure evocation. Uneven as they are, Zolotow's books possess a voice that is unitary and utterly recognizable. In the persona of the child it is wistful, uncertain, and replete with emotion; as the voice of an adult it is often strong and in control. As an editor and a writer Charlotte Zolotow has significantly shaped expectations about form and quality in the contemporary picture book. If she has at times been tempted to write too much, at her best she has written very well.

Afterword: Propaganda, Namby-Pamby, and Some Books of Distinction

Perry Nodelman
University of Winnipeg

There have probably been more books for children published in any given year of this century than in any entire decade of the century before it. There have probably been more books for children published in the United States of America in each of the decades of this century than in the entire world in all the years before 1900. Yet in relation to the small number of merely good, the sizable number of merely adequate, and the vast number of decidedly mediocre books, the great American children's books are surprisingly few. Why so much, and why is so much of it unmemorable? The reasons for the abundance also explain not only the general mediocrity but also what distinguishes excellent books from the rest.

There have been more human beings alive in this century than ever before, and therefore, more children to write for, more adults to write for them, more publishers to publish books for them. But there has also been more interest in childhood than ever before. Throughout this century, adults have taken for granted an idea that became popular only in the last century: that children see and think differently than adults do. Furthermore, what was a revolutionary attitude near the beginning of the nineteenth century had become a commonplace by 1900, an accepted idea by which all Americans live: childhood is not just different from maturity; in some ways, it is better.

In the last century, children were considered to be stylishly dressed in the pinafores of servants and the suits of ordinary seamen. In fact, the similarity throughout history between children's clothing and the workclothes of laborers has implied the inferior position children occupied in the scheme of things—a position explained by devastating childhood mortality rates that made it foolish to invest too much attention in those who might not live long and also by religious and philosophical systems that did not value childlike innocence. But in contemporary America, blue jeans, once the working outfit of laborers and then the standard uniform of children and teenagers, have become fashion for adults also. This reversal of the patterns of history implies

a deep worship of childhood and childlike things. Not surprisingly, much recent writing for adults has been a sort of fantasy once produced exclusively for children, and the most popular American movies tell stories like the ones that used to be found only in children's comic books. It is also not surprising that some contemporary pop therapists encourage adults to solve their problems by screaming like infants and by being as egocentric as children.

The American worship of childhood emerges from the American ideal of equality. If everyone can equally aspire to change one's position in life for the better, then everyone *can* equally change. The means by which one changes is education, and the time one learns best is childhood, when one is flexible, impressionable—still innocent enough to become better than one's parents. No wonder that adults wish to ape the hopefulness with which they invest childhood; and no wonder that twentieth-century America has produced so many children's books.

As part of a vast educational enterprise, these books are meant to make children better than they already are; consequently, they are as filled with educational propaganda as children's books of all times have always been. But paradoxically, their underlying admiration for the flexible innocence of childhood implies something quite different from earlier books—that innocence is in itself desirable. Therefore, many American children's books of this century have been mediocre for two contradictory reasons. On one hand, they belabor educational concerns with an unfailingly blatant obviousness; on the other, they suggest that infantile ingenuousness is "cute"; that is, they imply that children should be admired for being ignorant, immature, in need of education. The archetypal American children's story of this century, the one told again and again in countless books, sums up these contradictions. It is about a fuzzy, childlike animal who leaves home to see the world and learns that home is best. The animal is supposed to be adorable because it does not understand and cannot cope with the world it explores; but then that same ineptitude is also the means by which young readers are supposed to learn better. Such books imply that children are limited in their need for education, as well as wonderful because they are so limited.

The rare books that stand out avoid neither worship of childhood nor high-minded educational intentions; they inevitably include both. But in the best books, the two do not contradict one another. Rather, their writers find ingenious, innovative ways of balancing the two. Because their worship of innocence balances their condemnation of it, such books neither condemn nor worship. They merely describe innocence honestly.

For all its failings, Frank L. Baum's *The Wonderful Wizard of Oz* (1900) is such a book. Published in the first year of this century, it is the first important children's book of the century. Yet its language is undistinguished, its plot feebly organized. Dorothy simply walks through Oz, a pedestrian described in pedestrian prose, until Baum runs out of interesting places for the yellow brick road to pass through. Not only is Dorothy's trip episodic but it does not even have the purpose we expect of such trips. She learns nothing from her quest; in fact, one of the charming things about the book is that Oz hardly affects her unflappable common sense.

Nevertheless, Baum does *try* to teach his young readers something, the thing Dorothy knows all along: home is best, because the unfamiliar things we dream of are not just uncomfortable but nearly always disappointing. So Baum makes Dorothy spend all her time in Oz wishing she were back in Kansas; and he insists on making many of his wonderful inventions mere fakes. The lack of conviction Baum expresses in his own inventiveness is one version of the great paradox of American children's literature; Baum wanted both to indulge in childlike imagining and to condemn it, and rather than integrate the two, he merely let them sit side by side and contradict each other.

But they do not really contradict each other, because Baum's fresh inventiveness dwarfs the educational uses he pretends to find for it. Nevertheless, it is unfortunate that his vision was larger than his willingness or his capacity to express it, and that most people nowadays know Baum's Oz only through the grandiose M-G-M film of 1939, a more tightly conceived expression of Oz that gets rid of Baum's freshness along with the crudity of his style.

As Baum's difficulties suggest, fantasy is something of an un-American activity, an indulgence in impractical foolishness that interferes with the serious business of getting ahead by means of hard work and discipline. Few American writers have avoided either encumbering their fantasies with heavy superstructures of moral allegory or else defiantly indulging in wispy whimsies that avoid meaning altogether. Consequently, the great American fantasies tend to be quite unlike the vast mass of American fantasies; instead, they are Americanized versions of forms first established in other countries.

Wanda Gág's picture storybook *Millions of Cats* (1928), the one undeniably great American children's book of the 1920s, has the folksy charm of both European folktales and primitive European woodcuts; what is ingenious and refreshing is Gág's clever combination of the two. The blocky solidity of the pictures and the insistently memorable refrain control and allow the grotesque violence of a story in which "hundreds of cats, thousands of cats, millions and billions and trillions of cats" all devour each other. A similar infusion of vitality into old forms can be found in the remarkable *Jack Tales* (1943), collected by Richard Chase. These energetic American versions of European folktales show how old stories can come to reflect new cultural circumstances.

Numerous Americans have produced quite adequate literary fairy tales in this century, including writers as diverse as Carl Sandburg and John Gardner; but only two writers have produced distinguished work of this sort, stories that seem both American and like traditional fairy tales. In *Many Moons* (1943), James Thurber fuses clever *New Yorker* satire, unabashed Hans Christian Andersen sentimentality, and the usual American children's-book moral allegory into a story of great charm. In a more substantial series of literary fairy tales in recent years, in particular those in *The Girl Who Cried Flowers and Other Tales* (1974) and *The Hundredth Dove and Other Tales* (1977), Jane Yolen has shown that, despite their lack of detailed characterization, fairy tales can be both subtle and affecting. Many of the prolific Yolen's more than sixty books are ingenious experiments in adapting traditional European folk materials to contemporary forms; in the singularly undreamy *Dragon's Blood* (1982), her nuts-and-bolts descriptions of the care and maintenance of dragons make them far more believable to practical contemporary minds than most fictional versions of such beasts.

The European influence on Eleanor Cameron's work is transparent enough to amount to homage. In *The Court of the Stone Children* (1973), Cameron convincingly transplants to American soil the rich British tradition of children's fantasies about contact with people from the past; in *Beyond Silence* (1980), she reverses the pattern and takes a contemporary young American to Scotland for a different sort of contact with the past. Both these books are thoroughly American in the way they relate fantasy elements to the psychological needs of their main characters, so that what is delightful is also useful; both possess a refined psychological subtlety found also in Cameron's fine realistic novels, particularly in *To the Green Mountains* (1975).

Lloyd Alexander's five books about Taran of Prydain, beginning in 1964 with *The Book of Three*, are firmly grounded in the legends of ancient Wales; but the strength and also, far too often, the weakness of these books is that Alexander's young hero and heroine are very much contemporary Americans—just as the hobbits in J. R. R. Tolkien's books, another obvious influence on Alexander, are very much British academics. Somehow, short British academics do not seem out of place amid the wilds of Middle-Earth; but while the democratic exuberance of Alexander's Taran and Eilonwy breathes new life into the old Welsh stories, Taran's soul-searching sensitivity and Eilonwy's liberated motor-mouth frequently do seem out of place amid the pseudomedieval trappings of Prydain. On the other hand, Alexander's characteristic breeziness accords perfectly with the pseudo-Sufistic trappings of Abadan, the setting of *The First Two Lives of Lukas-Kasha* (1978); like much Sufistic wisdom, this witty book delightfully undercuts its own philosophic pretentions. In her trilogy of books about Ged, the wizard of Earthsea (*A Wizard of Earthsea*, 1968; *The Tombs of Atuan*, 1971; *The Farthest Shore*, 1972), Ursula Le Guin indulges in just as many pseudo-European trappings. But unlike Taran, Ged suffers, and suffers mightily, from his thoroughly American denial of tradition. The conflict between Ged's personality and his environment becomes an important theme of the three books, a theme explored most poignantly in *The Tombs of Atuan*, the second book of the three. Here Tenar's escape from the suffocating traditions of her gods leads her to a tortured exploration of the relationship between freedom and tradition. In their absolute integration of European traditions and American values, and in their elegant control of imagery that moves them past political allegory into profound expressions of Jungian archetypes, the Earthsea books are the most distinguished American achievement in the area of high fantasy.

But high fantasy is not necessarily a great American tradition. As *The Wonderful Wizard of Oz*

and many of the other books already mentioned suggest, American fantasies tend to be breezier than their English counterparts. They hide their serious intentions under layers of slapstick or whimsy, perhaps because of a democratic fear that seriousness is stuffy and aristocratic. Consequently, many of the masterworks of American children's literature are delightfully unstuffy, decidedly hilarious, and not at all profound.

Dr. Seuss has produced an astonishing number of such books. His first book, *And to Think that I Saw It on Mulberry Street* (1937), is not so wacky and frenetic as some later Seuss extravaganzas nor even so wacky as the less frenzied *Five Hundred Hats of Bartholomew Cubbins* (1938) nor so frenzied as the less wacky *Horton Hatches the Egg* (1940). But the integration of verbal and visual rhythms in *And to Think that I Saw It on Mulberry Street* is amazingly sophisticated for a book that comes so early in the history of its genre; Dr. Seuss understood how to lay out the pages of a picture storybook decades before anyone else even thought it mattered. While his later books are less ingenious in design, their exuberant pictures of, and words about, crazy beasts are impeccably nonsensical. The essence of Dr. Seuss's peculiar talent can be found in three very big books. *If I Ran the Zoo* (1950), *If I Ran the Circus* (1956), and, above all, *On Beyond Zebra* (1955) are of Wagnerian proportions; they express a deeply anarchic insanity in impeccably controlled verse. The limited vocabulary of the easy-to-read books Dr. Seuss produced later in his career, beginning with the revolutionary *The Cat in the Hat* (1957), seems also to have limited his imagination. While it is decidedly superior to most books of this sort, *The Cat in the Hat* is to *On Beyond Zebra* as commercial jingles are to grand opera.

Dr. Seuss's long career marks the fullest flowering of the interbreeding of children's books and cartoon art, but many other classics of American comic fantasy are also illustrated in cartoon style. As one of the few books not illustrated by its writer that actually achieves excellence, *The Story of Ferdinand* (1937) is a genuine rarity. Munro Leaf's words and Robert Lawson's pictures share a sly satirical wit that makes the propagandistic intentions of this pacifist story more than just bearable. The humor implies a more sensitive sort of machismo than the bellicose celebration of brute violence that Ferdinand himself so wisely rejects, and both words and pictures cleverly use small details to suggest further implications. While Lawson's work on his own as a writer was rarely so artful, his novel *Ben and Me* (1939) is another comic delight. The cartoonist's anarchist spirit emerges in both pictures and words, as the testy mouse Amos sends up the stodgy pomposity not only of his buddy Benjamin Franklin but also of the numerous stodgy novels for children about the American past that dominated publishing for children in the 1930s.

Ben is a mouse, Ferdinand is a bull, Dr. Seuss's bird-hatching Horton an elephant. Talking animals dominate American children's literature, which in this way decidedly belongs to the tradition begun by the fables of antiquity, a literature also devoted to equal doses of one part blatant propaganda and one part delight in the stupidity of fuzzy creatures. Not surprisingly, this most actively pursued of all genres of children's literature is also the most frequently clichéd.

In the context of countless cute bunnies and timid mousies, two wonderful books by E. B. White seem particularly noteworthy. The first of them is not really about an animal; *Stuart Little* (1945), a surprisingly accomplished first novel for children, describes a boy who merely *looks* like a mouse; but he can talk to birds. Stuart has horrified generations of adults, who have seen him as freakishly deformed. But children and oddballs, who can recognize in him their own feelings of alienation in face of a world designed for people more powerful than themselves, rightfully adore Stuart, the indefatigable Don Quixote of American children's literature. Wilbur, the less heroic pig hero of White's *Charlotte's Web* (1952), is even more widely and more deservedly adored. The cute animals who face silly domestic crises in most children's books do so with unfailing optimism, mostly because they are too innocent to know any better; but Wilbur, who started out being as ingenuous as all the rest, learns from his spider friend Charlotte a wisdom as great as Stuart Little's. Nor does Wilbur escape the occasional moment of justly merited despair.

In *Charlotte's Web*, White displays perfect control of diction and imagery, and an almost perfect understanding of the limitations and possibilities of children's literature as a genre. White's manuscripts, now housed at Cornell University, reveal that this book cost him much effort, that he rewrote it again and again. The result has the apparent effortlessness of all great art, a simplicity that resonates to great depths. Even very young children enjoy hearing the gracefully told and gripping story of *Charlotte's Web*; highly sophisticated readers find more and more in it as they read it again and again. It is certainly the most likely candidate for consideration as the greatest of all American children's books.

White's animals possess the characters animals might have, if animals actually had characters like human beings; Wilbur is piglike, and Templeton is a real rat. They represent one of the many ways writers have developed to describe those strange beings who look like animals, think like people, and act sometimes like one, sometimes like the other. Some writers merely use their characters' animal natures for the sake of distance—in order to tell children stories with human implications that they might find unsettling if the stories actually happened to humans. A fine example of such an approach is the series of books about Frances by Russell Hoban, begun in 1960. The illustrations for these books, first by Garth Williams and then by Lillian Hoban, are often the only indication that Frances and her family are badgers, not people; for Frances's problems are those of a human child. Furthermore, Hoban explores those problems with a light tongue-in-cheek irony that not only cheerfully undercuts Frances in her many moments of self-indulgence but also implies the deep emotional intensity both badgers and people often invest in theoretically minor upsets.

In another well-wrought book, this one about a toy mouse, Hoban makes more of the nonhuman nature of his characters. The windup father and son team of *The Mouse and His Child* (1967) must cope both with the rigidity of their lives as toys and with the violence of their lives as animallike creatures in the wild. Adults sometimes treat children like toys, adorable, quasi-human playthings that are rejected when they break down and stop conforming to preestablished patterns; and adults sometimes treat children like animals who talk, rude, uncivilized beings who try to act like *real* human beings. In *The Mouse and His Child*, Hoban explores the existential problems of creatures who are part toy, part animal, and part human, in terms of a clever parody of Samuel Beckett's gloomy plays. Whereas Beckett describes people who lose their vitality when they start acting repetitively like machines, Hoban describes machines who develop hope when they learn to act like people—an interesting message for children.

In his funny *Fables* (1980), Arnold Lobel's animals most often conform to the fable tradition, and their adventures provide hilarious allegories for human behavior. But the main characters in Lobel's limited vocabulary books *Frog and Toad are Friends* (1970) and *Frog and Toad Together* (1972), while always both funnier and more touching than they realize themselves, are at their best when they confront their paradoxical nature as animals who act like people. In "The Swim," for instance, Toad must realize how silly a toad looks in a human bathing suit.

In terms of more accurate zoological detail than any of the other animals mentioned so far, the bat in Randall Jarrell's *The Bat-Poet* (1964) is very much a bat. But he is also very much a poet, and his wonderful, strong poems about bats and mockingbirds are as good as any other poems for children written in this century. Not that there is much competition; far too many of the versifiers who set themselves up as children's poets indulge in weakbrained evocations of the world as theoretically seen through the eyes of excessively gentle children. Such poets evoke what is limited and childish, rather than what is significant and childlike; but the bat's poems *are* childlike, for Jarrell convincingly shows us what a thoroughly ingenuous nonhuman being might see. A similarly persuasive evocation of innocence appears often in the poems of David McCord (starting with *Far and Few,* 1952, and collected in *One at a Time,* 1977), almost never in poems written specifically for an audience of children; unfortunately, McCord is most frequently represented in anthologies by his least evocative and most childish poems.

The animals in Jarrell's brief, but beautifully wrought, allegorical book *The Animal Family* (1965) are even less human than his bat; they do not talk. In fact, what makes this book special is the poetic way Jarrell makes his characters seem alien. The animals, the mermaid, even the one human being, are all "different," to use a word that echoes so poetically through the book itself.

One final animal is also different—the highly cultured and very gentlemanly mouse of William Steig's *Abel's Island* (1976). Steig tells of this witty Edwardian gentlemouse in a delightfully quirky pseudo-Edwardian style. In a fascinating twist on a long-established convention, Abel is one humanlike animal who survives his confrontation with the wilds, not because, like Beatrix Potter's Peter Rabbit or Baum's not-really-cowardly lion, he gives up human postures and learns to act like his true animallike self but instead because he has a degree of civilization that keeps him regular, idealistic, and gentlemanly human no matter what horrors nature throws at him.

As a mouse from the past, Abel joins Lawson's mouse Amos as a representative of numerous historical characters in American children's literature of this century. Unlike most of those characters, however, Abel and Amos have some vitality; for most American historical fiction for children has been high-minded and stodgy, moral porridge thick with historical detail. The characters in these books are almost always courageous, honest, dutiful, patriotic, clearly not mice but men—even when they are women.

Nevertheless, there is one undoubted masterpiece of American children's literature about the past: the wonderful series of Little House books by Laura Ingalls Wilder, published between 1932 and 1943 and describing Wilder's own life as a child some decades earlier. These books are the most distinctly American of the great American children's books and the first important American children's books to be set neither in England, like Howard Pyle's *Merry Adventures of Robin Hood* (1883), nor in an invented land like Baum's Oz. In the earlier books of the series, Wilder described the events of her own frontier childhood with a carefully maintained double perspective. While the child Laura's perceptions are convincingly childlike (and not always admirable), readers with a more mature understanding can always see the mature implications Laura ignores in what she perceives. Each of Wilder's books is orchestrated thematically and in terms of carefully organized images in a way that makes them distinct from the others; but as a group, they each take their places as movements in a symphony, the whole being a detailed and cohesive portrait of a nation's and a child's maturing.

Two other interesting books about the American past suggest the problems American children's writers have frequently had with this genre. Esther Forbes's *Johnny Tremain* (1943) is pompous, spectacular, sentimental, uplifting—one of those books so persistent and so sincere in its pursuit of sheer trashiness that it is hard not to enjoy. Forbes clearly meant the fervid patriotism of this simpleminded M-G-M-movie-of-a-novel, which was set in the time of the Revolutionary War, to apply equally to the war Americans were fighting at the time of the book's appearance: World War II. Some decades later, another book about the Revolutionary War, *My Brother Sam Is Dead* (1976) by James Lincoln Collier and his historian brother Christopher Collier, also clearly applied to the war Americans were then currently involved in, this time the Vietnam War. The different places those two wars occupy in the minds of Americans say much of the differences between these two books. The quiet, searching questioning of *My Brother Sam Is Dead* is an elegant answer to the fireworks of *Johnny Tremain*. But it has none of the exuberance of *Johnny Tremain*; and *Johnny Tremain* has none of the bleak, documentary accuracy of *My Brother Sam Is Dead*.

In fact, few American historical novels for children have managed to balance accuracy and intensity, as British historical children's novels often do and as Laura Ingalls Wilder's books do. Possible exceptions might be Paula Fox's *The Slave Dancer* (1973), in which stripped-down prose communicates the horrific events aboard a slave ship with some of the intensity of good playwriting; the three novels on medieval Japan Katherine Paterson published in the early 1970s; and *Sing Down the Moon* (1970), in which Scott O'Dell writes of the "Long Walk" of the Navaho tribe in 1863 with a cool quietness that is deeply moving.

But the small American achievement in historical fiction for children is more than balanced by the many excellent books Americans have produced from the 1940s on about children coping with the more-or-less contemporary world. Such books often manage to integrate honest reporting with the usual educational impulses, both to describe childhood accurately and suggest how children might transcend their childishness.

A charmingly homey domesticity dominates the books about the Moffats, written in the early 1940s by Eleanor Estes, and about the Melendys and their friends and relations, written by Elizabeth Enright from the early 1940s through the 1950s. These have all the fresh wholesomeness of earlier domestic books like Eleanor H. Porter's *Pollyanna* (1913); but while Estes's stories take place at about the same time as do the saccharine events of Pollyanna's life, both Porter's and Enright's children act convincingly like children, rather than like the ethereal sparks of the divine fire that passed for children in the utopian domestic novels of earlier years. Similarly wholesome, but invested with a dry, taciturn wit that wonderfully evokes the small towns they are set in, are Robert McCloskey's *Lentil* (1940) and *Homer Price* (1943). The gentle satire of these books is accurate and loving.

By the time Beverly Cleary wrote *Henry Huggins* (1950), typical American children were more likely to live in suburbs than in small towns. But Cleary's children are just as wholesome, just as cutely trouble-prone and as craftily resourceful in getting out of trouble, and just as undisturbed by public anarchy or secret nightmares as had been their earlier counterparts. It wasn't until unflappable

Henry Huggins gave up center stage to the more sensitive Ramona Quimby, in the 1970s, that Cleary's young characters showed any sign of actually possessing ids or their environment any signs of the various social disruptions of the real world.

Other young characters in children's novels do not live such utopian dream lives. The hapless hero of Judith Viorst's picture book *Alexander and the Terrible, Horrible, No Good, Very Bad Day* (1972) faces a catalogue of domestic horrors with delicious deadpan bitterness. Harriet, the would-be writer of Louise Fitzhugh's cleverly acerbic *Harriet the Spy* (1964), has to cope not only with the implications of her own difficult character but also with an urban environment as uncomfortably filled with hostility, folly, and misunderstanding as the real one. *Harriet the Spy*, a paradoxical triumph of both comic satire and psychological truth, is one of the small handful of important American children's books because it is childlike only in the unflinching pleasure it takes in its young heroine's unflinchingly honest perceptions of the world around her. It was greeted with much controversy upon publication, for there are many adults who simply do not want to know that there are children like Harriet—children who not only can see through adult hypocrisy but who also have a few hypocrisies and other failings of their own. Fortunately, a lot of children are at least that human. Fitzhugh's real triumph is that she lets the book end without making Harriet into anything less than she already was.

The clever satire of *Harriet the Spy* is much more convincingly descriptive of the human condition than the presumably real but highly melodramatic grotesquerie of those novels of recent decades portentously labeled as the New Realism. The characters in these books, an army of clones of J. D. Salinger's Holden Caulfield, are all alienated, all living in nightmarish worlds dominated by malevolent adults, and all convinced of their own undoubted moral superiority. As satisfying wish-fulfillment fantasies, these books are without peer in the history of literature for young people; as realism, they obviously leave much to be desired. But Robert Cormier, whose *The Chocolate War* (1974) is just as luridly melodramatic and self-indulgent as the rest of these books, produced a genuine masterwork in *I Am the Cheese* (1977), a book that turns its genre inside out. Adam Farmer actually experiences the horrific alienation that characters in other young adult novels merely imagine in a craftily constructed plot that is enormously gripping. In comparison to the intensity of *I Am the*

Cheese, novels about children with life-shattering problems like obesity, annoying siblings, and the onset of menstruation seem more than a little self-indulgent.

Other less intense novels present just as convincingly accurate portraits of children. In an undeservedly unheralded series of autobiographical novels, Ilse-Margret Vogel chronicles young Inge's childhood in Germany with a gentle nostalgia that oddly suits and perceptively comments on the disruptive events these books describe: the death of a twin sister (*My Twin Sister Erika*, 1976), the visit of an insane aunt (*Farewell, Aunt Isabell*, 1979), and a competition between Inge and her mother for the affections of a young man (*My Summer Brother*, 1981). In *Drop Dead* (1965), which is either a realistic fantasy or a quite fantastic realistic novel, Julia Cunningham tells a horror story in a chillingly quiet way that mirrors the superficial quiet of her inwardly seething protagonist; and Claudia and James Kincaid of E. L. Konigsburg's *From the Mixed-Up Files of Mrs. Basil E. Frankweiler* (1967) do not seethe at all. In fact, they feel that their lives are devoid of excitement, and Konigsburg understands them well enough to allow them to choose for themselves the safest of all possible adventures: a stay in the exotic wilds of New York's Metropolitan Museum of Art.

Konigsburg's keen eye for the realities of suburban childhood and unfailingly ingenious narrative techniques are exemplified equally well in many other books, most notably an eccentric novel about concentric twins, *(George)* (1970), and a collection of wise short stories, *Throwing Shadows* (1979). Paradoxically, some of her impeccably understood safe Americans are the Renaissance Italian Leonardo da Vinci and the various medieval husbands of Eleanor of Aquitaine; for like most American forays into history, Konigsburg's historical fiction finds a past peopled with contemporary American types. Nevertheless, all of Konigsburg's books are filled with the deliciously snippy Konigsburg wit and an unfailing insistence on standards of personal morality that might make Henry James flinch.

Konigsburg is one of three American children's novelists of our time whose work is distinguished both by excellence and by a flexible willingness to explore new forms. The other two are Katherine Paterson and the astonishing Virginia Hamilton.

While Hamilton's first novel, *Zeely* (1967), is not as complex or as rewarding as her later books, it is still more complex and more rewarding than most children's books. But Hamilton really hits her stride with the ingenious *The Planet of Junior Brown* (1971), a book that makes unbelievable situations and characters seem chillingly real; and in *M. C. Higgins, the Great* (1974), she has produced her best book so far. Complex, psychologically searching, artistically integrated, this novel represents a new maturity in thinking about children's literature, not just for Virginia Hamilton but also for the many award committees that named it best book of the year in a unique sweep. Hamilton's books since *M. C. Higgins* have been a fascinating, and often fascinatingly flawed, series of experiments that attempt to combine various aspects of fantasy and realism; the most recent of these, particularly *The Magical Adventures of Pretty Pearl* (1983), suggest that the experimentation is bearing fruit and that another great book is on the way.

Taken together, the string of books Katherine Paterson published throughout the 1970s are almost as diverse as Hamilton's. But Paterson is not the innovator Hamilton is, and each of her novels is merely a fine representative of a recognizable genre: the historical novel in her three wonderfully evocative novels of ancient Japan and three different sorts of realism in the stark *Bridge to Terabithia* (1977), the comic *The Great Gilly Hopkins* (1978), and the sensitively delineated *Jacob Have I Loved* (1980).

It was the British Randolph Caldecott and Beatrix Potter who first showed how it might be possible to tell an interesting story in a combination of words and pictures. But it has been Americans, a people besotted by the rich visual imagery of motion pictures, snapshots, and comic books, who have explored the implications of the picture storybook, the most twentieth-century of children's genres, and who have discovered most of the significant technical innovations within it. The best picture storybooks have texts designed to be read aloud in the rhythms of well-ordered speech and pictures that communicate the tone the words should be spoken in. There have been more excellent picture storybooks than any other sort of American children's literature.

The list begins with Wanda Gág's feisty *Millions of Cats* and includes the wonderful books by Leaf, Lawson, and Dr. Seuss already mentioned. In the 1930s, there were also the charming *The Story About Ping* (1933), in which the rhythmic grace of Marjorie Flack's words is matched by the delicacy of Kurt Weise's pictures; the first of Ludwig Bemelmans's whimsical books about Madeline (1939); and Virginia Lee Burton's *Mike Mulligan and His Steam Shovel* (1939), a book less imposing but more fun than her spiraling monument of 1942, *The Little House*. In the 1940s, Robert McCloskey's exuberant pictures for *Lentil* were matched by his equally exuberant but more charming pictures for *Make Way for Ducklings* (1941), still one of the most interesting explorations of visual point-of-view in picture books; just as charming in a decidedly unexuberant way are Marie Hall Ets's delicate and poetic pictures for *In the Forest* (1944). The one book that stands out from the lively but undistinguished picture books of the 1950s is Lynd Ward's *The Biggest Bear* (1952). Ward's pictures depict his tall tale in a visual style that mixes equal amounts of inflated pomposity and deflating wit, perfectly complementing the text.

But the most interesting picture books of the 1940s and 1950s were almost always those with texts by Margaret Wise Brown—a fact that reveals how significant and how difficult a writer's contribution to a picture book always is. Few of Brown's books actually tell stories; but she realized better than anyone has before or since how pictures can support and amplify the very simplest of texts. Almost every one of her books conveys an ingeniously innovative idea in carefully chosen words that delight even the youngest of children. In her best texts, like the rhythmically insistent *Goodnight Moon* with illustrations by Clement Hurd (1947), Brown's text is like poetry itself and makes poetry out of otherwise undistinguished art.

The most important of American picture book artists, and perhaps the most important American practitioner of children's literature in this century, began his work in the 1950s. But Maurice Sendak really began to make a distinctive contribution in the 1960s, a decade in which he produced not only the dreamy, light-filled, impressionistic pictures that transform Charlotte Zolotow's pedestrian text for *Mr. Rabbit and the Lovely Present* (1962) into a quirky and decidedly paradoxical masterpiece but also many important books that he both illustrated and wrote. In 1963 he produced the most famous, and still, perhaps, the most significant American picture book—a book distinctly American in its Oz-like insistence on the relationship between fantastic places and real life. All by itself, *Where the Wild Things Are* is a catalogue of picture book technique; while the story of Max's encounter with some highly innovative grotesques is satisfyingly gripping, the book is a technical triumph as well as an emotional one.

In later years, *Where the Wild Things Are* (1963) turned out to have been the first book in a peculiar

trilogy. The next book in this improbable series on related themes is *In the Night Kitchen* (1970), a joyful celebration of Sendak's fascination with comic strips and other aspects of the rich American tradition of popular culture, including billboard art, Mickey Mouse, Laurel and Hardy—and, perhaps, the great popular tradition of sexual titillation, for Sendak's young hero is the first unabashedly naked child to immodestly reveal his all in a children's picture book. In the final book of the trilogy, *Outside Over There* (1981), nakedness abounds and so does complexity, as Sendak presents all his favorite motifs in concentrated form: bare skin, floating bodies, big feet, magical openings in secure enclosed spaces, ingenuous demons, the relationship between control and anarchy, and the music of Mozart. All of this is, quite magically, childlike enough both to delight young children and confuse middle-aged adults.

In addition to his brilliant and influential picture books, Sendak has made important contributions to every sort of children's book. His pictures of overweight and forbidding-looking medieval princesses idiosyncratically, but wonderfully, evoke the spirit of the Grimm fairy tales in *The Juniper Tree and Other Tales from Grim* (1973). His words just as capably describe the real life adventures of the ebullient and indefatigable girl Rosie in *The Sign on Rosie's Door* (1960) and the nonsensical fantasy adventures of the self-indulgent and indefatigable dog Jennie of *Higglety Pigglety Pop* (1967).

Other illustrators, less blessed by a multitude of talents, have often produced brilliant pictures for texts that are, to be kind, pedestrian. Ezra Jack Keats's interesting collages for *The Snowy Day* (1962) must fight his own boring text; his magnificent, brooding pictures for *Apartment Three* (1971) come to seem melodramatic in relation to the small story accompanying them. Gerald McDermott's showy pictures for *Arrow to the Sun* (1973) are a rich coalescence of Pueblo motifs and contemporary graphic design; they imply subtle details about the story that his choppy text does not even hint at. Leo and Diane Dillon are a little luckier in having Verna Aardema's quite tellable texts of African tales to illustrate in their fluidly sensuous pictures for *Why Mosquitoes Buzz in People's Ears* (1975) and the too much neglected *Who's in Rabbit's House?* (1977), a fascinating evocation of bodies in motion.

The other distinguished book artists of our time are often at their best when they use the least words, as do Peter Spier in his intricately detailed and comically honest pictures for *Noah's Ark* (1977) and Donald Crews in his vibrant and courageously simple books *Freight Train* (1978) and *Truck* (1980), or when they avoid the faddish ideas about childhood and illustrate the traditional words of the great European fairy tales, as do Nancy Eckholm Burkert in her cool, elegant pictures for *Snow White* (1972) and both Trina Schart Hyman and Susan Jeffers in many fine books. Hyman's pictures are distinguished by a fluid use of line and a dramatic fervor that is richly melodramatic; Jeffers's sophisticated combinations of intricate detail and white space are unfailingly elegant (but surprisingly similar in book after book). The 1970s and 1980s also produced two brilliant practitioners of illustration without color: David Macaulay in intricate books about buildings like *Cathedral* (1973) and *Unbuilding* (1980) and Chris Van Allsburg, whose almost photographic pictures in *The Garden of Abdul Gasazi* (1979) and *Jumanji* (1980) possess a chilling surface stillness that seethes with magical possibilities.

In *The Wreck of the Zephyr* (1982) and *The Polar Express* (1985), Van Allsburg proves that color pictures can be equally mysterious. This book, Sendak's *Outside Over There*, and fine novels by E. L. Konigsburg and Virginia Hamilton suggest how the great tradition of American children's books has continued in the 1980s. In the light of the conservative atmosphere of America in this past decade, it may not be surprising that these distinguished books have all been produced by established writers and illustrators. Thus far, the 1980s have been as unexciting a decade in children's literature as any in this century, and apart from those few books by writers with an already established reputation for surprising their readers, there have been no unsettling innovations, no major breakthroughs, no particularly new voices—at least none that have captured the interest of large numbers of children and large numbers of adults interested in children's books. The 1960s and 1970s may well have been a "Golden Age" for children's books in America; that age may be over.

American children's literature has grown more complex as the century has worn on, just as the lives of American children have. It may be for that reason that there have been more interesting and noteworthy books in recent decades—and it may be that the decidedly less interesting books of recent years result from adult attempts to hide the real complexity of life in our time from both ourselves and from child readers. Nevertheless, the great American children's books share certain qualities, no matter when they were written. They all balance admiration of the childlike with an honest perception of the limitations of childhood. Sometimes they do so by means of a double perspective, as in Laura Ingalls Wilder's books; sometimes by means of ambivalent portraits of humanlike animals like Frog and Toad, or of monsters that evoke ugly human emotions, like Sendak's wild things. Sometimes the expression of ambivalence is the balance between simple, childlike texts and complex, sophisticated pictures that typifies the great American picture books; sometimes, even, there is a final simple accommodation between what one desires and what one must put up with, as in the case of E. B. White's Wilbur and Virginia Hamilton's M. C. Higgins.

The great American children's books are almost all about children (or childlike animals) who are eternally hopeful and never really fulfilled, eternally open to change yet unchanging, eternally educable but never actually educated. Dorothy of Oz, the bull Ferdinand, the pig Wilbur, Burton's Little House, the girls Harriet and Claudia, and the boys Max and M.C. are all delightfully involved in the business of growing up—and they, none of them, grow up. They merely get older without becoming much different from what they were so charmingly in the first place. In this way, they express the great paradox of childhood in America and thus, of American children's literature: an abiding interest in how children are childlike, based on the conviction that the most childlike of all qualities is the ability to grow past the childlike.

Checklist for Further Reading

This bibliography focuses on studies that deal with twentieth-century American children's literature. Important general studies and critical works that have become standards in the study of children's literature have been included as well. Although major journals in the field of children's literature have been omitted from the list, they are valuable sources of further information on many of the authors covered in this volume. Among the best-known and most useful periodicals are: Children's Literature Association *Quarterly; Children's Literature,* the annual journal of the Children's Literature Division of the Modern Language Association; *Children's Literature in Education; Horn Book* magazine; *Phaedrus: An International Journal of Children's Literature Research;* and the *Lion and the Unicorn.* Articles from these and related periodicals may be identified in general and subject periodical indexes under headings related to children's literature.

Of interest to students of twentieth-century American children's literature are: *Children's Literature Abstracts,* no. 1- , May 1973- (Birmingham, England: International Federation of Library Associations, Sub-section on Library Work with Children); Virginia Haviland's *Children's Literature: A Guide to Reference Sources* (Washington, D.C.: Library of Congress, 1966) and its supplements; Suzanne Rahn's *Children's Literature: An Annotated Bibliography of the History and Criticism* (New York: Garland Publishing, 1981); Elva S. Smith's *The History of Children's Literature: A Syllabus with Selected Bibliographies,* second edition, revised and enlarged by Margaret Hodges and Susan Steinfirst (Chicago: American Library Association, 1980); W. Bernard Lukenbill's *A Working Bibliography of American Doctoral Dissertations in Children's and Adolescents' Literature, 1930-1971* (Occasional Paper, no. 103. Urbana: University of Illinois, Graduate School of Library Science, 1972); and Dianne Monson and Bette J. Peltola's *Research in Children's Literature* (Newark, Del.: International Reading Association, 1976).

AMERICAN BACKGROUND: HISTORICAL AND CRITICAL STUDIES

Attebery, Brian. *The Fantasy Tradition in American Literature: From Irving to Le Guin.* Bloomington: Indiana University Press, 1980.

Bingham, Jane, and Grayce Scholt. *Fifteen Centuries of Children's Literature: An Annotated Chronology of British and American Works in Historical Context.* Westport, Conn.: Greenwood Press, 1980.

FitzGerald, Frances. *America Revisited: History Schoolbooks in the Twentieth Century.* Boston: Little, Brown, 1979.

Haviland, Virginia, and Margaret N. Coughlan. *Yankee Doodle's Literary Sampler of Prose, Poetry and Pictures.* New York: Crowell, 1974.

Lystad, Mary. *From Dr. Mather to Dr. Seuss: 200 Years of American Books for Children.* Boston: G. K. Hall, 1980.

Meigs, Cornelia L., et al. *A Critical History of Children's Literature: A Survey of Children's Books in English.* Rev. ed. Macmillan, 1969.

Townsend, John Rowe. *Written for Children: An Outline of English Children's Literature.* Philadelphia: Lippincott, 1983.

SURVEYS AND CRITICAL STUDIES

Andrews, Siri, ed. *The Hewins Lectures, 1947-1962*. Boston: Horn Book, 1963.

Bettelheim, Bruno. *The Uses of Enchantment: The Meaning and Importance of Fairy Tales*. New York: Knopf, 1976.

Broderick, Dorothy. *Image of the Black in Children's Fiction*. New York: Bowker, 1973.

Brown, Marcia. *Lotus Seeds: Children, Pictures, and Books*. New York: Scribners, 1986.

Cameron, Eleanor. *The Green and Burning Tree: On the Writing and Enjoyment of Children's Books*. Boston: Atlantic/Little, Brown, 1969.

Carpenter, Humphrey, and Mari Prichard. *The Oxford Companion to Children's Literature*. New York: Oxford University Press, 1984.

Chambers, Aidan. *Booktalk: Occasional Writing on Literature and Children*. New York: Harper & Row, 1985.

Egoff, Sheila A. *Thursday's Child: Trends and Patterns in Contemporary Children's Literature*. Chicago: American Library Association, 1981.

Hazard, Paul. *Books, Children and Men*. Translated by Marguerite Mitchell. 4th ed. Boston: Horn Book, 1960.

Huck, Charlotte. *Children's Literature in the Elementary School*. 3rd ed. New York: Holt, Rinehart & Winston, 1979.

Hunter, Mollie. *Talent Is Not Enough*. New York: Harper & Row, 1976.

Inglis, Fred. *The Promise of Happiness: Value and Meaning in Children's Fiction*. Cambridge & New York: Cambridge University Press, 1981.

Kingston, Carolyn. *The Tragic Mode in Children's Literature*. New York: Teachers College Press, 1974.

Lukens, Rebecca J. *A Critical Handbook of Children's Literature*. 3rd ed. Glenview, Ill.: Scott, Foresman, 1986.

Meek, Margaret, Aidan Warlow, and Grieselda Barton. *The Cool Web: The Pattern of Children's Reading*. New York: Atheneum, 1978.

Paterson, Katherine. *Gates of Excellence: On Reading and Writing Books for Children*. New York: Elsevier/Nelson, 1981.

Rees, David. *The Marble in the Water: Essays on Contemporary Writers of Fiction for Children and Young Adults*. Boston: Horn Book, 1980.

Rees. *Painted Desert, Green Shade: Essays on Contemporary Writers of Fiction for Children and Young Adults*. Boston: Horn Book, 1984.

Rudman, M. K. *Children's Literature: An Issues Approach*. 2nd ed. New York: Longman, 1984.

Sale, Roger. *Fairy Tales and After: From Snow White to E. B. White*. Cambridge: Harvard University Press, 1978.

Savater, Fernando. *Childhood Regained: The Art of the Storyteller.* New York: Columbia University Press, 1982.

Sims, Rudine. *Shadow and Substance: Afro-American Experience in Contemporary Children's Fiction.* Urbana, Ill.: National Council of Teachers of English, 1982.

Smith, James Steele. *A Critical Approach to Children's Literature.* New York: McGraw-Hill, 1967.

Smith, Lillian. *The Unreluctant Years: A Critical Approach to Children's Literature.* Chicago: American Library Association, 1953.

Southall, Ivan. *A Journey of Discovery: On Writing for Children.* New York: Macmillan, 1976.

Sutherland, Zena. *Children and Books.* 7th ed. Glenview, Ill.: Scott, Foresman, 1986.

Townsend, John Rowe. *A Sense of Story: Essays on Contemporary Writers for Children.* Philadelphia: Lippincott, 1971.

Townsend. *A Sounding of Storytellers: New and Revised Essays on Contemporary Writers for Children.* Philadelphia: Lippincott, 1979.

Tucker, Nicholas. *The Child and the Book: A Psychological and Literary Exploration.* Cambridge & New York: Cambridge University Press, 1981.

Yolen, Jane. *Touch Magic: Fantasy, Faerie and Folklore in the Literature of Childhood.* New York: Philomel Books, 1981.

CRITICISM COLLECTIONS

Bator, Robert, ed. *Signposts to Criticism of Children's Literature.* Chicago: American Library Association, 1983.

Butler, Francelia, and Richard Rotert, eds. *Reflections on Literature for Children.* Hamden, Conn.: Shoe String/ Library Professional Publications, 1984.

Chambers, Nancy, ed. *The Signal Approach to Children's Books.* Harmondsworth, England: Kestrel, 1980; Metuchen, N.J.: Scarecrow, 1981.

Egoff, Sheila A., ed. *One Ocean Touching: Papers from the First Pacific Rim Conference on Children's Literature.* Metuchen, N.J.: Scarecrow, 1979.

Egoff, G. T. Stubbs, and L. F. Ashley, eds. *Only Connect: Readings on Children's Literature.* 2nd ed. New York: Oxford University Press, 1980.

Fenwick, Sara Innis. *A Critical Approach to Children's Literature.* Chicago: University of Chicago Press, 1967.

Field, Elinor Whitney, ed. *Horn Book Reflections: On Children's Books and Reading: Selected from Eighteen Years of the Horn Book Magazine, 1948-1966.* Boston: Horn Book, 1969.

Fox, Geoff, and Graham Hammond, with Stuart Amor, eds. *Responses to Children's Literature.* Proceedings of the Fourth Symposium of the International Research Society for Children's Literature Held at the University of Exeter, 9 September 1978. New York: K. G. Saur for the Society, 1979.

Fox, et al., eds. *Writers, Critics and Children: Articles from Children's Literature in Education.* New York: Agathon Press, 1976.

Fraser, James H., ed. *Society and Children's Literature.* Boston: Godine, in association with the American Library Association, 1978.

Haviland, Virginia, ed. *Children and Literature: Views and Reviews.* Glenview, Ill.: Scott, Foresman, 1973.

Haviland, ed. *The Openhearted Audience: Ten Authors Talk about Writing for Children.* Washington, D.C.: Library of Congress, 1980.

Hearne, Betsy, and Marilyn Kaye, eds. *Celebrating Children's Books: Essays on Children's Literature in Honor of Zena Sutherland.* New York: Lothrop, Lee & Shepard, 1981.

Heins, Paul, ed. *Crosscurrents of Criticism: Horn Book Essays: 1968-1977.* Boston: Horn Book, 1977.

McCann, D., and G. Woodard, eds. *The Black American in Books for Children: Readings in Racism.* Metuchen, N.J.: Scarecrow Press, 1972.

May, Jill P., ed. *Children and Their Literature: A Readings Book.* West Lafayette, Ind.: ChLA Publications, 1983.

Sutherland, Zena, ed. *The Arbuthnot Lectures: 1970-1979.* Chicago: American Library Association, 1980.

Tucker, Nicholas, ed. *Suitable for Children? Controversies in Children's Literature.* Berkeley & Los Angeles: University of California Press, 1976.

INTERVIEWS, PROFILES, AND BIOGRAPHICAL REFERENCE WORKS

Blishen, Edward. *The Thorny Paradise: Writers on Writing for Children.* London: Kestrel/Boston: Horn Book, 1975.

Commire, Anne, ed. *Something About the Author.* Detroit: Gale Research, 1971-

Cott, Jonathan. *Pipers at the Gates of Dawn: The Wisdom of Children's Literature.* New York: Random House, 1983.

Doyle, Brian, ed. *The Who's Who of Children's Literature.* New York: Schocken Books, 1968.

Hopkins, Lee Bennett. *Books Are by People: Interviews with 104 Authors and Illustrators of Books for Young Children.* New York: Citation Press, 1969.

Hopkins. *More Books by More People.* New York: Citation Press, 1974.

Kingman, Lee, ed. *Newbery and Caldecott Medal Books: 1956-1965.* Boston: Horn Book, 1965.

Kingman, ed. *Newbery and Caldecott Medal Books: 1966-1975.* Boston: Horn Book, 1975.

Kirkpatrick, D. L. *Twentieth-Century Children's Writers.* 2nd ed. New York: St. Martin's, 1984.

Wintle, Justin, and Emma Fisher. *The Pied Piper: Interviews with the Influential Creators of Children's Literature.* New York: Paddington Press, 1974.

Contributors

Alida Allison..*Palm Desert, California*
Marilyn F. Apseloff..*Kent State University*
O. Mell Busbin ....*Appalachian State University*
Nellvena Duncan Eutsler ....*East Carolina University*
Elizabeth Francis ....*University of Nevada at Reno*
Sue Garness..*Augsburg College*
Ophelia Gilbert..*Central Missouri State University*
Andrew Gordon ....*University of Florida*
Theodore W. Hipple..*University of Tennessee*
Karen Nelson Hoyle...*University of Minnesota*
Laura Ingram...*Columbia, South Carolina*
Sylvia W. Iskander ....*University of Southwestern Louisiana*
Marilyn H. Karrenbrock ....*University of Tennessee*
Hugh T. Keenan ....*Georgia State University*
Myra Kibler ....*Belmont College*
William E. Kreuger ....*Millican University*
Barbara Lovell...*Durham, North Carolina*
Francis J. Molson..*Central Michigan University*
Anita Moss...*University of North Carolina at Charlotte*
Alice Phoebe Naylor...*Appalachian State University*
Perry Nodelman ....*University of Winnipeg*
Marygail G. Parker..*Minneapolis, Minnesota*
Lesley S. Potts ....*Lee County Public Library, Lee County, Mississippi*
Philip A. Sadler ....*Central Missouri State University*
Elizabeth Segel ....*Pittsburgh, Pennsylvania*
Prabha Gupta Sharma................................*Randolph School Library, Huntsville, Alabama*
M. Sarah Smedman.............................*University of North Carolina at Charlotte*
Joe Stines.............................*Tampa-Hillsborough County Public Library, Tampa, Florida*
Douglas Street ....*Texas A&M University*
Grace Sulerud ....*Augsburg College*
Anita Trout ....*University of Tennessee*
Malcolm Usrey ....*Clemson University*
Kay E. Vandergrift..*Rutgers University*
E. Charles Vousden..*Bloomfield, Connecticut*
Mary Lou White ....*Wright State University*
Carol Wintercorn ....*Appalachian State University*
David A. Wright..*Bryan College*
Jane Harper Yarbrough ....*University of Wisconsin Center, Marinette*
Laura M. Zaidman ....*University of South Carolina, Sumter*

Cumulative Index

Dictionary of Literary Biography, Volumes 1-52
Dictionary of Literary Biography Yearbook, 1980-1985
Dictionary of Literary Biography Documentary Series, Volumes 1-4

Cumulative Index

DLB before number: *Dictionary of Literary Biography,* Volumes 1-52
Y before number: *Dictionary of Literary Biography Yearbook,* 1980-1985
DS before number: *Dictionary of Literary Biography Documentary Series,* Volumes 1-4

A

Cumulative Index

D

E

F

G

H

M

N

T

U

V

W

6761